Market Street looking west with old gas pump, circa 1920. From left, Braner Building, Auwarter home, Post Office, Auwarter store, 3-story building at southwest corner of Market and Main. Across on northwest corner: White Horse Hotel, Rieder's Opera House, Gebauer building with Texaco Motor Oil sign and Parrot Bread logo on side of building, Ford Sales and Service with man on ladder.

Market Street looking west, 1923. (l. to r.) Tom Millett near pole; Sollie Hampton; Earl Liles in football suit; Cecil Naylor; John E. Deimling Jr.; G.V. Conley; John H. Schmidt; Hy Miller Sr.; John "Red Jake" Deimling Sr. in white apron, butcher. Four Ford Model T cars. Business houses on left: Dr. Jim Adams' office; Rick & Joyce's Tavern; Braner Building. Background: "Castle Hall;" Masons Tavern; 3rd Floor Dance Hall; Troy's first gymnasium. On the right: Albert Rieder's Tavern; former Legion Hall; Taylor & Allen's Tavern; J.C. Gebauer's Hardware Store; Jim McLanahan's Ford Garage; John Jarvis' 75-foot maple tree.

Market Street looking east, summer of 1925. On the left: Rollie Porter, Dr. Schoeck; on the right side of the street: Sollie Hampton, Thomas Millett, Vorhees Conley, Charlie Hazzard (white apron).

From Border Street looking east on Market Street, 1943.

Troy, Illinois Area
History and Families

1803-2002

JARVIS TOWNSHIP   PIN OAK TOWNSHIP

This book is dedicated to all future generations of the City of Troy and the surrounding area in hopes that they will not forget to preserve the area's rich heritage. May this book be informative, educational and enjoyable to all who read it.

**Compiled by the
Troy Historical Society**

Turner
PUBLISHING COMPANY

Publishers of
America's History

Graphic Designer:
Thalita A. Floyd-Wingerter

Copyright © 2003
Troy, Illinois
Historical Society

This book or any part thereof
may not be reproduced without
the written consent of the Troy
Illinois Historical Society and
the Publisher.

The materials were compiled and
produced using available
information; Turner Publishing
Company and the Troy Illinois
Historical Society regret they
cannot assume liability for errors
or omissions.

Library of Congress
Control Number:
2002116933

ISBN:978-1-68162-028-2

Limited Edition of
600 copies
of which this book is
number_____ .

Contents

Foreword

With great pride and pleasure the Troy Historical Society presents this book to the Troy community. The first book to be published solely about the Troy area, it also commemorates the 145th year of the City of Troy's incorporation. More than this, however, was our purpose: to preserve the Troy area's rich history.

The production of this book has been a struggle from its inception in the fall of 2000 to its completion in the summer of 2002. The book project was new to all of us, and some in the community might have doubted our ability to pull it off. Sometimes, so did we.

Eventually, through continued publicity and hard work, both the community and society members worked together to reach this time - press time. Through adversity and frustration, through thunderstorms and 100-degree temperatures, through laughter and tears, this time-consuming project has come to fruition.

We want to especially thank all of those who have helped in any way to bring this great project from an idea to a product. We sincerely hope that future generations will enjoy reading, will learn from it, and will continue to preserve the area's history because of it.

The committee has made a strong effort to include as much history as was possible. An astounding 1,400 pictures were submitted, nearly 450 family and personal biographies were written, and 100s of articles were recorded on various aspects of the area's history. We sincerely thank the families who submitted their photos and biographies, and the current businesses, organizations and individuals who were so generous with their time and money.

We are especially grateful to the Jarvis Township Road District and to Commissioner James Grapperhaus for allowing us to use the district's conference room as our book office.

To the other individuals, organizations, entities, and businesses that have contributed in many other ways, THANK YOU. Special thanks goes to Jarvis Township, Troy Lions Club, Troy Fire Protection District, City of Troy, Bob Turley and St. Paul AAL for the very generous financial contributions.

As you read this book and look at the pictures, remember that volunteers handled every aspect of this book before it went to the publishers. We gave our best effort to bring you a quality book. We hope you enjoy it.

Mae Grapperhaus, President
Troy Historical Society
and members of the book committee

Acknowledgments

This book was written, edited and published entirely by members of the Troy Historical Society and volunteers from the community. The committee sincerely thanks those who were so generous to submit funding, biographies, stories and photos to make it a complete project. Thank you for your willingness to share with others.

The articles from the newspapers were written by Mae Grapperhaus and edited by Jeanette Dothager. Judy Little scanned all of the photos, and Joy Upton scanned the text, typed and served as manager of the project. Other articles were written by various members of the Troy Historical Society, including Pat Huck, Judy Little, Mae Grapperhaus, Reba Mathis, Marilyn Sulc, Pat Peverly, Millie Shaffer, Jeanette Dothager, Audrey Deeren, Joy Upton and Merrill Ottwein.

Record keeping, sorting, filing and typing were done by members Pat Huck, Linda Dunstan, Nancy Fischer, Marilyn Sulc, Diana Bauer, George Bauer and Ruby Schultze. Photographers included Judy Little, Mae Grapperhaus and Darrell Hampsten. Pat Huck, Mae Grapperhaus, Diana Bauer, Marilyn Sulc, Jeri Tellman, Earl Fischer, Gloria Mannz, Jeanette Dothager, Joy Upton and Linda Dunstan worked with fundraising.

Others who assisted with the book in a variety of ways included Gene Barnard, Bob Rogier, Mark Buske, Lisa Frey, Joyce Meyer, Nancy Malvin, Diana Shreve, Darrell Hampsten, Paul Ping, Vernon Little, Doug Little, Charmion Semanisin, Mr. and Mrs. Tom Tritsch, Jack and Dot Rees, Allen Holloway, Fran and Pete Gebhart, Jo-Ann Weiler, Pat Peverly, Wilma Edwards and the Tri-Township Public Library.

(l. to r.) Around the table: Reba Mathis, Linda Dunstan, Pat Huck, George Bauer, Marilyn Sulc (seated), Nancy Fischer, Gloria Mannz, Diana Schreve, Joy Upton, Jeanette Dothager, Diana Bauer, Mae Grapperhaus, Judy Little and Audrey Deeren.

(l. to r.) Front: Linda Dunstan, Marilyn Sulc, Jeanette Dothager, Joy Upton and Audrey Deeren. Back: Jeri Tellmann, Nancy Fischer, Judy Little, Reba Mathis, Mae Grapperhaus, Diana Bauer and George Bauer.

TROY, ILLINOIS

ENTRANCE TO YOUR GATEWAY OF OPPORTUNITIES

August 22, 2002

Troy Historical Society
PO Box 265
Troy, IL 62294

Dear Society Members:

In commemoration of the City of Troy's 145 years of incorporation, I would like to take this opportunity to express my gratitude to the Troy Historical Society for your hard work and dedication.

Through the years, the Historical Society has emphasized the importance of learning about our past to guide us in our future. They have educated our residents, recognized significant historical structures in our community and painstakingly recorded and preserved our heritage. And soon, our history will be easily accessible with the publishing of a book about Troy and the surrounding community—the first such publication in Troy's 145 years of incorporation.

As we continue to grow and develop as a community, our fate is uncertain. However, through the work of the Troy Historical Society, we can take comfort in knowing that our past has been maintained to aid the course of future generations.

Sincerely,

Tom Caraker, Sr.
Mayor

TC/lt

116 East Market • Troy, IL 62294-1599
Mayor/Administration: 618/667-6741 • Fax: 618/667-4009 • Public Works Dept: 618/667-9924
Building & Zoning Dept: 618/667-8734 • Website: ci.troy.il.us

4

History of the Troy Area

Ted Mersinger with team of mules and rake, circa 1945.

Levo Bakery and Mothers Way bread truck.

(Right) Troy Exchange Bank as it appeared after being dynamited by robbers on the night of November 25, 1899.

Powell Street located on the north end off Clay Street, circa 1900

Troy, Illinois, Area
History and Families

The Troy Area

The history of the Troy area is similar to the discovery and growth of the Illinois prairie. The Indians and the French explorers followed the many waterways and trails. With the French, came the development of churches and homes in nearby Kaskaskia and Cahokia.

Before the American Revolution of 1776, the English made plans to have a governor over the Illinois country. Land speculators wanted to purchase this land from the Indians and not the English. Settlers who were mainly from the southern states began to explore and build primitive lodging outside of the early French settlements. They began to come farther north into what is now Jarvis and Pin Oak Townships.

After George Rogers Clark with his group of Big Knives overcame the British at Kaskaskia and Cahokia in 1778, they attacked Vincennes, IN, and received the surrender of the British on February 25, 1779. The Illinois country became part of the state of Virginia. From 1780 until 1784, the original states surrendered their western lands to the United States. Congress ordered the survey of these public domain lands. Each township was to be six miles square. In 1809 Illinois became a territory separate from the Northwest Territory.

The French, the British, the land speculators and the squatters had land claims in the American Bottom. This lawless frontier began to have laws regarding land ownership. These early settlers lived in very primitive conditions with the hardships of traveling through swampy lands, sickness, Indian attacks, and the weather. Many thought the prairie would not raise crops because there were no bushes or trees growing on it. However, the American Bottom prairie soon became prized farmland with nearby water sources. Silver Creek was and is the largest water source that flows through Madison County. It enters Pin Oak Township in Section 1 at the northwestern part and flows south leaving in Section 35. In the southern portion of Section 13 the water of East Fork mingles with the waters of Silver Creek. It continues through the eastern portion of Jarvis Township. Canteen Creek begins in the southwest portion of the township.

Until the courts resolved the land claims, no public domain land could be sold. Thus, these settlers remained squatters. Eventually, the land was sold for $1.25 per acre. Small tracts of 160 acres were sold on credit. Jarvis and a portion of Pin Oak Township public domain land owners are listed by Section numbers. Not all purchased the entire section of 640 acres. Jesse Renfro lived in section 24 in 1811; Robert Seybold, section 8 in 1803, but they did not purchase the land. Some received land by a warrant issued for their military duty. The following data was taken from the web site of the Illinois State Archives in 2002. Spelling of names is listed as found.

Illinois became a state in 1818 and Troy was platted in 1819 by James Riggen and David Hendershott. They had paid John Jarvis $10 an acre for the ten acres of land in section 9 and had the land surveyed into lots. Before the purchase, the community was known as Columbia; but James Riggin named it Troy. By 1820, Troy Village had a total population of 120 persons, living in 17 households according to the U.S. Federal Census. (Spelling of names in all census listed herein are translated from the census taker's spelling and handwriting.) These hardy souls were Morgan Thompson, Walker Nichols, Thomas Baker, James Palmer, John Eberman, John Yaple, Daniel Fray (Frey?), John Ripper (Riggen?), Horatio McCray, Andrew Ellison, Harry Riggins, John Jarvis, Isaac West, Thomas Ranch and Josias Wright.

More information on these early Troy frontiersmen can be found in the other sections of this book and various Madison County history books listed on the bibliography.

In the beginning Troy grew slowly from John Jarvis' band mill, Calvin McCray's storehouse/log cabin, and Horatio McCray's frame structure built onto his brother's cabin for accommodations for travelers. Both Jacob C. Gonterman and Joseph Eberman had taverns.

By 1833, Troy had a post office with George Churchill as its postmaster. The town plat was finally placed on record on March 5, 1839. The National Road (old U.S. Route 40) from Vandalia through Troy to St. Louis was built. Illinois lacked funds at this time and toll gates were erected every ten miles to help pay for building the National Road.

Frontier Troy became the first stagecoach stop from St. Louis. Travelers got food at the taverns and blacksmiths took care of the horses. Coming from the east, the stagecoach would stop in the evening and the travelers would stay overnight. Wagon trains became a method of travel for those moving from one locality to another. Farmers rode their horses into town and tied them up at the railing or a post. So did the robbers. (See the photo of Troy's bank that was dynamited.) Guns were muskets which required ball and powder. Food and protection depended upon their use.

By 1850, Troy's population had grown to 250 inhabitants. Of these, 35 were foreign born with 30 from the British Isles. One hundred five were born in Illinois. This census was taken by Asst. Marshall F. F. Kraft on February 25, 1852.

Listed by occupation are some of the 250 inhabitants of Troy.

Blacksmiths: Dempsey Robinson, Joshua Long, Ferdinand Cornman, William Randolph, Russell Campbell

Boarding House Keeper: Ann Prior

Bricklayer: Warren Lenks

Brickmaker: Joseph Parker

Carpenters: Albert Radefelt, William Kehe, Charles K. Poor, John McCall, Isaac Holt, Andrew Mills

Carriage Makers: David Shaw, L. or S.R. Corman, Henry Meadley, Joshua Woodbury

Clergyman: Rev. John Padon

Farmers: Hollis Gillett, James Willow, James Paydon

Flour Miller: James McKay

Grocery Keepers: Isaac Howard, Charles Pickering

Gun Smith: George T. Cochran

Hatter: Moses Bardsley

Horse Trader: William P. Henderson

Hotel Keeper: John Wood

Laborers: John Holmes, Thomas Kuggler, Peter C. Cole, Albert Pribble, Patrick Conway, James Dean, Henry Langham, George Grover, Patrick Kerenian, Eli Prentice, Patrick Prannagan, John Laramie, Robert Stover, Henry Hobs

Merchants: Julius A. Barnsback, John Wilcox (Clerk), S. R. Swain, Charles Vaughn, Thomas Judy, And. J. Swain (Clerk), John Brady

None: Samuel Hunter, William Laramie, Robert R. Swain, Thomas P. Moore, William McCallister

Physicians: Joseph Gates, J.S. Dewey, George H. Dewey (Student of Medicine), F.W. Lytle, Charles Duponte

Plasterers: William Cormack, James Henderson, Frank Cornman

Saddlers: Morris Armstrong, Jacob Williams, William Cole, James Brown

School Teacher: J. McDonough Gates

Shoemakers: James Brown, Caleb Johnson

Stage driver: William Mason, John Padon, Solomon Abel, William Nix

Tailor: George Hulme

Teamster: Philip Gatch

Lower Part of Pin Oak Township

(* purchased more than 160 acres; + various tracts by many purchasers.)

30George Barnsback, Thornton Peeples, Abraham Prickett, Isaac C. Mott	29Abraham Prickett, George W. Teas, Paris Mason, Isacc C. Mott, Jacob C. Gonterman, Samuel McKittrick	28Jacob Gonterman, Rouland Shephard, +	27 Thomas Hilman, Jubilee Posey*, +	26 Rowland P. Allen, Pierre Menard*, Montgomery Bell*, +	25James Ground, Adrian Hegeman, Pierre Menard, John Shinn, Montgomery Bell*, +
31George Barnsback*, John Kain, +	32Joseph Burrough, Jacob Judy, John Robinson*, Matthias Handlon	33Jubilee Posey*, John Robinson,Calvin McCray, George W. Tease	34 Samuel Wood, Jacob Gounterman, William Padon, Jubilee Posey, Caleb G. Gonterman	35Rowland P. Allen, Pierre Menard*, +	36 John Campbell, William Sampson, Pierre Menard*, +

All of Jarvis Township

(* purchased more than 160 acres; + various tracts by many purchasers.)

6Abner O'Kelly,George Kinder, Jubilee Posey, Joel Whiteside, James Riggin, Samuel Reed +	5Henry Cook, Samuel Wood*, Calvin McCray	4 Titus Gregg	3 Field Jarvis, John Lewis, Calvin McCray, Charles McMicken	2Charles McMicken*, Josiah Caswell, William Vineyard +	1Pierre Menard, Laban Smart*, Jesse Rentfro, Antoine Peltier, Wiley Smart, Fletcher Jarvis
7 William F. Purviance, David Gaskill, Silvanus Gaskill, Robert Seybold*	8 George Churchill*, David Hindershott, Abrahm Vanhooser*, William Harned	9Field Jarvis, Joseph Eberman*, John Jarvis*	10James Simmons,Robert Stice, Charles McMicken, Calvin McCray, +	11Abraham Casteel, Jesse Rentfro, Gabriel Wats, Thomas M. Boson, +	12Andrew Black, Leonard Dugger, Jacob Husong, Field Jarvis, Louis Nolin, Jordan W. Jeffreys
18DavidGaskill, RobertMcMahon Julien M. Sturteuant, Jonathan B. Turner*	17 Henry Bick, GeorgeChurchill Gaskill*, +	16John Edwards Joshua Marsh Daniel Reece (Lot 1)	15Israel Turner, Abraham Vanhooser*, George Churchill, +	14Ignatius Anderson, Cleveland Hagler*, John Hagler*, +	13Robert G. Anderson, John Lindley*, Daniel Reece, Valentine Vanhooser
19Rivers Cormack, Joshua Rentfro, Elijah Renshaw, James Mason, Milton Hall, +	20Abraham Vanhooser, James Watt, John Conlee, Daniel Rece	21David Samples, Luther Druny, John Edwards, James Mason, +	22Harden Warren, Hardy Warren, Charles McMicken*, +	23 Laban Smart, John Wright, Valentine Vanhooser*, +	24 William Kingston*, William Parkison, +
30 William H. Bradsby *, William Hall	29 Daniel Reece *, William Hall, Abraham Vanhooser	28 multiple names 40 acre parcels	27 Robert Armstrong, +	26Joshua Armstrong *, John Briscoe, George Bridges	25 Joshua Armstrong, Curry Barnett, Mathias Chelton, William L. May, Green P. Rice
31 David Moore *, Samuel Winson	32William Baird, Absolom Baker, Job Robinson, +	33 Charles McMicken +	34Norman William*, John Riggen, Charles McMicken, James Mason +	35 John Briscoe, Abraham Kingston*, Simon Linley	36 William L. May, Joshua Armstrong, Andrew St. John Robert White

Wagon makers: Thomas S. Smith, Aaron Smith, Thomas Deck, John Rieser, William Roberts

There were stagecoach drivers, teamsters and wagon makers.

Troy continued its gradual growth during the next decade. It was officially incorporated as a village on February 18, 1857. The inhabitants brought more industry and small shops, but farming was still the main business in the township. Also, Troy's men fought in the Civil War during the 1860s. (See military section.)

Central Europeans came by boat up the Mississippi River to this area. In 1870, Troy had a surveyor – James M. Anderson; Sophie Kerns, a midwife; druggists David Pauchet and William T. Donohoe; physicians E.R. Owens, John Dewey, and Labin Franklin. Troy also boasted four broom makers and one ingineer (probably engineer). The village also had traders, manufacturers, merchants, five shoemakers, four teachers and one minister.

Muddy roads often caused wagons and stagecoaches to become mired. They did not hinder the growth of Troy which had a population of 650 in 1880. Of the foreign nativity, 100 were from the German area; six, England; 14, Ireland; one, Scotland; one, Holland; three, France; and 20 from Switzerland. Three hundred eighty-eight were born in Illinois, with the remaining 117 born within the United States.

Residing in Troy were 10 farmers with 15 farm workers and three retired farmers, but the other farmers resided on their farms in Jarvis and Pin Oak Townships.

Some women were noted as having specific occupations and some unusual occupations were recorded in the census. (Troy Genealogical Society has microfilm of all censuses for Troy.)

Occupation	Name
Hotelkeeper/ Johnson House	Johnson, Sarah
Post Mistress	Johnson, Mattie
Flour packers	Williamson, Robert
	Vetter, William
	Risby, Charles
Seamstress	Waldel, Sarah
	Burk, Mary
Dressmaker	Kersey, Sarah
Broom maker	Peterman, William S.
Huxters	Miller, Fred
	Caswell, Orson
Hemp maker	Polzaldt, Mosetz

Civilization was beginning to come to the area. Census records reflect the change in the lifestyles of Troy citizens. Blacksmiths were still needed but not as many harness makers, saddlers, stagecoach drivers, and wagon makers. Churches and schools now existed and needed personnel. Thrashing was a big business.

Immediately south of Troy was Brookside Village. There were seven households of 35 persons in 1880. They include the families of Milbank, Candell, Mulvany, Miller, Clepper, Frendman, Jorden, Moore and Hale.

Troy was incorporated as a city on April 12, 1892. By 1900 Troy had over 1,080 persons living within its city limits.

Occupation	Name
Boarding House	Wild, Eliza
Boarding House	Wreston, Martha
Dressmakers	Riebold, Kate
	Riebold, Rose
Huckster	Morgan, Mathew and his 2 sons
Milleners/Milliner	Grainger, Cora
	Kiesel, Lizzie
	Kiesel, Mary
	Houston, Lorinda
Music Teachers	Gerfin, Martha
	Jones, Ollie
	Risser, Maggie
Tinners	Gebaur, John
	Hampe, William
Type Writer	Kingston, Grace
Washer Women	Echerman, Alberta
	Kuch, Achura
	Melchoire, Mary
Well Digger	Peterman, Mackdon

One-third of the population was not born in Illinois, and 1 out of 10 were foreign born. The railroad had encouraged several immigrants to settle here. (See transportation section.) An equal number of taverns and schools was now present. Wood choppers were needed for clearing the land and constructing buildings for industry and more substantial houses.

Still a small city in the twentieth century, Troy continued its slow growth with small business and industry. Farming was still a major business and influenced the type of business that would flourish in Troy. In 1910, the railroad still employed a great number of Troy residents as did the local mines.

Occupation	Name
Drs. Office bookkeeper	Hagar, Irma
Milliner	Wilkinson, Rose
	Brown, Della C.
	Schotemayor, Mary
Tailoress	Hoope, Louise J.
Dressmaker	Kueker, Linda R.
	Bohland, Minnie
Sewer	Fressel, Rika
Asst. Postmaster	Millett, Lula F.
Boarding house keeper	Peters, May L.
	McGeachin, Sarah
Music teacher	Davis, Ruth B.
	Gerfen, Martha
Hack & drage	Purviance, George
	Purviance, James F.
Thresher/trvelinman	Friesland, Charles
Electric light plant	Sapp, Elmer
Contractor Emp.	Hindmarch, James E.
Rocket storekeeper	Snodgrass, Ouston

Coal Miners Living in Troy in 1910

Weaver, Peter
Morgan, Thomas D.
Morgan, Hopkins
Thomas, David
Thomas, William
Norbury, William
McDaniels, Henry
Norbury, John
Houston, Moroni
Norbury, Thomas
Walker, Dorice E.
Young, Ephraim
Kelly, Charles B.
Johnson, Moses
Worsman, James
Mederall, Frank S.
Cook, James
Evans, Joshua
Ramshell, William
Ramshell, William
Ramshell, Thomas
Monroe, George E.
Watts, John
Monroe, Walter
Llewellyn, Wm. S.
Llewellyn, Morgan
Pax, Herman
Bonsino, Frank
Jonina, Mike
Makovisa, James
Makovisa, Tony (age 16)
Morrow, Wm.
Heck, William
Heck, Conard
Smith, Charles
McCam, Forbus
Cazyhonni, Frank
DeBass, Henry
Chaystal, Otto
Mantle, Robert H.
Mantle, Charles
Hoenig, William L.

Rieder, Joe H.
Rarick, Philip W. (Manager)
Rarick, Philip J.
Horsley, Herbert W.
Porter, James A.
Frangon, Peter P.
Frangon, Wm. A.
Housman, August
Hess, Fred T.
Davis, James H.
Samuels, Henery
Wells, Wm.
Bernadine, Lav.
Healey, Wm.
Wilde, Albert E.
Horsley, Arthur R.
Hanke, Edward L.
Davis, Samuel
Wood, Wm.
Joseph, Edgar B. (blacksmith)
Neubaauer, Julius E.
Beutel, August, Jr.
Beutel, Joseph
Beutel, August
Wise, Philip
Campbell, Fred
Naylor, Thomas
Ward, Ralph
Ward, Herman
Schress, Charles
Ruff, John F.
Hampton, Earnest
Beboher, Henry
Bohnenstiehl, John A.
Lewis, William
Schroeder, William
Rother, Frank
Wilkinson, Walter
Wilkinson, John T.
Howgate,
Wilkinson, Percy
Tilly, William
Williams, Joe
Onselma, Andreas
Onselma, John
Domnich, C.
Combato, Matt
Ferdinand, Count
Andrews, Don C.
Monroe, William
Capelle, Paul
Myers, Arthur W.
Eiffert, Fred E.
Higgins, Thomas
Strong, A.
Hager, John L.
Hazzard, John
Bennett, Wm. L. (engineer)
Morgan, Solomon
Frame, Hugh (blacksmith)

Oreland, Charles
Capell, Alfred
Warner, Richard (engineer)
Guennewig, John
MacChanny, John
Peterman, John S. (carpenter)
Peterman, James R.
Nichols, John
Watson, Huey
Waldon, Axel
McKenna, John
Janchoi, Peter
Fesiro, John
Fellra, Joe
Canotto, Orstengo
Travasso, Joe
Cobetto, James
Rovetto, John
Schlott, Joe .
Maletz, Frank
Wild, Paul B.
Pg 20
Voelker, John A.
Allen, Milton A.
Belk, Elmar W.
Scott, Peter
Scott, James
Scott, William W.
Taylor, James
Vethmar, Charles
Vethman, Frederick C.
Vethmar, John (age 16)
Henderson, Robert
Taylor, James A.
Coons, Vinson
O'Conor, Martin
Riley, John
Liskey, Martin
Magilnski, Toney
Kegias, Joseph
Bolakonia, John
Davis, Mathews
Poleto, Charles
Bernini, Onuxi
Burniski, Toney
Grasman, John W.
Grasman, Patrick
Shankehi, Stan C.
Davis, David
Snodgrass, George
Elliott, Charles
Hultz, Charles
Hanke, Henry
May, S.
Andrews, Michel
Maden, Henry
Maden, Walter
Schliman, Fred
Carner, Frank
Coms, Lewis W.

Bothard, Fred
Bothard, August J.
Boston, James
Boston, Ralph D.
Boston, James
Barnes, Ellis L.
Samuel, John H.
Schotemayor, Henry
Schotemayor, Henry
Kinder, Lester M. (Foreman)
Kinder, Nelson R. (engineer)
McIntosh, John
Fritts, John W.
Snodgrass, Lawrence
Faires, Edward
Jones, Daniel G.
Ruff, William J.
Wild, William H.
Farnsworth, Moody
Carona, John
Primm, John
Fullers, Harry
Mick, Gottlieb H.
Chapman, Thomas
Wood, Henry H. (Foreman)
Giger, George, A.
Maxfield, Richard E.
Peters, McDonnel
Fegge, Louis H.
Beute, William
Snodgrass, Frank
Schlichtung, John
Frost, Alexander
Renfro, Rome
Jones, John T.
Jones, John T.
Horsley, George
Peyla, Jos.
Peyla, Albert
Raush, Charles
Lewis, Francis
McCormick, James
McCormick, Duncan
Winter, William

These miners lived in Troy or stayed at the hotel. Some married Troy girls and became active citizens. They built homes, attended church, joined organizations and helped to develop the uniqueness that is Troy.

Newspaper articles give a glimpse into the activities of the inhabitants of early Troy: in 1895, the city council met and approved dramshop bonds for Wm. Meiners, Julius Barth, August Peters and E.J. Lambert; land transfers; Vandalia Railroad Time Table for Troy Station; notices of societies' meetings, births, weddings, funerals, and accidents; Opera House performances;

announcements, such as, to parents to go to Jarvis' Grove during school hours and they would have the pleasure of meeting their own boys smoking cigarettes and chewing tobacco; and winners of the horse race held at the Troy Race Track.

Growth in Troy was slow at first. However, by the mid 1840s, its designation as a stagecoach stop provided the city with revenue and importance. Several mills operated in the 1850s, and the town was incorporated in 1857.

In the June 20, 1895, issue of the *Troy Call*, a reporter had stated, "…We would urge more of those wishing to locate in a city to look at the sites and locations here. We have as good building locations as any city of equal size; our taxes are low, and with good railroad facilities, cheap coal and all necessities of life Troy is as good a place to live as any in the world."

Eventually, people heeded his advice, for the population grew steadily in the following decades of the 20th century. New businesses and occupations were listed on the census every 10 years, showing how the citizens and their needs changed. By 1978 the Troy area was the 3rd fastest growing area in the United States. Its population increased 52 percent between 1970 and 1980.

At the beginning of the 21st century, Troy continues to develop and expand. New businesses open monthly, new subdivisions house a growing population, and the city often offers new services to its residents. Perhaps the quote from the 1895 *Troy Call* should be updated.

"We would urge those who wish to relocate to look at the sites and locations here. We have as good subdivisions and building sites as any city of equal size; our taxes are usually comparable to other towns our size; and with good interstate facilities nearby, Metrolink within a short drive, and two airports close by; fairly inexpensive utilities, and all the necessities of life, Troy is as good and convenient place to live as any in the world."

A Partial Bibliography of Troy

History of Madison County, Illinois. Edwardsville, IL: W. R. Brink & CO., 1882.

Centennial History of Madison County, Illinois and Its People, 1812 to 1912. Edited and compiled by W. T. Norton. Chicago: The Lewis Publishing Company, 1912.

Gazetteer of Madison County… Alton, IL: James T. Hair, 1866.

The Prairie State: A Documentary History of Illinois Colonial Years to 1860. Edited by Robert P. Sutton. Grand Rapids, MI: Wm. B. Eerdmans Publ. Co., 1976.

Edwardsville Intelligencer.

Madison County Genealogical Society Stalker. The Society, 1982.

The Armies and the Leaders. Edited by Francis Trevelyan Miller. New York: Castle Books, 1957.

Howard, Robert P. *Illinois: A History of the Prairie State.* Grand Rapids, MI: Wm. B. Eerdmans Publ. Co., 1972.

Various United States Federal Census from the National Archives.

The following Troy newspapers (microfilm copies), provided by the Troy Historical Society, are located in the Tri-Township Public Library District.

• *Weekly Call*
• *Troy Weekly Call*
• *Troy Call*
• *Times-Tribune*
• *The Troy Tribune*
• *The Troy Times*
• *Times-Tribune*

An Early History of Pin Oak Township

Pin Oak Township got its name from a grove of Pin Oak trees in Section 16. In the early days about half the land was timber and all of it would have been, except for the frequent prairie fires. With the increase of settlers and the consequent check of the fires, new groves of timber sprang up and flourished. Silver Creek and its branches flow through the township. Mainly an agricultural township covered with fertile farms, Pin Oak is bound on the north by Hamel Township, on the east by Marine Township, on the south by Jarvis Township and on the west by Edwardsville Township.

Joseph Bartlett, along with pioneers Lockhart and Taylor, were reputed to be the first settlers. They came in 1808 and began improvements in 1809. Bartlett became the first assessor and treasurer of Madison county, served in the War of 1812 and, also, in the Black Hawk War. Service in wars was common among pioneers as they had to defend their new homes or lose them.

Jubilee Posey, a native of Georgia, came in 1811 as a youth and lived to an advanced age. He provided a log cabin for the first school which was taught by Mr. Atwater.

Paul Beck came prior to 1812 and built a blockhouse and established a horse mill, which he later sold to George Coventry, an Englishman who came from Kentucky in 1813. This place and other adjacent lands were subsequently purchased by Gov. Edward Coles and remained in his possession until his death in 1868. In 1819 Coles, having freed his slaves, brought them to Pin Oak township and settled them on land he had purchased. He gave each adult male a quarter section. Among the slaves was "Uncle Bobby Crawford," a very able preacher who was renowned as a Christian among whites as well as blacks.

Other early residents were Thomas Barnett, Sylvanus Gaskill, Laban Smart, Col. Thomas Judy, James Tunnell, John Minter, Jacob Gonterman, Matthias and George Handlon, Samuel McKittrick, Edmund Fruit, James Keown, Thomas J. Barnsback, George Hutton, James Pearce, Alvis Hauskins and Robert McKee.

Today, Pin Oak Township is still mainly a farming area and does not have any incorporated towns. The nearest town is Troy, which is about 1/2 mile south of the Pin Oak and Jarvis Township line. Interstate 55 runs north and south and Interstate 70 runs east and west through the township. Illinois Route 143 runs east and west and Goshen Road, part of the old Goshen Trail, also runs east and west through the township. Bartlett Cemetery in Section 21 has burials from the early 1800s to the present.

Troy's Government

Troy was incorporated first as a town on February 18, 1857. It was organized as a village with the "Trustee" form of government. Elected trustees elected a "President" from among them.

In 1892, the "Town" was reorganized into a city, and the "Aldermanic" form of government was chosen. Since that time, a mayor and aldermen with ward responsibilities have been elected. That form of government exists today, subject to minor changes in State law.

Due to a fire in the early 1900s, a complete book of previous minutes was destroyed. But other records provide the following information.

(Left) Troy City Council, 1957. (l. to r.) Seated: Clerk Carl Embrey, Mayor Oscar Gindler and Alderman Leroy Flath. Standing: Alderman Robert Sliva, Alderman Joe Nemnich, Water Commissioner Harold Gaertner, Alderman Myrl York, Marshal Gus Suter, Alderman Walter Lauer and City Attorney Arthur Wendler.

(Right) Troy Municipal Building, 116 East Market, 2002.

Troy City Council, 1992. (l. to r.) Front: Alderman Sam Italiano, Mayor Velda Armes and Clerk Mary Chasteen. Back: Bud Klaustermeier, Public Works Supt.; Alderman Robert Dawson; Alderman Ron Schultze; Alderman Joe Lanahan; Treasurer David Roady; Alderman Dave Lauer; and Alderman Charles Nolan.

Troy City Council, Officials, and Dept. Heads, 2002. (l. to r.) Seated: Alderman Susan McTaggert, Ward I; Alderman Jay Evans, Ward II; Alderman Sam Italiano, Ward II; Mayor Tom Caraker Sr.; Tammy Mitchell, City Clerk; Alderman Rollie Reiss, Ward III; Alderman G.J. Lanahan, Ward III; and Alderman Jeff Soland, Ward IV. Standing: Police Chief William Brown; Treasurer David Roady; City Administrator Russell "Bud" Klaustermeier; Attorney Steve Wigginton; Keith Frey, Building and Zoning Superintendent; Robert Obernuefemann, Street Superintendent; Alan Secrest, Water and Sewer Superintendent; and Alderman Duane Hughes, Ward IV. Not pictured: Alderman Larry Tessaro, Ward I.

Mayors of Troy

Mayor Nelson Kinder

Mayor John Kelly, Sr.

Mayor David Rees

Mayor Rollie R. Moore

Mayor Carl Taake

Mayor Velda Armes

Mayor Oscar Edward Gindler

Mayor Ron Criley

Mayor Tom Caraker, Sr.

Presidents of the Board and Mayors

John Padon	(1857)
J.F. Clepper	(1892)
J.J. Brown	(1893-1894)
Elias Burk	(1895-1898)
S.W. Rawson	(1899-1902)
F.F. Miller	(1903-1904)
H. Stolte	(1905-1906)
F.W. Braner	(1907-1908)
C. Busse	(1909-1911)
Wm. Beutel	(Pro-Tem) (1912)
N.R. Kinder	(1913-1914)
James H. Davis	(1915)
W.J. Vetter	(1916)
George Liebler	(1917-1918)
R.L. Dawson	(1919-1924)
F.J. Michael	(1925-1926)
Thos. Millett	(1927-1928)
R.L. Dawson	(1929-1932)
John Kelly	(1933-1934)
Dave Rees	(1935-1936)
George Liebler	(1937-1948)
Rollie Moore	(1949-1952)
Oscar Gindler	(1953-1965)
Carl Taake	(1966-1980)
Ron Criley	(1981-1988)
Velda Armes	(1989-1997)
Tom Caraker Sr.	(1997- present)

U.S. Post Office in Troy

The U.S. Post Office for this community was originally established as Ridge Prairie on March 21, 1833. The name was changed to Troy on March 23, 1844. The Troy office changed from 4th class to Presidential shortly before January 30, 1905.

The Post Office was located at various buildings in Troy. It was at 107 East Market for many years, then moved to North Main Street into a

Postal Carrier Marcel Gebhart, 1972

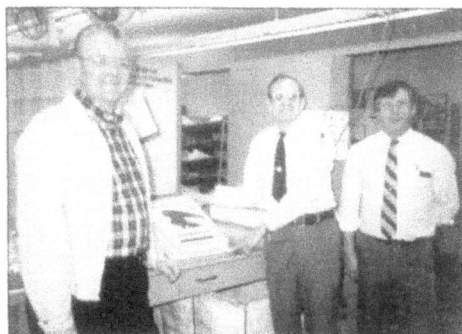

(l. to r.) Virgil "Pete" Gebhart, retired post-master; Marcel Gebhart; Don Way, postmaster, March 1990

new building in 1962 and from there to its current location on Edwardsville Road.

Information for this article provided by the Post Office Department (information after 1920), Troy Postmaster Donald Way (list) and a June 1994 issue of the Times-Tribune.

Troy Postmasters

George Churchill	Mar. 21, 1833
Thomas J. Brady	Aug. 16, 1842
John Brady	Apr. 28, 1843
Moses Bardsley	June 19, 1844
Thomas McDowell	Sept. 18, 1845
Michael Walsh	Dec. 8, 1846
Thomas Faherty	Aug. 23, 1847
John Wood	Dec. 16, 1847
Julius S. Barnsback	Jan. 9, 1850
William P. Renfro	Mar. 20, 1854
James A. Henderson	Mar. 29, 1855
James B. Edgar	Aug. 5, 1856
Caleb Johnson	Apr. 9, 1861
Miss Mattie Johnson	Jan. 20, 1875
Henry A. Risser	Feb. 25, 1889
Austin R. Snodgrass	Apr. 16, 1889
Samuel S. Avis	July, 1893
Marion W. Powell	July 27, 1897
Thomas Millett, Jr.	Jan. 30, 1905
August Droll	July 10, 1913
Fred L. Mosimann	Aug. 29, 1919
Fred S. Edwards	Nov. 15, 1919
Edward J. Wise	May 13, 1930
James Wheeler Davis	Nov. 6, 1933
Mrs. Myrtie Schmitt	June 30, 1953
Virgil Gebhart	Dec. 31, 1966
Donald Way	Jan. 14, 1989–current

Postal Employees, 112 N. Main Street, 1995

(Above) Troy Post Office, 112 N. Main Street, 1995

(Left) U.S. Post Office in Troy, 515 Edwardsville Road, June 16, 1997

Utilities
Electricity

Troy had its own electrical plant at one time; it was located on the east side of Main Street, across from the south end of the City Cemetery. It was started about 1892. On August 8, 1916, an election was held to ask the voters' permission to sell the power plant; 206 were in favor and 90, against. Bids were taken and Southern Illinois Light and Power was the only bidder at $6,100. The bid was accepted at the November 13, 1916, meeting. They not only purchased property, but also received a franchise to operate in the City of Troy.

Water

At the insistence of the Troy Commercial Club, the acting engineer of the state water survey of the University of Illinois came to Troy to investigate the possibility of securing an adequate and sanitary water supply in September 1916. In June 1933, a petition was presented to the City Council for a Water Works. On February 4, 1935, an agreement between the city and the Federal Public Works Administration was signed. On March 4, 1935, $65,000.00 in bonds was sold to pay for the city's portion of the work. The WPA's portion of the cost was $35,000.00. Water service was secured from Collinsville, and in 1954 Troy dug its own wells below the Collinsville bluffs, along Route 157.

Telephone Service

On March 24, 1897, the City of Troy passed Ordinance # 29, granting to the Central Union Telephone Company the right to maintain poles, wires, and fixtures in the City of Troy. Ordinance #44, on January 16, 1901, granted to the Kinloch Long Distance Company, the right to operate in the City of Troy. Ordinance #120 on September 17, 1913, gave the right to operate in the City of Troy.

The phone company was located on the second floor of the Braner Building. The first ads in the *Troy Call* with phone numbers were published in December 1909. In October 1916, Martin Arth sold the phone company to E.N. Michael of St. Jacob. The company had 236 subscribers, including 10 country lines. The phone company had direct connection with long distance lines of both the Bell and Kinloch systems. In 1920 F.J. Michael took over the telephone system from his father and on March 1, 1927, sold the system to Edwin C. Frey. The system was housed on the second floor of the Braner Building and had 427 phones and 11 country lines. His son, Clarence Frey, and Eno Petry were the linemen, and plant repairs were underway. Miss Lula Hoppe was the chief operator during the early stages of the phone company.

During the Depression in the 1930s, it was necessary to metallize the phone lines. The next improvement was to convert the entire plant to common battery. In 1940 a new building was built, and new inside equipment was installed.

Clarence Frey purchased the phone company from his father Edwin in 1941. The telephone operators were Lucille Auwarter, Irene Marchiando, Chloe Riley, Marie Dollinger, Florence Guennewig, and Bert Dettmar. Vera Buehlman was clerk, and Leroy Flath, lineman.

Clarence Frey, Troy Telephone Company, 1940s-1950s.

On May 11, 1951, dial phones began. Troy had dial phones before Collinsville and a large part of East St. Louis had them. At first, Troy only used 4 digits; then the exchange was Normandy, then Normandy 7, which converts to 667, the current phone exchange.

Mrs. Charles (Mae) Hanks made the first telephone call to her mother, Mrs. Ethel Capelle. The second call was made by Arthur H. Minor to Louis Smith, and the first incoming toll call was made to Wilbur (Mick) Wyatt. On May 17, 1957, Illinois Bell took over the system, which was then sold to Ameritech, which merged with Southwestern Bell.

Troy Police

The origin of the Troy Police Department is not precisely known, but "City Marshals" are named from time to time in news articles and on the federal census. In the early years they were called "City Marshals"– they most certainly were one-man departments – and, they were "on foot." One, Paul Taylor, is given credit for apprehending a thief in the 1920s and Earl Young apparently duplicated that in the 1930s with a different thief. In the second instance, the thief was turned over to Deputy Sheriff Deimling, also from Troy, for incarceration in the Madison County Jail.

Several life-long Troy residents remember Marshal Earnest Spencer in the late '30s and '40s who used only a bicycle

Troy Police Force, May 15, 1969. (l. to r.) Front: Cadets Steve Howe, Tom Guennewig, Bill Rapien and Vic Diepholz. Back: Gus Emmer, Juvenile Officer; Bill Pahl, John Wendzinsky, George Opolka, Dick Rogier, "Ike" Chasteen, Tony Caruso and Police Chief Bob Gereau.

Troy Police, 1977. (l. to r.) Mayor Carl Taake, Police Comm. Gus Emmer, Terry Brookman, Steve Howe, Norris Lutz, Chief Clarence Quinley, Sherman Boaz, Charles Wooliver and Brian Turley.

Troy Police Force. (l. to r.) Front: Chief Bob White, Tony Caruso, John Wendzinsky and Sherman Boaz. Back: Bill Pahl, George Opolka, Dick Rogier, Ike Chasteen and Ron Criley.

to keep the town free of crime. These memories center around a bit of a game — where false alarms, it seems, were alternately phoned in from opposite ends of town to see how many "laps" Marshal Spencer could do.

Walter Kurtz was the first Troy police officer to be uniformed and have a police car. The car was equipped with a radio for receiving police calls. He began his duties when he was appointed in 1949 to succeed Bob Henderson. A life-long

Walter Kurtz, age 60, 1950s.

Troy Police Department, 1990. (l. to r.) Front: Linda Lee, Kyle Geiger, Janet Alexander, Kathy Schroeter, Pam O'Donald, Pat Michaels, Pat Take and Chief Bob Noonan. Back: Rob Luttrell, Tom Recklein, Bill Brown, Kevin Woodring, John Carter, Bob Rizzi, Clarence Jackson and Charles Wooliver.

Troy Police Department, 2002. (l.to r.) Front: Chris Wasser, Patrolman; Chris Coyne, Detective; Michelle Schneider, Administrative Assistant; Pat Take, Telecommunicator; Linda Lee, Telecommunicator; Donna Markovich, Telecommunicator; Joe Girolamo, Telecommunicator. Back: Lenny Paparigopoulos, Patrolman; Bob Radosevich, Sergeant; Bill Brown, Police Chief; Charles Wooliver, Lieutenant; Robert Rizzi, Lieutenant; Rob Luttrell, Sergeant; Bud Jackson, Patrolman; James Newcombe, Patrolman; Brent Shownes, Patrolman; and Ryan Meier, Patrolman. Not pictured: Kevin Woodring, Patrolman.

Troy Police Department Special Reaction Team (SRT), circa 1999. (l. to r.) Front: Ryan Meier, Derek Davis and Sgt. Rob Luttrell. Back: Lt. Charles Wooliver, Lenny Paparigopoulos, Todd Huseky, Sgt. Bob Radosevich and Lt. Bob Rizzi.

Police Building, Kimberlin Street – used before move to City Hall in 1995.

16 years for the state highway department prior to being Troy's Police Chief.

The following men have been Troy's Police Chiefs: Walter Kurtz, Bob White, Bob Gereau, Norman Brown, Clarence Quinley (1974-1989), Bob Noonan (1989-1997) and present Police Chief Bill Brown.

The City of Troy has always provided its citizens with the best crime prevention by supporting the growth of its police department in accordance with the population's growth and demands, from primitive offices to a state-of-the art police office and jail in the new City Hall building.

Neighborhood Watch Program

A Neighborhood Watch Program was set up by residents in Troy and encouraged by the City of Troy in the late 1990s. They erected signs drawing attention to the program.

Troy Volunteer Fire District

According to early records, Troy did not have an organized fire department before 1884. That year fire did extensive damage to the business district and a residential area, and from that time forward, Troy has supported increasingly

resident of Troy area and an active civic leader, he served as the Republican committeeman for Jarvis Precinct Two. He was born on a farm between Troy and St. Jacob and spent his boyhood there. He married a member of the Busse family of Troy, and they had two sons, Dale and Homer. Walter worked

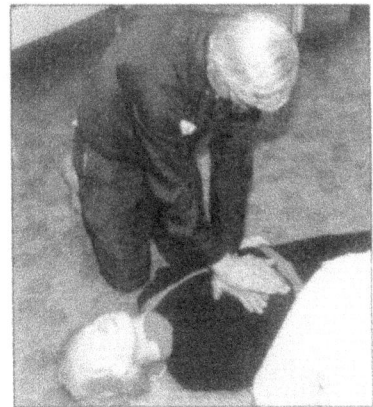

During a 1982 emergency service training of "Annie, Annie, Are You All Right?" George Schmerbauch is performing the life-saving practice.

15

Jule Smith in the first motorized Troy Fire Truck in the 1920s.

1927 Reo driven by Oscar Gindler in 1974 Troy Homecoming Parade.

sophisticated fire fighting ability and equipment. Even then, early equipment was limited to 50-gallon tanks of water, on two-wheeled carts, pulled to a fire by humans.

In 1900, the firehouse stood on the southwest corner of Center and Main Streets. It had a pumper fire engine. Firemen lifted the lid from the cistern on the Town Square and used the water from it. The cistern was in the center of Main and Market Streets. It is still there, but was covered when the new road was paved over it.

About 1915, shortly after they became available, Troy purchased automotive equipment for the first time, a Ford Fire truck with two 25-gallon chemical tanks, from the Ameri-

New Engine 92 pulled out of the firehouse following a snow and ice storm in 1985.

can LaFrance Company. It cost $6,766, and the volunteer company of some 40 men, headed by Thomas Scott until 1920 and by Joe Scott until 1927, began to sponsor homecomings in order to pay for the equipment.

Hazel Riggin and Ed Helmich served successively as fire chiefs from 1927 to 1951 and Troy added four men to its roster.

In 1929, the department was allowed by the City Council to purchase a Reo midship truck, provided the fire-fighters would sponsor homecomings and pay the installments on the engine. The apparatus was thus acquired without cost to the city.

When the city gave the fire department one room of its new city hall in 1930, firemen renovated the room at no expense to the city, and they financed installation of three cisterns in different parts of Troy. The only cost to Troy was the $2.00 per man fee when fire-fighters turned out to fight a fire.

In 1953, Troy purchased a Dodge front mount pumper at the cost of $9,316. In 1957, the present fire district was formed to include 62 square miles. In 1959, the year that Lester Adelhardt was elected chief, ground was purchased for a new firehouse. Two years later, a 500-gallon International pumper was acquired for $17,000.

In 1962, the new firehouse was dedicated. Built at the cost of $40,000, volunteer firefighters financed and worked themselves to install the kitchen and its fixtures, the floor coverings for the meeting rooms and the painting of the building. Trustees for the new district were Arnold Langenwalter, John Meier and Ed Helmich.

During this period, the Troy department was called upon to fight two large commercial fires in town. The first occurred in 1966, the year after Roy Lewis was elected chief, at the Modern Linen Laundry building located on Laundry Street just south of Route 162. The second happened in 1977 at the

Old firehouse on Kimberlin Street, by the Reo truck, December 22, 1935. (l. to r.) Standing: Melvin Marti, Monk Linch, Charles Peters, John Kelly Jr., Les Norbury, Oscar Gindler, Ed Guennewig, Walt Thompson, Ed Wise, Dan Liebler, Herman Polwort, Earl Young, Harry Taake, Melvin Schoeck and Arthur Clark. In truck, David Rees (passenger) and Ed Helmich (driver).

New white firetruck, 1950. (l. to r.) Kneeling in front: Dave Sims, Ed Brendel, Bill Dunstan and Ray Druessel. Standing: Ed Guennewig, Oscar Gindler, John Kelly Jr., Bob Baglin, Carl Taake, Ed Lesicko, Bob Dunstan, Russ Wiesemeyer, Walter Kurtz, Burl Porter, Melvin Marti and Tony Mersinger. Back, standing on truck: Orville Hecht, Herman Hanke and Jack Taylor.

Troy Firefighters in front of fire house on Kimberlin Street, 1950s. (l. to r.) Front: Dan Liebler, Ed Guennewig, Henry Rees, Dave Sims, Roy "Shorty" Lewis and Carl Taake. Second row: Harry Taake, Ed Helmich, Walt Thompson, Ed Lesicko, Bob Baglin, John Kelly Jr., Melvin Marti, Walter Kurtz and Gus Suter. Back: Oscar Gindler, Bill Dunstan, Jack Taylor, Bob Dunstan, Russ Wiesemeyer, Herman Hanke and Tony Mersinger.

In new fire suits, 1970s. (l. to r.) Back: Tony Frey, George Schmerbauch, Jim Rood, Ray Druessel, Gus Suter, Lee Suter, Sam Kueker, Clarence Adelhardt, Owen Brendel and Rick Gibbs. Front: Leroy Flath, Bud Klaustermeier, Jim Laughlin, Alvin Loyet, Carl Strom, Bill Kueker, Herb Lochman, Harold Gaertner and Jack Taylor.

Kitson Craft Boat Factory on West Market Street. The fire required assistance from the Collinsville and Maryville departments.

In 1974, the Madison County Firefighters Association pension plan began. It had an initial enrollment of 803 men countywide. A four man pension board was established. Its first members included Les Adelhardt of Troy, Lynn Rhoades of Rosewood Heights, Robert Volz of Alhambra and Bill Meehan of Venice.

The Troy Fire Department acquired a 750-gallon Ford pumper in 1973, and walkie-talkies and a movie projector and screen for training in 1974. New firefighting gear was purchased in 1975, and in 1976 acquisitions included a four-wheel drive International pumper, rescue equipment, a porta power tool and memorial flags. In 1978, the department obtained an additional monitor and a walkie-talkie. In 1979, a 1500-gallon tanker truck was purchased; in 1980, an equipment truck; 1982, a 35mm camera and new dress uniforms; and in 1983, a video recorder and radio system.

Although Troy is a small rural town, its firefighters have been called frequently for mutual assistance. In 1979, the department was commended for its work during an ice storm. Troy also has been the scene of large fires. One occurred at a furniture company in 1980. Troy firefighters were assisted by firefighters from Collinsville and St. Jacob. In 1981, a fire at a Troy bowling alley necessitated mutual assistance from Edwardsville, Collinsville and St. Jacob.

In the 1990s, an addition to the fire station was built, giving more room in the bay area and enlarging the administrative office area. In 2001, the fire district acquired additional property, the old Henry Stolte house, to the west of the firehouse, for future expansion.

In 2000, the Troy Volunteer Fire Department received a Class 4 Rating. The department's upgrading to Class 4 was for the superb work of the department firefighters, for the water supply and other operations of the Troy Department.

Information for this story was taken from Serving Together: 150 Years of Firefighting in Madison County, Illinois *written by Betty Richardson and Dennis Henson, and from Troy firefighters' recollections.*

Troy Volunteer Fire Department, 1992. (l. to r.) Seated: Trustees Dennis Petry, Walter Brunworth and Darwin Meier. Front row: James Rood, James Hampton, James Laughlin, Bud Klaustermeier, Leonard Baumgartner, Carl Strom, Gene Fayollat, Ken Lanahan, Bill Brown, Bill Kueker, Jim Simon, Lloyd Wood and Kevin Byrne. Back row: Lonnie Meier, George Schmerbauch, Ron Schultz, Lee Suter, Jim Krotz, Ron Boullion, Brian Huston (partially hidden), Sam Italiano, Dennis Bauer, Jim Brenkendorf, Fred Gilomen and Jim Grapperhaus.

2001 Troy Firefighters: Jim Hampton, chief; Tim Byrne, assistant chief; Rick McCurdy, assistant chief; John Ansley, captain; Dan Gonzalez, captain; Bob Hancock, captain; Bob Obernuefemann, captain; Scott Lochmann, captain; Dennis Bauer, Greg Becherer, Preston Becker, J Bryon Cook, Fred Gilomen, Dale Grapperhaus, Curt Klaustermeier, Jim Krotz, Kevin Manso, Paul McAllister, Paul Noll, Mike Pardue, Mike Rose, George Schmerbauch, Alan Siegrist, Jim Simon, Ed Smith and Ed Whittington. Not pictured: Justin Byrne, Roy Jarman, Harvey Meier, Alan Rose, Rich Saia and Ken Wiegmann.

Trojan Bowl fire on a very cold night in January 1980.

Hayman's Restaurant fire in August 1982.

Troy City Garage

Old City Garage, 1993.

The old Troy City Garage was located on the east side of Kimberlin Street prior to the Troy City Hall renovation. The bays faced Kimberlin Street and to the right was the side of the city hall. The building was the former Porter Garage.

In 2002, the city garage is located on Center Street.

Jarvis Township Road District

The township and the road district are two separate entities. Two separate meetings are held each month for each district. The road commissioner's job is to oversee all the work for the township roads including oiling and chipping, snow

Road Commissioner James Grapperhaus with wife Mae in new truck, 1999.

plowing, cleaning road storm damage, cleaning ditches and doing many other chores that are included in the job.

Several of the road commissioners are named as follows: John Schmitt, John Brendel, Norman Brendel, Henry Wilhelm,

Old Jarvis Township Road District Maintenance Garage, Collinsville Road, 1970s. In the 1980s, salt and cinder bays added.

Jarvis Township Road District crew by road grader inside new highway maintenance garage, 2002. (l. to r.) Phil Poletti, Ty Taake, Dan Broska and Jim Grapperhaus, commissioner. In cab, Dale Grapperhaus, foreman.

Road crew with trucks in front of the new Jarvis Township Road District Highway Maintenance Garage, located 7915 Collinsville Road, 2002. (l. to r.) Jim Grapperhaus, commissioner; Dale Grapperhaus, foreman; Dan Broska, laborer; Ty Taake, laborer; and Phil Poletti, part-time laborer. Part time laborer Alan Poletti was not present for the photo.

Henry Mannz and James H. Grapperhaus.

Grapperhaus is the longest running road commissioner in the history of the township, having been appointed in 1977 to fulfill the term of Henry Mannz, who resigned to take a full time rural mail carrier's position. Grapperhaus has been elected for six terms. In 2002, he is currently the Jarvis Township Road Commissioner. His full time road crew includes Dale Grapperhaus, foreman; Dan Broska and Ty Taake.

The information for this story was researched from the Jarvis Township Records and the Troy newspaper.

Jarvis Township Road District new Maintenance Facility, 2002. (l. to r.) Virgil Gebhart, trustee; Wayne Brendel, trustee; Jim Grapperhaus, Road Commissioner; and Alan Dunstan, township supervisor.

Troy City Cemetery, South Main, 2000. (l. to r.) Mayor Tom Caraker, and Troy Historical Society members Reba Mathis and Pat Huck.

- Gindler Cemetery
- Hall Cemetery
- Harris Cemetery
- Hoenig Family Cemetery
- Langenwalter Cemetery
- Loyet Cemetery
- Metz Cemetery
- Riggin Cemetery
- Schmidt Family Cemetery
- St. Jerome Catholic Cemetery
- St. John the Baptist Catholic Cemetery
- St. John Evangelical Cemetery (new)
- St. John Evangelical Cemetery (old)
- St. Paul Lutheran Cemetery
- Troy Cemetery
- Watt Cemetery
- Widicus Cemetery
- Wittman Cemetery
- Wood Cemetery

Area Cemeteries
Troy City Cemetery

The Troy City Cemetery was first established in 1849 and has served as a tranquil final resting place for many Troy citizens, including the McCray and Dewey families, donors of McCray-Dewey High School land, along with many military veterans and their families.

For many years, annual Memorial Day Celebrations were held here.

In 2000, the first formal identification sign was erected! Money through a tourism grant enabled the Troy Historical Society to have the sign made and the city installed it.

Jarvis Township, Madison County, Illinois, Cemeteries

- Bohnenstiehl Family Cemetery
- Canteen Creek Baptist Church Cemetery
- Edwards/Lemen-Edwards Cemetery
- Fehmel Family Cemetery
- Friedens United Church of Christ Cemetery
- Gilead Cemetery

Pin Oak Township, Madison County, Illinois, Cemeteries

- Bartlett Cemetery
- Daugherty Cemetery
- Fruit Cemetery
- Hagler Cemetery
- Hamilton Cemetery
- Moller Cemetery
- Smart Cemetery

Maps and directions to both Jarvis Township and Pin Oak Township cemeteries can be found in the Historical/Genealogical Room at the Tri-Township Public Library.

Memorial Day Parade, South Main at entrance to Troy City Cemetery, circa 1950s.

Notable Leaders of the Past
Mary Chasteen, City Clerk

Mary Chasteen, 1991.

Mary Chasteen served as Troy City Clerk from 1983 to 2001. She was married to Leroy "Ike" Chasteen, who served on the Troy City Council at one time. They are the parents of three children. Ike passed away in the 1990s.

Mary noted upon her retirement that she had worked for three different administrations and Troy Mayors, Ron Criley, Velda Armes and Tom Caraker and enjoyed all the time she spent working in the capacity of city clerk. She noted also that she had seen many changes in those years and had experienced many different situations, some of which were quite humorous.

The Honorable George Churchill

George Churchill lived on Ridge Prairie west of Troy in 1817. He was well thought of and respected by most of the citizens in the area. He had been born in Hubbardton, Rutland County, Vermont, in 1789. At first, George learned the printing business in Albany, NY, and later worked as a journeyman in New York City. He came west via Pittsburg, Cincinnati, Louisville, and Shawneetown, from where he walked to Kaskaskia. As a printer, he later worked for the first newspaper printed in St. Louis.

Supposedly, the view of the Illinois prairies made him decide to be a farmer. He bought land in Township 3, Range 7, on which he lived the rest of his life. Eventually, he owned over 600 acres, paying ei-

ther $1.25 or $2 per acre. Churchill helped form an agricultural society in 1822. He served as secretary of the society, which disbanded after 3 years. Although the society lasted a brief time, it set a high standard for future societies. He set a high standard in all he did, including his appointment as Troy's first postmaster in 1833.

Churchill was both a farmer and a respected government official. He never actually ran for office, but did serve when elected. He was a state senator (1839-1843) and state representative (1823-1833, 1845-1847) for 16 years, longer than anyone before him. He was one of the most active opponents of the movement for the introduction of slavery into Illinois in 1824. His votes against the slavery issue so angered his opponents that he and Nicholas Hanson, a fellow assemblyman, were burned in effigy in Troy.

Churchill was a good student and a fine writer, and paid great attention to detail. He amassed a large collection of historical data, especially of the early history of the county and this part of the state. Unfortunately, his papers were lost in the great Chicago fire, having been sent there after his death. George had vast political knowledge, too. As a Senator, he made short 5 minute speeches, containing all that he thought needed to be said. His talent as a writer enabled him to draft a considerable number of the bills sponsored by his side of the house.

He remained a bachelor and, supposedly, had eccentric and peculiar habits. In physical appearance, he was unprepossessing. He reportedly had a sallow complexion, lackluster eyes, and a dull expression. However, his lack of physical attributes did not detract from his great knowledge, writing ability, and dedication to government service. His many positive character traits made him a valuable and well-liked citizen of early Troy.

Captain I.W. Cook

Captain I.W. Cook was Troy's candidate for State Senator in 1902. He attended the Madison County Republican Convention in Granite City to select delegates to the State's Congressional and Senatorial convention. Eleven delegates accompanied him from Jarvis Township, and the Rex Orchestra of Troy also went along, making the Lauff Hotel their headquarters. J.W. Gornet of Troy was chosen as one of the delegates to the senatorial convention and Charles Wandling was an alternate.

A total of 321 delegates attended the convention. Captain Cook felt confident that he would secure the nomination for State Senator, and indications were that he would win.

Captain Cook lived in what later became the Herman Hecht house (now the site of the Russell Wiesemeyer Community Center (home of Jarvis Township Senior Citizens) located at the Tri-Township Park.

More information on Captain Cook and the election could not be found before publication. *Information was taken from a 1902 issue of the* Troy Weekly Record.

Sheriff Edward R. Deimling

Edward R. Deimling was born in Troy and served as Madison County Sheriff from 1922 to 1926. After purchasing 15-1/2 acres in Maryville in 1912, he and his family resided there in a two-story home that he had built between 1915 and 1919. The cost of its construction was $8,000 to $10,000.

He lived in the Maryville home while he was the sheriff. For a good number of years, he and his brother, John Deimling of Troy, raised cattle and hogs on the 15-1/2 acres, then took them to Troy to John's butcher shop and butchered them for the sale of processed meat.

In 1923, Sheriff's Deimling's wife aided the Joe Nemnich Sr. family during their house fire while they resided in Edwardsville. Mrs. Deimling brought a blanket to keep little Charmion Nemnich, their daughter, warm while the fire was ablaze.

Edward R. Deimling died in July 1937. The family occupied the Maryville home until 1946. It was sold between 1946 and 1948 to a Granite City family who gave it to charity to be used as a Assembly of God Children's Home. It remained a Children's Home until the 1970s when the state changed children's home regulations. At that time the State of Illinois acquired it. It lay idle for several years.

In the early 1990s, the Village of Maryville purchased the house and grounds around it, then remodeled the house to accommodate the village offices. The offices moved into the building in 1994.

Information from Village of Maryville Comptroller Marvin Brussati, The Troy Call*, the Madison County Sheriff's Department and a resident's recollection.*

Alan J. Dunstan, Madison County Board Chairman, Jarvis Township Supervisor

Alan J. Dunstan,
Supervisor and County Board Chairman

Alan J. Dunstan began his political career in 1978, when he was elected City of Troy Alderman. He served in that capacity until 1980 when he was elected Madison County Board member. He was re-elected in 1982, 1986, 1990, 1992, 1996 and 2000. In 2002, he was elected Chairman of the County Board.

He was elected Jarvis Township Supervisor in 1985 and re-elected in 1989, 1993, 1997 and 2001. He was elected Democratic Precinct Committeeman and served from 1978 through 1996.

He is a former member of the County Democratic Executive Committee and has been a Madison County Deputy Registrar since 1976, registering more than 1,000 voters in Jarvis Township.

His education includes a BS Degree in Government, SIUE, specialization in state and local government; a BS Degree in Business Administration, SIUE, specialization in economics and post-graduate courses in marketing and economics, SIUE.

Ray Johnsen, Delegate

Ray Johnsen of Troy served as an elected delegate to the Illinois Constitutional Convention of 1966. That important upgrade was quickly adopted by the state and remains its working constitution today.

Ray Johnsen was a popular figure around Troy for many years, serving as editor of the *Troy Tribune* during much of the period the *Tribune* was being published by

Ray Johnsen, Delegate to Illinois Constitutional Convention, 1966

Paul Simon. After coming to Troy at the request of Paul Simon, Ray subsequently married Nancy Watson, daughter of Mr. and Mrs. James Watson, owners of Watson Lumber Company. Both genial and popular figures, Ray and Nancy quickly became "leading citizens," enjoying wide friendships and significant community contributions. Ray and Nancy raised Steve, Sue and Jimmy. The family followed Paul Simon to Washington, D.C. where Ray managed Paul's offices. Both are now retired.

Merrill Ottwein, State Senator

Merrill Ottwein and Grace, his wife, 1969.

Merrill Ottwein, who grew up on a farm just outside of Troy, won a surprise victory in a special election held to fill the office of State Senator of the 53rd District which was vacated by Paul Simon, who had become Lt. Governor. Friends before and after, it created an interesting situation. Paul was a Demo-

crat; Merrill, a Republican. As Lt. Governor, Paul Simon also became President of the Senate, presiding over most sessions.

Merrill and his family and hosts of friends succeeded with a grass roots campaign that used a theme of "People Power," creating an unorthodox person-to-person campaign that was nearly non-partisan, and where hosts of people, and often kids, helped out.

After an enlightening Senate session, Merrill had to run again in the fall general election, where he lost to Sam Vadalabene. He claims all was an incredible experience, and that he could surprise the other side only once!

The Honorable Philip J. Rarick

Justice Philip J. Rarick

The Honorable Philip J. Rarick, Justice of the Appellate Court of Illinois, Fifth Judicial District, was appointed as Justice of the Supreme Court on May 13, 2002 to fill the vacancy left by The Honorable Moses W. Harrison II, who retired September 4, 2002.

Born in Troy in 1941, Justice Rarick received his BA degree from Southern Illinois University and his law degree from St. Louis University. He engaged in private law practice in Collinsville from 1966 until 1975, during which time he served as City Attorney for the City of Collinsville, Township Attorney for Collinsville and Jarvis Townships and Assistant State's Attorney in Madison County.

Justice Rarick assumed judicial office in 1975 and served as Chief Judge of the Third Judicial Circuit from 1985 to 1987. He also served as presiding judge of the Criminal Division in Madison County from 1982 to 1985 and from 1987 to 1988. He served as a member of the Illinois Courts Commission from 1992 through 1999, and as an alternate member from 1999 to the present time (2002).

From 1987 to 2002 he served on the Executive Committee of the Illinois Judicial Conference, and as chairman of the Complex Litigation Study Committee from 1988 through 2001. In addition, he served on a number of other Judicial Conference committees.

He also served as a member of the Board of Directors of the Illinois Judges Association. He was elected to the Appellate Court, Fifth District, in 1988, and was retained in 1998. He has also served on the Industrial Commission Division of the Appellate Court since 1992. Judge Rarick has participated as a faculty member for numerous education conferences and regional seminars as well as new judges' seminars.

Justice Rarick resides in Troy with his wife, Janet. They have one son, P.J., and one granddaughter.

Paul Riebold, Jarvis Township Supervisor, County Board Member

Paul Riebold graduated from McCray-Dewey High School in 1942. He was active in various Troy and Madison County organizations before he was elected Madison County Board Member and Jarvis Township Supervisor, serving from 1961-1977.

While in office he served on various committees, including Madison County Animal Control, Silver Creek Development, Madison County Welfare Services, and Southwest Area Study Commission. He also acted as vice-president of the Illinois Association of County Board Members from 1972-1975 and presided as president of the Illinois Township Officials Association.

Paul Riebold, Supervisor and County Board Member

tion, Zone 1, from 1968-1972. *Information from Chris Riebold and Reata McAllister.*

Charmion Semanisin, City Clerk

City Clerk Charmion Semanisin, Retirement Party, 1982

Charmion (Nemnich) Semanisin went to work in the Troy Water Department under City Clerk Helen Pahl. When Helen retired, then Mayor Carl Taake appointed Charmion to the position of City Clerk. She served for 8 years, was elected twice and retired in 1982.

She was a cheerful presence in City Hall and a friend to everyone in town.

John M. Shimkus, U.S. Congressman for the 20th District

John M. Shimkus was born Feb. 21, 1958. He married Karen Muth in 1987, and they have 3 children. The family resides in Collinsville, where John is active in various community groups.

John was appointed to the U.S. Military Academy at West Point in 1976. After graduation, he trained as an Army Ranger and paratrooper, later serving in West Germany and in the U.S. Currently, he is a lieutenant colonel in the U.S. Army Reserves. In addition to his degree in general engineering from the Academy, he has also earned a teaching certificate and a master's degree in business administration from other institutions.

After teaching high school government and history for a while, he was elected a Collinsville Township Trustee in 1989. In 1990, he became the first Republican county office holder elected in 10 years when he defeated a 12-year incumbent to become Madison County Treasurer. On

U.S. Congressman John M. Shimkus

Nov. 5, 1996, John was first elected to Congress; he was re-elected in 1998 and 2000.

John serves on various Congressional committees and caucuses, helping to introduce and pass legislation beneficial to all Illinois citizens, as well as to all Americans. Among the legislation he has been involved with is the designation of 9-1-1 as a national emergency phone number, the TREAD Act, and legislation changing the nation's alternative fuel policy. He is also responsible for many local projects in the 20th District.

U.S. Senator Paul Simon

In 1948, at age 19, Paul Simon left Dana College in Nebraska to purchase the *Troy Tribune*. He bought the paper with a loan underwritten by the Lions Club, becoming the youngest editor-publisher in the nation.

In addition to the usual functions of a weekly hometown newspaper, Simon used the paper to expose violations of state gambling laws by syndicate gambling interests.

Senator Paul Simon, 1987

Unable to get local action, Simon paid a visit to Governor Adlai Stevenson, who sent the state police to shut down several of the offending establishments.

Simon was later called as a key witness to

Paul Simon, 1990

testify on February 24, 1951, before the U.S. Senate's Crime Investigating Committee. He eventually built a chain of 14 weeklies. At one point, a partner in the newspaper business was Alan Dixon, later a U.S. senator from Illinois. Simon sold the profitable chain in 1966 to devote his full time to public service and to writing.

He enlisted in the U.S. Army in 1951. He was assigned to the Counter Intelligence Corps. Simon spent most of his two years as a special agent for the unit along the Iron Curtain in Europe.

In 1953, he declared his candidacy for the Illinois House. Given virtually no chance of winning 1 of 2 Democratic nominations, Simon ended up first in a field of 3 with a 9000 vote margin. He later won the general election and was re-elected to the House in 1956, 1958, and 1960. He ran successfully for the Illinois Senate in 1962 and was re-elected in 1966. During his legislative career, he received the "Best Legislator" award of the Independent Voters of Illinois, during each session he served. In his General Assembly career, Simon won passage of 46 major pieces of legislation. He soon earned himself a reputation as a progressive member of the Legislature.

In 1968, Simon became the first and only lieutenant governor of Illinois elected with a governor of another political party. As lieutenant governor, he established leadership in an office long regarded as a figurehead post only. He became the state's unofficial "ombudsman," answering an estimated 50,000 citizen requests during his 4 year term. He worked diligently to make state government more responsive and efficient.

In 1972, Paul Simon entered the Illinois Democratic primary for governor against Dan Walker. He was supported by most party leaders, endorsed by every major newspaper in the state, and expected to win. He lost by 40,000 votes out of 1.5 million cast.

Paul Simon helped begin the Public Affairs Reporting program at Sangamon

State University in 1973. This program was for journalists interested in covering government. He also taught history and government there. During the spring semester of 1973, he lectured at Harvard University's John F. Kennedy Institute of Politics.

In November 1973, Simon announced his candidacy for the U.S. House of Representatives from the 24th District of Illinois. He was elected to Congress in 1974 and reelected 4 times. In 1982 he was elected as one of Illinois U.S. Senators, where he served until his recent retirement.

Although he now resides in Makanda, IL, and teaches at SIU-C, the Troy community still regards him as one of its own. The Victorian house that he and his family lived in on Market Street is still referred to by many as "the Simon house." Many long-time residents still remember him as the young editor of the *Troy Tribune.* The weekly paper is now the *Times-Tribune;* it often carries stories of Troy's Senator Paul.

President Harry S. Truman in Homecoming Parade

Former President Harry Truman was in the 1962 Troy Homecoming Parade.

The afternoon of the homecoming, Truman was in Highland speaking at the Democrat Day at the Madison County Fair. He was scheduled to be in Granite City that evening for another political function. When Mayor Oscar Gindler heard about Truman coming along Route 40 en route to Granite City, he arranged for Truman's entourage to be halted at Blue Haven Service Station at Bypass 40 (now Route 162) and Route 40 intersection.

Being led by Troy Police, Truman's entourage traveled along the bypass route instead

President Harry S. Truman, Troy Homecoming Parade, July 18, 1962.

of new Route 40 and joined in on the parade in progress as it was going west on Market Street. People lined the streets and stretched their necks to see the former U.S. President.

Charmion Semanisin was watching the parade near 110 West Market when he passed by. "Tell Bess hello," she said. Truman answered and looked her straight in the eye as he pointed to her and said, "I'll do that."

Mae Grapperhaus was at the square holding her four-month-old daughter, Laura, while Truman passed by. Grapperhaus thought at the time, "This is the first time I have ever seen a U.S. President and my daughter is seeing him, too."

State Senator Frank Watson

After serving four years in the House of Representatives, Frank Watson was elected to the State Senate in 1982. He currently serves as the assistant majority leader and serves on the Agriculture, Conservation, Education and Executive Committees. He has distinguished himself as an Illinois lawmaker, playing a vital leadership role in several important areas, including welfare reform, economic development, employment opportunities, and school reform. He has consistently fought for more funding for edu-

Senator Frank Watson

cation at all levels, and has sponsored and fought for legislation to improve rural health care and transportation.

Senator Watson is a graduate of Purdue University and is a registered pharmacist and owner of Watson's Drug Store in Greenville, where he is a fourth generation pharmacist. Frank and his wife Susan live in Greenville. They have two children, Chad and Kami, who are both married. *Submitted by Senator Frank Watson.*

Jarvis Township Government and Supervisors

Jarvis Township government has records dating back to 1857 when police magistrates were taking care of local problems, fines and assessments. Records, in some instances, were difficult to read, and all were hand written in numerous large bound volumes. The names of the early magistrates are as follows: 1857 – R. Common; 1858 – Henry Leis; and Andrew Mills, who served beginning in 1860. Mills continued serving through 1886 as best could be determined.

On April 29, 1876, township government began with business dealing strictly with the roads in the community. Meetings were held only about twice a year. More than one commissioner served on the "Board of Highways Commissioners," whose main topic was the construction of roads and bridges. The first board of commis-

Jarvis Township Officials, 2002. (l. to r.) Carl Strom, trustee; Tammy Soland, assessor; Virgil "Pete" Gebhart, trustee; Bob Stonecipher, trustee; Alan J. Dunstan, supervisor; Barbara Wright, town clerk; Wayne Brendel, trustee; James Grapperhaus, road commissioner; and Darrell Hampsten, tax collector.

Walter Brunworth, long time Jarvis Township Clerk, circa 1990.

Lucille Schmalz, first woman tax assessor in Jarvis Township, circa 1970s.

sioners included James N. Jarvis, town clerk; James P. Anderson, chairman; George W. Mills; John Liebler; and J.G. Anderson.

Records revealed that a variety of purchases were made. A road scraper and plow were purchased for $34.00 from Henry Martin and Son. Stationery was purchased from H. A. Risser for 25 cents. In 1912, nineteen carloads of rock were received for construction of the first mile of township hard road.

Sometime during the year of 1876, the first supervisor, Ignatius Riggin, was appointed (or elected). At the September 23 meeting, a bridge was to be built over the "Brown Mound" Branch, no location noted. James A. Pelemer submitted the winning bid of $22.00 over W.E. Bisonhardt's bid of $24.00 to build it. In 1881, another bridge was built: a truss bridge across Silver Creek on the Collinsville and Looking Glass Road.

Town meetings have not changed; at least the laws governing them have not. In 1891 the township officials met at the Liebler School House. A moderator was chosen to preside, as he still is, and the time for the meeting had to be 2 p.m.

Beginning in 1892, the meeting was held at 2 p.m. unless it was changed by vote prior to the date set for the town meeting. This law is still in effect. (The time of the annual Town Meeting is always set and voted upon at the previous year's annual Town Meeting.) By 1886 meetings were held monthly. In September of that year the Town Clerk, G. W. Hassinger, attended his last meeting as he died shortly after. In the October meeting, a resolution was made in sympathy of Hassinger by the board, praising Hassinger for his dedication to the board of trustees.

The following list of Jarvis Township Supervisors is given in succession:

Ignatius Riggin	1876-1878
J.A. Barnsback	1879
J.N. Jarvis	1884
J.B. Bosenworth	1886-1887
W.E. Wood, Supv. Int.	1888
H.H. Padon, Aud.-Supv.	1888
George Schneider	1888-1894
H.C. Kersey	1895-1897
J.W. Gornet	1898-1902
George Liebler	1903-1914
A.T. Seligman	1915-1917
R.J. Auwarter	1918-1919
Fred H. Gornet	1920
George Liebler	1921-1925
Emory Kimberlin	1926-1944
Harry Taake	1945-1960
Paul O. Riebold	1961-1976
Glenn Gindler	1977-1984
Alan J. Dunstan	1985-present

The information for this story was researched from the Jarvis Township Records and the Troy newspaper.

Jarvis Township Officials, 1992. (l. to r.) James Grapperhaus, road commissioner; Virgil Gebhart, trustee; Barbara Wright, town clerk; Adrian Mersinger, trustee; Russell Wiesemeyer, trustee; Alan J. Dunstan, supervisor; and Wayne Brendel, trustee.

State Representative
Ron Stephens (R-Troy)
110th District
Assistant Republican Leader

State Representative Ron Stephens

The Illinois State Representative for the 110th District was born February 19, 1948, in East St. Louis, IL. He and his wife, Karen, have five children. He is a self-employed retail pharmacist. He received his education at St. Louis College of Pharmacy, receiving a BS in 1975.

He served in the U.S. Military in the Vietnam War, where he was awarded the Bronze Star and Purple Heart.

He was the Village of Caseyville Trustee from 1981 to 1984; Director of State of Illinois Emergency Management Agency (1990-1991) and State Representative from 1985 to 1991, and from 1993 to present.

He is a member of the Veterans of Foreign Wars, Shriners, Troy Chamber of Commerce, Metro-East Pharmacy Association, State and National Pharmacy Association, past chairman of Friends of Scouting of Troy, and past president of the Troy Kiwanis Club.

His committee assignments include Regulations and Registrations, Appropriations-Public Safety, Aviation, and State Procurement.

Tri-Township Park District

The Tri-Township Park District was formed by a special election held on February 25, 1967. The results: 573 for, 195 against. The district includes all of Jarvis Township and portions of Pin Oak and Collinsville Townships. The original elected commissioners were Russell Wiesemeyer, Milton Langenwalter, J.W. Dull, George Schmalz and Oscar Gindler.

On April 15, 1967, the district agreed to purchase a 44-acre tract of land on the west end of Troy for $70,000. This property was formerly the Herman Hecht farm. The Troy Civic Improvement Co., a branch of the Troy Lions Club, donated the amount of $35,000. The remaining funds came from a matching grant from the Department of Conservation.

Some of the original goals of the commssioners were picnic areas, softball and baseball diamonds, open air pavilion, swimming pool, tennis courts, playground with parking lots.

The Troy Lions Club, many other civic organizations and individuals made donations and volunteered services to help develop the park. By 1971, the park included a stocked fishing lake, playground equipment, over 200 trees and baseball diamonds where the Troy Khoury League played games.

The American Legion donated $5,500 toward the construction of the large pavilion. Shelters, picnic tables and grills were added in 1973. The large pavilion was completed in 1974. The Lee Leonard Building for storage was built and named for Leonard's dedication to the park.

In 1977 four tennis courts were built. The Troy Soccer Club was formed and used the park in 1979. The district received a $43,000 matching paving and lighting grant in 1980.

The Jarvis Township Senior Citizen Center was built on the east side in 1981, funded by community development program.

First Public Lake Fountain, Tri-Township Park Lake, 1996.

The park expanded in 1984 and purchased an additional 7.3 acres at a cost of $42,000. By 1988 talk of a swimming pool surfaced again. The issue was defeated 2,644 no, 1,088 yes. The Troy Homecoming moved to the park and the Tri-Township Baseball and Softball Association was formed and replaced the Khoury League in 1989.

The Cub Scout sponsored War Memorial was completed in 1990 and enhanced in the late 1990s by civic organizations/individual

ner and 5.1 acres were purchased for $75,000. The house is the park office.

The petting zoo was added in 1996. A summer day camp began and major expansion took place in 1998. The park purchased 32 acres on the west end of the park for $320,000.

In 1999 the Senior Center was renamed the Russell Wiesemeyer Community Center to honor Mr. Wiesemeyer for his 30 years of service.

In 2000 the park agreed to purchase 11.5 acres of land from the City of Troy on the east end of town for

Tri-Township Park Commissioners, 2002. (l. to r.) Norman Beck, Randy Wiesemeyer, Phil Loethen, Barbara Wright and Terry Ball. Not pictured: Louis Simpson and Todd Moore.

$225,000, funding from the Illinois First Grant of $450,000. State Rep. Ron Stephens secured the grant and later sponsored an additional $55,000 grant. Later the city and the park dissolved the contract, and funds used for 32 acres.

In 2001, a controversial $20 million "sports mall" was put on the ballot. It was defeated by a 9-1 margin. The election also produced five new commissioners.

The park hosted the Cancer Walk for Life in 2001 and 2002.

In 2002, the park received a matching Oslad Grant for the sum of $367,100. A total of $734,000 was to be spent on sewer lines, restrooms and the development of the 32 acres.

Troy Volunteer Fire District's donation of a truck cab and chassis to the Tri-Township Park District. (l. to r.) Terry Taake, Phil Hogue, Carl Strom, Bill Brown, Bud Klaustermeier (fire district trustees); Louis Simpson, Kevin Woodring, Dennis Kniser, Gary Jarman, Laura Wise (park commissioners); and Tim Greenfield, park superintendent.

contributions. In 1991 the popular walking path was constructed and the 4th of July Picnic began.

The park expanded again in 1993. A house at the southeast cor-

Andy Semanisin at the Park

Andy Semanisin worked at the Tri-Township Park for several years in the 1980s and 1990s. He was a dedicated worker and had the best interest of the park in mind at all times. He loved feeding the ducks on the park's lake. In 2000, the Tri-Township Park dedicated a plaque at one of the ball diamonds in his memory.

Andy Semanisin cutting the park's grass, 1990s.

Tri-Township Public Library District

Tri-Township Public Library District, 209 S. Main, 2002.

The library in Troy had its beginning as a WPA program 64 years ago and has evolved into a modern 13,440ft. building in 2002. The first library was funded by the Federal Government as a Works Progress Administration (WPA) project from December 1938 until about December 1940. It was housed on the second floor of the Braner Building, and Wilma Cline acted as librarian.

The second library in Troy was formed as the Troy Library Association. It operated from April 1964 until January 1972. The library was located in the G.A. Shaffer building at 211 S. Main Street. This building was eventually torn down, and the empty lot was purchased for $12,000 from the Shaffers.

Treasurer; Dee Gore, Secretary; Pat Huck, Librarian; Mary Halde, Jim Hunsley, Pat Merz and Sharon Smith. On December 20, 1980, the Library Board purchased the former Mateer Funeral Home (for $84,000) at 209 S. Main St. The Library Tax referendum passed in the city on April 7, 1987,

L-R, front: Pat Merz, Dennis Ashcraft, Jeanette Dothager and Pat Huck. Back: Joy Upton, Leo Lindsay, Valerie Meyer, Mary Rose and Judy Little.

and in the rural area, March 8,1988. The first election of trustees was held in April of 1989. Those elected were Julie Miller, President; Pat Huck, Treasurer; Judy Madison, Secretary; Pam Baker, Nancy Barsch, Jean Lenny and Pat Merz.

After much hard work and effort, the new Tri-Township Public Library District building (a $1,300,000 building) was opened July 16, 1995. It consists of two floors totaling 13,440 square feet. Today, the library offers the district the services of both a Director and Assistant Director/Librarian with Masters Degrees in Library Science, a computer room, internet availability, both children and adult programs, a history-genealogical research center, twice a month book sales, and a large community room available for rent.

Serving on the current Board of Trustees are Jeanette Dothager, President; Dennis Ashcraft, Vice President; Judy Little, Secretary; Pat Huck, Treasurer; Pat Merz, Leo Lindsay and Joy Upton.

Troy Library Association, circa 1964. L-R: Joey McDowell, Dale Juehne, Jim Bailey, Jeanne Simon and Millie Shaffer.

In 1975, as a project of the Woman's Club of Troy, a library committee was formed consisting of Ona Gilbreath, Leona Stunkel and Pat Huck. As a result, the Tri-Township Library opened June 16,1976, at 110 East Market. The first Board was made up of Ona Gilbreath, President; Evelyn Schmisseur,

Tri-Township Public Library, 209 S. Main, 1980.

Businesses of Yesterday

A stage coach stop, a brick factory, a combination funeral parlor and furniture store, a soda bottling plant, a blacksmith shop, a filling station – what do these have in common? They were all old businesses that provided Troy's citizens with services and products in the past. Some lasted for years; others, only weeks. A few were passed on to sons; others burned to the ground.

The old businesses provided the area's citizens with services and products necessary for everyday life, with items for basic survival and with luxurious merchandise for gifts and pleasure. They served as community gathering places and geographical markers. No matter the products or services, Troy's old businesses reflected the times and the people.

213 East Market

From approximately 1930 to 1960, the building was a grocery store owned and operated by Louis Struckhoff. The building's history prior to Struckoff's ownership is obscure.

In the 1970s and 1980s, Barbara Lowery operated Impressions Beauty Salon. Barbara lived next door to the building. Previously she had operated her shop from her home in another part of town and, at one time, operated a beauty shop at Sarah Street and Edwardsville Road in an old filling station building.

A few times, the building sat idle and unoccupied. In the mid-1990s, Happy Days, a beauty salon operated by Mary Ellen Elliott opened. Later Laura Gardner operated a beauty salon named Teasers. Teasers was in business for approximately six months.

Happy Days Salon was a beauty shop in existence for about two years in the late 1990s. The interior was decorated in a 1950s theme with photos of 1950s movie and recording stars, cars and other memorabilia decorated the walls.

In 1998 or 1999, Daryl and Lisa Harris purchased the building and did extensive remodeling. Lisa Harris moved her shop called Artworks and Framing into the building. She previously had run the shop in the Gebauer building at 110 East Market Street.

Happy Days Salon (213 East Market), April 1988

In 2000, Cindy Hewitt bought the building and redecorated it again. An east addition was built to accommodate seating and it was called East Market Street Cafe. The cafe offered noontime lunch. In addition, Cindy provided a catering service for a time. It was a cheerful addition to the East Market Street scene.

Currently the building is the headquarters for a major restaurant chain.

The building has been remodeled many times to accommodate the type of business that it housed and each business has a history of its own. *Information taken from the Times-Tribune and from local residents' recollections.*

320 East Center

320 East Center has been a busy commercial site for many years. Robert Voelker operated a service station and repair shop there before selling it to Brian Pfeil, who then ran the business. For a time, Brian's wife and daughters had a dance studio there, also. Emmett Pfeil ran

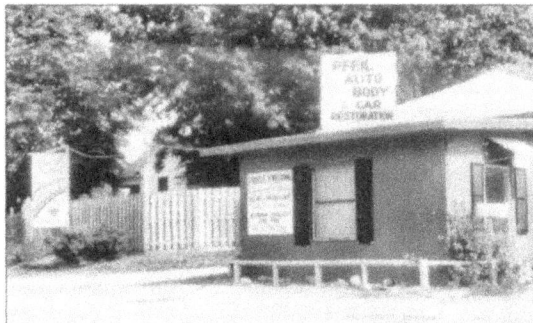

320 East Center

his welding business at the site, beginning in 1970. In 1975, Bobbie Pfeil opened an Oak and Craft Shop there. Today, a tire store occupies the site.

Adams Store

The Adams Store was the last of the old era of general merchandising in Troy. It closed in 1987. Originating as an ice business with an ice delivery service, James Adams began the store in 1932 in the old Klein building at 116 S. Main Street. Adams continued to sell large blocks of ice out of a refrigerated room at the east end of the building in addition to the general merchandising for another 25 or more years.

Adams married the former Mary Elliott. They had two sons, Dr. James Adams, who was a general practitioner in town for many years, and Gene Adams, who took over the business after his father's death.

Adams Store, Betty & Gene Adams, 1987

Gene married the former Betty Rood and had one son, John. Prior to their marriage, Betty owned a paints and gifts store across the street from the Adams Store. Betty then sold the business to James and Alma Rood who ran the store until they sold it to Russ and Audrey Klaustermeier. They named the business A&R Paints and Crafts. Later Russ's son purchased the business and moved it to another location down the street.

Betty and Gene ran the Adams Store until its closing in 1987. It was difficult to compete with the larger discount stores that were popping up in nearby cities. A large auction sale was held when the store closed drawing people from near and far. Many bought fixtures that had been in the store for over 50 years.

During its heyday, the store was a lively place for just about anything one would need in clothing, school supplies, games, toys, shoes, boots, candy, sewing notions, and much more. Every year a sidewalk sale was set up on the north and west sides of the store, drawing customers out for the bargains. Local youth groups (scouts, 4-H clubs, and school organizations) used the large windows during special times of the year to present information about their club or organizations. The second floor of the building was the Adams' home. After the store closed, the building stood idle for some time. Then Kim Cruse rented it as a florist shop, naming it Kim's Creations. Kim operated the shop for a number of years, then moved her business to Edwardsville Road in the former Floyd and Lee Cullop residence.

Following Kim's Creations' departure from the building, the first floor of the building was leased to Christian Wolf Communion Wafer Company, owned and operated by James Deeren. *Submitted by Mae Grapperhaus.*

Adelhardt's

In 1946, Les and Ruby Adelhardt decided to start their own business, and purchased a small market from local butcher Alex Martin, who operated a business in the Deimling Building at the northwest corner of East Market and Hickory Streets. The store changed locations and had a

Les Adelhardt behind meat counter, Foodland, circa 1960s

number of different names including Troy Market, Foodland, Troy IGA, and Adelhardt Foods. The last location was at 111 West Market Street, the former Gindler Studebaker dealership building. It continued to grow and serve the community for 40 years. Les ran the store until 1970 when Terry "Bud," his son, took over. Bud continued to run the successful business for the next 14 years. The store was sold in 1987. *Submitted by Sherry Smith.*

Arrow Post and Pole

Arrow Post and Pole dealt primarily in treated lumber, posts and poles. They sold some other farm-related items, but the lumber was the main thrust of the business. The business existed from the mid 1950s to the early 1960s and owned by Charles Knecht and Ben Zenk. Knecht joined the business in 1960, and it was located to the northwest of Troy on Zenk Road in the old Zenk farmhouse. Knecht's daughter, Rosemary Schultze, remembers when her Dad be-

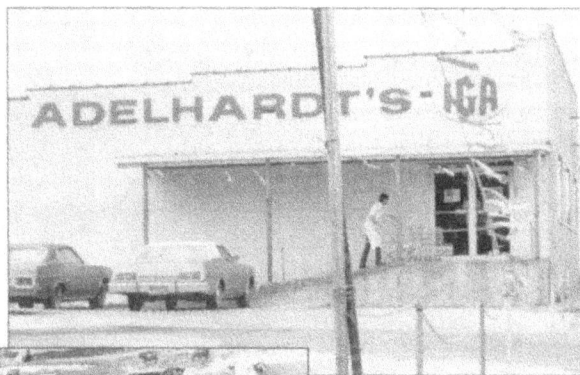

Adelhardt's IGA, circa 1960s

gan the business. She was learning to type and did the invoices for the business on a portable (non-electric) typewriter. After the company was dissolved, Charles Knecht went to work for his brother, Phil Knecht, at Edwardsville Machine Shop, retiring from that business. *Information from Rosemary (Knecht) Schultze.*

The Auwarter Building, pre-1900s

Auwarter Building

The Charles Auwarter family came to Troy in 1858. Charles bought the property site – Block 4 – in 1859 from Samuel Hunter. After the death of their father Charles, Martin F. Auwarter and his brother Charles started the store on Main and Market Street (101 East Market) in 1879.

Martin F. Auwarter married Mary Johnson in 1873. They had four children, Charles C. Auwarter; Robert F. Auwarter; Cora Auwarter; and John Auwarter, who died age 11. Mary Johnson Auwarter died in 1887. Martin F. Auwarter's second marriage was to Ella Osborn in 1890 or 1896. One son, Paul R. Auwarter, was born to them. Martin F. Auwarter died in 1931, leaving the property to his wife, Ella Auwarter.

The third generation to run the store was Robert F. Auwarter. He died in 1935, and the property was in Ella (Osborn) Auwarter's name. She rented the building to John Schoon, who ran a Rexall Drug Store there. After renting for several years, John and Edna Schoon purchased the building in 1956. Later, Bud Kamm ran the drug store there. Allen and Sue Holloway purchased the building from the Schoons in 1960 and ran Allen's Drug Store there before selling the business to Todd Evers in 1998.

According to an old photo, the store at one time had a second floor (around 1900 or before). No documents show when the building was made into a one story building as it is today. *Submitted by the Troy Historical Society.*

Barsch Shoe Repair

Not counting the time he served in the army during WWII, William "Nance" Barsch repaired shoes in Troy for 40 years, from 1936 to 1976. He learned his trade

William "Nance" Barsch, retirement, 1976

from his step-father, John Marshall. Marshall had operated the shop in the Rieder building, then in his home at 106 Kimberlin. When Nance inherited the business, he retained the Kimberlin Street location. *Information from the* Troy Tribune, *March 11, 1976.*

Bauer Water Service

Bauer Water service was owned and operated by George Bauer, also known as "The Water Man," of Troy. The business started in approximately 1975 with one truck and a 1,050 gallon tank to hold water. He serviced the rural areas of Troy, Maryville, Collinsville, Edwardsville, Hamel and Glen Carbon. As years passed and the population grew, he was able to have larger trucks with two 1,050-gallon tanks on each to service customers' water needs quickly and efficiently. Water was available to hundreds of rural residents with wells and was available for service for commercial needs at the time. The service was able to transport approximately three-million gallons of water a year, depending on the types of weather conditions. Many friends were made through the years and even though George retired in approximately 1998, people still know him as "The Water Man." *Submitted by Diana Bauer.*

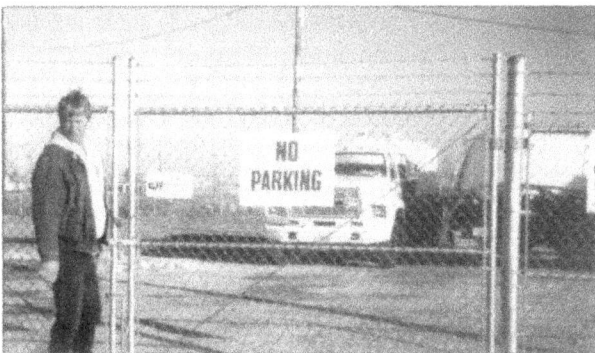

George Bauer (the Water Man)

Belladonna Beauty Salon

Belladonna Beauty Salon was operated by Brenda Wilkerson in the 1980s and early 1990s at 112 West Market Street in the Levo Building. Prior to her ownership, it was run by Terri (Gerstenecker) Hardesty and Debbie (Gerstenecker) Sheib who were twin sisters, the daughters of Edgar and Nell Gerstenecker. Terri and Debbie also had a nail shop along with the full service salon. Brenda worked for them and later bought the business. Terri and Debbie also ran a shop on West Clay Street for a time in the 1980s. *Submitted by Mae Grapperhaus.*

Troy Best, Barber

Troy Best was a barber for a little over 55 years in Troy, retiring in February 1976. After completing his training at Molar's Barber College in St. Louis, MO, he worked with Edward J. Helmich at 103 East Market Street for approximately 10 years, when he opened his own shop in the old hotel building on the wedge (Collinsville Road and Center Street). This was in the early 1930s, when there were four barbershops in Troy: Jack Gebauer and Jule Peters operated the other two. After about eight months, Best moved his shop to Main and Center Streets in the former Shell station building.

Troy Best, barber, circa 1940s

He stayed there for 10 years and then moved his shop to 111 South Main Street in 1940. In 1963, he went into semi-retirement and worked in that capacity until 1976. When Best started barbering, hair cuts were 40 cents; when he retired, they were $3.25.

After several years of retirement, Mr. and Mrs. Best (the former Bertha Kunart of Carlinville) lived in Troy. Soon after Bertha's death, Mr. Best moved to his daughter's home in North Carolina. He died there in the 1990s. *Information for this story was taken from the February 26, 1976, issue of* The Troy Tribune.

Blue Haven

Around 1941, Oscar Gindler bought the land on the corner of Route 40 and By-Pass 40. At that time, Route 40 was the busy highway that went from coast to coast. On this land, Oscar built a service

Blue Haven on U.S. Rte. 40

station, a large restaurant, and a motel complex. West of the businesses, he started a small subdivision. To take care of the sewage for the subdivision, he built on the south side of Route 40 the first privately-owned lagoon in the state of Illinois.

On the east side of the complex, he built a Mobil gas station, which he sold to Willard Maden. In 1971, Willard Maden sold it to Willard Gindler, Oscar's son. Willard got rid of the gasoline tanks and sold the inventory in 2000, but the building has not yet been sold. The restaurant was a long, arch-roofed building. Truck drivers hauling supplies, people traveling, and local family patrons made the restaurant a very busy place. The motel was managed by Jerome Gill, then Tony Mersinger. The restaurant was rented by Alex LaBelle, Walter and Katherine Bouscher, Maurice Wohlgemuth, and Charles Auwarter. For the motel complex, Oscar moved torndown barracks lumber from Scott Air Force Base to Blue Haven. When Interstate 70 was established and Route 40 became less busy, Oscar sold the restaurant and motel to Basil Luna. The Lunas had a cabinetmaking business in it until 1995. That property is still sitting vacant today, 2002.

Brookside Hotel

Brookside Hotel was built in the early days of Brookside (south of original Troy) sometime in the early 1880s. Its large hall was quite a social center and it also once housed a meat market. Previ-

31

William Norbury, inside Brookside Hotel

Brookside Hotel, 1900

ous to annexation by Troy in 1891, the village board also met there.

Located at the corner of Route 40 and South Main Street, it was near the railroad and accommodated many travelers who came in on the train. At one point Mr. Norbury owned the hotel. It was destroyed by fire on April 23, 1901.

Burk's Blacksmith Shop

Elias Burk, a blacksmith, built a two-story frame building in the late 1860s on the northwest corner of Clay and Staunton Road. When new, shortly after the Civil War, the building was Burk's blacksmith shop, where plows were made for farmers. It continued to serve in a later era when iron shoes were needed for mules in coal mines near the town and for horses that raced regularly at the Troy racetrack.

Standing near the shop to the west was the Burk family home, built about the same time. The house still stands (in 2002). Burk built both structures shortly after he returned to Troy in 1864 after serving with the Union Army in the Civil War.

Born in Germany in 1840, he came to this country when he was seven years old. He became an apprentice blacksmith at age 16; and when he was 20, he came to the St. Louis area. After the war, he married and built his business and his home in Troy, adding to the house as his family grew. Of the nine Burk children who reached adulthood,

two of his daughters were Mrs. Rose Peters and Mrs. James Bone. Three other children were John, Fred and Elias Burk (Jr.).

In addition to smithing, Burk also helped build the First Evangelical Church in Troy. He served intermittently as lay pastor, when an ordained minister was not available. The church still serves the community, but from a different building.

Hammering plows and horseshoes by day, the smith was on call around the clock as an amateur veterinarian. He was often called out in the middle of the night to save a sick animal. Well known, also, for his racehorse shoes, Burk won first prize for his entry at the 1904 St. Louis World's Fair. Often Burk would go to the mines at night to shoe the mules that pulled the coal carts, while running his blacksmith shop by day.

Burk was in and out of politics, serving as Mayor of Troy three times. One time he was elected without running as his daughter Mrs. Bone told a local newspaper. He knew nothing about his victory until a crowd gathered in front of his home.

A group of men in front of the Burk Blacksmith Shop, circa 1883, including Fred and John Burk.

The first floor of the old building served as a workshop, but the second floor saw varied uses. Sometimes it was a dance hall. A "Grand Holiday Hop" was held at Burk's Hall on December 30, 1880. A St. Louis string group provided the music. The second floor was used also to build wagons. The late Charlie Voelker, who was a life-long Troy resident, was in Wisconsin and came across a wagon, which looked familiar. With examination, he saw that it had been made at Burk's Shop.

Burk's Blacksmith Shop stood for many years vacant. It was torn down in the 1960s to make way for the apartment building located on the same spot.

Taken from a story by Peter A. Donhowe of the St. Louis Post-Dispatch *staff. It was printed in the July 25, 1957, issue of* The Troy Tribune.

Central Hotel

The Central Hotel was located on Market Street in Troy, between what is now 5 Star Billard's Parlor and Dr. Walter Zielonko's former office. Marshall and Gertrude "Ma" Dillingham purchased the hotel in 1916 from Mrs. Miners for $5,000. They operated it until 1933 when they moved to Alton, Illinois. Business at the hotel dropped off due to the Depression and the slow-up of work at the coal mine.

When Frank Adam Voelker died in 1924 at the age of 31, his wife, Vera (Dillingham) Voelker, moved back to the Hotel to live with her parents and to raise her two daughters, Dorothy (Donna) and Jane (Fisher). It was a grand place to grow up in, and afforded both sisters with many happy memories. Not many girls are raised in a hotel with both grandparents, their mother, and 15 or so boarders to take care of their needs and most of their whims.

The hotel had 13 bedrooms upstairs. Each room had a bedroom set of an ornately carved high back bed, a marble top washstand with basin and pitcher, a wardrobe and dresser, rocking chair, table with a clock and lamp, and a beautiful 9 foot by 12 foot rug. Either lace or shantung curtains hung at each window. And, of course, a china commode was under each bed. All these things are considered antiques now, but then they were considered normal furnishings.

The family living quarters were downstairs, consisting of three large bedrooms, a living room with an upright piano, large library table, leather couch and chairs. The dining room table was long and would easily seat 24, with beautiful tall back chairs and a big buffet. The kitchen was suited for commercial use, with a coal cooking range that had eight burners, a double wide warming oven, a huge oven, and a hot water reservoir.

The long wooden sink had an indoor pump direct from the cistern. The sink would be stacked with the miners' buckets and carbide lights. A large icebox was out in the hallway away from the heat of the stove and serviced by the iceman each day.

There was also a room called the "big room" on one side of the building. It may have been used as a store at one time, but the family used it to dry the washing in the winter time, and for storage. At one time relatives moved their three rooms of furniture into the big room, and used it as an apartment.

The front door to the hotel had a stained glass window. It opened into a large entry hall where the guest register, desk and telephone were located. A large, winding stairway led upstairs to the guests rooms. Many of the guests were permanent residents; most were coal miners who roomed and boarded there; some guests just stayed overnight. Many interesting people passed through, and the hotel even experienced some dangerous times, like the time some of the Shelton gang stayed overnight with machine guns and all. Another time a woman guest punctured her ear drum in hopes of getting morphine from the local doctor.

A large cellar housed the huge coal furnace, one that heated 19 rooms. No other place in Troy had one so big. The coal truck made many a delivery, and the children loved to watch the coal slide down the chute into the

Central Hotel

coal bin. The fruit cellar had many shelves filled with beautifully canned fruits, vegetables, chili sauce, catsup, apple butter and jelly. It took a lot of food to serve so many hungry people. Ma Dillingham's lady friends would come help her at canning time or during apple butter time. They made a fun job out of hard work. What was a busy time for them was a party time for the children.

The front of the hotel was built right on the sidewalk, and had two large sets of steps. A small grassy area existed between the sidewalk and the street. Ma planted red and yellow cannas that bloomed so beautifully in the fall there.

The yard contained several outside buildings. In the "shower house" residents could shower with water that bad been warmed by the sun, and stored in a huge barrel. There was also a washhouse. Ma hired local ladies to help with the laundry for 16 bedrooms. They used a wooden hand-wringer washing machine, rinse tubs, and a copper boiler filled with starch and bluing. She made her own lye soap in a large kettle over a fire. The ironing was also done in the washhouse with irons that were heated on the stove. What a hot job! There were two privies, one for men and one for ladies and children. A long red brick sidewalk led to these two outhouses.

Outside of the back door was a beautiful red brick patio. A trellis covered it, and grapevines entwined the trellis, dripping big juicy bunches of grapes. The well and pump were located here. Ma had a flower and herb garden off to one side. While walking on the winding path, guests could see roses, corn flowers, peonies, sweet peas, poppies

and four o'clocks. Ma decorated the bedrooms with all types of ferns and begonias. Her flower garden always furnished enough flowers to decorate the graves on Decoration Day. Toward the back of the yard was a large vegetable garden and several apple trees. The family even had a Jersey cow.

A two-seated covered swing was under a big shade tree, and a swing hung by ropes from a sturdy limb for the children and their friends. Most of the time the children played on the front sidewalk with their tricycles, roller skates, and wagons. The sidewalk was a great place to draw a hopscotch, or to play marbles. The children played house in the hotel, with each child having a room to herself. A bright red living room rug had a circle of flowers in the center, a perfect circle to play marbles in. The family spent many a musical evening in the living room around the piano. When the windows were open in the evening, a crowd often gathered outside just to listen.

It was fun growing up in "uptown" Troy. The bakery was directly across the street, and they sold redhots and other candy. Auwarter's grocery store was on the corner; the post office was down the street; Doc Schoeck's garage was along side the hotel; and Schmidt's car dealer, at the end of the block. The town jail sat at the end of the next block. Even though it was small, it scared the girls; and when the 8:30 whistle blew, they were in the house safe from the Constable.

The hotel was torn down after sitting unoccupied for many years. Many Troy town folks remember it as fondly as the family does. *Information given to the Troy Historical Society by Jane F. Fisher.*

Charlie Peters' Grocery

Charlie Peters' Grocery, corner East Clay and Hickory Streets, circa 1929. (l. to r.) Charlie Peters, behind the counter, Homer Polwort and Arline Kueker (niece).

Clover Farm Store

For a time the Adleharts operated the Clover Farm Store at Hickory and East Market Streets. It was located in the Deimling Building, which was on the site of the current Municipal Building's parking lot.

(Right) Clover Farm Store, early 1950s

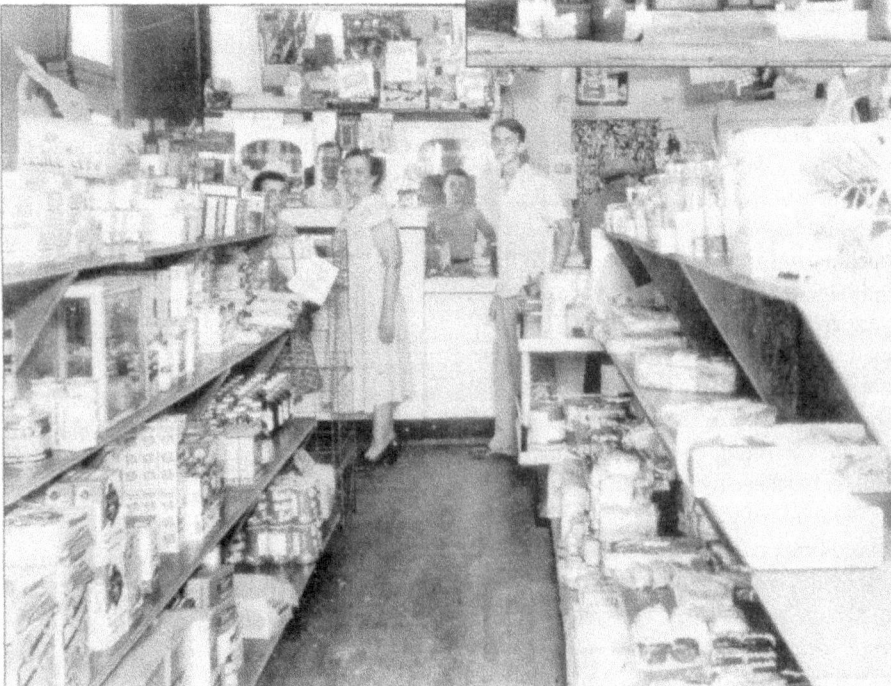

Inside the Clover Farm Store, 1950s. (l. to r.) Katie Plagemann, Les Adelhardt, Mrs. Plagemann, helper Dennis Kueker and George Plagemann.

Coal Mines of Troy

In 1880, Donk Brothers Coal Company of St. Louis built a railroad through Madison County and Troy, the St. Louis, Troy and Eastern Railway, used primarily to transport coal.

Three mines were located along the railroad line: Mine No. 1 in Maryville; Mine No. 2 in Collinsville; and Mine No. 3 in Troy. When the Vandalia-Pennsylvania Railroad system came through Troy in the late 1800s, Brookside mine began operation. Soon mines began to spring up everywhere. By 1889, millions of tons of coal were produced, and Madison County ranked fifth in the state's production.

Not only European immigrants and local men worked in the mines, but also mules were used to pull the loaded coal cars on rails that were then taken to the top. They were down in the darkness of the mines so long that they became blind. After they were no longer used, a man took the animals to live out their days in his pastures outside of Troy. Supposedly, they would often bump into each other because they could not see in daylight.

Working in the mines was a dangerous occupation. Unavoidable accidents occurred frequently due to falling coal, cave-ins, or explosions of gas and dust. These accidents led to serious injuries, loss of limbs, crippling deformities and, sometimes, death. Besides working under hazardous conditions, the miners also struggled for safer workings conditions and, of course, better wages. This struggle often caused strikes, for the miners were at the mercy of the coal companies.

Hundreds of Troy residents and area men were employed at these mines. Though the hours were long and wages low, people relied heavily on the coal production. At one time, bituminuous coal was the chief fuel in plants that generated energy with steam for manufacturing materials for finished products sold retail stores.

The mines were also very important for the Troy businesses. When the miners worked, they bought and spent their dollars. When they did not work, business slowed, and some businesses had to close their doors.

In 1894, a National Strike of Coal Miners started in the Eastern states and, finally in May of that year, it affected local area miners. Coal companies thought they could starve the miners out by not giving them a raise or better working conditions. How-

Brookside Mine

Troy Mine

Coal Company and an increase of its capital stock. Company leaders proposed to make it a Co-operative Company and to have as many employees as possible hold interest in the success of the mine operation. Forty men were solicited for this pur-

pose. In 1930, the state of Illinois continued to be the most productive in coal mining. During WW II years, the country depended on coal for factories and for making war supplies. Too, coal was needed for steel production.

All mines in Troy are closed and no longer do the men labor under ground in dangerous conditions. But many families have past memories and

ever, the miners stood together, and the newspapers covered the front pages with "If we must starve, we need not work at starvation wages," and " Down with 'The Millionaire Kings.'"

During this time, hundreds of miners from nearby towns marched to the Troy mines. Here they were met by armed guards. No disturbance of any kind was created. They waited until the men came up from the mines and informed them that a meeting would be held in "Rieders Opera House" that evening. That night, an overflowing crowd of miners was present. Many stirring speeches were made, and every miner agreed to strike and to remain out until a settlement was made.

The strike became so general that all manufacturing and large cities suffered severely from lack of coal. The striking miners were confident of early victory. They knew that the strike would be beneficial to the operators, also, as coal would greatly advance in price. Because of this price increase, they could have given better wages, and still made a millionaire's profit.

The strike lasted longer than they had planned. Many miners and their families lived in company-owned houses; sometimes, they even kept other miners to help pay rent. When the strike lingered on, they were threatened with eviction by the company superintendents. These were sad times, since miners were also suspended from their jobs. Eventually, the strike ended, but most of the miners felt defeated. Gradually, mine conditions became safer, wages better, but the veins were slowly running out of coal. In 1911, the Brookside Mine temporarily suspended operation pending a reorganization of the Brookside

Brookside Mine

Dollinger's IGA Grocery

Dollinger's IGA Grocery, 107 South Main Street, circa 1930s. (l. to r.) Les Becker and Irwin Dollinger, owner.

stories about friends and family who worked the mines. The coal industry in Troy remains an important part of Troy's history. *Some information taken from Nov. 3, 1911, issue of the* Troy Weekly Call. *Submitted by Marilyn Sulc.*

Cullops

Both of the Cullops owned and operated businesses in Troy. Lela Polwort Cullop ran Lela's Beauty Shop in the 1940s and 1950s. Her first shop was in the 201 East Market Street building. Her second shop was 106 North Main Street. Marian Schurman Lewis was a beautician at her shop. In the 1950s, her husband, Floyd Cullop, owned a hardware store on East Market Street, next to the Kroger store. He also sold bottled gas.

They built a home at 306 Edwardsville Road. At Christmas time, residents from surrounding towns would come to see the decorated Cullop home. Atop the roof was a radiant figure of jolly Santa Claus, bringing his group of reindeer to a halt. Rudolph was the leader, complete with his red-bulbed nose. Eight snowmen were grouped on the terrace, singing the chorus of "Silent Night, Holy Night." A beautifully decorated tree stood in the background. Inside the house, easily viewed through the picture window, a gold revolving tree sparkled.

The couple retired and lived in Mexico. Lela still resides there in 2002. *Information from* The Troy Tribune, *January 10, 1952, and a resident's memory.*

Cum-Bac Café

The Cum-Bac Café was located facing south on Center Street, just east of the Adams Store. The business was under different ownership through the years. A block building, beige or yellow in color, it was vacant for years before being demolished in the late 1990s.

Numerous businesses, most of which were foods related were housed there. Owners included Mr. Struckhoff, later Art Pahl; and Mr. and Mrs. Ostresh operated a bakery there in the 1950s. *Information provided by residents' recollections.*

Droy's Motor Service

Owner Fred "Freddie" Droy of Droy's Motor Service, which

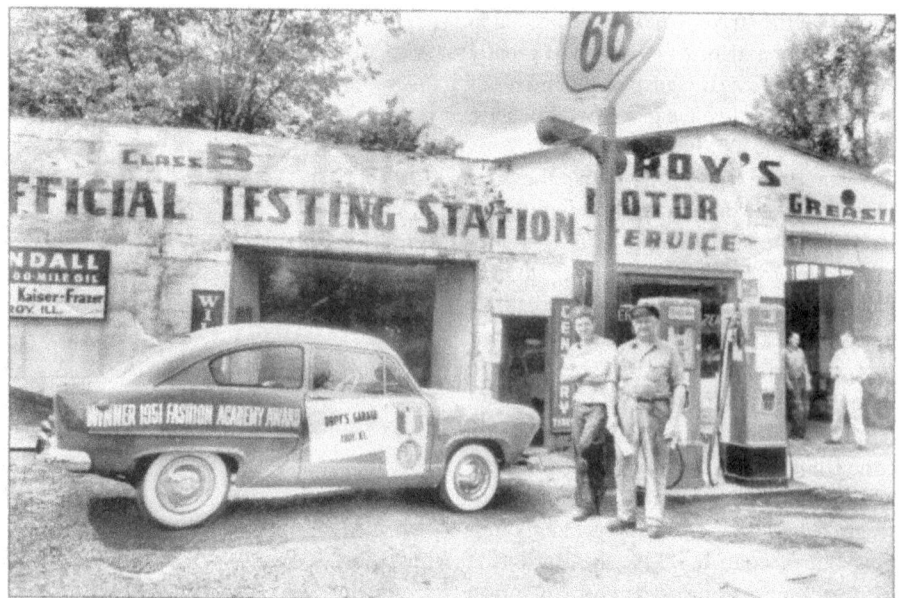

Dunstan's Market

(Right) City Market operated by William Dunstan on South Main (behind Allen's Drug), circa 1940s.

Interior of Dunstan's Market, located at the southeast corner of Main and Center Street. William Dunstan had his market on the north side of the same building as the Troy Frozen Foods, circa 1940s. (l. to r., center of photo) Rena Dunstan and Bill Dunstan, owners.

was located at 200 Collinsville Road, was a Kaiser-Frazer Dealer at the time. Droy also had the official testing station for trucks. The west end of the building was added before 1950s. Later, Bob Droy, Fred's son, took over the business and it became a Ford dealership.

Duckett's Lunch Room

Elmer Duckett owned a lunch room that was located facing south on Center Street across from the Adams Store (in the same block) and owned by the

Droy's Motor Service: Bob and Fred Droy out front; Henry J. by the auto section, 1950.

Eckert's Cider Mill

George Eckert's Cider Mill, south side of Clay Street near Washington Street, early 1950s.

Duckett family. The business flourished for several years (in 1930s and 1940s). The Greyhound and Vandalia bus stops were located there for several years.

Numerous businesses, most of which were food related, were housed in the building through the years. At one point it was called the Cum-Back Café. In the early 1950's Gretchen (Wheeler) Hodapp purchased the restaurant from Duckett and continue to have the Greyhound and Vandalia Bus Lines stop there. Later it was a bakery owned by Mr. and Mrs. Larry Ostresch.

Edwards Funeral Home

Jewel and Verna (Schultze) Edwards were married in 1932. In 1939, they bought the Heddergott residence, 205 Edwardsville Road, to establish the Edwards Funeral Home. They owned and operated the Edwards Funeral Home from 1939 until 1965. They had several neighbors and friends help with the ambulance runs for emergencies. The building is still in existence at this printing, and still is a funeral home. *Submitted by Verna M. Edwards.*

Embrey's Appliance

Carl Embrey began working for John Gebauer in the hardware business following high school in 1938. He began his own store in April of 1941 at 21, when he purchased the business from Gebauer at 110 East Market Street. He began the business with $7.00 in his cash resister. That summer, he was married to Fern Porter.

The store continued to be open and was managed by Walter Thompson while Embrey did his part in World War II. He served in "H" Company, 318th Regiment, 30th Infantry. He served in the Third Army under General Patton, was wounded twice, and received the Silver Star.

Following his discharge in 1946, Embrey moved his store to the Schoon building (located where Dr. Friederich's office is in 2002) on South Main Street. When he moved from the East Market Street address, he used a wheelbarrow because he did not have a truck at the time. Times were rough, and he admitted that he did just about anything to get the business started.

By 1959 Embrey expanded and bought the upholstery business at 125 East Market Street from Louis Grieve. Embrey Appliance business stayed at the Market Street location until his retirement in 1989.

Very active in the community, Embrey also served for 14 years as the Troy City

Embrey Appliance, 1988

Clerk. The Clerk's office was located right in the store. Fern helped Carl with the city water cards, as well as worked in the store. At first, the Embrey's carried all sorts of gifts and toys. It was Embrey's Hardware at first, but later they expanded it to an appliance store only. They sold televisions, stoves, refrigerators and other appliances for the modern home. Embrey's was the first to sell televisions in Troy when television was in its infancy in the late 1940s.

In April 1983, Mayor Ron Criley presented Embrey with a special Distinguished Service Award in appreciation for his 40 year business career in Troy. Embrey's Appliance had served four generations when Carl retired. He sold the business to Terry Giger on January 1, 1989. The new business is called Terry's Appliance Center. *Information from the January 5, 1989, Times-Tribune.*

Edwards Funeral Home. Jewel Edwards, proprietor, in front, 1940s.

Embroidery Works, early 1900s

Embroidery Works

The Embroidery Works factory did embroidery work on clothes, etc. At various times the building was a shoe factory, Moderne Linen Laundry, later Morgen Linen, and a furniture store when it burned in early 1980s.

Fairview Farm Dairy

George Ottwein, Sr., started a daily milk route in Troy around 1916. He hitched a horse to a buggy and drove up and down the streets of Troy with two ten-gallon cans of milk and a long-handled dipper. He then filled the tin containers that people brought out or hung on their picket fences. The price was $.04 a pint and $.08 a quart. Of course, the family had to care for and milk the cows first.

A few years later sons Oscar and George, Jr. took over the route, bought a bottling machine, and filled bottles with milk, added cardboard caps and delivered daily to the stoops and porches of Troy. The price for years was $.05 a pint, $.10 a quart and $.25 a gallon. One customer bought half a pint every day for $.02 1/2. If a family had problems and couldn't pay the milk bill, it still got delivery. "Grandpa" George said that children and babies need their milk! Sometimes the men of a family would help on the farm to pay off the milk bill.

When Oscar's son, Merrill, and nephew, Leslie Becker, got big enough, they "ran" the milk route before school in the mornings, standing on the running board and hanging on through the open window; this way two sides of the street got delivery at once. When refrigeration became more common and Troy got bigger, half the town got delivery one day, and the other half the next.

The family had a black cocker spaniel, Skippy, who "ran" the route behind the truck and who knew the route so well he would take short cuts and meet the truck on the next street. When he tired, he'd climb up on the fender for a free ride. For many years the milk truck or a hay frame was decorated and driven in the homecoming parade. When pasteurization became mandatory, the family sold its raw milk to O'Fallon Dairy and sold bottles of O'Fallon Dairy pasteurized milk to its customers. The business was sold to Wilbur Kleuter in the 1950s. *Submitted by Audrey Ottwein Deeren.*

Financial Institutions

Two early banking institutions were located in Troy in the late 1800s and early 1900s, the Troy Exchange Bank and the Troy State Bank. Both were eventually closed during the Depression, one for the usual reasons, the other in the midst of fraud and embezzlement charges. Later, a group of civic-minded citizens staked their money and their reputations to establish the Troy Security Bank.

File's Grocery

(l. to r.) George Ottwein, Jr., George Ottwein, Sr. and Oscar Ottwein, c.1944.

Ira P. File Grocery, southwest corner North Main and Clay Streets, circa 1900.

The Troy Exchange Bank began as a private bank in 1885 by W.W. Jarvis and H.H. Padon. Two years later, Jarvis purchased Padon's interest; and the bank continued as a private bank until 1910, when it was organized as a state bank. The bank was housed in two different locations: the Auwarter Building on Main Street, where it was dynamited by robbers on November 25, 1899; and the Braner Building at the corner of Kimberlin and East Market. D. Genevieve Jarvis, W.W.'s daughter, worked as cashier and served as president from 1894 to 1926. Both she and her father retired in April 1926. John Feldmeier became president and L.P. Wetzel became cashier then.

In May 1927 the bank purchased two large lots on the corner of Main and Market for $2500. The 2 lots had been swept clean by the huge fire which had destroyed the old opera house on Sept. 30, 1922. The bank announced plans to build a new bank building on the corner. However, the stock market crashed in 1929, the Depression followed, and the bank closed.

The building stood vacant for several years. In the late 1930s and early 1940s it housed numerous businesses and professional offices.

Located in the Braner Building, the Troy State Bank existed for a short time. Its closing, with rumors of fraud and embezzlement, was a source for headlines in 1929. The bank was closed on Feb. 8, 1929, by order of State Auditor Oscar Nelson, and examiners were sent to audit the bank's books. The embezzlement of $154,000, of which $112,000 was owed by the Troy Coal Company, occurred on February 5, three days before it had been closed.

Bank president A.F. Seligman and cashier Benton B. Miles were arrested and charged with the crime. Oddly enough, Seligman was also a principal stockholder of the coal company, and Miles was his son-in-law. Authorities discovered the money had gone to finance the Troy Coal Company and used mainly to meet the payrolls of the company which employed 150 men. After weeks of hearings and legal battles, action was filed to dissolve the bank.

After the Depression and WWII, the real need for a Troy bank became evident. James Watson convinced the men of the Troy Lions Club of this need, and soon translated words into action in 1948. He became the chairman of a banking committee appointed by the Lions. These members pledged their credit and their reputations. They offered their time and resources, sold stock and invested in it themselves, obtained necessary bank fixtures and equipment, and then installed the fixtures themselves. They pledged their own credit so the State Bank of Illinois would grant a charter to the Troy Security Bank. On May 8, 1948, the charter became a reality, thanks to the diligent work of these men.

The bank held the name of Troy Security Bank for over 25 years. During the early years of operation, a large memorial board, honoring the local residents who had served in WWII, was erected on the northeast corner of the lot. Close by stood a small bandstand where local bands often performed.

Later, the United Illinois Bank purchased Troy Security. For a brief time it became the Illinois First Bank, then Central Bank. Central was bought out by Mercantile; then United Illinois Bank and Firstar Bank occupied the site. Currently, US Bank conducts business there.

Numerous additions and remodeling projects have been made to the original building. The War Memorial and bandstand have given way to drive-up facilities and a parking lot.

Several banking institutions have existed in Troy over the years. Madison County Federal Savings and Loan of Troy was located on West Market. The firm was later purchased by the Bank of Edwardsville.

Landmark Bank came to Troy in 1987, located at 100 McDonald Blvd. It was purchased by Magna Bank, and Magna was later sold to another banking firm. Bethalto Airport Bank arrived in 1986, located at Bargraves and Rt. 162. Later, it was sold to another bank and has been remodeled, undergoing several name changes. With the growth of Troy, other banking institutions have established themselves. However, none will ever surpass Troy's early banks in influence and importance to the city. Taken from issues of The Troy Call and The Troy Tribune and the recollections of Troy residents.

The group of Troy Lions Club members who brought a bank back to the City of Troy in 1948. (l. to r.) William S. Schmitt, James J. Watson, John Schoon, Dan Liebler, Jewel Edwards, Oscar Ottwein, Clarence Frey, Oliver Spitze, Earl Schmidt, Oscar Gindler, Fred R. Wakeland, Clarence Henning, David Sims, Harold Schmidt and Rollie R. Moore.

This bank building at 100 East Market Street was built as the Troy Exchange Bank. It later became the Troy Security Bank, and, as time went on, many banking institutions have occupied the building.

First Chance Tavern

First Chance Tavern, late 1800s. Phil Schultze with hand in the air.

J.R. Fritts, Butcher

J.R. Fritts was a butcher in Troy. He was born in Tennessee on November 16, 1877, to William M. and Sarah C. Fritts. He received his education in the public school of Oliver Springs, TN, and also took a course in a private school. Upon completing his education, be became a coal miner until 1908, when he moved to Troy and opened a butcher shop in partnership with a local man. He bought his partner out in 1909, and he ran the business alone. In his shop, he carried a full stock of the finest meats, as well as a full line of staples and fancy groceries. His place was finely kept.

A staunch Republican, he was married to Rebecca S. Sheldon in Tennessee on August 29, 1896. They were the parents of six children, four boys and two girls. *Information from* The Edwardsville Intelligencer, *September 1912.*

Frosty Flavors

Bill Kindudis owned Frosty Flavors, located on Laundry Street, at one time. The establishment was open during the summer months for sweet tooth cool treats. Frosty Flavors flourished in the 1980s and 1990s.

In 1994, John Petras ran the shop. He added seating space and a fuller menu.

To the left is the former home of Floyd and Lela Cullop. It was Kim's Creation, a florist shop for about three years in the late 1990s, owned by Kim Kruse, who had moved her shop from the old Adams Store on South Main Street to this location.

The building was sold in 2002 to Joan Spencer and Mark Ponce. Spencer is opening a flower shop named "Every Bloomin' Thing" on the east side and Ponce is opening a custard business on the west, "J's Custard."

Gebauer Building

The Gebauer Building at 110 East Market Street has a long history. In the early days, it was a hardware and tin store and an undertaking establishment. J.C. Gebauer was the undertaker and was affiliated with Schroeppel and Company, undertakers from Collinsville. Through the years it has housed many businesses, including several taverns, a grocery store, a paper products store, a restaurant and a church. Lottie Lanahan ran a restaurant there in the 1960s and Bill's Tavern was there at one time.

George Langdon, who owns the building, married Anna Mae Gebauer, a descendant of J.C. Gebauer. In the fall of 1993, Mr. Langdon had the building's exterior renovated and removed the long-standing porch. In 2002, the first floor houses Alexandra's Collection on the west side and Bonnie Levo's Law Office on the east side. The second floor is leased out for apartments.

Gebauer Building, 1988.

Frosty Flavors, owner Bill Kindudis, 1986

Geo. C. Morriss City Feed Store

George C. Morriss City Feed Store. Located on Clay Street, early 1900s.

Gindler & Schurman
Dairy Store and Confectionary

Inside Gindler & Schurman Dairy Store, October 1937.

Grace's Grill and Noah's Ark

Grace's Grill and Noah's Ark Tavern occupied the same building at 116 West Market Street. Noah Hall ran the tavern on the west side of the building, while his wife Grace (Voelker) Hall, ran the grill on the east side. It was a friendly spot in town, and many organizations and boards met there for meetings and luncheons.

Grace's Grill was the subject one morning on St. Louis's Ed Wilson's radio talk show in the early 1950s. He and Russ David, another St. Louis celebrity, had come to the McCray-Dewey High School the night before to perform at a show. Before the show, both Wilson and David stopped at Grace's Grill for a bite to eat. The next morning Wilson told about Grace's good food.

Both Noah and Grace were well-liked business people in Troy during the 1940s, 1950s, and 1960s.

Hayman's Restaurant

Deb Hayman and Kurt Ackerman, children of Ken Ackerman, owned Hayman's Restaurant and the Roadhouse Inn. The restaurant was once one of four restaurants in the family chain of restaurants within a 25 mile radius. They included Ken-Don's Restaurant, owned by Ken Ackerman in Hamel; Ackerman's Restaurant at Route 143 and I-55, owned by Don and Elaine Ackerman; Randy's Restaurant on Cherry Lane near 1-55/70 in Troy, owned by Randy and Carol Ackerman; and Hayman's.

Ken-Don's was destroyed by a lightning strike in the spring of 1985; Randy's Restaurant was destroyed by fire in December of 1999; and Hayman's burned to the ground in August of 1984. Ackerman's was sold when Don and Elaine Ackerman retired. The Ackermans were fine restaurateurs and knew restaurant management, and they served delicious food.

Hayman's, as well as Ken-Don's, Ackerman's and Randy's, was a popular eating place in the area and drew people from many miles away. Hayman's was one of the first in the area to have a salad bar which was set within an antique bathtub.

The Roadhouse Inn was not damaged by the fire. Kurt Ackerman continued with the business for a time. It since has been sold and is under new ownership.

Grace's Grill and Noah's Ark, 1957

Edward Heinecke (at left) with his employees.

Heinecke Cigar Factory

Edward Heinecke was the owner of the Troy factory which produced the popular "REX" cigar. The cigars were from selected, well-seasoned tobacco and were noted for their purity, flavor and workmanship. The Rex cigar was a long filter article and sold for five cents in 1932.

Heinecke had operated a cigar factory business for several years in Marine, IL. In 1929, he opened the factory in Troy. Patrons from Troy, Collinsville, Maryville, Marine and other towns kept his establishment busy, filling orders. Mr. Heinecke reported a constantly increasing business in 1932.

Edward Wilhelm Heinecke was born and grew up in St. Louis, MO, and learned the trade there. He and his wife Bertha (Murphy) Heinecke had a son Edwin Rex Henry Heinecke, born to them on March 19, 1901. They also had two other children, Frederick Boyd Heinecke, born Oct 1902, and Margaret Edith Heinecke, born in 1906.

Information from the Troy Weekly Call, *February 1, 1932, and Edwin Heineke.*

Iola's Beauty Shop

Iola Kirsch operated a beauty shop from the basement of her home for 22 years. Iola, her husband John G. Kirsch and two children, Janet Ruth and John Walter moved to Troy in 1953.

She worked at the Troy Locker Plant for 5 1/2 years when Harold and Earl Schmidt owned it. She then decided to go to beautician's school. She began her shop in 1960, when she opened in the basement of her home at 310 South Troy Avenue. She then moved the shop next door to 312 South Troy Avenue in 1968. She operated her business for 22 years (1960-1982). *Submitted by Iola Kirsch.*

J.N. Jarvis Job Printing

James N. Jarvis erected this building in 1885 for his job printing and publishing business. It was located on East Market Street, where the J.C. Gebauer residence was later built. For many years it was a voting place in township and village elections.

(Left) J.N. Jarvis Job Printing. (l. to r.) Edward Deimling, John F. Deimling, David Llewellyn, James N. Jarvis, John B. Seep and Henry Stolte.

A. Heddergott Store

A. Heddergott store, Clay Street, circa 1900.

J.N. Jarvis Job Printing Shop

William Jackson, Tree Seller

William Jackson sold walnut trees. He took the tree stumps to the grain elevator to weigh. When he had a train carload, he would ship the walnut stumps to Ohio by rail. The veneer was in the stumps, according to his son Wilbur. Jackson's truck was not always large enough to haul some trees. He borrowed a larger truck from Harry Trost.

William and Wilbur Jackson loading walnut tree on Trost's truck, 1929 or 1930.

Jerry Dickman Milk Hauling

Jerry Dickman was the owner of a milk truck service, which hauled fresh milk from farms, in Troy, Marine, Hamel, Alhambra, Grantfork, and Edwardsville to the dairy. He started with his first truck in 1954, and increased to four trucks in the late 1950s. He picked up the milk in the early morning, seven days a week, sunshine or snow. In the

Four of Jerry Dickman's milk trucks, 407 Cook Avenue, late 1950s.

twelve years of hauling canned milk, Jerry told many stories of the challenge of picking up and delivering milk on time. He had to make sure every truck would be ready by 5:30 a.m. each morning. The narrow, unpaved country roads were soft in the spring and drifted shut in the winter. When the farm lanes would drift closed, he would drive across frozen fields, and would sometimes need a tractor to pull him through to the next farm.

In the 1960s farming changed with government regulations, and many farmers stopped dairying because bulk milk tanks were the trend. By 1965 the time was near to sell or change the way of hauling. Jerry found a buyer and sold the business. Later that year he started hauling grain for Russ Klaustermeier of Troy. *Submitted by Darlene Dickman.*

Jo-Nels Florist

Barbara and Ray Schuessler owned Jo-Nels for several years at the northwest corner of Center and South Main Streets.

Kiesel Building

The Kiesel Building at the northeast corner of Kimberlin and East Market Street was razed in 1919, but not before a story was written in the newspaper about its life. Built in 1845, it was erected by Colonel Thomas Judy who conducted a general store within its walls. Judy sold the business to William Mize and the business was continued under the firm name of William Mize and Son, the latter being John H. Mize.

Then it passed to the ownership of James B. Edgar who conducted a general store there until the Civil War broke out. Edgar then went to California. Edgar sold the building to Wiley Bryant, who also conducted a general store and he sold it in 1868 to Julius A. Barnsback and W.W. Jarvis who ran a hardware store there.

They sold it the same year to William Donoho who continued a hardware business and added a line of drugs – a rare combination in that day and age. Donoho sold the building to Dr. F.A. Sabin who continued to use it as a drug store and a printing office. The *Weekly Bulletin* was published there for a short time in the rear end of the structure. Dr. Sabin sold the building to Joseph Kiesel. After that, the building served a number of purposes.

Kiesel Building

S. Kingston ran a drug store there and A.R. Snodgrass used it as a confectionery and post office. George Kiesel had a general store in it for a number of years, as did J.H. Hallis. Its last occupancy was a grocery store owned by Theodore Gebauer.

It had been vacant for several years prior to its demise and was used as a storeroom by various parties. The taking down of the old building revealed the substantial manner in which it was built, another rarity in 1919. The heavy timbers were all of oak, hand hewn and in a good state of preservation.

This was not a complete history for the building, but as near as The Troy Call *could get at the time.*

Kiser's TV Sales and Service

Kiser's TV Sales and Service, located at 107 South Main Street, was owned by Gene Kiser who opened the business in the 1950s. Gene, his wife Fern, and their sons worked in the business. The business slogan was "It's wiser to call Kiser."

The building burned to the ground in February 2001.

Kiser's TV Sales & Service, 1991

Klein's Shoe Store

Edward H. Klein owned and operated a shoe store in Troy. He was born in 1877 in Troy, the son of Andrew and Bertha (Petzoldt) Klein. After attending Troy public schools, he took a course at the Bryant and Stratton Business College in St. Louis, and later worked in a shoe store there. He worked until 1901, when he returned to Troy and bought the business from his father, who had established it in 1867. In 1912, Klein's was the only shoe store in Troy.

Edward H. Klein, circa 1912

Klein was married in Worden, IL, in 1910 to Lena M. Dornseif. They had one son in 1912, Eugene Edward Klein. In 1912, Klein's store was in the Braner building at the corner of East Market and Kimberlin Streets. He later built a building on South Main Street. *This information from a 1912 issue of the* Edwardsville Intelligencer.

Klein Building on South Main.

Kroger Company Store

The Kroger Store was located in the west side of the first floor of the Braner Building at the corner of Kimberlin and East Market Street. It was managed by John Kelly in the 1940s and 1950s. The east side of the building contained Cullop Hardware Store. At the same time, City Hall was located on the second floor in a back room above the store. Most of the remaining second floor was occupied by the Legion Hall.

A fire originated in the basement of the Kroger Company Store, causing extensive damage to the floor with heat and smoke damage to the entire store. The fire caused an estimated $14,000 in damage to the stock, machinery and equipment. Fire Chief John Kelly, also Kroger's manager, determined the total damage to the building was $8,000. Of that amount, $1,000 was figured on the Legion Hall. Cullop Hardware Store's smoke damage was estimated at $200. City Hall's damage was over $22,000. The fire was believed to have been caused by faulty wiring in the basement. Ironically, a fire destroyed the building completely in 1992.

Later, the Kroger Company withdrew the grocery franchise in Troy, and Kelly opened the A.G. Market in the same location; but he expanded it to the entire first floor. When Mr. Kelly died, his son-in-law, Wib Klueter, took over the store. In 1982, the store was moved to South Main under the management of Mike Klueter, a grandson of John Kelly. It is now known as Kelly's Deli.

James Deeren, owner of Christian Wolf Inc., later bought the building and manufactured communion wafers there until fire destroyed the building in 1992. *Information from The Troy Tribune, February 21, 1952.*

Levo Bakery and Building

The bakery at 110 West Market has a long history. It stands on Lot 3, Block 3 of the original town of Troy in J.C. Gonterman's addition. The date of its construction is unknown; but, around 1903 Fred and Mary Riebold had a confectionery there. Later, Mary K. Kuntzmann owned a store there.

Other owners of the property included Henry Schwalm, N.M. Jarvis, Charley Schultze, W.S. Schmitt, Fred H. Gornet, Edgar H. Little and Darwin B. Schroeder. Around 1922, Peter Levo Sr. ran a grocery store in the building. Not until 1925 was the building purchased by Edward T. Levo, who began a bakery and named it the Mother's Way Bakery, the name coming from the best entry in a naming contest.

He sold the bakery to his brother Peter Levo (Jr.) in 1933, who operated it until the early 1960s, changing its name to Levo's Bakery. In the early 1960s, Pete Levo moved his bakery business to the basement of his home at Center and Ash Streets.

Edward T. Levo still owned the building, and leased it to several businesses over the years. In the late 1960s and early 1970s, it was Koch Dry Cleaners (pick up and delivery); and later it was Arview Heating and Cooling. After Edward's death in 1967, the building was purchased by Oscar Mersinger, Edward's brother-in-law.

Les' Ideal Spot

Les's Ideal Spot, northwest corner of Main and Market Streets, owner Lester Hazzard behind the bar, Duncan McCormick, and Troy's only policeman, Chief Ernest Spencer, circa 1940s.

Outside of Levo's Bakery, 1939. (l. to r.) Ike Wurtz, Paul Levo (age 3) and Pete Levo.

In 1973, Stoyan "Star" Stoyanoff made it into a bakery again. Stoyanoff had operated a bakery in E. St. Louis, prior to coming to Troy. He named the Troy facility Star Bakery.

Later, Stoyanoff retired, and his son, Mark Stoyanoff, ran the bakery. In 2001, Stoyanoff sold the business. *Submitted by Mae Grapperhaus.*

Levo's Homestead Tavern

Edward T. "Ed" Levo owned and operated Levo's Homestead Tavern at 108 West Market Street for over 30 years. His specialty was jack salmon sandwiches.

According to an old abstract, the lot which is part of lots 1 and 2 in the original town of J.C. Gonterman's addition. Platted by F.T. Kraft in 1839 and recorded before Troy was incorporated in 1857. Numerous owners have owned the property and it is believed that the log cabin, which is under the current siding and a portion of the present building, was built in 1855. The property has been sold many times through the years. In 1856, James M. Bailey sold it to William T. Robinson. It was then sold to Samuel Cowles. The names of Keisel, Mills, Harris, Schwalm, Jarvis and Schultze were among early owners.

In 1903, Mary K. Riebold bought it from Charley Schultze. During that time the ownership went back and forth for various reasons and according to the abstract there were mortgage deeds, quit claim deeds and release deeds. Riebold sold it to Mary Kuntzmann in 1906. It was sold back and forth again with various legal documents added to the abstract. By the 1930s Ed Levo bought it.

In approximately 1964, Levo had a stroke and could not care for the tavern any

Lions Theatre (inset: Sheldon Lending), 1949

more. He then moved to live with his sister and her husband, Louise and Oscar Mersinger. Later he resided at Rockwood Nursing Home where he died in 1967.

While he was incapacitated, Alice and Chris Rensing ran the tavern. The tavern was then sold to Al Ludwig, who ran an insurance agency. Since that time it has been sold numerous times and used for several different types of businesses. David Margherio owned it for several years. He owned the State Farm Insurance business. Later, the Shelter Insurance office was housed there. Currently a communion wafer manufacturer owns it.

The building was being used as a tavern and was an early stage coach stop. The building has a small apartment on the second floor, which is leased. The Levos, Ed's parents and siblings, lived in the building for a short time in the 1920s during the time they operated a store next door at 110 West Market Street (bakery building).

In the spring of 2002, the City of Troy designated it as a historical landmark. It is also designated as historically significant by the Troy Historical Society and was awarded a plaque in 2000. Shortly after the award was given to the building, it was sold to a new owner and the plaque was returned by the former owner. *Submitted by Mae Grapperhaus.*

Lions Theatre

Located at 120 East Market Street (now the parking lot of the Troy Municipal Complex), the Lions Theatre opened on June 14, 1949. The Troy Lions Club was instrumental in getting the theatre built and opened. The building was estimated to cost $52,000, with the fixtures costing an additional $25,000 to $30,000.

Sheldon Lending of St. Louis was the first manager. He was hired for the theater by the Troy Civic Improvement Company and began work in June 1949. Frank Mann became the new owner in June 1952. Lending, who also managed the O'Fallon Theatre, took a position with the U.S. Defense Corporation in St. Louis, Missouri.

The opening night performances were at regular admission price of 48 cents. Proceeds from these performances went to the Lions Club treasury to help pay off the building's $23,000 debt. Performances were scheduled for 7 p.m. and 9:30 p.m. The high school band played a few selections before the opening performances both evenings (June 14 and 15, 1949). The opening featured movie was " Miss Tatlock's Millions" starring Wanda Hendrix and John Lund. Approximately 110 people attended the grand opening. Four free passes were given away at the opening performances to Vera Mae Brown of Troy; Bill Ray of Edwardsville; Mrs. Theda Atwood of Troy and 0. E. Helmich of Troy. Helmich gave his pass to one of the small boys. On the first regular night of admission, Lewis Frey bought the first adult ticket and James Bowler bought the first child's ticket. Attendance brought people in from Edwardsville, Collinsville, St. Jacob and Troy.

The Homestead Tavern, 108 West Market, 1965.

The theatre project originally began in 1945, when William Schmitt, chairman of the Lions Troy Civic Improvement Company, made a verbal agreement with Dutel Braner of Collinsville for a business lot. A meeting was set for the Lions Club to finally approve the lot, but VJ day interfered with the meeting. When the Lions members did approve it the following week, Braner informed Schmitt the lot had been sold. Another one of several difficulties developed when it appeared no permit could be secured for building. However, after several trips to Springfield and a great deal of correspondence, a permit was secured, primarily through the efforts of Harry Taake, Jarvis Township Supervisor, who contacted State Representative Melvin Price. Then, the man who had a lease on the theatre died.

Later, when four different contractors had submitted bids for construction, all were too high for the money the Lions Club had in the project treasury. The deal was finally made with Modine and Company of Edwardsville. Members of the committee who worked with Schmitt on the theatre project were Jewel Edwards, Rollie Moore, Ted Guennewig, Tom Taylor, Estel Smith, Harold Schmidt, William Pitt and Wilbur "Mick" Wyatt.

The theatre flourished for 10 or more years. Then, as television became a major part of the family household, movie attendance dropped, causing the Lions Theatre to be remodeled and made into a bowling alley, joining the way of many small movie houses in the U.S. Following the theatre days, Trojan Bowl was a center of entertainment in Troy until the late 1970s when it burned to the ground in January during zero temperatures. The Lions club not only built the theatre, but also helped to bring the newspaper and the bank to Troy. *Information from the June 1952,* Troy Tribune.

Dan G. Liebler's General Merchandise

Dan G. Liebler owned and operated a general merchandise store on 107 South Main Street. His telephone number was 9. The store offered groceries, as well as general merchandise, in the early part of 1900.

Mr. Liebler was a civic-minded individual and was involved in the fire department and other civic organizations.

Ma's Café

Lumber Companies of Troy

Records show that Troy had a lumber business as far back as 1872. However, the first lumber company of record was that of Will W. Jarvis who had Chicago Lumber at the corner of Market and Hickory Streets. In 1890 the Troy Lumber Yard was in business and owned by H. H. Padon, Troy's first mayor. By 1895, the Troy Lumber Yard was owned by the Busse brothers. From 1899 to 1904, records show the Troy Lumber Yard owned by Chris Busse Jr., and it was located somewhere on South Main Street. Later, from 1908 to 1910, H.F. Kueker and Son owned it, and it was still located on South Main Street. By 1914, Stolze-Trares Lumber Company was located at Center and Washington Streets. Seligman and Keck owned and operated the lumber business at the same address for a number of years, beginning in approximately 1924.

A Mr. Schwartz was involved in the lumber company for a while, according to old timers. Then in about 1933, James Watson became owner of the Watson Lumber Company at Center and Washington. In the 1940s, James Watson brought in sons, Blair and Leeds, to run the store and yard at the same location. Later, James Deeren also became bookkeeper in the business.

Later, in the 1970s, Troy Building Supply owned by Dave Hart (and associates) was in charge of the business. By the early 1990s, R.P. Lumber Company, owned by R. Plummer, bought the facilities. The old building and sheds were razed in 2002. *Information from old Troy newspapers.*

Ma's Café

Ma's Café was owned and operated by Elsie "Ma" Polwort. The little restaurant was in the building at 201 East Market Street, then later, at the corner of Charter and South Hickory Street near her home.

Meyer Landscaping and Garden Center, March 1987.

The Miner's Store

Inside the Miner's Store located at 201 S. Main Street. William Dunstan worked there, circa 1900s.

Ma ruled with a firm hand. All the kids would gather in her café and respected her. She had the café-confectionery until she was up in years and closed it in the early 1980s. Customers could always get good hamburgers at Ma's Café.

Meyer Landscaping and Garden Center

Meyer Landscaping and Garden Center opened at 802 Sherbourne in the spring of 1987.

Jerry Meyer, owner and operator, had a landscaping business out of his home for 10 years prior to opening the store. Betty Daly was the manager and the company's landscape consultant. Meyer also owned Meyer Yard Service. Jerry died in the late 1990s, and the business was sold.

Modern Beauty Shop

The Modern Beauty Shop, at the southeast corner of South Main and Center Streets, was owned and operated by Virginia Wyatt from 1941 to 1945. Virginia was married to Wilbur "Mick" Wyatt, who was very active in the community and in the Troy Lions Club.

Moderne Linen/ Morgan Linen Service

Moderne Linen was owned by Harold Hosto, who sold it to Morgan Linen Service of St. Louis around 1978.

Newport Bottling Works

The Newport Bottling Works was founded by J. Erwin Hindmarch in the 1920s. His brother-in-law, "Babe" Elliott, worked with Erwin, helping to bottle the soda using a machine that filled one bottle at a time. The business began in Erwin's basement and later moved to a building on the south side of Route 40, east of Main Street, at 203 East Highway 40, previously the Union Dairy.

Earl and Harold Schmidt purchased the business from Erwin Hindmarch in 1929, changing the name to Newport Soda Company. Earl made deliveries and promoted the business, while Harold mixed the syrup and flavorings and bottled the soda. They soon graduated to a used "Shield" bottling machine, filling two bottles at a time. The business became difficult to operate, however, during World War II due to the rationing of sugar and bottle caps.

William "Bill" Pitt purchased the business from the Schmidt Brothers in 1944. Bill expanded the business to include new flavors and brands, introducing his own label, "Parpit."

Moderne Linen Service, 1950. (l. to r.) Billy Row, Charles Maedge

Moonlight Roller Rink and Cottages

(Right) The New Moonlight Camp Grounds, circa 1930s, owned and operated by Arthur and Irma Hartman.

The gang at Moonlight Roller Rink, early 1940s.

He installed a new automatic machine to speed up the bottling process. In the 1970s Pitt quit bottling soda but continued distributing compressed CO_2 gas, a still profitable part of the business. The glass Newport Soda bottles are now collector items. *Submitted by Harold Schmidt, Jr.*

Enos Petry, Local Electrician

Enos Petry, son of Philip and Mary (Probst) Petry, grew up in the Blackjack community. He lived in Shiloh, IL, with his wife Ella and their two children, Rita and David.

Enos was an electrician, but worked for the telephone company. His ad in *The Troy Call* instructed customers to leave orders at the telephone company for wiring or repair work. Enos did a lot of work for the farmers who were just installing electricity in the rural areas. He wired many barns and sheds after his regular day at the phone company was over.

Randy's Restaurant

Randy's Restaurant opened in 1980. It was located at 906 Cherry Lane and owned and operated by Randy and Carol Ackerman. The business flourished and served fine food. Randy's catering service also provided good food for many banquets and dinners in town.

Various civic groups held meetings and banquets there; and some held their regular monthly meetings there. Weddings, showers, holiday parties, school and family reunions, birthday parties and many other events were held at Randy's. If it were a large affair, it was held in the lower level, which was decorated with town scenes on all the walls. Dividers were used to separate smaller parties.

Upstairs was a formal dinning area on the east side and a smaller eatery with a lunch counter. On Sundays, a buffet was served in the luncheon area. To the west side of the building was a sports bar with a large screened TV. Randy's provided many wonderful times and lots of good food to local residents as well as out of town guests and travelers.

Residential Care Center

Residential Care Center, formerly known as the Professional Care, was located on Liberty Square off of South

Randy's Restaurant, May 1996.

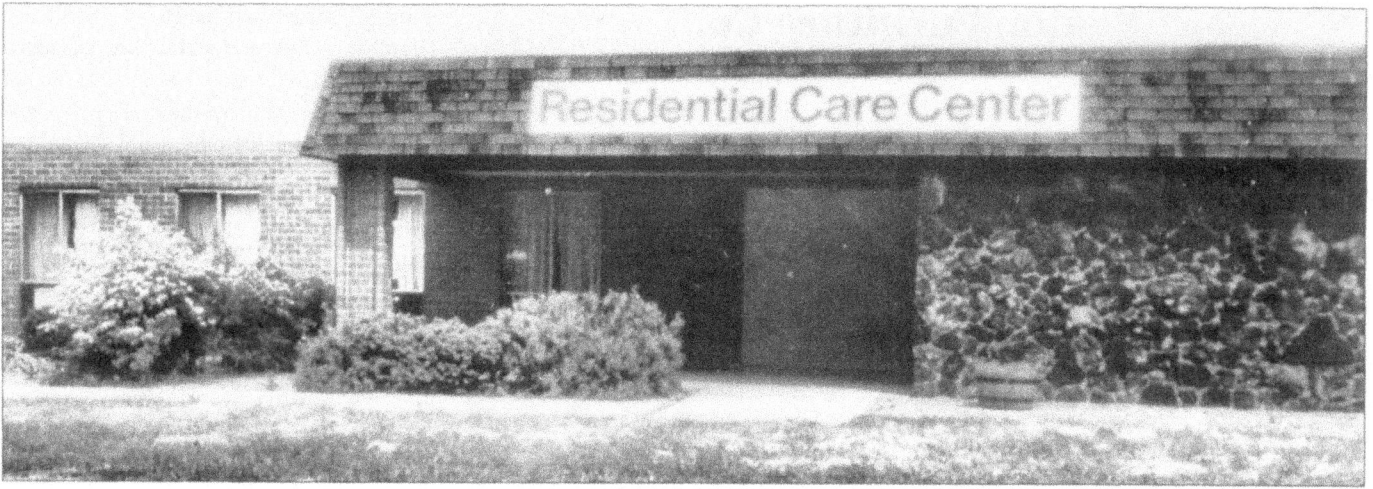

Residential Care Center, 1991

Main Street. The Center, a residential home for the handicapped, existed from the 1970s until the early 1990s under several ownerships. The building was vacant for a number of years before it was sold. A new structure was built as the Liberty Square retirement center.

Russ's Upholstery Shop

Russ's Upholstery Shop, located at 818 Industrial Drive, was owned by Russ and Renee Stark of St. Jacob. Russ, who was an expert on upholstering, also did convertible tops. The business thrived in the 1980s and 1990s. In the mid-1990s, the Starks visited their Electron Tops supplier. In addition to watching the demonstrations, they toured the factory to see how convertible tops were made. Russ and his employees installed new convertible tops for both domestic and foreign cars, in addition to running the upholstery business. Russ met with an untimely death in 2001.

Riebold's Blacksmith Shop

Doc Riebold's Blacksmith shop, corner of Collinsville Road and West Market Street, was in business in early 1900s. In 2002, the site contains an apartment building.

R & L Supply

R&L Supply, 440 Edwardsville Road, 1994. Ralph Jameson began R & L Supply in 1968 in part of the old Troy Mine complex. Later, the business was sold to his son, Ralph "Rusty" Jameson.

G.A. Shaffer Agency

In 1947, G. Allen Shaffer purchased the insurance business from J.E. Hindmarch, who had owned the business for over 50 years. Shaffer received his training in the insurance business by starting as an office boy in the firm of Ploeser, Watts, and Co. in St. Louis in 1940 and attending night school sponsored by the Insurance Board of St. Louis. He then worked for Marine Underwriters, an affiliate of Plouser Watts.

In January 1943, he entered the service during WW II. Upon his return in 1946, he rejoined Marine Underwriters and later became automobile underwriter with New Amsterdam Casualty Company in St. Louis. When the opportunity arose to assist the ailing Mr. Hindmarch in getting out his policies and eventually to purchase the business, "It was like a dream come true," said Mrs. Shaffer (the former Millie Collins). "For Allen had repeatedly stated he would like to have his own insurance business like Mr. Hindmarch's." In 1948, the Shaffers purchased the building at 213 South Main Street from Mrs. Hindmarch and converted it into office and living quarters. Mrs. Shaffer joined her husband in the office in 1949, after having been employed for several years by Bell Telephone in St. Louis. Mr. Shaffer added Real Estate Sales to his business activities in 1949. In 1963, the Shaffer Agency moved to 120 West Market Street to quarters in the new United Savings and Loan Association building. Shaffer had served as secretary-treasurer of that association since 1948. In 1964, Allen purchased the Harry Taake Insurance business when Mr. Taake retired.

Seaton Furniture Co.

Seaton Furniture, 300 Edwardsville Road, 1986.

Both Mr. and Mrs. Shaffer were born in Troy and received their education in the Troy schools. They were active members of the Troy Presbyterian Church and participated in many civic activities, including donating their former office space at 213 S. Main to the Troy Library. Their son, Bill, attended Millikin University in Decatur, IL. *Information from* The Troy Tribune, *September 7, 1967.*

Schoon's Drug Store

Formerly Kingston's Drug Store, Schoon's Drug Store stood at 112 South Main Street. Now, Dr. Mark Friederich has his dentist office there. Later, Schoon's was moved north to the corner of the block, where it remained for many years.

David Sims, Troy's Youngest Entrepreneur

David Sims, who started his climb in the business world at the tender age of 13, was perhaps the youngest entrepreneur in the history of Troy. Mr. Sims, a thrifty businessman, bought the store in 1902 and ran a general store in the Brookside Addition of Troy. The store was located at the corner of South Main and Barnsback Streets. His mother, Quinlan Hopkins Sims, had urged him to work in the store because she did not want him to work in the mines. Her first husband had died in the mines, and she did not want that to happen to young David. He ran the business until entering the army during WW I. After being injured overseas and hospitalized for over a year, David came back home and resumed operating the store.

Dave, with the help of his wife Maude, ran the store. Maude could be seen behind the counter with Dave. He was often in his truck picking up groceries and supplies. He and Maude were parents of one son, Paul Sims. After 50 years in the same location, he sold the business to Gordon and Sybil McFarland, Sr. and retired. The McFarlands ran it for a few years.

Sims had other interests in the community besides the general store. He was a director and officer of the Troy Savings and Homestead Association for 46 years and served on the board of directors at the Troy Security Bank for 26 years, serving as its vice president at one time. For a long time he was the oldest retired fireman in Madison County. He was a member of the American Legion, the Troy Lions Club, and the World War I Barracks 286. David died on February 1, 1981, at the age of 98.

Jim Hindmarch and John Schoon inside Schoon's Drug Store.

Sims Store building under renovation, 1985

Later, Bill and Donna Dawson purchased the old Sims Store building and renovated it by adding a second floor.

Dr. Donald Spencer, D.V.M.

Dr. Don Spencer (b. Sept. 28, 1942, d. May 31, 2000) was the only son of Warren and Della (Howard) Spencer. He had two sisters, Carol (Spencer) Deloney and Cindi (Spencer) Hoppes.

Dr. Don attended Troy schools and was in the first graduating class from the new Triad High School in 1960. He received his Doctor of Veterinary Science Degree from the University of Illinois in 1967, graduating first in his class.

He operated Troy Veterinary Clinic at 100 W. Throp for 33 years, becoming a well-known veterinarian in Troy and the surrounding area. He had a well-deserved reputation as an expert diagnostician with patients coming from hundreds of miles away to seek his expertise and services.

Dr. Don married Joan Dehler on Aug. 19, 1978, after her son Michael Dehler had earlier suggested that Don needed to meet his mother. Joan, with her great love of animals, often worked in the clinic with him. Together they made the Troy Veterinary Clinic a Troy landmark.

St. Louis Dairy Company

St. Louis Dairy Co. milk collection site, 1897. Sitting, Gus Droll.

Another Troy landmark honors Dr. Spencer today. The small memorial park at the corner of Center and Main Streets has been dedicated to Troy's own Dr. Don. *Information from Joan Spencer and written by Jeanette Dothager.*

Sunset Inn

The Sunset Inn was located on Route 162. Frieda Burian owned and operated it from the 1940s through the early 1990s. At one time she was the oldest licensed bartender in Madison County. She ran a tight ship and was strict in her tavern rules. The petite lady didn't like cigars smoked in her bar and did not welcome motorcyclists.

Various clubs and organizations held many dinner meetings there. The Troy Grain Company met there on numerous occasions in the 1940s and 1950s for meetings and banquets. Frieda always cooked a good meal for the dinners.

Frieda was in her 90s when she retired.

After the bar was sold, a number of other owners ran it. It partially burned in the mid 1990s and opened a short time later, but it was not as large as it had been before.

Dr. Donald Spencer, D.V.M.

Sunset Inn, 1992

Aerial view of Ackerman's Motel, Tasty Treet and Wash and Dry Laundry, circa 1970s.

Tasty Treet

The old Tasty Treet building, located at the intersection of Riggin Road and Route 162, was owned by Bill and Isabelle Ackerman, who operated the small restaurant in the 1950s. Tasty Treet served sandwiches, fries, and soft drinks. It became a hangout for the mid-1950s high school crowd. Later, the building became a laundromat, and in the late 1980s, it became a video rental store. Now a convenience store and gas station occupies the site.

The Hair House

The Hair House owned by Jean Furfaro was located on South Hickory Street. Formerly, she operated a beauty salon and a laundromat on Americana Drive near Route 40.

The "Shack" at Donk's Mine

In the early part of the century (1920s) John Wesley Wyatt operated a little restaurant-cafe at the Donk's mine west of Troy. The location was in the Riggin Road and Edwardsville Road (Route 162) intersection area. In this wooden building resembling an old chicken house, he would cook for the truckers sitting on stools at the counter. He sold hamburgers, coffee, soda, candy, and pastries and donuts from the local bakery to the men waiting to load coal.

Wyatt's daughter Emma believes that this was possibly the first fast food restaurant in Troy, serving a limited menu that was both genuine and tasty. Wyatt's motto was "No profanity in this place." "If there is profanity and bad language, you are out the door," he would say. *Information from Emma Wyatt Karmn.*

Tique Shoppe

When two friends with the same interest got together, they purchased the building at 107 East Market Street. Those two friends were Mae Grapperhaus and Doneise Strom who began the Tique Shoppe, an antique and collectible store. After redecorating the inside of the 87-year-old structure that was once the Troy Post Office, the business opened its doors around Thanksgiving in 1989.

Tique Shoppe, July 1992

Both owners had other full time positions and the store was open only about three days a week. Several friends and relatives helped run the store at various times. In 1995, the owners decided to close the store and lease out the building.

The building was leased to Dorsy Menendez and Julie Boucher who ran Twice As Nice, a consignment shop. Later, Dave and Sons ran a heating and cooling business. Other businesses that leased it were Vibrations and a motor sports store. It is currently a beauty salon.

Tri-County TV Sales and Service

Tri-County TV Sales and Service, located at 112 East Market Street, opened about 1970.

In 1974, Charles and Mary Hobbs, the owners of Tri-County TV Sales, bought the sales portion of the business from Gene Fayollat. The Hobbs announced a new line of products, including refrigerators, food freezers, washers and dryers, compactors, room air-conditioners, stoves, portable dishwashers, disposals, televisions and

The Hair House, circa 1986. Jean Furfaro standing on the left.

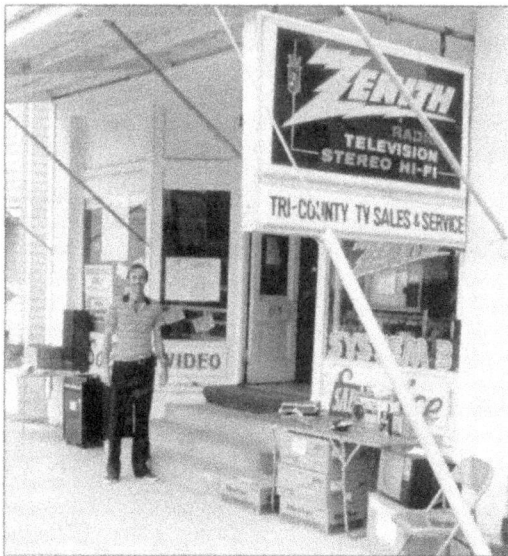

Gene Fayollat, Tri-County TV, 115 S. Main Street, 1985.

small appliances. Gene Fayollat, a certified technician, became the operator of Tri-County TV Services and took care of the television repairs.

Later in the late 1980s, Fayollat opened a shop on South Main Street. He and his wife, Joyce, owned and operated the shop under Tri-County TV Sales and Service for several years.

Trojan Bakery

The Trojan Bakery was started May 1, 1951, by Larry and Ruth Ostresch in the old Cum-Bac Cafe. Later, they purchased the Joe Nemnich building at 115 South Main Street for the bakery. The Nemnichs were residing in the building prior to it being sold.

When the bakery first opened, it was designed to serve meals and sell doughnuts. The doughnut business was so heavy the Ostresch's decided to eliminate meals and concentrate on doughnuts and other bakery goods.

Troy Building Supply, 1990s

Added to the doughnuts and pastries, the Ostreschs put their newest addition, a baker's oven, to work producing homemade bread. *Information from* The Troy Tribune, *July 19, 1951, and from recollections of Charmion Semanisin.*

Troy Building Supply

In the early 1990s, Troy Building Supply Inc. opened at 120 West Center Street.

Formerly, it was the Watson Lumber Company. Troy Building Supply was once owned by Dave Hart. Later the business was sold to a large conglomerate. The lumber company moved to a new location along Route 40 and Formosa Road. The old building was demolished in 2002.

Troy Center

The Troy Center opened its doors in August 1994 and was located at 300 Edwardsville Road, the location of the former Seaton's Furniture Store. Roland and Eileen Lataille were the owners/operators. The hall accommodated up to 450 people and was equipped with a kitchen. The facility was used for sit-down dinners, business conferences, weddings, and regular monthly meetings of civic organizations. The Troy Center closed its doors in October 2001, and currently (in 2002) the building is for sale.

Troy City Mills

Gustave Vetter was the proprietor of the Troy City Mills, according to the county history.

Other sources identify T. A. Throp and Company as the owner. Located on West Clay

Troy City Mills, late 1800s

Street, grain and flour were ground in this 4-story building. The mill could grind 40,000 barrels of flour per year. A 10 x 26 ft. cooper shop was attached to the mill and employed 15 coopers. The large mill pond near the mill extended to today's Watt Street area.

The mill burned in the late 1800s. A large millstone taken from the site now rests in the front lawn of McCray-Dewey School on Dewey Street.

The 1880 U.S. Federal Industrial Census lists both William Donoho and Gustave Vetter as having flour and grist mills. Donoho's had an elevator.

53

Troy Call

(Right) Troy Call. *B.W. Jarvis and John Healey.*

(Left) Troy Call, *circa 1904 (photo taken by J. Norbury). (l. to r.) Mack McConville, John Healey and B.W. Jarvis.*

(Right) Troy Call, *1949. Ben and Jim Jarvis.*

54

The Ottwein Confectionery, 1927. Behind the counter (l. to r.), Irma Ottwein, Mrs. Carrie Ottwein and Dot Becker. Customers: Mr. Auwarter and Mr. Bugger.

Front: Marie and Harold Schmidt. Back: Earl and Leola Schmidt. Wedding photo, April 4, 1931.

The Troy Confectionery

George (Sr.) and Carrie Ottwein operated this little restaurant from 1927 through 1929. They rented 1/2 of the building at 111 South Main (currently an insurance company) from a Mrs. Hampe and converted it to a confectionery. They bought a marble-topped soda fountain from John Schoon, Troy druggist. Their teenage daughters, Irma and Helen Ottwein, helped with the cooking and waitressing. They furnished full family style meals at noon for 35 cents, including home-made pie. The fountain served ice cream specialties and cold drinks, such as cherry cokes for 5 cents. At this time the railroad was being built south of town, and the workers came at noon for a fine home-cooked meal.

In 1929 the business was sold to Edna and Bob Sliva.

Troy Food Mart

Troy Food Mart (TFM) and the Troy Tidy Wash Laundromat, located at 504 Edwardsville Road, were owned and operated by Selda and Rollie Reiss. They ran TFM for nearly 20 years. Prior to the Reisses running the business, Don Svoboda had run the Dairy Mine at the same location. It was an early convenience store for Troy. The old Dairy Mine was razed for Reiss's Troy Food Mart built at the same location.

In 1994, Selda and Rollie turned over the business to Mary Evans and Craig Harris. Later, the building was sold to a banking institution that built a new bank on the property, after razing the existing buildings.

Troy Frozen Foods

Troy Frozen Foods, 200 South Main, was started by Earl and Leola Schmidt and Harold and Marie Schmidt with the grand opening on November 18, 1944. The building was purchased from Theodore Gebauer in 1944 and was the original site of the Hampton Harness Shop. In a portion of this building was Troy Frozen Foods and in the other portion, the Dunstan Grocery Store. The initial remodeling involved converting the store building to a freezer/cooler locker facility. The refrigeration equipment was purchased from National Refrigeration Company of St. Louis. Wilbur H. Kurtz of Collinsville did the remodeling work, and the wiring, C.W. Hirschi of Highland. The business opened during World War II and was endorsed by the War Production Board (WPB) and by the Triple A.

Initially there were 550 frozen food rental lockers available to the public; and on opening day, 430 had already been rented. A later expansion of the facility added additional locker units and, at one time, more than 1000 were available and rented. Troy Frozen Foods provided the public with freezer capabilities and the opportunity to purchase in quantity. Home freezers were rare at this time but later, as home freezers became more popular and available, the rental unit usage declined.

Earl and Harold sold custom-cut beef quarters, dressed hogs, chilled, cut, wrapped, and quick-frozen meat for home freezers. Home made sausages were also a popular item. During deer season, 300+ deer would be processed each year. Earl and Harold expanded Troy Frozen Foods to include the area occupied by the grocery store due to the increasing popularity of custom-cut freezer meats, and the business thrived.

Selda and Rollie Reiss, July 1994

Troy Frozen Foods, 1945

In August 1950, army officers from San Salvador flew into Scott Air Force Base and wanted to buy a quarter of beef, as good meat in their area was scarce. Officers at Scott recommended Troy Frozen Foods. After returning to San Salvador, they sent word to the Schmidt brothers to have six quarters of beef and two hogs ready for shipment. On a return trip to Scott, the officers stopped at the locker plant and picked up the meat. They returned to San Salvador, a 2500 mile trip, flying at a high altitude for about 15 hours so the meat would not thaw.

Many local people were employed at the plant over the years it operated, but most notable was Mr. Wilbur (Mick) Wyatt of Troy. He started in November 1945, just one year after the plant opened, and worked there for the Schmidts until they sold the business in November 1971, and continued working for the new owners until April 1972.

Troy Frozen Foods was sold to Mr. And Mrs. Donald Nihiser of Highland, IL, on November 29, 1971, 27 years and 11 days after the initial opening. The building was destroyed by fire on August 11, 1993. The Nihisers then relocated Troy Frozen Foods to 404 East Highway 40, where it remains in operation today. *Submitted by Carolyn Schmidt Golfin, daughter of Harold and Marie Schmidt.*

Troy Gifts and Flowers

Troy Gifts and Flowers, located on the lower level at 119 South Main with entrances from both the south and the east sides, was owned by Rita Youngman from 1975 to 1984. She purchased the business from Mr. McClintock. *Information from Rita Youngman.*

Troy Gifts and Flowers, 1984

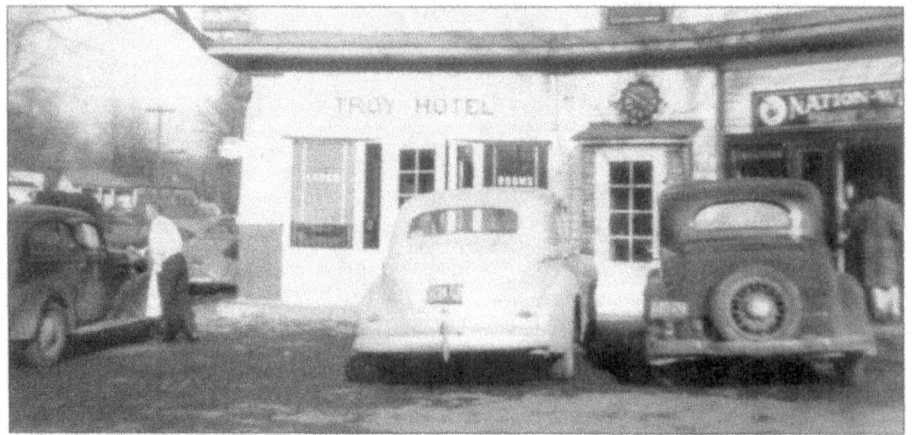
Troy Hotel and Nation-Wide Store, circa 1940s

Troy Hotel on the Wedge

Rollie R. Moore came to Troy in the spring of 1926. He purchased the property known as "the wedge" back then. It was located in the West End at the intersection of Border (later Collinsville Road) and Center Streets. The purchase was made from Dr. Edgar H. Little.

Moore, from East St. Louis, had 25 years experience in the restaurant business in St. Louis and East St. Louis and knew how to please customers. He planned to improve the property and add a modern gasoline filling station and restaurant on the north side of the building. In addition to the hotel and restaurant, he operated a Nationwide Store. After Rollie Moore's term as mayor (1949-1952), he went back into business at the store. He had leased the building to Harry Swanson for two and one half years. *Information from* The Troy Call, *Feb.19, 1926, and* The Troy Tribune, *July 3, 1952, issue.*

Troy House Furnishing Company

The Troy House Furnishing Company, house furnishers and undertakers was established and incorporated in 1910. The firm carried a stock of all that was necessary for a complete house furnishing. A feature of this firm was the undertaking and embalming department, which was in every way abreast of the times (in 1912) and was the only establishment of its kind in 1912. Henry C. Kueker was the only licensed embalmer in the township and ranked among the very best in Madison County.

A white and black hearse was carried, as were also all trappings suitable to the occasion. Henry F. Kueker was president of the Company and Henry C. Kueker, his son, was secretary and treasurer. Henry F. Kueker was born in Mandelsloh, Germany, in 1852; his parents were Christ and Louisa (Feddeler) Kueker.

After attending the public school in his native country, he worked on a farm and in a flour mill until he was 16 years of age, when he emigrated to the United States in 1868, entirely alone.

Henry C. Kueker, circa 1930

Arriving in Chicago without funds, he took whatever work was offered but in 1869 moved west, settling in Randolph County where he worked on a farm.

After he had enough money saved, he bought a farm in 1876. Three years later, he moved to Pin Oak Township, where he again took up farming, remaining there until 1892.

He then settled on a farm near Troy and later bought another farm. In 1905, he moved to Troy, where he started in the lumber business with his son, the firm being styled H.F. Kueker and Son. Finally, in 1910, the lumber business was disposed of and the Kuekers, father and son, opened the homefurnishing and undertaker business.

Of the Lutheran faith, Henry F. Kueker was a leading member. He was an openhearted, open-handed man who

Henry Kueker in his hardware store.

gave many young enterprises his encouragement and financial help.

He married Christina Dowel in Ruma, IL, on March 9, 1876. They had five children, Henry C., Louisa, Linda, Anna and Clara Kueker.

Henry C. Kueker was born in 1885 in Pin Oak Township. His grammar school education was received in Troy, then he took a course in the Scranton Correspondence School. His first employment was with his father on the farm, where he worked until 1905. He then moved to Troy with his parents. They started the lumber business and later launched the Troy House Furnishing Company.

In 1911, he took the course of embalming in St. Louis and in 1912 took the state examination at Peoria and passed. He married Lydia F. Helmich of Troy. *Information was taken from a 1912 issue of the* Edwardsville Intelligencer.

Troy Livery Feed and Stable

Troy Livery Feed and Stable was located west of 111 West Market Street at the corner of Washington and Market Streets. Mr. Kimberlin owned it. He advertised that he had "a hack line to and from the Vandalia depot. Horses and mules bought and sold. First-class turnouts." One of his competitors was the Star Stable owned by N.M. Jarvis, who also bought and sold horses. Mr. Jarvis advertised that he had new rigs and gentle horses. William Meiners, proprieter of the Central Hotel, advertised "A good stable in connection with the Hotel."

Kimberlin family in front of the Troy Livery Feed and Stable, circa 1900.

Troy Marine and Tackle

Troy Marine and Tackle, a boat and outboard motor dealership located on Highway 40 east, opened in June 1978, under the ownership and management of Gary and Becky Kueker. The dealership carried a line of aluminum boats from flat bottom johnboats to deluxe bass boats; a line of flake tournament bass boats and sleek 4-seater runabouts; and fiberglass boats from 26 foot cruisers to 15 foot ski boats. They also handled a complete line of fishing tackle and related equipment. The firm provided service facilities for engine repair and a shop for fiberglass boat repair.

The business flourished for about 10 years. *Information taken from the* Troy Tribune, *May 25, 1978.*

Troy Press Brick Company

A new industry was announced on the front page of the Troy newspaper in 1906. James E. Hindmarch, a brick layer, and Adolph Meyer teamed up to comprise the firm of Hindmarch and Meyer, a manufacturer of hollow concrete building blocks. They named it the Troy Press Brick Company. The business provided brick for the Troy community which was used in several buildings around town, namely the Braner Building at Kimberlin and East Market Streets in 1907.

Hindmarch was the grandfather of Dorothy Hindmarch Scott, who in 2002, resides in Troy. Dorothy is the daughter of James' son, John Irwin Hindmarch, an attorney. Later on, James Hindmarch worked for John Schoon at Schoon's Drug Store. No information could be obtained about Adolph Meyer.

Union Dairy Company

Union Dairy Company, near the Vandalia Railroad south of Main and Route 40, early 1900s

In 1916 John Feldmeier of the Exchange Bank sold the plant of the Troy Press Brick Company at a receiver's sale in front of the Troy Post Office. John F. Deimling auctioned the plant in front of a large crowd, including a number of attorneys present representing interested parties. However, Mrs. Augusta Gornet purchased the company with a bid of $2,000.

The Press Brick Company was located along the Vandalia Railroad east of the depot. It included 18 acres of ground and had originally cost about $12,000. The plant had not been in operation several years prior to the auction. As a result, the machinery, kiln and sheds were in poor condition. It was not known at that time what the future held for the plant. *Information from* The Troy Weekly Call, *September 15, 1916, and Dorothy Hindmarch Scott.*

White Horse Hotel

Built in 1853 by William Meiners, the White Horse Hotel was for travelers and their horses. It contained Les' Ideal Spot tav-

Troy Press Brick Company, circa 1900

White Horse Hotel

John Wyatt home and the business, Rooms for Rent, 116 Center Street, circa 1930s

ern, owned by Lester Hazzard, and other small shops. The hotel stood next to the Central Hotel at the corner of Main and Market Streets. In 1955, the American Legion Post 708 members and volunteers razed the building.

Wyatt's Rooms for Rent

A bright electric sign hung on the north side of the Wyatt house, at the southeast corner of Clay and Washington stating, "Rooms For Rent—Steam Heat." John Wesley Wyatt and his wife, Ora (Hurst) Wyatt, offered rooms for rent for weary travelers who came through Troy on the National Road. To

the south side of the Wyatt property was a garage with five bays for the travelers to park their automobiles while they stayed over night. One of the Wyatt daughters, Emma (Wyatt) Kamm, said that she remembers travelers coming and staying for breakfast the next morning before traveling on to their next destination. Kamm recalled that one of the boarders who stayed a while in the Rooms For Rent was a gentleman who enjoyed Ora Wyatt's delicious pies. He would always eat the pie first before the main course of the meal. The business existed for about three years in the late 1920s. The house was formerly the Dr. C.E. Molden home. *Information from Emma Wyatt Kamm.*

Medical History

Troy has been fortunate to have had medical services from trained personnel. In the spring of 1842, a Dr. Green was the only physician available. By 1850, he was joined by doctors Joseph Gates, J.S. Dewey, George H. Dewey (a student of medicine), F.W. Lytle, and Charles Dupont. Several served in the Civil War. In addition to Dr. John Dewey in 1870, Troy also had Dr. E.R. Owens, Labin Franklin, Midwife Sophie Kerns, and two druggists – David Pouchet and William T. Donohoe.

During the 1880s these physicians took care of Troy's sick: Dr. Fred Zenk, Charles Schott, Frank Schoon, Fred Zanders, J.J. Brown, F.A. Sabin, and John R. Whiteside. Dr. Frank Jackson was retired and S. Kingston was the druggist.

At the turn of the century, Frank Schoon and John R. Whiteside were no longer in Troy, but a Dr. Fred Brown was. Also, an undertaker, Charles F. Steinhaus, had come to town. In 1920, the first dentist was given as Caspar Pfaff and the veterinarian was John Schoeck. The druggist Sampson Kingston was still working at the age of 85.

A dentist was C. Miller. W.W. Billings was an M.D. and the County Coroner. In the past, funeral directors were Edwards, Mateer, Kueker, and Howell. Additional data is given below on those who served Troy's medical needs for a long time.

Dr. James Adams

Born in 1920 in Troy, Dr. James Adams was the son of James Matthew and Mary Elliott.

He attended Troy schools, Blackburn College, and the University of Illinois. He received his medical degree from the Medical School of St. Louis University.

He began his practice at the age of 28 and practiced for 32 years. He was a physician in Troy from 1957 until 1989. A debilitating disease prevented his continuing his practice.

James married Agnes Small and they became the parents of six children. *Information from his son Dr. James Adams.*

Dr. Fred W. Braner

Dr. Fred W. Braner, born in 1870, was a physician and surgeon who came to Troy in 1899. Before coming to Troy he studied and practiced medicine in Arkansas and New Athens, IL. He owned about 15 pieces of property in Troy. Braner Hall, at 113 E. Market Street, was named after him. It burned on June 10, 1992.

Dr. J. J. Brown

Dr. J.J. Brown, born in 1912, attended Shurtleff College in Alton, McKendree College in Lebanon, and Washington University in St. Louis. He graduated in 1879, and opened his practice in Troy in 1880. He also served many years as the Mayor of Troy. He married Rachel Ida Hardy in 1877 and had three sons.

Dr. George H. Dewey

Dr. George H. Dewey, brother of the prominent Dr. John S. Dewey of Troy, was a physician in Troy, Collinsville, and Marine at various times in his career. Like his better-known brother, John, George served in the Union Army during the Civil War. He died in Quincy, IL, in 1902.

Dr. John S. Dewey

Dr. John S. Dewey became a citizen of Troy in 1846, and stayed 33 years until his death. He was a surgeon and served with the Union Army in the Civil War. After the war, he served two terms in the Illinois Legislature. His wife, Angeline McCray Dewey, bequeathed the family estate to endow a high school in Troy named the McCray Dewey Academy.

Dr. Charles E. Molden

In 1907, Dr. Charles E. Molden, fresh out of Physicians and Surgeons College in St. Louis, MO, began a most outstanding medical career, dedicated to the health and welfare of the people of the Troy vicinity. When the young doctor stepped off the train at the Troy Depot, he began a service, which became a goal for any young medical man to follow.

Dr. Molden, who came to Troy, "Because I had no money and could make a start without going in debt, I became associated with Dr. J.J. Brown in Troy." Dr. Brown retired in 1919 and went to California. In those days with economic conditions as they were, a doctor was often paid in foodstuffs. All the events of those years which followed could never be told in a printed article, but Dr. Molden was a dedicated physician, answering any call, no matter the distance, the weather, or the circumstance.

He enjoyed recalling the days he made calls, first on horseback and later with a horse-drawn cart and then a prized second hand Model T Ford. During his career, Dr. Molden brought 1,285 children into the world. The first born was Freemont Schoeck. Among the many youngsters he treated was Bob Turley, Troy's famed baseball player.

But other things show what a well-rounded person Dr. Molden was. One could always speak with him on any current event or other topic. Everyone who went to his office knew his wonderful collection of all types of horses. He came by that love honestly; while attending high school, he did chores and cared for the horses owned by a Roseville, IL, doctor, Dr. E.L. Mitchell. A friend once stated that the reason Dr. Molden had such a love for horses was that as he combed and cared for the horses, he breathed enough hair and mud into himself that he could never lose their memory. It was with Dr. Mitchell that Dr. Molden had come into close contact with the medical profession. Second only to the desire to help and serve people, Dr. Molden recalled the day he decided to become a doctor so he could get enough money to purchase a handsome Chestnut mare. He remembered the surprised look on the faces of his parents back in Hume, MO, but they supported his choice. The young lad had also helped to care for the horses for the family doctor back in Hume.

In addition to his hobby of collecting horses, Dr. Molden found time to devote 40 years of active work and interest as trustee and board member of the Troy schools. He was instrumental in helping with the establishment of McCray-Dewey High School. Also, beginning in 1919, he was associated with St. Joseph's Hospital in Highland.

Dr. Molden's first wife, Nellie, died. He later married the former Irma Overman Wild. Mrs. Molden also was an active person and a leader in the Woman's Club of Troy, girl scouts, church work and other worthy projects. He was nominated by the Madison Co. Medical Association for "State Doctor of the Year" in 1952 and in 1950, he was named *The Troy Tribune* sponsored "Troy's Citizen of the Year." He was a charter member of the Troy Lions Club and was an avid gardener. Another of the great joys for Dr. Molden was his five children and 11 grandchildren. The children were Dr. C.A. Molden, physician and surgeon, St. Louis; Henry Molden, night editor of the Omaha, NB, *World-Herald*; Mrs. Lois Russel, Denver, CO, whose husband was a professor of education at Denver University; Mrs. Dellagene Karsner of Huntington Wood, MI, whose husband was associated with General Motors as a publicity man; and Dorothy Rotkis, Washington, DC, whose husband was stationed in the nation's capital with the Air Corps. *Information from The Troy Tribune, July 25, 1957.*

Dr. Walter Zielonko

Dr. Zielonko, or Dr. Z as many called him, came to Troy after obtaining his medical degree from Chicago Medical School. His friend and colleague, Dr. Shoemaker, was living and working in Marine and pointed out Troy to Dr. Z and his family. Dr. Zielonko began his medical practice in Troy on October 25, 1950.

He served in the Korea War where he served as a Captain in the U.S. Army Medical Corps. He served very near the battle zone near the end of the war. He was then sent to Japan where he worked for fourteen months, medically dismissing soldiers on their way home.

After his return to Troy in 1952, he actively pursued building a patient database. Many patients stayed with him over 50 years. He delivered over 1400 babies. He had many highlights in his career, including serving as Chief of Staff in 1984 and 1985 of Anderson Hospital.

During his later years, he directed his practice to geriatric care. After 51 years, he retired in 2001 and turned his practice over to Dr. Dorothy Loderstedt. He and his wife, Florence, have five sons and eleven grandchildren, plus his numerous Troy friends. *Information from The Times Tribune.*

2002

In 2002, the number of medical professionals has grown with the population. There are five physicians and two medical groups of physicians. Troy has seven dentists, two chiropractors, two optometrists, and two pharmacies. The citizens of Troy have access to good health care from these medical professionals and Oliver Anderson Hospital located nearby on Route 162.

Agriculture

In its early history Troy was known as a stagecoach stop on the National Road and a mining town with its own railroad service. However, the German farmers and other immigrants who came to America in the 1800s and built farms and homes in this area, contributed to Troy's development just as much as the businessmen and shop owners did. These men and women were

Wilber Edwards' "steam engine," circa 1920s.

pioneers turning the prairie into farms, the farms into homes, and the homes into part of the larger community – Troy. Although subdivisions have replaced farm fields and super highways cover old farm roads, the agricultural heritage remains an important part of Troy's own history.

Threshing time at the Knecht's Farm, north of Troy, 1920s.

Barns
A Barn Raising

A pole barn was built in one day on August 3, 1954. On July 3, 1954, Oscar Mersinger's dairy barn had burned to the ground with 1200 bales of hay inside. A

Oscar Mersinger is in front, the third from left standing. The man at the very top center on the rafters is Milton Flath. Workers throughout the day (some are not on this photo) included Henry Riebold, Arnold Langenwalter, Walter Mills, Erwin Loyet, Al Arth, Omar Bugger, Wilbur Bugger, Leo Bugger, Emil Mersinger, Paul Riebold, John Kranz, John Riebold, Leo Sedlacek, Merle Fohne, Oscar Riebold, Cornie Schmitt, Fred Heuiser, Pete Pelligrini, Guy Harris, Andy Roth, Jerome Roth, Ed Poletti, Ted Flath Sr., Ted Flath Jr. (on John Kranz's shoulders), Joe Lansing, Oswald Druessel, Herb Busse, Jim Gerstenecker, Melvin Niehaus, Arnold Niehaus, Carl Wendler, Ted Mersinger, Oliver Schlemer, Adrian Mersinger, Ben Mersinger, Dave Burgess, Gladys Burgess, Clara Flath, Erna Smith, Erwin Smith, Adelia Heuiser, Fern Gindler, Harold Gindler, Rose Siegel, John Siegel, Muriel Mersinger, Gil Mersinger, Mary Romeo, Carl Richter, Jo Lansing, Gladys Hall, David Hall, Bud Swanson, Bernice Arth, Ted Gunther, Frank Poletti, Harry Taake, Louise Mersinger, Mae Mersinger, Leo Petry, Dick Petry, Lawrence Mersinger, Joe Mersinger, Alvin Loyet and many others.

Joe Bugger's Barn, early 1900s. (l. to r.) John Schwend, Leo Bugger, Charles "Billy," Joe, Frank Bugger, Mary Emig, Adam and Ida O.

Aerial view of Mersinger Farm, circa 1950.

month later, neighbors, friends and family came to help construct this pole barn. About 100 people showed up throughout the day. Members of the Troy Grain Company Board of Directors and their wives helped cook for the workers that day. John Kranz supervised the men during the construction. The photo was taken after the noon meal.

Riebold Centennial Farm, circa 1904.

Farms
Riebold Centennial Farm

The Riebold farm received the distinction of a Centennial farm in 1972 from Gov. Ogilvie. The Johann Riebold family emigrated from Germany to Madison County in 1838. Johann purchased an eighty-acre farm located in Jarvis township, log cabin, and livestock for $700. Jacob, the youngest child was born on the farm in 1843. The farm has remained in the Riebold family for over 160 years. In the 1860s, Jacob built another log cabin on the farm. By 1900 it had been transformed into a Victorian farmhouse, covered with clapboard. The original log cabin was relocated to the current home site and used for storage. In 1948 the Victorian farmhouse was replaced with a brick home. This honor is given to farms that have been owned by the same family for at least 100 years. Since the 1970s the farm has been operated only as a grain farm. The Mark Riebold family currently lives on the farm located on E. Mill Creek Road.

Phillip Mersinger and family in front of barn, early 1900s.

Farm Animals

(Above) Phil Schultze is in back with Christ Schultze driving the mules, circa late 1800s.

August and Emma Schurman Barn, late 1930s.

(Left) Pete Pelligrini and calves, May 1939.

The John Henry Bauer "threshing machine"
crew, 1920s.

(Below) Adrian Mersinger on International-H
tractor pulling a McCormick-Deering combine
with Oscar Mersinger on top, 1948.

Threshing, early 1900s.

Farm Work

Joe Foucek on tractor at Sunnyside Nursery, circa 1950s.

John Brendel butchering a side of beef, circa 1930.

(Right) Wine-making, 1941.
Jim Romeo and Pop Levo.

Transportation

Today, many families find Troy an ideal place to live because of its physical location—close to St. Louis, near Scott Air Force Base, and in the midst of the I55-70-270 exchange.

Early settlers and townspeople found much the same situation. Troy sat on the National Road, was a stagecoach stop going west before St. Louis and the first stop going east from St. Louis, and had a railroad depot. When the automobile drove into town, several garages and dealerships soon opened to service and sell cars. From stagecoach stops to super highways, Troy has remained an important element in the development of the area.

Buggies

(Above) Clint Rood on sawhorses, Mary and little Charlie; and George Rood in buggy, early 1900s

The Kleins (owners) in buggy behind Klein Building

Streets and Roads
National Road

The National Road, later known as Route 40, passed through Troy. Over this road stagecoaches were driven between St. Louis, MO,

Automobiles

(Below) Levo, Goretti and Pelligrini families and friends showing off new touring cars which were open cars, with soft tops and side curtains, 1920s.

(Above) Auto in back of Henry Kueker's Funeral Parlor, early 1900s

and Terre Haute, IN. Troy, the first station out of St. Louis, was where the horses were changed and passengers would have their noonday meal. The stop was known as the "Johnson House," which was on the site later occupied by the Fred Auwarter home. The building at 108 West Market was said to have been

Art Hazzard's 1955 DeSoto Fireflite Sportsman, 1956

(Above) Lester and Nelson Kinder with one of the Morgan horses

the stagecoach stop, but its location is uncertain.

The stages going east left St. Louis in the morning and arrived in Troy before noon. Those going west usually passed through late at night. The arrival and departure of these conveyances were a great attraction and were always greeted by a throng of people. Julius A. Barnsback served as agent for this stage line in 1846.

When the East and West were connected by railroads, these stages became

Ella Nemnich, 1940 Ford DeLuxe, on S. Main Street, 1945

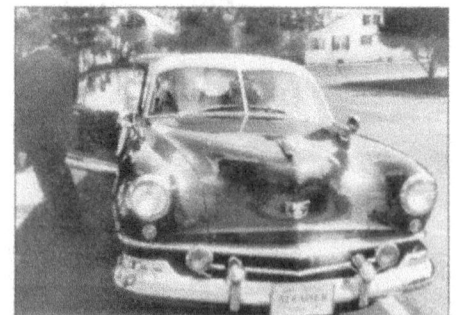

Henry J. Kaiser's personal car, a 1951 Kaiser Jade Dragon. Chauffeur and owner Bill Hubert of Troy, May 30, 1992.

outdated. A hack line from St. Louis to Highland was then established for carrying passengers and mail. This line also passed through Troy and was maintained until completion of the Vandalia Road from St. Louis to Highland in 1868.

The old stagecoach route or National Road between St. Louis and Terre Haute, IN, Troy stop, circa 1920. Now the convergence of Center Street and Collinsville Road.

South Main Street looking south near Padon Street and across from city cemetery, early 1900s.

Truck mired in Market Street mud.

New Hard Road to Troy

The Madison County Board of Supervisors in September 1927, adopted a resolution outlining a county hard road building program to extend over the next several years. Fourth on the list of roads designated to be included in the hard road program was one between Granite City and Troy by way of Peters Station and Glen Carbon.

Supervisor John Davis of Collinsville made an effort to have the route of the road from Granite City to Troy changed. He wanted the road to connect with the National Trail at Collinsville. His resolution was defeated 35 to 12.

A committee of three was appointed to handle the right-of-way for the proposed hard roads. If the right-of-way was not acquired by donation or other agreement, it would be condemned under the eminent domain laws of the state and paid for by Madison County.

Funds to build these new hard roads were to come from the Illinois Division of Highways and from the county's portion of the gasoline tax, which was estimated to be $175,000 annually.

Railroads

During the time that General William Tecumseh Sherman owned land south of town, Troy was already connected to St. Louis by railroad. Tickets were sold at the Vandalia Depot in Troy by L. P. Hale in 1895.

In 1888 a railroad was built between Madison and Troy by the Donk Brothers Coal Company. It was called the St. Louis, Troy and Eastern Railroad and was used only to haul freight and coal.

According to the census of 1910 the following railroad employees lived in Troy. Telegraphers were Franklin Baughman, Grant L. Elliott, Robert G. Godwin, Sidney R. Sweeney and Fred Clare. Switchmen were Thomas Ford and Jessie Meeker. Laborers were Erwin Spahn, Earl F. Foster,

Train engine on the Vandalia line in front of the Troy Station

William Chance, Filer C. Kennedy, Robert H. Vance, Daniel Carter and Fred J. Carner. Foremen were William M. Preston, Richard Foster, James Tierney and James W. Foster. Walter Meyer was an agent.

In 1912 Troy had two railroads: the Vandalia and St. Louis and also the Troy and Eastern. In December 1927, work was completed on a new Pennsylvania Railroad cutoff that had taken almost two years to complete. It started east of Collinsville, ran to just west of St. Jacob and passed about two miles south of Troy. About 12 miles of entirely new road was built, including 7.8 miles over the cut-off and about four miles of secondary tracks. The improvement cost $2,402,000. The track laying crew consisted of several hundred men divided into three camps – one in the Silver Creek bottom, one on the Kirsch farm south of Troy and the other one near Collinsville. The new route lessened the distance by 5600 feet and made

Train engine at the Vandalia Depot south of Troy

four slight curves of the previous 11 sharp curves. After completion of this project, only local passenger and freight trains would run over the old line through Troy.

At one time Troy had six daily passenger trains through the city. Three trains

went east and three went west. One freight train came from St. Louis each morning, bringing freight to Troy. It would pick up grain from the farmers' elevator, coal from the mine and livestock from the farmers. The Pennsylvania Railroad was offering a round trip ticket from Troy to St. Louis for the Lindbergh Reception on June 18, 1927, for 65 cents.

The Illinois Commerce Commission granted the Pennsylvania Railroad the right to discontinue four more trains in July 1927 as the result of a hearing held in Collinsville. No longer would a train run from Troy to St. Louis in the morning and none from St. Louis to Troy in the evening, and no train service at all on Sunday. It was the first time in the history of the railroad, built 60 years before, that no morning or evening train would run and no Sunday service would exist. This, of course, would make it impossible to make a trip to St. Louis and return the same day. The only accommodations offered would be to take a train into St. Louis at 2:24 in the afternoon and return at 7:57 the next morning.

The Pennsylvania, formerly Vandalia, Depot was a two-story building located on the south edge of Troy. When Grant Elliott was the agent, his family lived upstairs; he was also the last station agent to work at the depot. The main line of the railroad had been relocated two miles south of Troy in 1933, and the depot was then used for freight only. During the construction of the current Route 40, the depot was moved to the southeast corner of Route 40 and Troy O'Fallon Road. In 1945 Mr. and Mrs. Rudy Moravec purchased the depot and lived in it until about 1965 when they tore it down and built a new home.

The Interstate Commerce Commission held a hearing on December 6, 1951, at the Mark Twain Hotel in St. Louis, to hear the application by the Illinois Terminal Railroad to abandon the Troy spur, a two-mile stretch of track between Troy Junction (west of Troy) and the City of Troy. The railroad's contention was that the losses derived by the company versus the future expense of maintaining the track would render continued operation unprofitable. Attorney Arthur F. Wendler represented those protesting the abandonment who were Mayor R.R. Moore and Alderman Wm. Holshouser, representing the City of Troy; Watson Lumber Company, James L.

Pennsylvania railroad crew on handcart

Watson; Modern Linen Service, Harold H.H. Hosto; Troy Domestic Mining Co., James Smith and Harry Cooper; Troy Lions Club, John Schoon and Harold Peters; and the Cullop Bottled Gas Service, Floyd Cullop. Attorney Wendler stated that filing exceptions to the proposed report would be without merit, due to the fact that the Pennsylvania Railroad could service the users of the railroad to be abandoned. At that time the Pennsylvania still had a spur coming to the Troy Grain Company on the south side of Troy, parallel to Route 40.

Train chugging into Troy Station

Depot and Station House

Railroad section house near the Troy Station, south of Troy, later to be the Gene Elliott house.

Vandalia Railroad Station, Troy, IL, circa 1900

Vandalia Railroad Station, Troy, IL, circa 1900

Youngest Telegraph Operator

In 1902, Roy D. Elliott, at age 13, was the youngest telegraph operator in Troy, and perhaps in the entire business. Roy was the son of G.L. Elliott, station agent and operator on the Vandalia (Railroad) Line in Troy. He had a natural aptitude for the work and studied for only 8 months before taking the examination. He took the exam in Terre Haute, IN, not missing a single question. However, his father decided that the boy needed to remain at home and do relief work, and develop greater speed and perfection. *Information from the June 28, 1902, issue of* The Weekly Call.

Car Dealerships

In the past, Troy had several auto dealerships. One of the first was John Pistone in 1920.

In 1927 J.C. McLanahan had a Ford Garage; he also sold Lincolns, Fordson tractors, accessories and had a battery service. It stood where the City Hall and Police Department are now. In early December of 1927, he was one of the dealers showing the newest Ford car with many new amenities only found in luxury cars. It had a noticeable European touch with exterior beauty and interior roominess with convenience and luxurious appointments. The engine, which was practically vibrationless, could develop 40 horsepower. Anywhere from 20 to 30 miles to a gallon was expected, depending on driving speed.

The Reinheimer Garage sold Dunlop tires in 1927. Their ad in the *Troy Call* said every 2-1/4 seconds, someone buys a Dunlop.

Fred Droy, Oscar Gindler and William Schmitt, who all owned car dealerships in Troy, were named as local tire inspectors for the Tire Rationing Board for Jarvis and Collinsville Townships in February 1941.

The Porter Garage sold DeSotos and Plymouths. The owners also provided wrecker service and did body and framework repairs. On January 4, 1952, the new Plymouth was on display and the 1953 DeSoto, with 160 horsepower, was on display November 13, 1952.

Schmitt Chevrolet Company sold Chevrolets trucks and cars. The new 1952 Chevrolet car was on display January 19, 1952.

Droy's Garage advertised the new 1951 Henry J. Vagabond and the 1951 Kaiser Virginian would be displayed January 24, 1952.

In 1953 Julius V. Stogsdill operated a Skelly station in the wedge across the street from Wiesemeyer's Service Station. In the late 1950s he sold it to Vogt Oil Co., who then sold it to the Helmich Brothers. This location is now a lovely little park.

Gindler Sales and Service had the new Studebaker Starliner on display March 20, 1952. They also did general repairs, wheel balancing, steam cleaned motors and sold batteries, tires and other accessories.

Schmitt Chevrolet

William Samuel Schmitt and his brother John Schmitt began Schmitt Chevrolet automobile dealership in 1929 at 113 West Market Street. They received the associate Chevrolet dealership under the Eichmann-Lathrop Chevrolet Company in Collinsville. William S. bought his brother's interest in the business around 1940. William S. retired in 1958.

At this time, William's son, B.J. "Nobby" Schmitt, and son-in-law, Jack Weir, bought the agency. After one year, Nobby bought Jack's interest in the business. Jack Weir then moved to Nokomis to operate an automobile agency there with William's son, Jack Schmitt.

Schmitt Chevrolet

Chevrolet Dealership

Old Chevrolet dealership, corner of Center and South Main Streets, 1920s, Wilbur Kimberlin, owner.

In August of 1961, Nobby Schmitt bought the Chevrolet-Buick-Oldsmobile Dealership in Greenville, IL. He closed the agency in Troy and moved his family to Greenville. *Submitted by Kae Elliott Schmitt.*

Gindler Sales & Service
111 W. Market Street, Troy, IL
Normandy No.7-2281

Oscar Gindler sold Studebaker and Packard automobiles at his Gindler Sales & Service at 111 Market Street.

Mrs. Joseph (Fannie) Nemnich kept the books and sold parts. Her husband, Joseph J. Nemnich, Sr., was a mechanic, along with Herman Henke and Ramsey Mason. In 1960, an exchange mechanic from Denmark, Egon Jensen, spent a year working in the garage. His friend Velo Rasmussen worked at Schmitt Chevrolet, the brick building next door that later burned. Oscar and his family took Egon to the State Fair in Springfield, to see President Dwight D. Eisenhower, so Egon could return and say he had seen the President of the United States.

The block building is still in existence at this printing and is a billiard business.

Service Stations and Garages

Service stations and garages kept Troy's automobiles running.

The Shell Service Station, located next to Adams Store on South Main, was owned by Ray Matthews in 1952. Earlier it had been owned by Buel Koonce.

Wiesemeyer's Service Station advertised Mobil gas, Mobil tires and Mobil batteries in January 1952. It was located where Russ's Car Wash is now at 204 Edwardsville Road. In 1956 Russell Wiesemeyer built a new service station at 218 Edwardsville Road where it is still in operation. The service station located at 204 Edwardsville Road was owned by Paul Simon and Jerome Baumgartner in the early 1960s – at that time it was a Sinclair Station.

In 1977 St. Louis East Truck Plaza (Union 76 – now Amoco), Mid State Trucks Plaza (Skelly) and Country Plaza (Amoco) were all located at the intersection of Route 162 and Interstate 55/70.

The Blue Haven Garage owned by Willard Gindler, Len's Service owned by

Studebaker Dealership, Oscar Gindler, Proprietor, circa 1950s

Country Style Plaza, April 1996

Len Baumgartner, and Brookside Automotive owned by Rudy Moravec were all operating in 1977.

Kinkel Auto Supply at 802 S. Main in Troy had its grand opening in December 1977.

At 320 East Center Street, where OK Muffler & Tire is now located, was a service station owned by John H. Voelker. His son, Bob Voelker, later owned it and rented it to James Capelle. Brian Pfeil purchased it in 1970 and used it for a garage. In 1985 he sold it to Mr. McMackin, the Buick dealer from Collinsville, who rented it to Jerome Baumgartner, who later purchased it.

Country Style Plaza

The Country Style Plaza, 820 Edwardsville Road, was a truck stop with fuel and vehicle services and a restaurant. The restaurant was a popular eating place.

Originally, it was the Standard Truck Stop when it opened in the 1970s. After remodeling, it became the Country Style Plaza.

Droy's Garage

Fred Droy owned Troy Chevrolet or Droy's Garage, as it was commonly called. At age 30, Droy began his business at 200 Collinsville Road. In 1930, the garage featured a ramp on the right side of the building. Later, Freddie and Bob had a Kaiser-Frazer dealership and had the official testing station for trucks. The west end of the building was added before the 1950s. Later, Bob Droy, Fred's son, took over the business; and it became a Ford dealership.

Matthews' Shell Station

Ray Matthews ran Matthews' Shell Station for several years. Located next to Adams Store at the corner of Center and South Main Street, it had numerous owners before Matthews.

In the early 1930s, Lud and Gil Mersinger, brothers, ran the filling station. In the mid 1930s, Babe Elliott ran it.

Ray Matthews, Shell Gas Station, 1954

Droy's Garage, Elmer Levo and Fred Droy, owner, 1930

69

Midwest Paint & Body

Midwest Paint & Body, South side of Rt. 40 East, 1988. Owner Larry Decrevel, 1980s–early 1990s.

Gindler's Service Station

Oscar Gindler's Service Station, 1938

Reinheimer Garage

Reinheimer Garage, circa 1920s.

Wiesemeyer's Mobil Station

Russell Wiesemeyer, Mobil Station, 204 Edwardsville Road, 1940s-1950s.

Len's Service Station

Len's Service Station, owner Leonard Baumgartner, Edwardsville Rd.

Historic Homes and Buildings

Troy's rich architectural heritage is shown by the houses and buildings constructed in other centuries that still provide homes and business locations in 2002. The Troy Historical Society and the Troy Historical Commission have designated many of the sites as historically significant and historical landmarks. The Commission was formed in 2002 and has as members: Pat Peverly, president; Mae Grapperhaus, vice president; Diana Shreve, secretary; Marilynn Sulc and Mark Feazel.

To date (2002) the following buildings have been designated as historically significant by both the Society and the Commission: St. Paul's Lutheran School, 112 North Border Street; the Deimling House, 216 East Market Street; the Carney House, 306 East Market Street; the Jarvis House, 317 East Center Street; the Stage Coach house, 108 West Market Street. In addition, the Troy Historical Society has also designated the Padon House, 308 South Main Street; St. John's Chapel on Lebanon Road; and the 107 East Market Street Building.

The Historical Commission also selected the Stanek Home, 225 East Market Street; the Kennedy House, 105 West Clay Street; and the Troy Christian Church, 114 South Main Street.

Many more have been nominated, but had not been approved by the Troy City Council at the time this book was written. These landmark structures are included in a historical district in the old town sector of Troy.

103-105-107 East Market Street

These buildings have been a part of Troy since the early 1900s.

East Market Street Buildings. (l. to r.) Auwarter Home, Troy Post Office, Troy Call *Office and Ideal Barbershop, circa 1940s.*

The building at 107 East Market was built in 1902 in the group of buildings originally on the Auwarter family property. The building served as the Post Office until the late 1960s when the postal department moved to new quarters.

The building has undergone several changes over the years. An addition on the south was built several years ago. The rear of the building has a concrete floor and a wooden floor in the front. In the 1970s, paneling was added to the walls, and the ceiling was lowered. The early 1990s saw a rest room added and the flat roof repaired and rubberized. Now its brick exterior is white.

Many businesses and one church have occupied this historic space. In 2002, it received the Troy Historical Society Award for historical significance and has been designated as a city landmark.

The Troy Call (later called *The Troy Tribune*) occupied the center building (sign points down to door) at 105 East Market Street. The building has had a variety of businesses after the newspaper moved.

The small building at 103 East Market is Ed Helmich's Ideal Barbershop.

The buildings look like one building; however, they are three individual buildings, attached to one another. In addition, they are attached to the corner building (Allen's Drugs) at Market and Main Streets. The house at the left was the Auwarter residence. It has been razed, and the property is now a telephone company parking lot.

108, 110, 112 and 116 West Market Street, August 1993. This scene of the south side of West Market Street shows smoke from the fire at the Troy Frozen Foods building in the background.

112 West Market Street

Edward T. Levo built the 112 West Market Street building in 1958. He removed the front porch from his home and added a storefront to form a laundromat. Later, Bill Ackerman who had managed it for several years leased the laundromat.

In the 1970s, the laundromat was remodeled for a beauty shop, Belladonna, operated by Brenda Wilkerson. Later it was leased to another beauty salon.

In the early 1990s, it was again remodeled to allow the Troy Chamber of Commerce to have a small office on the east side. Bonnie Levo had her law office there at the same time. Levo used it for evening appointments when she was with Tognarelli and Levo law firm of Collinsville.

In 1995, the building was sold from the Ed T. Levo Estate Trust. It currently is an insurance office. *Submitted by Mae Grapperhaus.*

201 East Market Street

The historic building at 201 East Market Street has housed many businesses since it was built around 1900. Very early Herman Roeben and Fred Gerfen had a hardware and a blacksmith shop. In 1910, the partnership dissolved and Roeben was sole proprietor of the hardware store while Gerfen had the blacksmith shop. Mr. Steinhans, an undertaker, operated a funeral parlor and a furniture store on the first floor at one time. Apartments were on the second floor. In the 1920s and 1930s it was the Kueker Funeral home with a furniture store on one side and the funeral parlor on the other side. Kueker sold his funeral home business to Jewel Edwards and the building has been used for numerous businesses since that time.

In the 1940s Ma's Cafe and Lee's Beauty Shop were housed there. Fred "Happy" Liebler began a hardware store in 1948 and operated it until 1981. "Hap," as many called him, had everything and anything in his store (anything from bulk seed to harnesses and from wrenches to stovepipes.) Hap Liebler was one of a kind and worked hard at his business. He also did some carpentering and fixed screens and windows. The store was an experience to say the least. Hap could always find what the customer was looking for, but it may have taken a little time to find it. Hap Liebler passed away in 1990.

Terry Singler purchased the hardware store business in 1981 and continued with it until 1985. That year, Ewald "Wally" Hoffman and Leonard Suess purchased the building and the business and renamed it the Troy Hardware Store. In February 1985, *The Troy Times*, published by Paul Ping, began a newspaper in the east rear apartment on the first floor while the Troy Hardware had the front of the building. Hardware store employees included Bill Burgess, Jeff Suess and Bob Feldpausch. The Troy Hardware flourished for about one year.

In 1986, the newspaper office moved to the building's front east side. When the two newspapers, *The Troy Times* and *The Troy Tribune*, merged, the newspaper office remained on the east side. During that time the west side was remodeled to become a jewelry store while Vintage Classics, a dress shop, operated in the rear of the west side. In 1990, the newspaper office expanded to the west side. Chicago Hot Dog, a walk-in restaurant moved into the east side. It was in operation for almost one year.

In the mid-1990s, Cynthia Long conducted a theatrical studio and later Jeri Tellmann operated a consignment shop on the east side. In about 1998, the newspaper office took over the entire first floor on both east and west sides.

In 2002, the newspaper continues to occupy the space, while an apartment is in the east rear side. Five apartments within the building are leased. In 2000-2001, the building was re-tuckpointed and the trimming was painted. The covered porch still stands on the north side of the structure.

At the rear of the building is Wally Hoffman's barn. This barn was used back in the Kueker Undertaking days to house the horses and the horse drawn hearse. *Submitted by Mae Grapperhaus.*

Arth Log Cabin

Lewis G. Arth in front of Anton and Anna Arth's log cabin, circa 1957.

Braner Building

The Braner Building, located at 113 East Market Street, was completed in 1908 by Dr. F. W. Braner, a prominent and well-known physician. This handsome, new, two-story brick business building was the first substantial improvement to Troy during 1907. It was constructed on the former Martin property at the southeast corner of East Market and Kimberlin Streets. Dr. Braner had made a contract with Troy Press Brick Company for 175,000 bricks to be used in the construction. August Gerling, a local bricklayer, was the contractor for the work, which began about April 1,1907.

The front of the building was red brick with black brick trimmings and plate glass windows. The lower floor was comprised of two separate storerooms; and the second floor was a spacious lodge or meeting hall with two sets of office rooms, three on each side (toward the back or south end of the building). The offices were to be arranged so that a tenant would use one or two or the full suite as desired.

At one time, it housed Hampton Store and Millinery on the east side and Troy State Bank on the west side. On the second floor, meetings were held. Later it was a Kroger Store on the west side. Kelly's A.G. Market followed the Kroger store, and the entire first floor became a grocery store owned and operated by John Kelly.

During the Great Depression, the first Troy Library was located on the second floor. A WPA project from 1937 to 1940, the library was run by Wilma Cline. Later the area was used for the American Legion Hall; and many weddings, parties and anniversary celebrations were held there. Santa Claus was brought in by the Legion at Christmas time to give children candy and peanuts. The Troy Jaycees took the second floor in the late 1950s.

In the 1950s, on the east side of the first floor, Floyd Cullop owned and operated a hardware and bottled gas store. The building housed the old Troy firehouse, the Troy Police Department; and the telephone company was also located upstairs toward the back of the building for a time. The Troy City Hall offices were located on the second floor for several years, too, before a separate building was acquired by the city.

An old hose tower was located at the rear of the building for the fire department. That tower was there until the building was destroyed by fire on June 10, 1992. When it burned, James and Audrey Deeren owned it and operated the Christian Wolf Communion Wafer Company in it. *Information from the* Troy Weekly Call, *March 23, 1907, and from Troy residents' recollections.*

Braner Building, circa 1910

Burk House, 2002

The Burk House

The Burk House still stands on Clay Street. The house was built by Elias Burk, a Troy blacksmith, after he returned from the Civil War in 1864. Nine children were born to Mr. and Mrs. Burk.

Elias Burk was the mayor of Troy from 1895 to 1898. He also served as interim pastor at the Evangelical Church in Troy and helped to build the first Evangelical church in Troy.

The John Carney House

The John Carney House (circa 1870) is significant as an excellent example of Italian Villa architecture popular from 1830-1880. The outstanding feature of the Italian Villa style is the combination of the tall tower with a two-story T-shaped floor plan. The roof, windows, and placement of porches are all distinguishing features. The home is located at 306 East Market Street.

The home was included by the Illinois Historic Structures Survey done in 1974 as "architecturally important." Through the efforts of the current owners, the home was placed on the National Register of Historic Places in 1983. The Carney Home is designated as Troy's First Historic Landmark and remains a proud example to the diligent restoration efforts of its owners.

John Carney was born in Jennings County, IN, on September 22, 1820. He was the eighth child of Pleasant and Elizabeth Carney, natives of Pennsylvania and Virginia. In 1852, Mr. Carney was in business in Ste. Genevieve County, MO. In 1861 he moved to Belleville. He moved to Troy in 1863 and purchased an interest in an extensive mill property; and, in connection with Mr. T.A. Throp, conducted the operations of the mill nearly ten years. Upon the death of Mr. Thorp, he continued the business. The mill was one of the largest and most complete flouring mills in the West.

Mr. Carney was described as "a self-made man ... contributed more largely than any other citizen of his means to every enterprise that was calculated to benefit or in any manner add to the prosperity of Troy or her citizens." (*Biographical Sketches of Citizens of Madison County, Illinois*, 1873). John Carney owned the home until 1875.

Deimling Building, 1995

Other significant owners were Dr. Fred Zenk, who, with his sisters, owned the home from 1888-1944 (responsible for the "Zenk Addition" to Troy); and Senator Paul Simon, from 1959-1974. The present owners, David and Patricia Peverly, purchased the home in 1979.

Deimling Building

The old Deimling building was located on the northwest corner of East Market and Hickory Streets. It is now the parking lot for the Troy Municipal Complex.

It housed many businesses including Deimling's Meat Market; Martin's Market; Les Adelhardt's grocery store; the Troy Restaurant, better known as "The Greeks;" Kelly's Auction House; Table Tone exercise business; Howe's Funeral Home, owned by Steve Howe; and Christian Wolf Communion Wafer Factory. In the rear was a small apartment building.

It was used as a haunted "funeral home" sponsored by the Troy Jaycees during the latter part of its life. The last occupant was the communion wafer factory owned by Jim Deeren.

The Deimling House

The well-cared for home at 216 East Market Street has an unusual history in that it has had only four owners in its long history. The first owner was John Deimling, a prosperous butcher, who owned it from the late 1800s through the early 1900s. Next, the Leeds Watson family owned it and lived in it for several years. Leeds owned and operated Watson's Lumber Yard in Troy for many years. In December of 1975, the Ron Criley family moved into the house. Mr. Criley served 2 terms as mayor of Troy while he lived there. The house is now owned by Harold and Diana Shreve, who moved to Troy in 1994.

The house retains its original Victorian style, and the exterior paint colors are repre-

John Carney House, 2002

The Deimling House, circa 2002

sentative of the exterior colors used when the house was built. The home continues to be a landmark in Troy and on Market Street. *Submitted by Diana Shreve.*

The Edwards Home Place

The old John and Sarah Edwards home was located in Section 21 of Jarvis Township, southwest of Troy (in 2002 it is 7948 West Kirsch Road). The house burned to the ground in the late 1920s. At the time Mr. and Mrs. Wilbur Edwards lived in the home. Wilbur was on over night jury duty the night that it burned and his wife was staying with a neighbor.

The Edwards family owned a large amount of acreage in Section 20 and 21 of Jarvis Township. After the fire, the house site and farm stood idle for about 7 or 8 years. Kate Mersinger and her son, Oscar Mersinger, purchased it in 1936. Oscar built a new home there when he married Louise Levo. The couple lived there all of their married lives. It is now the home of Dale and

Kelly (nee Hasty) Grapperhaus. Dale is the grandson of Oscar and Louise Mersinger.

The people on this photo are not named, but they were members of the Edwards family. *Photo submitted by Betty Trihey. Narrative by Mae Grapperhaus.*

The Elliott House

The Grant L. Elliott House at 511 S. Main Street is presently owned by St. Jerome's Catholic Church and named "The Elliott House."

The Elliott House, 1920

The Foucek House

Foucek home at Sunnyside Nursery, Collinsville Road

The Gebauer Building

The Gebauer Building is located at 110 East Market Street. Here it stands, in 1988, as the United Pentecostal Church on the first floor and apartments on the second floor. The building has a long history. In the early days, it was a hardware and tin store and an undertaking establishment. J.C. Gebauer was the

Charles Edwards Homeplace, circa 1919

Gebauer Building, 1988

undertaker and was affiliated with Schroeppel and Company, undertakers from Collinsville.

Through the years it has been many businesses including several taverns, a grocery store, a paper products store, a restaurant, and a church. Lottie Lanahan ran a restaurant there in the 1960s and Bill's Tavern was there at one time.

George Langdon, who owns the building, married Anna Mae Gebauer, a descendant of J.C. Gebauer. In the fall of 1993, Mr. Langdon had the building's exterior renovated and removed the long-standing porch. In 2002, the first floor houses Alexandra's Collection on the west side and Bonnie Levo's Law Office on the east side. The second floor is leased out for apartments.

The Gerling House

The residence at 314 Montgomery Street belonged to Christian and Caroline Gerling (married 1885). The house was built by Gus Gerling, half-brother to Christian, in the latter half of 1909, and was finished and occupied in February 1910. By the 1930s a bungalow-style porch across the front of the house had replaced the small Victorian-style porch. After Christian Gerling died, Caroline con-

Hart House, about 1998

tinued to live there. When she died on June 10, 1942, her daughter and son-in-law, Deborah (born 1902) and Walter Brunworth (married 1930), purchased the house. They remained there until Deborah Brunworth's death in 1985, when the house was sold. The new owners undertook a restoration at that time.

A family story relates that the builders, apparently working from sketchy plans, used as the exterior dimensions of the house, the figures intended to be the interior dimensions. *Submitted by Suzanne Hansel.*

The Hart Home

The farmhouse of Carlton and Margaret (Kelly) Hart was located where the new Triad High School was constructed.

Carlton died a long time before Margaret. She, a long time teacher and principal in the Triad School District, sold her farm place to the Triad School District at a very reasonable price. The library in the new high school was named for her.

At the ground breaking ceremony for the new school, Mrs. Hart was on hand and said that when she lived on the farm, people would come with their children to pick strawberries there. Now with the new high school being built here, children will still come to that location. *Submitted by Margaret Hart and Mae Grapperhaus.*

Hecht Home *or* Captain Cook Home

The Herman Hecht family home was formerly the Captain Cook home. It stood on the site of the Senior Center building in the Tri-Township Park.

The Gerling House, 1910

Hecht or Captain Cook Home, 1978

Jarvis House

The Jarvis House

This house was built in 1872. In the photo above, B.W. Jarvis (child on the steps) is pictured with his grandmother, Mary Ann (Kinder) Jarvis, and his mother, Elizabeth (Donoho) Jarvis, standing on his right.

John F. Jarvis Home

In March 1879, the Jarvis family moved into the Throp House on Edwardsville Road. The Throp's had come to Troy from the East, and Mr. Throp had the house built on the edge of town. The old homestead was a large red brick home with green wooden shutters on the front floor-to-ceiling windows. The

(Right) John F. Jarvis Home, 311 Edwardsville Road

The John F. Jarvis family outside of the large red brick house they had lived in together.

house had four large rooms and a hall downstairs. Upstairs consisted of five bedrooms, a bathroom, and a hall. Land acreage also included the Mill Pond.

The brick sidewalk leading to the house started at the front gate and ran to the old Mill Pond. On each side of the brick walk were trees and holly bushes. Flower beds accented the left side of the pathway, and, at one time, wild blue bells and pink peonies bloomed there. A large orchard was on the south side of the acreage, while various berry bushes covered the other side. Encircling the huge yard was a hedge fence. The poplar hitching posts had chains between them. The beautifully designed front door matched the design of the staircase. It opened into an entry hall trimmed in oak woodwork with a magnificent winding, cherry wood staircase. Mr. Throp had had the staircase sent from Chicago in pieces and assembled in Troy by the builder. The ceilings in this old home were thirteen feet high; therefore, all the doors had transoms.

On the west side of the house was a large room, the parlor. White painted walls with a colored border and white enameled woodwork made a perfect setting. The parlor, also, featured a white marble fireplace.

Across from the parlor another big room, a sitting room, was also painted white. Its woodwork was Birdseye maple. In the bay window was a square arch called an aleover. Here Nancy Jarvis, only daughter in a family of seven children, and William Baglin exchanged wedding vows on June 25, 1902. Attendants were Mable (Jarvis) Sede and Benjamin Jarvis. This room featured a large fireplace, too.

Next to the sitting room came a large dining room. Walnut woodwork and white walls distinguished the decor here. Next to the dining room was a kitchen. Walls and woodwork were painted tan, and a double pantry adjoined the kitchen, with a cistern beneath it.

The cherry staircase led into the upstairs hall. On the west side, above the parlor, was the guestroom. White walls with a colored border and white enameled woodwork decorated the room. French doors opened into the back bedroom; it was identical to the guestroom in appearance.

Across the hall, on the east, were two very large bedrooms. Here the woodwork was made of light oak and the walls were white. Dark colored fireplaces heated these bedrooms.

Off the back stairs was a small bedroom called the servant's room. It was painted tan. Two downstairs rooms had frosted glass panes in the bottoms of the windows. A non-plumbing bathroom completed this homestead.

The outbuildings on the property were a barn and a smokehouse. The barn was partitioned into sections. One section was used as a buggy shed and the other, as an icehouse. In winter ice from the Mill Pond was cut and stored for future use for the family and customers. A smokehouse, with thirteen inch thick walls, cured their meats.

This home burned in 1928 after the Jarvis heirs had sold it to the Humphries.

This information was taken from a handwritten article submitted to the Troy Historical Society in the early 1990s by Hilda Ebl.

William W. Jarvis Home

The William W. Jarvis House at 317 East Center Street is located at the intersection of Center and Dewey Streets.

The Jarvis House was listed in the National Register of Historic Places on February 3, 1988. The Jarvis House was listed under the area of significant architecture for the period 1800-1899. Constructed in 1867 by William W. Jarvis, a businessman and civic leader in the Troy community, the house is a significant representation of Italianate architecture. It is the only remaining example in the community representing the features of the asymmetrical compound-plan subtype. The exceptional significance of the house rests in its long history as an Italianate style residence with its integrity intact. The original design characteristics and the materials of construction enable the house to convey its principal historic qualities and picturesque appearance.

The house has an Italianate style marble fireplace with full arched opening in each of the two parlors and a brick fireplace with a wooden mantel in the sitting room. A curved staircase features a large walnut newel post with turned spindles and a solid walnut handrail. A narrow stairway concealed within an interior wall leads directly to the maid's quarters on the second floor.

William W. Jarvis was the grandson of John Jarvis, an early Troy settler, who in 1814 made the first entry of land in what was to become the city of Troy. Jarvis Township is so named in honor of the Jarvis family. The property was originally a land grant given under President Monroe. William W. Jarvis was born in 1842 and was given a good business education in the Troy schools. After service in the Civil War, Mr. Jarvis took up farming, studied law, and in partnership with J.A. Barnsback, opened the first lumberyard in Troy. He eventually purchased his partner's interest. In 1865, with H.H. Padon as his partner, he opened the Troy Exchange Bank and became sole owner in 1887. Mr. Jarvis lived in the house until his death in 1927. The house was then occupied by one of his daughters, Bessie Jarvis Keller, who then sold it to Harold and Marie Schmidt in August, 1961. According to Mr. Schmidt, it took about three months to research and title the property because it had never been out of Jarvis ownership. There had never been a real estate transaction on the property since the original land grant. In 1994 the house was sold to Terri and James Drazen of Troy who continue to maintain both the integrity of the architecture and interior appointments

Langenwalter Home

The Andrew Langenwalter Home. Submitted by Edith Hock.

in keeping with the period. *Submitted by Carolyn Schmidt Golfin.*

The Lowery House

The Lowery House was located in the 200 block of East Market Street on the south side. It was the home of Barbara (Schrameck) Lowery for many years. She operated a beauty shop in the small building on the west next door.

The photo was taken November 22, 1997, shortly before it was demolished.

Lowery House

Mallett House: The White House on Lebanon Road

In the 1840s, German settlers came to this mid-American region and built homesteads. Industrious and determined families cleared the woods and carved out farmland in the rich soil near Troy. Today, only an old tombstone on a forgotten spot along the southern edge of

Madison County attests to the life of one such family: Andreas and Margaretha Fehmel and their children. The family grave is still there, marked with a worn marble obelisk and one small head stone that pokes a tiny bit out of the ground, now overcome with a hundred years of silt and overgrown with weeds and poison ivy.

The house built by these German settlers, still stands southeast of Troy. Lebanon Road and Illinois Power lines now intersect the original farm—which was once probably much larger, pre-dating both the automobile and electric power. The farm's three ancient wells, which seemingly never run out of water even in dry weather, attest to the fact that those first settlers knew how to pick a good spot.

Since before the Civil War, the farm has been home to men, women and children who grew corn and wheat, raised cattle and milk cows, pigs and chickens. The crops grown on the farm's rolling acres and the domestic animals bred and raised here provided sustenance for generations of families. At the same time, fox, deer, turkeys, loons and owls enjoyed the untouched woods, the deep creeks, and the meadows.

In 1961, Dave and Mamie Mallett, bought the property from a widower named Edward Trippel. Their 16-year-old daughter Annette thought her parents had lost their minds buying this old, run down place. But from the very beginning, she loved the land.

Dave had been a Ford dealer in Collinsville, but the farm quickly captured his imagination and he began to put all his energies toward it. The Mallets named it "Red Fox Acres" after the pretty little fox indigenous to the region. When they decided to resurrect the dilapidated and sagging farmhouse, they had pallets of similar, soft, hand-made orange brick trucked from a church demolition project in Anna, IL, in order to retain the vintage look of the architecture. Each brick was lovingly cleaned and acid-washed by hand. They installed new oak flooring and lathe and plaster walls into the 100-year-old solid brick structure, and they brought in architectural antiques and lighting fixtures from St. Louis estates.

With the help of a huge old D-8 bulldozer, Dave carved out four lakes and recovered the fields and pastureland. By 1972, he had fenced in enough land that 50 head of Black Angus cattle grazed here and

Mallett House

Mallett House, rear view

the fields produced good crops of beans and corn. He farmed the tillable land himself and continued to work the farm until age and health stopped him.

After Dave's death in 1995, Annette and her husband Lew Haines moved to the family home. By then, some painting and repairs were needed, and it took a few years to figure out the best use of the old barns and pastureland. In 1998, they discovered the Paso Fino horse. As their herd expanded, Lew fixed up the barns, cleared the pastures, and fenced them again for the first time in many years. Lebanon Road has long been a teen-age drinking road and many staid and successful 50-somethings have told the Haineses they remember driving past this landmark house in their "glory days." Some say they thought it was haunted.

The house, of course, needs continual maintenance. The old wooden double-hung windows need glazing and painting every couple of years; the brick needs regular tuck-pointing. Since it does not have a foundation, ground water wicks up through the thick brick walls and challenges Annette to keep wallpaper and paint on certain spots. This old house is not cheap or easy to live in. But for her, it is worth any effort.

Today, Red Fox Acres continues to provide a beautiful home for animals and people, alike. Annette and Lew sincerely hope that American farmland and little farms like theirs can continue to survive – supported by agricultural use. *Submitted by Annette Mallett Haines.*

The Mersinger Log Cabin

The Mersinger log cabin has a long story attached to it. This log cabin home came into the Mersinger family in 1859. It was then that Frederich Mersinger purchased the property on which it stood for many years (along Troy-O'Fallon Road, about five miles south of Troy) from John Adam Bugger. No one really knows when the cabin was built because the property changed hands four times before the Mersingers purchased it.

James Watt bought the land from the U.S. Government in 1838 and later sold it to his son, Samuel, in 1841. The land was purchased by John Flory in 1847 and sold once again to John Adam Bugger in 1856. Bugger held the property for only three years before selling it to Frederich Mersinger.

Family members are not sure which one of them had the cabin, but it is believed that the cabin was moved from a nearby hill to the Troy-O'Fallon Road location. It was visible to passersby for just 21 years. In 1880, Frederich Mersinger and his family de-cided to build onto the home, so they constructed a larger, more modern, wooden home around the cabin.

Frederich died in April 1894, leaving his property to his widow, Anna, and their eight children. Anna then transferred the land to son, Phillip, who died in 1945. Two years before Phillip's death on October 17, 1943, Theodore "Ted" Mersinger, the youngest son of Phillip and his wife Helen, moved into the home, and Ted's mother moved to Collinsville. Ted and Helen remained in the home until 1972, when they moved into a modular home about 50 yards from where the log cabin home stood.

In 1977, as Ted and Helen and family were tearing down the old home, they found the log cabin. It has only three sides, as Frederick had torn the fourth side off to attach it to the new addition.

Through the help of the Madison County Historical Society, the log cabin was disassembled and transported to the society's museum back lot with the intention to rebuild it there. However, due to a lack of room and man power, the log cabin laid on the lot for three or four years. It was never assembled on the museum lot.

It was then donated to Southern Illinois University at Edwardsville, where a professor received a grant for a pioneering class. Students reconstructed it on the campus. The logs for the fourth wall were received from Fred and Arlyn Heuiser of Troy. The log cabin stood there unattended for about 21 years.

In the fall of 1999, the Troy Historical Society received information, that the cabin was going to be razed and destroyed, because SIUE could not afford to maintain it or keep it any longer.

With the help of volunteer family members and friends, the cabin was again disassembled in May of 2001. It was then

Log cabin being torn down, September 27, 1976, by Ted and Gary Mersinger at their homeplace.

Millet Building, 1995

The wall of the old jail

The Padon House, 1970s

transported to the Tri-Township Park in Troy where it is hoped it will be rebuilt again in 2002. *Submitted by Mae Grapperhaus.*

Millett Building

The Millett Building, at the northwest corner of South Main and Center streets, has a long history of various businesses. Currently (in 2002), it is an apartment house. Built by Mr. Millett in the 1800s, it once housed three separate businesses in the building, plus the upstairs apartments. Millett died in 1963.

In the 1940s and 1950s, the building served as a boarding house, a restaurant (Gretchen Wheeler), a Greyhound bus stop, Rebekah's organization meeting place, a television repair business, and a library, just to name a few of the tenants. Later in the 1960's through the mid 1990s, it served as apartments, Troy Books and Gifts (McClintock's), Troy Gifts and Flowers (Youngman's), Jo-Nel's Florist (Barb and Ray Schuessler), the Jewel Box (Paulette Darlington), a motor cycle shop, and a resell it shop.

On the west side of the building, currently stands an automobile detailing shop. Previously, the building was used as part of Jo-Nel's Florist. At one time it was used as an auto body shop owned by Curt Wood. *Submitted by Mae Grapperhaus from information acquired from Ardell Luna and Rita Youngman.*

The Old Jail

David Seligmann and his wife conveyed 20' x 20' of a corner of lot number 8 in Mechanicsburg to the town of Troy for a jail. The only remaining picture of the old jail is this side view of the red brick building, taken from the Gindler's back yard, in 1953.

(Right) Ottwein Home, 1893

Ottwein Home

The home the Ottweins moved to was already an historic home built in 1860 by the Julius Barnsback family. Julius was a prominent citizen in the 1860s and '70s, serving as an officer in the Civil War, returning to a prominent life as Sheriff of the County and a member of the House of Representatives. He also owned a nearby sawmill and the Troy Stagecoach Station, located on what was then, "The Collinsville Plank Road," later to become U.S. Route 40, or the "National Trail." Mr. and Mrs. Barnsback raised a family of seven girls in the big farmhouse, several marrying into prominent Troy families. After Julius' death, the farm came to be owned by the Jarvis and Weber families who sold it to the Ottweins in 1911. *The drawing came from the* Madison County History and Plat Book *of 1893. Submitted by Merrill Ottwein.*

The Padon House

John B. Padon, who was the first president of the Village Board of Trustees when Troy was organized as a city in 1892, built the Padon House in 1877. He was also proprietor of the Troy Steam Saw Mill.

The home is located at 318 South Main Street on the northeast corner of South Main and Padon Streets. The home has gone through several significant changes; but in the last several years, owners, Belinda Habiger and Greg Roberts have been restoring the home to the French Colonial style with ornate soffit work and porches. The bay window that was removed is to be rebuilt.

The bathrooms and radiator heat system were added whenever that type of heat became available. The original fireplace was dated 1911 and was converted from wood to gas after 1950.

A central heating/cooling system was installed in 1998. The bay window and front porch were replaced sometime after 1944. The east lot was sold in 1952 reducing the property in size. A simulated slate roof was added in 2002. The home's exterior color and surface is brick painted white.

A curved walnut stairway remains, as well as the original casing in one upstairs bedroom. The downstairs rooms have high ceilings with decorative features.

The Padon House received the Troy Historical Society's award for being historically significant in 2002. It has also been nominated in 2002 to become a City of Troy Landmark.

The Schott Building on the Square

J ohn S. Peterman built the Schott building at the southwest corner of Main and Market in 1887 for the Highland Brewing Company. He used 7 carloads of lumber in the construction, most of which was white pine of the best quality. The site was formerly known as the Henderson corner and was the scene of one of Troy's biggest fires.

After the Schott building was constructed, the first floor was used as a saloon; the second, as living quarters; and the third, a hall, occupied for many years by the Knights of Pythias Lodge; and for social functions. Other owners, after the Highland Brewery's ownership, were Cicero Ogle of Collinsville, and A.F. Seligman and F.J. Michael of Troy, who had purchased the building in 1925. The last tenant was James Mason who was charged with a violation of the Volstead Act (the policy of prohibiting the sale of intoxicating liquors or the enforcement of this policy by an act of Congress passed in 1919 and repealed in 1933). As a result, the building was padlocked for a year by government authorities.

In May of 1926, the building was razed by the Michael Lumber and Hardware Company of St. Jacob, having been unoccupied for a year. Because of the building's massive frame construction, it had long been regarded as a fire hazard. It had been on fire several times, but the fires had been discovered early enough to prevent serious damage. The other building to the south on this same site was most likely the building which later housed Kiser's TV, which was destroyed by fire in February of 2000. *Information taken from the May 7, 1926, issue of the* Troy Call.

The Sprick House

L izzie Sprick lived in the house for several years. Then, Edward Maedge and his family lived there for 35 to 40 years. It faced Washington Street. The house was demolished for Troy Fire House expansion.

Sprick House, 2000

The Stanek Home

T he Stanek Home at 225 East Market Street was designated historically significant and a plaque was awarded on June 20, 2001, by the Troy Historical Society to owners Eugene and Altheda Stanek. The two-story frame structure is located on the east half lot two in Block 46 of the Wesley Jarvis Addition to Troy.

There were eighteen owners of the property and although the abstract does not designate a date when the home was built, there is evidence that it was originally a log house.

According to documentation, the original owners of lots one and two in Block 46 were Wesley and Mary Jarvis, who sold it to Ferdinand and Elizabeth J. Cornman in April 1846. In August of the same year, the Cornmans sold it to Jacob M. Gonterman. In February 1847, Abraham B. Harris bought it from Jacob Gonterman. In October 1853, Harris sold it to Dewitt C. Putnam, who in August 1855 sold it to James B. Andrews. Andrews

owned it until 1868 when it was sold to William and Hannah P. Donoho. The Donohos sold the east half of Lot Two to Elizabeth L. Good in 1872.

The following people owned the house after that: John S. Dewey, William Reeder, Joseph Granger, trustee for William A. Meiners Sr., William B. Reeder, William J. Vetter, and John Bohland. Research indicates that the Bohlands were the administrators of the estate and occupied the home until 1939 (the longest time for a single-family occupancy).

The Bohland family sold it in 1939 to Dan Weir who sold it to John J. Howard in 1952. Later Fred H. Gornet owned it and then sold it to Cora L. Edwards in 1957. Edwards sold it to Ora G. Edwards in 1958. In 1962, the house was sold to Herman Roeben. The house lay vacant until September 2, 1970, when Eugene G. and Altheda M. Stanek bought the property.

The house was built in sections, one added to another, and the interior of the house has had numerous repairs and renovations. *Submitted by Mae Grapperhaus from the June 28, 2001, issue of the Times-Tribune.*

The Stolte House

H enry Stolte, a contractor and builder, was born in Pin Oak Township in 1858, the son of Herman and Bernadina Z. (Schottemeyer) Stolte. He

Stanek Home, 2001

The Stolte House, Border and Clay streets, early·1970s

ness until 1887, when he entered the general merchandising business.

He received an offer from John W. Gornet and again went into the building and contracting business. He did a large amount of work all over the county and in St. Louis, MO.

Mr. Stolte married Hannah Gerfen in 1892. He built his bride a new home on Clay Street upon their marriage. He built two porches on the house on the north side, one for the morning sun and one for the evening sun. The house had fancy "bric-a-brac" at the top around the eaves.

Through the years several families occupied the home. In about 2000, the Troy Fire Protection District purchased the home from the Struckhoff family, the last owners of the home. The house was razed in the spring of 2001 for the fire department engine house and parking lot expansion.

was educated in the public and parochial schools of Troy and worked on the farm until he was nineteen. Soon after, he went to St. Louis and worked as a carpenter for a time. He returned to Troy in 1879 and went into the building and contracting busi-

The Wild House

The Wild House, 314 South Main, 1903. (l. to r.) Emogene McCormick, Eliza Wild, Mable Baglin in buggy, Nancy Jarvis Baglin, Duncan and Bill McCormick, and Bill Dunstan.

Sports

The sports history of Troy includes a variety of activities, ranging from fishing and sack races to a championship high school football team and a New York Yankee pitcher. School sports have always occupied an important part of the sports scene, but historically, the community sports and teams were just as valuable. They provided entertainment, generated community pride and spirit, and offered recreation to participants and spectators alike.

Baseball
Owen Brendel, Troy's Own Cardinal

Owen Brendel, at the age of 21, signed a contract with the St. Louis Cardinals Baseball team on July 27, 1947. This was before the "big time." He received only $150 per month for his work, but said, " I'd have played for nothing." Brendel was signed by scout, Buddy Lewis and was sent to Salisbury, MD. Later he was transferred to Lynchburg, VA, for training and he finished the 1947 season there. In the spring of 1948, he was sent to Albany, GA, to play on a team owned by the National League Cardinals. As a first baseman, he received much of his experience playing for the Highland Merchants team, beginning at the age of 16. He also played for the old Troy Advertisers, a member of the Southwestern Illinois Inter-City Baseball League. He hit .295 during his three months with Troy. He batted and threw right-handed. His chances were very good. Brendel, who grew up on a farm south of Troy, had the support of his parents, the late Mr. and Mrs. Ed Brendel who always encouraged him.

He was signed up at old Sportsman's Park on Grand and Springer in St. Louis, traveling there on a bus and then, by streetcar to the park. He went on a Thursday and signed on Friday. Twenty-one hundred young men were trying out; only three were signed. The other two were from St. Louis. Buddy Lewis, not main scout Walter Shannon, brought him back to the farm following his signing on

Owen Brendel, when he signed with the St. Louis Cardinals Baseball Team, 1947.

that last day of tryouts. At his first training, he remembered that it was "strictly business" and had no recollection of anything unusual or funny happening.

The next year on the last day of spring training in Albany, he failed to make the last cut. He was supposed to go to Johnson City, TN, but that never happened. Upon his return to Troy, his Dad had sold the farm, so he had to make other plans for employment. With plans to marry, he began working for the Edwardsville Creamery. He worked there for 20 years and later worked for and retired from Prairie Farms Dairy in 1988.

Never forgetting or wanting to forget baseball, Brendel kept up with the game by joining the newly formed Troy Red Birds. He played first base, but in a pinch he'd play third, but never really liked that position.

He and his wife, the former Sally Kniepman, have six children (four boys and two girls). They have always been supportive of their children's sports activities. Brendel was one of the first men to organize a Khoury League in Troy and was elected Troy's first Khoury League "commissioner" in the late 1950s.

Coaching many a game, he is still very interested in baseball and other sports as well. Brendel enjoys gardening (a farm boy at heart) and helping out at his church, St. Jerome's Catholic in Troy or at any of the Troy Knights of Columbus functions. He retired from the Troy Volunteer Department after 20 years of service. *Information from* The Times-Tribune, *July 1997.*

Khoury League

Although many fathers and other interested persons have helped with Khoury League ball teams in Troy, the first organizers were Owen Brendel, Leeds Watson, Blair Watson and Dr. W.L. Zielonko.

Owen Brendel and Dr. W.L. Zielonko met Mr. Khoury in St. Louis in 1958 to ask his advice on beginning a league. Brendel made three trips to St. Louis, concerning the league. Games were played on the McCray-Dewey High School campus. The divisions included the Bantams, the Atoms and the Juvenile/Midgets. The Bantams played on the location where the Molden School in 2002 stands; the Atoms

Dennis Little, circa 1975

Bobby Blasnic, circa 1975

played on the diamond east of the McCray-Dewey School; and the Juvenile/Midgets played at the northeast corner of the field.

When the league began, Owen's sons, Jerry and Bob Brendel, were in the Atoms and Bantams respectively.

The Troy business people donated funding for the Khoury League uniforms. *Information from Owen Brendel.*

Troy Red Birds

The Troy Red Birds baseball team was in existence in the 1930s through the 1970s. The home games were played on Moonlight Diamond next to the Moonlight Roller Rink on Collinsville Road. Many young men participated in the league and played against teams from many surrounding towns. In 1952, they were leaders in the Red Division and hosted the Edwardsville VFW Braves in a twin bill. The team was a member of the Southwestern Illinois Inter-City Baseball League.

Troy Call Baseball Club

The Troy Call Baseball Club, summer 1907. Philip Rarick, John Healey, William Schlichting, Arthur Gornet, Paul Gerfen (manager), William Ramshaw, J. Irvin Hindmarch, Russell P. Jarvis (mascot, about 2 years old), Arthur Sprick, Ray Rawson and Duncan McCormick.

Troy Grade School Varsity Basketball Team 1948-1949

(Right) Troy Grade School Varsity Basketball team, 1948-1949. (l. to r.) Kneeling: June Lindquist, Lynn Zenk, Captain JoAnn Robertson, Mary Jo Brown and Sharon McFarland, cheerleaders. Row 2: Bob Dollinger, Charles Mayer, Captain Hugh Harrigan, Bill Humphries, Co-captain Robert "Tony" Hunsche, Bill Murphy, Bob Baglin and Bob Atwood. Row 3: Manager Jack Schmitt, Bill Atwood, Bud Schmerbauch, Paul Levo, Don Marchiando, Ernie Nemnich, Bucky Wadlow, Jim Holshouser and Coach and teacher, W.S. Freeman. Row 4: Ed Jarvis, Dale Hosto, Bob Wheeler, Ed Holshouser, Jim Bowler, Bernie Rapien, Len Herbst, Jerry Ames and Dale "Ping" Wille. Not pictured: Jack Rees.

Fishing at Silver Creek

Lutheran Ladies Bowling League

(Left) Lutheran Ladies Bowling League, circa 1940s. (l. to r.) Front: Mildred (Martin) Galloway, Frances (Smith) Gebhart, Marge (Thomas) Porter, Lillian Howe, Fritz Blasé, Maxine (Deterding) Flath, Ida Brunworth, Audrey (Dunstan) Vesci, Dolly Rosetti and Pearl (Schildmeier) Haase. Middle: Thelma (Kueker) Yurock, Hazel (Maden) Kueker, Frieda Flath, Jerry (Barbee) Kueker, Fern (Kueker) Taake, Laverne Howerton Holshouser, Evelyn (Porter) Harrison, Arlene (Hecht) Gerling and Katherine Bouscher. Back: unidentified and Shirley (Beutel) Fischer. Information submitted by Clara Richter.

(Left) Fishing at Silver Creek near Troy. (l. to r.) Unknown, Adam Voelker, Gus Voelker and unknown.

Triad High School Varsity Cheerleaders State Champs

Triad High School Varsity Cheerleaders, State Champs 2001. (l. to r.) Row 1: Emily Tillman, Jessica Ivie, Emily Mayhew, Kara Kunz, Cyndi Foehrkolb and Stephanie Windham. Row 2: Sara Pani, Nikki Moreland, Kaitlin McNamera, Jenny Lyerla and Jessica Eyrich. Row 3: Coach Kim Morrison, Jenna Shellenberg, Missy Burns, Amanda Hanafin, Lindsey Lucas and Coach Kelly Grapperhaus. This was the first time a Triad Cheerleading Team won a State contest.

Triad High School Varsity Cheerleaders, State Champs 2002. (l. to r.) Row 1: Amanda Hanafin, Jessica Eyrich, Valerie Lewis, Nikki Moreland, Jenny Lyerla, Sara Pane and Kaitlin McNamera. Row 2: Rachel Straube, Amanda Long, Jenna Shellenberg, Kelly West, Megan Boucher, Erica Windham, Lindsey Lucas and Jenna Underwood. Row 3: Coaches Dave Vanderbelt, Kelly Grapperhaus and Becca Severit.

Triad High School Football Team, 2001

The first Triad High School Football team to ever make it to quarterfinals. The following are the players numbers then the name: 2-Tyler Yates; 3-Mike Huffman; 4-Rob Cange; 5-Chris Miller; 9-Shane McBride; 10-Pat Brannon; 11-Mike Drazen; 12-Travis Tillman; 14-Phillip Barras; 20-Jacob Stein; 21-Eric Keil; 22-Dave Kleeman; 23-Brian Simmons; 24-Garrett Whitt; 25-Dan Ramsey; 32-Brendan Mutchek; 33-Maurice Huffman; 35-Kellen Johns; 36-Todd Smith; 38-Zach McDonald; 39-John Nanney; 40-Ken Scroggins; 44-Chris Thomas; 45-BJ Krieger; 51-Dustin Johns; 53-Scott Hurst; 54-Brad Carril; 58-Rob Woodward; 60-Tyler Bulva; 61-Brian Jordan; 62-T.J. Schwartz; 64-Andy Evans; 65-Mike DaCruz; 67-Tristan Burris; 68-Josh Muniz; 69-Greg Vadnal; 70-Jared Reilson; 71-Mike Wade; 72-Jeremy McCurdy; 73-Eric Robinson; 75-Trent Dittmer; 76-Chris Norm; 78-Tim Drazen; 79-Jared Hampton; 80-Luke Smith; 81-Dave Porter; 82-Chris O'Dell; 84-Chris Porter; 89-Ryan Eberhardt. Coaches: Paul Bassler, Mike Georgeoff, Ken Deatherage, Josh Ackerman, Ric Johns, Rus Witzig and Mr. Perry.

Troy Racetrack

The late Charlie Voelker, a long-time Troy resident, as a youth used to climb a tree to watch the races that were held on Saturday afternoons at the Troy racetrack. Large crowds came to see the horse, buggy, mule and foot races featured, which were held at least once a month in the spring and summer. The track was located on the western edge of town. It was owned by John Jarvis in the late 1880s and was behind his home just east of the Troy United Methodist Church on Edwardsville Road. *Information from the* Troy Tribune, *July 25, 1957.*

Edwardsville Gun Club

Founded May 16, 1879, the Edwardsville Gun Club is the oldest continuously operating gun club on the North American continent. Its first officers were W.E. Wheeler, president; E.B. Glass, vice president; Herman Ritter, secretary; J.R. Brown, treasurer; with H.E. Bayle and F. Mumme serving as board members. The purpose of the organization was to establish social trapshooting matches among its members and to promote the preservation of game and fish in the State of Illinois.

The club has had several shooting sites over the years, the original of which was on the W.H. Bohm farm west of Edwardsville. After many other locations, the club purchased a 40-acre tract which includes two lakes in Pin Oak Township, north of Troy on October 9, 1987.

As in the past, members volunteered labor and building materials. The footings for the clubhouse were poured on March 22, 1988. Although the building shell construction was contracted, members and friends provided all the labor for finish work and for the five trap fields, walk ways, and trap houses. During the next 10 years, membership continued to grow and the grounds, lakes and facilities were maintained and in some cases improved by volunteers.

On February 5, 1999, a fire totally destroyed the clubhouse. Fortunately, the office trailer used for shooting activities was not harmed and club operations continued from the trailer until the completion in 2000 of a new 3,600-square-foot clubhouse. In April 2001, after a sixth trap field was constructed, the club hosted the 2001 Illinois Southern Zone Shoot.

Current officers and board members are Bill Kreutzberg, president; Bob Grosze, vice president; Charlie Russell, secretary; Mark Peterson, treasurer; immediate past president, Kate Schneider; Steve Lexow, Allen Holloway, Steve Kirsch, Lloyd Hutchinson, Brian Peterson, Andy Nalefski and Gary Gan, directors. *This brief history was submitted by members of the club.*

Jim Mersinger, Vineman Triathlon in Sonoma Valley, CA, fall 2000. He competed in this Triathalon for his 40th birthday year.

Jim Mersinger, The Ironman

James Joseph "Jim" Mersinger, who is often nicknamed "Ironman," has entered many Triathlons in his life. Always enjoying bicycling and running, in his 30s he began training for the Ironman Distance Triathlon. He began with the triathlons in 1990. He entered the Canadian Ironman twice. He also went to Kona, Hawaii, the big Island of the Hawaiian Islands, after being selected from thousands of entries. A former Triad High School athlete, Mersinger also traveled to Florida for the Great Floridian, to Ohio, California, and Utah to compete.

He stands at 6'2" and weighs around 205 pounds. He placed fourth in the Clydesdale category (a category for men over 200 lbs.) both at Vineman (12:18) and at Great Floridan (12:43) and third at Pineman (14:42).

A Triathlon is an endurance event where participants compete in running, bicycling and swimming. Jim has beaten his previous records in most of his events. At the Great Floridian, he set new Ironman PR's for each of the disciplines. His swim time was recorded at 1 hour, 13 minutes; bike time, 6 hours, 25 minutes; and run time 4 hours, 47 minutes.

Jim, who grew up in the Blackjack community south of Troy, and his wife Rozann have two children, Joseph and Molly. They live in Maryville. *Submitted by Jim Mersinger.*

Judy Ulrich Run for Life

The Fun Run/Walk for Life was held several years in the early 1990s following the death of Judy Ulrich, a well-loved physical education teacher in the Triad School District. The Troy Jaycees sponsored the activity.

Troy YMCA

The Troy Lions Club was instrumental in getting a YMCA activity program in the Troy Community. The Lions donated $4,000 to the new YMCA to get plans started for the project. Classes were offered in swimming at local home pools, namely the Don Callahan residence and the Jim Merrell residence. Swimming divisions included water babies, water bugs, polliwogs, guppies and adults.

Classes in gymnastics, cheerleading, pompon, baton, karate, intermediate gymnastics, and basketball and tennis instruction were held. In addition a story hour and open gym were provided. The locations for these classes and activities were at McCray-Dewey Jr. High School gym and at the Tri-Township Park. Pat Barker was the YMCA-Troy Branch director, as well as an instructor.

Ralph Jameson of R and L Supply Company supplied the office for the YMCA-Troy Branch. Terry Taake, David Bess, Ron Harbison, Tim Greenfield, Ralph Jameson, Stu Savage and Pat Barker helped get the YMCA started. It only flourished for approximately one season. *Information for this story was taken from the June 13, 1985, issue of the* Troy Times *and from local residents' recollections.*

Mayor Velda Armes (left) starts the one-mile Judy Ulrich Fun Run/Walk for Life.

Triad High School Girls Soccer Team, 2002

The 2002 Triad Girls Soccer team made it to the State play-offs and was the Section Champion. Members of the team were Lori Harvey, Eva Karpowicz, Melissa Barger, Ashley Switzer, April Eilering (keeper), Jessie Bayne, Amy Dix, Krissi Rengel, Amy Mayes, Alaina Lacopo, Chrissy McCauley, Erin Dix, Jenna Shellenberg, Meghan Massey, Elizabeth Ball, Nicole Chappell, Annie Shauster, Stephanie Meier, Natalie Jameson (keeper), Abby Bohnenstiehl, Jordan Stuart, Jessica Cook, Erin Spotanski, Nikki Martin, and Erin Cullipher (keeper).

The team had a 22-2-2 record, with a state record of 168 goals scored and just seven allowed; 20 shutouts (most in the state); conference champs, fours years in a row; regional champs, third straight year; and first ever sectional championship.

Junior midfielder Jessie Bayne was named to all-state team for the third straight year, also to First Team All-*Chicago Tribune*, as well as first team All-Metro (*St. Louis Post-Dispatch*). Alaina Lacopo (sophomore forward) was named to the all-sectional team. Abby Bohnenstiehl (junior back) was named to the all-sectional team for the second straight season and to Third Team All-Metro. April Eilering (junior goalkeeper) was named to second team All-Metro. *Information furnished by Derek Crain of the* Times-Tribune.

Triad Girls Soccer Team 2002

Troy Soccer Club

The Troy Soccer Club (TSC) was incorporated in August of 1989. The Club was formed when existing Troy participants, who had been playing in the Collinsville Soccer Association, organized and created the new Troy Soccer Club.

The organization has experienced steady growth over the years. The original divisions were restructured and the number of participants has increased from the initial size of around 300 to the current level of over 700. Additional fields have been added over the years to handle the increase in players, along with additions and improvements to the concession stand. *Submitted by Bill Beguhn. Paid for by the Troy Soccer Club.*

Troy Soccer Club

BOB TURLEY

Young Bob Turley

Bob Turley was born in Troy, on September 19, 1930, the son of Henrietta (Maden) and Delbert Turley. As a youngster, he moved to East St. Louis, but always had ties with Troy. He had relatives in Troy and visited there often. When he was growing up, he would spend several weeks a year in Troy with relatives, fishing and hunting and enjoying the Troy area.

Always an athlete, Bob became a star baseball player. He appeared on the major league roster for the first time on September 29, 1951, and changed the quality of the sport forever. From that debut, he went on to make his mark with the most legendary team of all time, the New York Yankees. Bob became known as "Bullet" Bob because of the speed of his fast ball. He was already a legend when he became the first and only player ever to win both the Cy Young Award and the Hickock Award. The Cy Young Award was for both leagues in 1958 as the best pitcher in major league baseball. The Hickok Award is the symbol for the best professional in any sport. He was also named the Most Valuable Player in the 1958 World Series. His most notable pitching performance came during 1958 when he pitched three games of the World Series to lead the Yankees to a World Series title. He is considered a legend for all time.

As for coaches, Bob Turley had some of the best. Two coaches, Casey Stengel and Art Williams, were among the most influential people in Bob's life. In 1974, Bob's baseball career was over, but he didn't find a "replacement" career that satisfied him. That year, Art Williams, a former Georgia football coach, was doing exciting things at a company called Waddell and Reed. As one of the first six-figure earners, Bob collected his $100,000 ring to go along with his World Series rings. Bob was on hand in September 1984 for the ground breaking of the new International Headquarters in Duluth, Georgia.

When he and a handful of other Waddell and Reed people left that company to form their own special company, "Primerica," he knew his life was going to change. He had found a new team, and the rest was history. In 1987, the original RVPs of that era, known as the Original Seven, rejoined for a special appearance on EPN-TV.

Bob and Carolyn Turley were married November 11, 1981, and she has been instrumental in his success and an unbelievable partner throughout the years.

For his 70th birthday, a large party was held in his honor at Chateau Elan in Braselton, GA. It was also the occasion of his retirement from Primerica. He still keeps close ties with the company from either his home in Hideaway Beach on Marco Island, FL, or at his Georgia home.

Information for this article was obtained and written by Mae Grapperhaus per telephone interview in 2000 after Turley's 70th birthday and in 2002 for this book.

Bob Turley family. (l. to r.) Back: Don, Bob and Terry. Front: Kathy, Carolyn and Becky (Turley) Salyer.

Above: Bob Turley in action as a pitcher for the New York Yankees.

Left: Bob Turley with his Cy Young trophy in late 1958.

Entertainment

The entertainment history of Troy may not include famous composers, actors, or musicians, but it can claim famous magician Roy Mayer. Troy can, also, proudly claim a quality and variety of performers and performances unusual to small towns. The Troy Opry house, various community bands, singing groups, and even rock bands have given Troy a unique entertainment history.

(Above) Troy Band, circa 1900 or earlier. In back standing, second from right, Dan Liebler; leaning on tuba, Bob Dawson. Carl Davis is thought to be in the photo.

(Right) Dorothy Ludwig Gindler, Majorette

Bert Weber, Majorette

(Right) McCray-Dewey Grade School, Arbor Day Parade, April 22, 2002

McCray Dewey High School Band, circa 1930s

Gene Adams in his typical piano-playing pose: very upright and animated and always smiling, circa 1960s.

Gene Adams, Pianist

Genial Troy pianist Gene Adams owned and operated Adams Store in downtown Troy, but his beloved avocation was playing the piano. He studied with Miss Gussie Miller, but developed his own improvisational and jazz style. He was not only well-known about town, but also played with several area dance orchestras and had guest appearances on some radio shows. *Submitted by Merrill Ottwein.*

Aebel's Dance Hall

The Aebel's Park, located just south of Route 40 to the east of Troy-O'Fallon Road, was a well-known place for young couples to go to dance in the 1920s and 1930s. It had a beer stand on the outside of the hall for summer use.

Blackjack Brass Band, with Henry Riebold on bass drum, early 1900s

Band Stand, Memorial Day, 1946

Band Stand

McCray-Dewey High School Band was probably assembling for a 1949 Memorial Day concert in the little city park which was located where the U.S. Bank drive-through is currently located in 2002. Louis Philippe was the director. Members furnished their own white shirts and trousers, and the school furnished black wool capes, lined with orange satin, and black wool hats.

Blackjack Brass Band

The Blackjack Brass Band circa 1880s or 1890s. Not much is known about this handsome group. Henry Riebold is on the bass drum, and the Mersinger brothers-Valentine, Adam, and Phillip- and Adolph Boulanger are believed to be in this picture. When the roads were bad, they used to practice over the telephone, by getting the operator to open the party lines.

Fairview Four Quartet

The gentlemen in the Fairview Four Quartet (named after the Ottwein Fairview Farm Dairy where they often practiced) started singing together when they attended McCray-Dewey High School in the 1940s. After interruptions for college and military service, the group started performing again in their spare time, eventually being heard widely in the local St. Louis area and making

appearances all over Illinois. Members are the Rogier brothers – Dick, Robert and Floyd, Jr. – and Merrill Ottwein. Soprano Audrey (Ottwein) Deeren and pianist Gene Adams often appeared with them for a short variety show. *Submitted by Merrill Ottwein.*

Fairview Four Quartet, (l. to r.) Dick Rogier, Robert Rogier, Audrey Deeren, Floyd Rogier, Jr. and Merrill Ottwein, singing selections from "The Music Man" at the Madison County Sesquicentennial Celebration.

Johnny's Jokers/ X-I tations/Palace

The original band, composed of John Schmitt, accordion; Mike Klueter, saxophone; and Dean Huston on a snare drum borrowed from the Troy band director, Darwin Schmitt, started in 1964 when they were in the 7th grade. Their first "gig" was at Adelhardt's Pizza and Ice Cream Barn, located on the parking lot of Adelhardt's Grocery Store (111 West Market St.). Mike Sexton, Rick Box, and then Chris Hentz the following year, were added on guitars, and the name was changed to X-I tations. Teen dances were held on Saturday nights at

X-I tations Band, March 1967. (l. to r.) Mike Sexton, guitar; Rick Box, guitar; Dean Huston, drums; John Schmidt, accordion; and Mike Klueter, saxophone.

the Jaycee Hall, and they were paid $25 per night to perform.

Parents of the band members chaperoned, collected $1 admission at the door and "kept the peace." The police station was next door, and officers did a nightly walk through, so the kids were always aware of their presence. Angelo's Restaurant at the north west corner of West Market and Hickory Streets, remained open until after the intermission so the youngsters had a place to buy refreshments.

High school graduation and college plans put an end to the X-I tations. In the mid 1970s a new band, "Palace," was formed. It consisted of Dean Huston on drums (a full set this time), Steve Kueker, and Dave Blackard on guitar, Steve Eaton on bass, and Dave Young, vocals. They played weekly anywhere from Rolla, MO, to Neoga, IL. Marriages and families were the reasons for the end of Palace. *Submitted by Thelma Huston.*

Roy Mayer, Troy's Famous Magician

To see Roy Mayer perform his three-linking ring routine, his billiard balls manipulation and his "Miser's Dream," where money appears all over the place, was to see a master of his art. It was as smooth, witty, effortless and graceful as the patter that went with it. When he was about 10 years old, Roy learned magic from a kit and was soon performing for his friends at the north St. Louis home where he was born on November 3, 1906. By the

age of 12, he was entertaining Scout troops and church groups. Will Lindhorst, one of St. Louis' leading magicians, lived near Roy, and he soon became Lindhorst's assistant. By age 17, he performed on his own at small clubs and banquets.

Later, Roy met Bernice Schultze, adopted daughter of Sophie and John Schultze of Troy, who became his wife and assistant. The couple lived in Troy for the rest of their lives, raising their 2 sons, Roy and Charles, here.

Roy worked at various jobs to make a living, and magic was a sideline. As a Beech Nut candy salesman, he was tapped by the Skoura brothers, operators of a chain of St. Louis movie houses, to perform magic, then pass out candy between movies. He was one of the first to do magic with a commercial tie-in and became known as the "Beech Nut Magician."

Just as his magic career was becoming financially successful, the Depression struck, and the entertainment business declined. But Roy Mayer worked at various jobs and honed his skill wherever he could. World War II brought economic rebirth; and Roy was sought after to play many of the new St. Louis night clubs springing up. Agencies began to book him; and at the age of 42,

he became a full-time professional. He hit the road with Bernice at his side. Roy's career blossomed. The school show route covered the central and eastern states, averaging 3 to 4 shows daily. In the next 13 years they traveled over 390,000 miles by car! Roy's fame and skill as a magician became widely known. He turned down offers from the big shows in places like Las Vegas to work from his home and family base in the midwest.

After about 25 years of touring, the Mayers decided to slow down. In 1961 his friend and fellow magician, Gabe Alberici, hired Roy as a safety engineer where he helped the J.S. Alberici Construction Company receive recognition for an outstanding safety record. Roy continued to perform his magic in his spare time and only illness slowed him down in the last years of his life. Roy died in 1991.

Bernice continued to live quietly in Troy, and died in 1996. Son Roy, who graduated from Valparaiso University, worked most of his life as an industrial chemist in St. Louis where he is now retired. Son Charles graduated from University of Illinois and Ohio State University in electrical engineering. He was in the Navy and later joined the C.I.A. Sadly, Charles was killed in an airplane crash in Iran in 1968 while working for the government.

Roy was well known in the magic world. He was active in the International Brotherhood of Magicians and the Society of American Magicians. Harry Houdini, president at the time, signed his membership card.

Roy's skill was tremendous, but adding to his success was surely his warm and

Roy Mayer, Magician

McCray-Dewey High School Band

First McCray-Dewey High School Band, 1932. (l. to r.) Standing: Hank Ford, tuba; Virginia Flake, saxophone; Miss Sonnenberg, instructor; Joe Mersinger, saxophone; Homer Polwort, saxophone. Seated: Raymond Bress, trumpet; Dorothy (Ludwig) Gindler, violin; Matilda Maden, piano; John Gerfen, saxophone; Jerome Davis, saxophone

winning personality plus that of his charming wife. In later years, Roy and Bernice were known among magicians as "The Old Smoothies," a tribute to their effortless style and grace. Roy performed for groups in Troy many times over the years and was considered a hometown treasure. *Information from* The Times Tribune, *January 1995.*

High School Band Directors

Popular band director Louis Philippe taught at McCray-Dewey Township High School for about 10 or 12 years in the 1940s and 1950s.

Darwin "Shorty" Schmitt was another band director who had great influence on many young Troy musicians. He taught in the Triad district for about 15 years. After retirement he opened Schmitt Music Stores in Highland, Glen Carbon and O'Fallon, selling instruments and music.

Some band directors who received their early training from Louis Philippe or Shorty Schmitt and attained some prominence in their field are Ted Fedder, Eddie Fulton, Norbert Meier, Robert Rogier and James Druessel.

Other band directors who taught at the high school for short periods of time were Charles Cordeal, Roger Junk, Mark Buske, and Robert Rogier.

John Malvin is the current director at Triad High School. He has been in the district over twenty years.

Gussie Miller

Miss Gussie Miller was a renowned piano teacher in Troy from the 1920s through the 1950s. Not only was she the piano teacher for hundreds of young people in the Troy area whom she regularly presented in recitals, but she put together some memorable Music Week Concerts, featuring talented individuals and groups from all over the community. She was a fine pianist, a graduate of the Kroeger School of Music in St. Louis. Miss Gussie was a gentle, refined presence in the lives of her students, many of whom would not have had music lessons but for her, especially during the Depression years. Many became fine musicians and remember her gratefully. *Written by Audrey Deeren.*

Gussie Miller, long time music (piano) teacher, 1950s.

Joseph Mersinger and the Modernaires

Joseph Mersinger, pictured at the piano below in 1955, played instruments for years in area dance bands including the Al Alseman Orchestra, The Bob Taylor Band, The Favorites, The Fred Fischer Orchestra, The Art Clark Orchestra and The Modernaires. *Submitted by Joseph J. Mersinger.*

Louis Philippe, 1940s

Darwin Schmitt

The Modernaires, 1955. (l. to r.) Joseph Mersinger (piano), John Ozella (trumpet), Robert Goebel (drums) and Chuck Bedard (saxophone).

Schultze Brothers Band. (l. to r.) Seated: James N. Jarvis (Instructor), John H. Hagler, Fred Kuhlman, William Long and Ben Schultze. Standing: Pete Bour (bass drum), Chris Schultze, Fred Metzger, John Smith, Charles Schultze, Phillip Schultze and William Wittman (snare drum).

Schultze Brothers Band

The Schultze Brothers Band of Troy, circa 1895, is shown above at the Modern Woodmen's picnic at East St. Louis where they won a cash prize and had their picture taken. They were popular at Troy events and often played at Rieder's Park, south of Troy, for dances and other events.

Troy Community Band

Community bands have played a big role in America's cultural heritage. In the tradition of the story in "The Music Man," amateur musicians have brought this bit of Americana to life in Troy in a long line of bands, many mentioned in this history book.

The 2002 Community Band got its start in the late 1980s under the direction of Darwin Schmitt, then the local high school band director. Currently Bob Rogier, retired Triad school superintendent and music teacher, is the director. The band plays at a variety of local events, including summer concerts in the park.

Bob Rogier is in a great position to reminisce. His grandfather, Robert Dawson, was a renowned tuba player (as well as bass singer), and Bob remembers him playing in several bands, including the Miner's Union Band. (Bob Dawson was not a miner, but the best tuba player around so he was recruited. Bob Rogier also claims, grinning widely, that he was a world class cusser. A fixture around Troy for many years, Bob Dawson represented Illinois Power locally, and Bob remembers his grandfather running service calls with a wheelbarrow.)

One band member tells about an ancestor in a group of young men from the "Spring Valley" area southwest of Troy wanting to start a band and ordering a bunch of instruments via mail-order catalog. When they came, they each reached in the big crate and whatever they came up with, they played. They called themselves the "Spring Valley Band" but not much more is known of them!

Membership in the Troy Community Band varies from season to season, but some members have been in the band since its start. Ages of members have ranged from talented 14 year-olds to beloved senior citizens Virginia Kraft and Irwin Dollinger,

who played in their 80s. As of the summer of 2002, the members are Susan Schmidt, Debbie Wiese, Elaine Schuette, Becky Fischer, Cindy Hill, Trudy Mollet, Melora Becker, Rebecca Barr, Bonnie Schuette, Cindy White, Debbie Pyles, Ryan Gilmore, Murray Cornelius, Kevin Wiese, Mark Liszewski, Elizabeth Liszewski, Patti Take, Travis Rosenthal, Richard Martin, Sharon Jasper, Dawn Stillwagon, Audrey Deeren, Merrill Ottwein, Darrell Burnett, Robert Viviano, Nathan Gilmore, Eric Allard, Howard Schuette, Kurt Schuette.

Troy Drum and Bugle Corps

The Troy Drum and Bugle Corps, whose members were young women in their teens or twenties, began about 1929 or 1930. Mr. Hufford, principal of the Troy Grade School, helped the group get started. He was assisted by versatile area musician Bert (Weber) Loyet, who was the first majorette. Later, Dorothy (Ludwig) Gindler and Anita (Schneider) Jarvis were also majorettes. Most of the music and drum cadences were taught by ear as few members could read music. The group was extremely popular and played in drum corps competitions, homecoming parades, centennial events, political and union parades, and other civic events in Troy and surrounding towns and as far away as Decatur, Springfield, Carbondale and St. Louis.

Mr. Hufford also taught two Troy girls, Anna Mae (Gebauer) Langdon and Alma (Capelle) Rood, to twirl batons to add to the show. This was a new and novel idea and became very popular. The group also performed simple drills. The first uniform consisted of a black cotton gabardine jacket trimmed in gold with matching pillbox hat, white box-pleated gabardine skirt, white gloves, silk stockings and spectator pumps with 1 1/2 inch heels – not very comfortable for hot summer parade marching! Later, a summer uniform of a white blouse and elbow cape with black buttons and a cloche hat was worn.

Some members of the group were Charmion (Nemnich) Semanisin, Olivia Mersinger, Margaret (Kelly) Hart, Mary (Kranz) Zinkgraf, Faye (Snodgrass) Cassens, Esther Mersinger, Laverne (Porter) Crompe, Julia (Knecht) Taake, Gladys (Conley) Blaney, Pauline (Naumer) Steinmeier, Margarite (Fox) Tackas, Pearl (Wyatt) Sury, Evelyn (Elliott) Kimberlin, Lucille (Bysbe) Schindler, Hilda (Wetzel) Elam, Norma (Rood) Jackson, Grace (Shaffer) Roth, Edna (Shaffer) Linder, Norma

Troy Community Band at the St. Jacob Strawberry Festival, May 2002.

Troy Drum & Bugle Corps, 1936

(Shaffer) Stephen, Wilma (Shaffer) Cline, Tillie (Maden) Hess, Beatrice (Arth) Klem, Margarite (Arth) Lucido, Ardith (Kimberlin) Lory, Erna (Norbury) Lewis, Emma (Wyatt) Kamm, Bernadine (Dellamano) Lombardi, Iona (Jackson) Moser, Dorothy (Molden) Rotkis, Melba (Hart) Paul, Helen (Capelle) Hildreth, Esther (Schurman) Guttersohn, Gladys (Gornet) Heckel, Thelma (Kueker) Yurock, and Florence (Gornet) Reiss.

A marvelous photo of the Troy Corps was taken from an office building window in downtown St. Louis in the late 1930s. The huge parade was part of a national American Legion Convention held in the city. The parade route was several miles long and the day was very hot, of course, the young ladies were in full uniform and marched, as usual, in their high heels! Dorothy Ludwig was the majorette.

Troy Junior Drum and Bugle Corps

Following the success of the Troy Drum and Bugle Corps, a Junior Corps was formed. It existed for several years in the mid-1930s. These young ladies wore white dresses with red sashes and pillbox hats. Lynette Pritchett and Anna Mae Gebauer were majorettes.

The group was greatly in demand, especially at all the homecoming parades around. They played at the Illinois State Fair, at Sportsmen's Park, and won quite a few competitions. The girls were taught by Troy musician Carl Davis, who was an army bugler, and Barrett Niedlinger of Collinsville, who taught drumming.

Here is a partial list of girls who were members: Millie Marie Collins, Lynette Pritchett, Dorothy Davis, Anna Mae Gebauer, Virginia Schramek, Margaret Moore, Edith Lochmann, Edna Lochmann, Evelyn Virgin, Dorothy Manley, Laverne Capelle, Dorothy Dee Hindmarch, Fern Kueker, Arlene Kueker, Anna Marie Flake, Mildred Martin, Pauline Schmerbauch, Alice Pranaitis, Pearl Wyatt, Gladys Drique, Verna Drique, Betty Rood, Martha Kueker, Darlene Arth, Ann Taylor and Jean Wise.

The Troy Opry House

Clifton "Clif" Patterson, Illinois State Harmonica Champion, owned the Troy Opry House located at 704 Edwardsville Road in the early 1980s. He won the state championship five times at the Illinois State Fair, as well as winning awards all over the country for his playing.

While he owned the Troy Opry House, he lit up that part of town every Friday evening with a down-home type country music and comedy show. He was joined by sidekick Paul Tinnon, one of the top fiddlers in the area. *Information for this article was taken from a February issue of the* Times Tribune *and the recollections of Mae Grapperhaus.*

Troy Swiss Band

A German band formed around 1941, playing polkas, waltzes,

Troy Junior Drum Corps, 1934

95

marches, and pop songs at dances and other community affairs. The stresses of WWII and the fact that Director Art Kamm was of Swiss descent precipitated a name change to Troy Swiss Band.

Arthur Kamm, married to Emma Stein of Troy, was also known for his huge bass voice. He is the father of Jule "Bud" Kamm of Nokomis and Arthur "Swiss" Kamm of Troy.

(Right) The Troy Swiss Band. (l. to r.) Jule "Bud" Kamm, Oliver "Bud" Arth, James Cravens, Robert "Red" Taake, William "Bill" Holshouser, Omar R. Hampton, Eugene Schrameck and Arthur E. Kamm, Director.

Troy United Mine Workers Band

(Left) Troy United Mine Workers Band, circa 1915. (l. to r.) Front: Jule DeVries, David Sims, Henry Maden, George Raber and John McMullen. Back: Charles Schrameck, William Frangen, William Llewellyn, Harry Belcher, Tom Lewis, Carl Davis and Bob Dawson. Information from the Troy Tribune, July 23, 1957.

Parades and Events

Alpine Festival

The first Alpine Festival was held in August 1956, at the southwest corner of Main and Market (square). Main Street was usually closed off. It was initiated by the Troy Jaycees. Members and wives dressed in Alpine dress (Bavarian type) and served the people beer in a garden situated around the dance floor.

The festival was held for about 9 years. Many years it rained, so one of the last festivals was held in June to see if the rain could be avoided. It rained in June, also. Those who attended and the Jaycees themselves had a lot of fun during those years.

In 1958, a parade was held during the Alpine Festival.

Due to weather and disinterest, among other problems, the festival was discontinued in the mid-1960s.

Jaycee Alpine Festival, Vic and Vera's Tavern located in the old hotel at N. Main and Market, 1956. (l. to r.) Standing: Vic Wesemann, tavern owner, Dale Rose and Ray Maden. Seated: Irene Maden, Dot Holshouser (with head in lap) and Marge Klueter.

Troy Homecomings

(Below) Henry Kueker, second from left, Homecoming Float, early 1900s

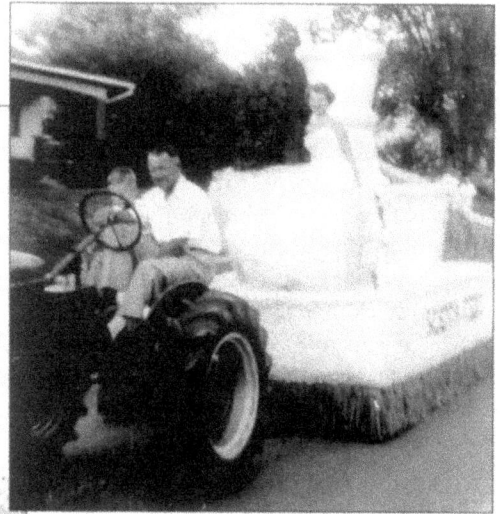

Marilyn Edwards on Schoon's Drug Float, Troy Homecoming Parade, 1953

(Right) Triad High School Marching Band, Troy Homecoming Parade, 1986

American Legion Color Guard. Third from left, Art Hazzard bearing the American Flag, Troy Homecoming Parade, 1956

Troy Centennial 1957

Memorial Day

(Below) Memorial Day, Tri-Township Park, 1999

Art and Irma Hartman, Troy Centennial Parade, 1957

Troy Parks

The earliest mentioning of a Troy park was in the 1882 edition of *History of Madison County* published by W.R. Brink and Co. A Troy Park Association was founded in February 1882, with the purpose of procuring and preserving a public square or park. The Association had a capital stock of $100, divided into shares of $25. A square of ground immediately south of the schoolhouse had been purchased. It is likely that it was south of the W.S. Freeman School (in 2002) on the Clay Street side. The ground was to be laid out into a park. The officers of the association were Dr. F.A. Sabin, president; William Freudenau, vice president; Henry H. Padon, secretary; Frederick Gerfen, treasurer; and David Seligmann, member. Another park of sorts was the racetrack at the John Jarvis residence on the west end of Troy. (See Troy Race Track.)

A small park was established in the late 1930s-early 1940s to the rear of the bank building on 100 East Market Street. A bandstand was built and also a large memorial board listing all area WW II service men and women. Band concerts and several speaking events were held there before it was demolished in the 1950s.

In the late 1950s, the Troy Jaycees purchased some land in Brookside, near the creek, and for several years, it was hoped that a Jaycee Park would be built there. Later, in the 1960s, the Troy Jaycees purchased land in the vicinity of the 1500 block of Troy-O'Fallon Road at the first curve. Later, David Skeens Sr. bought it and built a home on the property, and the Troy Jay-

cees abandoned the idea of having a park. In the meantime in the 1960s, the Troy Lions Club was planning a park on the western side of Troy on the Herman Hecht farm.

Earlier, before the present Tri-Township Park (see story) was begun on the Hecht farm, the Troy Lions Club held some land along Route 40, just west of the Troy Grain elevator. That too, was later sold for industrial use.

In the mid 1990s, a small park was established on Meadow Drive. The park was an open piece of land that lies on a pipe line. Since no residential homes can be built over the utility, it was made into a park.

As it disbanded, the Troy Optimist Club gave the City of Troy funding from its treasury to place benches on the site.

Time, weather and vandalism destroyed the lawn furniture. Currently the City is planning to revamp the old Optimist Park.

In addition, the City is planning Klaustermeier Park to the east edge of Troy, just west of Twin Lakes subdivision on the old Neustadt property.

In 1997, the City of Troy purchased the property at West Clay and Edwardsville Road known to many as "the wedge," from Helmich Brothers Equipment. Prior to that, it had fallen into disarray. The Troy Main Street organization worked to make a park. In 2002, the city and Downtown Revitalization, Inc. took the project over. It currently is a pleasant little park with a gazebo, lamps, landscaping and fencing.

Dr. Donald Spencer Memorial Park

Dr. Donald Spencer Memorial Park is located at the southeast corner of Center and South Main streets. It was erected following the death, in 2000, of Troy's longtime veterinarian, Dr. Spencer. The park was sponsored by memorials, the City of Troy and grants.

Main Street Park

This gazebo sits in the Main Street Park at Edwardsville Road and West Clay. It was placed in the park in June 2002. Since this photo was taken, the park has been completed with lamps and landscaping.

Rieder's Park

Chris Schultze is at right at Rieder's Park, located on Lower Marine Road east of town.

Catastrophes
Kitson Craft Fire

The Kitson Craft building fire occurred during daylight hours. Due to its sporadic explosions and the heavy black smoke, the fire fighters were unable to remain close. These dramatic photos were taken by professional photographer Bob Little as he was driving through Troy.

(Left and Below) Kitson Craft Fire, early 1970s. Photos from Bob Little.

Fire at Troy Baptist Church

On January 14, 1940, the Troy Baptist Church, the second oldest in the city, was destroyed by fire which originated from an overheated furnace in the basement. The loss was estimated at about $10,000 which was only partially covered by insurance.

The Bible School had just assembled and members were in different locations within the church and annex when the smell of smoke was detected. An investigation was made with a result that the fire was found to have already gained considerable headway.

Pastor W.J. Richardson calmly advised all present to leave the building quickly but in an orderly way. About 80 persons, mostly children, filed out without panic or injury. Within a few minutes the entire frame structure burst into flames and none of the church furniture could be saved.

The Troy volunteer fire department responded promptly and soon had three streams of water on the flames, but it was apparent early that the church building was doomed.

Near zero weather and a strong west wind hampered the firefighting; and when surrounding property was threatened, the Collinsville fire department was summoned and aided materially in checking the flames. The Peters' residence immediately east of the church, occupied by M. Dillingham and family, caught fire several times but was saved from destruction. The Theodore Gebauer business on the north and the Scott residence on the east were also threatened for a time.

Ordinarily, without an adequate water supply, the frame building would have been entirely consumed in less than half an hour, but with five streams of water pouring on it, rapid progress was checked and the flames were fought for nearly two hours.

At times in the earlier stages of the fire, it appeared as though the church might be saved, but all that remained was a portion of the annex and parts of several outside walls of the church that was erected in 1876. *Information from* The Troy Call.

Troy City Mills Fire

Ruins of the Troy City Mills, destroyed by fire on Friday night, November 19, 1892. Located near the old Mill Pond off Clay Street.

Troy Baptist Church on fire, Main Street, 1940

Interesting Stories
Blackjack Community

The Blackjack settlement located about five miles south of Troy is unincorporated. It was founded as a German farming community and still is in 2002. New residential homes are added each year; however, it is still agricultural.

Two churches were prominent in the community in the late 1800s. They were St. John the Baptist Catholic Church and school located on Lebanon Road near Blackjack Road and St. John's Evangelical Church located at Lebanon Road (and what is in 2002 Troy-O'Fallon Road).

St. John's Evangelical Church and school was destroyed by a tornado in 1939; however, St. John's Catholic Church prospered until 1992, when it was closed by the Springfield Diocese in a consolidation effort.

Many farm type businesses prospered for a time in Blackjack. Although they were not close in distance, they were working for a time. Most of the businesses were on or near farms located there.

A brick yard was located north of Erwin Loyet's place on Lebanon Road. Frank Mersinger was involved in that business for a time. There was a tavern there and a horse stop of sorts, with a cellar on a hillside nearby. Also, in this area was a creamery operated by Pete Minier.

Blackjack flour mill thrived for awhile. It was located near Blackjack and Mill Creek Roads. At the northeast corner of that intersection was the Blackjack School. It was also called the "Hen Peck" school.

Two cemeteries are located within the boundaries of the community. They are St. John Evangelical Cemetery located on Lebanon Road near Troy-O'Fallon Road and St. John the Baptist Catholic Cemetery located on Lebanon Road east of Blackjack Road.

In the 1930s and 1940s, Arthur Rock had a filling station at the southwest corner of Blackjack and Lebanon Road, located near Rock's house. Rock offered soda, candy, as well as gas and oil for the automobile.

In horse and buggy days, a blacksmith shop was at the same corner. Nearby was a mail carrier stop: the rural carrier stopped at noon to feed his horse. Jake Herbst was the proprietor.

In 1993 the Troy Knights of Columbus purchased the former St. John the Baptist Church property. Various activities are held on the grounds, including chicken dinners in April and October; concerts in St. John's Chapel; K.C. meetings and family activities in the hall; and the St. John the Baptist Country Festival held in June on or near St. John the Baptist's feast day.

The area is still a quiet, peaceful and scenic area and is still known as Blackjack. *Information for this story was submitted by Mae Grapperhaus who held an interview with Joseph J. Mersinger, and from personal recollections.*

Carl Richter's Bet

During the 1968 World Series, when the St. Louis Cardinals played the Detroit Tigers, a hot bet was going on between two Troy men. Carl "Snap" Richter, a farmer from southwest of town, bet Russ Klaustermeier, who worked at the Troy Grain Company, that the Tigers would win. The bet was made between the two men, that, if the Tigers won, Klaustermeier would push Richter from the Troy Grain Company to the Troy square at Main and Market (one mile in distance). And if the Cardinals won, Richter would push Klaustermeier the same distance and location.

The Tigers won and the bet came to fruition. Russ pushed Carl all the way up South Main to the square and dumped him out there, while Frank Fritz, a brother to Loretta Keck, played the concertina. It was a funny sight. Traffic stopped to see the event on South Main, while other motorists just drove on by. Fritz walked a block or two with his concertina then took a ride the rest of the way, but the two main "characters" went all the way north on Main Street from Keck's Tavern.

(l. to r.) Russ Klaustermeier pushing Carl Richter, in the wheelbarrow, Frank Fritz-musician, 1968

After the much-talked about event, all went back to Keck's Tavern near the Troy Grain Company to celebrate.

Memories of Old Troy Town

Troy is fortunate to have recollections from the early days collected by citizens who lived then and are willing to share their memories. They offer a personalized look at the town and its citizens as they went about their daily lives.

The screenline of the Troy Post Office on East Market was wedge shaped. At the point of the wedge was the General Delivery counter where customers waited at a small window, and the postmaster handed them their mail. Mail boxes were located along the side of the wedge. People had their own keys for their boxes. On the east side of the building, people bought stamps or mailed and received packages.

On the corner of Main and Market stood Auwarter's General Store. Upstairs, in the then two story building, was the location of the *Monitor* newspaper office. Later Schoon's and Kamm's Drugs were located on the ground floor. School books were sold at Schoon's. Parents could take their used books there, and Schoon bought and sold books for grades 1–8.

At one time the jail sat at the corner of Border and Clay. It stood in front of Peddler Leet's place. The small brick jail had three tiny rooms with two cells.

An early firehouse was on the southwest corner of South Main and Center Streets. Firefighters would lift the lid of a

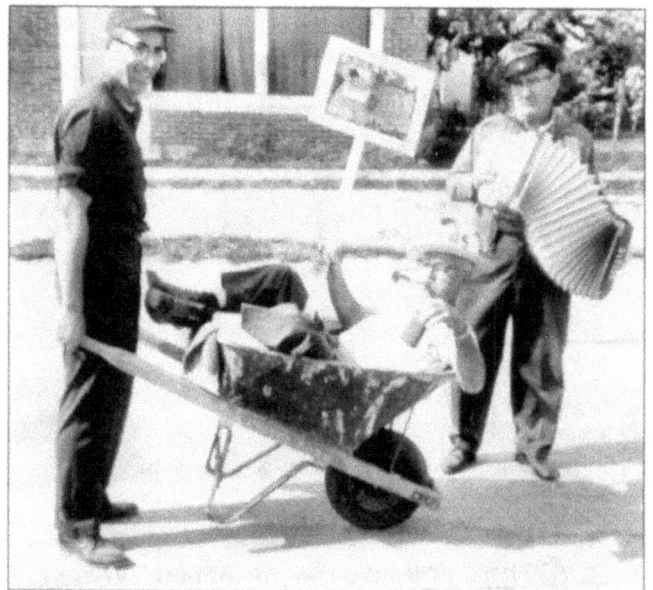

cistern on Main and Market, and using buckets, put water in the man-pulled pumper. The firehouse moved to Kimberlin Street, and in the 1960s the new firehouse was built. The cistern(s) have since been covered by buildings and roadways.

Homecoming celebrations were originally held in the downtown area. A highlight of those occurred in 1962, when former President Truman led the parade.

Troy had its own type of notoriety. A tavern named the Bloody Corner stood on Main Street. A murder was reported to have taken place there, thus, the name.

In 1978, Troy was nationally named one of the fastest growing cities in the US. By then the days of roller skating on Market Street, a one man police force, a hack to take passengers to the depot, blacksmith shops, the Troy Opera House with its silent movies and piano players were long gone. Troy continues to grow rapidly, but many still miss the hometown of their youth. *Information compiled from the writings of Clara Kirsch and Charmion Semanisin.*

A War Bride's Story

When Harold Gaertner brought his war bride, Greta, from Germany in 1948 to the home of his parents, Kate and Jule Gaertner, and his siblings, Doris, Carl and Gladys, it must have seemed to her a safe haven at last. Although Greta was fluent in both Czech and German languages, she spoke limited English. However, Kate and Jule spoke a little German and she soon felt at home with this kind and loving family.

Margaret "Greta" Milota was born in 1927 in the industrial city of Brno, Czechoslovakia, where her parents, Margaret and Joseph, had emigrated to find work on the advice of her step-sister, Marie, who had married a Czech. Her father was German and her mother, Austrian. She had a younger sister, Angela.

In 1939, the Nazis invaded Czechoslovakia without firing a shot. They totally controlled everything. In a "new" German-speaking school (6th-9th grades), Greta was trained to be a Technical Draftsman, designing machinery for factories. As the war progressed, living became very hard. Food and clothing were rationed. Toward the end of the war, they were often hungry and subsisted on soup and bread.

In 1944, the Allies began to bomb their factory city. Greta says it was ter-

rible running to the shelters, so afraid, and wondering if their parents' factories would be destroyed. Indeed, one day her father never returned from work. Many children roamed the streets not able to find their parents.

In 1945, the war ended. The Czechs were happy to be delivered from their Nazi captors, but the country was immediately taken over by the Russians who turned out to be worse in many respects. The soldiers were less disciplined, were largely illiterate, and raped and robbed the Czechs at will, pulling watches off of arms and earrings out of ears. Margaret Milota would often hide her two young daughters.

In the chaotic post-war political climate, Czech communists ruled, puppets of the Russians, who decided to deport all of Austrian descent. The three Milotas were forced to leave their small apartment, taking only what they could carry, and join others in a group which was forced to walk 60 miles to the Austrian border. They were given bread and water twice daily and fish-head soup for lunch, always guarded by armed soldiers. The old and infirm who could not stand the walk were shot.

Greta's mother had a sister in Austria who lived on a farm another 25 miles away, so they decided to keep on walking, asking for food from farmers. Finally, the exhausted family fell into their surprised relative's welcoming arms. Their peace was short-lived, however, as the Russians soon occupied Austria due to a post-war agreement with the Allies. Again there was terrible harassment from the illiterate Cossack soldiers, who were mainly drinking, raping and stealing. Many times Greta's mother had the girls jump out of the back window of the farm house and hide in the corn fields when they heard the horseback soldiers coming. Eventually, the farm was taken away from the family and everyone was required to work in the fields, guarded by a husky Russian woman who watched them from the edge. One day Greta's sister, Angela, didn't feel well so just stayed in bed. The guard went after her, beat her and forced her to work. Angela was not healthy and often fainted, so was sent to work in the kitchen. The women also had to wash lice-filled, filthy clothes for the Russians, boiling them in tubs and scrubbing them by hand.

Greta's mother heard that the Americans treated people very well and, miraculously, was granted permission to get on a boxcar heading for American occupied Germany. Right after the war, there was chaos and hunger with homeless people everywhere, and each country seemed glad to send people to the next one. The Milotas were taken to a suburb of Heidelberg (which was not bombed because of its historic value) where the American occupying forces were trying to cope with thousands of such refugees and surrendered German soldiers. There were shortages of food, clothing, housing and jobs, but eventually they were given housing with a German family and jobs. Eventually, Greta found employment in the Army PX where she met many young American soldiers, among them a tall, lanky corporal from mid-America named Harold Gaertner. Both Greta and Harold are somewhat quiet and reserved, but a friendship blossomed which quickly turned into romance. Harold bought her food, soap and other supplies from the PX. When Harold was scheduled to return to the states, they were married by the Burgermeister (Mayor).

The couple was now assigned passage on a troop ship sailing from the port of Bremerhaven – the servicemen on the lower decks and the war brides occupying the upper deck. After a difficult goodbye to her mother and sister, Greta sailed away to a new life.

Harold brought his bride to his family in Troy but had to return to camp in Maryland to finish three months of service. Finally, he arrived back home and set up housekeeping with his pretty bride. Harold worked a while for Hap Liebler Hardware, then for the City of Troy, and eventually found a career with the U.S. Postal Service where he stayed for 27 years. He had given six years to the U.S. Army. Drafted in 1942, he spent three years in active service in the armored infantry, saw action in the Battle of the Bulge, and spent three years as part of the American Occupation Troops in Germany.

Greta worked at her first job in Troy at Hosto's Laundry, and then secured an office job with Hartford Insurance Company in St. Louis, where she worked for 18 years.

It was to be nine years in America before the couple was able, with the help of Catholic Relief organizations, to send for her mother and sister, who by then had a 4-year old son. Sadly, Greta's mother, who courageously got her children through such perilous times, died two years later of a heart attack. Greta's sister suffered many health and emotional problems in her life and is now in a care facility. Compassionate Harold and Greta became legal guardians for her sister's child, and also adopted a little girl. Strong family ties and their strong faith have sustained them through life's ups and downs. They are members of Friedens Church, the V.F.W. and Auxiliary, and live a quiet life in retirement at their home in Troy.

In 1972 Greta and Harold were able to visit her half-sister, Marie, in Brno, Czechoslovakia, which was still behind the Iron Curtain. Renting a car, they drove a road lined with barbed wire and passed guards armed with machine guns. They visited her childhood haunts, where she spent the first 13 years of her life. An emotional trip, indeed!

Greta, who became a U.S. citizen in 1949, says she is telling her story in the hope it will help people remember the value of the freedom they have in this country and those who fought to sustain it. Her pride in her adopted country and its democratic system has caused her to volunteer to be an election judge many times. Of her terrible war experiences, she says, " I try not to dwell on them but we must not forget them, either. I believe God was on our side and pulled us through. Now, I'm proud to be an American."

More About Troy... Odds and Ends

The first Justice of the Peace in Troy was Joseph Eberman, who was appointed after the War of 1812.

Troy had its first post office in 1833. George Churchill was the first postmaster.

John Jarvis, one of the founding fathers of Troy, is buried in the Barnsback Cemetery, located somewhere around Wayland Ave. His slave is buried at the foot of his grave. John Jarvis' wife, who died in 1851, is buried in the City Cemetery.

Gebauer's Hardware was in business beginning in 1857.

John Carney came to Troy in 1861 to stake a claim. The Troy City Mills was early co-owned by Mr. Carney and Mr. Throp.

Adam Mersinger owned the White Horse Hotel between 1880 and 1900. The hotel was located on the north side of West Market Street. It was later called the Central Hotel and was run by the Dillinghams.

In 1897 the Troy City Mills was destroyed by fire.

Kuntzmann's Bakery was in existence in Troy in 1901.

Subscribers to *The Weekly Call* were paying $1.00 in advance for a one year's subscription in 1901.

The Blue Goose Motor Company, the forerunner to Greyhound Buses, had a route through Troy in the early 1900's.

In 1902, members of Kaskaski Tribe No. 126, Improved Order of Red Men, went to Belleville and Greenville to witness the installation of new lodges of the order. They also attended a big meeting of the order in Edwardsville.

Also in 1902, M.W. Powell laid out a new residential section in the north end to be known as Powell's Addition.

The Mt. Zion Working Band was in existence in 1902. It was apparently affiliated with the Mt. Zion Methodist Episcopal Church located south of Formosa Road on West Kirsch Road.

In 1905, Walter Wilkinson took charge of the Green Tree Saloon on the northwest corner of the square. A Postal Savings Bank designated for Troy by the Post Office Department began business in February of 1912. At the beginning there was no great rush to deposit money.

A huge snowstorm struck the area in February of 1912 and continued for 24 hours, establishing a new record. It was declared to be the heaviest in 30 years.

The Heddergott General Store was in business on West Clay Street at the turn of the century (1900). The telephone number was Kinloch 13.

In 1906, J.L. Griffin discontinued the Green Tree Hotel. Also that year, J.H. Steinhans and Sons added a new hearse to their undertaking business.

In 1912, several of Troy's many saloons changed hands as George Liebler purchased the saloon of George Raber in the south end of Troy, Harry Blecher bought the saloon of Fred Metz in the Braner Building, and Herman Kueker took charge of the saloon from H.E. Prott in the Central Building.

In 1916, Gebauer's Hardware Store was in business at 110 East Market Street;

George W. Flake was advertising Headlight Union Made Overalls in his store for $1.85 a pair; Dan G. Liebler had a general merchandise store; E.T. Levo was proprietor of Mother's Way Bakery on West Market Street; and Charles F. Peters was advertising Festal Hall Milk at three cans for 25 cents.

Also in 1916, an advertisement in *The Weekly Call* pictured all sorts of shoes at the business of Edward H. Klein, Troy's Oldest Exclusive Shoe House (located on South Main in what is now known as the Adams Store building). Walter W. Meiners had a shoe repair shop and also sold shoes, location unknown.

On February 22, 1916, The Gem Theater (formerly the Troy Opera House at or near 108 East Market Street) run by Joseph Rikli of Highland opened with a special photoplay production never before seen in Troy. Movies were also shown on the second floor of the Braner building for a time. A Mr. Novero of Maryville showed movies at the Show House at the corner of Washington and West Clay in the 1930s and 40s. He came on Saturdays and showed 16 mm movies for a 10-cent admission. This was before the Trojan Theater was built by the Lions Club in the late 1940s.

In 1924, William S. Schmitt owned the Troy Transfer Line. It met all trains at Vandalia Station and carried passengers, express, baggage and freight. Also in 1924, Col. D.A. Macklin was a public auctioneer in Troy. Those needing his service were to apply at the train depot. In 1924 Dr. Thomas F. Dillon was a dentist in town and Dr. Charles E. Molden and Dr. W.W. Billings were physicians.

In June 1924, a few famous people were seen passing through Troy on the National Trail in automobiles. Barney Oldfield of automobile racing fame was driving a car of his own to Los Angeles, California, and James Montgomery Flagg, a well-known artist, was spotted in a Kissel Sport Model roadster with his newlywed wife on a honeymoon tour.

In the 1920s, H.C. Riggin ran Riggin Auto Salesroom on the first floor of the Odd Fellow's building at the corner of South Main and Center streets. Mr. Gerfen owned the Star Automobile dealership at 125 East Market before the building housed the powdered milk factory. This building is currently Terry's Appliances.

In 1927, the Red Line Motor Company made a regular schedule run through Troy from Vandalia to St. Louis.

In June of 1927, the old Deimling residence adjoining the meat market on East Market Street (city parking lot in 2002) was moved to the north end of the lot. The residence that was moved was erected in 1877. Professor and Mrs. R.C. Hufford, who lived in the Deimling residence for several years, moved to the home of Mrs. Louise Joseph on Market Street.

Also in 1927, John H. Voelker, proprietor of the East End Filling Station, was purchasing gasoline in carload lots and established a receiving station on the Troy and Eastern Railroad near the Troy Brass Works. A tank truck was purchased for the purpose and William Heck, Jr., was employed to run it.

In 1926, Charles E. Voelker purchased the Silver Creek Inn located east of Troy on the National Trail from Mrs. Nellie Paulet. The place was operated by Conde Smith, but had been closed for several years.

In 1930 the following businesses existed in Troy: M.F. Auwarter sold general merchandise on the square; Duckett's Confectionery and Greyhound Bus Lines stop; Troy Exchange Bank, John Feldmeier, president, D.G. Jarvis, vice president, and L.F. Wetzel, cashier; McLanahan's garage on East Market Street; August Droll, cash grocer, on South Main Street; Cottage Grocery and Meat Market, George Warma, proprietor; Mrs. Hattie Call owned a cleaning and pressing business. The Shell Filling Station at Main and Center was managed by Herb Beutel. Peter J. Craney was an attorney in the 1930s with an office in the Eckert Building on Clay Street.

Also in 1930 Emory Kimberlin had a truck hauling business which included hauling livestock. The Troy Dairy was organized in January of 1930. Its trustees were F.W. Langewisch, Edward Kueker, Edward Gerstenecker, Eldon Engeling, H.W. Tegtmeyer, Oscar Gindler and Leonard Schurman.

F.G. Reinheimer sold his garage to Fred Droy in June 1930. It was located on Collinsville Road approximately where Thermo Door is located in 2002.

Harry Taake was manager of the Troy Grain Company in 1930.

John Deimling owned the City Meat Market in 1930; Hampton's Store sold shoes, and ladies and gents furnishings in the Klein building, later, the Adams Store building. Henry J. Miller did clock, watch and jewelry repair in the Liebler building on Main Street. R.R. Moore owned the building at the point of Center and Collinsville Road furnishing rooms, meals, and groceries. A.W. Sparks managed Troy Lumber Company at Center and Washington streets. Porter and Preston owned a wrecker and auto repair service. Electra Shoe Repair shop was owned by Louis Morgan. Kueker's Dairy was owned by Herman Kueker. It advertised pure country milk and cream. The George Eckert Cider Mill was located on Clay Street, where the fire station is in 2002.

Also in the 1930s, Mrs. Fred (Cora) Edwards ran a restaurant on Collinsville Road, at the corner of Sarah Street.

In 1936, Alex Martin, who occupied the residence property of Henry W. Riggin on Clay Street, was making preparations to open a new meat market in the Deimling Building at East Market and Hickory Streets (city parking lot in 2002).

Brookside Dairy building was located at Fitch and South Main, across from what is now the 4-0 Quick Shop.

The Brookside Hotel was destroyed by fire in 1936. It was owned at the time by Highland Brewing Company and operated by Frank C. Raber, Sr.

In 1936 construction of the tower for Troy's new waterworks system was begun by a force of eight structural steel workers who worked for the Chicago Bridge and Iron Works.

In 1942, John W. Schmitt purchased the Shell Service Station operated by Buel Koonce. Also in that year, Edwin Guennewig, who operated a meat market and grocery store for a number of years in the Hampe Building, purchased the I.G.A. Store of Irwin Dollinger in the Liebler Building on Main Street.

John and Edna Schoon purchased 101 E. Market Street in 1945 from Martin Auwarter. The Auwarters had closed their store in 1934.

In January of 1942 Roland Porter purchased the interest of Burrel Preston in the Porter and Preston Garage and purchased the former McLanahan Garage and residence property on Market Street at Kimberlin from the First National Bank of Collinsville.

William Dunstan had a grocery store from 1944 to 1951.

Gene Adams played piano in the Boots Wilhawk Orchestra in the 1940s.

In 1947 Mr. and Mrs. Buel Koonce sold their interest in the Blue Haven Restaurant east of Troy to Mr. and Mrs. Alex LaBelle.

Ted Guennewig opened a dry goods store on July 29, 1949, at the southwest corner of South Main and Center street (across from the Troy Frozen Foods).

Chuck Reed painted the WWII Honor Board that once stood behind the bank at the northeast corner of Main and East Market Streets. It stood for many years; however, it was in disarray and later demolished.

First prize was a ton of coal according to an advertisement for an American Legion card party in 1949.

Walter Fischer Plumbing began in April of 1951 on East Market Street.

Matsel Dry Goods and Furniture Store was located in the Odd Fellow's building on the southwest corner of Center and South Main Streets in the 1950s and '60s. It was a Western Auto Store and later Gary Nottingham took over management. Later, Mr. Tschannen, then Roy G. Halleman, managed it.

John McMullen owned the Ideal Restaurant on Market Street in 1952 in the Voelker Building. His specialty was fish sandwiches.

In 1956, Mr. And Mrs. Jerome Gill, former operators of the Blue Haven Tourist Court, located near the intersection of Bypass 40 and New Route 40 east of Troy, moved to California to operate a 32-unit motel.

Jake's Emporium was located in the 200 block of Collinsville Road west of Droy's Garage. Jake Schlimme owned it in the 1940s and '50s. Later, Ralph and Shirley Turley ran it as Turley's Place. It was also known as the Dug Out at one time.

Keck's Tavern, owned and operated by Louie and Sis Keck in the 1940s and '50s, was located on the southwest corner of South Main and Route 40. Later, Sis died and Louie married Loretta. When Louie died, Loretta ran the tavern alone until the 1980s. At one point, Bud Swanson leased the tavern. Gloria Warsala ran the business from 1984 to 1989; Don and Lynn Sonnenberg owned and operated it from 1989 to 1992. At one time it was called "Moose's Bar." It is still a tavern today.

In 1952, the following Troy taverns had purchased a new federal $50 gambling tax stamp: Sunset Inn, Frieda Burian; Agnes Sartoris Tavern, Clay Street; Bill's Tavern, William C. Heck, 200 block of East Market Street; Moonlight Gardens, Arthur W. Hartman; Dominic Sartoris Tavern, Collinsville Road; Troy Hotel Tavern, Thelma Groeteka, Center and Collinsville Road (the wedge).

Windy Hill and Taylor Addition were annexed to the city in 1951.

Trojan Bakery and Lunch (formerly the Cum Back Café) opened in May of 1951.

In the 1950s, Cullop Hardware was located on the east side of the Braner Building at Kimberlin and East Market Streets. Floyd Cullop, who also sold bottled gas, owned it. The west side of the building was the Kroger Store owned by John Kelly, Jr.

George E. Hartley Sr., was the last man to work on the railroad in Troy. He pulled out the last car of equipment from the Troy Mine with Engine No. 752 in early 1952 when the mine closed. In 2002, Mr. Hartley is the last living man to bring a train out of Troy on the Illinois Terminal. On that last train, George Lobster was engineer, Bob Thomas was a fireman, Bill Sherman was conductor, Lloyd Master was brakeman, and George Hartley was the head brakeman.

Bill's Place was located in the Gebauer Building at 110 East Market during the 1960s.

The Clay Street Tavern was owned by Jim Sartoris. Later his daughter ran it.

The Sartoris family owned the tavern from the 1940s through the late 1990s when it burned to the ground.

Whistling Pete's Tavern was located on Collinsville Rd. west of Sunnyside Nursery. It was owned by Pete Sartoris. Later, the business was moved east on Collinsville Road to his son's (Dominic Sartoris) home, who built a block building next door for it which he called "Dom's Place," which he operated for many years. Later it was Woody's Woodpecker Inn. Woody had a collection of ball point and other writing pens strung over the bar. He sold the business to Guy and Mary Lou

Italiano who changed the name to Mary Lou's. In 1985, Josephine Sartoris Kueker and Shirley Huston Sartoris operated The Bait Shop there.

The Troy Republican Club flourished in the 1960s and 70s.

The Troy Democratic Women's Club flourished in the 1960s after Paul Simon ran for Governor of Illinois. It later became the Troy Democratic Club.

The Troy Democratic Men's Club was in existence for several years during the 1970s.

Prior to Randy's Restaurant at the I-55/70 and Route 162 intersection, Ivan and June Schroeder operated a cheese shop to the west of Randy's. This was in operation in the late 1960s and early 1970s.

Also in the 1960s and 70s, Brookside Automotive was owned and operated at 810 S. Main Street by Rudy Moravec.

In 1967, Norman Holloway and Ray Ulrich took over the ownership of Bud's Barbershop from Milton "Bud" Klaus.

In the 1970s, Skelly's Mid-State Truck Plaza opened. It was on the northwest corner of the I-55/70 and Route 162 intersection.

In 1972, Sam and Jean Furfaro ran the Trojan Coin Laundry on American Drive. Jean also had a hair salon in the same building.

In 1977, the 4-0 Quick Shop (formerly The Villa) opened for business. It was owned by Joan Harrison and Betty Jo Wiegers.

Also in 1977, the United Savings and Loan and G.A. Shaffer Agency, Insurance and Real Estate, was located at 122 West Market Street; Hayman's Restaurant and Lounge opened on Route 162 with a good smorgasbord; Wood Auto Body was located on the west bay of Len's Service Station with Gene Wood the operator; The Villa was owned and operated by Earl Pratt, Sr.; Albright's had a drive-in food place; Faye's Stop and Go was located at 117 East Market.

Troy Cycle Parts was a business on South Main St. in the 1970s.

In January of 1977, a fire at the A-1 Carbonic Company and Clean Coverall was being investigated. The fire destroyed both businesses which were located in the former Newport Bottling Company building on the south side of Route 40.

In the 1980s, Homer and Pat Gum opened "This Is It Lounge" on Route 162 west. The business flourished for 10 years or more. It is currently a bar and lounge.

In 1987, Mercantile Bank replaced the Bethalto Bank at Bargraves Blvd. In the same year, Landmark Bank, with James B. Watt as chairman, broke ground for a new facility.

The Olde Fashioned Fourth of July celebration was begun in 1991. Rich Eberhardt and the Troy VFW were instrumental in getting it started.

Kim's Creations opened in February 1992 at 116 S. Main St. in the Adam's Building. From that location she moved to West Market (Edwardsville Rd.) in the former Cullop home. Kim Cruse was the owner/designer. She closed the business in 2001. In 2002 Joan Spencer and Mark Ponce opened "J's," a custard shop and Every Bloomin' Thing, a flower and gift shop, in the location.

In 1992, the old jailhouse on Kimberlin St. got a much needed face-lift.

In 1995, Mike Beckman opened The Movie Company in the former Ackerman Laundromat at Riggin Road and Edwardsville Road; and D.W. Brown Realtors opened a Troy office with Kathy Bertels, the broker-manager.

The City of Troy bought the old Neustadt place on East Center Street in 1995.

P'N'T Specialties Shop was located in Westbrook Center on O'Hara for about two years in the late 1990s. Owners were Pat and Tara Rothman.

Mary Sheroky Miller and Emily Pfeil owned Vibrations, a dance studio at 105 East Market Street in the mid 1990s.

C.A. Henning, a former Triad School District Superintendent, and a long time member of the Troy Lions Club, was Grand Marshall in the 1998 Troy Homecoming parade. Parade officials sought out a stagecoach and he rode "shotgun" for the parade.

Carroll J. Lanahan, Illinois Territorial Ranger

Carroll J. Lanahan is a member of the Illinois Territorial Rangers, Seventeenth Regiment, Company B. The Illinois Territorial Rangers were formed by an act of the U.S. Congress in 1811 and are still active and have never been decommissioned. Lanahan has been actively trying to establish some sort of a land marker at the Augusta Cemetery location to recognize Fort Chilton.

The history of Fort Chilton is important to the Troy area. The first settlements made in the St. Jacob area were made along the east side of Silver Creek by some hardy pioneers from Kentucky and Tennessee in 1810. The families of John Lindley of Augustus, TN, and William and Cyrus Chilton of Harrison and Smeltzer lived there until the war with England in 1812, when the Indians began to show themselves as hostile.

The Chiltons and their neighbors, who lived in this and adjoining townships, built a fort and stockade for defense. The fort stood in the northwest corner of Section 17, near where

Augustus Chilton settled. Major Isaac Ferguson and Captain Abraham Howard commanded the fort. The Indians never attacked this fort, although eleven families received shelter there the first year. In 1814, a dozen rangers were placed on guard there under command of Samuel Whiteside.

When the highway made way for its path (overhead) near the Augusta Cemetery along Route 40, it covered the place where the church and fort used to be. However, Lanahan said the fort markings are still slightly visible in the ground near the cemetery.

In 1820, a town was laid out near the fort and called Augusta, but the plat was never recorded. No lots were sold, and the town existed only in the imagination if its originators.*

Lanahan goes to various schools in the Troy community and presents his story and displays various artifacts while he is in full Ranger uniform. He has been doing this for many years.

Recollections of Charmion

I've seen many changes in Troy. It's called progress! I remember when the population was 1,150. I was part of the fast growing Troy when I was City Clerk. In 1978, we were written up in national magazines as one of the fastest growing cities in the USA.

At one time Troy had two all girl Drum Corps – the senior corps and the junior corps. The senior corps had 32 marching members and the drum majorette and two baton twirlers. They were attractive in black and white outfits. I belonged to the senior corps.

I remember roller skating on Market Street and riding on a bicycle-built-for-two; Jim Jarvis taking us riding on his bike; and homecomings on the streets uptown. Two busses passed our house when we first moved

Carroll J. Lanahan and artifacts, McCray-Dewey campus, late 1990s

to the West Center location. They were the Greyhound and Vandalia bus lines.

We had one policeman, Ernest Spencer, then Max Groeteka. I remember Eli Burk's Blacksmith shop with a hitching rack for horses. I remember the Baptist Church fire and the Presbyterian Church that burned. I played in that empty basement area.

I recall the Auwarter's store where the Evers (Allen's) Pharmacy is in 2002; Mr. Schoon's Drug store was in the location of Dr. Friederich's office in 2002. My grandmother sent me to Mr. Schoon's Store to buy a "good pair of glasses" for $1.00.

I got my hair cut by Mr. Helmich, the barber. Troy Best had a chair in Helmich's shop, then later had his own barbershop and cut my sons' hair.

My most treasured memory is when President Harry S. Truman led the Troy Homecoming parade in 1962. As he passed where I was standing I yelled, "Say hi to Bess for all of us." He looked right at me, pointed his finger and said, "I'll do that." That was a thrill.

I also have fond memories of Carl Taake as Mayor for three terms and before that he was City Treasurer for four terms – almost 30 years of serving Troy.

Andy and I had two sons, Robert and David, and five grandchildren: Daniel Lee, Susan Lorraine, Mary Ann, Thomas, David and Leslie Marie. God's been good to me. *Submitted by Charmion Semanisin.*

Troy Memories

From the 1950s until the present day, my family (the Stockglausners) would spend countless holidays with our cousins, Oscar and Louise Mersinger and daughter Mae. Their farm was a place for picnics, hikes, horseback rides and 4th of July celebrations.

When my sister Eileen and I were approximately 10 and 12, we made our way by bus from St. Louis to visit our cousins. The rest of the family was already spending the weekend there, but our mother and father had come down with colds and couldn't go. So, very early in the morning, we took a bus to downtown St. Louis and then, another to Troy. We walked from Troy all the way to Oscar's farm. It was quite an adventure.

Another memorable occurrence was during the 4th of July holiday in 1954. The whole family was again gathering at Oscar's farm. Everyone was outdoors, when one of my uncles shouted that there was smoke coming from the barn. Sure enough, the hay, which had been so laboriously stacked into the barn loft, had spontaneously erupted into a blazing fire. Some of the relatives rushed to toss hay from the loft in an effort to save it or slow the fire, but in just moments, they had to beat a hasty retreat. The barn was a blazing inferno with a waterfall of mice and rats jumping from the loft. When Oscar went to call the fire department on the party line, the people talking wouldn't get off! He really had to yell at them to make his point. Even with the rapid response of the firefighters, the barn was totally lost. The pond was nearly pumped dry in fighting the fire. Neighbors came from near and far since they could all see the smoke. Fortunately, no one was injured and the cows were all out to pasture.

The farm in Troy was where I learned to ride horses, fish in the pond and gather eggs for Louise. We spent hours hiking in the woods, and finding persimmons and berries to eat. For a city girl, this was heaven! *Submitted by Nancy (Stockglausner) Burchianti, daughter of Lester and Florence (Mersinger) Stockglausner.*

Troy's German Immigration

Troy's "All American" population reflects people from all origins and backgrounds, but historically, it has also reflected immigration patterns common in the Midwest. In the first half of the 1800s, records reflect that the majority of Troy's population originated in the British Isles, probably having lived on the east coast before coming to the Midwest. In the early 1900s, small numbers of immigrants came from Italy and the Slovak countries of Europe to work in the mines. As a result, several outstanding families came to Troy. But, the most recognizable direct immigration came from Germany. Starting in the 1830s with a trickle, it reached a flood in the mid-1800s, tapering off in the last quarter of the century.

Germans especially came directly to the farmlands around Troy and increasingly, to city businesses as well. Much of Troy's existence, it was easy to conclude that, "All the farmers around Troy were German!" An historic statement can be made about these people and their contribution to the character and history of Troy, aside from the usual characterizations of "industrious, hard working, organized and persistent."

The first owners of Illinois land were generally not Germans. Many received "first-titles" to land in the area by virtue of their service in the War of 1812. Nearby Edwardsville became a "Land Office" for the U.S. in 1812, six years before Illinois became a state. "Speculators," too, abounded. Some bought land directly from the U.S. Government, for a few dollars per acre, or more commonly, from those initially receiving it for military service, so that these speculators came to own much of the agricultural land in southwest Illinois. Many never farmed the land, and some never even saw it.

This growing wave of German immigration came to purchase the land from "first owners," and to farm it seriously. Land prices were modest – from $5 to $20 an acre. Germany's "revolution" of 1848 triggered the greatest numbers of immigrants to America. Obviously, conditions would have to be really bad to even consider leaving one's homeland. Furthermore, the trip itself was daunting, expensive, and had to be prepaid.

The reports of great opportunity in the U.S. by many early immigrants, many from Germany itself, contributed to the decisions to emigrate. Family members in America often sent back first-person "proof," encouragement, employment promises, and actual money, which made the risks seem bearable.

A typical scenario at the height of the immigration era would have been similar to the following. A farm family from Blackjack would write to the folks back home (letters took three months or more) in Germany, telling them what ship to get on to come to New Orleans and what it cost, what steamship to take up the Mississippi to St. Louis, and in which hotel to stay. They were instructed to stay there until someone from Blackjack came weekly with a horse and wagon to carry new arrivals back to Troy, where they would live with relatives until they became acclimated. Although probably as many immigrant stories exist as immigrants, this scenario, or something similar, was probably enacted countless times. This would explain how citizens from the same town or area in Germany would come to an enclave of relatives and friends from the same area of the old country.

It still was a horrendous decision to make. A total uproot would occur, leaving families and friends, and towns and country behind. It would risk life and limb. All of the family's resources, and some more borrowed, were put at risk. Emigrants knew they were never coming back to a life that they and generations before had known and loved.

It's easy to assume that these immigrants were "peasants," and even poor. They were, in fact, mostly commoners, but they weren't necessarily poor, by standards of the day. They had to pay the equivalent of several years of income to prepay their way. Obviously, they helped each other, and once a family member came, he offered encouragement and, usually, money to those following. Nor were they without skills. These farmers from Germany looked for land to farm.

South of Troy, in Blackjack, "Low Germans" congregated, Germans from south and southwest Germany. Low German communities were also established around St. Jacob and Marine, and around O'Fallon.

The German community that developed north of Troy and around Edwardsville, however, came mostly from northern Germany, "High Germans." These two groups came from the same country, but the customs and the language were still somewhat different. However, as English became the common language, these differences ceased to exist.

Communication, therefore, between the new country and the old was probably more common than believed, at least during the early years of residency, although slow. Two documents exist that describe important characteristics of the immigration process: the agony of decision, with the encouragement and help offered, and the travel process itself. They incidentally describe what life might have been like for immigrants. The first is several excerpts from letters written by Olaf Magnus Norling back to his parents in Sweden. Olaf was a sailor on the ship that brought the Langenwalter family from Germany to America. He fell in love with one of the Langenwalter girls, left the ship and married her. First settling in Blackjack, they later moved to the Effingham area.

In 1852, in a letter from Troy to Sweden: "...I now am home with my brother-in-laws's parents in Illinois where I have been several times before.

Around here the land is good and he has a big farm which he bought the year before I came here and paid $1400 for only the land. He has a big garden with 83 fruit trees – apple. His oldest son and a girl are married since I came here. I have the oldest of the girls. Her name is Elizabeth Langenwalter. She is now 24 years old....

... I wish I had you all here in America, because here is a good country and a man can earn more and live much better here than by you. So I wish I had you all with me here. And if you will come or at least any of you, I could if I am alive, help you to get land. If so, write to me. I will now give you information on how you can go....

P.S. Here I send a bill of exchange for 250 Mark Banco and you can take this to a merchant or a banker and he will give you money for it, to help you to come here. If my father could come it will be my wish, but if father don't come, he has the right to take some of the money for helping himself. Farewell, live well, and write as soon as you can."

In a letter from Troy in 1863:

"Beloved parents, brothers and sisters,

It is a long time since I wrote to you and therefore I will once again let you know that I and my family have good health for which we thank God....

...I have seen in papers that Sweden prepares for war, perhaps against Russia. Here in America we have had war in three years but thank God mostly in the southern states and here in Illinois we have not yet any war, so you should not think we have war in all of America.

...Times here one can say are good. The prices are very high for all things and money is not hard to have. Wheat costs near 50 cents per bushel. Oats and corn or maize cost about 35 cents per bushel. I threshed 1180 bushel wheat and 350 bushel oats this year. My corn I have not yet harvested. I think I will have 1000 bushels. I have 100 acres land and have more horses than any farmer in Norum's parish. Land here costs from 30 to 50 dollars for each acre. Four years ago I built another house. It cost me $700. I had thought that any of my brothers would come here to me, for here you can live better than in Sweden, and if so, write to me soon....

Olaf Magnus Norling"

The last document relating is a letter that was written in 1851 from Rudolph Bardelmeier in Lienen, Prussia, to his brother, Ernst, who had already settled in Hamel Township.

"Dear Brother,

I received your letter and saw that things are going well with you which gives me great joy. ...It probably will not be long until we will be able to speak to each other personally. Dear Ernst, you write to me that everything is so good, that I am hoping you are not telling me an untruth. You write that I can get 16 dollars per month, which I can hardly believe....you write that if I thought that my brother was true and sincere with me, then I should write you, and that you would send me the money. So I went to rely on God and you and follow your advice. This will be my last letter; you can realize that I have the desire to come there – since I have here no father, nor mother, nor brother nor sister; but if you are not sincere and earnest with me, then leave us here; but if you will promise me faithfully that everything is true, and you are not writing me any untruths, then I will want to come; but write soon and send the money; ...Write exactly how I can get on the ship, and when I arrive there if you will meet me, and what I must do here and in short, everything....

Rudolph Bardelmeier
c/o W. Wesselmann
Zu Westerbeck
Lienen, Muenster"

Information compiled by Merrill Ottwein.

107

I Remember...

I can remember when Troy had no street lights. Everybody had wells. No one had a refrigerator or a deep freeze. The ice truck came by, every day. There were very few cars in Troy. I lived on Powell Street and we could play ball on the street because no cars came. We played out until dark and went to bed because very few people had electrical lights. The house behind our house had gangsters living in it. You didn't see them during the day but they were there at night. Many a night my Dad would put us on the floor away from the window.

The center of town was "The Square" – now the corner of Main and Market. The Central Hotel was on the northwest corner – really a boarding-house for miners by the 1920s. Across Market Street was the old stage coach depot, in the '20s a tavern, now offices. The northeast corner held the Exchange Bank, with a little park behind it. Auwarter's Grocery Store stood on the southeast corner where the drugstore is now. Directly east of that was Helmich's Barber Shop, then the *Troy Call* office, the Post Office, and Auwarter's house.

Also, when I was a child, we had one road into Troy. It was Old Route 40 that ran past the old roller rink and on Center Street and then out east of town. We had no route by the grain company and no Route 162, or 55 or 70. When it snowed deep we were cut off.

But the whole town was closer. Everyone talked to each other and everyone helped each other.

I'm 82 and lived my whole life in Troy. *Submitted by Mildred (Taake) Huston.*

Walking Tour of Troy, circa 1887

Clara Kirsch wrote the following information from the remembrances of her grandma with some of the details clarified in later years by Eli Burk, a long time resident. Clara was born in Blackjack to Gustav and Emma Kirsch and spent her entire life in Troy, serving as a schoolteacher in the area for 43 years. She first taught in country schools, then at the Troy Public School.

"On the corner of Clay and Staunton Road stood the gray brick school house known as the Troy Grade School. Across Clay Street stood Ed Jarvis' barn, where he kept a hack to take people to the depot. Dr. Zenk owned the land and lived in the big house on Market Street (the Carney House).

Across Staunton Road from the school was Burk's Blacksmith Shop. Down Clay Street to the east was the Dewey Estate, which later became the McCray Dewey School.

Coming east on Rt. 162 at the Troy Methodist Church was the Throp home. John and Nancy Jarvis had purchased it in 1879. Around the corner on Clay was Voelkers. On the south side was Droll's Tavern (later McCormick or Pistone's). Next was Seligman's home; Peddler Leet was next, then Eckert's Grist Mill (present Troy fire house).

Across Main Street was a tavern called Bloody Corner. At the intersection of Clay and North Main was John G. Jarvis' home, later Art Gaertner's home.

Going east on Clay: Mrs. Apple's Bakery and the Williamson home; then, at Clay and Staunton, was Burk's Blacksmith shop.

At Market and Collinsville Rd., Riebold's Blacksmith shop stood. Next, east was the Peterman House, then the Keissel Hat shop and cobbler shop.

Continuing east was the bakery building (the stagecoach stop). Auwarter's store was on the southeast corner of Market and Main. Upstairs, Fred Miller ran the *Monitor* newspaper.

Going east, Johnson's Post Office and Fred Auwarter's home were seen. Across Kimberlin Street was Martin/Jarvis Boarding House; then came Healey's Tavern and G. Gerfen's Blacksmith Shop.

Across Hickory was Steinhans furniture/funeral home; later, Henry Kueker owned it.

On Steinhans' back lot lived a teacher named Badgley; and toward the front of the lot was a well digger; east was the Julia Fielder home and Mantle home.

At Border and Clay was the small brick jail. It sat in front of Peddler Leet's place." *Submitted by Sherry Smith.*

Market Street looking west, circa 1900.

Map of Troy, Illinois
(circa 1906)

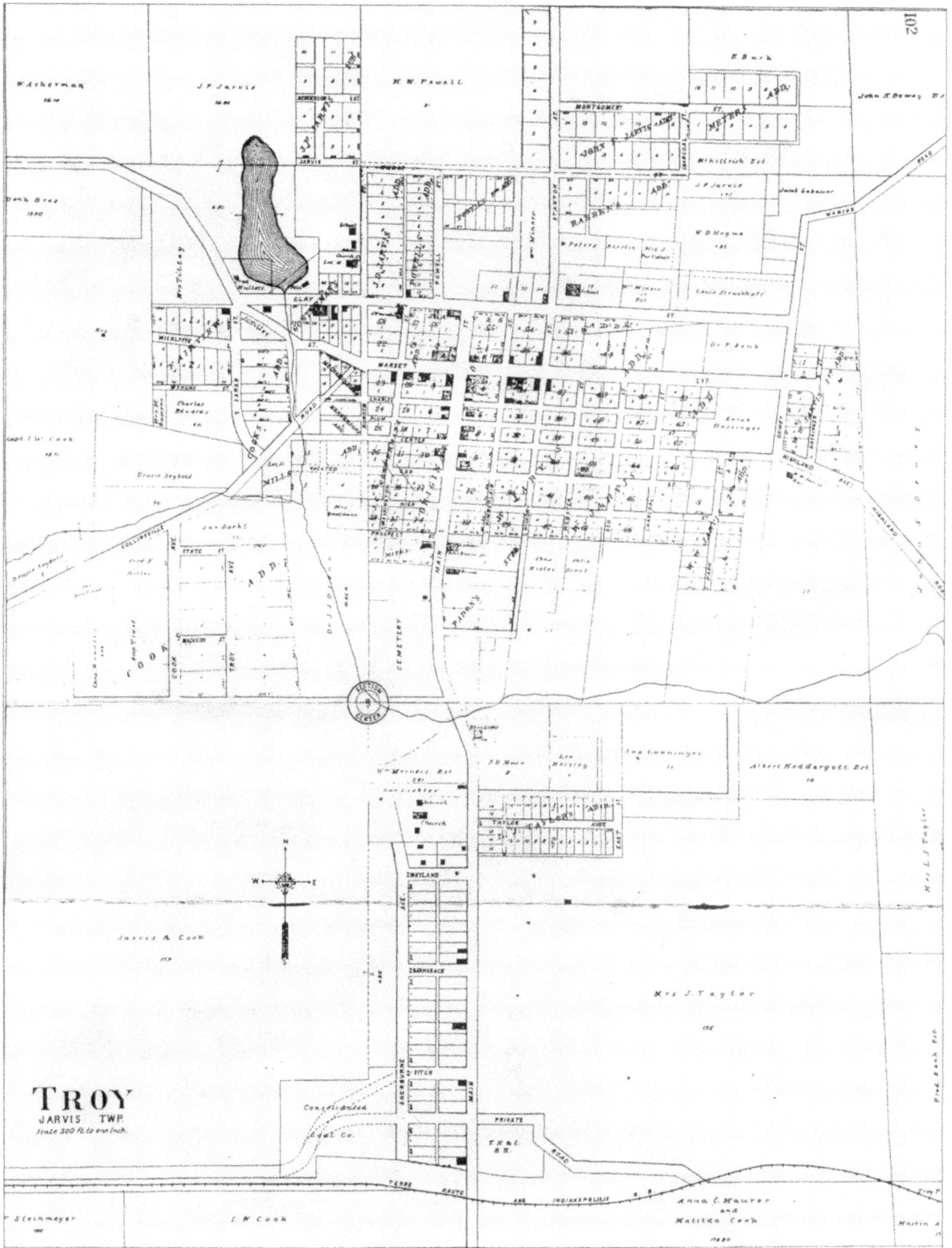

Residential section of Troy before streets were paved.

The wrecking ball from demolition equipment at the Braner Building across the street crashed into the brick wall of the Troy City Hall on Market Street in 1992.

Churches

Friedens United Church of Christ

St. John the Baptist Catholic Church, Blackjack, 2002

(Below) St. Paul's Lutheran Confirmation Class, 1918. (l. to r.) Front: Estelle Niebruegge, Evelyn Gerfen, Theodora Gerling, unknown, Clara Fedder, Hulda Schlaefer, unknown. Middle: August C. (Jack) Brunworth, Dale Peters, Benny Schultze, Emil Eisenberg, Arthur Flath, Oscar Schlimme. Back: Edward Schultze, Pastor Lange, Bernard Sudhoff.

Evangelical and Reformed Church (Friedens), early 1920s

(Left) Methodist Episcopal Church, after 1870

Introduction

From the earliest times, the Troy community has always found a place to worship, whether in private homes or in a building dedicated to that purpose. Early county churches, simply constructed, served the early settlers as religious, educational and social centers. In town, early churches grew from home study groups and storefront centers to sturdy, permanent structures, and, eventually, to religious complexes, housing worship centers, educational wings, recreational facilities, and social halls. Whatever the building, whoever the congregation, whenever the era, the Troy community churches have been a vital and necessary part of this area's history, and its future.

Abundant Blessings Church

Abundant Blessings Church is non-denominational and is charismatic. Weekly services are held on Wednesday and Sunday.

Pastor and Mrs. Jack Walter at the entrance of the Abundant Blessings Church, 200 A Collinsville Road, late 1990s.

Bethel Southern Baptist Church

The Bethel Southern Baptist Church began on January 23, 1955, when a group of 20 dedicated Christians met in a store building owned by Walter Fischer. Dr. Archie Brown of Vandalia met with the group and gave them what help he could. The Mission continued to meet on Sunday afternoons in the store building with Dr. Brown and the Rev. Ross Davidson preaching and teaching.

On February 20, 1955, the Mission held its first Sunday school and morning

Bethel Baptist Church, 1990s

worship service. Rev. Ross Davidson became the Mission pastor. Events moved quickly after that: evening worship services were held; Training Union was organized; the first Wednesday prayer meeting was held on February 22, 1955; a W.M.U. with eight charter members was organized; Sunbeams, GA's and RA's were organized; and, a few months later, a men's Brotherhood with six charter members began.

The Vandalia church continued to help the Mission until September of 1955 when the Rev. Arba Capron of Woodriver extended an invitation for them to become a Mission of their church. The Troy members accepted the invitation. Since the Woodriver church was in the same association, the Woodriver church continued to help the Troy mission until December 9, 1956, when the Mission was constituted into the Bethel Southern Baptist Church with 42 charter members. In 1976, 17 of these were still members of the church.

On February 6, 1957, the church purchased several lots on Throp Street for $750.00. On March 31,

1957, a ground-breaking ceremony was held with Pastor George Sinquefield and Mr. Luther Hall, chairman of the building committee, breaking ground first. They were followed by the entire congregation who participated in the ceremony.

The first addition of the educational building was dedicated on June 22, 1958. This addition was used for worship services and Sunday school until the second addition was finished on October 7, 1962. Only five years later, on December 3, 1967, the Rev. Noel Hutchings and the members held another ground breaking ceremony for the new sanctuary. On September 8, 1968, the first service was held in it.

During the summer of 1974, the church acquired the Schmidt property directly east of the sanctuary. A new three-bedroom parsonage was built facing North Charcoal Street in 1975. In 1986 the corner lot at 217 Staunton Road was purchased. The congregation continued to grow over the years, and a new, larger church became necessary. A building program was soon under way.

On Sunday, April 6, 1997, the last service was held at the Throp Street building. The members caravaned to their new church site to sing and pray. On Sunday, April 13, 1997, they had the first worship

Bethel Southern Baptist Church, 2002

service at their new location at 7775 Collinsville Road. In the fall of 2000, the congregation occupied their newly constructed educational building.

The Throp Street building was sold to the Triad School District to be used as the district offices. *Taken from information given by Nan Stogsdill.*

Canteen Creek Baptist Church

The Canteen Creek Baptist Church formally came into existence on June, 17, 1817. Early church records indicate the charter members had been meeting before then, but no one knows for how long. Now they applied for membership in an association of other Baptist Churches called the Illinois Association and were accepted in September 1817. They met the fourth Saturday of every month, probably at the home of Robert and Mary Seybold, but they quickly planned a new meeting house. The site was in Section One of Collinsville Township, on 2-1/2 acres of land donated by the Seybolds. In April 1818, they announced plans to raise the walls of a 25 foot square building. Members were instructed to deliver logs from their property to the new church site but not enough logs arrived and construction was delayed. A year later, in April 1819, the meeting house was finally occupied. The church grew rapidly in the 1820s. A new, larger, meeting house was occupied in February 1822. By late 1825, this building was also being used as a school. In the mid 1830s, membership stabilized, and after that, it began to fall. The Canteen Creek Baptist Church served as the mother church for other Baptist congregations, and sent a number of new preachers into the community.

However, in the 1830s, the land adjacent to the church fell into the hands of a new owner, and the church and its new neighbor apparently did not agree. The differences continued until, in January 1844, church members Daniel Reece and his wife Polly donated land in Section 16 of Jarvis Township for a new church cemetery. Not much later, the church abandoned its original site and moved to the new property. In 1870, Andrew Woods donated a tract of land adjacent to the site in Section 16, for those whose, "ancestors or kin have been buried in the adjoining tract, (which was) conveyed in 1844 to the Trustees of the Canteen Meeting House for a burial ground." In both deeds, the grantors were paid $1.00 for their land.

Fewer records were kept in the church's later years, and it apparently operated only sporadically. However, it was not dissolved until 1901, a full 83 years after its initiation. It was a rigorous church. Members were often called to account for their behavior; and if they were not properly repentant, and willing to beg forgiveness, they were summarily "excluded" from membership. If members did not attend regularly, a committee was established to visit them and "invite" them to the next meeting. Squabbling members were called before the church leaders and ordered to settle their differences forthwith. In 1820, member George Harlin was charged with playing "real tunes on a fiddle with the world for carnal amusement." His response was found to be unsatisfactory, and he was "excluded" from membership on the spot! It's a wonder the church lasted as long as it did!

Note: The research for this article was done by members of the Madison County Genealogical Society, and previously published in that organization's journal named *The Stalker*.

These records are probably the oldest original minutes records of any church in Madison County. Some Troy family names who were members of the church and/or buried in the cemetery are Seybold, Anderson, Gunterman, Wood, Whiteside, Vanhooser, Sims, Armstrong, Howard, Long, Padon, Reece, Riggin, Thompson, and Samples. Canteen Cemetery is still accessible from the Troy-O'Fallon Road.

First Baptist Church

The First Baptist Church in Troy has a long history. Organized by Elders James and Joseph Lemen in 1833, it began with 15 members who met at the home of John Lemen near Silver Creek. It was then called the Baptist Church of Christ, Friends of Humanity.

In 1840 the church was moved into Troy to its present location at 204 South Main Street.

Built under difficult circumstances, the first meeting place in Troy was finally dedicated in 1849, with James Lemen preaching the sermon.

The number of members had increased to 100 in 1870, and another church was built and occupied by 1876. Dr. Bulkey preached the dedication sermon. (However, tragedy struck on January 14, 1940. During Sunday school, the church and all the furnishing were entirely destroyed by fire. Other churches in Troy offered their buildings for use, but the church members, not wanting to interfere with the other churches, chose to rent the Theodore Gebauer building until the new building was completed.)

On Sunday, September 1, 1940, a service was held for the laying of the cornerstone of the present church. Reverend Will-

First Baptist Church, 204 South Main, 1991

iam Richardson was pastor at the time and had been since October 1937. Reverend Clarence Henson officiated at this service and was assisted by Pastor Richardson, Percy Ray, Clarence Anderson and Troy Best. It was renamed the First Baptist Church of Troy.

In June 1941, the dedication service for the church was held. The pastor was Reverend Delmer Walker. The church voted to leave the Northern Baptist Convention in July 1945 and voted to associate itself as an independent, fundamental Baptist Church with the General Association of Regular Baptist Churches.

In 1962, the property was purchased at 108 Prospect Street to be used as a parsonage. Reverend William Blake was pastor. By March 1967, the church was ready for extensive remodeling, and the parsonage was also remodeled. Sunday school rooms were constructed in the basement and the basement floor was tiled. New carpet was laid in the sanctuary, the foyer was enclosed, and the front of the church was completely redecorated. Rev. John White was pastor during the renovation.

On October 6, 1968, the church called Rev. John Taylor as pastor. Under his leadership many were lead to the Lord, and several new missionaries were added to the budget. Pastor Taylor and his wife Junie were there until July 1973.

In 1978, under the leadership of Rev. T.B. Frazine, the AWANA Youth program was initiated, and children's church ministry was begun by the pastor's wife. Reverend Frazine remained as pastor for 14 years until 1991. Reverend Harry W. Logan was called to serve beginning in 1992. In 1993, a 160 year anniversary service was held. Reverend Don Proesser is pastor in 2002. *Taken from history submitted by John Cline.*

Friedens United Church of Christ

Friedens United Church of Christ was formally organized on December 13, 1874, under the name of "Die Evangelische Frei Protestant Gemeinde" (The Evangelical Free Protestant Congregation) after having services in homes. The first Constitution was signed by the following charter members: Elias Burke, Rudolph Hoge, Johann Riebold, Charles Metzger, Julius Nill, Adam Feldner, Friedrich Hoge, Jacob Mahler, Henry Mumme, Frank Heddergott, Peter Bernhardt, Frank Holtgrave, William Schultz, Phillip Gross, Fritz Schuler, and William Freudenau. In January 1875, the first congregational meeting was held in the local Presbyterian Church. Until a small church could be built, services were held in the local Baptist Church. The first resident pastor, the Rev. Dietrich Peter Cammann, came in 1876 and held regular services in German, conducted a Sunday School, and built the first parsonage with his own hands.

In the next few years, pastors stayed for short periods as they were mostly "free" pastors and not members of a denomination. The church then directed a plea for a pastor to the German Evangelical Synod of North America. The Synod sent a graduate of Eden Theological Seminary, the Rev. Ernst Riemeyer, in 1887. The local church joined the Synod and was reorganized as the German Evangelische Friedens Gemeinde (German Evangelical Friedens Congregation). The Rev. Riemeyer was succeeded by the Rev. N. Hansen in 1891. He was succeeded by the Rev. G. Plassman in September 1895. At this time, there were 38 active members and 25 to 30 families

interested. The Sunday School had 100 pupils and 10 teachers, and a Young Peoples' League and a "Frauenverein" (Ladies Society) were organized. A German Summer School was held during the months of April through September. Several student and supply pastors served Friedens for the next few years.

In 1912, the first choir was organized, and the present parsonage was built. At this time, English gradually began to be used in the church instead of German. Eventually, all the services were in English except for the Good Friday Communion Service, held in German until the early 1940s.

In 1909, a three-acre plot one-half mile east of Troy was purchased and landscaped for a cemetery, "for members to have a well-deserved resting place, but not restricted to the Friedens congregation." After complaints about the condition and upkeep of the cemetery, a committee of three ladies took charge of it in May 1919. They posted signs and published a notice in *The Troy Call*, prohibiting livestock from grazing in the cemetery.

In 1920, a Daily Vacation Bible School began, drawing great interest. In July of 1921, the congregation voted to replace the small frame church with a larger brick structure at a cost around $22,000. For several years after that, short-term pastors served the church until the Rev. Richard H. Mornhinweg, from Hookdale, Illinois, came in January of 1932, and remained for 43 years.

In 1934, the Evangelical Synod of North America merged with the "Reformed Church of the United States." The local congregation became Friedens Evangelical & Reformed Church. Friedens' sister church, St. John's Evangelical Church in

Friedens United Church of Christ, 2002

the Blackjack community, was destroyed by a tornado in 1938. These members gradually joined Friedens, greatly strengthening the Troy congregation.

Many changes took place in the ensuing decades as the church grew and thrived. In the early 1950s, the large two-story parsonage was moved one block south onto the property purchased from Mrs. E. Breve. The church was then expanded to fill the entire block. During renovation, worship services and Sunday School were held in the Lions' Theatre. Again, the Presbyterian Church offered its rooms for meetings.

In 1957, the national E. & R. Church merged again, this time with the Congregational Christian Churches. The local congregation was now called Friedens United Church of Christ. Through numerous name changes, the name Friedens, which means "Peace" in German, has been retained. Pastors in the 1970s and 1980s used monetary gifts as seed money for the Troy interdenominational "Ministries Unlimited." A new Christian Education Wing was built for $375,000. From the beginning, many improvements to the property were initiated, often completed with the hard work and labor of members and paid for by fund-raising efforts. When the "new" church was built in 1922, it had no indoor plumbing. Members hauled all water needed down winding stairs from an outdoor well. Eventually, plumbing and heating were modernized, and air-conditioning and an elevator were installed.

The Women's Guild (formally the "Frauenverein") worked long and hard from the earliest days, catering meals for groups, holding "White Elephant" sales, and doing sewing and quilting projects. A Men's Brotherhood, likewise, was very active.

The Rev. Jane Hillman began her ministry at Friedens in December 1990. The church began providing a field education placement for Seminary students from Eden Seminary in 1994. Pastor Hillman accepted a call to Ohio in 2001 after a busy 10-year tenure.

The church today has active youth and adult activities and its facilities are used by community groups. Friedens also supports many mission and outreach programs, both locally and abroad. Now considering the calling of a new pastor, the congregation is continuing its tradition of worship under the able and compassionate ministry of its interim pastor, the Rev. Carol Tag.

Methodist Episcopal Church, 114 S. Main Street, 1890s.

Methodist Episcopal Church

The first Methodist circuit riders, or traveling preachers, appeared in Madison County in 1803. They organized societies, or class meetings, which met in the homes of early settlers.

The first Methodist Society at Troy was organized in the home of John Jarvis in 1820, where regular meetings were held. Later, the society constructed a small, square frame building about 2 miles east of Troy called Gilead. It was covered on the outside with rough clapboard, and the inside walls were plastered. The benches were made of logs split in two, with pins fastened into the round side for legs. It was the first known religious building erected in the immediate area. The building was later used as a school house. Among the early preachers were John Dew and J.H. Benson. The Society grew and prospered,

at one time having more than one hundred members. Subsequently, the group occupied a brick school house on Section 11, near the home of Jesse Renfro, when he was a local preacher and school teacher.

The Society in Troy was reorganized with 17 members in 1843, and a building was erected. Some of the members of the Gilead Society came in from the country to join the new congregation. The group began to grow, and numbered 45 by1844. William Barnsback was class leader and steward. In 1847 a bell, which had belonged to a sunken steamboat, was purchased from James Eads of St. Louis and placed in the church building. Several years later, it was removed and given to the Troy Public Schools where it was installed.

In 1864 the Society erected the Jubilee Church, a neat frame structure on a brick foundation. The building's dimensions were 34 by 24 feet, and it included substantial seating, pulpit and bell. The Troy

Society was materially assisted in this project by John C. Dugger and others of the Gilead Society. This new facility served the group for only a few years, and the members decided to build a larger building at a more convenient place.

A lot located on the east side of Main Street was purchased in 1867 for the sum of $600. In 1870 a handsome brick church was erected during the pastorate of Rev. D.B. Van Winkle. Much of the work and financing can be attributed to William Barnsback and William Donoho. Dr. William Cartwright, one of the early circuit riders in Illinois, dedicated this new Methodist Episcopal Church building in 1872. In 1876 the Gilead Society moved its membership to Troy. The church grew and was made a station. The membership increased to 105 during the pastorate of Rev. C.J. Tolle.

The building was remodeled in 1939. Rev. George Hayden was the pastor at the time, and was assisted by Rev. William P. Ludwig, who was retired. A basement was dug and the floor raised. The windows were repositioned (to accommodate the higher floor level) and stained glass was installed.

A new pipe organ was purchased in 1951, a new piano in 1953, and new carpeting (purchased by the Fidelis Circle) was installed in 1957. In 1955 a house located at 308 E. Market Street was purchased from Mrs. L.P. Wetzel for the price of $11,000, becoming the church parsonage.

In 1957 plans began for an educational facility to be located behind the church building. Forrest Piper, Leeds Watson, Vic Sansing, Milton Strong, Jim Lybarger, August Emmer, and James Marsh were named to the Building Committee. The project was finished in 1965. In recognition of a bequest of $25,000 from the estate of long-time member Ora G. Edwards, the building was named in her honor in 1970.

Soon, more space was needed for worship services. The Methodists moved to their new building on Edwardsville Road, and it was named Troy United Methodist Church in keeping with the name change which had occurred in 1940, at that time the Methodist Episcopal Church had become the Troy United Methodist Church. *Information supplied by Rev. Dennis Price and Robert Rogier.*

Mt. Zion Methodist Church

In 1827, Mt. Zion Church was built three miles east of Collinsville on land now located at West Kirsch Road in Jarvis Township. Prior to the church being built, a society had been formed. A preaching place had been held at the home of Robert McMahan in the earliest history of the county. It had been used until the building of Zion Church. This very early settlement of McMahan, Seybold, Halis, Gaskill, Gillet, Teter, and others was the place where, under the efforts of Joshua Auwarter in 1809, the Benevolent Association in Illinois Territory was formed. The object of the association was to provide for the necessities of the poor and indigent "without distinction to race or color, and more particularly for the families of those engaged in defending the frontier settlements from Indian hostilities." A preaching place also existed at the home of Sylvanus Gaskill, about three miles north of Zion Church. This was one of the larger churches on the Edwardsville Circuit in 1844, with 60 members participating.

The present Zion Church was built in 1902 during the pastorate of Rev. C.S. McCollom. Circuit riders and assistants

Mt. Zion Methodist Church, circa early 1900s

served the Edwardsville Circuit, which included the Troy and Mt. Zion Churches. The property was sold in approximately 1970, and the Christophasons now use it regularly for services. The church still stands with a current addition. *Most of the content of this story is taken from the November 4, 1993, issue of the* Times-Tribune.

New Assembly of God

The latest church in Troy is the New Assembly of God located at 8965 State Rte. 162.

New Christian Fellowship Center

In 1977 the New Christian Fellowship Center was established with John Polizzi as Pastor. Located along the North Frontage Road on the east side of I-55/70, the building had a seating capacity of 600. It existed for about 10 years.

St. Jerome Parish

St. Jerome Parish was established in 1870. Early masses were said in a small rented hall above the former Burk's Blacksmith Shop on the corner of Clay Street and Staunton Road. Asst. Pastor of St. Paul's Highland, Rev. A. Kersting, built the first church in 1883, at the Staunton Road address, and it was named St. Jerome.

Rev. Wimor Oberdoerster bought 12 lots from the Highland Brewery Company on Main Street in the Brookside Addition of Troy. The church was then moved to this property. A rectory was built at a cost of $1,584. In 1892 Rev. Oberdoerster was appointed the first resident priest and pastor of St. Jerome.

The second pastor was Rev. August Forster. The cornerstone of a new church was laid on Thanksgiving Day, 1895, and the church was dedicated in 1896. This was the brick church just taken down in 1986, having been used for nearly one century. In 1895 there were 22 families in the Troy parish, and 33 in St. John the Baptist in Blackjack.

Rev. A. Wieneke was sent to St. Jerome in 1899 and remained until September 1914. From September 1914 until July 1920, St. Jerome had four as-

St. Jerome Catholic Church and Rectory, 1985

signed pastors: Frs. B. Montrushio, C.T. Stolze, William A. Pachelhofer, and A.M. Jaschke.

In July 1920, Fr. J.J. Klaes was appointed, and during this year St. Jerome Grade School was closed. He was succeeded by Fr. George Hobbs in 1928 at the beginning of the Depression. The families of St. Jerome supported the church and kept out of debt, donating all of their work. Fr. Hobbs served St. Jerome for 19 years.

Fr. Joseph V. Dineen arrived September 18, 1946, to take charge, remaining here 34 years. During these years the church saw complete redecorating, a new roof and much-needed repairs, plus the many changes brought about by the Second Vatican Council in the 1960s.

Fr. Donald Knuffman came to St. Jerome on July 1, 1980. The parish again had undergone many necessary changes, amidst growing with the City of Troy. Groundbreaking for a new church was held on May 7, 1986, and the first mass in the new church was celebrated on June 7, 1987, with the formal dedication on October 4, 1987.

Fr. Dean Probst was installed as Pastor of St. Jerome Church on May 1, 1990, and served as pastor until February 1996.

On February 27, 1996, the present pastor, Fr. Steven Janoski, took on the duties at St. Jerome Parish. The parish now con-

sists of about 600 families. It is very active in many phases of the church today and continues to grow. *Submitted by Gladys Weider.*

St. John the Baptist Catholic Church

The Blackjack settlement, located about 4-1/2 miles south of Troy on the Lebanon Road, was first known as Black Hawk. Some claimed it was named after the chief of a tribe of Indians.

Others say that the present name, used since 1833, was given to it because much of the land was covered by trees which cast a dark shadow over it.

In 1842, missionaries from St. Louis came on horse back 3 or 4 times a year to conduct services for the settlers. By 1843, the community was comprised of four Catholic families. Later, it would grow to 17 families, and they were still without a church. In 1853, Rev. P. Limacher of Highland took charge and soon took steps to build a frame church. It was completed in the spring of 1853, erected at a cost of $500, on one acre donated by Mr. Gietermann. Father Limacher visited them until 1858, when the rapidly growing Highland parish claimed all of his services. From 1858 through 1872, nine priests from Edwardsville, Collinsville, and Highland served the congregation.

Beginning in 1873, the parish was without a priest for five years. The 25

St. Jerome Church, 2002

St. John the Baptist Catholic Church in Blackjack, Sisters House and School, before 1904

Catholic families were asked to consolidate with Troy's Catholic Church. But after donating $2000 for a new Troy church, the consolidation plan was abandoned.

In 1877, the Rev. F. Reinhard took charge, and the little country parish once more begain to flourish. Services were held regularly every two weeks. For four years Reinhard made the trip to Troy, staying for three days, where some members from Blackjack would receive him. However, the little frame church had fallen into serious decay.

In 1882 Rev. A. Kersting of Highland took charge of the congregation. Soon, the congregation decided to tear down the old church and to build a new brick structure. Kersting appointed a building committee and served as the president himself. This committee was to collect funds, provide the necessary material and supervise the erection and completion of the church. Bishop Bates laid the corner stone on May 1, 1883. The new church was erected at a cost of $3300.

Everything necessary for the inside of the church was quickly provided. Parish member John Petry made and donated the three beautiful altars and the pews. The married ladies collected for the organ and other articles. The John Mersinger and the Frederick Mersinger families and a teacher,

Goeltz, donated statues. Franz Bertram donated eight acres of ground to be used for the cemetery.

Bishop Bates dedicated the bell on April 30, 1884. The next day, the Bishop blessed and dedicated the new structure under the title of St. John the Baptist. In 1885, European stained glass windows were purchased for $300.

In August of that year, Rev. Joseph Jele succeeded Father Kersting. Later in 1888, Rev. Wimar Oberdoerster succeeded Jele. At first, he visited the congregation regularly. When he became pastor of the newly erected Troy parish, Blackjack was annexed to Troy as a mission.

He built a Sisters house in Blackjack in 1891 for $897.85 In 1893, he built a new school for $849.65. He organized several societies in the parish before being transferred to Pierron in 1899.

He was succeeded by Rev. A. Wieneke, who had the church renovated for $500 in 1901. After 15 years, he was transferred. After he left, various priests served the parish through 1920. One of these was Rev. J. J. Klaes, who came in July of 1920. Four years later, the church was decorated at a cost of $800 by Max Autenrieb of Germany.

Another was Rev. George E. Hobbs, named pastor in 1928. Even through the

Depression, he was able to keep the school open and the parish out of debt. In 1946, Father Hobbs was appointed pastor of Ss. Simon and Jude Church in Gillespie.

Rev. Joseph V. Dineen arrived in September of 1946 to take charge of the parish. The sister's house and the school were torn down in 1952, and a new parish hall was built over the site. The hall was completed in 1953 at the cost of $3718.

Through the years an annual church picnic had been held on the first Sunday of August. Families donated home raised chickens and home grown vegetables for the chicken dinner. In addition, various stands were enjoyed. In earlier times a dance had been held outside and, later in the church hall. In 1973, the tradition was broken when the last picnic was held. After 34 years of service to the parish, Father Dineen was appointed pastor to St. Patrick Parish in Grafton.

On July 1, 1980, Rev. Donald Knuffman was appointed pastor. He organized a parish annual fall festival held each October. In 1983, Father Knuffman and others coordinated a large Centennial celebration, held on the first Sunday in August. However, in 1990, Father Knuffman was transferred to Effingham, and Father R. Dean Probst became pastor.

Since priests were becoming scarce, the church was closed in March 1992. The long historical tradition of Blackjack and the Catholic church there was finally at its end.

The Troy Knights of Columbus Council 9266 purchased the church and grounds from the Springfield Dioceses for $20,000. The K.C. membership has brought the church and grounds back to life again with various social functions and meetings. *Information taken from a history written by Rev. J.J. Klaes and submitted by Mae Grapperhaus.*

St. John's Evangelical Church (Blackjack)

The church, school and parsonage stood at the northeast corner of Lebanon road and the current Troy-O'Fallon Road (4-1/2 miles south of Troy). All were destroyed by a tornado in 1938 or 1939. The cemetery was the only part not destroyed by the tornado.

(Left) St. John's Evangelical Church

St. Paul's Lutheran Church

The congregation of St. John's Lutheran Church at Pleasant Ridge clearly saw the need for an organized congregation in Troy so 15 members (all men) were released by them in their annual voter's meeting on January 1, 1867. On January 25, 1867, this new church was organized under the name of "Die Deutsche Evangelische Lutherische St. Paul's Gemeinde, U.A.C., zu Troy, Madison County, Illinois." In May of 1867 St. Paul's became a member of the Lutheran Church Missouri Synod and has remained with the Synod ever since.

When the church building became too small in 1865, a new building was erected and dedicated on August 26, 1888. By 1900 both German and English were used in worship services. On April 4, 1948, the new organ named "Peace Memorial" was dedicated in honor of those who served in World War II; it was dismantled and reassembled in the new church. The last service in the white frame church, that had served the congregation for 73 years, was held on June 18, 1961. During construction of the new church, worship services were held in the school auditorium. Within the east wall

The Evangelical Church Parsonage in Blackjack, circa 1930s

St. Paul's Lutheran Church, 1961

St. Paul's Lutheran Church, Interior

of the front entrance to the new church is buried the cornerstone from the old church bearing the inscription "A.D. 1888." The dedication of the new church was held on February 10, 1963. In 1999 a new addition to the church, along with an elevator, was completed.

A Christian congregation though is much more than simply buildings and other material things - the true story is about how its members strive to be faithful to God's Word, unite in worship, love one another, share their faith and serve the needs of all people in Christian love.

Troy Presbyterian Church

Troy Presbyterian Church was organized October 2, 1842, by Revs. William Chamberlain, Thomas Lippincott, and C.E. Blood with thirteen members: Dr. J.K. Reinger, Cyrus Scott, Benjamin Posey, Mrs. E.C. Reiner, P. Scott, G.W. Scott, James Perigo, S.A. Scott, E. Davis, Cintha Scott, I. Perigo, E. Scott and E. Goodwin. It was received into the Alton Presbytery on October 13, 1842. This was the first church organization of any kind in the city of Troy. The limited period of eldership was adopted in 1845.

The first house of worship was a frame building which is still occupied as a residence. It was moved from an adjoining lot to a site at the northeast corner of Center and Hickory Streets. These faithful Presbyterians financed the construction of a small frame building (24 x 30 feet) which

was made of poles for studdings which were then covered with split boards one foot wide. The old oak seats were the gift of the Collinsville Presbyterian Church. In 1871, this property was sold and a new brick church was erected on South Main Street. This building was dedicated on May 3, 1872, and was used as a house of worship until August 23, 1926, when it was struck by lightning and destroyed by fire.

For almost two years the congregation was without a permanent meeting place but

Troy Christian Church

Troy Christian Church, 114 South Main, 2002.

Presbyterian Church, 1872

Troy Presbyterian Church choir, early 1940s. (l. to r.) Row 1: Fern Hood, Imogene Auwarter, Joyce Sherlock. Row 2: Mildred Martin, Millie Shaffer. Row 3: Geneva Patton, Evelyn Gerstenecker, Kathy Gerstenecker. Row 4: Omar Hampton, Bob Matthews, Gene Adams, Charles Auwarter.

was able to keep its organization intact through the good will of other churches in the community who graciously offered their facilities to the Presbyterian congregation. On April 1928, ground was broken for a new building, the cornerstone of which was laid with appropriate ceremony on June 17, 1928, and dedicated on February 17, 1929, with some of the furnishings salvaged from the fire.

Ministers who served the congregation were Revs. William Chamberlain, Thomas Lippincott, J.R. Dunn, Calvin Butler, John Gibson, Lawson A. Parks, Socrates Smith, James B. Darrah, Caleb J. Pitkin, William Ellers and J.D. Gehring. Elders included John McKee, Dr. Franklin A. Sabin. The last full-time resident pastor was John Heller who left in June 1940.

From then on the pulpit was filled with interim pastors, both ordained and lay people. At one time, the congregation numbered many. In 1988, the church disbanded due to dwindling membership. All the church records were turned over to St. Louis leadership and the building was sold. *Submitted by Millie Shaffer.*

Troy United Methodist Church

The Methodists met in their former church on South Main Street until growth required more space for worship services.

In 1979 the church received 2-1/2 acres, located on Edwardsville Road at the west edge of Troy, from Mr. and Mrs. Harvey Schultze. In 1981 an additional acre of land was purchased for construction of a new building. In January 1983 Bishop Hodapp officiated at the consecration services for the new church sanctuary. The final cost of the building alone was $540,000.

More construction soon followed. In 1993 construction began on a 12,000 square foot facility called the Family Life Center, housing a gymnasium used extensively in the church ministry and for community functions. In 1998 two more acres of land were purchased and a new parking lot installed. A new parsonage, located in Taylor Lake Estates, was purchased in 1999.

The membership, which was 698 in Jan 2002, has more than doubled since the relocation of the church in 1983. The old building on Main Street is now owned and used by the Troy Christian Church. The Ora Edwards Education Building is operated as the Early Childhhood Center.

More than 50 pastors have served the church since 1868. These include Everett Hayden (1927-39), Nate Turner (1941-43), Eugene Scruggs (1947-49), and since 1950: Gerald Weiss, Robert Walker, Harmon Dycus, Bill Cummins (1955 and 1959-63), Carroll Morris, Charles Tindle (1964-68), Gary Scheller (1968-78), Edward Weston (1978-85), William Cooper (1985-88), Dennis Price (1988 to present). *Information supplied by Rev. Dennis Price and Robert Rogier.*

Troy United Methodist Church, 2002

121

The United Pentecostal Church of Troy

In August of 1973, The United Pentecostal Church of Troy was founded by Rev. Howard and Mrs. Anna (Zellars) Bradshaw, in the living room of their home at 105 Prospect Street. The family had relocated to Troy in 1967 from E. St. Louis, Illinois. Prior to starting the church in Troy, Rev. Bradshaw entered into the ministry in 1962, serving as the Assistant Pastor to Rev. E.M. Lowery at Calvary Tabernacle, 4108 State Street in E. St. Louis. Rev. Bradshaw is currently an ordained minister with The United Pentecostal Church International (UPCI) located at 8855 Dunn Road in Hazelwood, MO, and his wife Anna is local licensed minister as well.

In the fall of 1973, the congregation moved to 107 E. Market Street. As the congregation grew, it purchased 105 and 107 E. Market Street locations, and rented 110 and 112 E. Market Street. All of these buildings have a rich history in the city of Troy, but were occupied by the United Pentecostal Church from 1973 until 1989. During this time, the church made religious radio broadcasts each Sunday morning, and bought several vans and buses to transport people to church. Rev. Bradshaw also served as a Chaplain at Oliver Anderson Hospital, and along with Lucille Schmalz, formulated and made the first deliveries for Ministry Unlimited. Two acres of land were purchased on east Route 40 with the intent of building new facilities for the church, however in December of 1988, the Presbyterian Church in Troy was sold to the United Pentecostal Church. The congregation moved into the building at 312 S. Main Street in June of 1989, and purchased the adjoining property at 308 S. Main Street shortly after that. The Rt. 40 properties were sold.

In 1993 Rev. Howard Bradshaw encountered health problems, and his son, Rev. Brian and Mrs. Lori (Hutchinson, of Tower Hill, Illinois) Bradshaw, became the Pastor, with Rev. Howard Bradshaw becoming Senior Pastor and Rev. Anna Bradshaw becoming the Associate Pastor. Rev. Brian Bradshaw is an Ordained minister with UPCI, having been in the ministry since 1983. Rev. and Mrs. Brian Bradshaw had served the church throughout the years in various capacities, such as Sunday school teachers, Youth Pastors and Assistant Pastors. His wife is currently the Minister of Music at the church. In 1998 Rev. Howard Bradshaw was made Bishop of the church, with Rev. Brian Bradshaw becoming the Senior Pastor. Under their combined leadership, the congregation purchased two adjoining properties, 316 S. Main Street and 313 S. Hickory Street. Currently the church is considering relocating or building new facilities at its present location.

The United Pentecostal Church of Troy, 2002

Schools

McCray-Dewey High School Alumni present a donation in honor of Dr. C. E. Molden to Molden Elementary School Principal in the fall of 2001. (l. to r.) Sharon Schlaefer, Thelma Huston, Mae Grapperhaus, Norma Jenks, Tal Fisk, Louise Rinkel.

Gilead School

St. Jerome Catholic School, circa 1910. Child is holding Palmer Penmanship Award penant. Photo submitted by William Schroeder.

(Left) May Pole, Lutheran School, 1910. (l. to r.) Front: Gertrude Miller, Augusta Bohland, Professor C. Kellermann, Martha Burmeister, Bertha Heddergott, Helen Peters, Frieda Fedder. Back: Namio Neunschwander, Gussie Schlimme, Elinore Wendler, Freda Peters, Lillie Schlaefer, Amanda Trost, Lydia Gerling, Clara Gornet, Frieda Niebruegge, Frieda Bohland.

McCray-Dewey Academy, late 1800s

Troy, Illinois, Area
History and Families

The Schools of Troy and Surrounding Area

Local history does not record the actual starting of the first school in Troy, but evidence reveals that three "pay" schools existed in the 1800s. One was located on North Main Street, where a barber shop is now located, and another on South Main, where the Dr. Spencer Memorial Park is now located. Sources also report that the Independent Order of Odd Fellows erected a hall at the corner of Center and Main Streets. The lower story of the building was occupied as a schoolhouse for seven years. No other information is known about this school. Currently, A&R Paints and Crafts is located there. Another school was on Market Street. The exact location of the Market Street school is not shown in early records, but it is known that this school was for girls only. The first known school in Madison County was taught in 1824 at the Gilead Church east of Troy.

In the 1800s schools in the Troy area were opened and closed quite often because of lack of funds. The original public school was erected in Troy in 1856, a time when schools began to appear everywhere. The first public school was large: it had 4 rooms!

By 1930, Jarvis Township had nine schools. They were the Gilead School, Formosa School, Blackjack School, Spring Valley School, Liberty School, and St. John's Catholic School. Three others are still in operation — the Troy Public School (now called Freeman Elementary School), St. Paul's Lutheran School, and McCray-Dewey High School (now an elementary school). In 1930, the nine schools employed 21 teachers. Five of the teachers were in the McCray-Dewey High School; the others taught elementary students. The total enrollment in the township was 565, 75 of which were high school students. The total salary for the 21 teachers in 1930 was a mere $20,620.90. *School section compiled by Jeanette Dothager.*

Blackjack School

Blackjack School was located on Blackjack Road near Mill Creek Road, south of Troy. The building still stands today, but it has been converted to a taxidermist shop. The school was the typical white frame schoolhouse with a coal stove that had to the stoked at night by the teacher. A storm cellar was available to the school population, but, fortunately, it was seldom used. As with most country schools of the period, a well and a bucket with dipper provided the students' drinking water inside. The customary out door toilets completed the physical plant.

Two big events during the school year were the box social in the fall and the big picnic on the last day of school. The pro-

Blackjack School Dist. No. 65

ceeds from selling the fancy box lunches went to buy school supplies. The end of school picnic featured "bought" ice cream and home made cakes.

Ruth Druessel Stock, who taught at Blackjack during the 1941-42 school year, remembered that it snowed the morning of her last day picnic. However, the weather warmed, and the picnic went on as planned on that April day,

Mrs. Stock remembered the school fondly, as both she and her father had attended there. During her year as teacher, she had 10 or 11 students, and received $90 a month as salary. Seventh and eighth grades were taught on alternate years, and these students, too, had to take a graduation test in Edwardsville and pass it before they could go on to high school. Later, as the districts consolidated, Blackjack students attended the Troy schools. Mrs. Stock later became a kindergarten teacher in the Troy school system. *Material taken from an oral interview with Ruth Druessel Stock.*

C.A. Henning Elementary School

The C.A. Henning Elementary School was dedicated on October 2, 1988. Robert Rogier was Superintendent at the time, and William Hyten was its first principal. The innovative design featured a media center, large multi-purpose room, and over 20 classrooms in two separate wings, as well as the usual cafeteria and kitchen areas and offices. Its location at 520 East Highway 40 is convenient for the Creekside families and buses from other areas of the district. *Submitted by Jeanette Dothager.*

Blackjack School, 1917: Alma Holt, Dora Langenwalter, Oscar Gindler, Arnold Holz, Walter Busch, Elsa Holz, Walter Gindler

C.A. Henning Elementary School, 2002

Formosa School

Formosa School was located on Formosa Road near Route 40, near the current I70-55 interchange, not too far from the state salt dome. The school building was moved by Art and Irma Hartman to a location on Collinsville Road, next to the present Jarvis Township Building. It is now a home on Holly Busch Farm.

Gilead School

Gilead School was located a few miles east of Troy, on the north side of Rt. 162 and just north of the old Blue Haven Restaurant, which was at the juncture of old Rt. 40 and Rt. 162. The building was a square, measuring 20 or 30 feet per side. The outside was weatherboarded with rough clapboards, and the inside was plastered. It was the first school in Jarvis Township, and the first classes were held in 1824. The school year lasted six months at that time and records show that teacher Jesse Renfro furnished the books. Mr. Renfro received $100 for the school term, or about $16 a month. During the last year of his teaching, Jesse had 40 pupils for six months. The school building later became a residence and was eventually torn down. *From the biography of Jesse Renfro and from material submitted by Helen Noll.*

Liberty School

Liberty School was located south of Troy on South Liberty Road. Like the other country schools of its time, it was an important part of the rural community. Ora Edwards was a teacher for several years there, and one of her students, Merle Gerstenecker Triska, remembered making soup at school on top of the furnace. Two other teachers that taught there were Martha Borst and Helen Gerstenecker Siefferman. The school closed when the districts were consolidated. The building has since been converted to a house, and Dale Willimann now lives there. *Information from an interview with Jim and Mary Catherine Gerstenecker and Merle Gerstenecker Triska.*

Maple Grove School

Maple Grove School's property was on both sides of the road. The south parcel was used as a ball diamond and playground. On the north stood

Formosa School, circa 1935. (l. to r.) Front: Harvey Heinlein, unknown, Glenn Kleuter (?), Rosemary Heinlein, Irene Frey, Roy Mayer, Julius Waitukaitis. Middle: Florence Kleuter, unknown, Irene (Schlemer) Droy, LaVerne (Schlemer) Stein Renaud, Leon Mayer, unknown, Earl Mayer, Robert Kleuter, Edward Frey (in back). Back: Caroline Vebeloque, unknown, Dorothy Heinlein, Teacher Clara Kirsch, unknown, John Henry Wilhelm, Juanita Webb.

Gilead School. (l. to r.) Front: James Loyet, unknown, Emma Bell Cook, unknown, Bernice Niehaus, Bernadine Niehaus, Marcella Niehaus, Elinor Loyet. Back: unknown, Francis Loyet, unknown, Victor Diepholz, Melvin Niehaus, Teacher, Loraine Niehaus, Ethel Keck, Dorothy Keck, unknown, unknown, Marie Loyet.

Gilead School, 1925. (l. to r.) Front: Arnie Cline, Robert Porter, Helen Porter Hagemann, Helen Schmitt Noll, Virginia Schmitt Horn, Otmar Schmitt (5 yrs. old). Middle: Rudy Schmitt, George Schmalz, Zelda Cline, Charles Hoenig, Rugene Schmitt, George Cline. Back: Evelyn Nobs Flath, Florence Schmitt Wuench, Elsie Hoenig, Leo Cline, Melvin Burcham, Cleon Schmitt, Sallie Burcham, and teacher Edna Keck Sliva.

(Left) Liberty School 1952, last graduating class. (l. to r.) Front: Eva Hall, Shirley Harris, Doris Willimann, Dorothy Braunsderf. Back: Teacher Mrs. Alma Gebauer, Joe Grodzicki, Edgar Pratt, James Gard, Alvin Wagner, John Grodzicki.

Liberty School Building

Liberty School, February 14, 1912. Teacher Ora Edwards.

the school building, two out-houses, and a storm cellar. One of the teacher's duties was to start the fire in the coal burning basement furnace each morning and to carry out the ashes from the previous day. Drinking water was carried in from the outside well and put into a container in the schoolroom.

In 1930, eighteen students attended, and the school owned 294 library books, valued at $180. School started the Tuesday after Labor Day and ended the last day of April so that the older children would be able to help plant crops. Teacher Marie Fields earned $100 a month at that time.

By 1931, the library had grown to 345 books valued at $212. In 1934, Helen Ellis (Gansmann) taught for $65 a month. Other teachers employed later were Mary Catherine Kinder (Gerstenecker), Margaret Kelly (Hart), Iona Jackson (Moser), Harry Bartlett, and Grace Scheibal. Mary Catherine Gerstenecker remembered that during her two years there, she helped her students put on a play. Several characters needed to wear fur coats as part of their costumes. Mary Catherine was able to borrow only one, from Mrs. Wilma Dull. They solved the problem, however, by handing the coat out of a window on one side, having a boy run with it to the other side of the building, and handing it through another window to the next character to wear it on stage. Students and parents "were like family and became lifetime friends."

The building still stands on Maple Grove Road, north of Troy. It was sold after neighborhood children began attending the Troy School. The building has been re-

Maple Grove School, 1940s

modeled and is now a residence. *Information submitted by Thelma Huston from the Maple Grove School Register from 1930-35 and from an interview with Mary Catherine Kinder Gerstenecker.*

McCray-Dewey Academy

In her will, Angeline McCray-Dewey specified that if there was not enough money in her estate to build the McCray-Dewey Academy, the executors should allow funds to accumulate until they were sufficient to do so. Actually, when all the accounts were settled, the available cash in the estate came to a little more than $3,000, not enough, even in 1880, to build much of an academy. Her trustees were

Julius A. Barnsback, William W. Jarvis, Oliver Reid, Dr. Frank A. Sabin and Samuel Rawson. They followed her instructions and allowed the money to accumulate until 1886. That year they refurbished a building on the McCray farm and hired Professor Edward Bigelow as headmaster. On September 6, 1886, they opened the academy. The curriculum was roughly equivalent to that of a modern high school, including classes in English, German, Bookkeeping Commercial Law, Economics, Arithmetic, and Science. The science portion was broken into General Science, Botany, Zoology, Physics and Geography. There was also something called Household Science. There was even an athletic program featuring basketball and tennis teams for both boys and girls. Attendance was free to residents of Troy under 26. Graduation required 16 credits, with one course for one year constituting a credit.

In four years, the academy was out of money and closed. This was not the only time that would happen. After reopening in the 1890s, the academy closed again in 1901. It reopened in 1905 and continued until 1917, when it closed for the last time. In 1929, the Township High School District 143 filed suit to condemn the ten-acre tract and building. The suit was successful, the academy was demolished and a new high school built there. The courts awarded the estate $4,000 for the building and the ten acres.

In 1931 the courts determined that the academy could never open again, and emphatically dissolved the McCray-Dewey Academy Trust. The directors were ordered to sell the tenant farms that had supported the academy and apply the funds to retire

Madison County Special Education Cooperative

Madison County Special Education Cooperative, Market Street, 2002

McCray-Dewey Academy. (l. to r.) unknown, Cecil Friesland, James Wilkerson, Paul Auwarter, Wiley Bryant, Wilber Gebauer, Irwin Scotti, Otto Feldmeier, unknown

bonds issued by the trust to build and operate it. All that was left was the name. The new school was named The McCray-Dewey High School.

McCray-Dewey Junior High School

On July 1, 1954, the Troy, Marine, and St. Jacob Public Schools formed what would later be called the Triad Community Unit School District #2. With the completion of the new high building in 1959, McCray-Dewey High School became the McCray-Dewey Junior High School, housing Troy's 6th, 7th, and 8th grades. Today with the housing of Triad Middle School on the old high school campus on old 40, McCray-Dewey is one of the elementary centers in Troy.

McCray-Dewey Township High School

In 1917 when the community felt a need for a new township high school, the trustees of the Dewey estate leased the land to the township trustees and the name of the Academy was formally changed to McCray-Dewey Township High School.

Then on December 15, 1928, a bond issue was passed for $70,000. Ten acres of land were purchased and the present McCray-Dewey School was built at a cost of $64,816.30. The building was completed in April 1930. It contained 12 classrooms, several offices, and a combined auditorium-gymnasium. The three-story building contained 294,000 cubic feet. F.L. Eversull was the first principal of the new high school. It was dedicated on May 2, 1930, complete with a school holiday, downtown parade, a program of music and speeches, and a visit from the state superintendent of schools, Frances G. Blair of Springfield. The event was a "gala day in the school history of Troy and the township."

The school served as a high school until 1959 when Triad High School was built. It then became Mc-Cray-Dewey Junior High School. Today, with the construction of the new Triad High School and the housing of the Triad Middle School in the former high school building, McCray-Dewey is an elementary center. It shares its campus with the Molden Elementary School and the Wakeland Center. *Information taken from* The Troy Call, *May 2, 1930.*

1935 Class, circa 1932-33. (l. to r.) Row 1: Gladys M. Conley, unknown, unknown, E. Julia Knecht, unknown, Virginia Flahe (Flath?),unknown. Row 2: Homer H. Polwort, Carl H. Taake, Maden?, unknown, Dugger?, unknown. Row 3: Dorothy L. Molden, Bernadine Hall, unknown, Erna A. Norbury, unknown, unknown, unknown. Row 4: Henry J. Wendler, unknown, Dale H. Kurtz, Joseph J. Mersinger, Donald Taylor, unknown, Edgar A. Schultz?, unknown.

Molden School

Molden School was completed in 1965. This unique round building was named after Troy physician Dr. C.E. Molden, who practiced medicine in Troy for 50 years. Molden School, located at the north end of the McCray-Dewey campus next to the Wakeland Center, houses elementary classes today. *Information taken from the* Times Tribune, *July 23, 1992.*

St. Jerome Catholic School

St. Jerome Catholic School was in session for a short time only. Records do show that the Benedictine Sisters taught there, and enrollment was small. The school closed in 1920 when it became financially impossible for the parish to continue to support it. *Submitted by Mae Grapperhaus.*

St. John Evangelical School

This school was located to the west of the St. John Evangelical

McCray Dewey Junior High School, late 1980s

Molden School, 2002

Church in Blackjack, across the "snake turn" from the church. The school, church, and parsonage were destroyed by a tornado in 1939. *Information submitted by Marie Dollinger.*

St. John the Baptist Catholic School (Blackjack)

As early as 1864, St. John the Baptist Catholic Church in Blackjack had a Catholic school. It was a log cabin, but it reflected credit upon the parents of the time who wished to give their children a religious education. The little congregation could not always find a Catholic teacher, the first of who were men, and at times the children had to at-

tend the Blackjack Public School, not far down the road. Early teachers were of the old school: men who did not spare the rod. Often they received scant remuneration ($45.00 per year) for the services rendered.

This practice continued until Father Oberdoerster came to the parish and succeeded in obtaining the Precious Blood Sisters from Ruma, Illinois. He built a Sister House in 1891, which was nearly completed, when the three sisters arrived.

In 1893 a frame structure was erected. The building was provided with a stage on which the children often gave plays. The sisters' house and the school were erected at the cost of $1,850.

Benedictine Sisters succeeded the sisters of the Adorers of the Blood of Christ of Little Rock, Arkansas, after nine years. From 1914 through 1918,

Sister Bridget, Sister Louisa, and Sister Casper taught the students. They remained until 1919 when WWI caused a shortage of sisters, and they were withdrawn. However, the sisters, by their good example, had a lasting effect upon the community, as well as the children. At least seven girls took the veil and joined the religious order.

Although 40 children attended the school, the expense of operation became too great for the small community; the school was closed in 1944. *Information was taken from* The St. John Centennial Booklet, *from* The Diamond Jubilee Booklet of the Springfield Diocese, *and from reflections of community members.*

St. Paul's Lutheran School

A number of Lutheran families living in the Troy area during the days of the Civil War belonged to St. John's Lutheran Church in Pleasant Ridge. They wanted to give their children a good Christian education, but transportation to Pleasant Ridge was difficult and it was impossible to walk. During the winter and spring, the children often missed school, so in 1864 a parcel of land, consisting of five acres, was purchased in the northwest part of Troy for $600 by Fred Zenk, George Struckhoff and Herman Taake for the purpose of establishing a Lutheran Christian Day School.

Already located on these five acres was a small brick building, 16 x 18 feet, consisting of one room. Other interested Lutherans in the Troy area approved of the school and paid a share of the purchase price. An additional room was built on to serve as a combination school and teacherage.

St. Jerome Catholic School 8th Grade Graduating Class, 1918

St. John Evangelical School, early 1900s

(Right) St. Paul's Lutheran
School Building

(Below) 1931-32. (l. to r.) Roy W.,
Wilford Meier, Arthur K.,
Laverne, Marie, Virginia, Fern,
Ethel, Betty. Teacher Arthur
Stahmer, Janitor Henry Kueker.

(Above) St. Paul's
Lutheran School,
Grades 1-8, 1951-
1952

(Right) Early
Classroom,
possibly
Homemaking Class

(Below) St. Paul's
Lutheran School,
1930s

(Below) Classroom,
St. Paul's Lutheran
School, 1935

With the assistance of the pastor at Pleasant Ridge, an instructor was found and began his duties in June of 1864. Thirty-nine children were enrolled for this first term, 21 boys and 18 girls. As it became evident that more room was needed, it was decided to build a new building that would serve as both a place for worship on Sunday and as a school. This building was dedicated in September 1865; but, after a time, it was found to be inconvenient having one building serving as both church and school, so in 1873 a new school building was erected.

In a strong demonstration of faith by the congregation, the present St. Paul's Lutheran School was built in 1911 and dedicated on Pentecost Sunday in 1912. This brick structure, with four classrooms, is still serving the current classes, although a number of changes and renovations have taken place.

Spring Valley School

This country school's name was not always Spring Valley. Originally, it was named Ridge Prairie, probably so named because of the lay of the land in surrounding fields and timbers. Later, it was renamed Spring Valley, shortly before the present building was built. The name was given because the community had many springs located in the valleys between the many small hills to the north, east, and south of the school yard. The springs are still there, as well as the valleys.

John and Sarah Edwards, who lived southwest of the school's current location,

Spring Valley School, located at 8004 West Kirsch Road, 1949-50. Current owners are Mae and James Grapperhaus.

Spring Valley School, 1910. Teacher, Sally Anderson. (l. to r.) Front: Anita Schmitt, Christine (Schlemer) Loyet, Clara Kirsch, Jim Joseph. Back: Viola Schmitt, Amelia (Hoenig) Burkan, Olinda (Kirsch) Galli, Agnes (Schlemer) Mayer, unknown, Oliver Schlemer, Bertha Schmitt, Frieda Schmitt.

donated the land for Spring Valley School. The abstract, dated August 20, 1853, stated that the property, "shall be kept and occupied for school purposes where the English language shall be the medium communicator." The land was deeded to Andrew Wood and John Lebora, trustees for the Ridge Prairie School.

A frame building housed the first school, which was in need of major repairs by 1903, when a new school building was erected. The first school was transported with horses east on West Kirsch Road to the Gus Kirsch farm near what is now (in 2002) Troy-O'Fallon Road. Former student Joseph Mersinger remembers that, as a child, he played in the old school building on the Kirsch farm. He recalled that it had a slate blackboard attached to the wall; and even after it was placed at the Kirsch's, he remembered seeing that it was still attached.

The old school was sawed in half, so it would more easily cross a narrow bridge on West Kirsch Road, and transported by horses and wagon to its new location. The old school could have been removed after the close of school at the end of April, and the new school constructed the same summer before September when the next school year began, Mersinger remembered. "In those days, neighbors helped to build it, and it didn't take too long for such a building," Mersinger said.

Valentine Mersinger (Joseph's brother) was on the Spring Valley School Board at the time of the construction. He and many

other neighbors helped build it. Valentine was one of three school board trustees. The other two were Mrs. James (Kate) Gerstenecker and Mrs. George (Cora) Edwards.

As the years went by, several other neighbors in the district held the position of trustees. At the time of the consolidation in 1950, Oscar Mersinger, Oliver J. Schlemer, and Edmund "Dick" Petry held the positions. During the last years the school was open, a number of students had dwindled, and the last year there were only six: David Burgess, Bill Mills, Patty Burgess, JoAnn Wuench, Carol Wuench, and Mae Mersinger. The next year all of the country students in the district were bused into Troy. In December 1950, the school and the acreage around it were sold at auction. Oscar Mersinger, the sole bidder, purchased the school, storm cellar, coal shed, privies, and land for a mere $1800.

A list of teachers dating back to 1907 include the following: Emma Wittman, Sally A. Anderson, Mary Pritchett, Ora Edwards, Serafina Bertorello, Pauline Naumer, Florence Richter, Jennie Miller, Olive Hall, Louise Steinkoenig, Vesta Schoeck, Ruby Kirsch (Adelhardt), Jennie Haywood, Lillian B. Welch, Laura Favre, and Rose Snadden. *Submitted by Mae (Mersinger) Grapperhaus from memory, the* Times-Tribune, *Joseph Mersinger's recollections and legal documents of the Edwards family. Paid for by the Friends of Spring Valley School.*

Spring Valley Country School, 1920. (l. to r.) Front: Ray Bress, Edna Bress, Marie Schlemer, Wynona Bress, Loretta Schlemer, Alvera Zaganelli, Ruby Kirsch, Wilbur Butcher. Back: Annie Brendel, Marie Wuench, Harold Butcher, Agnes Petry, Augusta Hoenig, Lois Edwards, Clara Petry, Carl Wuench, Louie Zaganelli and Leslie Butcher. Ora E. Edwards, Teacher. Not pictured: Philip Petry, Director.

Spring Valley School Interior, 1930s. Teacher, Ruby Kirsch. Students: Alma Schlemer, Joe Waitukaitis, Earl Bress, Eddie Longhi, Arthur Bress, Aaron Cook, Evelyn Virgin, Ken Brendel and Norman Brendel.

(Left) Spring Valley School, late 1930s. (l. to r.) Front: unknown, unknown, Rich Longhi, unknown, Mrs. Jennie Haywood - teacher. Middle: Jim Brendel, Cora Mae Detienne, Ken Brendel, Bert Longhi, unknown. Back: Owen Brendel, unknown, Irene Schlemer, Maynard Brendel, Dorothy Detienne, and Ralph Wiesemeyer.

Jim Brendel on his horse, circa 1940. When he was about ten years old, Jim would take his horse and cart to transport all the students who lived along the route to Spring Valley School.

(Below) Spring Valley School, October 17, 1929.

(Left) Spring Valley School, December 9, 1930. Teacher Mrs. Vesta Faitz.

(Right) Spring Valley School, 1947-48. (l. to r.) Front: David Burgess, Bill Mills, Patty Burgess, Gordon "Mac" McFarland, Jr., Mae Mersinger. Back: Sally Burgess, Melvin Schlemer. Teacher, Mrs. Lillian Welch, took the photo.

Sylvan Hall School

Sylvan Hall School sat at the juncture of Lower Marine Road and Maple Grove Road, northeast of Troy about 3 1/2 miles. It was a typical country school with a pot-belly stove to warm the room, and no electricity to lighten cloudy days. Water was carried in a bucket into the school, and students shared the ladle, later getting their own "folding" cups. In the early days the long desks seated three students side by side. Later the individual desks arrived. Eventually, the school also received a piano. The piano was used for the teaching of music and, undoubtedly, for the Christmas program, the Box Social, and the program and picnic held on the last day of school each year.

In the 1930s the teacher's salary was $70 per month. She had to buy her own extra supplies and materials for special projects. She taught 10 subjects that varied from agriculture to morals and manners. School was never closed for snow days, as some students would ride horses through the snow, and the teacher was expected to be there. Teachers usually did the janitorial duties, including hauling in the coal for the stove, unless one of the "big" boys did it.

Before the 8th graders could graduate, they had to take a test and pass it with a grade no lower than 75%. Only the country students were required to take this test.

When the schools incorporated, Sylvan Hall was closed, and the students sent to Troy to be educated. The school is now a residence. *Information taken from an interview with Mary Kranz Zinkgraf, teacher at Sylvan Hall from 1932-38.*

Triad High School, 2002

Triad Middle School, 2002

Triad High School

The new Triad High School building was dedicated on October 30, 1999. The new facility is a state-of-the-art design, that includes a 16,500 square-foot gymnasium with mezzanine and seating for 2300 people; a commons area that includes a 2,640 square foot performance stage; seven science labs and seven industrial/technology labs; a large library; and a total of 67 classrooms. The total building square footage is 218,700 square feet. The community is quite proud of this new home of the Knights!

Triad Middle School

Starting in the 1991-92 school year, Troy's McCray-Dewey junior high students moved to Molden School and joined with grade 6 to form the Molden Middle School. In 1999, upon the completion of the new Triad High School, the Triad Middle School was established on the campus of the former high school. All 6th, 7th, and 8th graders from Marine, St. Jacob, and Troy now attend classes there.

Troy Grade School

The first school building in Troy was built at the corner of Staunton Road and Clay Street in 1856. It began with four classrooms, and as the town's population grew, additions to the school building became necessary until it was decided to build a new building. The original Troy Grade School stood until the current building was completed in 1939. The school was renamed the William S. Freeman Elementary School in 1988 after its long time principal. It still is used as one of the elementary centers in the Triad District.

Sylvan Hall School, about 1930-31. (l. to r.) Front: Clem Talleur, Jr., Charles Hunsche, Alvin Helmich, Clarence Butcher, Kenneth Engeling. Middle: Ruth Kuhn, Edna Prott, Wilma Gieseking, Fern Porter, Viola Feldmeier, Lucille Prott. Back: Mary Knecht, Paul Helmich, Tildon Helmich, Julia Knecht, Ruth Miller, Eldon Smith, Ellen Porter, Norma Prott.

(Above) Troy Public School, early 1900s

(Right) Troy Grade School. Left, teacher Adda Matthews, circa 1910, taught for 39 years and quit before 1938. Principal Arthur Canedy (?) at right.

Troy Grade School, circa 1917. Al Schultze, "Buss" Hart, Verna Schultze, Etta Schultz, Eli Burk, Mary Thomas, Robert Baglin, Bill Callan, Barsch, Weider.

Troy Grade School, circa 1920s. (l. to r.) Front: Paul Frangen, Norm Wilkerson, Johnny McCain, Frank Enrico, Johnny Bertorello. Back: Mary Eliz. Rees, Mabel Porter.

(Left) Troy Grade School 1925, Grade 4, Teacher Mary Kelly (Peggy Hart's sister). (l. to r.) Row 1: Laverne Edwards, Russell Manley, Norman Frangen, Joe Lesicko, unknown, Wilfred Schultze. Row 2: Jim Mersinger, Francis DeVries, William Llewellyn, James F. Davis, Vincent Schroeder, Charles Norbury. Row 3: Annie Struckhoff, Marie Hertsinger, Marie Graef, Lena Wyatt, Melba Vetter, unknown, Norma Shaeffer. Row 4: unknown, H. Morgan, Helen Hegren, Naomi Bohrmeister, Ruth Rieder, Harry Hazzard, William Schroeder.

(Right) Troy Grade School, First Grade, 1937. (l. to r.) Front: Mae Meta (Capelle) Hanks, Fern (Hood) Mateer, Margaret (Kelly) Kleuter, Marian (Schurman) Lewis, Ruth (May) Loyet, Viola (Schmerbauch), Colleen (Haukapp) Gorham. Middle: Roy Mayer, Wilbur Harris, Leslie Becker, Armin Shadwick, Tommy Nemsky, unknown, Eugene Rapien, Edgar Gerstenecker, Jack Preston, Bobby Wille. Back: Teacher Adda Matthews, Betty (Carter) Bazaillion, Rae (Hodson) James, Beatrice Tuell, Audrey (Ottwein) Deeren, Carol (Hart) Jaggers, Verna (Bour) Albertina, Alice Scully, Betty (Snow) Foster. Note: Picture taken on the north side of the old grey grade school building.

(Left) Class of 1949. (l. to r.) Front: Paul Levo, Bob Atwood, Frieda Maedge, Dorothy Schmerbauch, Jim Holshouser, Jo Ann Robertson, Bucky Wadlow, Shirley Hersht, Bob Baglin. Middle: Mrs. V. Edwards, Bill Humphries, Robert "Tony" Hunsche, Bill Murphy, Don Marchiando, Hugh Harrigan, Ernie Nemnich, Charles Mayer, Bob Dollinger, Principal and teacher W.S. Freeman. Back: Mary Jo Brown, Joyce Arone, Darlene Finny, Mary Ellen Schmidt, Lynn Zenk, Betty Lou Gregory, Shirley Huston, Gerry Brenkendorf, Nelda Galli. Missing were Jack Rees, Jupe Mueller, and Ruth Faitz.

W.S. Freeman School, 2002

135

Wakeland Center

Wakeland Center, located on the McCray-Dewey campus, was dedicated on May 16, 1976, when C.A. Henning was superintendent. It was one of seven projects made possible by a successful bond election held in November of 1974. At its dedication the center had two special education classrooms, rooms for vocal and instrumental music, and facilities for speech therapy, psychological and counseling services. The building is still in use today and stands between the McCray-Dewey building and the Molden Elementary School. *Submitted by Jeanette Dothager.*

Wakeland Center, 2002

Troy School Personnel

Harold Wentz, teacher, taught 6th grade and music at Troy Grade School; Musical director at McCray-Dewey High School; and taught art at Triad High School until his retirement.

Viola (Morriss) Edwards, 1948-49, teacher, taught high school English and also 7th and 8th Grade

Clara Kirsch, teacher, taught 43 years in Blackjack, Formosa, Troy Grade School

Emil Isenberg, custodian, McCray-Dewey High School

Frances Wilhelm, teacher, age 90 years old on November 17, 1983

(Below) Troy Grade School Faculty, 1958-1959. (l. to r.) Front: Harold Wentz-5, Harold Schwehr-6, Alma Gebauer-1, Clara Kirsch-2, Flora Gebauer-3, Imogene Auwarter-5, Bill Freeman-8, Bob Evans-7. Back: Mary Zinkgraf-1, Peg Hart-6, Katherine Werder-7, Helen Siefferman-3, Mary Gerstenecker-4, Ona Gilbreath-8, Marian Stowe-4, Julia Taake-2.

Art Hazzard, School Crossing Guard at Clay and Hickory Streets near W.S. Freeman Elementary School

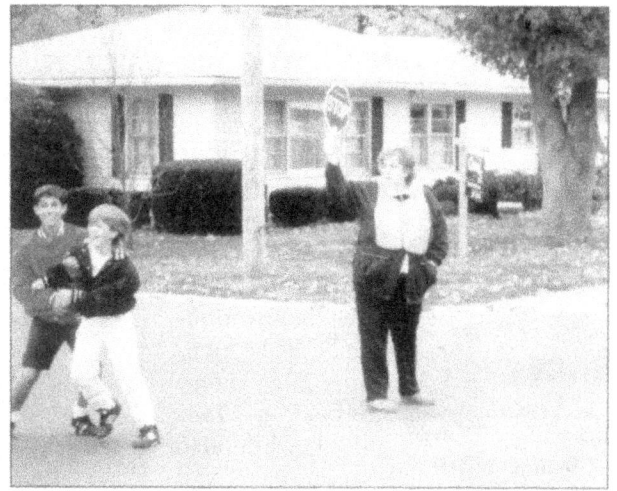
Becky Hanser, School Crossing Guard at Dewey and East Clay Streets, 1980s-1990s

Triad School Superintendents

Fred R. Wakeland, Superintendent

Fred Wakeland

Fred R. Wakeland came to the Troy community as superintendent of McCray-Dewey High School in 1945. He continued as superintendent of the Triad unit when it was formed in 1954 until his retirement in 1962. After his retirement at 71, he became the Madison County Assistant County Superintendent of Schools and served in that position for 13 years. In memory of his dedication to Triad's schools, the special education unit in Troy was named the Wakeland Center in May of 1979. *Taken from* Troy-Tribune.

C.A. Henning, Superintendent

C.A. Henning

Clarence Henning served as superintendent of Triad Community Unit # 2 from 1962-1977. During his tenure, Triad grew considerably. All-day kindergarten began, reading specialists were employed, and new buildings were added. All bond issues and tax referendums were passed during this period. The C.A. Henning Elementary School on Rt. 40 was named in his honor. *Information provided by Kay Korte.*

William S. Freeman, Assistant Superintendent

William S. Freeman

William S. Freeman was instrumental in the development of many educational programs and curricula for the Triad Schools. He was a dedicated educator who wanted the best for the students and the community. After his retirement he worked for the County Superintendent's office. He, also, continued to serve on many committees for community betterment. Bill died in 1988, but he is still remembered as townspeople pass by the William S. Freeman Grade School (formerly the Troy Grade School) named in his honor. *Taken from sources supplied by Mary June Freeman and Scottie Freeman.*

Robert Rogier, Superintendent

Robert Rogier, a long time Troy resident, replaced C.A. Henning as superintendent in July of 1977, after serving as Assistant Superintendent for one year.

During his tenure as superintendent the district continued to grow in enrollment.

Robert Rogier

Several building additions were completed, and a new elementary center – the C.A. Henning Elementary School – was constructed and opened in Troy. After retirement in 1989, he returned part-time to direct the high school band for one year, and served for six years on the McKendree College Board of Trustees. *Information supplied by Robert Rogier.*

Billy Tracy, Assistant Superintendent

Bill Tracy

In July of 1977, Bill Tracy was appointed Assistant Superintendent of the Triad District. He had been serving as principal of the Troy elementary schools for the previous 10 years, and had also served as principal of St. Jacob Grade School.

Bill died in December of 1999. He was widely respected as an outstanding educator. His sense of humor, ready smile, and sincere love for children and people in general will be remembered by those who knew him.

137

William Hyten, Superintendent

William Hyten

William (Bill) Hyten came to Troy in May 1981 and worked as part-time principal and teacher at Troy Primary School. He was the first principal at the Henning Elementary School in 1988-1989, while also serving on the unit curriculum committee with Bill Tracy. In May of 1989 he was named District Superintendent, and served in that capacity for 13 years, retiring in June of 2002. *Information supplied by Bill Hyten.*

Mike Loftus, Assistant Superintendent

Mike Loftus was principal at Marine Grade School for three years before his appointment as Assistant Superintendent in 1991. Previously, Mike taught Head Start, kindergarten, 3rd and 6th grades, and served as principal of Marine Grade School. *Information supplied by Mike Loftus.*

Mike Loftus

St. Paul's Lutheran School, Arthur Stahmer's Class, 1930-1931

Troy Grade School

(Right) Formosa School, circa 1933. (l. to r.) Front: Carolyn McDonald, Irene (Schlemer) Droy, Harvey Heinlein, Leon Mayer, Earl Mayer, LaVerne (Schlemer) Stein Renaud, John Henry Wilhelm, Juanita Webb, Dorothy Heinlein. Back: unknown, LaVerne Blumberg, Caroline Beveloqua, Edward Frey, Teacher Clara Kirsch, Lois Heinlein, Blanche Frey, Jack Blumberg, Alice Blumberg, Agnes Wilhelm.

Clubs and Organizations

*Bill's Gang at Rieder's Park,
circa 1920s*

*(Left) MWA Organization,
circa 1900.*

*(Right) Christmas in April, 1990s. During the Christmas in April
project, spearheaded by area realtors and later resumed by the Troy
American Legion, volunteers assist in repairing homes around Troy.*

Introduction

Various clubs and organizations have kept Troy citizens involved and active for many generations. Too numerous to mention all of them in this book, these groups have served to educate, to entertain and to serve the community. A political club or a service organization, a nationally affiliated group or a local club, each has contributed to Troy's history in its own unique way.

Local 4-H Clubs

The Troy and Pin Oak area has had 4-H Clubs since the l930s under the guidance of the University of Illinois 4-H Extension division. The following are names of clubs and leaders (past and present) as recalled by local residents: Troy Merry Makers – Mrs. Melba Bohnenstiehl, Mrs. Bernice Arth, Mrs. Edna Meier, Mrs. Maxine Flath, Mrs. Fern Gindler, Mrs. Marcella Lindsey, Carol Meier and Yvonne Meier. Three Troy Merry Maker Clubs eventually evolved: Troy Senior Merry Makers, Troy Midi Merry Makers and Troy Mini Merry Makers.

The Cloverleaf Ag 4-H Club leaders were Charles Bangert, Howard Knecht, Joyce Schuerger, Mae Grapperhaus, Gayle Stahlhut, Betty Rinkel, and Cori Frerichs. Among the oldest clubs in Madison County, it was begun in the 1930s.

Other clubs during the 1930s included the Blackjack Pig Club, Blackjack Clothing Club, Formosa Clothing Club and the Pin Oak Pig Club. Other clubs that were in existence through the years were Liberty Hustlers – David Hall; Pin Oak Willing Workers – Mrs. Oliver Spitze; Pin Oak Ag Club – Virgil Bardelmeier; Troy Ag Club – Walter Mills, Evelyn Schmisseur; Progressive Farmers – Louis P. Dauderman; Acme 4-H – Carl and Clara Richter; Southern Stars – Glenn Gindler; Guys and Dolls 4-H; King's Kids – Kelly Wilhelm, Darlene Clark, and Joe and Pat Girolamo.

Cherokee Trail Riders

The Cherokee Trail Riders, a horse club, had a clubhouse along By-Pass 40 (Route 162 in 2002) at the west end of Troy. Horse shows were held on the property and club meetings were held in the clubhouse. The club existed during the 1950s. Fred Meier owned the property.

Eagle Scout Paul Jarvis

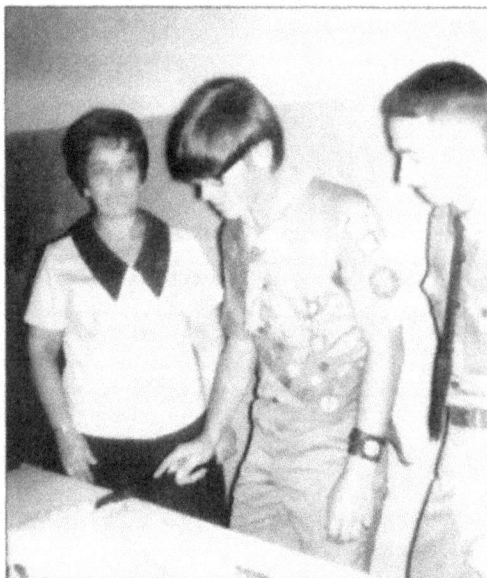

Eagle Scout Court of Honor, Boy Scouts Troop 38, Troy American Legion Hall, October 13, 1969. (l. to r.) Jane Jarvis, Paul Jarvis and Scoutmaster Gerald Vecez.

Friends of the Library

The friends group may be small in number, but it does big things. Started when the Tri-Township Library was housed in a store front on Market Street and then later in the former Mateer Funeral Home, the group began helping financially with a quilt stand at Homecoming. From that successful venture, they have grown to weekly quilting sessions and successful book sales held on the first Friday and third Saturday of every month on the library's lower level. The Friends were responsible for most of the finishing of the basement level, including a well-equipped kitchen. They have also continued their contribution to the mortgage payments, helping to considerably diminish the principal on the Mateer building and the new facility.

Nita Gulley served as the first president of the group. Joyce Hill now leads the Friends and has made the book sales an area wide event twice a month. Membership rolls have included Pauline Lewis, Martha Swillum, Mary Tonelli, Marie McConnell, Judy Madison, Pat Merz, and Ruth Stock among those that have worked with the group in

the past or currently do so. *Information provided by Pat Huck and Pat Merz.*

Friends of the Park Troy, Illinois Association

The Friends of the Park was begun June 9, 1998, when a group of friends got together to discuss what could be done to enhance the Tri-Township Park and improve the environment in all the parks in the Troy community.

The Friends of the Park was chartered in March 30, 2001. Fundraisers, including the dollar campaign, have been held at the Troy Homecoming and at other events at the Tri-Township Park. The first officers were Laura Wise, president; Mary Klitzing, vice president; Linda Mead, secretary and Esther Prater, treasurer.

Members in 2002 are Ellen Abbott, Mary Anne Barkley, Diana Bauer, Sherri Fickinger, Darrell Hampsten, Phyllis Hardesty, Gary Jarman, Sharon Jasper, Mary Klitzing, Lori Konsky, Doris Lading, Elizabeth LaKamp, Pam Bohnenstiehl, Kay Lanfersieck, Linda Mead, Margaret Merrell, Mary Kmetz, Carol Meyers, LeAnne Olmstead, Jan Phelan, Esther Prater, Annie Ratliff, Dawn Rowane, Louis Simpson, Jerri Tellmann, Lisa Wilcox, Stephanie Williams, Laura Wise and Kevin Woodring. Friends of the organization are Kelly Burke, Kara Kennedy and Cindy Mitchell. *Information submitted by Laura Wise.*

Girl Scouts

Girl Scout Troop in Troy, December 1955.

Jarvis Township Senior Citizens

The senior citizen organization in Troy was initiated in the late 1970s. First called the Troy Senior Citizen Club, it was incorporated in May of 1978. The group met in various places because they did not have a meeting place of their own. Supervisor Glenn Gindler and resident Pat Huck attended the Tri-Township Park District Board of Commissioners meeting in October of 1977. Pat Huck explained that the senior citizen organization was proposing the erection of a 50 X 150 foot building for which they were making application through Thompson Associates to the Madison County Community Development Program for funding in the amount of $185,000.

The building site selected, as an economy measure, was that of the Herman Hecht farmhouse on the park district property. The preliminary plan whereby the senior citizen organization, under the sponsorship of Jarvis Township, would apply for community development funding to erect a senior citizen center on the site of the Hecht property was approved by the park commissioners at that meeting. The Troy Senior Citizens Club met for about three years under that name. Then in December of 1980, the name was changed to Jarvis Township Senior Citizens. For a short time there were two senior groups, the Troy Senior Citizens and the Jarvis Township Senior Citizens. Grants were received from the Madison County Community Development Depart of Aging, the Troy Lions Club, Jarvis Township and the City of Troy. The center is now located where Hecht's house once stood. The building was dedicated on September 2, 1981.

Many changes came through the next few years as the seniors struggled to keep the center maintenance up. Jarvis Township assisted with funding to help the seniors on numerous occasions; however, it was still a hardship for the organization. In the mid 1990s, the Tri-Township Park district took over the maintenance of the building to further assist the seniors in their plight. The building was under the jurisdiction of the park commissioners and the park district handled rentals and maintenance. The seniors had full right to the building as in the past, but did not have the responsibility of its maintenance. The Troy Lions Club volunteered its services both financially and in labor. Lions Club volunteers assisted in redecorating the inside of the center.

Later, the name of the Jarvis Township Senior Center was changed and named the Russell Wiesemeyer Community Center in honor of Russell Wiesemeyer, who was the first Tri-Township Park District Board President. Irene Kotzman was the first director for the Troy Senior Citizens.

Kotzman remained the director until the two organizations divided. For a time, both organizations met on a monthly basis. Laura Shamhart was the first nutritional director at the center.

Sandy Johnson O'Mohundro then was hired as director. In 2000, when O'Mohundro retired, Sherry Brendel became the center director. Since the center's beginning, numerous fundraisers have been held: a weekly daytime bingo, a homecoming quilt raffle stand, bake sales, food stand at the

Kiwanis President Neil Goodwin, Ben Keefe and Ron Stephens.

Old Fashioned 4th of July Picnic in the park, and craft sales.

Kiwanis Club of Troy

The Kiwanis Club of Troy was chartered on August 6, 1991, with the assistance and guidance of Bob Sedlacek of the Kiwanis Club of Glen Carbon. The club met at Randy's Restaurant at 7a.m.on Tuesday mornings. The active organization supports youth and gives scholarships most years to the Triad High School senior worthy of the award. The club also sponsors Peanut Day Collection and the annual Halloween party for the area youngsters. At Christmas time, the club gives to a needy family. Currently, Matt Kotzmann is president.

Knights of Pythias Mentor Temple No. 104

The Knights of Pythias was a fraternal order in Troy during its early history. Information is scarce about the organization, but it has been found the meetings were held on the third floor of the building located on the southwest corner of the square (Main and Market Streets).

The Mentor Temple No. 104, the ladies auxiliary of the Knights of Pythias, was organized in Troy in the spring of 1902 by Mrs. Nancy Williams, deputy grand chief, of Salem. The new order started with 44 charter members and the following were its first officers: Mrs. M.A. Cartwright, P.C.T.; E.A. Hindmarch, M.E.C.; Mary

Russell Wiesemeyer Community Center, 1985.

Volunteers from Ministries Unlimited, The Pantry, June 2002. (l. to r.) Patricia Merz, Margaret Lee, Sue Tracy, Reverend Jack Walter, Lola Jameson, Judy Madison, Pat Cheney and Mabel Bradshaw.

Lewis, E.S.T.; Minnie Bain, E.J.T.; Elizabeth Samuel, M.of F.; Margaret Hughes M. of R.C.; Kate Harvey, M. of F.; Ida Sculley, P. of T.; and Mattie Mendenal, G. of O.T.

Ministries Unlimited

Ministries Unlimited began in 1978 with Moments for Meditations. It used that name until 1984, when it became Troy Ministries Unlimited. It was comprised of ministers from the Troy churches, who began a transient fund. Each person who applied for assistance was given $30 from the fund. Lucille Schmalz was one of the early proponents for MU, spending many hours for the cause. Other workers who had a very large part in its development included Billy and Sue Tracy, Margaret Lee and Pat Merz.

Activities and location of Troy Ministries Unlimited changed over the years. MU has sponsored the Ema Smith Poetry Contest, Christmas for the less fortunate, and given food vouchers to those in need.

After being located in various buildings, the Pantry soon found a permanent home. The construction of the building by volunteers with donated materials began and soon the new Pantry building at 310 Collinsville Road was completed and dedicated in January 2000. The Troy Lions Club played a large part in backing the donations and the volunteers for the project; many other community volunteers also helped.

Churches who are active in MU in 2002 are Abundant Blessings Church, Bethel Baptist Church, Troy United Methodist Church, Friedens United Church of Christ, St. Jerome Catholic Church, Troy Assembly of God, St. Paul's Lutheran Church, New Life Assembly of God, United Pentecostals of Troy, Troy Christian Church and Troy First Baptist Church. Christmas for the less fortunate is prepared at different churches that have space and delivered the Saturday morning before Christmas.

In 2002, Reverend Jack Walter of Abundant Blessings is president; Margaret Lee is secretary; and Sue Tracy is treasurer. The Pantry hours are Tuesday from 10 a.m. to 11a.m. and on Thursday from 1p.m. to 2:30 p.m. Recipients may contact any church for information. *Information was submitted by Sue Tracy.*

Odd Fellows and Rebekahs

Neilson Lodge No. 25 of the Independent Order of Odd Fellows (I.O.O.F.) jurisdiction of Illinois was instituted on February 29, 1847, and received its charter on July 14, 1847, only 28 years after Thomas Wildey instituted the Order of Odd Fellowship on the American Continent in 1819 in Baltimore. This charter was issued at the request of local residents J. K. Reiner, T. J. Brady, John S. Dewey, Thomas McDowell and Andrew Kimberlin. By 1848, the Lodge had grown rapidly and it was necessary to find a permanent hall; therefore, a building committee was appointed. A deed of the lot for the Odd Fellows building (at Center and South Main Streets) was obtained in 1848. Madison Jitton constructed the original part of the present building during the next spring and summer. The hall was dedicated in 1849.

Over the years, the Lodge rented its hall to a variety of groups including the following: the Masonic Lodge of Troy, the Masons, the Troy District Court of Supreme Court of Honor, the Modern Woodsmen of America, and the Methodist Sunday school. The first tenant of the store on the lower floor was J. M. Gates. At various times since then, the ground floor was leased out including: Charles Lyon for the sale of soda water and ice cream in 1872; The Royal Purple Temperance Association and Reading Room; the post office in 1893; the city hall; Bolman Mercantile Co.; Percy Division's store; the Miners' store; William Dunstan's store; Chevrolet Sales Agency; Gussie Roosh's Garage; Silas Prichett's Garage; Illinois Power and Light; Moderne Cleaners; Mrs. Polwort's Soda Fountain; Guennewig Furniture Store; Matsel's Dry Goods and Furniture; Western Auto (several different managements including Mr. Nottingham, Mr. Tschannen and Roy Halleman and others). In 2002 it is a paint and crafts store.

Santa's House

Santa's House was built by volunteers from the Troy Chamber of Commerce in the early 1990s at South Main and Center Streets. In the mid 1990s the house was moved to the Troy Plaza. Presently, it is located at "The Wedge."

Santa's House, 1990s

The "Hearts" Travel Club. Some of the women pictured here are (l. to r., front) Mrs. Schlimme, "Ma" Polwort, Mrs. Gerfen, Hulda Becker, Mrs. Wehmeier, Carrie Ottwein, Barbara Wiesemeyer, Mrs. Keck, Louise Gebauer (mother) and Louise Gebauer (daughter), Elizabeth Ottwein.

The "Hearts" Travel Club

The "Hearts" Travel Club was a group of women from Troy who got together for many years in the 1940s and 1950s to celebrate each other's birthdays. They played the game of Hearts and had a great time together.

Troy Chamber of Commerce

After failing to form a strong local chamber of commerce in 1980, a group of Troy business owners interested in assisting the growth of Troy decided to try to resurrect the chamber in May 1987. After several meetings, and with the funds from the first chamber, the reorganization occurred. With the help of the Collinsville Chamber of Commerce, a Troy chamber was formed by the end of the year. Several monthly meetings were held, and

Triad High School Future Farmers of America

The Triad High School Future Farmers of America (FFA), 1967. (l. to r.) Row 1: Ted Flath, Jerry Alvis, Paul Widicus, Bob Kruckeberg, Gary Mersinger, Rich Grodzicki and Chapter Sweetheart Mary Gwin. Row 2: Ralph Luna, Harold Frey, Don Miller, Don Becker, Kenny Frutiger, John Hess, James Gieseking, Robert Porter and Bill Huston. Row 3: L. Hess, J. Straube, J. Mick, D. Iberg, J. Haegle, A. Kapp, Bob Obernuefeman, Larry Helldoerfer and E. Klenke. Row 4: Tom Schmisseur, Ted Krauskopf, Larry Astrauskas, Paul Strong, Mike Moore, J. Black, J. Iberg and A. Keller. Row 5: Mike Pfeil, Irvin Kassing, M. Astrauskas, Mark Poletti, Don Mersinger, W. Lafferty, J. Ashford and S. Tabor. Row 6: Al Flath, Larry Kampwerth, Dale Stock, L. Hoenig, Dave Reinacher, Robert Voegele. Delmer D. Launius, Vocational Instructor, not pictured.

by early 1988 it was decided to publish a newsletter to the members who had joined. Bill Keeler was the first editor of the monthly newsletter.

It soon became obvious that help was needed to take care of the mounting paper work. Mrs. Lois Byrd was hired as a part-time (20 hours per week) executive director. The Troy Building and Homestead Savings and Loan provided office space inside the lobby at 100 W. Market Street for the chamber office.

Most of the early meetings were held at noon time with full membership present, but a few of the meetings were held at 7 a.m. in the morning. The first places for regular meetings were Randy's and St. Louis East Truck Plaza Restaurant, and a few were held at Tony's Restaurant in Maryville. Later meetings were held at Hardee's in Troy, and currently (in 2002) are being held at various businesses. "Business After Hours," begun as an every other month activity, now meets monthly.

A variety of community related projects have been sponsored by the chamber over the years. The first major project completed by the chamber was the sponsorship, and partial funding, of a feasibility study for a possible regional airport at Shafer's Metro East Airport in St. Jacob. Another project sponsored by the chamber was a Santa House, constructed and donated by Lanahan Construction Company in 1989. The chamber also took over the Oktoberfest.

Already started a few years prior by merchants at the Center and South Main Streets intersection, the chamber expanded it, and eventually had three locations for the Oktoberfest at the same time. Later, it was decided to keep it in one place or at least rotate the Oktoberfest between Troy Plaza and Old Town. In 1992, the chamber initiated and assisted in placing a "Welcome Sign" in front of Country Plaza on Route 162. The sign was a joint effort with several organizations contributing: the Troy Jaycees, Troy Knights of Columbus, Troy VFW, Troy American Legion, Woman's Club of Troy, and the Troy Lions Club. In April 2002, the City of Troy gave funding to take the Troy Main Street as a branch of the chamber.

The chamber office was moved to 112 W. Market Street into the Levo Building; and, later, it was moved to its current location at 535 Edwardsville Road. The following ladies were executive directors for the organization: Lois Byrd, Carol Pigg, Sally Koval, Jeannine James, Valerie Tindle, and, currently (in 2002), Dawn Mushill.

Troy Chamber of Commerce presidents were H. Ed Broderhausen, Kevin Roth, Dr. Kevin Fallis, Ray DeLuca, Tom Caraker, Bill Thompson, MaeDel Trione, Kathleen Bertels, Kerry Baugher, Dr. Tom Unger, Cathy Cassot, Neil Goodwin, Gerry Eckert, and, currently (in 2002), Jeff Maclin.

From a few interested business people, the chamber has grown to 200 members strong.

Troy Democrat Clubs

The Troy Democratic Women's Club was begun when Paul Simon ran for Illinonis Lieutenant Governor in the early 1970s. The club's main purpose was to get Paul Simon elected. Membership numbered about 35 at the beginning. The club flourished with just women members until the late 1980s. Club members met at the home of its members each month and sometimes at the Jaycee Hall at 112 South Main Street.

Political rallies were held at various places in Troy several times prior to elections and fund-raisers were held at the Troy Homecoming for a few years.

In 1987, when Simon ran for the U.S. Presidential nomination, the club raised $10,000 for his campaign at a political banquet held at the Highland K. of C. Hall. Jeanne Simon, Paul's wife, was the guest speaker and Madison County Board Member Alan J. Dunstan was Master of Ceremonies. About 100 attended the dinner.

Men were accepted into the club in 1988, and the name was changed to the Troy Democrat Club. The club continued until about 1994 and was disbanded due to the lack of members.

The Troy Democratic Men's Club was formed in the mid 1970s with about 15 members. Meetings were held at the Jaycee Hall located at 112 South Main Street. After about five years, this club disbanded, also.

Troy Historical Society

The Troy Historical Society was the brainstorm of Mae Grapperhaus, who had talked to several people who were in agreement that a society should be formed to preserve the area's rich heritage.

The first meeting was held at Randy's Restaurant February 18, 1993. Those present for that meeting were Mae Grapperhaus, Elizabeth Donati, Reba Mathis, Pat Huck, Patricia Merz, Claudia Carmichael, R.T. Bamber and Suzanne Phegley.

The next month, an organizational meeting was held at the old Tri-Township Library (former Mateer Funeral Home). The first order of business was to elect officers. They were Mae Grapperhaus, president; Walt Raisner, vice president; Suzanne Phegley, secretary; Reba Mathis, treasurer; Frank Ebl, Hilda Ebl, Pat Huck, Pat Merz and Bonnie Levo, trustees. The by-laws were established and the proper documents for a not-for-profit organization were sent to the state within the first few months.

The purpose or mission of the society is to collect and preserve historical information and artifacts about Troy and the surrounding area; to educate both youth and adults about Troy's rich history; to promote the historical value of the Troy community; to provide a museum for students and the public; and to present historical facts and photos through displays and talks at various public meetings, events and activities.

Troy Historical Society Officers, 2000. (l. to r.) Jerry Sizemore, president; Diana Shreve, secretary; Mae Grapperhaus; vice president; and Marilyn Sulc, treasurer.

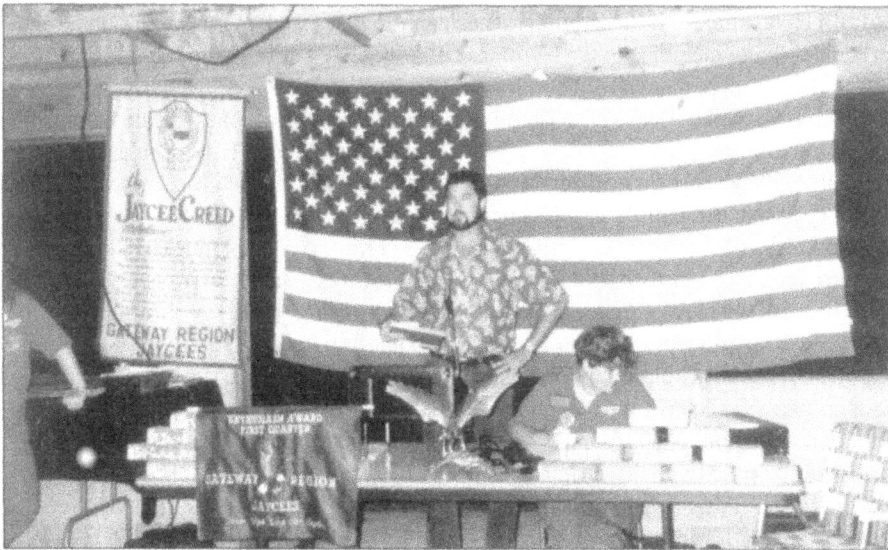

Troy Area Jaycees President Dave Fults, presides at the microphone at a Gateway Region Jaycees held at the Tri-Township Park in Troy in the late 1980s. Members of the Gateway Region included Troy, Aviston, St. Jacob, Highland, New Baden, and Bethalto.

The society has published two brochures about Troy; initiated a plaque program for historically significant Troy buildings; published a calendar of historic photos; given talks to school students and organizations in the community; displayed old photos in several places in Troy; secured a sign for the Troy City cemetery; maintained a room in the library for display in conjunction with the Troy Genealogical Society and published this history book about Troy. In addition, the society is in the process of reconstructing an 1860s log cabin to be used as a mini museum and has had all the newspapers since 1872 and many school attendance records and some church records microfilmed. The microfilm is on loan to the Tri-Township Library. Many other historical activities have been produced by the society.

The society currently meets on the third Wednesday of each month. Its annual banquet/meeting is held on the third Wednesday of June each year. Dues are $5 per year. *Submitted by Mae Grapperhaus, president.*

Troy Jaycees

The Troy Jaycees has a long and sporadic existence. The first Jaycee organization was formed in the late 1950s. The organization initiated the Alpine Festival, held on the square in the open space prior to the construction of Troy Homestead Savings and Loan. The streets were blocked off and a dance was held. All the Jaycees and their wives, Jaycettes, dressed in Swiss costume for the event. The Troy Jaycees were formed by the wives of the Jaycees and assisted the Jaycees in their projects.

In the mid 1960s, the organization sold Christmas trees on the same lot as a fundraiser and also manned the Skilo stand (while bingo was illegal at the time) at the Troy Homecoming.

The second floor of the Braner building at the corner of Kimberlin and East Market Street served as the Jaycee Hall in the 1960s. The back of the second floor was the Troy City Hall. Later, the building at the northeast corner of South Main and Charter Street served as the Jaycee Hall.

In the early years, ground was purchased on South Main to the south of the Troy City Cemetery for the purpose of erecting a Troy park; however, the park never materialized. Later, ground was purchased along Troy-O'Fallon Road on the south side of the first curve. Dave and Gladys Skeens purchased the ground from the Jaycees and built a home there.

Some of the early members included: Bob Holshouser, Paul Riebold, Norman Brendel, Dale Juehne, Swiss Kamm, Dave Skeens, Leonard "Butch" Amann, Ed Bernreuter, Ray Schindewolf, Jim Bash, Ron Schultze, Jim Grapperhaus, Harold Schwehr, Paul Ping, Ike

Chasteen, Dave Vincent, Terry Roderick and Fred McDowell.

Dances, hayrides and other activities were enjoyed by the group. They also attended state conventions and district rallies. The Jaycettes initiated a Valentine bunco that was held in the Jaycee Hall in the Braner Building. The event was held for several years.

In 1992, the Troy Area Jaycees, spearheaded by Dave Fults, joined a community effort to erect a new "Welcome to Troy" sign, west of Troy along Route 162 near the intersection of Route 162 and I-55/70.

Members who helped erect the sign were Dave Fults, Larry Sims, Steve Dawson, Duane Hughes, Keith Frey, Alan Heuiser and several of their children.

As time went on, the group was disbanded and has been resurrected several times.

Troy Knights of Columbus Council 9266

The Troy Knights of Columbus Council 9266 was organized on April 6, 1986. Members who organized the Troy council formerly were members of the Maryville Knights of Columbus. Forty transfers and 25 new members were included in charter membership.

After the St. John the Baptist Church closed in Blackjack, the Troy K.C.s pur-

The first Troy Knights of Columbus 9266 installation of officers at St. John Chapel. (l. to r.) Back: Mike Coulson, Al Novich, Andy Swillum, Wayne Brendel and Richard Smith. Middle row: Bob Sheroky, Stu Weider and Dan McAley. Front: Pete Schumacher, State K.C. representative; Art Gremaud; Art Capelle; Father Don Knuffman; Owen Brendel; Brad Meyer; and Elmer Bernhardt, State K.C. officer.

chased the church, hall and grounds in 1994 from the Springfield Diocese for $20,000. They currently hold their monthly meetings in the hall and have various prayers in the St. John Chapel.

A chicken dinner is held in the spring and fall. Proceeds from the dinner help to pay off the property and maintain it. The K.C.s began St. John the Baptist Country Festival in June of 1998. The festival is always held around St. John the Baptist Feast Day in June.

The K.C.'s helped to sponsor the Old Fashion 4th of July Picnic for a few years and helped at the annual Troy Homecoming. They serve the Mother's Day breakfast for the mothers and their families on Mother's Day and also assist with other functions of St. Jerome Catholic Church.

Men who have served as Grand Knight are Art Capelle (first), Brad Meyer, Owen Brendel, Maurice Tebbe, Doran Rakers, Ken Wiegmann, Randy Gall, Russ Sillery, Dennis Petry, Jim LeClerc and Dan Hellrung.

Troy Main Street

Troy Main Street was organized in 1999, after a group called "Take Pride in Troy" was formed. Deb Brendel spearheaded that group with a Christmas Lighting contest in 1998. Mayor Tom Caraker and several other key people in the community pursued the organization.

The first part time director was Chris Berg. The first president of the organization was Kathryn Murray; Bonnie Levo was vice president; Linda Dunstan, secretary;

and Bill Hyten, treasurer. In addition to the officers, original members of the board included, Mae Grapperhaus, Bill Thompson, Fred Parsons, Mike Yates, Deb Brendel, Eileen Lataille and Sally Dempsey. The Mercantile Bank (later Firstar) donated the office space in the bank's basement for Main Street's use.

Jeri Tellmann, who served as secretary of the board of directors, volunteered her services in the Main Street office. In November of 2001, she was hired on a part-time basis to be the executive director. Besides Berg and Tellmann, other executive directors were Sally Koval, Sally Dempsey and Tanya Richter. Although the organization was short lived, it had several accomplishments. In 2000, it purchased a stage coach, Troy's symbol. Many fundraisers and activities were held; among them were a downtown merchants' breakfast, Hoot'n' Holler, Troy Main Street stickers and banners, and serious efforts to complete the Troy Main Street Park on the wedge.

In the spring of 2002, the Troy Chamber of Commerce took the Troy Main Street group under its wing with money supplied from the City of Troy tourism funds, and the new groups was named Troy Downtown Revitalization Inc.

Troy Optimist's Club

The Troy Optimist's Club was organized in approximately 1985

and met at Randy's Restaurant on a regular basis. The Optimist's slogan was "Friend of Youth." In the early 1990s, the club disbanded, and the treasury was turned over to the City of Troy to be used for the Optimist's Park that was established on Meadow Drive.

The Troy Optimist's Club sold Christmas trees from a lot on Edwardsville Road as a fundraiser for about four years. The "Big Red" Bus, owned by Dave Hart, was used to carry fans to St. Louis Cardinals Football games and to keep workers warm. *Information from Don Sonnenberg.*

The Woman's Club of Troy

The Woman's Club of Troy had its beginning on Jan. 31, 1924, when 25 ladies of the community met at the Troy Public School and organized as a "Mother's Club," with being a mother as one of the requisites of membership. Officers were Mrs. A.F. Seligman, President; Mrs. C.E. (Nellie) Molden, Vice President; Mrs. L.P. Wetzel, Secretary; and Mrs. R.C. Ford, Treasurer. These ladies were the wives of locally prominent gentlemen, banker, doctor, school supt., and high school principal, respectively.

At the second meeting in Feb. 1924, members decided to join the 22nd District Federation. In 1927 the club affiliated with the Illinois Federation and with the General Federation of Women's Clubs. Changing its name to The Women's Club of Troy, the organization dropped the motherhood requirement.

Over the years, the club has endeavored to be deeply involved in community projects, particularly those concerning the youth. Some of their activities have included health exams for grade school children, books for the high school library, swimming lessons, many Red Cross blood drives, contributions to the local library which had its nucleus through efforts of the club many years ago, contributions to local Boy Scouts and Girl Scouts, as well as many others. They have also contributed to some national projects. Their funds are raised by bake sales, garage sales, and an annual Fashion Luncheon.

In 2000, the club withdrew from GFWC and is an independent club and continues its efforts as Troy's oldest service club, welcoming all Troy ladies as members who also wish to serve their community.

The Stage Coach, the wedge at West Clay Street and Edwardsville Road, April 28, 2000. (l. to r.) Standing, Mr. Thurnau; in windows, Jeri Tellmann, Monica Wright and Chris Berg; riding shotgun, Bob Ramsey and unknown.

Troy Genealogical Society

The Troy Genealogical Society was organized 25 February 1997 for the purpose of preserving family and local records for posterity, making more people aware of this need to preserve their family history, and making that information available to others.

The founding officers were Judith Little, President; Reba Mathis, Secretary; and Pat Huck, Treasurer. Other founding members included Kathy Buckman, Lois Davis, Eileen Edwards, Mae Grapperhaus, Gloria Mannz, Sharon McAley, Barb Reeves, Jim Richter, Susanne Richter, Peggy Riley, Michele Skabialka, Marilyn Sulc, Joy Upton and Ethel Wright.

One of the early goals of the society was to provide a computer for genealogy use at the library. In November 1999 a combination silent auction and chili supper was held to raise funds. With the success of this event, a computer, printer, and over a hundred CDs were purchased.

On 7 March 2000 the Tri-Township Public Library Board of Trustees voted to allow the Troy Genealogical Society and the Troy Historical Society to use the room originally designated for this purpose when the library was built in 1995. This room, located on the lower level, is equipped with many research aids. Along with the computer, which is connected to the internet, there is a printer, CDs, books, quarterlies, a microfiche reader and various other items. Many of the items were donated and a number of new books were purchased with a donation from the Aid Association for Lutherans.

Meetings are held the first Wednesday of each month at 7:00 p.m. at the library with many interesting and helpful programs presented. A quarterly newsletter has been published since August 1998.

– *Submitted and paid for by the Troy Genealogical Society.*

Troy Genealogical Society Charter Officers, 1997. (l. to r.) President Judy Little, Secretary Reba Mathis and Treasurer Pat Huck.

American Legion Auxiliary Post 708

The American Legion Auxiliary Post 708 was chartered in 1922. The charter members were Mrs. Myrtle Schmitt; Mrs. J.E. Gebauer; Mrs. Anna B. Gornet; Mrs. Cora L. Edwards; Mrs. Kathleen Bertorello; Mrs. John Gebauer, Jr.; Miss Vernetta Schmitt; Mrs. John Schoon; Mrs. Dan G. Liebler; Mrs. Sarah Duckett; Mrs. Louise Moore; and Miss Florence Thompson.

The first elected officers were Mrs. Myrtle Schmitt, president; Mrs. John Gebauer, Sr., vice president; Mrs. Anna B. Gornet, secretary; and Mrs. Fred Edwards, treasurer. Miss Kathleen Moore, Mrs. John Gebauer, Jr. and Mrs. Vernetta Schmitt served on the executive committee.

The Auxiliary had a large membership and actively supported the Legion. Meetings were held on the second floor of the Kroger store which later became Kelly's market. When the present post home was built in 1959, the Auxiliary furnished the new kitchen with appliances and dishes.

The current members of the Auxiliary are Estelle Bayer, Nancy Barsch, Sharon Briggs, Maxine Carson, Terry Cook, Margaret Dennis*, Aloma Edwards, Adeline Frederking, Frances Harber, Beverly Husted, Evelyn Jackson, Catherine Kiefer, Niccole Kiefer, Robin Kane, Margaret Lee, Terri L. Long, Lydia Miller, Lisa Muench, Joan Niebruegge, Mrs. Roland Porter*, Mary Sackett*, Charmion Semanisin, Glena Strom*, Jeri L. Tellmann and Sondra K. Wilshire. (* indicates recently deceased members)

– *Submitted by Nancy Barsch.*

(l. to r.) Front: Nikki Kiefer, president; Nancy Barsch, secretary; Estelle Bayer, treasurer; Maxine Carson, vice president. Back: Aloma Edwards, chaplain; Charmion Semanisin, Evelyn Jackson, sgt. at arms; and Margaret Lee.

American Legion Post 708

Troy's American Legion Post was chartered on February 8, 1921. Theodore Gebauer served as the first Commander. The charter members were Henry E. Thompson, Roy Lewis, James J. Moore, James R. Peterman, Bernard J. Moore, Edward J. Wise, Theodore J. Gebauer, August C. Beutel, Clarence E. Walden, Abe May, Robert Sliva, Duncan McCormick, William S. Schmidt, F. J. Michael, and Elmer Hoenig.

In 1957 the organization purchased the property at 103 Market Street. The present post home was built there and dedicated in 1959. Since that time it has been used for post, civic and private functions. Office space in the building was leased to Dr. Walter Zielonko since the building's opening.

As it has since its inception, Post 708 participates in many civic functions and continues to honor its purpose to foster and perpetuate Americanism and to preserve the memories and incidents of the Great Wars. The post's honor guard performs 21-gun salutes for funerals. Also for many years, the post gave each child who came to see Santa Claus a large bag of nuts, oranges and candy.

(Above) American Legion Post 708 Hall, 103 W. Market, 2002.

(Left) Adjutant Don Barsch and Commander Bill Long outside Legion Hall, Mid 1990s.

Present officers of the post are Commander John Wilshire, Senior Vice-Commander Bill Long, Junior Vice-Commander Alice Anderson, Adjutant Donald Barsch, Finance Officer Ben Harber, Service Officer Jesse Foley, Chaplain Dan Muench, Sergeant-At-Arms Dexter Kane, Judge Advocate Donald Niebruegge, Jr.

– Submitted by Donald Barsch. Paid for by the American Legion Post 708.

Troy American Legion Post 708 members, January 2002. (l. to r.) Front: Dale Kurtz, Bob Llewellyn, Delmer Launius and Arthur Wendler. Back: Alice Anderson, Dan Muench, Commander John Wilshire, Donald Barsch and Donald Niebruegge, Jr.

Past Commanders

Barsch, Donald	1990-91
Caruso, Tony	1957-58
Diepholz, William	1945-46
Druessel, Ray	1949-51
Dunstan, Bob	1951-52
Foley, Jesse	1997-99
Ford, Ray C.	1926-27
Frederking, Paul	1955-57, '59-60, '62-63, '64-65, '75-80
Gebauer, Theodore	1921
Hanks, Howard	1923-24, '38-39, '48-49
Hausmann, Dr. Charles	1925-26
Hogg, Robert	1981-89
Humphries, Thomas	1935-37
Isenberg, Glenn	1947-8
Jackson, Doug	1952-55, 63-64
Ketring, William	1940-42
Levo, Ed	1931-32, '43-44,
Long, William	1996-97
Lorenzen, William	1924-25
May, Abe	1921-22
McCormick, William	1944-45
McFarland, Gordon	1969-74
Niebruegge, Don, Sr.	1967-68
Ponder, Frank	1989-90
Ruckreigle, Marvin	1960-61
Schlimme, Walter	1939-40
Schrameck, Frank	1929-30, '37-38
Schrameck, Fred	1966-67
Schroeder, Vincent	1965-66, '74-75, '80-81
Scott, Donald	1946-47
Scott, William	1930-31, '33-34
Scully, Alvin	1934-35
Sliva, Robert	1942-43
Smithers, Roman	1961-62
Strom, Elmer	1958-59
Walden, Clarence	1922-23
Wilshire, John	1999-01
Wise, Ed	1928-29, '32-33

Troy VFW Post 976

(Left) Troy VFW Post 976, March 2002. (l. to r.) Front: Wilbur Jackson, Jack Graham, Corky Parton, Delmer Launius and Gene Rainbolt. Row 2: Ron Long, Alice Anderson, Sam Italiano, Rich Miller, Dean Donley, Bill McNamee, Rudy Wagner, Don Clark, Rick Sullivan, Bill Hellon, Jack Kraft, Mike Straube and Steve Goodried. Row 3: Jim Farmer, Commander Roger Alons, Bob Struckhoff, John Wilshire and Ron Goehlich. Not pictured: Marvin Wray, Jim Holshouser and Dale Gardner.

(Right) Troy VFW Post 976 Auxiliary, March 2002: Connie Donley, Christean Long, Sandra Howell, Betty Holshouser, Carolyn Lee, Sharon Wells, Susanne Miller, Rhonda Clark, Charlotte Rainbolt, Lea Long, Sandra Hanser, Maxine Scott and Sharon Patton.

The Troy VFW Post 976 was charted in October 1987 with 33 members. Homer Pettus was the first commander. The VFW (Veterans of Foreign Wars) is a service organization for veterans and widows and children of the veterans.

One of the first fund raising events by the organization was a booth in the 1988 Troy Homecoming. It was located in the vicinity of Bernhardt's Food World on West Market Street.

Before the Troy VFW Post 976 had a permanent home, the members met at various places. In 1994, the organization purchased the corner lot formerly occupied by the Troy Frozen Foods at Center and South Main Streets.

The members also a purchased a 21-foot long food trailer that they moved around town. One of the locations in which the trailer was used was on the Frosty Flavors lot at 306 Edwardsville Road. The trailer was also used for various functions in the city including the Fourth of July Picnic, Zip Code Day on June 22, 1994, and at other events. Later the trailer was moved to the new lot and fish fries were held there for about five years. At Christmas time, the lot was used to sell Christmas trees.

In 1999, the VFW purchased the building on West Market Street, formerly the laundromat and dry cleaning establishment.

– Paid for by the Troy V. F. W. Post 476.

(Left) VFW food trailer, Frosty Flavors lot, April 1994. (l. to r.) Rich Miller, Susanne Miller, Marvin Wray and Dale and Martha Gardner.

(Below) Dedication of the new Troy VFW Post 976 home on West Market Street, 1999.

Troy Lions Club

Troy Lions Club officers, restaurant at Route 40 and Route 4 in St. Jacob, 1991. (l. to r.) Tim Greenfield, Sam Elder, Dennis Alvis and Virgil "Pete" Gebhart.

Troy is very fortunate to have the Lions Club. This active and supportive group has consistently contributed money, time, work, and sponsorship to a variety of community and educational organizations. Without the Lions, many community activities would not have occurred, including Homecoming. The club was chartered in 1938 and ever since, it has given generously to the Troy community. Below is a brief account of a few of its many contributions, listed by decade.

In the 1930s: Arthur Hartman was the first president. The club supported the town library and the Boy Scouts; took in $92.95 at Homecoming stand; bought first park site at Market and Main; put up road signs and built a bandstand.

In the 1940s: It co-sponsored the Homecoming; began effort to pave By-pass 40; began caring for city cemetery; sent *Troy Call* to all area servicemen; gave to USO, war relief, war bonds and Red Cross; purchased lot for Troy theatre for $825; formed Troy Civic Improvement Company (TCIC); gave away two cars at Homecoming; financed *Troy Tribune* and Troy Security Bank (136 stockholders, mostly Lions members); awarded theatre contract for $36,497.70; painted street parking lanes; and donated to city to turn on street lights every night.

In the 1950s: The Lions transferred $5,500 to TCIC; discussed discontinuing Homecoming – no action taken; transferred $15,300 to TCIC; purchased and installed 200 street signs; leased park area to Troy Security Bank; sponsored Bob Turley Day; donated $100 to each of city's churches; led United Fund; donated $1,030 to city; installed new theatre heating system; gave new Corvette away at Homecoming; celebrated 20th anniversary; and bought 10 acres for an industrial park site.

In the 1960s: The club sold the Lions Theatre; acquired President Harry S. Truman for homecoming parade; opened library; donated $1,000 for high school band uniforms; purchased Christmas decorations; purchased city mosquito spray equipment; sponsored St. Jacob Lions Club; purchased acreage from railroad right-of-way; purchased 44 acres for park (individual members signed $35,000 loan note); donated $20,000 to TCIC; granted $2,500 to park district for legal fees; sponsored high school athletic banquet; celebrated 30th anniversary; held auction and purchased park picnic tables and barbecue pits.

In the 1970s: The club donated 10 trees to park and $160 to library; donated park benches and $2,500 to Anderson Hospital; put up park shelters; donated $14,400 to park pool fund; supplied water service to Industrial Park and built road to it; donated $6,000 for park shelters; donated to

(Below) Troy Lions Club members, photo booth at the Troy Homecoming, 1950s. (l. to r.) Paul Sims, Rollie Moore, Howard Carson and Oscar Gindler.

Troy Lions Club 15th Anniversary in the St. Paul Lutheran Hall, 1953. (l. to r.) Seated: Dr. Charles E. Miller, William S. Schmitt, Dan G. Liebler, James L. Watson, John H. Schoon, Rollie Moore, J. Wheeler Davis, Oscar E. Gindler, Harry Taake. Standing: Harold A. Schmidt, John Kelly Jr., Oscar J. Ottwein, Harry Cooper, Clarence E. Frey, Earl L. Schmidt, Arthur W. Hartman, George Krite (Collinsville guest) and L.E. Morris (Collinsville guest).

Charter members of the Troy Lions Club at the 40th anniversary of its charter, October 18, 1978. (l. to r.) Seated: Oscar Ottwein, Harold Schmidt, Earl Schmidt, Wheeler Davis. Standing: Oscar Gindler, L.E. Morris (District Governor), George Krite (1938 president of Collinsville Lions) and Joe Foucek.

Scouts; donated $2,978 to pool fund; $15,000 to park for tennis courts; gave 1,000 trees to park and funds to library; boasted 102 club members; donated $1,678 to pool fund; donated to handicapped Lions Camp; gave $2,500 to soccer club; purchased new Christmas decorations; pledged $25,000 to Illinois Lions Eye Research Center; donated $21,500 to Troy Senior Citizens Center; donated $15,000 for Tri-Township Park tennis courts and main baseball field lighting; donated for Troy Khoury League soccer fields; Triad High School band uniforms; gave money for tone pagers for Troy Fire Department and six walkie-talkies for City of Troy; two buses for Triad students to Lions International Convention; donated for child's eye surgery; and for eye glasses to school student.

In the 1980s: The club donated to Tri-Township Library; purchased 2 CPR dummies for the high school and community; donated to Legion baseball team; purchased park land for $35,350 and spent $6,500 for Boy Scout Troop #38's bus; sponsored 2 Khoury League teams; donated $1,000 to Junior American Legion League and Boy Scouts camp; donated $1,500 to Jarvis Township Senior Citizens Center; purchased Girl Scouts flags; donated to Troy Khoury League; gave $500 to Ministries Unlimited; re-finished Triad wrestling mats.

In the 1990s: The Lions donated $500 Senior Citizens Center for driveway sealing; gave $300 for lights on flag pole at Tri-Township Park; sent $100 to Eye Research Institute; donated $25 to Leader Dogs; gave $500 for Tri-Township Park bridge; spent $400 on bullet-proof vests for Police Auxilary; donated $100 to Friends of the Library; sent $400 to the Lady Knight Spikers; donated $800 to Triad Middle School "Odssey of the Minds World Finalist;" spent $1,000 on Triad High School Volleyball Nets & Standards; gave $2000 for 4 Scholarships; provided glasses and examinations for 10 people. The Lions gave $1,000 for 4th of July celebration; gave $200 for Christmas in April; gave $50 to Madison County Humane Society; donated $1,000 for new tents for Troop 38; gave $600 to Jarvis Senior Citizens TV/VCR; gave $100 to Lions of Illinois Foundation; donated $184 for McCray-Dewey playground equipment; gave $200 to family after home fire; $350 Triad After Prom; $2,000 for 4 Lions Club Scholarships; and provided glasses and examinations for 2 people; constructed Ministries Unlimited building and donated $1,000 to its Building Fund; gave $200 to Triad Exchange Student; $1,112 to American Diabetes Association; donated $1,500 for Veterans Memorial in Tri-Township Park; donated money for "News in the Classroom" to Triad Students; gave $1,000 for Triad Athletic Booster Club "paver"; gave $5,500 to a child with cancer from a fundraiser; spent $300 on a wheelchair for child; and donated $2,000 to Troy Historical Society for Troy history book.

The Lions do not confine their generosity to just one donation to a group during a decade, but supported various groups continually. For examples, over the years they have given over $16,000 in scholarships, hundreds to the After Prom party, hundreds for eye exams and glasses, and thousands to the Senior Center and the park. Their motto, " We serve" is quite evident in every activity. They do, indeed, serve the Troy community.

– Information and photos submitted by Wib Klueter, Audrey Deeren, Carolyn Golfin, Arthur Hartman and current Troy Lions Club members. Paid for by the Troy Lions Club.

TROY LIONS CLUB PRESIDENTS

1938	Arthur Hartman	1969	Carl Taake
1939	Dr. C. E. Miller	1970	Robert Converse
1940	John Kelly, Jr.	1971	Paul Levo
1941	Oscar Ottwein	1972	Owen Brendel
1942	James L. Watson	1973	Virgil Gebhart
1943	Earl Schmidt	1974	Jack Rees
1944	William Schmitt	1975	Robert Purcell
1945	Oscar Gindler	1976	Gene Thomas
1946	Harry Taake	1977	Robert Cadagin
1947	Tom Taylor	1978	Terry Taake
1948	Clarence Frey	1979	Ray Bean
1949	R. R. Moore	1980	James D. Laughlin
1950	Harold Schmidt	1981	Rev. Erwin J. Kolb
1951	John Schoon	1982	William Shaffer
1952	Leeds Watson	1983	Terry Adelhardt
1953	C. A. Henning	1984	Stewart Savage
1954	Dr. H. H. Glenn	1985	Duane Zobrist
1955	Arthur Wendler	1986	David Peverly
1956	Wilbur "Mick" Wyatt	1987	John Thomas
1957	Jewel Edwards	1988	Tim Greenfield
1958	G. A. Shaffer	1990	Don Hamilton
1959	Walter Kurtz	1991	Dennis Alvis
1960	William Pitt	1993	Sam Elder
1961	Jimmie Lybarger	1994	Robert Converse
1962	William Freeman	1996	Gary Jarman
1963	Wilmer Carson	1997	Granville Templeton
1964	Forrest Piper	1998	Todd Nihiser
1965	Raymond Druessel	1999	Sam Elder
1966	Les Adelhardt	2000	Roger Tegmeyer
1967	Russ Wiesemeyer	2002	John Nehrt
1968	James Smith		

Sack Races, July 4, 1999. The sack races were among the sporting events provided by the Troy Lions Club at the Old Fashioned Fourth of July held at the Tri-Township Park each year. Here are a group of younger contestants trying their skill at the race as the adults cheer them on. Russell Wiesemeyer Community Center, home of the Jarvis Township Senior Citizens organization, is in the background.

Labor Day picnic, 1911

Memorials

Dunstan family, circa 1962. (l. to r.) Back: Robert Dunstan, Dorothy (Dunstan) Folkerts, Audrey (Dunstan) Vesci, Billie Dunstan. Front: Grandpa Dunstan, Grandma (Rood) Dunstan.

Mersinger family, circa 1950s. (l. to r.) Back: Ed, Emil and Bena Mersinger. Front: Rich and Joann Mersinger.

Rood family, circa early 1900s. (l. to r.) Clinton Esau Rood, Hilon Rood (on Clinton's lap), Ancil Rood, Rena (Rood) Dunstan, Adella (Sinclair) Rood, Winnie Rood (on Adella's lap).

Troy, Illinois Area
History and Families

In Loving Memory of
Albert A. Arth

Below: Albert A. Arth, First Communion

Albert A. Arth (1913-1985)

Albert A. and Bernice E. Arth, circa 1970s

(Left) Albert Arth, son-in-law Vincent Kauhl, and his son Barry, age 16, in 1982 after pheasant hunting.

(Above) Four Generations – Anton Arth, great grandfather; Lewis G. Arth, grandfather; Albert A. Arth, father, Sylvia E., daughter, March 1942, at the Anton Arth farm, which later became the Ray Poletti Farm.

Albert and Bernice Arth Farm, aerial view, 1969

David F. Mallett
In Memoriam

My father, Dave Mallett, was born May 13, 1910, and grew up in East St. Louis. He started out as a journeyman electrician and an automobile mechanic. During the Depression, he and his wife Mamie tried various things: they owned a small hardware store; and after his election as Clerk of the Appellate Court, 5th District, they lived at the Court House in Mount Vernon for several years. Starting from zero, they created a series of automobile dealerships culminating in *Collinsville Ford* and *Dave Mallett Ford* in Collinsville.

Dad made a long sojourn into politics. In 1952 he was the Democratic candidate for State Treasurer and in 1956 ran again for Secretary of State. Both times were presidential election years with Adlai Stevenson heading the ticket. Both were Eisenhower landslides, and Dad lost the Secretary of State race by a few precincts in Cook County (whose vote counts were held out for four days after the election).

On the left, Estes Kefauver and Adlai Stephenson. On the right, Dave Mallett. (1956)

He had been so close to victory, but this race gave him a glimpse at a level of political fraud and corruption that was so disheartening he left state politics for good.

He was a 32nd degree Mason, a Jester and a Shriner. He was Potentate of Ainad Temple in 1961. As a child, I especially remember the Shrine Parades, Circuses and Rodeos.

He was involved in the building of the new *Shriners Hospital* in St. Louis and was founder and first president of the *Bank of Edgemont*.

Dad dedicated the last 25 years of his life to the creation of *Red Fox Acres*, our farm in Troy. There, he renovated a 100-year-old farm house, cleared acreage and farmed corn, beans, wheat and hay. He dug ponds and fenced pastures in the woody areas for horses and Black Angus cattle.

Some of my parents' best memories may well be of hillsides full of wild violets, rope swings and grandchildren, barbecues and starry nights at Red Fox Acres.

Dad, we miss you... .

David and Mamie Mallett

Annette Mallett Haines

In Loving Memory of
Oscar and Louise Mersinger

Oscar and Louise in courting days. Taken in St. Louis' Forest Park, early 1930s.

Their wedding day, January 30, 1937.

Oscar as a baby, about one year old.

Oscar, Louise and daughter, Mae, in 1977.

The couple farmed their entire married life on a farm on West Kirsch Road, southwest of Troy. *Submitted by their daughter, Mae.*

(Above) Their new home that they built on the farm.

(Above) View of farmhouse from top of silo, 1954.

Aerial view of their farm, 1970s.

The barn they built in 1937. It was destroyed by fire in 1954. Oscar by wagon at haymaking time.

Oscar Mersinger and new 1951 farm truck.

In Memory of
William S. and Louise Schmitt

William S. and Louise Schmitt

In Memoriam
John Somraty III and
Gertrude Estelle Powers

Troy Radio and Television Service, Telephone Exchange #2851, was established in June 1952 by John Somraty. A new sign advertising the Troy business was placed on the family truck. The repair service location was in the Old Central Hotel on Route 162 near the Main Street intersection. There was a pub or tavern a few doors from the business at the corner of Main Street and Route 162. The hotel was remodeled and eventually removed. As late as 1952, the old hitching posts could be found outside the building.

In early 1952, John Somraty completed training in a radio and television repair course, and received certification. The repair shop existed approximately twelve plus months. John Somraty had health complications, one of which continued to plague him, a childhood leg injury.

His two oldest daughters, Rose Marie Somraty and Mary Jane Somraty, age four-

John Somraty III

(Left) Mary Jane Somraty

(Above) Helen June Somraty shows off a new sign advertising the Troy business placed on the family truck.

(Left) Rose Marie Somraty

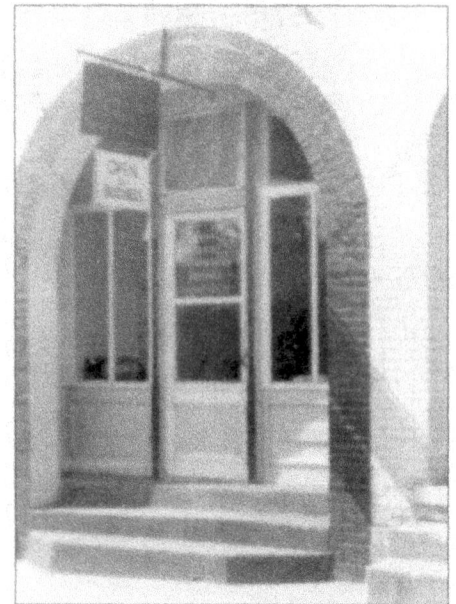

teen and twelve respectively, were given the responsibility of running the office. His younger daughter, Helen June Somraty (standing in front of sign), who was ten years of age, accompanied the older girls occasionally. His daughters worked in the summer and weekends during the school year.

The two older sisters met Paul Simon, who had purchased the local Troy newspaper. Paul Simon's newspaper office was located past the corner drug store on Route 162, and before Hickory Street. Rose and Mary would visit Paul Simon at his newspaper office. He was always patient with the two curious, teen sisters, who asked a lot of questions. The sisters admired the confidence and boldness of his beliefs and ideology. They were intrigued by his tenacity and aspirations to better society, as well as his intellectual capacity and willingness to share knowledge and ideas. The result is that Paul Simon, unknowingly, influenced and contributed to their evolving vision of their social and political world.

Although Troy Radio and Television Service was in business for a short time period, the positive influences by the Troy community, the office experiences and the technical exposure resulted in profound lasting effects on the Somraty family. The entire family had an opportunity to experience at some level, the technical and electronic aspects of the business through observations and absorption. The children became familiar with the TV supplies and sophisticated electronic equipment for that time period. A small eight inch television, that their father repaired, provided the children with an expanded vision to the outside world, which few rural families had available then.

These unique experiences influenced the Somraty children in ways that they could not imagine at the time. A ripple effect was felt by John and Gertrude Somraty's family. This effect produced children, grandchildren and great grandchildren with engineering degrees, science and education degrees, computer science careers, business careers, medical careers, military careers, business owners, and educational careers involving both national and international services.

Thanks to Mary Powers Somraty Aegerter. Submitted by Rose Powers Somraty Yarbrough (see biography).

Troy TV Service, 1952.

In Loving Memory of
Russell Wiesemeyer
Troy's Long-Time Civic Leader and
First Tri-Township Park District President

Russell Wiesemeyer, born June 21, 1920, and died April 26, 2000, was a pillar of the community and a true gentleman. The following is a portion of the story written in the *Times-Tribune* following his death:

A true Troy Trojan, he will be missed immensely by his family, his many friends and all whose lives he touched. Wiesemeyer died in his sleep following a long illness, but his memory will go on forever in Troy.

He was a dedicated civic leader; a true and honest businessman and a loving husband and father who didn't know a stranger. He was a Troy legend.

Wiesemeyer's determination and strong dedication was what it took to accomplish the major milestones in this community through the years.

He was one of the founding fathers of the Tri-Township Park District and served as the district's first president from 1967 until his retirement in 1996.

Tri-Township Park Director Tim Greenfield, who was formerly on the park board said Wiesemeyer was like a father to him.

"Russ was the one who talked me into being on the park board," Greenfield said. "He was like a Dad to me. He treated me like one of his sons. Whenever I had something to talk over with

him, he always gave me good advice. He always looked to improving the park."

Remembering him fondly, Greenfield added, "There was only one Russ Wiesemeyer."

Russell Wiesemeyer

Russ loved Troy and it showed in everything he did. When Russ said he was for something or he was going to do something, you could bet he would come through.

A member of the Jarvis Township Board of Trustees since 1972 until his

retirement in 2000, Russ had the community at heart in all he did.

Supervisor Alan J. Dunstan said this week he is shocked upon hearing about Wiesemeyer's death.

"When I had problems, I'd ask him his opinion. He always gave good advice," Dunstan said.

Longtime Jarvis Highway Commissioner, Jim Grapperhaus, who served with him as a township official, said, "I never heard a bad word against him or about him."

Reverend Steve Janoski, pastor of St. Jerome's Church knew him only a short four years.

"Not once did he complain about his health problems," Janoski said during the funeral homily, adding, "I have never heard one wrong word about him."

Troy Mayor Tom Caraker said, "The residents of Troy have lost a true friend, humanitarian, a kind and gentle person who donated his entire life to the betterment of the community. Mr. Wiesemeyer will never be forgotten; his traditions will be carried forward."

Russ Wiesemeyer was married to the former Stella Howard. They were the parents of six children: Gary, Linda, Patty, Jim, Rick and Randy.

He was a WWII Veteran, a member of the Troy Lions Club, St. Jerome Catholic Church and many other civic organizations.

"We miss you, Dad," your son, Jim.

In Loving Memory of
Troy Friends
Who Have Gone to Eternal Life
January through June 30, 2002

Erwin Loyet (1912-2002), Longtime St. John the Baptist Cemetery Sexton (Over 20 years)
Raymond Druessel (1917-2002), Retired Troy Volunteer Fireman
Leroy Z. Bugger (1929 –2002), Longtime Blackjack resident
Josephine "Josie" (Sartoris) Kueker (1921-2002)
Diana (Bugger) Messina (1958-2002)
Wendell "Jean" Grimaud (1929-2002), Founder of Moccasins and Longtime Boy Scout Supporter
Marian (Rakers) Montroy (1948-2002), Wife of Gerald Montroy
Zdenka "Zea" (Fiala) Foucek (1911-2002), Longtime owner/operator of Sunnyside Nursery
Ronald D. Schultze (1934-2002), Former Troy Volunteer Fire Chief/Troy Ward One Alderman
Stella (Howard) Wiesemeyer (1920-2002), Widow of Russell Wiesemeyer
Faye (Kimberlin) Gibbs (1934-2002), Owner/Operator of Moonlight Tavern
Alma (Capelle) Rood (1921-2002), Widow of James Rood
W. "Jerry" Sizemore (1927-2002), Troy Historical Society Member/Past President
Roy G. Halleman (1931-2002), Longtime Troy businessman
Darren Curnayn (1974-2002)
Lorine (Niehaus) Bugger Tonnies (1923-2002)
Dolores "Dee" (Thiess) Loomis (1921-2002)

Submitted by Jim and Mae Grapperhaus

Donk Brothers Coal Mine

Troy's Own Doughboy

War heroes have come from many small towns, but not every small town can claim "The Outstanding American Doughboy of World War I." Troy can. He was Walter E. Gaultney, who joined the army in 1917.

In a short time he became Corporal Gaultney, 11th Infantry, 5th Division in the American Expeditionary Forces located in Germany. He was wounded in action; and after recovery, he insisted on returning to the front lines with his "buddies." One of his proudest moments was marching in the parade as a personal Honor Guard to General John J. Pershing under the Arch of Triumph in Paris the day the Armistice was signed to end World War I. After the Armistice was signed, he also marched in the Ticker Tape parade in New York. This was a thrill for him as was the parade in Washington, D.C. Both times he walked along side his commander General John J. Pershing. He was selected by Gen. Pershing and the war department as "The Outstanding American Doughboy of WW I." On his retirement from the railroad, Congressman Melvin E. Price invited him to Washington, D.C. to see his portrait that hangs in the Smithsonian Institute entitled "Outstanding American Doughboy of World War I." It is also noted in the official Congressional Record of Honors.

Walter was chosen for a series of paintings to be done by Joseph C. Chase,

Walter E. Gaultney, Corporal U. S. Army, World War I

the artist commissioned by the War Department for a pictorial record of WWI. His picture is in the following books: *History of the World War*, volume 5 by Frank H. Simmons; *Deeds, Heroism and Bravery* by Rupert Hughes and Elwyn Barron in 1920; *The Doughboys* by Laverne Stallings, published by Harper and Row in 1963. Here the caption reads, "He was selected by his commander as an example of his finest type of soldier, being alert, ingenious, speedy and heedless of personal danger." Corporal Gaultney's picture was featured on the front page of *Leslies Magazine*, March 29, 1919, and the *Saturday Evening Post* in 1928.

War of 1812

Benjamin Hagler

Benjamin Hagler, veteran of the War of 1812, is buried in Gilead Cemetery. He donated the ground on the which the cemetery is located.

World War I

(Above) Paul Capelle, World War I, U.S. Army. Military funeral in July 1947 in St. Jerome Catholic Cemetery. Father George Hobbs and Father Joseph V. Dineen officiated.

(Left) Robert Sliva, World War I

Martin Hecht, Pvt., World War I, El Paso, TX, 1917

Bill Diepholz, World War I

Nemnichs in War. On the left: Joseph Nemnich, Jr., World War II, 1943-1946. On the right: Joseph Nemnich, Sr., World War I, May 1918.

Charles Guy Harris, World War I, U.S. Army

Rollie Porter, World War I

Leo Petry, World War I, Company cook

World War I

(Left) Peter Mersinger, World War I, France, 1918-1919

Edward T. Levo, World War I, 38th Div. Regiment Hdqtrs./G.

On the right, Joseph Gerling, World War I, May 20, 1918, near Prospect, KY.

World War II

Victor Diepholz, World War II, 1940s

Delmer Launius, U.S. Air Force Pilot, World War II, 1942

Elmer C. Levo, U.S. Army, World War II. Killed in action, Normandy, Vire, France, August 8, 1944. Buried in St. James Cemetery, near Rennes, France.

Arthur Wendler, left, kneeling, World War II, U.S. Air Force B-24 Pilot, 1944

World War II

Gilbert H. Mersinger, U.S. Navy Fireman First Class, World War II. Awarded the Presidential Unit Citation Star aboard the USS Lexington *for heroism displayed in action against enemy Japanese forces in the air, ashore and afloat in the Pacific war area.*

Veronica Mersinger, World War II, U.S. WACS, 1942

William "Billie" Romeo, U.S. Navy, World War II

Gene Sury, World War II, Machinist Mate 1 C-Seabees, 1942

Earl "Foots" Kueker, World War II. Killed in service, 1943.

Andy Semanisin, World War II, South Pacific, 1944

World War II

Korean War

(l. to r.) Walter and Kenneth Lyons, U.S. Navy, World War II.

(Below) Joe Potter, World War II, U.S. Army, 1944

Merle Hansel, Korean Conflict, Military Police, 1953

(l. to r.) Gene and Kenneth Lyons, U.S. Navy, World War II.

Vietnam War

Kenneth A. Gaultney, U.S. Army Sgt., Vietnam War

Gary Mersinger, Vietnam War

Robert A. Semanisin, Vietnam War, U.S. Army, 1967-1969

Todd Mersinger, U.S. Army Pvt. 2nd, serving in Germany, 2002

Honor Roll

The Honor Roll was constructed in the early 1940s and was located in the Lions Park once on Market Street. It stood 12 feet high and stretched 23 feet wide, resembling a monument.

The substantial frame construction was illuminated at night by neon lighting, controlled by a time clock. The memorial was designed by Charles Reed of Troy and constructed by Wilbur Kurtz of Collinsville for $500. The names of men and women who had served in the various branches of the armed services during World War II were inscribed, including the names, written in gold (denoted by asterisks in this list), of those who had died in the service of their country.

Later, when the bank expanded its driveway and the sign needed repair, it was quietly torn down.

Revolutionary War

Baker, Absolom
Bridges, George
Hagler, Benjamin
Hall, William
Smart, Laban

Black Hawk War

Whiteside, Michael

Mexican War

Henderson, James A.
McDowell, Thomas
Seybold, James, M.
Mize, William
Gerstenecker, Gottlieb
O'Brian, Margaret
Loyd, Joseph

Civil War

Appel, G.M.
Armstrong, Silas A.
Baird, John
Baird, John L.
Baird, William
Baird, William H.
Baker, Samuel
Barber, Norman C.
Barnes, Stephen G.
Barnsback, Julius A.
Barnsback, Julius A. Jr.
Bartly, James
Bass, John
Becker, George
Blake, Charles W.
Boes, Anthony
Boling, Silas
Briscoe, James B.
Brown, Charles W.
Brown, William L.
Burk, Elias Sr.
Buttiker, Louis
Canna, John

Carrol, Jeremiah
Comstock, Elihu B.
Cornman, Ferdinand A.
Cornman, Horatio
Cornman, Horatio O.
Cornman, Monroe A.
Cox, Nelson
Crisley, Robert
Crowson, W.M.
Davis, John C.
Dawson, Thomas W.
Deck, Asbury M.
Deck, John W.
Devlin, John
Dewey, Dr. J.S.
Dewey, Dr. John S.
Dogal, Joseph
Dolan, Patrick
Dollinger, Ignatz
Donaho, William
Donaho, William T.
Dooley, Joseph
Droll, Felix Sr.
Dunlap, John
Eller, William

Ensminger, John
Evans, Thomas
Farmer, Lemuel J.
Farmer, William
Farrer, John W.
Fohne, Joseph
Frederick, Anthony
Freeland, John
Fuller, Heaston
Garnet, George
Gaskill, Joshua O.
Gates, George W.C.
Geers, William L.
Gerstenecker, Gottlieb
Gerstenecker, William
Gilham, Orsemus
Gillett, Albert P.
Glenn, John M.
Gornet, George
Granger, Joseph L.
Grimm, Joseph
Growson, William M.
Hall, W.M.
Hall, Alfred
Hammock, Andrew J.

Harker, Hiram
Harrison, David
Hasting, William G.
Hat, Edward M.
Hawley, Francis S.
Hawley, Francis S.
Hawley, John
Hays, Oliver
Hays, William P.
Heddergott, Frank
Helm, S.W.
Henderson, James A.
Hewett, Walter
Hocher, Joseph P.
Holcomb, Mahlon D.
Holley, John
Hollis, John
Holloway, Marshall
Jacobs, R.E.
Jaka, John
Jarvis, Sidney B
Jarvis, William W.
Johionson, David
Johionson, James N.
Johnson, James

Johnson, Joseph	Lytle, Francis W.	Paul, William	Snodgrass, Edward	Woodbury, George
Johnson, Sidney L.	Mantle, Joseph	Paul, Oliver	Snodgrass, Kilburn M.	Woodbury, George
Jones, John	Martin, John	Perry, Ebenezer	Stevenson, Joseph P.	Young, Ephram
Karnes, Harvey C.	Mc Clanahan, James	Perygyn, Benjamin	Stewart, Joseph W	Younghaus, Henry
Keegon, Edward R.	Mc Farland, Jesse	Pfeiffer, Frank	Stice, George	Zanders, Edward
Kennedy, James H.	Mc Kinley, George S.	Pline, Leonard	Stice, George W	Zanders, Frederick W.
Kensey, Levi	Mc Kittric, Francis	Porter, Joseph	Swain, Robert B	Zanders, S. W.
Kersey, Harrison C.	Mc Lanahan, George C.	Prentice, John E.	Swain, Robert R.	Zeis, Henry
Keyser, Ambrose	Mc Mahan, Hugh	Price, Robert L.	Swartz, Frederick	Zolph, Simon
Kimberlin, Charles B.	Mc Mahan, Martin L.	Purviance, William H	Taughney, James	
Kincaid, W.S.	Mc Neill, James T.	Purviance, Joseph H.	Tegtmeyer, Fred	
King, Andrew J.	McDowell, Thomas	Radon, Henry	Thomas, James B	## Spanish American War
King, Martin B.	McLanahan, James	Reed, John	Throp, Bernard	
Klein, Andreas	Meier, John H.	Rees, Henry	Tilley, Rev. Jordan	
Kluge, Augustus	Miller, Andrew	Richter, August	Tollhurst, David	Bohland, Fred
Kruger, Frederick	Miller, Henry	Riggin, Jackson	Tompkins, John T.	Bohnenstiehl, John A.
Kyle, David	Miller, John H.	Riggin, William H	Voelker, Adam	Bohnenstiehl, John D.
Lamb, James	Mills, Albert	Ritcher, Augustus	Vohringer, George	Boston, James Jr.
Lamborn, William	Mills, Albert	Roberts, John	Warner, George	Young, David A.
Land, John	Moore, George W.	Roberts, Peter S.	Watson, Samuel	
Lang, James	Morris, John	Rollins, David	Watt, Harvey T.	
Laturno, Joseph M.	Morris, Peter	Sanders, Frederick W.	Webster, Horace	## World War I
Leasure, Chesner	Morrison, Lorenzo	Sauer, Henry	West, Charles	
Leasure, John	Muehlenburg, Henry	Schall, John	Whalen, John	Ackerman, Carl W.
Leonard, Alvin	O' Bryan, Daniel	Seaver, Theodore J.	Whitlock, Robert W.	Arth, Fred M
Lewis, C.C.	Padon, Henry H.	Seitz, Lawrence	Wilcox, William	Arth, Walter
Lewis, Columbus C.	Padon, James	Seybold, Samuel	Williams, David	Bast, Roy H
Linderman, Abraham	Padon, Judson	Shornick, Samuel	Willis, George	Belcher, William R.
Lloyd Joseph	Padon, William	Skelton, John S.	Willoughby, John H. B	Blakey, Eugene E.
Loyd, Joseph	Palmer, Frederick	Smith, Jacob	Willson, John	Bohland, Frederick
Lytle, Francis W.	Parker, William	Smith, Pliny	Womack, William	Bohland, John

Honor Roll, 1940s

Bohnenstiehl, John A.
Boston, James Jr.
Beutel, August C.
Bugger, Zeno
Busse, Erwin
Capelle, Paul Jr.
Collins, Julius F.
Conover, Jasper E.
Converse, Charles
Cullen, John W.
Deluca, Rose
Dettmar, Fred C.
Dettmar, John
Diepholz, William F.
Drique, Leo
Droy, William
Druessel, John
Dugger, Stillwell
Dunstan, William W.
Edwards, Keith L
Elliott, Roy
Engeling, Fred C.
Esenberg, Edward F.
Faitz, Elmer
Folkerts, Charles D.
Gaultney, Walter E.
Geiger, Erwin, J.
Gerling, Christian III
Gerling, Joseph F.
Gerstenecker, Wilbur
Gornet, Arthur A.
Grimm, Charles
Hanke, Henry R.
Hanks, Howard
Harris, Charles G.
Heuer, William
Hoedebecke, Fred
Hoenig, Elmer
Hollis, William B.
Howard, George V.
Hudson, Edward
Kirsch, Arthur F.
Kirsch, Beno P.
Kirsch, Edward
Kirsch, Edward F.
Kirsch, Ernest J.
Kirsch, Otto
Klostermeyer, William
Koenig, Henry D.
Koonce, Buel J
Kueker, Earl
Kuhlmann, Henry G
Kurtz, George
Langewisch, Theodore M.
Langenwalter, Arnold
Levo, Edward T.
Lewis, Roy
Liebler, Walter G
Lindley, Clyde
Llewellyn, Bob

Llewellyn, Morgan
Llewellyn, Richard
Llewellyn, William
Lorenzen, William F.
Lyons, Fred S.
Marti, George
Marti, Melvin
May, Abraham
McCluske, Louis
McCormick, Duncan
McCormick, William G.
Mersinger, Phillip
Mix, Samuel N.
Moergen, Ervin
Montague, Harry
Moore, Bernard J.
Moore, James J.
Moore, William P.
Morgan, Lewis
Mueller, Joseph F.
Nemnich, Joe
Nickolaus, John P
Paul, Dale
Polk, Luther
Porter, Roland L.
Preston, Howard J.
Price, Walter
Ruff, Carl J.
Schlichting, William M.
Schlimme, William H.
Schmitt, John W.
Schmitt, Val
Schmitt, William S.
Schrameck, Frank
Schrameck, Fred
Schultz, Edward
Schwear, Joseph F.
Scott, Alexander
Sliva, Robert W.
Spies, Clarence J.
Steinhage, Ernest
Tilley, William A.
Turner, Restore H.
Voelker, Frank A.
Voelker, Gustave
Wakeland, Fred
Watkins, William E.
Wessel, Louis
Wilkinson, James H.
Wise, Edward J.
Wrigley, Charles H.
Wrobel, Joseph K.

World War II

**Arth, George
**Freeman, Chester
**Hanke, Henry
**Hickman, Albert

**Kueker, Earl
**Kunkel, Philip
**Levo, Elmer
**Loyet, Eugene
**Maden, Walter
**Rogers, Darrel J.
**Rood, Neal
**Shipman, Michael
**Snodgrass, Robert
**Sprick, Arthur
**Stock, Marvin
Ackerman, Donald
Adelhardt, Clarence
Aebel, Cleo
Anderson, Meridith
Anderson, Robert J.
Arth, Oliver
Auwarter, Alfred
Auwarter, Charles
Barry, Harry
Barsch, William
Belcher, Arthur
Berniski, Adam A.
Berniski, Thomas
Bertorello, James
Beutel, Joseph
Beutel, Leslie
Bohnenstiehl, James
Bohnenstiehl, Walter
Bone, James
Borst, Gillie
Brendel, Aloys
Brendel, Harold
Brendel, Lester
Bress, Arthur
Brunworth, Paul
Burniski, Adam
Burniski, Thomas
Buske, Melvin
Bybee, Francis
Callen, Bruce
Callen, Richard
Capelle, James
Capelle, Paul
Capello, Frank
Carter, Morse
Cherry, William
Cline, Arnold H.
Cline, George R.
Collins, J. Morriss
Cook, Orville
Cravens, James
Creed, Joe
Cullop, Floyd
Davis, James
Davis, Jerome
Dawson, Robert
De Maria, Jackie
De Tienne, Richard
De Vries, Francis

Deck, Maynard
Dellamano, Albert
Dickman, Joseph
Diepholz, Victor
Druessel, Raymond
Dugger, Don
Dugger, Floyd
Dugger, Neal
Dunstan, Billie
Ebl, Anthony
Ebl, Michael
Ebl, Frank
Elliott, Roy D., Jr.
Embrey, Carl
Enrico, Frank
Esenberg, Frank A.
Esenberg, Glen
Esenberg, Leonard
Faitz, Earl
Fleming, Paul
Fleming, Richard
Ford, Henry
Ford, John
Fox, J. William
Fox, James
Frangen, Clyde
Frangen, Lester
Frey, Edward
Frey, Ottmer
Friedli, Forrest
Friedli, Leonard
Fritz, Earl
Gaertner, Charles
Gaertner, Harold
Gebhart, Virgil
Geiger, Bernard
Gerling, Joseph
Gerling, Ronald
Guennewig, William
Hall, Charles
Hall, Roland
Hampton, Omar
Hancock, Brandford
Hanke, Delbert
Hanke, Ralph
Hanke, Roy Arthur
Harrison, Oscar
Hart, David Arthur
Haukapp, George
Haukapp, Robert
Hazzard, Arthur
Hazzard, Harry
Hecht, Martin
Heck, Orville
Heck, Warren
Helmich, Tilden
Herrin, Earl
Hoenig, Cecil
Hoenig, Melvin
Holshouser, William

Hood, Charles
Hood, Leonard
Hunsche, Charles
Huston, Louis
Isenberg, August
Isenberg, Elmer
Isenberg, Frank
Isenberg, Victor
Jackson, Wilbur
Joseph, Tilghman
Kamm, Jule
Ketring, Coleman
Ketring, Eldon
Kibikas, Vernon
Kibikas, William
Kinder, Morrison
Kleuter, Florence
Kreutzberg, Lucille
Kueker, Arnold
Kueker, Merrill
Kueker, Walter
Kurtz, Homer
Langenwalter, Floyd
Lewis, Earl
Lewis, Francis
Lewis, Leslie
Lewis, Paul
Lewis, Roy
Lewis, William
Liebler, George
Liles, Carl
Lindley, Clyde
Llewellyn, Bob
Llewellyn, Morgan
Llewellyn, William
Lloyd, John
Lochman, Harold
Lochman, Robert
Lochmann, Roy
Loehring, Eldon
Loyet, Edward
Loyet, Francis
Loyet, Herbert
Loyet, Myron
Loyet, Robert
Lyons, Gene
Lyons, Harry
Lyons, Kenneth
Lyons, Walter
Maden, Raymond
Manley, Russell
Marks, Antone
Maurer, Charles
May, Lester
May, Marvin
Mayer, Arthur
Mayer, Earl
Mc Cain, Charles
Mc Cain, George
Mc Cain, Robert

Mc Dowell, Glen
Mc Dowell, Leland
McFarland, Gordon
Merkel, Frederick
Mersinger, Gilbert
Mersinger, Veronica
Molden, Charles
Moore, Francis
Moore, Robert
Mueller, Gilbert
Nater, Arthur
Nemnich, Joseph
Nemsky, Thomas
Norbury, Lester
Norbury, Theron
Pavlisin, John
Polwort, Homer
Porter, Burl Lee
Porter, Freeman
Porter, Robert
Potts, Harry
Preston, Burrell
Primm, Walter
Primm, William
Pritchett, Stanley
Rawson, Robert D.
Reiss, William
Richter, Florence

Riggin, Carl
Riggin, Paul
Roach, Clemen
Roach, Demen
Rock, Randall
Rood, Earl
Rood, James
Ross, Kenneth
Sartoris, Dominic
Sartoris, James
Schleeter, Donald
Schlimme, Walter
Schmerbauch, Charles
Schmerbauch, Marcus
Schmitt, Billy
Schmitt, Harold
Schmitt, Robert
Schrameck, Eugene
Schrameck, Francis
Schroeder, Vincent
Schultze, Wilfred

Schultze, Erwin
Schultze, Vernon
Schurman, Hilbert
Scott, Donald
Scott, Henry
Scott, Joe

Scott, Robert
Scully, Alvin
Semanisin, Andy
Sesock, Eddie
Sesock, John
Shaffer, Allen
Shaffer, James
Sights, Byron
Snodgrass, Edward
Snodgrass, Willard
Spencer, Warren
Spies, August
Spiro, Erich
Stein, Engene
Stoces, Henry
Stock, Orlo
Struckhoff, Elmer
Sury, Eugene
Taake, Raymond
Taake, Robert
Taake, Russell
Taylor, J. M. (Don)
Taylor, John T.
Taylor, Robert
Thompson, Bill
Voelker, Robert
Voruz, Nelson Louis
Wakeland, John M.

Walden, Allen
Watson, Blair
Watson, James
Weir, Jack
Wendler, Arthur
Wendler, Henry
Wendler, Herbert
Wieder, Alfred
Wiesemeyer, Russell
Wiesemeyer, Wilbur
Wille, Edgar
Williams, Clem
Willman, Floyd
Wittmann, Roy
Wittmann, William
Wohlgemuth, Marvin
Wohlgemuth, Mearl
Woods, Charles
Wright, Franklin
Wurtz, Joseph
Wurtz, William
Wyatt, Wilbur

Korean War

Gebhart, Marcel
Harris, Wilbur
Lochman, Arthur
Pahl, William, R.

Partney, Jack, W.
Rapien, William
Rogier, Floyd Jr.
Rogier, Richard
Rogier, Robert
**Schmerbauch, Daniel L.
Wiesemeyer, Kenneth

Vietnam War

Alons, Roger
Baumgartner, Otto
Brendel, Keith
Cullop, Roger
Eberhardt, Rich
Faitz, Dennis
Italiano, Sam
Mayer, Charles
Obernuefemann, David
Obernuefemann, Robert
Tedrick, Joe
Tessaro, Mike

Gulf War

Anderson, Alice Y
White, David

The Saudi Arabian Gulf War ("Desert Storm") Parade, February 1991

Family Biographies

Friends that hung out at Ma's Café

Henry and Anna Gindler with the catch of the day. Henry with fish and Anna with fowl. (circa 1920s)

Sunday School Picnic Parade going south on Main Street, July 4, 1906.

Troy, Illinois Area
History and Families

JAMES MATTHEW ADAMS - James Matthew Adams was born in 1893 to Joseph and Sarah (Taylor) Adams. James M. married Mary Mix Elliott of Troy (see Grant L. Elliott) around 1931. They owned the Adams' Store (a general department store) on Main St. in Troy. Mary and James M. had two sons: James Grant and Gene Albert.

James M. and Mary (Elliott) Adams, 1920

James G. (b. Mar.6, 1920-1989) became a medical doctor and practiced medicine on Market St. in Troy all of his career. He married Agnes Small from Chicago, IL. They had six children: James Elliott, Clara Dee, Mary Beth, Carol, Nancy and Thomas.

James E. (b. July 6, 1945) and his wife, Marcia, had two children: Heather (b. June 4, 1975) was married to Cameron Bennett on Oct. 9, 1999, and lives in Kansas City, MO; and James "Jamie" Brenden (b. Sept. 20, 1981). James E. and his family live in Jerseyville, IL, where he practices dentistry.

Clara Dee (b. Oct. 1, 1950) and husband, Roger Lubben, live in Auburn, IL. They have three children: Todd (b. Nov. 7, 1976), Ashley (b. April 23, 1984) and Sarah (b. Sept. 21,1981).

Mary Beth (b. Dec. 13, 1955) and her husband, Mark Chestnut, live in Chesterfield, MO, with their two children: Michelle (b. Oct. 27, 1985) and Daniel (b. Oct. 25, 1990).

Carol (b. Feb. 13, 1958) and her husband, Don Sternaman, live in Collinsville, IL. Carol has a son Randy Cooper (b. Aug. 5, 1980).

Nancy (b. Aug. 5, 1960) and her husband, Mike Pinksterhaus, live in Troy with their children: Michael (b. May 27, 1988), Kyle Adam (b. Feb. 9, 1992), Christopher (b. Dec. 5, 1997) and Lauren (b. Feb. 3, 1999).

Thomas (b. Nov. 24, 1962) and his wife, Mary (Sulc), live in Merrimack, NH, with their children: Kelsey (b. June 6, 1989) and Grant (b. May 12, 1992).

James M. and Mary Adams' second son, Gene Albert, (born Feb. 1927-1990) worked in the family store in Troy. He continued to operate Adams' Store after his parents died. Gene married Betty Rood of Troy around Dec. 1964. Their son, John Alan (b. Feb. 1970), lives in the area. *Submitted by James E. Adams and Kae Elliot Schmitt.*

BUD AND TAMI ADELHARDT - Terry Lee "Bud" Adelhardt was born in Troy on March 15, 1946, to Lester and Ruby (Kirsch) Adelhardt. He grew up in the family home on Staunton Road with his two sisters, Karen and Sherry,

under the watchful eyes of his parents, and his aunt, Clara Kirsch. As a high school student at Triad, he competed on the basketball, track and cross country teams, and also worked at his father's grocery store.

While attending Southern Illinois University, Bud met Tameysin Dell Souther of Springfield, Illinois. The two graduated in 1967, Bud with a degree in business, and Tami in commercial art. That same year, Bud joined the U.S. Air Force Reserves, serving 19 months active duty at Scott Air Force Base as a medical records officer. When he returned from basic training, he and Tami married August 26, 1967.

Tami was born in Springfield on October 1, 1946, to Chase and Dell (Colby) Souther. She grew up there with her four brothers, George, Tim, Latham, and Tom. Throughout her childhood, Tami spent as much time as possible on horseback at the local riding stables, as well as practicing her artistic talents.

Terry "Bud" and Tami Adelhardt, 1994

After marrying, Bud and Tami moved to a house on Elmer Street. Once his tour of duty with the Air Force ended, Bud returned to work at the family store. In 1970, he purchased the store from Les and managed it for the next 17 years. Tami worked as a commercial artist, first for Stix, Baer, & Fuller, then for the National Peace Officers' Press. She later worked as bookkeeper at the Adelhardt grocery store.

On October 26, 1969, Bud and Tami celebrated the birth of their first child, Chad Alan; their second child, Krista Marie, followed on March 14, 1973.

Throughout their early years together, the two were active members of the community. Bud served on the Board of Directors of the United Savings & Loan Association. He also belonged to the Troy Lions Club, serving as Treasurer, Vice President, and President, and is currently a member of the American Legion. Tami was active in the Sunday school, nursery, and Bible school at Friedens U.C.C. and for several years was the volunteer coordinator for the Early Childhood Screenings in town.

In 1987, the couple decided to sell the grocery store, but soon returned to the Troy business community when they opened Tub & Tumble Laundry & Dry Cleaning in 1989. They successfully operated the laundromat until 1991, when Bud began working for the Keebler Company where he is currently a sales representative, serving local stores. At about the same time, Tami decided to return to school. She graduated from SIUE in 1995 with a masters in

speech pathology. She is currently working in the Hazelwood, MO, school district as an early childhood speech/language pathologist.

Bud and Tami's son, Chad, graduated from University of Illinois in 1995 with a degree in psychology. He is currently working toward a second degree in graphic art, and is a faculty member of the art department at Meramac Community College. In 1996, Chad married Yati Hasnan of Kuala Lumpur, Malaysia. They now live in St. Louis.

Krista graduated from Webster University in 1995 with a degree in biology/animal behavior. After graduating, she spent time working at the Saint Louis Zoo, and later worked at the Purina Pet Care Center. She currently works at City Animal Hospital in St. Louis. *Submitted by Krista Adelhardt.*

JOHN ADELHARDT - John Adelhardt (1858-1952) of Marine married Anna Shermann (1866-1957) of Caseyville in the mid 1880s. They lived in the Marine area until they moved to Troy. In Troy they lived in what was recently the Schmisseur home on Troy-O'Fallon Rd. They raised nine children: Frank, George, John, Elmer, Val, Mayme, Louise, Anne, and Sophie.

Frank Adelhardt (1889-1978) married Carrie Frey (1892-1976) of St. Jacob in 1912. They first lived in Edwardsville; and then in 1919, they rented the Barnsback farm west of Troy. In 1922 they moved to the Fred Schoon farm also west of Troy where they raised three children: Lester, Clarence, and LaVern. In 1948 Frank and Carrie retired from farming and moved to Hazel Street in Troy.

Adelhardt family, 1930-31. (l. to r.) Front: Clarence, LaVern. Back: Frank, Carrie, Lester

Lester Adelhardt (1913-1980) married Ruby Kirsch of Blackjack (Troy) in 1935. Just after marriage they lived in Troy, then moved to Edwardsville for a short time, and then moved back to Troy. Les and Ruby lived in several homes in Troy before settling on Staunton Rd. Les worked at the Common Wealth grocery store during the war and then bought the grocery business from Butcher Martin in Troy and spent the next 35 years owning and operating the store. Ruby was a teacher in several of the area's country schools: Mt. Zion, Quercus Grove, and Spring Valley, and then worked as a substitute teacher in the Troy Public School system. They raised three children: Karen (Cookie), Terry (Bud), and Sherry.

Clarence Adelhardt, born in 1917, married Jane Southard of Poag (Edwardsville) in 1942.

Adelhardt Children. (l. to r.)
LaVern, Clarence, and Lester

Clarence served his country during WWII in the Army. When he returned, Clarence and Jane lived in Edwardsville for a short time, and Clarence worked at the Common Wealth. In 1948 they moved to the farm and took over the operation for Frank. They continued to farm until 1984 when they retired and moved to Glen Carbon. Clarence and Jane raised three children: Carol Sue, Cindy, and Christi.

Adelhardt family, circa 1940. (l. to r.) Front: Anny (Shermann) and John. Middle: Mame, Louise, Sophie, Ann. Back: Frank, George, Valentine, Elmer.

LaVern Adelhardt born in 1924 married William Buehrer of Granite City in 1944. They lived in Granite City for a short time then moved to Hazel Street in Troy. They raised two daughters, Debbie and Diane. *Submitted by Sherry (Adelhardt) Smith and Sherry Brendel.*

LESTER AND RUBY ADELHARDT - Lester George Adelhardt was born on February 22, 1913, to Frank and Caroline (Frey) Adelhardt. He grew up on the family farm just west of Troy with his younger brother and sister, Clarence and Laverne. As a young man, he helped his father work the farm until 1935, when he married another Troy resident, Ruby Marie Kirsch (1912-1994).

Ruby was the daughter of Gustav and Emma (Lueke) Kirsch, and grew up with brother, Elmer, and sisters, Olinda and Clara, on their family's farm, which was situated around what is now the intersection of Troy-O'Fallon and Kirsch Roads. As a young woman, Ruby received a teaching certificate from McKendree College, and taught at several country schools near her parents' farm, including Quercus Grove, Mt. Zion, and Spring Valley before marrying Les.

After they married, Les worked for a time as a firer at Richards' Brick Company in Edwardsville, then later became a burner/welder at Commonwealth Steel in Granite City. When World War II began, Les and his co-workers at the Mill quickly learned to make artillery and other supplies for the U.S. troops.

In 1943, Les and Ruby were blessed with their first child, Karen "Cookie," who was followed by their son, Terry "Bud," in 1946, and second daughter, Sherry, in 1955.

In 1946, the couple decided to start their own business, and purchased a small market from local butcher, Alex Martin. The store changed locations twice, and had a number of different names (Troy Market, Troy IGA, Adelhardt Foods), but continued to grow and serve the community for 40 years. Les ran the store until 1972, when Terry took over, continuing to run the successful business for the next 14 years.

Les was an active member of the community in many ways. He belonged to the Oddfellows Lodge, the Loyal Order of Moose (Edwardsville), the Board of Friedens U.C.C., and also the Troy City Council. He served as chief of the Troy Volunteer Fire Department for three years, and, as a member of the Madison County Fireman's Association, was instrumental in acquiring the MCFA Hall in Collinsville, and, also, in starting a retirement fund for MCFA members. Les was also very active in the Troy Lions Club for many years, and worked with others in the Club and community to establish the Troy Boy Scouts and Khoury League. When the Lions Club wanted to develop a community park, it was Les who convinced Herman Hecht to sell his land to the club. This land is now Tri-Township Park.

Lester and Ruby Adelhardt, 1935

Ruby was also an active member of the Troy community. Besides caring for Les and their three children, she belonged to the Friedens U.C.C. Guild, in which she actively participated for many years, and also worked as a substitute teacher in the Troy schools.

Lester and Ruby were married for 35 years before he died in 1980. They had 7 grandchildren at that time. Ruby lived to see that number grow to 9, plus 2 great-grandchildren. Since she died in 1994, four more great-grandchildren have been added to the family, with two more on the way. *Submitted by Krista Adelhardt.*

WILLIAM AND LOIS ADOMITE - The Adomite family settled in Tilden, IL, after coming from Lithuania. John had a son John Frank (b. Jan. 17, 1912) who married Rose Eileen Dusek (b. May 8, 1915) in Fairmont City. Her parents were Alois Dusek (b. Mar. 20, 1887) and Mary Dolezal (b. Jan. 13, 1892).

Alois, whose father was Josef Dusek, and Mary came separately through Ellis Island to America from Daruvar, Bohemia, in 1911-1912.

John and Rose Adomite resided at 2514 N. 34th St. in Fairmont City and had a son, William John Adomite, who was born in East St. Louis on August 18, 1950. Bill graduated from East St. Louis High School in 1968. Bill married Lois Jean Lenny (b. Oct. 29, 1951) on March 23, 1971, at Holy Rosary Catholic Church in Fairmont City. Her parents are Paul and Jean Lenny. Paul (b. Mar. 7, 1927 in East St. Louis) married Norma Jean Doussard (b. Feb. 15, 1930 in East St. Louis) on Jan. 16, 1949.

Adomite family, wedding photo, 2002
(l. to r.) Pamela, Paul and Jean, Susan and Allen, Lois and Bill, and Gordon

The Lenny family originated in Glasgow, Scotland. John Wallace Lenny (b. Mar. 28, 1822) traveled alone to Philadelphia at age twelve. He eventually founded Ogden, IL, in Champaign County, and settled there, marrying Mary Margaret Poage (b.Dec. 18, 1842) on June 3, 1859. Their son George Townsend Lenny (b. Jan. 18, 1861) married Mary Etta Simms (b. Sept. 26, 1866) on Oct. 17, 1885, and moved the family to French Village. Their son George Wallace Lenny, Sr. (b. Oct. 6, 1886) and Florence Viola Schuchman (b. Dec. 17, 1903) were married March 8, 1924, and lived at 1240 North 89th Street in Edgemont Station (now East St. Louis).

Norma Jean's parents were Raymond George Doussard (b. Dec. 6, 1896) and Vashti Lena Whitsell. Paul and Jean raised Lois at 9916 North Road in Fairview Heights. Lois graduated from Belleville East High School in 1969.

Bill and Lois bought 2 acres just north of Troy in 1970 and moved into their new home in February 1973. In 1976, Paul and Jean Lenny moved to Troy. On June 14, 1975, Allen Paul Adomite was born at St. Joseph's Hospital in Highland. Pamela Rose Adomite was born at Anderson Hospital in Maryville on October 26, 1977. Bill has worked for Union Electric since 1968. Paul retired from Bell Telephone in 1991 after 43 years service.

Allen graduated Salutatorian from Triad High School in 1993, completed his Bachelor's in Journalism from the University of Missouri School of Journalism in 1997, and completed his Master's of Public Administration from SIUE in 2002. Allen married Susan Lynn Parker (b. April 7, 1976) at Manchester (MO) United

Methodist Church on May 4, 2002. Susan graduated with her Master's of Accountancy from the University of Missouri in 1999.

Pamela graduated from Triad in 1995. Pamela married Gordon James Hulten at Troy United Methodist Church on September 1, 2001. Pamela and Gordon both completed their Bachelor's of Political Science degrees from the University of Illinois. *Submitted by Allen Adomite.*

JANET (KIRSCH) ALBERTINA -

The first child of John Gustave and Iola (Fulton) Kirsch was Janet Ruth (Kirsch) Albertina (b. 06/23/

Wedding photo
(l. to r.) Iola (Fulton) Kirsch,
Bridget (Munn) Albertina, Kyle T.
Albertina, Janet (Kirsch) Albertina

1935). She was an English/speech/journalism teacher at Mascoutah High School from 1957-60 and Collinsville High School from 1960-74. She then worked as an SSA teleservice representative in St. Louis, from 1981-1998, and is currently retired. She had one child, Kyle Todd Albertina (b. 08/07/1974), served in the U.S. Army, currently studying aviation mechanics at SWIC. He married Bridget Munn (b. 03/04/ 1978). *Submitted by Janet Albertina.*

DENNIS AND MARY LOU (GINDLER) AMMANN -

Mary Lou (Gindler) Ammann, daughter of Oscar and Dorothy Ludwig Gindler, was born February 2, 1948. She attended school in Troy and graduated from Triad High School in 1966. Playing the piano was a great love in her life, and she studied piano with Audrey Deeren, and later at McKendree College in Lebanon.

On May 20, 1967, she married Dennis Ammann of Highland at the Friedens United Church of Christ in Troy. Her husband was in the carpentry business, and in 1968 they opened a very successful restaurant business in Mascoutah, IL. They operated this business until about 1973. In May of 1970, Mary Lou and Dennis purchased and restored an Italianate Victorian home at the corner of Monroe and St. Louis Street in Lebanon, IL. In 1975, after the birth of their son, Christopher, they moved to a historic home on Mill Hill in Highland. In 1984, they built a new home in the country and still reside there. In 1995, they added a theatre pipe organ to their home in a little theatre that seats 60 people so that others could come enjoy the music that Dennis and Mary Lou play. They have hosted many groups and been able to help raise money for various not-for-profit groups

including the Troy Historical Society and Christian outreach ministries. Dennis performs many theatre organ concerts at the Lincoln Theatre in Belleville. For the past 15 years, they have been in the insurance business in Highland.

They are the parents of three children. Christopher Scott was born on April 12, 1975. He graduated from Highland High School in 1993 and then attended SIUE. He graduated with a degree in accounting in 1997, and received his CPA designation shortly thereafter. On September 5, 1997, he married Tamara Kay Flack of Hartford, IL. Tamara will receive her CPA designation later this year. They have just built a new home in Edwardsville.

Ammann family, circa 2000
Front: (l. to r.) Tamara, Mary Lou, Sara
Back: Christopher, Kevin, Dennis

Sara Elizabeth was born on October 29, 1976. She also graduated from Highland High School in 1994, and attended SIUE. She graduated in 1998, with a degree in Biology and Chemistry. In 2001, she received her Master of Science in biology degree from SIUE and now teaches Advanced Chemistry 2 at Triad High School. She has been the youth director at First Congregational Church in Highland for 6 years. She is also a very talented vocalist, who performs in the shows at the Lincoln Theatre in Belleville, and some of the churches in the area.

Kevin Garrett was born on February 27, 1980. He also graduated from Highland High School in 1998, and is attending Southwestern Illinois College in Belleville and Granite City. *Submitted by Mary Lou (Gindler) Ammann.*

ALBERT AND BERNICE (KLEIN) ARTH

Albert Anthony Arth (b. 1913, d. 1985 on the Matthews farm) married Bernice Elisabeth Klein Songer (b. 1916 in Manhattan, KS). They married February 20, 1941, at St. Henry's Catholic Church in East St. Louis. Bernie was widowed and had two daughters, Roberta June Songer and Glenda Marie Songer.

In 1942, they moved into Anton Arth's farm along Longhi Road and lived there for 6 years. In 1942, Sylvia E. Arth was born. When Lewis G. Arth retired, Albert, Bernice and daughters moved to the Vance - Arth farm in 1948. Alicia Ann and Teresa Kay were born after this time – 16 years after Sylvia. Currently there are 2 grandchildren and 2 great-grandchildren.

When the couple lived on the Anton Arth farm, along with farming grain, they raised cattle, pigs, chickens, geese, and ducks. A

troublesome goat even lived there with an ample supply of family pets.

Living on the farm was not as convenient as living in other home places. They had no running water, nor an indoor bathroom. The laundry was done in a wash house and hung up to dry on the outside lines. The family always planted a huge garden and canned many vegetables and fruits each year. The Arth daughters attended the nearby Formosa School.

Wedding photo, Feb. 20, 1941
(l. to r.) Albert Anthony Arth, Bernice
Elizabeth (Klein) Songer Arth, Beatrice
M. Klem (sister to Albert), and Carl
Welker (cousin to Bernice) of Mascoutah.

Albert also helped his father farm his land, once the old Vance farm. The couple bought a 116 acre farm, previously owned by Maurer, Cook, then Pejokovich. Thinking they would move there, they found it was almost impossible to live in the house, because it needed much work to make it habitable.

When Mary Arth became ill and the farm became too much for Lewis and Mary to manage, they decided to retire and moved to the three acres and a house they owned near Collinsville, across the road from Maack's addition along U.S. Hwy 40. This three acres Louis and Mary's daughter Marguerite inherited after her father's death. After her death, it went to her daughter, Nancy Lynn Lucido.

In August of 1957, Albert rented 226 acres from Mrs. Edith (Emery) Windsor of Elmhurst. She was the sister of Irwin Maurer, whose father

Bernice Arth, 1990s

was Charles Maurer. (He was married to a Cook.). They owned many farms located around the Troy-Collinsville area. Adam Kraft was the previous farmer before Albert Arth. Albert farmed until September 1983, when he turned the land over to Arnold Flath to farm.

After Albert's death the acreage on the home place (Vance-Arth farm and the acreage in Wilson Heights) went into the Albert A. Arth Estate belonging to his five daughters. In 1998 they sold the land to RP Lumber Company. The house and four acres belonging to Bernice A. Arth was then sold to RP Lumber Co. in 1999. The Pejokovich farm (about 91 acres) now belongs to the Bernice E. Arth Trust. In later years, a portion in the back where the pond was located, was sold for a housing development. Roberta (Songer) Rode and her husband, Louis Rode, lived there while Louis helped Albert in farming. After they moved to Edwardsville, the house was rented and later razed. By 1960, the old house had been torn down to make way for a new home. The Arth family lived in the upstairs above the smokehouse while the new house was being built, and the old kitchen still stood while the new house was being erected.

A lot of memories have been made in the old house. At one time it was a stagecoach stop over, and General William Sherman supposedly slept in one of the upstairs bedrooms, probably the middle one. Many remember butchering days on the farm. Bernice's family always came for this event. The family enjoyed a lot of joking and teasing as they made many different types of sausages. When it came time to butcher the chickens, the women got that job. The feathers went flying and, regardless of all the work involved, everyone had a good time. The chickens were a lot of work, but they provided many good meals.

Another good memory was the card games. The families would get together and play cards till all hours of the morning, usually Rummy. The family would gather at each other's houses most weekends. The many visits to Bernice's sisters and brother's houses also provided many memories. The children had fun playing together, since there were so very many of them.

Albert was an avid hunter and fisherman. He enjoyed these activities with his buddies and family. He came home with an abundant supply of duck, fish, geese and deer. In later life he went hunting with his son-in-law Vincent and grandson Barry. They shot many pheasants and always brought home several. Albert loved anything to do with the timber and wild life. He would go mushroom hunting and come home with sacks of them.

He belonged to the Democrat Club, the Knights of Columbus, the Tri-Township Park Board and did miscellaneous other jobs as a volunteer. Many times Albert would assist someone by giving him a short job to earn some money. Often he would just help someone out that was in need and give him a new change of clothing, food and a couple of bucks in his pocket and send him on his way.

Bernice was a homemaker and a 4-H leader. She belonged to various card clubs, home extension, Woman's Club of Troy, Troy Democratic Women's Club, St. Jerome Altar Society, Daughters of Isabella, and participated in many church activities and loved volunteering for various church functions. She never failed to have enough food for a stranger to have a plate full, should he stop and be hungry. Back at the Poletti farm, it was nothing for a hobo to come off the train, which came by near the house, and ask for something to eat. Of course,

she had something for them and maybe a lunch for the road. One Thanksgiving on the farm, the house and stomachs were full, when a man stopped in on his way from CA to FL. He said he had noticed all the cars and wondered if here was some spare food. "Of course," the family said, "come on in, we have plenty." The man came on the porch and ate till he was full and had a sack packed for the road. He was delighted and looked as if he needed some kindness shown to him as well. Albert and Bernie said, "I've never been hungry and it would be hard for me to refuse anyone of some food, especially if we had some to share."

The generosity shown by Albert and Bernice during their lifetime is unknown to many people. They have always given more of themselves than what was ever expected of them. Many people will never know of the kindness they have shown to others. What a fine legacy they leave behind them in their history of life. Medals were not given for their valor, nor would they have expected any. *Submitted by Sylvia Kauhl.*

ANTON ARTH - Adam Kraft took over the farming at the Maurer, Cook, Windsor farm and moved into the house. Anton had retired from

Anton and Anna (Strauss) Arth with son Oscar, 1910

farming and wanted to move to Collinsville, into the house with three acres that he owned; but Anna wanted to live in the log house in Wilson Heights. This was located off the frontage road of US Highway 40. They lived there until Anna died of a stroke in 1929, at the age of 62. Albert Arth, 22, was on his way to pick up his grandmother with a horse and buggy to take her to the school picnic, when he found out she had died of a stroke. Anton moved in with his son, Anton "Tony" V. Arth Jr. on Anton's farm, until the death of Tony in 1940. (The home place where Ray Poletti lives in 2002 along Longhi Road). Tony was married to Emma Ellsbeck; they had no children. When Tony died, Emma moved to Florida, and Anton moved in with Lewis and Mary Arth. *Submitted by Sylvia Kauhl.*

GEORGE FRANK ARTH - George Frank Arth was born on January 15, 1908, in OK, and died on Mothers Day, May 13, 1945, in Mindanao, Philippines. The plane in which he was a passenger was going to land at the base in a fog.

President Franklin D. Roosevelt had died, and the U.S. Flag was being flown at halfmast. The plane came in too low and clipped the flag

pole, causing it to crash; and all the passengers and pilots died.

George was married to Mildred (unknown) Arth. They had no children. He graduated from McCray-Dewey High School in Troy. George Arth was the Godfather of Sylvia Elaine Arth Kauhl. *Submitted by Sylvia Kauhl.*

LEWIS GEORGE AND MARY (MICKLAUTZ) ARTH - Lewis George Arth (b. 1885, d. 1968) married Mary Micklautz, daughter of Anton and Marguerite (Preloger) Micklautz in Ss. Peter and Paul Catholic Church, Collinsville, in 1907. The couple moved to a farm in Hunter, OK, that had been purchased by his father Anton, traveling there by train with all their belongings. George Arth, their first son, was born there. Mary also suffered a miscarriage while opening the cellar door when the wind caught it, causing her to fall. The times were so difficult in Oklahoma because of the very dry land. They had very few neighbors; in fact, the closest one was many miles away.

Lewis George Arth and Mary Micklautz Arth, wedding photo, 1907.

After five years, Lewis sold the farm for his father Anton and they moved back to IL. When they returned home, they moved to the Mathews farm where Albert Anthony Arth was

Lewis and Mary Arth, 50th Anniversary photo, 1957

born. Because of the poor ground, Lewis did not prosper. He discovered that the Vance farm was going to be rented, so Lewis talked to owner Nancy Vance, and rented her farm of 160 acres. Later, Lewis bought the house place from her where Marguerite and Beatrice were born. In 1967 on Thanksgiving Day, Lewis G. Arth became seriously ill. This was the year he and Mary Arth had been married for 60 years. After his illness, he seemed to improve in health, but

Lewis and Mary Arth's children
(l. to r.) Marguerite (Arth) Lucido,
Beatrice (Arth) Klem, Albert A. Arth

died of a massive stroke in July 1968. Mary Arth became seriously ill after she fell and broke her hip at the nursing home. Later, she celebrated her 92nd birthday in October 1977. She became extremely ill, was hospitalized, and died not long after. *Submitted by Sylvia Kauhl.*

LEWIS LUDWIG AND MARIA USRSULA (LUDOVICI) ARTH -

The first generation of the Arth family to come to America was the Lewis Ludwig and Maria Ursula (Ludovici) Arth family. Ursula was the daughter of Adam Strauss. Lewis' family had served in the French army before him. Lewis and Ursula came to America in 1872 and moved to the Cook farm in 1874. They had four children, Mary, Joseph, Anton and Raphael. These children were born in Eberhadt, Alsace Lorraine, France (East Germany). Mary Arth, 19; Joseph Arth, 15; Anton Arth, 12; and Raphael Arth, 17, had come to America together before their parents arrived.

Anton Arth family, 1893
Back: Anton and Anna. Front:
Lewis G., Oscar Adam, Anton V., Jr.

Mary married a Schwarts in the U.S. and lived in Granite City, IL. Little is known about her. Joseph "Sep" (b. 1857 d. 1947) was a carpenter. He married Rose Miller. Nothing else is known about him.

Anton Arth (b. Aug. 18, 1860 d. in 1948) married Anna Strauss (d. 1929) in 1884. He became a farmer in the Troy area, the beginning of the Arth family history here. They moved to the Charles Maurer farm, and Anton farmed a lot of land, hiring farm hands. Anna had hired help for household chores as well. Anton and Anna had six sons. Lewis George(b. 1885 d. 1968) married Mary Micklautz, daughter of Anton and Marguerite (Preloger) Micklautz, on Jan. 24, 1907, in Collinsville. John died in

infancy. Another son John died from being thrown from a horse. Anton V. Jr. "Tony" (b. 1887) married Emma Ellsbeck and had no children. He died in 1940 on Thanksgiving Day after falling down stairs at a friend's home. Oscar Adam (b. June 25, 1902 d. Nov. 4, 1984) married 3 times: Nellie, Florence from Troy, and Estella Conrad from Marine. He had no children.

Raphael (b. 1855 d. 1922) moved to St. Joseph, MO, and became a jeweler. There, he married Emma Williman (b. 1866 d. 1947). They later moved back to Collinsville. Raphael and Emma had a son, Rudolph "Rudy." He wanted to become a priest, but the study was too difficult for him. He never married. Their daughter Cecilia Ursula (Arth) Sullivan (b.1897 d.1981) gave birth to a daughter, Marguerite (Sullivan) Dunn. She married George Duane Dunn and had five children. Cecilia Sullivan also had a son named Robert. The only information about him is that he lived in Florida.

Ray Arth married Edna Griesebaum from New Baden, IL. They had two children, Norbert and Betty. Norbert married Grace Miller of Highland, IL. They live in Lafayette, IN. They had four sons; only two are known. Tom Arth married Annie, and they have 2 children. David married Karen; they have one son and live in Battle Ground, IN. Norbert and David Arth own pharmacies in Indiana.

Catharine Selsum, sister to Ursula, died 1895 at Ursula's home. *Submitted by Sylvia Kauhl.*

JACOB AND ANNA ELIZABETH LANGENWALTER BAER -

Jacob Baer, born 29 May 1818, at Obersulzen, Germany, came to the United States in 1844 with his parents, Jacob and Margaretha Gerlap Baer, and siblings, Christian, Johannes, Elizabeth, and Daniel. Jacob's father purchased Ogle farm land in Ridge Prairie, St. Clair County, IL. This farm was located about ten miles southwest of the Widicus and Langenwalter farms in Blackjack, IL.

A double wedding ceremony, performed by Minister A. Danz, took place on 28 March 1849, in the Jacob Baer, Sr., home in Ridge Prairie. The two couples were Jacob Baer and Anna Elizabeth Langenwalter and Jacob Langenwalter and Elizabeth Baer. Both newlywed couples resided on farms near the Baer homestead.

In 1850 Jacob purchased farm land adjoining Anna Elizabeth's parents' farm in Blackjack and they moved there.

Jacob and Anna Elizabeth's children were Jacob, b.17 February 1850, d. 26 February 1865, buried Langenwalter Family Cemetery; Katharina, b. 30 September 1851, d.12 July 1852, buried Langenwalter Family Cemetery; Maria, b. 25 August 1853, d. 5 August 1863, buried Langenwalter Family Cemetery; Elizabeth, b. 21 February 1855, d. 16 September 1858, buried Langenwalter Family Cemetery; Katharine, b. 27 December 1856, married 25 February 1883; John Hirstein, d. 24 January 1940, buried Summerfield Cemetery, Summerfield, IL, had eight children; Anna, b.16 June 1858, d. 6 September 1858, buried Langenwalter Family Cemetery; Samuel S., b. 6 October 1859, married 2 August 1885, Elisa K. Reibold, d. 7 October 1944, buried

Summerfield Cemetery, Summerfield, had ten children; Daniel, b. 25 January 1862, d. 12 November 1862, buried Langenwalter Family Cemetery; Daniel E., b. 29 September 1863, married 4 November 1894, Anna L. Dahlem, d. 20 March 1937, buried Summerfield Cemetery, had two children; John L., b. 12 February 1866, d. 11 January 1892, buried Summerfield Cemetery; Barbara K., b. 31 March 1869, married 4 November 1894, to David Samuel Ruth, d. 20 January 1919, buried Summerfield Cemetery, had five children; Jacob A., b. 2 June 1872, married Myrthe J. Pletscher, d.16 September 1947, buried Summerfield Cemetery, had four children.

Jacob Baer, 1880   *Anna Elizabeth (Langenwalter) Baer*

In January 1880, Jacob purchased 158 acres of land south of Summerfield and moved there to be nearer the Mennonite Church in Summerfield, of which they were members.

Jacob died 12 November 1903. Anna Elizabeth died 6 May 1904. Both are buried in the Summerfield Cemetery. *Submitted by Edith Hock.*

JIM AND VIRGINIA LUDWIG BAILEY

Virginia Ann Ludwig was born February 16, 1935, in Troy. Her parents were Albert and Irma Ottwein Ludwig. (see: Albert and Irma Ottwein Ludwig) The Ludwigs moved to Jacksonville, IL; Oak Park, IL; and Jefferson City, MO. Virginia graduated from William Woods College in Fulton, MO.

James Charles Bailey was born August 22, 1935, in Anderson, MO. His parents were James Lester and Olline (Elliff) Bailey. Jim grew up in southern Missouri in Anderson, Doniphan and Jefferson City. Jim attended Missouri University in Columbia, MO.

Jim and Virginia met in high school and dated throughout high school and college. Jim and Virginia were married November 24, 1955, in Jefferson City. They have 2 children: Cynthia Diane Bailey, b. September 21, 1956, and James Ludwig Bailey, b. September 27, 1959. At this date there are 2 grandchildren: Emily Eden Brennan, b. August 8, 1994, and Michaela Elliff Brennan, b. June 1, 1996. Cynthia and children live in Fort Worth, TX. Cynthia is a gemologist and owns her own jewelry store. Jim spends most of the year in California, where he works in the movie industry.

Jim, Virginia and children moved to Troy around 1960. They lived with Virginia's parents on Wayland. The Bailey family moved to Center St., in the house where Virginia's grandparents,

W.P. and Laura Ludwig, had lived at one time, and where her grandfather passed away. The Baileys moved to Market St., across the street from Hulda and Lester Becker, Virginia's aunt and uncle, and Carrie Ottwein, Virginia's grandmother. Jim worked in St. Louis at International Shoe Company and Beidermans Furniture Company. He was a computer programmer and systems analyst.

(l. to r.) Front: Virginia (Ludwig) Bailey, Cynthia (Bailey) Brennan, Michaela Brennan, Emily Brennan. Back: James L. Bailey, James C. Bailey

While in Troy, Jim and Virginia were active in the Troy Jaycees. Virginia was active in Friedens United Church of Christ and Troy PTA. Jim and Senator Paul Simon, then owner of the *Troy Tribune* newspaper, were instrumental in starting the Troy Library.

Cindy started school at the Troy Grade School. Jimmie has many fond memories of riding his tricycle down the sidewalk to Mr. Liebler's hardware store on Market Street. He would join the men, sitting on a bench in front of the store, watching what was going on in town.

After leaving Troy in 1964, the Baileys moved to Jefferson City, MO. During the years they have lived in Omaha, NE; Ayer, MA; Littleton, CO; and are currently living again in Jefferson City.

After moving to Jefferson City in 1983, Jim worked for the State of Missouri as a systems analyst. Virginia owned and operated a frame shop and art gallery. Jim and Virginia are now retired. Virginia is active in the community theatre and local art club.

Troy has always been an intregal part in Virginia's life as a child, then as an adult where she introduced her own family to the life of a small town. *Submitted by Virginia Bailey.*

BANGERT FAMILY - In 1811, Jubilee Posey, approximately 17 years of age, a native of Georgia, came to Madison County. He had been a ranger during the War of 1812. The U. S. Government granted acreages in the Sections of 32, 33 and 34, Pin Oak Township to Jubilee Posey for services rendered in guarding the settlers during that eventful period.

It has been reported that Mr. Posey started the first school in a log cabin in Pin Oak Township. He married twice and was survived by seven children at his death on August 4, 1878.

A son Benjamin is listed as one of the original thirteen members of the Presbyterian Church in Troy. (October 6, 1842)

The Bangert Home in Pin Oak Township (about 1930)

After his death the land then went to George Handlon, a grandson, who borrowed money on 406 acres of this land at 8 and 10 percent interest. The bank forclosed on the property and on January 6, 1886, the property was sold on the court house steps to the bank. On December 10, 1889, John Stolz bought 160 acres for $4800 and on May 8, 1894, Carl and Catherine Bangert bought 80 acres from Stolz.

Carl and Catherine (Mehrmann) Bangert were both born in Ft. Russell Township and married on April 5, 1888. They had two children, William (Clara Gieseking) and Wilhelmina (Minnie – Arthur Gaertner) when they moved to the Troy area. They later had Catherine (Katie – Julius Gaertner) and Charles (Edna Herren). They were affiliated with the Friedens Evangelical and Reformed Church. They had ten grandchildren.

At their deaths, the farm was purchased by Charles and Edna Bangert and is now known as the Bangert Subdivision off Riggin and Maple Grove Roads. Two of Carl and Catherine's grandchildren, Thelma and husband Chester and Gladys Gaertner Huston live on the old Bangert farm, along with 2 great grandchildren, Tona Huston and Stan Huston and three great great grandchildren – Crystal Huston, Tanner Riden and Lukas Skalisius. *Submitted by Thelma Bangert Huston.*

BARDSLEY - An early family settling in the Troy area of Madison County were the Bardsleys. Napthali Bardsley and his wife Hannah, great great grandparents, were both born in England, Napthali, b. 30 Sept. 1817, d. 11 Dec. 1891, IL, probably, Jasper County.

They migrated to the United States, prior to 1841. Early on Moses Bardsley, the father of Napthali, was found in Madison County, indicating that he probably migrated from England with Napthali and Hannah. Children of this union were Mary Jane, b. 2 September 1841, Newark, New Jersey; Napthali, b. 1843, New Jersey; Edmund, b. 1845, Madison County; Moses, b.1848, Madison County; Letitia Perlina, b. 22 October 1853, IL. By the location of the births of the children, it would appear that the family perhaps immigrated to New Jersey and moved from there to Madison County. Mary Jane married Henry Leturno. They moved from Pocahontas, IL, to Newton, Jasper County, IL, in 1872. Henry died in 1888; Mary, in 1935; and both are buried in the Slate Point Cemetery near Newton. Their children were William E., b. Wheeler, IL; C.R. (Cash) b. Wheeler, IL; Joseph, Shunoway, b. IL; Naphtali, b. Altamont, IL; and Truman, b. Blue Island, IL. Mary's

father, Napthali, apparently moved to Jasper County as he is buried in the Slate Point Cemetery near Newton. Details of the death and burial of Hannah are not known.*Submitted by Vernon L. Lacey.*

BARNSBACK FAMILY - The Barnsback name was originally Berensbach. It was created by joining the names of two families together: the family of Berens, from Zellerfield, and the family of Bach, originally from Gosler, Germany. Later it was shortened because the English people in the U.S. could not pronounce the original. The family dates back to the 1600s. A book was translated from German to English in 1842. The book was written and compiled by Major August Barnsback in Hoyershausen in 1818, and translated in 1842. A street in Troy in the Brookside section is named after the Barnsbacks.

Valentine Berens, originally of the family of Berens in Zellerfield, was adopted as a boy by his mother's brother, Andreas Bach, who had one of the highest commissions in the mining district called in German "Oberbergmeister." This Bach had no children, and he made the above Berens his heir, out of courtesy. He supposedly called himself Berensbach from that time on, and it has been the family name ever since. He had a son born at Zellerfield in 1640 named Justus Andreas Berensbach. His oldest son, Heinrich Thomas Berensbach, was born in 1668. He married Anna Christine Hattorf in 1712. None of the other children of Justus Andreas Berensbach were found in the church register at Willershausen, due to a church fire. Henry Thomas Berensbach had nine children: Esther Dorothea, Sophia Johanna, Christian Friedrich, George Theodore, Justine Andres, Ernestine Wilhelmne, John Henrich, Juluis August and Henriette Christine. In 1818, there could not be found any one living descendant in the male line of all the children of Henry Thomas Berensbach. It is possible that some of them might have become very poor and were living unknown as laborers.

In 1793, there was living in Gottingen, a Captain-Lieutenant of the Hanoverian army; but he left no descendants. Of the female line, there was one married to a certain Lieutenant Colonel Von Falkenberg. Justus Andreas Berensbach, the father of the above named Henry Thomas, had a son born, supposedly in a second marriage. His name was Johan Otto Bernsbach, who is the ancestor of the present family (in 1818). *Submitted by Mae Grapperhaus.*

GEORGE FRIEDERICH JULIUS BARNSBACK - George Friederich Julius Barnsback married Mary Ann Minter and immigrated from Germany to Illinois in 1809. They had 10 children: Jacob J., George J., William J., John J., Thomas J., Hannah J., Henrietta J., Marianna J., Julius J., and Isabella J. George Friederich Julius found that when he came to the U.S., it was very difficult for people to speak the name Berensbach, so he changed the name to Barnsback. The children married as follows: Jacob J. married Emily McCoy, first, then his second wife, Elizabeth Primm.

George J. married Damaris Yowell and had one child who died in infancy.

William J. married Nancy S. Watt and they had six children.

John J. married Rebecca Holt and had three children.

Thomas J. married Nancy Montgomery and had three children.

Hannah J. married Shadrack R. Gillham and had five children.

Julius J. married Jane Davis. Their children were Isabelle, who married William Donoho; Cora, who married John Whitesides; Jaca, who married J. B. Willoughby; and Lula, who married Alfred Helgerson.

In 1879, a Julius A. Barnsback served as Jarvis Township Supervisor. In the Troy Historical Society's research, nothing could be found about Julius A. Barnsback, but it is supposed, he was a direct descendant to one of the aforementioned Barnsbacks. Many of the family members married people whose names are familiar in Troy and in Jarvis Township. *Submitted by Mae Grapperhaus.*

JULIUS L. BARNSBACK - Julius L. Barnsback, son of Ludwig Berensbach and Caroline Brauna, was born at Lautenthal in the Kingdom of Hanover (Germany).

At the age of six, he lost his father and his mother. He was educated by his aunt in Uslar. At 19, he began his career in the mining district of Germany in the Hertz Mountains.

His health was not sufficient to continue his business, so in the company of a Mr. Ernst, he emigrated in the 1820s to North America. He settled in Illinois where his Uncle George was then residing.

He bought land and followed farming as his occupation until 1836 when he made a voyage to Germany. He returned in 1837 and with some funds; and since he was not able to bear the hard work of farm life, he settled in Edwardsville as a merchant. He was elected four times as Justice of the Peace. He was engaged in many kinds of occupations in America. He was considered as having lived a useful and inspirational life.

He also commanded a company of mounted riflemen as Captain in the campaign of 1832, against the Blackhawks, and was four months a captain in the U.S. service at that time.

He married Mary M. Gonterman, daughter of Jacob Gonterman, in Ridge Prairie in 1827. They had six children: Elizabeth, Lewis, George, Mina, Henry and Julius G.

This information was taken from *The History of the Family of George Friedrich Julius Barnsback* published in 1909. *Submitted by Mae Grapperhaus.*

RALPH AND LISA BARRAS AND FAMILY
Ralph and Lisa Barras and sons moved to Troy in December of 1999, from Altus, OK. Ralph left active duty in the Air Force to accept a job with the Illinois Air National Guard at Scott Air Force Base. Ralph was raised in New Iberia, LA, and Lisa was raised in Oklahoma City, OK. Phillip was born in New Iberia, LA: Kyle in Sacramento, CA; and John Tyler in Wichita, KS.

When they found out they were moving to the area and that it was a permanent move for their family, they looked over the different communities. It didn't take them long to choose Troy. They felt that Troy was the best for their family because of the size of the town, the people they met and the Triad School District. Even though it has just been two years, they really feel at home here and their boys love it. Immediately after they moved here, their boys became active in sports, giving the family a wonderful opportunity to meet several Troy families in a short amount of time.

Barras family, Dec. 2001
(l. to r.) Front: Kyle, John Tyler
Back: Ralph, Lisa, Phillip

In October 2000, Lisa began working as a sports reporter for the *Times-Tribune* newspaper. It has been a quick way to learn about the area, the people and the history of this area, not to mention all of the young athletes. She has also enjoyed her time volunteering for the Triad Athletic Booster Club.

Phillip is 15 years old and a freshman at Triad High School where he has been active on the football, basketball and baseball teams. He represented Troy in the summers of 2000 and 2001 as a member of the Troy Reds baseball team at the USSSA World Series. He was a quarterback for the first eighth grade football middle school team, which only had one loss during the season, and the first undefeated freshman football team at Triad High School.

Kyle is 12 years old and a sixth grader at Triad Middle School. He has been active on the Troy Trojans baseball team for two years, participated in the Troy Little Knights basketball program for two years and was a member of the Troy Titans Football team during its inaugural season in the fall of 2001.

John Tyler is six years old and a first grader at C.A. Henning School. He has played baseball for the TBSL for two years and basketball for the YMCA. He attends several Triad sporting events and looks forward to the time when he will be a Knight.

On his time off, Ralph enjoys golfing but spends most of his time attending sporting events. He has enjoyed being a coach for TBSL and at the YMCA.

The Barras family looks forward to continuing to enjoy being active in the community and local organizations, while enjoying the family atmosphere in Troy. *Submitted by Lisa Barras.*

DONALD AND NANCY (MILLS) BARSCH
Donald Barsch and Nancy Mills were married June 24, 1967, in Friedens United Church of Christ in Troy. Don, born April 21, 1943, is the son of John and Martha (Sinskey) Barsch.

Nancy, the daughter of Walter and Florence (Ward) Mills, was born August 19, 1947.

Both are graduates of Triad High School. Don entered the Army in 1965 after completing his Carpenter Apprenticeship and served until just prior to their wedding in 1967. He has worked for contractors as a commercial and residential carpenter. Don also worked at Scott Air Force Base where his experience and skills were put to use renovating buildings listed on the National Historical Register. Nancy worked at Gardner Advertising Company in St. Louis where she began as a secretary and was promoted to Supervisor of Word Processing. Eventually deciding it was time for a change, she went to work at KSDK-TV where she worked first in the Personnel Department and then as Assistant to the General Manager.

Nancy and Don Barsch

Don has always been very active in community service, including spearheading the first Old Fashioned Fourth of July Picnic. He remains active in the American Legion where he holds the office of Adjutant. Nancy focuses her energy on her family and spends her free time "antiquing" and writing. *Submitted by Nancy Barsch.*

JOHN AND MARTHA (SINSKEY) BARSCH - Two of the earlier families in Troy were the Barsch and Sinskey families. Both emigrated from Poland and Lithuania, settling first in Pennsylvania where the men worked in the coal mines.

John and Martha (Sinskey) Barsch,
wedding photo, 1927

There Barbara Haluch married Joseph Barsch and they had four sons. Joseph was killed in an accident and Barbara eventually married John Marshall. Barbara and John had one son.

The family later moved to Troy where they both had relatives and John Marshall worked in the coal mine.

John Barsch, one of Barbara and Joseph's sons, enlisted in the U.S. Marines in 1922. After serving three years, he returned to Troy where he met Martha Sinskey. They were married at St. Jerome's Church in 1927. Of that marriage, seven children were born, all delivered by Dr. Charles Molden. The children, four girls and three boys, are Barbara Waters, Adeline Frederking, Mary Jay Sackett, Joan Niebruegge, John, and twins Donald and Ronald. Though John and Martha are both deceased, they had 21 grandchildren and seven great grandchildren.

For many years John Sr. worked in the coal mines, but at one time he and Martha operated a tavern where "My Brother's Place" is now. Two of their children were born there.

William "Nance" Barsch, one of John's brothers, operated a shoe repair shop on Kimberlin Street where he lived with his stepfather, John Marshall. That house has been converted into an apartment building.

John and Martha lived near the coal mine in a mine-owned house and later bought the house at 301 Edwardsville Road where Dr. Lopatin's office is now located. They purchased the house from the Voss family after the coal mine closed.

Of John and Martha's seven children, Barbara, Joan and Don still live in Troy. Adeline lives in Glen Carbon, Mary Jay lives in St. Jacob, John "Buck" lives in Nevada and Ron lives in Minnesota. *Submitted by Nancy Barsch.*

GEORGE BAUER - The Bauer family of rural Caseyville Township traces its beginnings to the 1840s -1850s when George Bauer (1819-1899) came to the United States from Bavaria, Germany. The reason he left Germany, according to family folklore, was that he and two friends had "killed a rabbit."

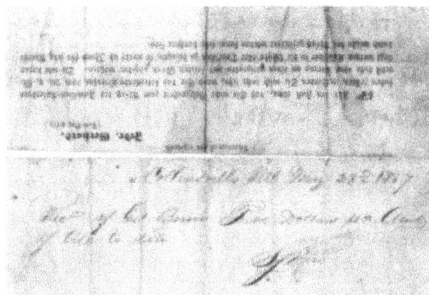

Documents of George and John Bauer.

During that time, this was verbotin. All three men, George Bauer, John Feig, and John Malter, decided to come to America to avoid the unpleasant consequences.

George Bauer settled in St. Clair County in land adjacent to the Madison County line. The deed for the land indicates it was purchased January 19, 1853, from Henry Baierlein. The first tax receipts date back to 1855 and describe the location of forty acres. Here, he built log barns and a house.

Although we do not know her name, George Bauer did marry, producing three children: John, Margaret and Kunigunda. He became a widower between 1863 and 1870. Upon George's death March 14, 1899, George's son John inherited the family farm of eighty

acres. Forty of the acres had been added in February 1892. John continued to enlarge the farm until it was nearly five hundred acres at the time of his death in 1928. His widow Kunigunda (Krauss Sanna Weiss Bauer) retained ownership of the farm until her death in 1945. At that time the farm was divided into parcels and sold at public auction. Of the four Bauer heirs – Peter, Katherine, John Jr., and William – only Bill and John, Jr. bought parcels. John Jr. is now deceased and his son John III occupies a small portion of the John Bauer, Sr. farm.

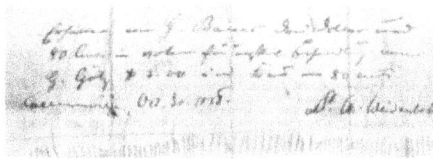

Documents of George and John Bauer.

Great-grandparents of George Bauer were Johann Georg Bauer July 8, 1809-March 14, 1899; great-great-grandparents of George Bauer were Johann Bauer December 8, 1773-January 8, 1845; great-great-great-grandfather of George Bauer was Christoph Bauer (birth unknown and death unknown).

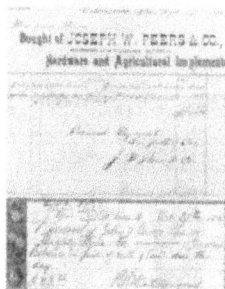

Documents of George and John Bauer.

As research continues, records go back as early as the 1600's. George Bauer's grandfather, John Bauer, Sr., was one of the first to introduce the thrashing machine in the State of Illinois, according to family records. George D. Bauer is married to Diana (Waline) Bauer and resides in Troy. George is a Lab Technician by trade in the dairy industry. He has three sons and four grandchildren. Interests include fishing, camping, boating and cooking. Many thanks to Aunt Doris Bauer for her many, many years of research on the family name and ancestors. *Submitted by George D. Bauer.*

OTTO AND GERTRUDE BAUMGARTNER
Otto Anthony Baumgartner and Gertrude Anna (Feldt) Baumgartner were married on July 28, 1936, in Pierron. Otto was born on November 29, 1911, to Otto and Christina (Kreiter) Baumgartner of Beaver Prairie near Carlyle. Gertrude was born on February 7, 1918, to Henry and Anna (Rasch) Feldt of Trenton.

Otto grew up in Beaver Prairie near Carlyle, and Gertrude, in Clinton County near Trenton. After their marriage, they lived in Millersburg-Pierron for eight years, Grantfork,

Highland, and then moved to Troy in 1952. They were blessed with eleven children: Leonard (b.1937) married the late Betty Heller; Esther (b.1938) married Donald Miller; Jerome (b.1940) married Rita Lewis; Mary (b.1942) married Charles Hobbs; Christina (b.1943) married the late Kenneth Friess; Henry (b.1945) married Carolyn Felton; Otto (b.1946) married Sharon Daiber; Anna (b.1948) married Richard Mersinger; Agnes (b.1950) married Frank Raine; Theresa (b.1953) married Robert Deak; and Paul (b. in 1955) married Mary Jo Drees.

Otto and Gertrude were also blessed with 37 grandchildren, 46 great-grandchildren and one great-great-granddaughter.

Otto Anthony worked over 23 years for Illinois Power and was still working for the power company, especially around the Granite City area, when he died on February 6, 1966.

Five generations of Baumgartners, 2000 (l. to r.) Front: Jennifer Forrester, Kayln Forrester, Gertrude Baumgartner. Back: Leonard Jr., Leonard Sr.

Baumgartner family circa 1970 (l. to r.) Front: Theresa, Mary, Agnes, Anna, Christina. Back: Paul, Henry, Leonard, Gertrude, Esther, Jerome, Otto

Wedding photo, July 28, 1936 Otto and Gertrude Baumgartner

Betty and Leonard Baumgartner and oldest daughter, Tammy Mitchell, center, in happy times. Other children not pictured are Leonard, Michael, Julie and Danny. Photo taken January 7, 1986, on Leonard Sr.'s birthday.

Otto was a member of St. Jerome Catholic Church in Troy, and Gertrude is still an active member of St. Jerome Catholic Church and St. Ann's CCW. Gertrude loved gardening and canning for her large family. She babysat for several of the grandchildren over the years. She loves growing flowers, feeding the birds, going to garage sales, and walking daily on the walking trail at the Tri-Township Park. Gertrude loves large family gatherings. Her children take turns taking her to church every Sunday and visiting with their families. *Submitted by Sharon Baumgartner.*

OTTO AND SHARON BAUMGARTNER

Otto Baumgartner of Troy and Sharon (Daiber) Baumgartner, of Alhambra made their home in Troy after their marriage on November 15, 1969, in Grantfork.

(l. to r.) Michelle, Laurie, Susan, 2000

Otto was born on October 4, 1946, to Gertrude (Feldt) Baumgartner and the late Otto Baumgartner of Troy. Sharon was born on February 6, 1949, to Quentin Daiber and the late Josephine (Wolbert) Daiber of Alhambra.

While growing up in Troy, Otto worked for Levo's Bakery and purchased his first bicycle from Western Auto in Troy with his earnings. He graduated from Triad High School in 1965. Otto worked for McDonnell Aircraft before and after serving in the United States Army. He is a veteran of the Vietnam War and belongs to the American Legion and VFW in Troy. Otto worked several years for his brother Leonard Baumgartner, who owned Len's Gulf and Len's Service in Troy. Otto and Sharon purchased the business in 1992 which is now Troy Tri-Auto, Inc. Otto is the manager and Sharon is the secretary for the business. Sharon graduated

from Highland High School in 1967 and worked there as a secretary. Because Sharon loves to work with children, she has been a school bus driver for the past several years.

Otto played softball for over twenty-five years for Troy teams including Allen's Drugs and Eberhart Heating and Cooling. He bowled many years and played horseshoes. Otto was a stock car driver at Highland Speedway and pit crewed for his brothers. Otto is an avid fan of the St. Louis sports teams and the late Nascar driver, Dale Earnhardt. Otto loves hunting, boating, Nascar racing, and, especially, golfing. Sharon was a Girl Scout leader for several years and helped coach girls' recreational soccer and softball. Sharon loves bowling, reading, craft fairs and traveling.

Otto and Sharon Baumgartner, 1996

Otto and Sharon were blessed with three daughters, Michelle (1970), Susan (1972) and Laurie (1978). They have one grandson, Maverick Michael (2001). Otto, Sharon and family belong to St. Jerome's Catholic Church in Troy.

Michelle Baumgartner graduated from Triad High School in 1988. She earned her BSN at SIU-Edwardsville (1992) and her MSN at St. Louis University in Missouri (1998). She is employed by Washington University as a Cardiothoracic Clinical Nurse Specialist. Growing up, Michelle was active in Girl Scouts, 4-H, soccer, volleyball, band and a member of the Triad Pom Pon Squad. Michelle loves rollerblading, biking, photography, and going to Blues' Hockey games.

Susan (Baumgartner) Mazur graduated from Triad High School in 1990. She graduated from BAC-Belleville and earned a BS in Mathematical Studies with Secondary Education at SIU-Edwardsville (1995). She is a math teacher at Hazelwood East High School in Missouri. Susan married Brandon Mazur of Glen Carbon in 1996 in Maryville. They have a son, Maverick, born on January 4, 2001. Growing up in Troy, Susan was active in Girl Scouts, 4-H, soccer, gymnastics, track, cross-country, band and cheerleading.

Laurie Baumgartner graduated from Triad High School in 1996. She graduated from Western Illinois University-Macomb with a BS in Physical Education/Athletic Training on May 5, 2001. Laurie earned a $5000 scholarship for graduate school. She hopes to obtain her master's degree while continuing to work as an athletic trainer. Growing up Laurie loved sports. She played soccer, softball, and basketball. Laurie was in Girl Scouts and loves swimming, water-skiing and snow skiing.

All three daughters graduated with honors. Otto and Sharon are proud of their three daughters' accomplishments. They hope to have more grandchildren like Maverick to love and share stories with of their lives here in Troy. *Submitted by Sharon Baumgartner.*

MARTHA MERSINGER BAYER - Martha was born on August 28, 1894, at the family home on East Mill Creek Road in Blackjack. She was the oldest of nine children of Adam and Elizabeth (Ella) Riebold. She was baptized at St. John the Baptist church in Blackjack where she attended school.

Martha (Mersinger) Bayer on her 90th birthday, 1994

She would ride to school in a horse-driven sleigh in winter with neighbor children, throwing a blanket over their heads to keep warm (and probably sharing germs which caused so many epidemics).

She left school after the third grade to help with responsibilities at home. When her mother passed away in July 1909, her responsibilities increased. Their neighbors, the Ottweins, helped as much as they could, but much of the burden was on Martha's shoulders. By this time, Martha was driving a horse and buggy with aplomb. About two years later, Adam thought it might be easier for him to raise his family in St. Louis.

When she was nearing 20 years old, she went to work as a bookkeeper in a small, local shirt factory owned by her future mother-in-law. This is how she met her husband, Joe Bayer. They were married in August 1916.

Among her many talents, Martha was noted for her quilting abilities. She died in April 1995, at the age of 100 years and 8 months. *Submitted by Arlene Vien.*

MINNIE RIEDER BEAVER - Minnie Rieder was born to August and Margaret (Christman) Rieder on December 13, 1898. Her mother died when she was two years old. After that time she and an older sister were sent to live with her uncle and aunt-Albert and Emma Rieder. They lived on a farm in Blackjack for a number of years, and later in a house at the edge of Troy.

She was married to Charles Beaver. They had three children: Helen, Albert, and Arthur. She died on November 29, 1979.

Her daughter, Helen Dorothy (Beaver) Dresch, was born on December 27, 1920. She recalled that her mother was quite progressive for her time, and that she was either the first or one of the first young women in Troy to drive a car.

Mrs. Dresch died in October of 2000. *Submitted by Pat Rehg.*

EMIL BECHERER - Emil Becherer was born March 16, 1904, to Henry and Elizabeth (Mersinger) Becherer and died December 3, 1987. He married Agnes Kalmer on February 12, 1941, at St. Damians Church in Damiansville, IL. Agnes was born in Damiansville on November 27, 1911, to Henry and Bertha (Heckenkemper) Kalmer.

Emil and Agnes Becherer

The Becherers settled on a farm in the Blackjack Community about five miles south of Troy. They have two sons and three daughters. The eldest son is Henry Joseph, born March 13, 1942. (See The Henry Joseph Becherer Family for additional information.) James Emil, born August 17, 1944, resides with his wife June (Scheibal) in Summerfield, IL. Eldest daughter Mary Elizabeth Kolo was born July 21, 1945, and resides in Collinsville, IL. Theresa Marie Kohlmiller was born October 24, 1946, and resides in Edwardsville with husband Ronald. Jo Ann Leitz was born June 21, 1953, and resides in Kirkwood, MO, with husband Robert. They also have 11 grandchildren and 12 great-grandchildren.

Emil farmed in Blackjack until his retirement when son Jim took over to work the family farm. During retirement Emil pursued his hobbies of whittling and broom making. Agnes was an avid quilter and spent countless hours piecing, marking and quilting quilts. She is a resident at Maryville Manor in Maryville, IL, and will celebrate her 90th birthday in November. *Submitted by Mary Ann Becherer.*

HENRY JOSEPH BECHERER - Henry Joseph Becherer was born in Highland, IL, on March 13, 1942, to Emil and Agnes (Kalmer) Becherer. He grew up on a farm in the Blackjack community south of Troy and was a member of the first graduating class of Triad High School in 1960. While serving with the United States Army from 1962 to 1965, he spent 2 1/2 years in Germany. After his discharge he went to work for AT&T in December 1965, retiring in March 2001.

On November 12, 1966, he married Mary Ann C. Norbury at S. S. Peter and Paul Catholic Church in Collinsville, the first wedding to be held in the new church. Mary Ann was born in East St. Louis, IL, on July 8, 1947, to Charles William and Agnes Ann (Petry) Norbury and grew up in the neighboring community of Collinsville, graduating from Collinsville High

School in 1965. They lived in that community until 1970 when Henry moved his family to Troy. In 1980 they moved to the farm in the Blackjack community where Henry was reared.

Henry and Mary Ann have four sons and seven grandchildren. Christopher Allan Becherer was born August 26, 1967. He is a supervisor with Raytheon Aerospace LLS in San Antonio, TX. On August 3, 1991, he married Lisa Hayes. Lisa, born October 2, 1967, is an X-ray Technician. They reside in Cibolo, TX, with their children Brenden Christopher (b. November 19, 1992), Cody Allan (b. April 2, 1997), and Christa Lynn (b. September 4, 1998).

Scott Wayne Becherer was born May 30, 1967. He and Loralee West were married on November 20, 1993. Loralee, a housewife, was born April 14, 1966. They reside in Twentynine Palms, CA, where Scott is stationed with the United States Marine Corp. He has a stepdaughter Alexandria Lee Whalen (b. October 13, 1990) and a son Tyler Scott (b. June 9, 1994).

Henry and Mary Ann Becherer, 1998

Curtis Michael Becherer was born September 29,1971. He married Angela Crawford on September 11, 1998. Angie, a housewife, was born December 13, 1968. They reside in Jenkinsburg, GA, with son Drew Michael born August 14, 1999. Curt is a flight mechanic with Delta Airlines.

Gregory Joseph Becherer was born January 18, 1974. He and Emily Pfeil, born November 5, 1973, were married on January 9, 1999. They reside in Troy with their son Gavin Reece, born February 13, 2000. Greg is a sheet metal worker with Westerheide Sheet Metal, and Emily is a student at Southwestern Illinois College.

Through the years Henry and Mary Ann have been actively involved in the Troy community. They are active members of St. Jerome Catholic Church. Henry is also a member of the Troy Knights of Columbus. The Becherers are avid campers and plan on traveling now that Henry is retired. *Submitted by Mary Ann Becherer.*

LESLIE AND MELORA BECKER - Leslie G. Becker was born July 2, 1930, in Highland, IL. He is the son of Lester and Hulda (Ottwein) Becker of Troy, IL. He attended Troy Public Schools, graduating in 1948. 217 E. Market was where they lived, but he preferred the farm, so he stayed out with his Aunt Hilda and Uncle Oscar Ottwein, helping on the farm and playing with his cousins. He has a lot of fond memories of gatherings out on the farm. Family members

are still celebrating special occasions out there. As he got older, he was employed by them to help with the farming. He also helped deliver milk for the Ottwein's Fairview Farm Dairy.

Leslie and Melora Becker

On November 5, 1951, he entered the service as a Marine, spending most of his time at Camp Lejeune, NC.

Melora Sackett Becker was born June 27, 1930, in Highland, IL, the daughter of Melvin and Lenora (Schrumpf) Sackett. Her father was a life insurance salesman and they moved frequently, finally settling in Edwardsville where she graduated in 1948.

They were married November 20, 1954. She worked for Shell Oil Co. until the family started to arrive. Leslie worked for Watson Lumber Co., Madison Service Co., Cottonwood Station Corp. and McDonnell Douglas. They lived at 308 Franklin in Troy for 5 years and then moved to Edwardsville, IL.

While living in Troy they attended Friedens United Church Of Christ. He served 8 years on the church board. He also was co-leader of the Troy Acme 4-H club for several years. They now attend Eden United Church Of Christ where he served 3 years on the Church Council, and was president of the brotherhood for several years. Scouting has been his main interest. He has received many awards including the Silver Beaver and recently the God and Service.

Melora was a homemaker until the children were grown, then she worked at SIU dining service for 16 years. She was a Girl Scout leader for 10 years and taught Sunday School for 25 years. She plays flute in the Troy Community Band, and loves to work on genealogy.

They have 4 children: Terry, Yvonne (Ginter), Kenneth, and Dianne (Stricker), 7 grandchildren and 3 stepgrandchildren.

They are both retired and enjoy an active family, church and community life. They enjoy traveling, especially to Denver, CO, to visit Yvonne, Ringo, Eric and Marisa Ginter and to Fountain Hills, AZ. to visit Dianne, Michael, Jessica, Brett and Jennifer Stricker. *Submitted by Melora Becker*

LESTER AND HULDA BECKER - Lester C. Becker was born May 10, 1901, in St. Louis, MO, the son of Louis and Minnie Berkenkamp Becker. The oldest of seven children, he quit school at age fourteen to help support the family, and later attended night school to finish.

Lester's grandmother Catherine Becker was a friend of Hulda Ottwein's grandmother

Hulda and Lester Becker, 1974

in St. Louis. Both came out to visit the Ottweins in Troy. When Lester was eighteen, they brought him along to visit the Ottweins.

Hulda (Ottwein) Becker was born November 20, 1901, on a farm near Maryville, IL. She was the oldest of the five children of George and Carrie (Wilhelm) Ottwein. She lived at home on the Ottwein farm just west of Troy until she married Lester on June 8, 1926, in the Ottwein home. They had no honeymoon and no money. The next morning they attended Uncle Adam Petry's funeral, which had been postponed because of the wedding.

They moved to St. Louis, MO, for one year, then back to Troy, moving in with the Ottweins at 217 E. Market.

Their son Leslie was born July 2, 1930. They shared the house with Helen (Ottwein) and Milton Voss until 1934, when they moved back to St. Louis for one year, later moving back to the house on Market Street and staying.

Lester was employed at the Busy Bee Candy Co. in St.Louis until 1942 when he started to work for Irwin and Elma Dollinger as a grocery clerk at their Troy IGA Grocery. Irwin sold out to Ed Guennewig, and Lester worked for him until August of 1948. He then started to work for John Kelly at the Kroger store. He worked there until 1952 when he started working at the Troy Security Bank, working there for 22 years and retiring in 1973 at the age of 72.

Lester served on the Friedens Evangelical Church council and was church school superintendent for 17 years. He was an alderman in Ward 3 for 12 years, and a Lions Club member holding several offices.

Hulda worked for a short time at Hugs Processing Co. and then 4 years at Schmidt's Locker plant. She and her mother did a lot of quilting (2 a month) for people all around the country. She taught Sunday school at Friedens for over 50 years and also held several offices in the Friedens Ladies Aid. She was a longtime active member of the Troy Republican Club. At age 67 she started oil painting, creating many beautiful scenes for family and friends, becoming a member of the Gateway East Artist Guild. Lester died September 30, 1989. Hulda lived in the house on Market Street until 1993 when her granddaughter Dianne Becker married Michael Stricker. They moved into the house, and Hulda moved to her son Leslie's in Edwardsville. Strickers moved to Arizona, and the house was sold in 1997, having been in the

family 70 years. Hulda died ctober 25, 1997. *Information taken from Hulda Becker's memoirs. Submitted by Melora Becker.*

ARLENE BELLMANN - Arlene Bellmann, longtime employee of the *Troy Tribune*, worked for 40 plus years and was an Editorial Assistant.

Arlene Bellmann

THE BLISS FAMILY OF TROY - Older residents will remember Gladys Bliss working in Kelly's Kroger store for 9 years. The store had no air-conditioning in the summer, and a potbelly stove in the winter. When everyone got busy, the fire went out. Workers had to add all the sales by hand.

At that time, half the building was Cullop's Hardware. The firehouse was in back, and the *Tribune* office housed Hap Liebler's Hardware. Across the street was Adelhardt's store. Porter's garage was where the City Building is now. Lucille Auwarter was the switchboard operator in the telephone building. Schoon had the drug store, and, yes, it had a soda fountain. In between, Wheeler Davis was Postmaster in the little post office.

Lester Bliss was teaching cadets to fly for the army at Parks Area College in Dupo. After the war he taught St. Louis businessmen to fly; among them were Von Gontard, President of Anheuser-Busch and Charles Stookey, radio farm announcer on KMOX. He took Ed Wilson, another announcer, up in a Piper Cub. He was so fat, Les couldn't get the wheel pulled back far enough for take-off. They almost hit the power lines. They never tried that again. He also taught Father Walsh and Father Cartier of E. St. Louis to fly so they could fly in and out of the Hudson Bay Country. They were the first flying priests.

The Bliss family bought 34 acres east of Troy and moved his folks, Rose and Melvin Bliss, down here. The family had come from St. Paul, MN, in 1941. In 1948 they purchased 3 1/2 acres out front from Cora and Fred Edwards. Fred had a gas station next to it and his wife had a small restaurant. The Edwards also had 3 small cabins.

The Bliss family built their house and were proud to be living on a short stretch of the "Old National Trail West." The road was a brick road.

Twin sons Lloyd and Larry were born June 11, 1952. They were Dr. Zielonko's first set of twins. They were in the first kindergarten class Troy started, but the class was at the new Marine school.

About this time they decided to tear up the Old National Trail to straighten it, taking one half acre, leaving the Bliss home on a bank. The

address has changed 5 times, but the family has never moved.

Gladys was a den mother when her sons were in Cub Scouts. They graduated from Triad High School in 1970. They graduated from Ranken Technical School in 1972. Lloyd took carpentry. He worked for Gravois Planing Mill in St. Louis, but the work was never steady. He took a job at Triad High School temporarily. Larry took Industrial Electricity. He worked at Crunden Martin. When Anderson Hospital was built, he put in his application and still works there. They get a kick out of people who don't know they are twins. Some think they are holding down 2 jobs. People see them in stores and wonder why they don't recognize them. They have to explain it must have been their twin.

Melvin Bliss worked a while at the Troy Elevator and also at Watson Lumber Co. He passed away with a heart attack in 1958. Jewel Edwards took his body up to Iowa for burial after the funeral here.

Mr. Henning offered Gladys a job in the cafeteria of the new Molden school. She worked there 3 years before going to United Savings and Loan Association and Shaffer's Insurance. She retired after 17 years. She has enjoyed retirement and has done a lot of traveling. She likes camping, hiking and bike riding. She loves to quilt and has quilted for years at Friedens church.

Bliss family, 1962
(l. to r.) Front: Lloyd, Larry
Back: Gladys, Lester

Gladys has seen a lot of changes in the last 60 years. There was no Twin Lakes, only corn fields to the east. The farm fields west of Troy have disappeared, too.

In November of 1981 their home was hit by a tornado. They lost their double garage and 11 trees. Luckily, the house was spared. The bay window was blown in, shingles torn off, but most of the home was preserved. *Submitted by Gladys Bliss.*

ROB AND LOU BOHNENSTIEHL - Robert Arthur Bohnenstiehl (1891-1966) married Louise Jane Wilhelm (1890-1985) in January 1914. Robert was born and raised in the Blackjack area; and Louise, in the Formosa School area. Rob boarded with George and Carrie Ottwein and worked in the Troy Mine. Before their mariage, Lou worked for her sister Carrie Ottwein, helping care for the children. They farmed what is now known as Country Village on the Frontage Road west of Troy. Supposedly, Rob crossed a frozen Mississippi River with a team and wagon to deliver potatoes and other items to St. Louis. He was a fine horseman, sometimes breaking horses for other people. Most Saturdays he was busy butchering beef for others. He also had a trucking business, delivering chickens and livestock to the E. St. Louis stockyards. (Arthur Riggin bought the business.)

Robert and Louise Bohnenstiehl, 1964

Louise was born on the farm she and Rob eventually purchased from her parents. However, as newlyweds, they lived in the house at Foucek's Nursery, later moving to the Kirsch farm in Blackjack and, eventually, to the "home place," living there until 1945.

Their only son, Lester Wilhelm Bohnenstiehl, was born Dec. 30, 1914. He married Melba Klueter (b. 1915) in 1939, and their first home was at the corner of Oak and Webster Streets. A foster son, Elmer Eckert, 16, came to live with them from the Hoyleton Home. The first day he arrived, he stuck himself with a pitchfork and had to work in the house, helping Lou with housework. Things improved rapidly and Elmer never thought of anyone else as his parents. Elmer served in the military, received a degree from U of I, and became an ag engineer. He married Sheri Norris in Troy in 1964. Both Elmer and Sheri have died and are buried in Troy. They had no children.

In 1945, Rob and Lou and Melba and Les traded houses, when Les and Melba took over the farming operation, and Rob retired. Rob worked for Watson Lumber Co. during his retirement and as Evangelical Cemetery caretaker. He still helped with "butchering" at many area farmsteads. A charter member of the Lions Club, he worked the hamburger stand at the Homecoming. Louise was active in church Ladies Aid, especially quilting and White Elephant Sales. When the Feldmeier house (circa 1930 at 219 East Market Street) sold, Rob and Lou happily purchased it. They enjoyed being close to relatives and close to church.

Two children were born to Les and Melba, Rosalie Bohnenstiehl Brackebusch (b. 1940) of Divernon, IL, and Darwin Bohnenstiehl (b. 1942) of Milner, GA. Both attended Troy schools and graduated from the University of Illinois.

Les and Melba divorced and Les married June Franz in 1973. Their first home was in an apartment in Troy; later they purchased a home in Highland, IL.

Melba built a home in Cottonwood and married David Hunker (1913-1988) in 1976. She now resides in Auburn, IL. *Submitted by Rosalie Brackebusch.*

ALOYS HENRY AND LEONA SUE (RUSSELL) BRENDEL - Aloys Henry

Brendel was born in Troy, IL, on August 14, 1916, the son of George and Mary (Gogel) Brendel. He married Leona Sue Russell (born on April 15,1917) of Waverly, TN, on January 30,1937. Leona was the daughter of Emma Jane (Cochran) and Dee Dixon Russell. Leona passed away March 10, 1981, and is buried at Friedens Cemetery in Troy.

As a teenager, Al worked in St. Louis at the stock exchange. He became good enough in the sport of boxing to win the Golden Gloves in St. Louis, the welter weight division in 1936 and the light weight division in 1937. Al served in the U.S. Navy during World War II on the LST 888, as a cook. After serving in the Navy, he eventually became a machinist helper, then machinist, working at several steel plants in Granite City, retiring in 1978. He enjoyed gardening, pinochle, traveling and wood working, making lamps and bowls. Leona enjoyed pinochle, reading, helping with the vegetable and flower garden, knitting and crocheting. They moved to Troy in 1952 from St. Louis.

Brendel family 1959
(l. to r.) Front: Keith, Doug
Back: Leona, Don, Al

They had 3 sons: Donald, Keith, and Douglas. Donald Lee Brendel was born July 17, 1938, in St. Louis. Don married Kathleen (Kay) Schulz on April 6,1963, at Pilgrim United Church of Christ in St. Louis. Don and Kay have 3 sons, Kent David (July 18, 1964), Steven Jeffrey (Januay 11, 1967) and David Jay (June 14, 1976).

Keith Aloys Brendel was born October 3, 1946, in St. Louis. He married Donna Marie Weber, daughter of Wilbur and Alberta Weber of Marine, IL, on October 2, 1971, at the United Church of Christ of Marine. Donna was born June 10, 1953. They have two children, Nichole Lee (Feb. 1, 1977) and Todd Allen (June 3,1981).

Their third son, Douglas Russell Brendel, was born August 14, 1952. He married Deborah Joy Mesle, daughter of Kenneth and Joy Mesle of Highland, on March 19,1978, at Highland United Church of Christ. They have two children, Carrie Joy (Sept. 22,1979) and Douglas Alan (August 16,1981).

Al married Marie (Kueker) Bode on April 3,1982, at St. Paul Luthern Church in Troy. Marie passed away December 31, 1986, and is buried at St. Paul's Cemetery in Troy. *Submitted by Kay Brendel.*

DONALD AND KATHLEEN (KAY) BRENDEL - Donald Lee Brendel was born

in St. Louis, MO, on July 17,1938, to Aloys and Leona (Russell) Brendel. He has two brothers, Keith Aloys Brendel of Highland, IL, and Douglas Russell Brendel of Troy, IL. His family moved to Troy from St. Louis in 1952. Upon graduating from McCray-Dewey High School, he entred the U.S. Navy, serving as a sonar technician. After 4 years in the military, Don worked for Potter Electric, installing alarm systems; St. Louis Car; General Steel Castings in Granite City; Purex Co.; and McDonnell-Douglas (now Boeing) in St. Louis as a maintenance electrician.

On April 6,1963, Don married Kathleen (Kay) Evelyn Schulz, daughter of Charles and Evelyn (Moeller) Schulz at Pilgrims United Church of Christ in South St. Louis. Kay and her twin brother, Raymond Charles Schulz, were born at St. Mary's Hospital in St. Louis, on November2, 1942.

Don and Kay have three sons: Kent David, born July 18, 1964; Steven Jeffrey, born January 11, 1967; and David Jay, born June 14, 1976. Kent and David reside in Troy. Kent drives a semi for CRST and David is a cook for Tippin's in South County, Missouri. David has a daughter, Bryanna Michelle. Steve is married to Monica (Skalisius) Brendel and they reside in Collinsville, IL. They have 3 sons: Andrew, Jesse and Seth. Steve is a welder, working in St. Louis, and Monica is a manager for Denny's Restaurant in Fairview Heights, IL.

Kay worked in the secretarial/clerical field for Farmer's Insurance District Office in Collinsville and operated her own business as a greeter for 17 years, welcoming new residents and newlyweds to the Troy community. Kay currently works for Jarvis Township Assessor as a deputy assessor. Her community activities include serving as an election judge, being a member of Friedens United Church of Christ in Troy, serving on the library board for 8 years, being a member of the Woman's Club of Troy and the Gateway East Artist Guild, and working in the Troy Chamber of Commerce when doing Troy Welcomes You.

Brendel family 1981
(l. to r.) Front: Steve, David
Back: Kay, Kent, Don

Don retired from Boeing in 2000. He enjoys traveling, St. Louis Baseball Cardinals and Rams games, the history channel, crossword puzzles, pinochle, music concerts, and helping Kay love and spoil their grandchildren. Kay enjoys art classes in oils, acrylics, watercolor, and pastels, reading, sewing, crafts, music concerts, pinochle, traveling, cooking and computer technology. *Submitted by Kay Brendel.*

DOUGLAS RUSSELL AND DEBORAH JOY (MESLE) BRENDEL -
Douglas Russell Brendel was born August 14,1952, to Aloys and Leona (Russell) Brendel who had just moved to Troy from St. Louis. Doug married Deborah Joy Mesle, daughter of Kenneth and Joy Mesle, on March 19,1978, at the Evangelical United Church of Christ in Highland, IL, where her father was pastor. They have two children: Carrie Joy, born September 22, 1979, and Douglas Alan, born August 16, 1981. They are active members of Friedens United Church of Christ.

Brendel family, 1993
(l. to r.) Front: Carrie, Doug
Back: Debbie, Doug

Doug graduated from Triad and received his teaching degree in elementary education from SIUE. He has been teaching sixth grade and coaching track and field in the O'Fallon school district since 1975. His interests and hobbies are family and sports oriented. He especially likes basketball and baseball.

Debbie received her nursing degree from SIUE. She works as a Nurse Case Manger for SSM Rehab. She has enjoyed music all her life and is currently an organist, accompanist and vocal soloist at Friedens Church. She is active in the Troy Main Street organization and plays clarinet in the Community Band.

Daughter Carrie attended the Troy schools and received a degree in Environmental Biology from SIUE. She currently works in the Pathology Lab at Washington University. She, also, has studied music and has a semi-professional career as a singer. She enjoys all kinds of music — country-western, contemporary Christian, musical theater and classical.

Son Doug also attended the Troy schools and is currently attending classes at SWIC in Belleville. His hobbies mainly involve sports, especially golfing.

Deb and Doug have thoroughly enjoyed living in Troy and raising their kids here. The life of this busy family revolves around family, church and civic affairs, music and sports, and lots of good times at their country home in Forest Ridge. *Submitted by Kay Brendel.*

GEORGE & ANNA (FUCHS) BRENDEL
George Brendel was born in Berlin, Germany. He married Anna Fuchs, who was born in the state of Bavaria, Germany, March 17, 1855, and

died December, 1947. Both are buried at St. Jerome's Cemetery in Troy. Her great-grandson, Donald Brendel, remembers Grandma Anna as loving her beer and playing pincohle.

They had nine children: George Brendel, b. 7/1/1884 in O'Fallon, IL, d. 2/7/1952, married Mary Ann Gogel, September 15, 1908, both buried at Resurrection Cemetery in South St. Louis County; Valentine (Dick) Brendel, b. 1895, d.1941, buried at Friedens Cemetery in Troy; Joe Brendel, b. 1888, d. 1960, his wife, Anna W., b. 1890, d. 1958; John Brendel; Henry Brendel, (Uncle Dutch), b. 1890, d. 1956, his wife Anna Mae b. 1904, d.1978, buried at Friedens Cemetery; Margaret Brendel, married Tom Sliva, b. July 17, 1897, d. May 7, 1967, buried at Friedens Cemetery; Anna E. Brendel, first husband, Louis Wells, second husband, Louis Capelle, d. 2/1/1973, buried at St. Jerome's in Troy; Mathias (Uncle Mott) Brendel, b. 5/6/1900, d. 09/14/1975, buried at Friedens, first wife, Estelle Zobrist, b.1901, d. 1933, buried Friedens, second wife, Dora Miller; William (Uncle Willie) Brendel. *Submitted by Kay Brendel.*

JOHN AND ANNA BRENDEL -
John Brendel was born on March 12, 1865, in Germany. He came to the United States in 1882 at the age of 17 and became a citizen in 1892. It is not known if John came to the U.S. alone or with others.

Brendels 1924: Titus, John, Edwin, Ann, Emil, Olivia, Albert, Anna and John.

Anna Schwartz was born in Madison County, IL, on February 15, 1871. Anna was a member of St. John the Baptist Church at Blackjack and a charter member of the St. John's Altar and Rosary Sodality formed around 1890.

John and Anna were married about 1890. They made their home on a farm at 1116 Troy-O'Fallon Rd. They were the parents of seven children: Titus Henry (b. July 8, 1892), Albert Joseph (b. April 16, 1894), John Andrew (b. October 19, 1897), Olivia Lee (Brendel) Arth (b. October 21, 1898), Edwin Conrad (b. February 23, 1902), Emil Peter (b. December 21, 1904), and Ann Marie (Brendel) Haukapp (b. November 28, 1907). John and Anna became members of St. Jerome Catholic Church. John donated a stained glass window pane to the old St. Jerome Catholic Church, which was built in 1895-96 and torn down in 1987. "John Brendel" was written at the bottom of the pane. He may have helped to build that church. John and Ann are buried at St. Jerome Catholic Cemetery on Troy-O'Fallon Rd. *Submitted by Sherry Brendel.*

GEORGE AND MARY ANN (GOGEL) BRENDEL -
George (M) Brendel, son of George and Anna Brendel, was born 7/1/1884 in O'Fallon, IL. He died 2/7/1952. He married Mary Ann Gogel on September 15,1908, at St. Jerome's Catholic Church in Troy. She passed away 1/25/1977. They are both buried at Resurrection Cemetery, South St. Louis County, MO. Her daughter, Viola, used the middle initial of M, like her father, but had no middle name. Mary Ann enjoyed quilting and was excellent at it.

Brendel family circa 1940s. (l. to r.) Front: Viola Ann, George, Mary Ann, Helen Edna. Middle: George John, Wilma Marie, Mary Alberta, Verona Francis, Margaret Alberta. Back: Antony Frederick, Aloys Henry, Charles Joseph, Ernest Joseph.

They resided in Troy until 1928, moving to St. Louis. George worked in the coal mines when living in Troy. They had 12 children: Gertrude Brendel, died in infancy; George John Brendel, born 2/14/1910 (deceased, date unknown); Verona Francis Brendel (Smith), born 1/3/1912 (deceased, date unknown); Margaret Alberta Brendel (Ries),born 4/8/1914, died 1/22/2001; Aloys Henry Brendel, born 8/14/1916; Anthony Frederick Brendel, born 1/16/1918, died 1/10/1988; Wilma Marie Brendel (Cusumano), born 4/11/1920; Mary Frances Brendel (Halley), born 6/16/1921; Viola Anna Brendel (Tacchi), born 12/6/1922; Charles Joseph Brendel, born 10/11/1924; Ernest Joseph, born 4/12/1927, died 3/16/1951 in Korean War; and Helen Edna Brendel (Whittington), born 6/26/1928 (deceased date unknown).

At the time of Mary Ann (Gogel) Brendel's passing, she left behind 38 grandchildren and 35 great-grandchildren. *Submitted by Kay Brendel.*

JOHN AND LOUISE BRENDEL -
John Andrew Brendel, son of John and Anna (Schwartz) Brendel, was born in Troy on October 19, 1897. John grew up on his parents' farm at 1116 Troy-O'Fallon Rd. along with four brothers, Titus, Albert, Edwin, and Emil and two sisters, Olivia and Ann. John was a farmer. John served as the Jarvis Township Road Commissioner in the early 1940s until his death on April 8, 1958.

Louise Margaret (Adelhardt) Brendel, daughter of John and Anny (Shermann) Adelhardt, was born April 11, 1903, in Marine, IL. Louise lived her early life in Marine along with her four brothers: Frank, George, Valentine and Elmer; and three sisters: Mame (Adelhardt) Frey, Sophie (Adelhardt) Purcell and Ann (Adelhardt) Rouse. The family moved to the Troy farm at 1260 Troy-O'Fallon Rd.

The farm that John grew up on and the farm that Louise's family moved to, are situated next to one another. Probably, John and Louise first met as neighbors. After John and Louise were married, they made their home across the road at 8333 Kirsch Rd. on an 80-acre farm. John helped to build the first bridge over the railroad tracks at Kirsch Rd. on Troy-O'Fallon Rd. He was the only person in the area who owned a team of horses to help him do the work.

John and Louise were married April 14, 1920. John and Louise had two sons, Norman George born May 5, 1922, and Kenneth Elmer born April 27, 1927. When Norman married, he moved his new bride Doris to the farm, and John and Louise built a home in Troy on Throp Street. They were members of St. Jerome Catholic Church in Troy.

Louise died on March 4, 1984. John and Louise are buried at St. Peter and Paul Cemetery in Collinsville, IL. *Submitted by Sherry Brendel*

Wedding day, October 19, 1897. Taken at Adelhardt farm. (l. to r.) Front: Anny (Shermann) Adelhardt, Anna (Schwartz) Brendel. Back: John Adelhart, Louise (Adelhardt) Brendel, John A. Brendel, John Brendel.

John Brendel and Louise (Adelhardt) Brendel wedding. Both sides of family taken at Adelhardt farm.

KEITH ALOYS AND DONNA MARIE (WEBER) BRENDEL -
Keith Aloys was born October 3,1946, in St. Louis, MO. He married Donna Marie Weber, daughter of Wilbur and Alberta Weber of Marine, IL, on October 2, 1971, at the United Church of Christ in Marine. Donna was born June 10, 1953. They have two children: Nicole Lee, born February 1, 1977, and Todd Allen, born June 3, 1981.

Keith attended and graduated from the Triad High School in 1966. After high school graduation, he enlisted in the United States Navy, serving in Vietnam on a river patrol boat. After being released from service, he worked at St. Louis Car, Magna Fab and Tower Automotive. Keith is an active member of the Woodsmen of the World and Highland VFW Post 5694.

Brendel family 1983-4
(l. to r.) Front: Todd, Nicole
Back: Donna, Keith

Donna Marie graduated from the Triad School District in 1971. After graduation she worked for National Peace Officer Press in Troy for 6 years. Donna currently owns and operates a child care facility out of her home in Highland. She enjoys doing crafts and has been active in the Woodsmen/Ladies of the World organization for 20 years.

Nicole Lee Brendel is a certified nurse assistant, working in New Baden for Clinton Manor. She is interested in learning the many facets of the computer.

Todd Allen graduated from Highland High School in 1999. He is currently attending ITT in Earth City, MO, and is majoring in electronics. His hobbies and interests are computers and building things electronic. *Submitted by Kay Brendel.*

LARRY AND ANNA MAY BRENDEL
Larry Dean Brendel, son of Norman George and Doris Louise (Kiser) Brendel, was born March 26, 1949, in East St. Louis, IL. Larry and his younger brother Wayne grew up on the Brendel family farm at 8333 Kirsch Road. Larry attended Troy elementary and junior high schools before graduating from Triad High School in 1967. He received a Bachelor of Arts (BA) Degree in Political Science at Southern Illinois University-Edwardsville in 1971, before beginning a career in public service in Springfield, IL, working for the Division of Vocational Rehabilitation, Disability Determination Services (DDS).

Larry met his wife, Anna May (Caufield) Brendel, while employed with the DDS. Anna May, daughter of James Caufield and Barbara Frances (Brown) Caufield, was born on May 20, 1952, in Springfield, IL. Anna May grew up in Standard City, IL, with one brother, Clyde C. Caufield, and attended Carlinville, IL, district schools. She graduated from Carlinville High

Brendel family, 2001
(l. to r.) Matthew, Anna May, Larry, Timothy

School in 1970. Anna May attended Lincoln Land Community College in Springfield and began working as a secretary with DDS in 1972. The couple was married at St. Mary's Catholic Church in Carlinville on May 18, 1974.

Larry and Anna May resided in Springfield until April 1977, when they moved to the Chicago area where Larry worked for the Federal Department of Health and Human Services (DHHS) and Anna May worked for Federal Sign and Signal, Inc. Later, in 1977, the couple moved to Garland, TX. Larry currently works as program manager of DHHS Administration for Children and Families in Dallas, and Anna May is business manager at St. Joseph Catholic Church in Richardson, TX. Larry and Anna May are very active in parish activities at St. Joseph's, including Larry's long time membership in the Knights of Columbus.

Larry and Anna May are the parents of two sons: Matthew Dean Brendel, born April 21, 1978; and Timothy Loren Brendel, born August 2, 1982, both born in Dallas, TX. Matt and Tim both graduated from L.V. Berkner High School in Richardson, TX. Matthew graduated from Texas A&M University in August 2001, earning a Bachelor of Business Administration degree in accounting and Master of Science degree in finance. Tim is currently attending Texas A&M University in College Station, TX, where he is a member of several organizations and the Kappa Alpha fraternity. *Submitted by Larry Brendel.*

NORMAN AND DORIS BRENDEL
Norman George Brendel, son of John Andrew and Louise Margaret (Adelhardt) Brendel was born May 5, 1922, in Troy, IL. Norman grew up on his parents' 80-acre farm, 8333 W. Kirsch Rd. (the corner of Troy-O'Fallon Rd and West Kirsch Rd. just outside Troy). Norman had one brother Kenneth Elmer, born April 27, 1927. Norman attended Spring Valley School to the 8th grade. He left school to help his dad on the farm. He also helped erect the electric poles from Troy to the area and was paid 50 cents a pole.

Brendel family, 1973
(l. to r.) Wayne, Norman, Doris, Larry

Norman farmed the family ground until 1969. The farm ground was subdivided into what is now known as Norman-D Acres and K A Acres. While a farmer, Norman also sold Moews Seed Corn. After the death of his father in 1958, Norman took his father's position as Jarvis Township Road Commissioner. He held

Wedding day, January 21, 1948
Norman and Doris Brendel

that position until 1971. He drove a meat delivery truck for 14 years until 1983. He retired at 61 due to health reasons. Norman was a 4th degree charter member of Troy Knights of Columbus. Norman passed away on August 20, 1997, and is buried at St. John's Cemetery, Blackjack. He was a life long member of St. Jerome Catholic Church.

Doris L. (Kiser) Brendel, daughter of Frank Ira Kiser and Iva Mae (Culley) Kiser-Jarvis, was born in E. St. Louis on January 26, 1926. Doris was raised in E. St. Louis along with one sister, M. Geraldine (Kiser) Harris. Doris graduated from E. St. Louis High School in 1944. She was a member of Delta Zeta Nu Sorority. After graduation Doris worked for the government as a secretary during WW II and later for a private company until she married in 1948. She was a charter member and president of the Troy Democratic Women's Club in the 1970's. She bowled on a league and belonged to a pinochle club. Doris was a member of St. Jerome Catholic Church and St. Ann's Altar Society. She passed away June 27, 2001.

Paul Riebold introduced Norman and Doris to one another at a fish fry held at Mel Niehaus' summer cottage in early spring of 1947. They were married at St. Joseph Catholic Church in E. St. Louis on January 21, 1948. They made their home on the Brendel family farm and lived in the old farmhouse until 1969. The old farmhouse burned in the mid 1970s. The barn and out building are still standing. The next owner built a new home on the site of the old farmhouse. Norman and Doris built a new brick home on the northeast corner of the farm at 1177 Troy-O'Fallon Rd. They sold that home and in 1988 they built a log home on Norman-D Acres, where they lived until Norman's death in 1997. They were the parents of two children, Larry Dean Brendel, born March 26, 1949, and Wayne F. Brendel, born February 28, 1955. *Submitted by Sherry Brendel.*

WAYNE AND SHERRY BRENDEL
Wayne F. Brendel, son of Norman George and Doris Louise (Kiser) Brendel, was born February 28, 1955, in East St. Louis, IL. Wayne and his older brother Larry Dean Brendel grew up on the Brendel family farm at 8333 Kirsch Road. Wayne attended Triad Schools where he graduated in 1973. He has been employed by AA Hotel and Restaurant Supply as a meat cutter for the past 25 years. He is a member of Meat Cutters Union Local No. 88. Wayne is a charter member of the Troy Knights of Columbus. Since 1981 he has held the office of Jarvis Township

Trustee. Wayne was a representative for Heritage Log Homes from Gatlinburg, TN, from 1989 until 1997. He enjoys camping, fishing, hiking and yard work.

Sherry Diane (Miller) Brendel, daughter of John Edward Miller and Janice Gay (Weaver) Miller, was born on December 5, 1958, in Pittsfield, IL. Sherry grew up in the Pleasant Hill, IL, area along with 3 sisters, Christine Lynn (Miller) Riebold, Gail Elaine (Miller) Anderson, and Ellen Kay (Miller) McDade. Sherry graduated from Pleasant Hill High School in 1977. She attended Pima College in Tucson, AZ, and SWIC in Belleville, IL. Before their first son was born, Sherry worked as a bookkeeper and office manager in Illinois, Missouri, and Arizona. Sherry is a parish school of religion catechist at St. Jerome Catholic Church where they are members. She enjoys reading, gardening, canning, cooking, hiking, and camping.

Brendel family, 2001
(l. to r.) Front: Adam, John
Back: Sherry, Wayne

Wayne and Sherry were introduced by her sister and brother-in-law, Mark and Christine Riebold on Memorial Day at a BBQ held at Riebold's home in 1990. Wayne and Sherry were married at St. Jerome Catholic Church in Troy May 25, 1991.

Wayne and Sherry built their log home on one acre of the Brendel family farm known as Norman-D Acres, named after Wayne's parents.

Wayne and Sherry are the parents of two sons, John Andrew Brendel, born January 5, 1994, and Adam Lowell Brendel, born July 21, 1995, both born in Belleville. John and Adam attend Triad Schools. They both enjoy video games, bike riding, bug/rock collecting, and going camping, fishing, and hiking with Mom and Dad. *Submitted by Sherry Brendel.*

BRUNWORTH FAMILY - August George Brunworth was born near Pleasant Ridge (close to Maryville) to Ernst and Mary (Hartbeck) Brunworth (August dropped the double "n" in Brunnworth). They later moved to Troy on Staunton Road near Throp Street and August took up the carpentering trade of his father. In the 1890's August married Lena Schildmeier, who died some years later leaving a daughter, Clara. He bought a house and five acres of land at 333 Staunton Rd.

In October 1898, he married Sophia Langewisch (see Wilhelm and Johanne Langewisch entry). They had five children: Norma (11/19/1899 - 6/19/1987) married Rev. Walter Biesenthal and moved to Ontario,

Wedding photo, October 1898
August and Sophia (Langewisch) Brunworth

Canada; Walter (4/17/1902 – 7/30/1994) married Deborah Gerling and remained in Troy; August (Jack) (8/12/1904 – 1/15/1981) married Henrietta Reuben and moved to St. Louis; Ida (1/17/1907 – 1/24/2003) remained in family home until removed to custodial care in 1994; Paul (6/10/1910 – 10/26/1993) married Josephine Heitmeyer and moved to Collinsville.

All the Gerling and Brunworth children were educated at St. Paul's Lutheran Grade School. They were taught in German until WWI when it was prudent to convert to the English language. The church continued to have German worship services as well as English through the 1940s.

Walter Brunworth and Deborah (Mutz) Gerling were married in November 1930. Six months later, due to the Depression, they moved into three rooms of the Gerling home as just Caroline and her son, Joseph, were living in the seven-room house. June 1934, Walter Gerling Brunworth was born and lived two days. Sharon was born in June 1936. They became owners of the Gerling home when Caroline died in June 1942. In August Joe, a WWI veteran, enlisted in the Army and Lydia Gerling Hecht with her daughters, Bethel and Carolyn, moved into half the house. When Martin retired after 30 years in the Army, he, Lydia and Carolyn moved to a farm near Fredericktown, MO. When Joe Gerling returned from WWII, he lived with Walter and Mutz and worked at the Army Depot in Granite City.

During WWII Ida Brunworth became employed at Myer Bros. Drug Co. in St. Louis. She was very active in the Lutheran Church both locally and regionally. She loved to bowl.

Walter also was very active in the Lutheran Church and was also an avid bowler. He worked for Bruno's Bakery from 1934 until retirement in 1964. He served on Troy's Fireman board for over 20 years.

Wedding photo, November 1930
Deborah (Gerling) and Walter Brunworth

Sharon married Arthur Repp in 1959 and moved to the St. Louis area. She became an RN and worked for DePaul Hospital for 22 years. Her husband taught theology at Lutheran High School North in St. Louis for 36 years. They have four children and 8 grandchildren. *Submitted by Sharon (Brunworth) Repp.*

SEBASTIAN AND MARY BUGGER

Sebastian Joseph Bugger and Mary Annie Dennler were married 14 November 1871, by Rev. P. Peters in Highland, IL. Sebastian was born 20 February 1850, to Adam and Katharina (Walier) Bugger. He died 11 June 1922, and is buried in St. John the Baptist Cemetery in Blackjack, Jarvis Township, Madison County, IL. Mary Annie Dennler was born 23 July 1852, in Jarvis Township. Her mother was Anna Marie (Mary) Dennler and her father was Joseph Schwend, also known as Anton Schwendemann. She died 13 April 1935.

Bugger family, 1911
(l. to r.) Adam, Charles (Uncle Billy), Frank, Zeno, Sebastian (Joe), Mary Emig, Leo, Ida Obernuefemann

Sebastian and Mary had 11 children. The oldest was Adam J., who was born 11 August 1872. He died 7 July 1953, and is buried in St. John the Baptist Cemetery, Blackjack. Anne Maria (Annie) was born in Blackjack on 2 August 1874. She married Peter Munier 23 February 1897, at St. John the Baptist Church in Blackjack. She died 12 July, 1950, in O'Fallon, IL, where she is buried. Caroline Ann (Carrie) was born 1 September 1876, in Blackjack. On 3 September 1901, she was married to William L. Joseph. She died 3 May 1960, and is buried in St. Joseph Cemetery in Lebanon, IL. A second son, John Adam, was born 7 September 1878. He married Louisa B. Fohne 16 September 1902. He died 20 June, 1936, and is buried in St. Joseph Cemetery in Highland, IL. Ida Barbara was born 10 November 1880. On 20 September 1910, she married David F. Obernuefemann. She died 18 May 1972, and is buried in Mt. Calvary Cemetery in Shiloh, IL. Mary Barbara, born 19 December 1882, married Elmer F. Emig on 20 November 1912. She died 1 January 1959, and is buried in St. Mary Cemetery in Trenton, IL.

Frank Joseph was born 14 February 1885. He was married 19 November 1912, to Edna L. Trippel. He died 11 November 1964, and is buried in SS Peter & Paul Cemetery in Collinsville, IL. Charles William (Bill) was born 30 May 1887. He married Rose VanCleda Obernuefemann on 6 May 1919. He died 16 March 1971, and is buried in Mt. Calvary

Cemetery in Shiloh, IL. Lee Anthony, born 4 September 1889, died 3 March 1974, and is buried in St. John the Baptist Cemetery in Blackjack. Zeno John was born 9 March 1892. He married Katherine P. Fritz on 24 June 1919. He died 20 June 1951, and is buried in St. John the Baptist Cemetery in Blackjack. Adella Apolonia, born 20 June 1894, married August A. Bieg, Sr., on 13 June 1917, at St. John the Baptist Church in Blackjack. She died 24 September 1977, in St. Louis, MO, and is buried in SS Peter & Paul Cemetery. *Submitted by Babe Papproth.*

JOHN ADAM BUGGER - In the autumn of 1844 Joannes (John) Adam Bugger arrived in America from Bellheim, Germany, with his second wife, Katherina Walther, and his 4 older children. The family made their way to the Blackjack area to become prominent farmers.

The oldest son, Charles Carl, was the only child of John Adam and his first wife Elizabeth Boehm. Elizabeth died just 2 weeks after his birth. In 1858 Charles married Louise Schwartz. They lived with his folks. In 1801, the couple and 7 children moved to Lick Mountain, AR.

After Louise died, Charles married again. He lived out his life in Arkansas, but his children moved to California, Oregon, Utah, Missouri and Arkansas.

Barbara was the first born of John Adam and Katherina. In 1858 Barbara married Phillip Schwartz (brother to Louise). They farmed in Jarvis Township where they raised 8 children.

Anna Agatha, the next child, married Frederick C. Mersinger in 1858. They were married in the old log St. John Baptist Church at Blackjack. Anna and her husband were farmers and also lived in Jarvis Township. They raised 9 children. Six stayed in Madison County, but 3 of the daughters became nuns.

Appolonia, the fourth child, married Adam Bechtlofft in Lebanon at the St. Joseph Church. They bought the old Wastfield Farm near O'Fallon where they raised their 6 children. The farm lately has been known as the Mansion at Lakepointe-an upgrade restaurant.

The fifth child was born in America and named John. In 1869 he married Elizabeth Wittmann. They became parents of 12 children. They also farmed in Jarvis Township. Two of the children died as infants, three became nuns, six became farmers and one lived in Belleville.

Bugger family, 1911
(l. to r.) Front: Mary and S. Joseph Bugger
Middle: Adele, Carrie, Anne, Ida, Mary
Back: Adam, John, Frank, Charles, Leo, Zeno

The youngest child, Sebastian Joseph, (known as Joseph) also became a farmer. In 1871 he married Mary Annie Schwend. Their farm sided the Johns' farm. The property is now being developed as the Castle Ridge Estates. Joseph and Mary had 11 children.

Adam, the oldest, never married and lived his entire life at home.

The second child, Anne-Maria, married Peter Munier. They farmed in the Blackjack area. Peter also picked up the milk and cream from the farmers and transported it to The Munier Bros. Creamery in O'Fallon. (They made the first ice cream in the area.) Their first child was stillborn.

Then they adopted Aurelia Schilling, a 10 year old. Alphonse, their only son, was born in 1910. In 1918 they moved into O'Fallon.

Caroline (Carrie), the next child, married William (Bill) Joseph. They farmed just northwest of Lebanon. They had 2 sons and 3 daughters.

John married Louisa Fohne. They farmed in the St. Jacob area, where they raised 3 sons and 3 daughters.

Ida, the fifth born, married David Obernuefemann. Their farm was just west of O'Fallon, where they also logged. Five sons and two daughters were born to them.

The next child was Mary. She married Elmer Emig. They farmed southeast of Trenton. All their children, one daughter and four sons, became farmers.

The seventh child was Frank, who married Edna Trippel. Most of their married life was spent in Collinsville. They raised 2 sons and 2 daughters.

Charles (Billy) also lived in Collinsville. He and Rosa Obernuefemann (sister to David) married and had 5 sons.

Leo was to remain single and live with his brother Adam.

Zeno, the youngest son, married Katie Fritz. They lived in Blackjack with their 1 daughter and 3 sons. One son had died as an infant.

Adele, the youngest child, married August Bieg. They made their home in St. Louis. Adele and Gus had 15 children, six sons and nine daughters. They lost their son, Joe, during WWII.

In 1935, Mary died, leaving 43 grandchildren and eight great grandchildren. *Submitted by Babe Munier Papproth.*

GRACE MAE (DAVIS) BURGESS - Grace Mae Davis moved to Troy in 1903 from Vandalia, MO, with her parents, James Henry and Sue Emma Davis, and her two brothers, Carl and J. Wheeler, and sister, Ruth Bell. All of the children were born in Mexico, MO. She was born 1 December 1890 and died 18 September 1985 in Highland, IL.

She taught grade school in Johnston City, Highland, and Troy. Grace belonged to the Troy United Methodist Church, Pride of the West Rebekah Lodge 544, Veterans of WWI Ladies' Auxiliary of Troy, and White Shrine of Collinsville. She married Hugh Burgess 7 Sep 1918 in Johnston City, IL. He died in 1944. They had one daughter, Shirley (Burgess) Martin (b. 11 Jan 1921 in Johnston City, married

James Oscar Martin 10 May 1942 in St. Louis, MO). Shirley had five children: Terry Douglas, James Burgess, Marianne (Martin) Nabrotzky, Adrianne (Martin) Poole, and Allan Francis. *Submitted by Shirley (Burgess) Martin.*

HENRY AND GESINA BUSKE - August and Albertina (Dagler) Buske were the parents of 9 children. The family came to America in 1870. Henry Ferdinand was born Jan. 3, 1881, in Litchfield, IL. He was married on June 17, 1911, to Gesina Frances Engelmann, who was born Nov. 2, 1892. Her parents were John M. Engelmann and Ida R. Johnson who were married March 3, 1889. They had eight known children. John and Ida are buried in Mt. Olive, IL. Ida's ancestry can be traced back to the early 1700s in Germany.

Buske family, circa 1940s
(l. to r.) Front: Leona (Buske) Prott, Arlene (Buske) Vosholler, Norma (Buske) Schumacher, and Erna (Buske) Smith. Back: Vernon Buske, Elmer Buske, Henry and Gesina Buske, Melvin Buske, Lester Buske.

Henry and Gesina (Engelmann) Buske rented a farm just north of Troy during the 1940s and 50s. They had ten children. Two died as small children, Irene and Herbert. The remaining eight children are Elmer Henry (b. 23 June 1915) married Henrietta Cornelia Hamann (8 children); Ida Abertine Erna (b. 2 April 1917) married Erwin Ray Smith; Melvin Edward (b. 14 Sept. 1919) married Doris Jean Federer (1 child); Lester Edward (b. 27 Sept. 1921) married Eileen Esther Gilomen (2 children); Mabel Leona (b. 30 Aug. 1924) married Eldon Otto Prott (4 children); Norma Helen (b. 8 Feb. 1927) married Gervase Bernard Schumacher (7 children); Vernon Edwin (born 27 Sept. 1931) married Dolores Marie Hoffman (2 children); Arline Mae (born 20 July 1935) married John Edward Vosholler (5 children). The family attended Friedens E & R Church. Henry and Gesina are buried in Friedens Cemetery, Troy, IL.

Erna and Erwin Smith remained in the area most of their lives. During the last ten years of her life, Erna was bedfast and spent much of her time writing poetry. Those poems inspired "The Poet's Corner," a weekly feature in the local newspaper, the *Troy-Times-Tribune*; "The Poet's Corner" ran during the 1970s.

Vernon and Dolores purchased a farm near Alhambra, IL, where they still live. After retiring, Vernon and Dolores enjoy traveling and entertaining friends and family.

They have two children, Mark Edward Buske and Janet Lynn Buske. Mark returned to Troy in 1987 to teach vocal and instrumental music for Triad Community Schools, teaching at both the elementary and secondary levels and directing many musicals and programs. He holds a Bachelor and Master of Music Education from SIUE and is employed as a vocal music specialist by the Ft. Zumwalt School District, O'Fallon, MO. He has sung on several European choir tours. He currently lives in St. Peters, MO. Janet also attended SIUE and has a Bachelors degree. She is still in the area, living in Edwardsville and working for the May Company in St. Louis. *Submitted by Mark Buske.*

KEVIN AND LINDA BYRNE - Kevin Byrne and Linda Schlaefer were married April 18, 1980, at St. Jerome's Catholic Church. Kevin is the son of Thomas and Carol (Hawkins) Byrne. He was born March 8, 1956, in Granite City, IL. Linda is the daughter of Larry and Sharon (McFarland) Schlaefer. Linda was born Jan. 13, 1959, in Highland, IL.

Kevin attended schools in Granite City before moving to Troy in 1971. He graduated from Triad High School in 1974. Kevin has his own business, Byrne's Home Improvement.

Kevin has many interests and hobbies. He enjoys hunting, especially ducks and geese and deer. He likes to fish, play softball and coach ball. For many years, he coached his two sons' baseball teams. He's a retired Troy Fireman and has served on the Troy Park Board.

Linda graduated from Triad High School in 1977. For a short time she worked at Highland Farmers and Merchants Bank and in 1978 became employed at the Troy Post Office. Linda was the first lady letter carrier at the Troy Post Office. She has carried mail several years. Linda is kept very busy with her two sons' high school and college sports events, and is Triad Athletic Booster's treasurer.

Kevin and Linda have two sons. Shawn was born Jan. 16, 1982, and attends McKendree College where he will be a sophomore and will be playing basketball for the McKendree Bearcats. He played basketball at Triad High School and holds the record for #5 on all time scoring list with 1172pts. Shawn likes to hunt with his father. Ryan was born May 14, 1985. He attends Triad High School and he also plays basketball and played varsity as a sophomore. He began his assault on the record books with 350pts, in his first varsity season.

Kevin and Linda have lived in Troy since their marriage, first at 108 Hassinger and now at 333 Bass. *Submitted by Linda Byrne.*

Byrne family, 2001
(l. to r.) Shawn, Kevin, Linda, Ryan

ARNOLD H. CLINE - Arnold Harold Cline was born on 11 July 1920 in Troy, IL, to Loyd Valentine Cline and Minnie Casey, the sixth of six children. Loyd farmed at several locations along Silver Creek, his children going to Sylvan Hall Grade School; then, the family moved to a farm on the edge of Troy.

Arnold H. Cline and Lillian (Cline) Hand, 1943

The children attended Troy Grade School. After Loyd's wife Minnie's early death on 5 March 1928, he gave up farm life, moved to Maryville with his children, and began work on the Illinois Terminal Railroad on 15 June 1929. During the Depression, in 1935, he started work on the Pennsylvania Railroad and moved to Prospect St., then to Lebanon Rd. in Collinsville. He retired from the railroad, dying on 15 April 1956.

Arnold H. Cline went from Troy School to Webster School in Collinsville. He then was employed by the Pennsylvania Railroad. Arnold married Theresa Kasino on 8 Feb. 1941, and a son, Kenneth Arnold, was born 5 Sept. 1943. During March 1943, Arnold was inducted and entered service in the Army, training at Camp Wolters, Texas. In late August 1944 he was shipped to Scotland, then France, and on to Belgium before reaching Germany. Arnold was assigned to the 4th Infantry Division, in the 22nd Infantry Regiment. In early Sept. '44 they penetrated the Seigfried Line. The offensive was halted in the face of German counterattacks.

Making slow progress through October, fighting hedge row to hedge row, town to town, the division moved forward. Arnold had written home of the vicious house-to-house fighting.

On 6 Nov. 1944 the 4th Inf. Div. entered the Huertgen Forest, just a few miles southeast of the ancient city of Aachen, which had a special meaning to the Germans as it had been the seat of the Holy Roman Empire for more than five centuries. Charlemagne's birth and 32 subsequent emperors and kings were crowned at Aachen. Hitler regarded himself as their successor. In the three wet, cold incredibly miserable months from mid-September to mid-December 1944, the fighting covered almost every inch of the entire forest mass. It was more than a forest; it was a special grim way of fighting a war. The Huertgen Forest was a chamber of horrors, combining the most difficult elements of warfare, weather and terrain. A major offensive was renewed 22 Nov., achieving a spectacular gain. It was on this cold, snowy, sleety, and muddy day of 22 Nov. 1944, that

Arnold H. Cline, the reserved young man from southern Illinois, died near the juncture of the dirt roads to Grosshau and Kleinhau.

In the spring of 1948, Arnold Cline's body was removed from the US military gravesite "Netherlands American Cemetery and Memorial" near Maastricht, Netherlands, and buried on 26 May 1948 at the Smart Hagler Cemetery near Troy, in the family plot of Loyd V. Cline. *Submitted by Richard L. Cline.*

GEORGE R. CLINE - George Russell Cline was born 17 Mar. 1917, to Loyd Valentine Cline and Minnie Casey in Troy, IL, the fifth of six children. Loyd, his father, farmed at several locations along Silver Creek, his children going to Sylvan Hall Grade School, then moved to a farm on the edge of Troy.

George R. Cline, 1944

The children, including George, attended Troy Grade School. After Loyd's wife Minnie's early death on 5 March 1928, he gave up farm life, moved to Maryville with his children, and began work on the Illinois Terminal Railroad on 15 June 1929. During the Depression, in about 1935, he started work on the Pennsylvania Railroad and moved the family to Prospect St., then to Lebanon Rd. in Collinsville. He retired from the railroad, dying on 15 April 1956.

George R. Cline married Gladys Graham and later had a daughter JoAnn.

After the Japanese invasion of Pearl Harbor, George was quickly inducted into the Army on 27 Jan. 1942, at Scott Field, IL, and spent the rest of WW II fighting the Japanese on the Pacific islands' beachheads in an amphibious tractor battalion attached to infantry divisions. Boot Camp was at Lake Charles, LA, amphibious tractor training at Fort Ord, CA, then he was shipped from near Bellingham, WA, on the *USS Calvert* to Hawaii. At New Caledonia in the Pacific, he received intense combat training, marching 10-12 miles every day, firing many different kinds of weapons, etc. George then went into combat in the Solomon Islands at Bougainville, encountering his first fights with the MI rifle. He then went to Angor, and on to Guadacanal for the long, intensive combat after the first beachhead battles. At Palau they stopped over for supplies. At Yap he arrived with an infantry division after the battle had just begun. Then, on to the Gilbert Islands, and Saipan to Tinian. In the Philippines he landed in the big invasion on Luzon with Co. B 720 AMPH TRAC BN. They moved south with many jungle clean up fights into Quezon City, the Navy helping with bombardments. They

continued down for the long, tough battles of Mindanao. During the mostly jungle fighting, there was intensive shooting. They then fought up the other side of the Island to the Bataan Peninsula onto Luzon Island, where George was when the war ended.

He was shipped immediately to Japan, landing in Yokohama, then sent by train to Shimbasha Station and on to Hiroshima. There they walked only on cleared roads where the Atomic bomb had exploded, and touched nothing on the road sides, since everything was radioactive. It seemed the entire city was flattened. George then returned to the states and was discharged at Jefferson Barracks, MO, on 24 Jan. 1946.

George operated a salvage business in Collinsville from the late 1940s until the late 1990s in Collinsville. *Submitted by Richard L. Cline.*

JOHN GODFREY CLINE - John Godfrey Cline's grandparents, Johann Klein (b. 1795-d. 1873) and his wife Henrietta (b. 1803-d.1883) (Frey), and their 5 children left Rockenhausen, Rheinland Pfalz in the German Confederation and landed in the USA in 1853. Johann soon bought acreage in rural Troy.

Their 2nd child, Volentine Cline (b. 6 Oct. 1835) and Parmelia Etheridge (b. 11 Dec. 1834) were married in Greenville 30 Sept. 1860, and eventually took over his father's farm. Volentine and Parmelia had 5 children, three of whom lived in the Troy area all their lives. Their second child was John Godfrey (b. 21 July 1863) who married Elizabeth Voris in 1881, had 11 children and lived all their life farming in the rural Troy/ Silver Creek area.

John Godfrey's and Elizabeth's 11 children, all born in the Troy area, were as follows: Lula, b. 16 Sept. 1885, m. Louis Butcher 3 Apr. 1902, and had 8 children – Everett, Helen, Sis, Clarence, Wilbur, Harold, Louis, Lester; Loyd Valentine, b. 17 Sept.1887, m. Minnie Gertrude Casey in Oct. 1908, had 6 children – Lillian, Leo, Mary Ellen, Rozell, George, Arnold; Mindora, b. 6 Nov. 1889, m. Barney Porter 28 Mar. 1907, and had 9 children – Freeman, Fernetta, Maybell, Edith, Nola, Ellen, Evelyn, Elmer, Roland; Fred, b. 5 Oct. 1891, m. Eva Borst Oct. 1920, and had 6 children – Harold, Mary, Elizabeth, John, Roger, Annie Mae ; John W., b. 3 Oct. 1893, m. Bertie Casey Oct. 1916, had 2 children – Homer, James ; Oren Wilbur, b. 1 Sept. 1895, m. Lillian Hall 22

Cline family, 1912
(l. to r.) Front: John Godfrey, Ruth, May, Ellen (Voris).
Middle: Lula, Ethel, Sylvania, Mindora.
Back: Minnie, John, Fred, Loyd, Oren

Mar. 1918, had 1 child – Wayne, then married Lucille Tyler; Minnie Arvelia, b. 3 July 1897, m. Arbie Nesbit 25 Feb. 1918, had 5 children – Arlie, Wilma Fernita, Willard, Arbie, Larry; Sylvia, b. 30 Sept. 1899, m. Riggin Borst 2 Feb. 1922, and had 2 children – Dorothy, Edgar; Ethel, b. 30 Aug. 1901, m. John O. (Buoivus) Smith 20 Aug. 1924, and had 3 children – Robert, Leona, Dale; May, b. 2 Mar.1904, m. Percy Buhr 9 Oct. 1924, and had 3 children – Verna, Nina, Kenneth; Edna Ruth, b. 4 May 1906, m. Jacob Davis 2 Jan. 1923, and had 3 children – Bernice, Robert, Arnold.

Buried in the Dugger Cemetery about a mile north of St. Jacob are Volentine Cline, d. 2 Oct. 1910, Parmelia, d. 5 Aug. 1904, Joseph Cline, d. 2 Oct. 1955, John Godfrey Cline, d. 30 Apr. 1937, and Elizabeth, d. 22 Feb. 1944. Many other Cline descendants are buried in the Smart Hagler, Riggin and Friedens Cemeteries near Troy.

This family was very close and their children remained so all their lives. They kept in contact and remained close friends. The descendants of these 11 children still continue to have an annual Cline Family Reunion. The 47th continuous reunion will be held on the first Sunday after Labor Day in 2000. *Submitted by Richard L Cline.*

LOYD V. CLINE - Loyd Valentine Cline was born on 17 Sept. 1887 to John Godfrey Cline and Elizabeth Voris on a farm in rural Troy. He was the second child of eleven born to this family. Loyd married Minnie Casey (b. 14 Oct. 1891) in Oct. 1908. They had five children, all born in rural Troy. Loyd continued farming until his wife Minnie's death on 5 March 1928, then gave up Troy farm life, moved to Maryville with his children, and began work on the Illinois Terminal Railroad on 15 June 1929, for 8 hours per day at 40 cents per hour. During the Depression in 1935 he worked on

Loyd V. Cline, 1908

Minnie Casey, 1908

the Pennsylvania Railroad and moved to Prospect St., then to Lebanon Rd. in Collinsville. He retired from the railroad, dying on 15 Apr. 1956.

Their first child Lillian (b.1908-d.1992) married Don Hand and moved to New Jersey, having a daughter Geraldine in 1935.

Leo Wilbur (b.16 Nov. 1910-d. 13 Dec. 1987) married Martha G. Pontel (b.17 May 1912) on 23 June 1932, had 3 children, then in 1945 moved from Maryville to Collinsville. He was a machinist at Granite City Steel until retirement. He always considered Troy his home. He died 13 Dec. 1987. Their children were Richard Loyd Cline, Leona Ann, and Samuel George.

Mary Ellen was born on 10 Dec.1912, and died on 15 Dec.1916, in an accident.

Rozell (b. 23 Oct. 1914) moved to Duluth, MN, married, and had three children, Richard A., Jack R., and Jerry.

George Russell (b. 17 Mar. 1917) married Gladys Graham and later had a daughter, JoAnn. After the Japanese invasion of Pearl Harbor, George was drafted into the Army on 27 Jan. 1942, and spent the rest of WW II fighting the Japanese on the Pacific islands beacheads with Co. B 720 Amphibious Tractor Battalion. George was on Luzon Island in the Philippines when the war ended, was shipped to Hiroshima and eventually was discharged. George operated a Collinsville salvage business until the late 1990s.

Arnold Harold Cline (b. 11 Jul. 1920) married Theresa Kasino on 8 Feb. 1941, and a son, Kenneth Arnold, was born 5 Sept. 1943. Arnold was employed by the Pennsylvania Railroad.

During Mar.1943 Arnold was inducted into the Army, training at Camp Wolters, Texas. In late August 1944 he was shipped to Scotland, France, and on to Belgium before reaching Germany, being assigned to the 4th Infantry Division, in the 22nd Infantry Regiment. Arnold died on 22 Nov. 1944, in the intense Huertgen Forest battle near Aachen by the juncture of the dirt roads to Grosshau and Kleinhau. In the spring of 1948 Arnold Cline's body was removed from the Netherlands and buried on 26 May 1948, at the Smart Hagler Cemetery near Troy in the family plot of Loyd V. Cline. *Submitted by Richard L. Cline.*

VOLENTINE CLINE - Volentine Klein was born in Rockenhausen, Rhineland Phalz, Germany, on 6 Oct. 1835, the oldest child of 5 born to Johann Klein and Henrietta (Frey). Leaving Germany with his parents, Volentine arrived in the USA at age 18 in New Orleans on 9 Dec. 1853; and after a steam paddle-wheeler boat trip up the Mississippi River, the family arrived in the St. Louis area. They spent several years around Greenville, Marine, and St. Jacob, then settled in Troy since many other German families had gotten their start there. Johann bought acreage in the rural area between Troy and St. Jacob.

Volentine Cline and Parmelia Etheridge (b. 11 Dec. 1834, in Millersburg) were married in Greenville 30 Sept. 1860, and eventually took over his father's farm. Volentine and Parmelia

Volentine and Parmelia (Etheridge) Cline, 1885

had 5 children: Henrietta, b. 1861, married Charles A. Cox on 2 May, 1876, and settled in the Keyesport area; John Godfrey, b. 21 July 1863, married Elizabeth Voris in 1881, lived all their life in the rural Troy-Silver creek area and had 11 children: Lula, b. 1885, Loyd, b. 1887, Mindora, b. 1889, Fred, b. 1891, John, b. 1893, Oren, b. 1895, Minnie, b. 1897, Sylvia, b. 1899, Ethel, b. 1901, May, b. 1904, and Edna, b. 1906; William Henry Klein, b. 1865, married Martha Ann Williams (7 Oct. 1888), lived in the Edwardsville/Granite City area and had 7 children: Louis, b. 1890, Charles, b.1891, Orville, b. 1894, Raymond, b. 1898, Edward, b. 1901, Monroe, b. 1904, Bertha, b. 1907; Elizabeth Laura, b. 1870, married John Howard in 1886, lived near Troy and had 7 children: Simon, b. 1888, George, b. 1896, Lee, b.1899, Allen, b. 1901, Benjamin, b. 1904, Gilbert, b. 1906, Viola, b. 1908; and Joseph, the youngest, b. 8 Aug. 1871, never married and lived all his life farming in the St. Jacob/Troy area.

Buried in the Dugger Cemetery about 2 miles north of St. Jacob are Volentine Cline (d. 2 Oct. 1910 in Troy), Parmelia (d. 5 Aug. 1904), Joseph Cline (d. 2 Oct. 1955), John Godfrey Cline (d. 30 Apr. 1937), and Elizabeth (d. 22 Feb. 1944). Many other Cline descendants are buried in the Smart Hagler, Riggin and Friedens Cemeteries near Troy.

As there are many descendants in the area, there is an annual Cline Family Reunion on the first Sunday after Labor Day at the Troy Tri-Township Park, with the attendance averaging about 60. The 47th continuous Reunion will be in 2001. *Submitted by Richard L. Cline.*

JOHN H. COLLINS - John H. Collins and Ethel Wright Morriss were married on June 2, 1913. Prior to her marriage, Ethel had been teaching country school northwest of Troy (Liberty School) in Pin Oak Township, traveling back and forth by horseback and buggy.

Ethel and John Collins, 1913

John went back to the coal mines. In 1914 they had a son, Julius Morriss Collins, and continued to live with Ethel's grandmother. They lived in that same home for more than 50 years. They had a daughter, Millie-Marie, in 1923. Ethel occasionally did substitute teaching in the Troy Grade School (since married women could not hold a full time teaching position in those days). John was active in the community,

*Collins family, circa 1930
(l. to r.) Front: Millie Marie
Back: J. Morriss, John H., Ethel*

serving on the school boards for many years, as an elder in the Presbyterian Church, a member of the AF&AM Lodge, Troy Lions Club and the VFW. Ethel went back to full time teaching during the teacher shortage of WW II, starting in the country school known as Qui Vive (near Triad Middle School) and later in Maryville, IL, from which she retired. Ethel and John shared almost 63 years of marriage, which ended at her death in Apr 1977 and his in Apr 1978. She was 86 and he was almost 94.

Morriss married Mary Ellen Brown of Lebanon, IL, on May 23, 1937, and they have two sons, John Cameron Collins of Rhode Island and Mark Hampton Collins of Littleton, CO. John and his wife, Debra Ciano, have two children, Christopher and Erica. Mark has a daughter, Paige. Morriss died in November 1998; and Mary E., in March 1999.

Millie Marie married George Allen Shaffer of Troy on June 18, 1944; and they have one son, William Allen Shaffer of Burleson, TX. Bill married Carolyn Hingle on November 23, 1974. They have two children, John William and Stephanie Diane. Allen died on February 11, 1988.

WILLIAM AND MARY (LANG) COLLINS
William Collins and Mary Lang, born and married in Devonshire, England, came to the United States with their year old son, William, in 1850. After settling in Troy, they had three more sons: James, John and Franklin. James moved to St. Louis; John, to St. Jacob; and Franklin spent most of his adult life working for local Troy banker, W.W. Jarvis, and his family as groundskeeper and handyman.

The eldest son, William Collins, worked in the Troy coal mines and married a local girl, Ida McMakin. To this union were born two sons, John Henry and Julius Franklin. Ida died at 29, leaving a 5-year old and an infant. Needing mother's milk (before the days of bottle feeding), the baby was sent to nurse with Mrs.

Wm. Gebauer, who's son Teddy was the same age. This was a common practice in those days, apparently, and was called "wet nursing."

William later married a widow, Caroline Riggin, who had four adult sons: Lawrence, John, Bert and Henry. In 1917 Mr. Collins was killed in a tragic accident in the Donk Bros. Mine in Troy.

Julius graduated from the local high school and went to work in St. Louis where he married Audrey Wolf in July 1918. He then went into the army as a member of U.S. Forces serving in France, where he was killed (Troy's first casualty of that conflict). Before his death, he wrote a very compelling piece, "A Soldier's Creed," which was published nationally.

John graduated from the Troy Grade School and immediately went to work in the local coal mine, residing with his father and stepmother until one of her sons came back to Troy.

John then boarded with a neighbor, Mrs. Fannie Morriss, who had a comely granddaughter living with her, Ethel Morriss. In 1909 John went into the U. S. Navy and sent many letters and postcards from his Pacific Fleet travels – China, Hawaii, South America, Central America (where he suffered a slight leg wound from a sniper's bullet while on uprising-quelling duty in Nicaragua).

When discharged from service in March 1913, he returned to Troy and his former abode with the Morriss ladies. In June 1913, he and Ethel married and remained in that same house for almost 60 years together. *Submitted by Millie (Collins) Shaffer.*

AGATHA MERSINGER CONLEY - In a farmhouse on East Mill Creek Road on February 8, 1898, the third child was born to Adam and Elisabeth Riebold Mersinger. Her name was Agatha. (See Adam Mersinger Family story.) She was baptized and attended school at St. John the Baptist Catholic Church on Lebanon Road in Blackjack.

Her mother died when Agatha was only eleven years old and the family moved to St. Louis two years later, in 1911. She spent much of her time helping her father, Adam, and sister, Martha, in the chore of raising the six younger children.

As she grew into adulthood, she worked for the priests at the rectory of St. Anthony of Padua near her home in south St. Louis. Her relationship with God was nourished here; and as it grew within her all of her later years, she openly shared God's love with her family.

Agatha Mersinger and
Edward J. Conley, 1924

She met and married Edward J. (Bud) Conley. Though they had no children, Agatha had a full life. She studied for and was certified in Swedish Massage and had a nice business for quite a few years.

In the early 1930s when most of her brothers and sisters married, the family home was sold and her father, Adam, moved in with her and Edward. She cared for Adam until his death at 89 in 1957.

Edward died in 1969 while they were living in their home in south St. Louis, and Agatha lived on until January 17, 1976, when she died from a massive stroke. She is buried beside her husband in Resurrection Cemetery in St. Louis. *Submitted by Dorothy Mersinger Bartnett*

B.F. AND MATTIE MAY (HAMPTON) CRAMER - Suzanne Hansel's maternal grandmother, Fanny Pearl (Cramer) Gerling, was the daughter of B.F. (Benjamin Franklin) Cramer (b.1858-d.1932) and Mattie May Hampton Cramer (b.1861- d.1944). (See photo.) Suzanne does remember visiting their home on 208 Throp Street, Troy, which still stands. The house was sold in 1946 to a Mr. Ed Breyer for $2,020. Fanny had two sisters, Mabel Margaret (b.1894-d.1975) and Ruth Alberta (b.1900-d.1967), and three brothers, Clifton F. (b.1883-d.unk.), Fred Z. (b.1885-d.1915) and Newton Jolly (b.1903-d.1963). All the children were born in Troy, and all are buried in Troy except Newton

B.F. and Mattie Cramer

who is buried in Cuba, MO. Suzanne's great-grandmother Mattie seemed very reserved to her as a child. She remembers going a few doors down on Throp Street and visiting with the Schlimmes. Something interesting found in the history of the Troy United Methodist Church was that B.F.Cramer's parents, Newton and Mercy Cramer, sold the lot on South Main to the Methodist-Episcopal Church for $600 in 1867, and the church was built and completed in 1870.(See photo) The church was remodeled in 1939 and looks more like it does today. The Christian Church purchased the property after 1983 when the new Troy United Methodist Church was built on Route 162. Just a few added bits of information : Mattie Cramer's father, Frank L. Hampton, was a saddler and harness maker and a Justice of the Peace in Troy. Suzanne's grandmother, Fanny, weighed only three pounds when she was born, and they carried her around on a pillow.

Suzanne remembers when her great-grandmother Cramer died. She was living

Four generations, 1941
(l. to r.) Front: Suzanne. Middle: Mattie
Cramer, Ruth (Gerling) Smith. Back:
Fanny (Cramer) Gerling

in the house on Route 143, Edwardsville, where she had been born. When her great-grandmother became ill, she came to live with her daughter, Fanny. The family put a bed for her in the living room. The night she died, they made Suzanne leave the room and shut the door. Great-grandmother Cramer was carrying on something fierce and yelling like crazy. For a short time all was quiet and then Suzanne heard a strange sound. Later she was told it was called the "death rattle."

Suzanne had memories of going with her grandma Fanny to Cullop's Beauty Shop in Troy, located in the old *Troy Times* newspaper building on North Main. To pass the time she used to take a magnet on a stick and pick up all the dropped bobby and hair pins. It was during World War II and that was a time when nothing was thrown away or wasted.

When the family moved in 1946 from Edwardsville to Glen Carbon, the house was down in a hollow with a creek branch running along side of the property. Suzanne's grandmother Fanny had a 410 shot gun that had been given to her by her son, Paul. Fanny wasn't strong physically but she sure had a lot of guts. Suzanne remembers she shot a rat that came up on the back porch and left a hole in the floor. Then there was the time birds were going crazy. She got her shot gun, looked up in the tree, shot, and down came a big black snake. She shot it a couple of more times after it hit the ground just to be sure. They never worried about critters with Grandma around. Years later when the "Beverly Hillbillies" was popular, Suzanne fondly compared her to "Granny" on that show.

Grandma and Grandpa always had chickens. Suzanne would sometimes gather the eggs. The family enjoyed having fresh fried chicken and all the yeast breads, coffee cakes and other goodies Grandma made. Of course, when the hens wanted to set, Grandma would throw them off the nests, at the risk of injury, but a few of them would sneak away. Then after a few weeks the proud mama hen would appear with her little chicks trailing behind. Suzanne told her kids that they would never see such a sight again. That was really special. *Submitted by Suzanne Hansel.*

RON CRILEY - Conrad Criley (1730-1777) lived in Chester County, Pennsylvania, where he and wife Civilly had seven children during 1750-1775. He died at the Battle of Brandywine.

Peter Criley (1774-1828), the 6th child, lived in Chester County as a wheelwright, making wheels for carriages and stages. He and wife Susannah Hanks had seven children, and left an estate of 70 acres.

Samuel Criley (1804-1875), the 4th child, and wife Margaret Dampman had seven children. They traveled the National Highway to Vandalia, IL, and settled in Clinton County.

Samuel served on the committee that proposed a new road across Illinois; this became Route 50.

Carroll Criley (1837-1910), the 3rd child, and wife Mary Woods had 10 children. He lived in Clinton County, was a prizefighter and blacksmith. He accumulated several tracts of adjacent land. His estate included a large family farm.

Earl Criley (1874-1955), the 9th child, and wife Myrtle Allen had six children. He lived in Clinton County, was a farmer, breeder of livestock, and an oilman. His estate included 3 farms.

William Criley (1894-1978), the 1st child, and wife Winifred Roper had five children. He lived in Clinton County, attended Brown's business school, and was a prizefighter, railroader, and farm manager. His estate included two farms.

Robert Criley (1921), the 3rd child, and wife Betty Chambers had two sons. He drove fuel trucks for tanks during WW2, was an over the road trucker, and now helps manage a family farm. Robert moved his family to Madison County, IL, in 1959.

Ronnie Criley, the first son, and wife Betty Schiber lived in Troy from 1965 to 1994 where they raised two sons, Devon and Aaron. Betty worked at the library and for Oncology Care at Anderson Hospital.

Ronnie graduated from SIUE. He worked with geometry calculations for construction of the St. Louis Arch to assure the legs would meet at the top. He worked with computer simulations for the Mercury, Gemini and Apollo Space Missions; he worked for the French Government to design oil locator and oil pipeline systems for the Middle East and Northern Africa; he developed a computer system and network for worldwide linking of Christian church workers.

Ronnie was Mayor of Troy from 1981 to 1989 when it was "the fastest growing community in Illinois." He was a Jaycee, Lions Club member, Madison County Deputy, Troy Policeman, and City Council alderman. While mayor, the city pursued a course of no new taxes while it reorganized city government; implemented a new code of ordinances and developed a personnel policy; upgraded streets, sewer and water; and pursued economic development where the priority was to protect residential areas from creeping commercial development. The city was also active in upgrading area health care and education facilities.

Ronnie and Betty are retired, live near Marine, IL, where they, their sons and their families all have adjacent rural land tracts and homes within sight of each other. *Submitted by Betty Criley.*

KIRK AND SUSIE THOMPSON CROFFOOT - Kirk, a native of Belleville, IL, graduated from Belleville West High School

Croffoot family
(l. to r.) Front: Katelyn.
Middle: Kirk, Susie. Back: Kristel

in 1977. In 1979 he graduated from Ranken Technical College with a degree in HVACR. Susie was born in Champaign, IL, but has lived in Troy since kindergarten. She graduated from Triad High School in 1979 and received her degree from Belleville Area College in 1988.

After he was laid off from a firm in Granite City, Kirk and Susie decided to start their own business. They began it in 1981, giving what they felt was honest and dependable service to their customers. They were the first to utilize photographs of themselves, and later their children, on a billboard in Collinsville to advertise their business. They have enjoyed a prosperous business and, especially, have enjoyed meeting new people and having customers who have been with them since the beginning.

Croffoot children
(l. to r.) Katelyn, Kole, Kristel

Kirk and Susie now have 3 children: Kristel (high school graduate in 2003), Katelyn, and Kole. The family has lived south of Troy, just off the Troy-O'Fallon Road, for several years. *Submitted by Susie Croffoot.*

JOHN WILLIAM AND IRENE ADA CULLEN - John William Cullen, son of Luke and Mary Foster Cullen of Pennsylvania, and Irene Ada Brown, daughter of Simon and Bertha Brown of Pocahontas, IL, were married at Pocahontas on June 24, 1923. John was an electrician at the coal mine in Pocahontas, and later became the mine manager. Irene worked for her parents in a grocery store there and was a homemaker.

A couple years after their marriage, the couple moved to Hammond, IN, where John worked as an electrician in a large electric motor shop.

In the late 1920s they moved to Troy, and rented a home on Powell Street. John began work at the Donk Brothers Mine in Troy, and Irene was a homemaker.

On April 19, 1932, Elinor Marie Cullen was born at St. Joseph's hospital in Highland, IL.

In 1935, John and Irene bought a home at 500 S. Main St. in Troy, and this became their home for the remainder of their lives.

In June of 1945, Dorothy June Diveley came to Troy and became the couple's second daughter.

The Cullen's were members of the Troy United Methodist Church. Irene was also very active in the ladies organizations of the church. She was also a member of the Troy Women's club. Irene had the distinction of having had an airplane ride with the famous Charles Lindbergh, during his barnstorming days, prior to his history making flight across the Atlantic ocean. John, a U.S. Army veteran of World War I, was a member of the American Legion. He was also a member of the Pocahontas Masonic lodge, the Scottish Rite Bodies, and the Shriners.

John William and Irene Ada
(Brown) Cullen, 1923

Their daughters, Elinor and Dorothy, attended the Troy Schools. Elinor graduated from McCray-Dewey High School in 1950, and Dorothy graduated in 1956.

In 1952, Elinor married Earl W. Hall, the son of David and Gladys Hall south of Troy. They had two daughters. After farming south of Troy for several years, they moved to a farm at Pocahontas, IL. Their daughters, Mary Lou and Kathryn, grew up there and attended school in Pocahontas and Greenville, IL. Both daughters now live in Highland. Kathy is married to Richard Porter, and they have two children. Earl Hall died March 6, 1994. On February 13, 2000, Elinor married Marvin Stille. They live on a farm north of Alhambra, IL.

On October 26, 1957, Dorothy June married John William Rees. Their history is in another entry.

John and Irene Cullen enjoyed gardening. John also enjoyed woodwork and Irene belonged to several quilting groups. After Dorothy was married, John and Irene spent the winter months in southern Texas.

John died in November of 1964 and Irene died in April of 1989. They are buried in the Brown Cemetery in Old Ripley, Bond County, IL. *Submitted by Jack Rees.*

FLOYD AND LELA (POLWORT) CULLOP
Floyd and Lela (Polwort) Cullop had one son, Roger, who died in an accident March 1986.

Lela Cullop, 87, at the McCray-Dewey Alumni Reunion in August 6, 2000, the day of her birthday. She was born August 6, 1913.

Lela Cullop, the daughter of Fred and Elsie Polwort, owned a business in Troy for many years. She opened in the 1940s, a beauty shop in the Kueker Building, then she bought the building that later housed the *The Troy Tribune* on North Main Street.

Floyd Cullop opened Cullop Hardware Store on East Market in the Braner Building. After he sold the store and Gas Company, Floyd went to Arabia to install a gas line to the sea.

Lela spent some time in Arabia, too, but when Floyd heard of "rumblings" in Arabia, they moved to Tucson, Arizona.

After they finished their home there, Floyd received a wire to come to Vietnam to work in construction (again in the desert), but after the TET Offensive, in which Floyd spent 10 days in a French bunker, he got a job in Libya. Then when Qadhafi took his passport and said he "must carry guns for Libya," Floyd decided it was enough. Getting his passport back, he came home and the couple traveled to Europe, Yugoslavia, Canary Islands, Africa, Egypt and many more interesting places.

Widowed, Lela Cullop now (in 2002) resides in Chapala Jalisc, Mexico. *Submitted by Lela Cullop.*

JAMES HENRY AND SUE EMMA DAVIS

James Henry Davis (b. 30 March 1861 in Barry, IL, d. 19 Dec 1919 in Troy) married Sue Emma Bunstine (b. 4 July 1861 in Wadsworth, OH, d. 27 Dec 1943 in Troy) on April 2, 1882, in Taylorville, IL. His parents were Hezekiah and Adra Ann ((Beal) Davis. Sue Emma's parents were John Jacob Bunstine and Catherine (Noff) Bustine.

James Henry and Sue Emma had four children: Carl Everett (b. 2 March 1884 in Mexico, MO, d. 27 April 1966 in Troy, m. Mayme Schrameck 18 July 1911); James Wheeler (b. 3 Aug 1885, in Mexico, MO, d. 23 Dec 1980 in Troy); Ruth Bell (b. 29 Oct 1888 in Mexico, MO, d. 10 Nov 1979 in St. Paul, MN, m. Willard Rawson); and Grace Mae (b. 1 Dec 1890 in Mexico, MO, d. 18 Sep 1985 in Troy, m. 7 Sep 1918 Hugh Burgess).

The family moved to Troy in 1903 from Vandalia, MO. Earlier they had lived in Mexico, MO. The family lived on Windy Hill (which is now known as Troy Avenue) in the second house next to the Kelly house. In the 1930s the Wise family lived on the other side, and in the next house lived the Rees family. Across the street

lived the Beutels, Capelles, and Burniski families. They attended the Troy United Methodist Church. James Henry served as mayor for a time, resigning in 1916.

Many family members are buried in Troy cemeteries. Carl and Mayme Davis and their daughter, Dorothea Marie Davis Taroli, and her baby, Billie, are buried in the cemetery one mile off the Troy-O'Fallon Road, across from Steelcrest Subdivision. Troy City Cemetery on Main Street contains the remains of James Henry and Sue Emma Davis, J. Wheeler Davis, Ruth B. (Davis) Rawson and son, Glenn Rawson, and Grace Mae (Davis) Burgess.*Submitted by Shirley Burgess Martin.*

JAMES WHEELER DAVIS -

James Wheeler Davis (b. 3 Aug 1885, d. 23 Dec 1980) was born in Mexico, MO, to James Henry and Sue Emma Davis. He lived there and in Vandalia, MO, before moving with his family to Troy in 1903. The family lived on Windy Hill, now Troy Aveue, in a neighborhood filled with the Wise, Rees, Beutel, Capelle, and Burniski families. Wheeler attended the Troy United Methodist Church with his family, and his father served as mayor of Troy at one time.

J. Wheeler Davis, circa 1950

One of Wheeler's first jobs was as a coal miner. He was an active and influential member of the union for many years, serving as secretary of the local union for a time. He was also secretary and treasurer of the District Council of the Common Labor Union of St. Clair and Madison counties and vicinity.

Wheeler also was interested in politics. He acted as precinct committeeman for four years. Wheeler was an active and untiring party worker for the Democratic Party, serving on the Democratic County Committee for two years.

However, his greatest impact on Troy was serving as postmaster from 1933-1953, when failing eyesight forced him to retire. He became postmaster of Troy on Nov. 6, 1933. He was noted for discharging his duties in a prompt and able manner for 20 years. He and his mother shared a home; and later, he and his sister, Grace Burgess, lived at 123 East Charter Street during his tenure as postmaster.

He participated in many community organizations. He took particular pride in being a charter member of the Troy Lions Club and was the club's first secretary. Also, he was happy to be the Lions' official greeter. Wheeler enjoyed membership in Neilson Lodge #25 of Troy for over 60 years, having been initiated into the lodge in Feb. 1918. He served as its

chaplin for over 15 years. He was also a member of Pride of the West Rebekah Lodge #544. Like most of his family, he was a member of the Troy Methodist Church.

Since he was a popular member of the community, Wheeler's birthdays were often celebrated in special ways by his friends and family. Of special note were parties and celebrations on his 85th, 88th and 95th birthdays. He was often surprised by friends and family "who thought of me (Wheeler) in such a marvelous way. . . ."

James Wheeler Davis died 23 Dec. 1980 at St. Joseph's Hospital in Highland. He is buried in Troy City Cemetery along with other members of his family. *Submitted by Shirley Burgess Martin, The Troy Tribune, and Vol. III of* Illinois Democracy.

RICHARD L. DAWSON -

Richard L. Dawson, Sr., was born in Troy on December 19, 1909, to Robert L. Dawson (b. Troy, d. 1948) and Kate Horsley (b. England, d. ?). He had 3 sisters and 1 brother (Ada Marie Dawson Rogier, Verna L. Dawson Lacquement, Dorothy Dee Dawson, and Niel Dawson), all born in Troy. Richard attended Troy public schools, and graduated in 1928 from McCray-Dewey High School. During high school he played basketball and other sports. His father was mayor of Troy for several terms.

Richard worked for the Troy Telephone Company until 1935 when he moved to South Bend, IN, and worked for the Studebaker Corporation until World War II. He then worked for the Bendix Corporation until the end of the war.

He met and later married Martha Ahlgrim Reinking on October 12, 1940. She had 2 children from a former marriage-Marlo Joan Reinking and James Arthur Reinking. Richard and Martha had 3 children of their own – Richard L. Dawson, Jr., Carol M. Cortrite, and Pat Wilhelm. The family moved to Longmont, CO, in November of 1949.

Richard was employed by the Dow Chemical Co. which operated the atomic plant for the United States. He worked there for 20 years until his retirement in December of 1972. Martha retired from Beech Air Craft in March of 1973. They spent the next 25 years traveling by R.V., and lived 25 years in Yuma, AZ, until Martha's death. They had been married 57 years when she died.

At this writing, Richard is 91 years old and lives with his daughter Patricia Wilhelm in Thornton, CO. He suffers with diabetes and osteoporosis. He must use a walker to get around, but, in his own words, "hope to live a few more years." *Submitted by Richard L. Dawson.*

DAWSON FAMILY -

Rev. T.W.B. Dawson, his wife Sarah, and their children Emily and Thomas arrived in Troy from Connecticut in the 1840s.

Rev. Dawson served as pastor of the Baptist Church for several years, and remained active in the church and community affairs. He also worked as toll gate keeper at the junction of the old Troy Road and Maryville Road. His wife died in 1867, and he lived alone in a cabin located on the site of the present Friedens Cemetery. In 1898 his cabin burned and he was found dead in the ruins. Foul play was suspected but never proved. The area was called 'Dawson Hill" for many years.

His daughter, whose married name was McCoy, died in childbirth in 1851. She, together with her infant son, is buried next to her parents in the City Cemetery.

His son, Thomas, attended McKendree College and in 1862 was recruited into the "McKendree Regiment." He served in this unit throughout the Civil War and was discharged in 1865. He married Fannie Bostick, daughter of James and Catherine Bostick, who had arrived with her parents and six siblings in Troy from Delaware in the 1840s. Thomas and Fannie were the parents of Robert (b. 1868) and Laura (b. 1870). Thomas was confined to the Old Soldiers Home in Quincy during his later years and died there in 1924. Fannie died at Troy in 1930. Laura Dawson never married and died in 1957.

In 1901 Robert Dawson married Kate Horsely, who emigrated from England with her family in 1882. They had five children: Marie, who married Floyd Rogier, had three sons — Robert, Floyd, and Richard. She died at Troy in 1969.

Verna married Frank Laquement. She had a son, Jean, and a daughter, Helen. She died in 1999.

Dorothy, after retiring from business and government work, served as Troy City Clerk for a number of years. She died in 1980.

Richard married Martha Reinking. They were the parents of five children – Marlo, James, Richard, Carol, and Patricia. He still lives near Denver, Colorado.

Neil, who was wounded and a P.O.W. in World War II, married Maxine Bridwell. They were the parents of Glenda and Michael. Neil died in 1997, Maxine still lives in Glen Carbon.

Robert Dawson was a skilled carpenter, plasterer, paper hanger, bricklayer, cigar maker and wood craftsman. He operated the old power plant located in Brookside. Later, when Illinois Power began to supply Troy's electricity, he worked as their agent. For many years he managed the office, read meters, collected payments, replaced street lights, and repaired damaged power lines. He never drove a car, but transported all his tools and equipment by wheelbarrow. He remained an active employee until his death, and was still climbing utility poles at the age of 79.

Robert Dawson served as mayor of Troy for several terms, played tuba in the old Troy Band, and had a renowned bass singing voice.

He died in 1947 at the age of 79. His wife, Kate, died in 1971 at the age of 90. They are buried in Friedens Cemetery. *Submitted by Robert Rogier.*

JAMES AND AUDREY (OTTWEIN) DEEREN - James Deeren and Audrey Ottwein were married on June 19, 1954, at Friedens United Church of Christ by Rev. R.H. Mornhinweg. The summer was one of the hottest and driest on record, and the couple remembers sweeping part of the lawn instead of raking to spruce things up. James, born on November 28, 1929, the son of William and Bertha (Prater) Deeren, is from Taylorville, IL. He at-

tended schools there and then graduated from the University of Illinois with a degree in business. Upon graduating from college in 1952, he was drafted into the U.S. Marine Corps, where he served two years. He met his future wife at a U. of I. homecoming weekend where he dated Audrey as a favor to his friend, Merrill Ottwein, who wanted his girlfriend, Grace, and his sister, Audrey, to come up from Troy for the homecoming dance and football game.

Wedding photo, 1954
James and Audrey Deeren

James worked a number of years with the Watson Lumber Company of Troy, and then entered the banking business, first with Boatmen's National Bank of St. Louis, then with St. Louis Union Trust Company. During his banking career he was concerned with investment research and account management. In the early 1970s he acquired Christian Wolf, Inc., which manufactured communion wafers, moved the St. Louis factory to Troy, and eventually came to manage the company full time.

Mr. Deeren retired in the summer of 2000 and enjoys his leisure time at family events, reading, watching the stock market and spectator sports.

Audrey Deeren was born in Troy on August 7, 1930, the daughter of Oscar and Hilda (Bardelmeier) Ottwein. She attended the Troy schools and Millikin University and received degrees from Southern Illinois University at Edwardsville and Webster University in Music Education and Vocal Pedagogy. Audrey studied piano with Miss Gussie Miller in Troy from the age of six. She taught music in the Troy schools for 12 years where she directed many concerts and musical programs. Memorable, she says, are production of "Oklahoma," the first musical in Triad High School's history, and a musical circus starring 90 first graders.

She also enjoyed a career as a choir director, directing choirs at Friedens Church in Troy, Eden Church in Edwardsville, Evangelical United Church of Christ in Highland, South 7th Street Baptist Church in Springfield, and the Highland Civic Choral Society. She was soprano soloist at many church, collegiate and community events. She has been teaching voice at Webster University for over 20 years. Semi-retired, she still directs choirs and has private voice and piano students. Audrey enjoys reading, gardening, scrapbooking, genealogy and playing the trumpet in the Troy Community Band. She is a member of Friedens Church, Delta Kappa Gamma, and the National Association of Teachers of Singing.

Mr. and Mrs. Deeren have two daughters, Deborah, married to Kevin Wiese, and Carrie, married to Gary Metze. They have three grandchildren, Katie and David Wiese, and Kyle Metze, who have crowned their lives with joy. *Submitted by Audrey Deeren.*

DEMPSEY FAMILY - Jeff Dempsey was born in Quincy, IL, and reared in Pittsfield. He attended Millikin University in Decatur, IL, where he received his bachelor's degree in Industrial Engineering. He also met his wife, the former Sally Schneider from Alton, IL. She was in the process of obtaining a nursing degree at Millikin also. Prior to moving to Troy, the family lived in Bartlesville, Oklahoma, where their daughters Andrea and Laura were born. They moved to Troy in 1988 and Andrea was immediately enrolled in first grade. Troy is the children's first memory of home.

Sally was a co-founder of "Take Pride in Troy," an organization that became part of Troy Main Street. She has been an active volunteer in Troy Main Street since 1998 and continues to work on improving Troy's downtown. Her first project is creating a visual park in the area we all refer to as the Wedge.

Jeff Dempsey family, 1990
(l. to r.) Jeff, John, Andrea, Sally, and Laura

Andrea graduated from Triad High School Class of 2000 where she was Drum Major of the Triad Band, and Valedictorian. The Class of 2000 had a record 13 Valedictorians that year. She was also a member of "The Saxie Ladies." The group, a saxophone quintet, performed at many events like the Troy Main Street designation in June of 2000. Andrea also is a committed pianist and is studying to teach Music Education at the University of Missouri- Columbia.

Laura is presently a senior at Triad High School. She is a member of the Class of 2002. Her greatest contribution to Troy came in 1999-2000. She was selected to be one of 10 student ambassadors to travel with Dr. James Kerr to set up and teach Model United Nations tactics to students in Kazakhstan. This program was one of great honor, as the United States Department of State selected Triad to be one of 12 schools to participte in this diplomatic mission of friendship. As a result of their great success, Triad was the only school sought to follow up with another visit to Kazakhstan. Laura hopes to be one of the returning members of this diplomatic mission.

John was born in Troy in 1990 and is currently attending Triad Middle School as a sixth grader. He is a member of the Little Knight's Basketball team and hopes to someday play for the Triad Knights. He has a promising future in this fine city that we call home. *Submitted by Sally Dempsey.*

MARY (HULTZ) DENISON - Mary Elizabeth Hultz was born on September 24,1933, in Troy to Helen Mary (Mueller) Hultz and Louis Philip Hultz. Mary Elizabeth attended Troy Grade School and McCray-Dewey High School, where she participated in the Glee Club and the band. During her junior and senior years she worked at Mason's Nursing Home. At 18 she went to work at Ralston Purina General Offices in St. Louis, working first as a messenger and later in William Danforth's office. He was the founder of the company and impressed the young Mary as a very nice man.

She met Charles Douglas (Doug) Denison at a dance in Highland, while he was stationed at Scott AFB. They were married on December 18, 1954, and in the following spring he was transferred to Barksdale AFB. Mary stayed behind and worked in St Louis until daughter Carol Diana was born on November 22,1955, at Highland's St. Joseph's Hospital. Carol died May27, 1956, in an auto accident in Louisiana. However, the family was blessed with 6 more children: Cathy Dianne, born at Ft. Polk, LA; Charles Dean, born in Shreveport, LA; Carl David, born in Atlanta, GA; Christopher Dale, born at Chanute AFB, Rantoul, IL; Cindy Doreen, born at Recife, Brazil; and Clifford Donald, born at Edwards AFB, CA. From Edwards the family moved to Fairbanks, Alaska, for 2 years. In 1968 Doug retired, and the family moved to Chula Vista, CA, where the children grew up and still consider their home. Mary worked as a Certified Nursing Assistant for 8-1/2 years in California.

Doug and Mary moved to Monmouth, IL, after Doug's heart attack in 1982. The children were grown and chose to stay in California, and David was living in Germany. Mary started working for Warren Achievement Industries as a caregiver, and worked for 3 years as a teacher's aide substitute at a school for handicapped children. Doug passed away in February 1985. Mary is now enjoying her grandchildren in several states: Justin and Clifford in CA; Doug and Carol in Lisbon, ND; Kalisha, Richard and Jamie in Rutland, ND; Tobias in Kaltenbrunn, Germany; and Jacob and Tiffany in WA; and her first great grandchild Keora, in Bellingham, WA. *Submitted by Mary E. Denison.*

JOHN AND ANGELINE (MCCRAY) DEWEY
According to a 1915 issue of the *Troy Weekly Call*, John Stanley Dewey arrived in Troy in the year 1846, a clock peddler. However, he had bigger plans. He disposed of his inventory, moved to St. Louis and attended medical school. After graduating he returned to Troy to open his practice and soon he became Troy's leading physician.

He was married in Troy to Carrie Berkey of Collinsville, but she died shortly after their marriage. Several years later he married Miss Angeline McCray, whose family owned a farm at the north edge of Troy. They first built a house on Market Street and later a home on McCray-owned property at the edge of town where they lived the rest of their lives.

Dr. John S. Dewey, 1877

Dr. Dewey served in the Union Army during the Civil War as a surgeon. He was twice elected to the Illinois Legislature. The Deweys had one child, who died at a young age. Angeline inherited the McCray property which included about 325 acres north of Troy and 40 acres in Pin Oak Township. All of this property was farmed by tenants.

Angeline (McCray) Dewey, 1877

Dr. Dewey died in 1879 and his wife died just a year later, on May 7, 1880. In her will, Angeline (McCray) Dewey provided for the support and maintenance of a niece, Georgie Belle Dewey, until she reached 21 years of age, died or got married, whichever came first. She also provided for the support of her mother, Catharine McCray, who was still alive. The rest of her estate was to be applied to the construction and operation of a school for Troy residents, which was to be named the McCray-Dewey Academy. *Submitted by the Troy Historical Society.*

GERALD AND DARLENE DICKMAN
Gerald (Jerry) Dickman, son of Leonard and Francis Dickman of Maryville, was born May 12, 1934. Darlene Dankenbring, daughter of Robert and Violet Dankenbring of E. St. Louis, was born February 16, 1935. On May 4, 1957, Jerry and Darlene were married. They moved to 407 Cook Ave., Troy.

Jerry was the owner of several milk trucks and ran a business that hauled fresh milk from the farm to the dairy. He started with his first truck in 1954 and increased to four trucks in the late 1940s. Later he worked for several other places. For 3 1/2 years he drove a tractor-trailer, hauling grain. He then went to work for Flagg Surveyors and Cottonwood Development. In 1983, he started to work for Truck Center of Troy until he retired in 1997.

Darlene has worked as a cashier for Triad School District from 1984 to the present.

In 1970, Jerry and Darlene moved to 8656 Schmalz Road. They built a house and a small farm on 17 acres. They have four children. The oldest son, Terry, was born January 30, 1960, and was very involved in the agriculture program at Triad High School and the FFA program. He is now employed by E. F. Trucking in Highland, IL. He married Sue (Adams) Kelly on September 15, 1984. They have five children: Dawn Kelly, born August 31, 1975; Shawn Kelly, b. October 14, 1979; Teresa, b. June 12, 1985; Joe, b. January 12, 1987; and Sarah, b. January 8, 1991. Terry and his family reside near Alhambra, IL.

Dickman family, 1991
(l. to r.) Randy, Dan, Jerry Darlene, Lynn, Terry

Dan, b. July 14, 1962, was also involved with the Triad High School FFA. He is now employed by Triad School District in the maintenance department. He married Sharon Daiber on July 11, 1987. They have three children: Todd, b. September 10, 1988; Adam, b. November 2, 1992; and Lisa, b. February 15, 1997. Dan and his family reside near St. Jacob, IL.

Randy, b. January 25, 1965, also was involved with the Triad High School FFA. He taught agriculture and coached four years at Triad High School. Randy is now self-employed as a landscaper and is still involved with education. He married Therese Zoski on August 5, 1994. They have three children. Andrew was born on April 4, 1995; Christopher was born on November 1, 1997; and Jonathan was born on August 18, 2000. Randy and his family reside near Highland, IL.

Lynn, b. April 30, 1970, was very active in sports at Triad High School. Lynn is now employed by TiAA-Cref in the trust tax department. She married Mike Renspurger on August 2, 1997. They have one child, Brooke, b. September 23, 1999. Lynn and her family reside near St. Jacob, IL.

Jerry passed away on October 27, 1999. Darlene now resides in Highland, IL. *Submitted by Dan and Sharon Dickman.*

CHRISTIAN DIEPHOLZ - Christian Diepholz was born in Kreis Minden, Westphalia, Germany, on September 1, 1856. Prior to emigrating to America, Christian served in the German Army for eight years in heavy artillery. After arrival in this country, Christian came to the home of his brother, Frederick, and worked with Fred in farming and clearing timber from the land that Fred had purchased. Christian later went to Pin Oak Township to live and farm. Their parents,

195

Wedding photo, 1890
Christian Fredrick and
Louisa (Kleimeier) Diepholz

Christian and Louise (Oberman) Diepholz, were born in Germany and died there.

On February 17, 1885, Christian married Louise S. Bode (b. Sept. 12, 1857, in Germany). Their children were Emma C. (b. Dec. 5, 1885, and d. Dec. 5, 1885) and Lisette C. (b. Mar. 8, 1887, and died July 6, 1887). Louise died Mar. 14, 1887, from childbirth, and perhaps home sickness for her native Germany.

Christian later married Louisa Kleimeier (b. 1863-d. 1956)about 1890. From this marriage were born the following children: William (b. Jan. 19, 1891, in Troy, d. Feb. 19, 1990) m. Susan Keck; Carl (b. Sept. 29, 1896, d. April 14, 1984, in IA); Herman (b. Dec. 28, 1898, in Troy, d. Dec. 31, 1978, in Boulevard, CA) married Elizabeth (Betty) Mary Nazy (b. Nov. 29, 1900, in New Haven, CT, d. Aug. 22, 1997, in San Diego, CA) in May 1944 in Las Vegas, NV; Hanna Marie (b. Dec. 5, 1900, in Troy, d. Sept. 15, 1972, in Highland) married Val (Valentine?) Edward Schmitt (b. Mar. 11, 1891, d. June 1, 1974, in Troy) on May 11, 1922, in St. Louis.

Christian died in 1930 in Troy of natural causes. He is buried at St. Paul's Lutheran Cemetery. Louise died in 1956 in Greenville. She, too, is buried in St. Paul's Lutheran Cemetery. *Submitted by Ruth E. (Diepholz) Azari.*

DIEPHOLZ FAMILY - Christian and Louise (Oberman) Diepholz of Germany had five known children. Christian and Louise were born and died in Germany.

Frederick Wilhem Diepholz (b. Sept. 8, 1832 in Kreis Minden, Westphalia, Germany, and d. April 25, 1923, in Glen Carbon, IL) married on Nov. 24, 1857, in Madison County, IL, Christina Buesking (b. May 18, 1832, in Westphalia, Germany, and d. June 17, 1903, in Glen Carbon). They had seven children.

Christian Diepholz

Heinrich "Henry" Diepholz (b. Sept. 11, 1840, in Petershagen, Prussia, Germany, and d. Jan. 29, 1923, in Strasburg, Shelby County, IL) married on Dec. 31, 1864, to Wilhemine Caroline Wirth (b. Dec. 14, 1846, and d. Jul. 7, 1927). They had six children.

Christina Diepholz (b. June 21, 1848 in Germany and d. Dec. 7, 1912) married August Traue (b. Feb. 10, 1839, and d. May 29, 1919). They had eight children.

Herman Chris Diepholz (b. Dec. 16, 1851, in Esslingen, Germany, and d. Aug. 16, 1937, in Louisville, KY) married in Germany Lazetta Christine Bradenmeir (b. March 1848 in Germany and d. Jan. 16, 1921, in Louisville). They had four children.

Christian Diepholz (b. Sept. 1, 1856, in Kreis Minden, Westphlia, Germany, and d. 1930 in Troy) married on Feb. 17, 1885, in Troy to Louise S. Bode (b. Sept. 12, 1857 in Germany and d. Mar. 14, 1887). They had two girls. He then married Louisa Kleimeier (b. Jan. 20, 1863, and d. 1956 in Greenville, IL). They had four children. *Submitted by Ruth E. (Diepholz) Azari and Emma L. (Diepholz) Suessen.*

FREDERICK DIEPHOLZ - Frederick Wilhelm Diepholz was born on Sept. 8, 1832, at Kreis Minden, Westphalia, Germany. His father was Christian Diepholz, and his mother was Louise Oberman. Both were born and died in Germany. Before he emigrated to America, he served in the German Army under Kaiser Wilhelm I as a coachman. His training influenced him years later when he would permit no team of horses to be harnessed unless the team was curried first.

Diepholz family, 1870
Christina, Henry A., Frederick

Frederick supposedly came to America in 1857. By Nov. 1857, he had been to East St. Louis, Staunton, and, finally, to Collinsville to the Henry Buesking farm. He supposedly farmed and lived in the Hecht place near Maryville and the present Rt. 162.

On Nov. 24, 1857, Frederick married Christina Buesking in Madison County. Frederick became a naturalized U.S. citizen on Sept. 26, 1869; and three years later, on Aug. 19, 1872, he purchased 60 acres of land from the William Kinder estate for $39 an acre. This land is located today on Rte. 159 near Glen Carbon Crossing. Seven children were born to this union: Sophia (b. Feb. 1, 1858 and d. Sept. 23, 1858); Maria Dorthea (b. Oct. 31, 1859), Charlotte Louise "Dorothea" Wilhelmine (b. Sept. 11, 1862), Elise Louise (b. Sept. 4, 1864), Friederick Wilhelm (b. Oct. 22, 1866 and d.

Sept. 21, 1870), Heinrick August (b. Apr. 8, 1869), Friederick Christian (b. Oct. 12, 1871). All seven children were baptized at Pleasant Ridge Lutheran Church.

Both Christina and Frederich lived long lives. Christina died on June 17, 1903, after being confined to her bed for three weeks, probably dying of heart disease. Frederich died at his home near Glen Crossing on Apr. 5, 1923, of myocarditis. Both Christina and Frederich are buried in the Troy Lutheran Cemetery.

Frederich had lived in this area for over 60 years. Until about two years before his death, he was able to get around well. Then an attack of rheumatism in his legs made walking difficult. When he died, he had lived in his home for 46 years.

Frederich was a devout Lutheran, who would drive his family each Sunday to Lutheran services in Troy. This journey took 1 1/2 hours by horse and buggy. Often, after services they would visit with his brother Christian who lived in Troy. *Submitted by his granddaughter Emma L. (Diepholz) Suessen and Ruth (Diepholz) Azari.*

WILLIAM F. AND SUSAN LOUISA (KECK) DIEPHOLZ - Susan Louisa Keck was the second of seven children born to Martin Jr. and Emma (Hobein) Keck. She was born December 4, 1897, in Troy and died July 31,1972. She married William F. Diepholz on June 9,1920, in Troy. He was the son of Louise (Kleimeier) and Christ Diepholz. "Bill" was born December 4, 1891, in Troy and died February 19, 1990, at Jefferson Barracks Veteran's Hospital in St Louis, Missouri.

He was a veteran of the U.S. Army and served during World War I. He was the last survivor of the 148 Troy WW I veterans and was a 68 year member of the American Legion Post 708. Bill was a member of St Paul Lutheran Church. He did street maintenance and worked

Bill and Susie Diepholz, 1968

for the Illinois Department of Transportation before retirement. "Susie" was a member of the American Legion Auxiliary 708 and the World War I Auxiliary Barracks 296, both of Troy. She was a member of Friedens United Church of Christ. They lived at 309 E. Center, Troy. Susie and Bill are buried in Friedens Cemetery in Troy. Susan and William Diepholz had one child. Victor William Diepholz married Margaret Maly on June 12, 1948, and had four children: Victor William Diepholz, Jr., who married Kathleen Haas August 2, 1980; Janet Marie Diepholz, who married Gregory Klaus on July 29,1978; (Janet and Gregory have two children: Emily and Erin.); Trudy Lynn Diepholz; and Gary James Diepholz. *Submitted by Pamela Keck.*

MARSHALL AND GERTRUDE DILLINGHAM

*Dillingham family
(l. to r.) Gertrude, Gordon, Vera, Marshall*

VERA A. DILLINGHAM (VOELKER, PRICE) -

Vera was born July 14, 1901, in St. Louis, MO, daughter of Gertrude Francis Peters (1878-1942) and Marshall Marcellus Dillingham (1875-1941). She had two brothers, Gordon Marcellus Dillingham (1913-1989) and Homer LeRoy, and one sister, Dorothy Katherine.

Vera moved to Troy in 1910 and helped her parents in the operation of the Central Hotel and in 1916 the White Horse Tavern. The 19 room hotel housed 35 boarders and Vera helped make the lunch buckets for the miners going to work.

Vera married Frank Adam Voelker on August 17, 1919, at the Central Hotel. Frank was a WWI veteran and was at the Argonne Forest in France. Frank got sick from a fishing trip at Silver Creek and died July 18, 1924 (31 years old). Vera and Frank had two children,

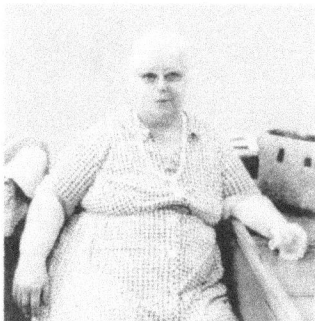

Vera Augusta Dillingham (Voelker, Price)

Dorothy Ellen, born on December 20, 1920, and Jane Frances Voelker, born on January 2, 1923. Vera married Walter Price, a WWII veteran on May 5, 1945. Walter died January 3, 1951, and Vera never married again. Her grandchildren were Gerald and Babett Donna, children of Dorothy and Larry Donna; John Marshall, Paul Gordon, Nancy Ellen, and Allen Francis Jarvis, children of Jane and Ernest Jarvis.

Vera was the piano player at the Rebekah Lodge in Troy, worked at the Alton Mental Hospital, and Scott AFB in Base Supply, visited the sick and needy, and was well-liked as a kind and loving person. She lived years at 320 Staunton Road in Troy, and would wave to friends from the front porch. She loved Christmas and always knew how to decorate for any holiday.

Vera died January 31, 1975, at the Alton Memorial Hospital of a brain aneurysm. She was a member of the Bethel Baptist Church and was buried at the Friedens Cemetery in Troy. *Submitted by Paul Jarvis.*

REVEREND JOSEPH V. DINEEN - Reverend Joseph V. Dineen, pastor of St. Jerome Catholic Church in Troy and St. John the Baptist Catholic Church in Blackjack from 1946 to 1980.Photo taken in early 1950s. *Submitted by Mae Grapperhaus.*

Reverend Joseph V. Dineen

IRWIN DOLLINGER - Irwin was born the first child to Maria Gindler Dollinger and George Dollinger at home in the Blackjack rural area of Troy (4 miles southeast), on July 14, 1906. At times he ice skated to school. He also practiced on the clarinet while cultivating corn. Irwin didn't go to high school. In those days boys were supposed to stay home and help farm.

It was very easy for him to court his wife as she lived across the street from his grandparents in Collinsville. Irwin married Elma Elbe on Oct. 31, 1930. They had four boys: Daniel, Robert, Gary and Joel (stillborn). Irwin always loved to entertain people. He played with a number of local bands – Joe Ladd, Shorty Schmitt, Happy Aces and Watt Schlemer. He also played in the Edwardsville Municipal Band, Troy Municipal Band, Collinsville Municipal Band and the R.S.V.P. from Belleville. Once he was to audition for the Paul Whiteman Orchestra, but he turned this down to be with his family.

Irwin worked in East St. Louis at a stove company when he and Elma were married. He then went to work for Dan Liebler in the grocery part of the grocery/dry goods store. In 1938 he

purchased the grocery store from Dan Liebler. In 1942 he sold the store to Ed Guennewig.

During World War II, he worked at Scott Field. Since he was a small man, he worked on the inside of airplane wings. In 1945 he went to work at Shell Oil in Wood River. He moved his family there in the fall of 1945. In 1948 he took over the farm from his parents. Unfortunately, there was a drought in those years. While farming he also worked at Wick's Organ Co. in Highland. In 1954 he went to work for Madison County Farm Supply from which he retired. Yes, and over the years he was still playing music.

In his retirement years he took up bowling, which he and Elma both enjoyed. They also took bus trips and they did visit family, who by this time were scattered about the state. He also became a Mr. Fix-it man; he especially liked to repair musical instruments. This was very handy for middle and grade school students as he lived across the street from their schools.

When Elma became ill in late 1980's and early 1990s, he took care of her. It was hard on him as he saw her slipping away. She passed on in 1992.

He still kept going to bowl and to play music, as he would say, "For The Old Folks." One of his most enjoyable moments was at his and Elma's 50th Wedding Anniversary when he played his sax along with a drummer named Neal, his grandson. He is also remembered as the candle man at Friedens Church where he made sure the candles would never go out on Sunday morning.

In Oct. of 1993 Irwin met his master as he was murdered in Edwardsville after bringing a friend home from a dance job. Why, no one will ever know. He is now repairing music instruments and entertaining at a better place. *Submitted by Dan Dollinger.*

MARIE L. DOLLINGER - Marie L. Dollinger born to George and Maria Gindler-Dollinger on March 12, 1913.

She grew up on the farm four miles southeast of Troy and went to Blackjack school. She had three brothers – Irwin, Carl and Paul.

She learned to play the piano from Bert Weber, who was a neighbor.

She helped with farm chores until she went to work at the Troy Telephone Company. When the phone company was sold, she went to work at Ralston Purina from where she retired.

She played the organ at Friedens Church for approximately forty years. She also played the piano for the Edwardsville Moose Auxiliary.

As a member of Friedens Church she quilted, made bed pads, and helped at suppers as long as she could. She enjoyed going on many bus trips and even organized them.

She always had to stand outside and wave as guests were leaving. It seems as though it was a tradition in her family. *Submitted by Dan Dollinger.*

JEANETTE E. DOTHAGER - Jeanette was born in Vandalia, Illinois, on November 17, 1942, to Earl Dothager and Dolphaline (Dot) Reavis Dothager. Her father Earl was a construction worker, former Cardinal pitcher, and avid hunter and fisherman. Her mother Dot was a

Jeanette Dothager, 1991

homemaker, employee of DeMoulin Brothers in Greenville and avid baseball fan. Earl died in 1994, and Dot now lives in Greenville. Jeanette has one brother, Stan, of Greenville and a sister, Lorri Garrison, also of Greenville, and three nieces and two nephews. Raised and educated in Bond county, Jeanette attended Pleasant Mound Grade School, Mulberry Grove Junior High, and graduated in 1960 from Mulberry Grove High School. Her family lived until 1956 in the small town of Pleasant Mound, close to grandparents and other relatives. In 1956 the family moved to a new house in the country, not far from Pleasant Mound.

In the fall of 1960 she entered SIUC, majoring in English education and minoring in speech and theater. After graduation in June of 1964, she accepted a position teaching English I and II at Triad High School. During the summers she attended graduate school at SIUC, receiving her Masters degree in Speech Education in the fall of 1969.

Her entire 30 year teaching career was spent at Triad High School, where she taught all levels of English, speech, and drama. She served as English Department Chairperson for many years and directed many plays and 12 musicals. For most of the productions she designed the stage sets and costumes. With the help of wonderful volunteer moms, dads, and faculty, the musicals were quite professional and colorful. In addition she co-sponsored many classes, sponsored National Honor Society, Drama Club, and English Club, and served on various administrative and Triad Education Association committees. In 1994 she took advantage of the early retirement plan offered by the state of Illinois. She likes to say, "I was able to retire while I still liked teenagers and had good health!"

Since retirement, she has spent three weeks in Europe in the spring, cruised the Caribbean in September, visited New Orleans in March, and seen the Colorado aspens in the fall-trips a teacher would be unable to make. These trips, plus others, have kept her busy, but she still finds time to attend art workshops and classes, to paint in watercolors and acrylics, to create original stained glass designs, and to paint a nursery mural for a client. She continues her membership and involvement with Delta Kappa Gamma and joined Illinois Association of Retired Teachers upon her retirement. Jeanette is also a member of the St. Louis Watercolor Society and Friends of the St. Louis Art Museum, enjoying special programs, workshops, and exhibits. She is currently serving on the Tri-Township Public Library Board and

acting as its president. Jeanette has, also, helped in the research and writing of this history book. Retirement has given her the opportunity to travel, to pursue her art career, and to spend more time with family, friends, and Gabby, her Bichon Frise puppy. *Submitted by Jeanette Dothager.*

GEORGE AND WILHELMINA (KLOS-TERMEIER) DRESSEL - In 1860, George Dressel was born, probably in Germany. As an adult, he married Wilhelmina Klostermeier. In

Wilhelmina and George Dressel, circa early 1900s.

1896 they purchased land and established their farm in the northeast corner of Jarvis Township. They had three daughters, Fredricka, Mamie, and Louise. Fredricka married Fredrick Spies and had one daughter, Mamie. Unfortunately, Louise died as a teenager. However, Mamie married Richard Schmalz and had one son George. *Submitted by Terry Giger.*

IRENE AND OSWALD "JIM" DRUESSEL
Irene was born July 8, 1912, to Henry and Anna Gindler of the Blackjack community south of Troy. She was one of five children. She had four brothers: Oscar, Walter, Harold, and Elmer.

Jim was born Jan. 13, 1898, to John and Kate Druessel also of the Blackjack community. Jim had 3 sisters and 4 brothers. They were Amelia, Edna, Lydia, Fred, Simon, John and Edward.

Rev. Richard H Mornhinweg married Jim and Irene Oct. 8, 1933, at Irene's home. At the time they were both members of St. John's Evangelical Church in Blackjack but were unable to have the wedding at the church because the old church was deemed unsafe and they had been having services at the school house.

Irene was organist at St. John's Church for a couple years and played for the men's choir. The choir members were Elmer and Clarence Faitz and Jim, Simon and Fred Druessel.

Irene and Jim were farmers and lived on Jim's home place. Irene and Jim had two children, JoAnn, born July 9, 1935, and James, born March 13, 1939. JoAnn and young Jim went to school at the Blackjack School and both graduated from McCray-Dewey High School.

Oswald "Jim" passed away Sept. 4, 1958, and is buried at St. John's Cemetery in Blackjack.

JoAnn married Richard Longhi of rural Collinsville on June 29, 1957. They were married at Friedens United Church of Christ in Troy by Rev. R.H. Mornhinweg.

Rich was employed by Brooks Foods and JoAnn worked at Basler Electric in Highland.

Brooks Foods moved from Collinsville and Rich opted not to move with them so he then found a job at Monsanto in Sauget, IL.

JoAnn quit work to raise a family. Rich and JoAnn had two daughters, Karen Jo and Kathy Sue, both born on Feb. 17, Karen in 1960, and Kathy in 1962. The girls attended schools in the Triad school district. Karen is now a registered nurse and Kathy is a homemaker.

Karen is married to Gary Kronk and they have two children, David and Michael. They live in St. Jacob.

Kathy is married to James Patton and they also have two children, Dylan and Emily. They live in rural Collinsville.

The family members are all lifetime members of Friedens United Church of Christ.

Jimmy Druessel, as he was fondly called, went on to college at Millikin College in Decatur, IL. He was a very good musician and wanted to be a band director. He graduated from Millikin, met Peggy Jo Good in Decatur, and they were married April 15, 1961.

Jim taught school for 15 years and then decided he wanted to make more money than school teachers made. He went into real estate for awhile and then took over his father-in-law's furniture store in Decatur.

Jim and Peg had three sons, Jeffrey, Timothy and Stephen. Jim passed away Aug. 14, 1998, at the age of 49. He is buried in Decatur.

After Oswald's, (Jim's) death, Irene and young Jim moved from the farm into a mobile home on JoAnn and Rich's property. Irene went to work at the TB Sanatorium in Edwardsville.

After a couple years there she met Anton "Carl" Kotzman from Staunton. They dated, went to lots of dances and then decided to marry. They continued to live at Irene's home. They were only married for three years when Carl had a stroke, and Irene became his caretaker until the time of his death on Nov. 24, 1979.

Irene moved to an apartment in Troy in 1981. *Submitted by JoAnn Longhi.*

ALAN AND LINDA DUNSTAN - Alan Dunstan and Linda Jean Mersinger were married July 29, 1994, at St. Nicholas Church in O'Fallon by Father Bill Hitpas. Alan, the son of Bill, deceased, and Loretta (Hellwig) Dunstan, was born in Highland, Illinois on August 28, 1957. Linda, who is the daughter of Emil and Irene (Vosholler) Mersinger, deceased, was born in Highland, IL, on January 2, 1953.

Alan is a General Agent for the Knights of Columbus, Jarvis Township Supervisor since

Alan and Linda (Mersinger) Dunstan, circa 2000

1985 and is also Chairman of the Madison County Board. He has served on the Madison County Board since 1980. Alan enjoys deer hunting and fishing and cooking for family and friends.

Linda works as an accountant for Highland Machine & Screw Products Co. in Highland. She is currently a member of the Troy Main Street and the Troy Historical Society. Linda enjoys planting flowers, playing softball and photography. *Submitted by Alan and Linda Dunstan.*

WILLIAM DUNSTAN - Thomas J. Dunstan (1857-1901) traveled to America alone from England, but later sent money to his wife, Sarah (1863-1943), to make the journey. Thomas and Sarah had eight children: Henrietta, Ethel, Della, Homer, William, Leona and a boy that died in infancy. Thomas managed a tavern in Brookside; but when he died, Sarah took boarders in her home to make a living. She lived in the small house on old route 40 (now Center Street) northeast across from the former Watson's Lumber Yard location.

The Freys, May 2001
(l. to r.) Ron, Lisa (Vesci), Jessica, Tanner (grandson), Angie, Luke

One of the sons, William Whitford Dunstan (b. 11/29/1893), married Rena Rood (b. 12/3/1898) on June 27, 1920, and managed the Miners store in the Odd Fellows building (currently where A&R Paint Store is located). They had four children: Billie (deceased), Audrey (Vesci), Dorothy (Folkerts), and Robert. He then moved his family to Dupo and then St. Louis to work at different meat markets. (They were living in St. Louis during the 1927 tornado. Billie's school was hit by it and his class was one of the last ones out before the corner fell.) Eventually, he returned to Troy and worked on road construction of bypass 40 (now 162). He then worked as a butcher at a store on Main Street (where Allen's Drug Store is located). The man who owned the store left, and William took over the store and paid 50 cents a week to pay off the other man's debts. The store was renamed Dunstan's Market and was run by the entire family. William was then asked if he wanted to rent another building (where the Spencer Memorial is currently located, formerly the Locker Plant). This store was the first grocery store in Troy where customers used pushcarts. In late 1950, the owners of the building wanted to expand, so William had to vacate the property and sell his grocery stock.

William and Rena passed away on July 7, 1964, and August 7, 1975, respectively. Billie

Dunstan married Loretta Helwig, and they had five children (Ronnie, Lanita, Jay, Alan and Elaine). Audrey married Ralph Vesci, and they had four girls (Pam, Babette, Jo Ann, and Lisa). Dorothy married Ralph (Jasper) Folkerts, and they had four children (Linda, Vicki, Sarah, Billy). Robert married Meryl Boulware, and they had five children (Randy, Lee, Betty, Rena and Marty).

Only two of the grandchildren are stilling living in Troy – Alan Dunstan and Lisa (Vesci) Frey. *Submitted by Lisa (Vesci) Frey.*

EDWARDS FAMILY

Emery and Anna Edwards family in 1930s
(l. to r.) Front: Edna, Lois. Back: Anna, Emery.

Anna Edwards holding Rita Trihey, February 1947

Emery Edwards holding
Rita Trihey, February 1947

CHARLES AND MARGARET EDWARDS

(l. to r.) Row 1: Charles Edwards, unknown child, Margaret (Kimberlin) Edwards. Row 2: unknown girl, unknown boy, Ora Edwards, Grace Haury, Keith Edwards. Row 3: unknown man, George Edwards, Dora Edwards, Blanche Edwards, Fred Edwards, Cora Edwards, Emil Haury, Emery Edwards, Anna Edwards, Wilber Edwards, Elizabeth Edwards. Row 4: unknown man, Joe Edwards, unknown man.

CHARLES AND MARGARET (KIMBERLIN) EDWARDS - Charles Frank Edwards married his second wife, Margaret Kimberlin (b. April 4, 1840 – d. Jan. 9, 1916) on March 12, 1861. They had five sons.

Edwards-Kimberlin family
(l. to r.) Front: Charles, Margaret
Back: George, Joe, Fred, Emery, Wilbur

George (b. Aug. 9, 1866) married Dora Riggin on June 1, 1892. They had one son Ora, who was born on Aug. 25, 1893.

Their second son, Joseph, (b. Oct. 28, 1868) married Blanche Baker on Sept. 26, 1899. They had no children.

Fred S., the third son, was born two years later on Nov. 2, 1870. He married Cora Auwarter on Nov. 24, 1896. They had a son, Keith, born March 21, 1899.

Emery was their fourth son. He was born on June 7, 1874. On March 17, 1903, he married Anna Harris. They had two daughters, Lois (b. May 4, 1913) and Edna (b. July 16, 1916).

Their last son, Wilbur, joined his brothers on Aug.14, 1876. He married Elizabeth Geers on April 18, 1906. They had one son, Lester A., who was born Oct. 29, 1916. *Submitted by Betty Trihey.*

JEWEL AND VERNA EDWARDS - Jewel Simpson Edwards was one of seven children born to Clarence Peter Edwards and Effie May (Simpson) Edwards. Clarence Edwards was born July 22, 1868, near Troy, and Effie Simpson was born May 13, 1874, near Lebanon, IL. They were married March 4, 1896, in Edwardsville, IL. Jewel Edwards was born October 2, 1903, in Troy.

Verna (Schultze) Edwards was one of eight children born to August W. Schultze and Louisa (Wendler) Schultze. August Schultze was born July 22, 1862, near Troy, and Louisa Wendler was born November 23, 1875, near Troy. They were married November 1, 1896, in Troy. Verna Schultze was born September 22, 1909, near Troy.

Jewel and Verna were married April 16, 1932, in East St. Louis, IL. They bought the Heddergott residence in Troy to establish the Edwards Funeral Home in the spring of 1939. Jewel was employed by the Lahey Funeral Home in Madison, IL, for eight years as a funeral director prior to moving back to Troy with Verna and their daughters, Marilyn and Vivian.

They owned and operated the funeral home until retiring in 1965. They lived in Troy until 1978 when they moved to Eden Village Retirement Center, Glen Carbon, IL, where

Verna is presently residing. Jewel passed away on December 20, 1986.

Marilyn Edwards married Clyde Spitze on March 20, 1954, in Troy, and they live in Las Vegas, NV. They have two children, Susan (Spitze) Ross and Steven Spitze, both who live in Nevada. They also have two grandchildren, Justin and Alyssa, children of Susan.

Vivian Edwards married James Heinemann on April 16, 1960, in Troy, and they live in Alton, IL. They have three children, Michael, Todd, and Lisa, all living in the Alton/Godfrey area.

They also have three grandchildren: Jeremy, son of Todd and Annette; and Mallory and Natalie, twin daughters of Lisa (Heinemann) and Rance Long.

Marilyn retired from the Las Vegas Convention and Visitors Authority in 1994 after 21 years of service. Clyde is employed in Las Vegas as a civil engineer. Vivian retired from Smurfit/Stone Corporation in 1999 after 23 years of service, and Jim retired from SIUE in 1998 after 30 years of service. *Submitted by Vivian Heienemann.*

VIOLA MORRISS EDWARDS - Viola Morriss, born Oct. 8, 1900, the daughter of George C. and Caroline (Sprick) Morriss, of the Formosa area, graduated from the Troy Grade and McCray-Dewey High School and attended college at Normal, IL, a state college for teachers. After a year there, she was employed as the teacher at the Formosa country school west of Troy. She later became a teacher of English in the high school, constantly working towards her teaching degree by taking classes at Shurtleff College in Alton during the summer and at night. She achieved her Masters degree from the University of Illinois many years later.

She married Keith L. Edwards, son of Fred and Cora (Auwarter) Edwards of Troy. During her married years she did private tutoring, and then went back to full time teaching when she was widowed. She taught in the Troy Grade School and later taught in the Granite City public school system and also at the St. Elizabeth parish school. Viola traveled extensively with her sister and brother-in-law, Gladys and Alfred Pape. The three traveled both here and abroad during her lifetime. She always traveled with the thought of expanding the horizons of those she taught through her own experiences.

She died on February 24, 1990. *Submitted by Millie (Collins) Shaffer.*

Keith Edwards and Viola Morriss, circa 1927

EISKANT FAMILY - Kenneth (Butch) Eiskant was born August 10, 1960, in Centerville, IL, to Kenneth and Thelma Eiskant. He attended Collinsville High School. Diana West, was born January 1, 1962, in Belleville, IL, to Judith Buxton and Charles West. Diana also attended Collinsville High School and graduated in 1980. In 1981 she went on to join her father in a small insurance company in Collinsville. Kenneth has worked as a carpenter since high school. On October 4, 1985, Kenneth and Diana were married in Collinsville, IL. In 1989 Kenneth and Diana moved to Troy with their child, Nathan, who was born in 1981. Their second child, Danielle, was born shortly after moving to Troy in 1989. Both children attend the Troy schools. Nathan graduated in 2000 from Triad High School and Danielle will graduate in 2007.

Eiskant family, 2000
Front: Danielle. Middle: Diana, Kenneth. Back: Nathan.

From 1981 to 1995 Diana ran an insurance agency with her father. In 1995 Diana decided to leave the agency and start D.L.E. Insurance Agency Corp. Since that time, the Eiskant family has become a part of the community. With the business booming and the children's school and church activities, they have made many friends in Troy and surrounding areas, and are currently building a new home (which will also house the insurance agency) on Troy-O'Fallon Road. It is to be completed in Fall of 2002. *Submitted by Diana Eiskant.*

GRANT L.AND CLARA (CADE) ELLIOTT
Grant L. Elliott, born May 9, 1867, in Nebraska, IN, was the sixth of seven children born to Daniel and Mary (Huckstep) Elliott. Their children were Taylor, Robert, Victor, Mary, Henrieta, Grant and Alice. Grant grew up on a farm near Altamont, Effingham County, IL, where his father served as justice of the peace for a number of years.

He began his employment as a clerk in a general store. He then became a section hand on the Vandalia Railroad at the age of 19. In 1885, after one year's work, he had saved enough money to study telegraphy under agent W.B. McHenry in Troy, IL. When his studies were completed, Grant returned to his native state of Indiana and served as a night operator for the railroad in Reelsville, IN. After three months, he was appointed as the station agent. He was also Postmaster in Reelsville for three years. He remained in Reelsville for five years before he was transferred to Staunton, IN. He

Grant L. and Clara (Cade) Elliott, 1935.

remained there for six years. He was sent to Troy, IL, in 1896 to fill a similar position with the Vandalia Railroad. He worked for railroads in this area for all of his employment.

Grant L. Elliott married Clara Cade on June 14, 1888. She was the daughter of Daniel and Pauline (Capen) Cade of Altamont, IL. Clara was born on June 15, 1870, in Sedalia, MO. She was educated in the public schools and graduated from high school there.

Grant and Clara had three boys and three girls: Roy Daniel (see Roy Daniel Elliott,Sr.), Jessie Capen (see John Irwin Hindmarch), Grace Dee (see Samuel Mix), Mary Mix (see James Matthew Adams), Jean Raymond (see Jean Raymond Elliott), Merrill Capen (see Merrill Capen Elliott). Mrs. Clara Elliott was a member of the Presbyterian Church.

Grant Elliott belonged to the Ancient Free and Accepted Masons, Troy Lodge #588. He also had been a member of the Troy board of aldermen for two years.

He and Clara spent the remainder of their lives at 511 S. Main Street, Troy, which is now property of the St. Jerome Catholic Church. It is known as the "Elliott House". *Submitted by Kae Elliott Schmitt.*

JEAN RAYMOND ELLIOTT - Jean Raymond Elliott (b. May 30, 1901, d.1969) lived in Troy with his first wife, Gertrude Richter. Jean operated a milk route in the rural Troy area for years. Later, when he lived in St. Louis, MO, he worked for and retired from St. Louis Dairy.

Jean and Gertrude had two children: Pauline (b. June 2, 1928) and Donnie (b.1930-1935). Pauline married Alan Bode of Collinsville, IL, on April 18, 1948. Alan worked as a telephone supervisor and they lived in Collinsville. Their four children are Patty (b. Jan. 19, 1949); Michael (b. May 22, 1951); Peggy (b. Aug. 2, 1959) and Penny (b. Jan. 2, 1962).

Jean R. Elliott, 1930

Patty Berndt lives in Collinsville. Her children are Wendy (b. Jan. 5, 1970) Stephens; twins, Kent and Chad (b. May 1, 1971) Stephens (Chad had son Justin); and Matthew (b. Dec. 2, 1985) Berndt.

Michael and his wife Wanda live in Collinsville, IL. They have a daughter, Michelle (b.July 10, 1971).

Peggy and her husband, Patrick Lange, live in Collinsville. Their children are Tiffany (b. June 15, 1980), Jessica (b. June 2, 1987) and Anna (b. Dec. 6, 1989).

Penny and her husband, Nick Ceretto, live in Collinsville. Penny has a daughter, Heather (b. May 23, 1982) Kohlhaas.

Jean Elliott's wife, Gertrude died at age 43 in 1947. Jean later married Wilma Bachmann in November of 1949. They lived in St.Louis. Wilma had two children: Jack and Dona Bachmann. *Submitted by Pauline Elliott Bode.*

MERRILL CAPEN ELLIOTT - Merrill

Capen Elliott was born July 29, 1903, and died Jan. 27, 1981. He was the youngest of Grant L. and Clara Elliott's six children – he was known as "Babe" Elliott.

Babe worked as a telegrapher; he operated a Shell station next to Adams' Store; and he later worked as sales manager for Bitzer Motors in E. St. Louis, IL, and Collinsville.

Merrill "Babe" and Selma Elliott, 1968

Babe married Selma Kueker on Nov. 10, 1925. Selma was born May 17, 1902, the daughter of Ferdinand and Margarita Kueker of Troy. Babe and Selma lived in Babe's family home and cared for his mother, Clara, until her death in 1954. Babe's sister, Grace "Dee" moved in with Babe and Selma in 1955. The Elliotts resided in this home at 511 S. Main St. until around 1985. Their house is now the property of St. Jerome's Catholic Church and named "The Elliott House."

Babe and Selma had two daughters: Blanche and Judy. Blanche was born Feb. 11, 1928. She married Lowell Taake (b. July 31,1929, d.1973) on July 3l, 1954. They had three daughters: Linda, Carol and Donna. Linda (b. Aug. 1, 1955) married Ewald Hoffman and lives in Troy. They have two daughters: Amy (b. Oct. 14, 1975) and Mindy (b. Aug. 22, 1979). Carol (b. July 20, 1958) lives in Troy with her husband, Michael Hollingshead. Donna (b. Aug. 23, 1959) and her husband, Mark Sanders, live in Troy. Donna has one son, Chad Burgess (b. Dec. 15, 1981).

Babe and Selma's second daughter, Judy (b. Feb. 10, 1943), married Leonard John Melchoir Suess (b. Dec. 8, 1940) on Nov. 9, 1963. They live in Troy near Judy's family home. Judy and Leonard had two sons: Jeffrey Elliott Suess (b. Jan. 7, 1965, d.Feb. 4, 1988) and John Eric (b. June 3, 1968). John married Michelle Kathleen Campe on Oct. 3, 1992. They live in Troy and have two children: Eric John (b. Feb. 23, 1996) and Molly Elizabeth (b. Nov. 13, 2000). *Submitted by Judy Elliott Suess and Kae Elliott Schmitt.*

ROY DANIEL AND ADA (HOGE) ELLIOTT - Roy Daniel Elliott, Sr., was born

on June 22, 1889, in Reelsville, IN, to Grant L. and Clara (Cade) Elliott. He moved to Troy, IL, in 1896 with his family. His father became the station agent at the Troy Depot for the Vandalia Railroad. Roy became fascinated with the decoding of the "dot and dash" system of telegraphy when he visited his father at work at the depot. At age 13, he was proficient enough to take the telegrapher exam in Terre Haute, IN, before Chief Train Dispatcher J.L. Davis. Roy was then employed by the Vandalia railroad to do relief work at the Troy station where his father was an agent. It is not documented as to the length of his telegraphy career, perhaps to 1930. Roy served as a Corporal in the U.S. Army, in France during World War I.

The Famous-Barr Store, in St. Louis, MO, employed Roy around 1930. He became a merchandise traffic manager until his retirement in 1950. At that time, he began working as a clerk for his brother-in-law, James M. Adams (sister Mary's husband), at the Adams Store in Troy. He retired from that job around 1962, and spent the remainder of his life south of Troy, next door to the home he had lived in across from the old Depot, where he first learned telegraphy. He died on September 26, 1978, at the age of 89.

Ada and Roy Daniel Elliott, Sr., 1975

Roy married Ada Elizabeth Hoge on August 5, 1911, in Springfield, MO. Ada was born on January 22, 1891, in Alton, IL, to William Vickers and Sarah Elizabeth Price Hoge. William V. Hoge ws a jeweler and photographer. Ada was working as a telephone operator when she met and married Roy. She spent her time as a homemaker and her hobbies were gardening, sewing and quilting. Roy and Ada had three children: Evelyn Lucille (see Wilbur Emery Kimberlin), born June 2, 1912, in Springfield, MO; Mary Dean (see Louis Jean Grieve), born June 23, 1915, in Troy; and Roy Daniel, Jr., born September 27, 1927, in Tulsa, OK (see Roy Daniel Elliott, Jr.). *Submitted by Kae Elliott Schmitt.*

ROY DANIEL ELLIOTT, JR. - Roy Daniel

Elliott, Jr., was born September 27, 1927, to Roy Daniel and Ada Elizabeth (Hoge) Elliott. He graduated from McCray-Dewey High School in 1945. He served in the U.S. Navy during World War II.

Gloria and Dan Elliott, 1999

Dan married Gloria Arlene Hensley *(see Otho Garrett Hensley)* June 18, 1949. He worked as an automobile mechanic at Porter's Garage on Market Street in Troy, and later at Bitzer Motor Co. in E. St. Louis and Collinsville, IL.

In 1955, Dan began night classes at St. Louis University in St. Louis, MO. Later he transferred to Washington University at St. Louis, MO, to complete his doctorate degree in Dental Surgery in 1962. Dan established his dental practice in Edwardsville, IL, in August 1962. In 1993, Dan sold his practice and semi-retired. He continued to treat patients in Highland, IL, for two years until his retirement in 1995.

Dan and Gloria lived in Troy until 1980 when they moved to Edwardsville. After Dan's retirement, he and Gloria moved to Hilton Head Island, SC, where they live today.

Gloria was a homemaker for Dan and their three children: Kae, Gail, and Roy Daniel, III. Kae Ann (b. May 3, 1950) married Steven Samuel Schmitt (a Troy native) on June 11, 1971. They have two children: Sara Marie (b. Sept. 25, 1975) and Steven Samuel, Jr. (b. June 17, 1978).

Gail Marie (b. April 1,1954) married Richard Gillig of Edwardsville on October 9, 1976. Gail and Richard had two sons, Travis Ian (b. Jan. 15, 1980) and Tyler Grant (b. Aug. 25, 1981). The boys live with their mother in Edwardsville.

Roy Daniel, III, was born on May 20, 1961. Dan currently lives in Houston, TX, with his wife, Elise, and her daughter, Taylor Gilchrist. Dan has a daughter, Anne-Marie, born Feb. 9, 1994, from a previous marriage. She lives in Boston with her mother. *Submitted by Roy Daniel Elliott Jr. and Kae Elliott Schmitt.*

JOE AND JACQUELYN (MORNHINWEG) ESTES - Joe and Jacquelyn (Mornhinweg)

Estes were married by her father in 1962 at Friedens United Church of Christ. They lived in Collinsville and moved to Troy in 1968. Their son Joe Mornhinweg Estes was born in 1963 and Jeffrey Milton Estes was born in 1965.

Joe Milton was born in Kentucky and moved to Tennessee when he was a senior in high school. After completing a stint in the U.S. Navy,

Estes family, 1985
(l. to r.) Front: Jacquelyn (Mornhinweg)
Back: Jeffrey Milton, Joe Milton, Joe Mornhinweg

he attended and received a degree in mathmatics from Austin University in Clarksville. Joe was employed at the mapping center St. Louis which was called Defense Mapping Aerospace Center. Most maps for the Lunar and other space project were made there. Joe did present a paper at a cartographers' convention. Some of his work was quoted in a publication in England. He retired in 1989.

Jackie attended Troy schools and graduated from SIUC with a degree in elementary education. She taught in the primary grades in the Triad school system from 1968 until her retirement in 1989.

Joe and Jackie enjoyed traveling. They have visited 47 states. A favorite vacation was a January cruise to the Carribean.

Their elder son Joe lives in Glen Ellyn, IL, with his wife Ellen (Paulin) Estes and their children Matthew and Lauren. Joe, employed by A.G. Edwards & Sons, is a VP in the Naperville office.

Jeffrey lives in Troy with his wife Vickie Moore Estes and their children, Scott and Jennifer. Jeffery is employed as a defense lawyer for the State of Missouri, specializing in death penalty litigation. *Submitted by Jacquelyn Estes.*

EVELYN EMMA (KECK) AND LEO FEHMEL -
Evelyn Emma Keck was born January 23, 1905, to Martin Jr and Emma (Hobein) Keck of Troy. She was the fifth of the seven children born to Martin and Emma Keck. She married Leo Mathias Fehmel, son of Jacob and Caroline (Noll) Fehmel of St. Jacob, on May 14, 1923, in Troy.

Leo was born April 19, 1903. They lived on a farm south of St Jacob, before purchasing their own farm at 10505 Keck Road north of St. Jacob. They lived and worked on the farm until Leo's death June 11, 1972. At that time, Evelyn moved to 510 Mill St., St. Jacob, until her death, September 26, 1988. They are buried in Keystone Cemetery. They had three children.

Dale L. Fehmel, born on August 15, 1926, married Genevieve Chipley on November 17, 1956, and lives in Florissant, Missouri. Dale and Genevieve have three children, Scott, Sandra and Cindy. Scott married Laura Franer and has one son, Ian Scott Fehmel. They live in Florissant, MO. Sandra married Michael D. Mrkacek and lives in Las Vegas, Nevada. Cindy works in a library and lives in St. Louis, MO.

Betty J. Fehmel, born December 10, 1931, married Eugene Steffes (1930-1999) September

29, 1962. They made their home in Rancho Palos, California. Betty and Gene had one child, Beth, who lives in Portland, Oregon.

Larry B. Fehmel, born February 23, 1939, married Sharon Keck on August 23, 1963. They live in St. Jacob, IL, and had two children, Linda and Tim. Linda married John Sedlacek on September 3, 1994, and has one son, Jacob William Sedlacek, born January 27, 2000. They live south of St. Jacob. Tim currently lives in Savannah, Georgia . *Submitted by Pamela Keck and Sharon Fehmel.*

EARL FISCHER FAMILY (1951-1955) -
Earl Fischer opened a plumbing business in Troy, IL, the summer of 1951 at 127 East Market Street under the name Walter F. Fischer Plumbing and Heating, which was located at 302 East Main Street, Collinsville, IL. Earl Fischer, born February 26, 1916, was the son of Walter F. Fischer. It was a family business, which included Earl's brothers: Walter Fischer, Jr., and Charles P. Fischer.

Since the city of Troy was putting in the sewage system in 1951, Earl felt this was a good opportunity for his business. In addition to plumbing and heating supplies, Earl's business sold Hotpoint appliances and Panda paints. It didn't prove profitable, so he closed his business after 11 months, continuing to work in the family business in Collinsville. The empty plumbing shop was used as a Baptist Church for services for a small congregation, and then it became Rosalie's Dress Shop.

When moving to Troy, Earl brought his wife, Veida Lacquement Fischer, born June 23, 1916, and sons, Earl Walter (13), and Thomas (2), and daughter, Susan (7). They lived across from the Lion's Theater in the brick home. John and Rosalie Petri traded Earl the house and adjoining business for a home in Collinsville that Earl Fischer owned.

Earl and Veida had many friends and enjoyed their life in Troy. Veida was a Brownie leader and Earl was active in the community. Earl Walter was active in Trojan sports, playing basketball, track, and cross country at McCray-Dewey High School. Susan was active in Brownies and Girl Scouts. Tom was the scourge of Market Street in his pedal fire engine. After school, he would try to run into as many students as possible who were walking on the sidewalk. The Fischers had a pool table in their basement, which made it a popular recreation spot for teenagers.

Fischer family, circa 1960
(l. to r.) Front: Thomas, Susan, Virginia
Back: Earl, Veida, Earl Walter

In 1955, Walter F. Fischer moved to another residence in Collinsville, requiring Earl to move his family back to 302 East Main Street, above the plumbing shop. Earl sold the residence and business to James Adams, who was beginning the practice of medicine.

Earl Walter Fischer regretted leaving his good friends and fellow athletes. He had grown up watching Collinsville Kahoks play basketball, and thought he had the ability to play Kahok basketball. He realized his dream by playing for them in 1955 and 1956, also lettering in cross country and track.

Earl Walter Fischer and Thomas Fischer each came back to marry Troy girls. Earl Walter married Nancy, Oscar and Dorothy Gindler's daughter, and Tom married Victoria, George and Verna Ottwein's daughter. *Submitted by Nancy Fischer.*

EARL WALTER AND NANCY FISCHER
Nancy Fischer was born on January 29, 1941, to Oscar and Dorothy (Ludwig) Gindler. She was born at home in her parents' bedroom. She was placed in a towel-lined bedpan and put on the radiator for warmth. Her birth took place at 203 Edwardsville Road in Troy, IL, which is now a flower shop next to the funeral home.

Earl Fischer family, Nov. 11, 2000
(l. to r.) Back: John, John Daniel and Laura Vandersand, Jennifer, Carmen (bride), Jeffrey (groom), Earl, Melanie. Front: Brooke Oberto, Nancy, Kathy Oberto, Greg Oberto, Ashley Oberto.

Earl Walter Fischer was born on August 19, 1938, to Earl and Veida (Lacquement) Fischer, at St. Mary's Hospital in East St. Louis, Illinois. The family moved to Troy when Earl Walter was in the 8th grade.

Nancy was in the last graduating class from McCray-Dewey High School in 1959. The next year Troy was consolidated with the St. Jacob and Marine students to attend Triad High School. Nancy attended 3 semesters at Illinois State Normal University, Normal IL, worked for Dog n Suds, Inc., and the University of Illinois School of Music, both at Champaign IL, St. Francis Hospital, Peoria IL, and Scott AFB IL, where she retired in February 2001 after 21 years of government service.

Earl graduated from Collinsville High School, attended Southern Illinois University, Carbondale, and graduated from McKendree College, Lebanon, IL, in 1960. He then did graduate work at Southern Illinois University, Edwardsville. He started teaching school in

Nashville, IL, his first year, and then taught 37 years of elementary education in Collinsville, IL, where he retired in June 1998.

Earl and Nancy were married on March 26, 1970, at St. John United Church of Christ, Collinsville where they have been active members for 31 years. They lived in Troy for two years and then bought the old Kinder place west of Troy. They renovated the brick home built shortly after the Civil War, and lived there 13 years. They then built a cedar log home on part of the property.

Earl and Nancy have five children. Greg Oberto's family lives in Waterloo IL, and he is employed by Eastside Lumberyard, East St. Louis IL. He has two daughters, Ashley and Brooke Oberto. Laura Vandersand and her husband, John, and son, John Daniel, live in Highland IL. John works for the City of Highland, and Laura is a homemaker and a Discovery Toys consultant. Jennifer Fischer lives in Elmhurst IL, and is a supply chain customer service coordinator for Kraft Foods. Jeffrey Fischer lives in Manchester, MO, with his wife, Carmen. Jeffrey is a project engineer for McCarthy Construction Company, and Carmen is a registered dietitian for the Rockwood School District. They have one son, Kyle Walter Fischer. Melanie Fischer lives in St. Louis and teaches 3rd grade for Hazelwood School District. *Submitted by Nancy Fischer.*

CHARLES AND JANE FISHER - Charles E. Fisher was born and raised in Southern Illinois. He graduated from Benton High School. He enlisted in the Army during World War II, serving in Europe. After the War, he attended SIU-Carbondale and then moved to the Metro-East. He retired from Nestle Tea Co. in Granite City in 1986.

Charles and Jane Jarvis (nee Voelker) were married July 31,1971, by Rev. Noel Hutchings at Bethel Baptist Church in Troy.

Jane was born in Troy to Frank and Vera Voelker (nee Dillingham). She graduated from McCray-Dewey High School in 1940. She worked for Civil Service both in St. Louis and at Scott Air Force Base. She retired in 1975 with 28 years service.

Both Charles and Jane are Emeritus Members of Anderson Hospital Auxiliary and are members of Meadow Heights Baptist Church in Collinsville, IL.

Jane was previously married to Ernest A. Jarvis (deceased) and has four children-three sons, John, Paul and Alan all of Troy, and one daughter Nancy of Bradenton, Florida.

Charles and Jane Fisher, 1975

The Fishers have eight grandchildren-Natalie Hall, Nathan Rowe, John R. Jarvis, Amanda Jarvis, Laura Jarvis, Adam Jarvis, Nicholas Smith and Abbie Lynn Jarvis. They have two great-grandchildren, Gaige Alan Bailey and Paighton Jane Hall. *Submitted by Jane F. Fisher.*

TOM FISCHER - Tom Fischer was born June 21, 1949, in Collinsville, IL, to Earl and Veida (Lacquement) Fischer. He graduated from Collinsville High School (1968). Victoria Ottwein was born April 12, 1946, in Troy, IL, to George and Verna (Gaertner) Ottwein. She is a graduate of Triad High School (1964).

Tom and Vicki both attended McKendree College, Lebanon, IL. Tom graduated in 1972 and Vicki in 1968. Tom majored in Physical Education, playing basketball under Coach Harry Statham. Vicki majored in business.

Fischer family, 2000
(l. to r.) Tom, Victoria, Rebecca

After graduation, Tom taught Physical Education at St Peter and Paul Grade School, Collinsville, IL. He taught collision repair and auto mechanics at Collinsville High School for one year. He then went to Beck Area Vocational Center, Hecker, IL, teaching auto collision repair for ten years. He is now at Collinsville Area Vocational Center, teaching there for 12 years.

Vicki worked at Hawthorne Animal Hospital for 27 years. She is now financial secretary at St. John Evangelical United Church of Christ, Collinsville, IL, having worked there for ten years.

They married on November 3, 1979, at Friedens United Church of Christ, Troy, IL, and built a house on the farm that was owned by Vicki's grandfather, George Ottwein, Sr. Their daughter, Rebecca, was born February 2, 1983.

Rebecca attended Troy schools, graduating from Triad High School in 2001. She is attending St. Louis University, Parks School of Engineering, in St. Louis.

The Fischers enjoy camping, boating, and flying their airplane. Tom holds a private pilot's license. They hanger their Piper Cherokee 180 airplane at Shafer Metro-East Airport in St Jacob.

Vicki enjoys genealogy, scrap booking and reading. Becky played clarinet and bass clarinet in the high school and community bands, and enjoys theatre and reading. She is a Gold Award Girl Scout. *Submitted by Victoria Fischer.*

EDWARD AND LAURA FOPPE - Edward J. Foppe (b. May 6, 1968), the son of Herb and Marian (Moss) Foppe, and Laura Susanne Richter (b. Oct. 25, 1966), daughter of James Lee

Foppe family, 2002
(l. to r.) Ed, Katelyn, Laura, Anna

and Susanne (Drayton) Richter, were married April 24, 1992, in Collinsville. They are the parents of Katelyn Susanne (b. April 17, 1996) and Anna Victoria (b. August 10, 1997).

Ed and Laura have good educational backgrounds. Both graduated from Belleville East High School, Ed graduating in 1986 and Laura, in 1984. Laura graduated from Southern Illinois University, Carbondale, IL, in 1988 while Ed graduated from Embry-Riddle Aeronautical University in Daytona Beach, FL, in 1991.

The couple lived in Atlanta, GA, from 1992 to 1999, moving to Troy in October, 1999. Here Ed began Genesis Computer Networks, Inc. in January 2000. The family keeps busy with work and family activities and hobbies.

Among Laura's interests are reading, running, and physical fitness. Ed enjoys NASCAR racing, golf, and softball. Of course, Katelyn and Anna are tops on their parents' priority lists. *Submitted by Ed and Laura Foppe.*

FOUCEK FAMILY - Zdenka Fiala and Joseph Foucek were married on June 7, 1933. They had no honeymoon, for the day after the wedding, the new Mrs. Foucek was sent out to hoe the sweet potatoes. In the early years the young couple truck farmed, raised pigs and chickens to make ends meet, pay off their debt, and buy the various trees and shrubs to start their nursery. In 1941 Mr. Foucek put up 2 greenhouses with the help of his brother. The business soon expanded to include another farm in Glen Carbon in 1945.

Wedding day, June 7, 1933
Joseph and Zdenka Foucek

Mr. and Mrs. Foucek had 3 daughters, 2 of whom still run the business today. He was a charter member of the Troy Lions Club and an avid supporter of the Tri-Township Park. Mr. Foucek passed away in 1987. Mrs. Foucek, in her nineties, still lived in the same house she moved into as a bride until her death in 2002. *Submitted by Doris Gause*

WILLIAM S. FREEMAN - Bill Freeman and his wife Mary June (Howdeshell) Freeman married April 29, 1941. Daughter Scottie was born on Oct. 17, 1942 and son Bob arrived on Aug. 5,1944. (He eventually married Karen Lybarger of Troy on Aug. 19, 1963.) The family moved to St. Jacob, IL, in the summer of 1946 because no houses were available to rent in Troy where Bill was to become the new principal of the Troy Grade School. The family moved to the area from Kampsville, IL, where Bill had been principal of that and another small community school in the area. Both Bill and Mary June's families came from nearby Calhoun/Pike County, IL, farming communities.

Freeman family, 1980
(l. to r.) Front: Mary June, Scottie J., Tracy Dell
Back: Connie Lynn, William S., Robert E.

A year later when a two-family home became available in Troy, the Freemans moved to Troy. The other family occupying the home was the Bob Taylor family, long time residents of Troy. A few years later the Freemans took up residence in a home on what was called "Windy Hill." They needed a little room for expansion as they were increasing the family number to 5 with the birth of Constance (Connie) Lynn on Nov.14, 1956. Another move to a home on Watt Street and another increase to 6 family members occurred in 1961 with the birth of Tracy Dell on Jan. 27.

Bill was a very dedicated educator whose concern was what was best for the students and the community. He went on to become Assistant Superintendent of the Triad District and, upon retirement, worked for the County Superintendent's office. Bill died on April 29, 1988, and is not only remembered with great affection by his family, most of whom still live in the area, but is also remembered by the community as it passes by the Troy Grade School on Staunton Road, renamed the William S. Freeman Grade School. In addition to his dedication to youth, Bill was also an active member of the Troy Lions Club and leader in the Troy Methodist Church. He had a wide range of interests including motorcycle riding, golfing, fishing and, most of all, laughing with and enjoying people, jokes, and life in general.

From her current home on Willow Drive just outside Troy, Mary June continues to be a dedicated mother, grandmother, and great-grandmother to her family. The reaches

of her love and care go out to grandchildren-Kristan Freeman (Mrs.Warren) Byrd, Kyle (Amy Strong) Freeman, Kane (Jennifer York) Freeman, Jessica Foehrkolb, Daniel Foehrkolb, Joseph Foehrkolb, Jennifer Baumgartner (Mrs. Chris) Forrest and Ashley Weaver- and to great-grandchildren Caitlin Byrd, Devynn Byrd, Cali Byrd, Kalyn Forrest, and Jake Freeman. *Submitted by Scottie Freeeman.*

EDWIN AND MARY BACHMANN FREY
Edwin Christian Frey and Mary Louise Bachmann were married on December 8, 1898.

Edwin was born on a farm near St. Jacob, Illinois, December 18, 1875, to Samuel Paul Frey, Jr. and Elizabeth Frutiger Frey. He had three brothers, Jacob, Arthur, and Oliver, and two sisters, Anna Francis Schoeck and Ella C. Gansman. Mary was the daughter of Jacob and Gertrude Schrepfer Bachmann. Her two sisters were Mrs. Gustav (Pauline) Bleisch and Mrs. Fred (Bertha) Oswald. She was born on June 20, 1878. Edwin and Mary had three children, Florence Elizabeth Schmidt Guennewig, Alma Pauline Langenwalter and Clarence Edwin Frey.

Edwin received his education in the public school and then began farming for himself on his farm ground south of St. Jacob. Edwin and Mary's three children attended the Frey school which was located right across the road from their home. Edwin continued farming until 1922 when he purchased the Home Telephone Company in St. Jacob and conducted that business for the following four years. In 1926 he purchased the Troy Telephone Exchange of Troy, IL, from E. N. and Fremont Michael. Edwin and Mary purchased their two story white frame home on Troy Avenue (called Windy Hill) in Troy, IL, which was built by Mr. and Mrs. Arthur Seligman. The home was on six acres and included a barn, smoke house, chicken house and out house. Edwin kept a few head of cattle and had an orchard with fruit trees and raised and sold red and black raspberries.

Edwin Christian and Mary
Louise (Bachmann) Frey, 1938

He was an active member of the Friedens United Church of Christ, a member of the Lions Club and at one time was one of the directors of the Highland Dairy Farms Company. He died at his home on October 6, 1941, after a short illness. Funeral services were held at his residence and interment was at the Keystone Cemetery at St. Jacob, IL.

After Edwin's death, Mary continued to live in the family home. Eventually she sold the

Edwin and Mary Frey home on Troy Avenue
(Windy Hill), 1943

home and went to live with her daughter and son-in-law, Mr. and Mrs. Theodore Joseph Guennewig in Troy. She spent the last year of her life as a resident of the Hitz Memorial Home at Alhambra, IL. She died on February 7, 1972, at the age of 93. She was a member of the Women's Guild of the Friedens United Church of Christ. Interment was in the Keystone Cemetery of St. Jacob, IL.

She was survived by her three children and six grandchildren: Grace Schmidt Ottwein, Lewis Edwin Frey, Carol Langenwalter, Jenny Bell, Marybeth Frey Connor, Jane Frey Miller and Sara Frey Chamberlain. Her second grandson, Lynn Harold Langenwalter, died in infancy. Her nine great grandchildren are Ann Marie, Amy Sue, Paul John and Emily Carol Ottwein, Samuel Lee and Susan Lee Jenny, Thomas Nelson and Amy Sue Connor and Jason Wade Miller. *Submitted by Carol Langenwalter Bell.*

CLARENCE AND BETH FREY - For a good part of its long history, Troy enjoyed a private telephone company, called The Troy Telephone Company; and two generations of the Frey family, first Edwin C., and then Clarence, operated it. It was started in the early part of the 1900's, by E. and Fremont Michael, but Edwin bought it in 1926, and Clarence purchased it in 1942. It was sold to Illinois Bell in 1955, and remains in their system today. "Central," the office that handled equipment and, of course, manual operators, was located downtown, at the corner of Market and Kimberlin where the company still is located. During this important period, the lives of the whole Frey family and even their neighbors were intertwined with the telephone company. Edwin and Mary Frey occupied a large two story home on Windy Hill, right across the street from Tom and Minta Lewis.

Edwin and Mary Bachman Frey had three children: Florence (Roland Schmidt, Ted

Frey family, circa 1950
(l. to r.) Back row: Lewis, Clarence, Beth, MaryBeth
Front row: Sara, Jane

Guennewig), Alma (Harold Langenwalter) and Clarence.

Among the 3 Lewis children (see Tom and Minta Lewis family) was Beth. Beth married Clarence Frey, the neighbor boy, in 1933, and built a classic brick bungalow next to the Lewis home and raised their own family there until leaving Troy in 1955. The extended family enjoyed life on Windy Hill for many years.

Clarence and Beth had three daughters and a son: Mary Beth, Jane, Sara and Lewis, all of whom attended the Troy High School. The family was social and active in the town's activities. Clarence was a charter member of the Troy Lions Club and became a charter director of Troy Security Bank, helping organize the first Troy bank since the Great Depression. In the Lions Club and elsewhere, he was a part of an infamous fun-loving group known for practical jokes on each other and on the town. The family was active in St. Paul Lutheran Church. Beth was an accomplished pianist and organist, furnishing entertainment for a multitude of community functions, and served as organist of St. Paul Lutheran Church for many years.

In 1955 the telephone company was sold; and, to support Beth's health, the entire family moved to Fort Lauderdale, Florida, where Clarence became involved as a real estate investor. Clarence died in 1982. Beth and all of the children still reside in that vicinity, enjoying children and grandchildren of their own. Lewis continued to work in the telephone business there until retiring several years ago.

And no story about the Troy Telephone Company would be complete without the mention of Leroy Flath, a long term employee first of the Troy Telephone Company and then Bell until retirement. Leroy and his wife, Maxine, became integral parts of the "telephone company family," serving Troy's important communication for many years. *Submitted by Beth Lewis Frey and M. Ottwein.*

FREY FAMILY - Many of this Frey family are from the St. Jacob area and are buried at Keystone Cemetery. A lot of them lived in Troy and were all great citizens. Family names associated with this Frey family are the following: Frutiger, Ottwein, Langenwalter, Sauls, Kassing, Gansmann, Clark, Fehmel, Noeltner, Binger, Hug, Brendel, Keck, Buehrer, and Spengel.

Samuel Frey I is buried in Keystone Cemetery. He was born in 1785.

Samuel Frey II was born 11-1-1810 in St. Jacob. He married in 1832 and died 9-2-1888 in St. Jacob. His first wife was Frederika Weirich who was born in 1840. Francis Gruenenfelder was his second wife who died 8-17-1845 and is buried in Keystone also. Samuel had two children: Lena who married George Schoeck and Katie who married a Julius and then married Hoffman Mohr.

Peter Frey was born 7-4-1859 and married in 1884. He died 4-12-1912 and is buried in Keystone. He married Katherine Gobleman who was born 8-4-1860 in Germany. Her father was Jacob. She died 9-29-1944 and is buried in St. Jacob. They had nine children.

1. Peter married Anna Isaac.

2. Edward (b. 2-11-1888 in St. Jacob-d. 7-11-1965 in Highland) married on 7-21-1910

Alvin Frey

Mayme Adelhardt (b. 9-2-1890 in Collinsville-d.9-2-1988 in Alhambra, IL). Her parents were John Adelhardt and Anna Miller. Edward worked for the Illinois Terminal Railroad for 17 years.

3. George (d. 1921)

4. Walter (d. 1953)

5. Kate (d. 1954, married Dan Carter)

6. Ida (b. 12-7-1883, m. George Keck 2-24-1901, d. 8-10-1964)

7. Linda (b. 1895-d. 6-6-1962 in New Athens, IL, married Ed Bailey)

8. Carrie (b. 3-19-1892 in Marine, m. Frank Adelhardt 3-24-1912, d. 6-9-1976)

9. Alice (b. 10-11-1898, m. Walter Spengel 4-17-1917, d. 10-10-1985).

Edward's children are given below.

1. Raymond (b. 1-2-1911 in Marine, m. (1) Alma Dubach, (2) Edna Warecke, d. 2-15-1986 in Highland)

2. Alvin (b. 6-14-1913 in Marine, m. 2-9-1933 Louise Morgan b. 10-13-1913- d. 4-30-1992 in Troy). His son Charles (b. 7-30-1934) married (1) Virgina Cashmirkosky and (2) Sharon Sparks. Grandchildren are Peter Frey and Lori McCurdy; great-grandchildren are Joshua and Jeremy Neilson. Alvin is a 50 year member of the Odd Fellow Lodge 25, a 50 year member of the Moose, a director for 30 years of the Collinsville Building and Loan, a member of Friedens United Church of Christ, and Troy's Senior Citizens. He had a home built in Troy, which he shares with Lillian Bensa.

3. Ottmar (b. 11-12-1915 in Marine, m. (1) Dorothy Rohrkaste, (2) Valerie Weider, sons-Kent, Tony, John, Andy, d. 7-15-1989, Belleville).

4. Irene (b. 7-6-1917, m. Pete Hardy 1938, d. 1982 in St. Louis).

5. Blanche (b. 6-3-1918, m. Walsch Bayer 1945, daughters Joann and Susan)

6. Edward (b. 1-17-1924 in Pin Oak, m. Ella Howard, a triplet, in 1947.) He received the Good Conduct Medal May 4, 1943, the Purple Heart and 3 bronze stars. He died 10-2-2000, and is buried in Friedens);

7. Marie (b. 11-24-1929 in Collinsville, m. Lester Gentry in Troy, d. 8-18-1986 in Highland, children – Wayne and Janell Gelly). *Submitted by Lillian Bensa.*

PETER FREY - Peter Frey (1854-1912) of St. Jacob married Kate Gobbleman (1860-1944) in the mid 1870s. They lived in the St. Jacob area near what is now Triad Middle School. They raised nine children-Peter, Ed, George, Walter, Alice, Linda, Kate, Ida, and Caroline.

Caroline Frey (1892-1976) married Frank Adelhardt (1889-1978) of Marine in 1912. They first lived in Edwardsville, and then in 1919 they rented the Barnsback farm west of Troy. In 1922 they moved to the Fred Schoon farm also west of Troy where they raised three children, Lester, Clarence, and LaVern. In 1948 Frank and Carrie retired from farming and moved to Hazel Street in Troy.

Peter Frey family, circa 1920s

Lester Adelhardt (1913-1980) married Ruby Kirsch of Blackjack (Troy) in 1935. Just after marriage they lived in Troy then moved to Edwardsville for a short time and then moved back to Troy. Les and Ruby lived in several homes in Troy before settling on Staunton Rd. Les worked at the Common Wealth grocery store during the war and then bought the grocery business from Butcher Martin in Troy and spent the next 35 years owning and operating the store. Ruby was a teacher in several of the area's country schools – Mt. Zion, Quercus Grove, and Spring Valley and then worked as a substitute teacher in the Troy Public School system. They raised three children, Karen (Cookie), Terry (Bud), and Sherry.

Peter Frey family, circa 1940

Clarence Adelhardt, born in 1917, married Jane Southard of Poag (Edwardsville) in 1942. Clarence served his country during WW2 in the Army. When he returned, Clarence and Jane lived in Edwardsville for a short time and Clarence worked at the Common Wealth. In 1948 they moved to the farm and took over the operation for Frank. They continued to farm until 1984 when they retired and moved to Glen Carbon. Clarence and Jane raised three children-Carol Sue, Cindy, and Christi.

LaVern Adelhardt, born in 1924, married William Buehrer of Granite City in 1944. They lived in Granite City for a short time then moved to Hazel Street in Troy. They raised two daughters Debbie and Diane. *Submitted by Sherry Smith.*

FRIEDERICH FAMILY - It all began one summer day, in 1969, at the SIUE library. Kay Kimmle, a sophomore from O'Fallon, IL, had just left her seat to do some research; and when she returned, there was a stranger talking to her friend and sitting in her seat. Little did she know then that the stranger, Mark Friederich from Granite City, would become her husband. Mark and Kay were married at SIUE in the Religious Center in Dec. 1971. Mark continued school at SIUE and entered the first class of the SIU Dental School located in Alton the summer of 1972 and graduated in 1975. Kay began her career in 1971 as a speech therapist in the public schools.

Friederich family, 1999
(l. to r.) Front: Andria, Kay, David
Back: Mark, Stephen

Mark and Kay moved to Troy in the fall of 1976. They purchased the house of Sheik and Eppy Maden on Windy Hill. In the spring before the birth of their first son, Stephen, the Friederichs joined Friedens UCC. In 1979, Andria was born and in 1982, David.

Mark moved his dental office to Troy in 1980. He and his father helped to remodel the old hardware store into the dental office located in downtown Troy on Main Street. In 1983, Kay joined the teaching staff of the Triad School District as a speech therapist. *Submitted by Kay Friederich.*

ARTHUR AND MINNIE (BANGERT) GAERTNER - Arthur Gaertner, born February 5, 1893, in Belleville, and Wilhelmina (Minnie) Bangert, born May 3, 1895, in Pin Oak Township, were married on April 30, 1916. Arthur was the son of John and Margaret (Bohnenstiehl) Gaertner, and Minnie was the daughter of Karl and Catherine (Mehrmann) Bangert.

Arthur was a carpenter by trade and was involved in much construction and renovation in the Troy area. The two were members of Friedens Evangelical and Reformed Church and

Minnie and Arthur Gaertner, 1943

were very active in its activities, Arthur in the men's brotherhood, church council and choir. He sang in a quartet with Les Becker, Oscar Ottwein and Carl Esenberg at church and community functions. Minnie was active in the Women's Guild where she held offices, was a quilter, and served at the many dinners at the church.

Arthur and Minnie had one son, Albert, who died in 1999; a daughter, Verna, married to George Ottwein, Jr.; one granddaughter, Victoria Ottwein Fischer, and one great-granddaughter, Rebecca Fischer. *Submitted by Verna Ottwein.*

JULIUS GAERTNER AND CHARLES ROW FAMILIES - Julius Gaertner was born Nov. 6, 1894, the son of John and Margaret (Bohnenstiehl) Gaertner. He married Catherine (Katie) Ester Elizabeth Bangert, who was born on Oct. 11, 1897, daughter of Carl and Catherine Bangert. They settled on the Bangert farm north of Troy until 1941, when they moved into Troy. They had 4 children: Harold, Doris, Carl, and Gladys. Katie died Feb. 12, 1955. Jule married Hilda Clayton on April 4, 1959. Jule died Aug. 24, 1982.

The Gaertner family, circa 1940s
(l. to r.) Front: Julius, Gladys, Catherine (Kate)
Back: Carl, Doris, Harold

Their daughter, Doris Katherine Margaret, was born June 27, 1925. She married Louis Schmitt who was born Sept. 29, 1921, in Grantfork, son of Wendeline and Caroline Schmitt, on Nov. 21, 1942, at Friedens Church in Troy. They had 4 children: Karen, Gerald, Bob, and Richard. Doris died May 11, 1992, and Louis died June 30,1997.

Karen was born Feb. 18, 1945, and married Charles William Row, born Jan. 8, 1943, son of Charles and Emma Row. They had 5 children: Julie Katherine, Kathi Lynn, Wendy Sue, Sheila Roxanne, and Clifford Louis (Chip).

Julie, born Sept. 28, 1963, married Rudy Moravec, son of Rudy and Verla Moravec, on June13, 1981. They had a son, Jason Dean, born May 16, 1982, in Omaha, NB. They divorced and Julie married George Ray Barker, Jr., son of George, Sr., and Carolyn Barker. George has three daughters: Amy Marie, born March 1, 1977; Samantha Renee, Nov. 25, 1981, and Ashley Ann, born February 7, 1983. George and Julie have a son, George Roy, III, born May 22,1985. George also adopted Jason.

Kathi Lynn, born May 18, 1965, married John Sorbie, son of John, Sr., and Janet Sorbie, on Dec. 1, 1984. They have one daughter, Heather Nicole, born May 9, 1985. They

divorced and Kathi married Kenneth Harris, son of Kenneth and Linda Harris, on May 26, 1990. They have 2 sons, Dylan Scott, born Aug. 4, 1991, and Cody Dalton, born Aug. 21, 1992.

Wendy Sue, born Aug. 14, 1966, married Larry Allen Ellis, Jr., son of Larry, Sr., and Maxine Ellis, on Aug. 20, 1985. They have two sons, Larry Allen, III, born May 8, 1985, and Christopoher Charles, born Sept. 8, 1987. Wendy and Larry divorced, and Wendy married Curtis Haller on March 10, 1990. They had a daughter, Kayla Mae, born Jan. 24, 1991. Wendy and Curt divorced.

Sheila Roxanne, born Oct. 1970, in Elgin, IL, married Jeffrey Bast on Nov. 4,1989. They divorced. Sheila married Randy Gene Waggoner, son of Charles and Juanita Waggoner, born Oct. 26, 1971, on May 1, 1999. They have one son, Brady Thomas, born July 28, 2000.

Clifford Louis (Chip) was born Oct. 2, 1972, and married Erin Nichole Habermehl, daughter of Ron and Holly Habermehl, on Sept. 13, 1997. They have one daughter, Jadyn Nicole, born Oct. 20, 2000. *Submitted by Karen Row.*

ARTHUR AND DRUSILLA GARLAND
Arthur "Sport" Garland was born in Fillmore, IL, in 1889 to Jesse Garland and Addie (Hinton) Garland. Arthur had 1 brother and 2 sisters. Jesse, his father, came to America from England in 1889.

Drusilla (Mashek) Garland, circa 1905

Drusilla (Mashek) Garland was born in Glen Carbon in 1893. Her parents were Frank Mashek and Anna (Primas) Mashek. Drusilla's mother Anna died when she was 2 years old and she was raised by her grandmother Mary Primas. Her father Frank Mashek moved to Missouri, remarried, and had 5 children. Drusilla's parents came to America from Bohemia.

Arthur and Drusilla had one daughter, Sybil Anastasia (Garland) McFarland.

Arthur "Sport" Garland worked as a proprietor of a livery in Troy as a young man and was quite the gentleman when he was driving the horse and buggies around town. He got his nickname "Sport" because of this. Later he worked in the Troy coal mines. Sport died in 1965.

Drusilla was a homemaker and died in her early 40s from cancer. Her granddaughter Gay (McFarland) Hinnen was 2 years old at her death.

Sport and Drusilla lived in Troy all their married life. *Submitted by granddaughter Sharon Schlaefer.*

WALTER AND GLADYS (ISLAND) GAULTNEY - Walter and Gladys were married in E. St. Louis, IL, on Dec. 24, 1924. In

Gaultney family, about 1954
(l. to r.) Front: Walter, Sr., Phyllis, Francis, Walter, Jr.,
Gladys. Back: Virginia, Irene, Frieda, Kenny, Betty.

1929 they moved to Troy Junction (an Illinois Terminal Rail Road Station, 2 1/2 miles west of Troy). The big 1 1/2-story house was painted bright orange and was just 4 feet from the railroad tracks. The company owned it.

Gaultney children
(l. to r.) Front: Francis, Irene, Phyllis, Kenny
Back: Virginia, Betty, Frieda, Walter Jr.

Walter was a foreman on a "section gang" which kept the tracks in good repair and safe for the trains to run between Troy and Edwardsville. He worked for the railroad for 33 years. In 1950 they built a house on Dale Ave. in Wilson Heights, and the "orange house" by the railroad tracks was torn down. The memories of that house will last forever for the four older children who grew up by the "tracks." The other four siblings did not come along until ten years later. Walter and Gladys had eight children: Betty Wilke, Frieda Sponemann, Virginia Niebruegge, Walter Gaultney, Jr., Alfred "Kenny" Gaultney, Irene Kohl, Frances Kohl and Phyllis Weatherspoon. They attended St. Paul's Lutheran School and church. This was a 2 1/2-mile walk each way. Sometimes the older four would get lucky because the train would

Gladys Gaultney, age 90

stop and pick them up when it was on the way to the Troy coal mine to pick up cars of coal. If they were a little late, they would get to ride in the "red caboose."

Walter joined the army in 1917, and served his country well. A highlight of his army career was being selected as "The Outstanding American Doughboy of WWI." Walter died in March 1966 at age 70, and Gladys died December 2000 at 95. Their 8 children, grandchildren, 5 great grandchildren, and 5 great-great grandchildren survive them. *Submitted by Frieda (Gaultney) Sponemann.*

WILLLAM GEBAUER - William J. Gebauer was born in Troy on September 23, 1864, the son of Mr. and Mrs. Jacob Gebauer. He was a barber by trade and operated a barbershop in Troy. His nickname was "Jake" Gebauer.

On June 22, 1892, he married Louise D. Hartung of Edwardsville. She preceded him in death on November 24, 1950. Nine children were born of this union. They were Wilbur, Alfred, Louise, Alma, Flora, Leona Watt, Sylvania Mantle, Marie Hazzard, and one twin son Arnold, who died in infancy. Seven grandchildren and four great-grandchildren also survived him. Mr. Gebauer was a member of Friedens Evangelical and Reformed Church of Troy; Neilson Lodge No. 25 1.0.0. F, Pride of the West Rebekah Lodge No. 544; and the Barbers Local Union No. 605 at Edwardsville. He died in February 1951 and is buried in Friedens UCC Cemetery in Troy. *Information for this biography was taken from William J. Gebauer's obituary in the* Troy Tribune *dated February 1951.*

MARCEL GEBHART - Marcel Gebhart was born Oct. 30, 1932, in Trenton, IL, to Charles and Medora Gebhart. He was one of 4 children. The family moved to Troy in 1939. Marcel attended the Troy schools and graduated from Troy High School in 1950.

Gertrude Hoffmann's parents, Wm. and Lena Hoffmann, lived on a farm in Collinsville, IL, where she was born Sept. 26, 1937. She was one of 10 children. Gertrude went to school at SS Peter & Paul Catholic School, and graduated from Collinsville High School in 1956. Marcel and Gertrude met through a friend. They were married on May 10, 1958, at SS Peter & Paul Catholic Church in Collinsville. They moved to Belleville, IL, for a short time before returning to Troy in 1959. They started a family in 1959. A daughter Loretta Marie was born February 20, 1959. Another daughter Karen Sue was born June 3, 1961. A son was born Oct. 8, 1964; they named him Michael Lawrence.

Marcel and Gertrude have 4 grandchildren and 1 great grandchild. Loretta married Ralph Leach Jr. July 12, 1979. They had a daughter Amy Marie born Nov. 25, 1979. A son Joseph Steven was born March 21, 1982.

Michael Lawrence married Debra Ellen Nungesser of St. Jacob, IL, on Nov. 4, 1989, at St. Jerome's Catholic Church in Troy. A son Christopher Michael was born Oct. 14, 1992. A daughter Katelyn Michelle was born Sept. 17, 1997. A great-granddaughter was born on Sept. 30, 2000. Crystal Marie was born to Amy Leach and Doug Nelson.

Karen Sue Gebhart has no children.

Marcel and Gertrude are members of St. Jerome's Catholic Church. Gertrude is active in the church, and belongs to St. Ann's Council of Catholic Women of St. Jerome Catholic Church. Marcel worked at McDonnell Aircraft; then he worked at Dow Chemical until Feb. 14, 1961, when be became a mail carrier for the City of Troy. He was one of two carriers delivering the town's mail. The other carrier was Ray Maden. Marcel's route was the east side of Market St. north of Troy to Windy Hill. He walked 18 miles a day, before his day was done. He loved delivering the mail back then, especially to the elderly. When they saw him coming, they would ask him to bring them stamps the next day. When his day was done, he would get the stamps and make a special trip to their home to be sure they got their stamps. He also reported a fire to the fire department while be was walking his route. The people of Troy were very kind to him. He then changed routes and had very little walking. As the routes got bigger, more carriers were hired. Marcel retired after 30 years in March 1990.

Gebhart family, 1998
(l. to r.) Front: Gertrude. Back: Marcel,
Loretta, Michael, Karen.

Gertrude was a housewife, raising their family. She was employed at Triad Community District #2 as a noon-time aide, then she was a cashier for 16 years. She took the job as crossing guard for the City of Troy for 6 years. She retired in June 2000. She moved back to Collinsville after the death of Marcel, who passed away Oct. 4, 1999. *Submitted by Gertrude Gebhart.*

VIRGIL AND FRANCES GEBHART - In the spring of 1939, Charles Gebhart Sr. and his wife Dora brought their four children from Alton, IL, to their recently purchased home on Montgomery Street in Troy's north end.

Charles Jr. was enrolled as a sophmore in McCray-Dewey Township High School and Virgil entered the freshman class. Ruth and Marcel attended Troy Grade School.

Having lived in Trenton, Alton, Woodriver and Roxana, IL, Charles and Dora preferred to raise their children in a smaller community. Charles Jr. (Chuck) remained single and gained a reputation as a very good bowler until his sudden death at the young age of 47 in 1971.

After serving in the U.S. Army Air Force, Virgil (Pete) married Frances Smith in 1947 in St. Jerome Catholic Church. They are parents of James, born in 1950, and Jane Ann, born in 1952, and Mary Andrea, born in 1957. Virgil

207

began employment in the U.S. Post Office Department (now the U.S. Postal Service) at the Troy Post Office in 1950, serving as Postmaster from 1966 thru 1988.

Ruth married James Palovich and lived in the Collinsville area during most of her married life. She had one son, James Jr. Ruth died of cancer in 2000, age 70.

Marcel served in the U.S. Army during the Korean Conflict and later married Gertrude Hoffman of Collinsville in SS Peter and Paul Catholic Church in Collinsville in 1958. Their three children are Loretta, Karen, and Michael. After long service as a mail carrier in the Troy Post Office and later delivering water softener salt for Kamm Soft Water Service in and around Troy, Marcel passed away in October 1999, only a few days more than a month after his last day of work. He was almost 67 years old. *Submitted by Virgil and Frances Gebhart.*

HENRY AND CAROLINE (ASPELMEIER) GERFEN

- Henry C. Gerfen was born on July 3, 1844, in Frotheim, east of Minden in Westphalia, Germany, as Cord (Conrad) Heinrich Gerfen, the fourth of five children born to Anna Marie Charlotte Reichmann and Carl Ludwig Gerfen, a cottager. Before taking on the responsibility of a family, Henry fought in the Danish War in 1864. On October 14, 1866, Henry married Caroline Marie Aspelmeier, daughter of Maria Elizabeth Brundhorst and Christian Friedrich Aspelmeier, a farmer, in her hometown of Hille. Their first five children were born in Hille: Carl Heinrich "Henry" on October 3, 1867, Marie Louise on October 27, 1870, Wilhelmina Sophie on June 24, 1875, and Christian Friedrich "Fred C." on February 22, 1878. Henry C. Gerfen served in the Austrian-Prussian War and the Franco-Prussian Wars in 1870-1871, after which he settled into farming. In 1880, he left his family in Germany and came to America to investigate its possibilities, returning before the end of the year. The following year Henry brought his family to settle in Troy where he followed the blacksmithing trade he had learned in Germany. Their sixth child, Carl August, was born in 1885. The 1890's began with sorrow when Sophia died on October 9, 1890, followed by her mother on February 22, 1897. Henry later remarried Helena Roeben, who survived his death on August 13, 1926.

Henry Gerfen, circa 1900

Carl Heinrich "Henry" Gerfen and his wife, Maria Taake, had four children, Herman Heinrich Paul "Paul," Lena, Arthur, and

Raymond William Julius. Lena had one daughter, Marie Liermann. Raymond and his wife Irma Crescent Born had five children, Marjorie Marie (Mrs. Emil C. Schneider), Raymond Frederick, Neal Stanley, Ruth Irene (Mrs. Edward Froidl), and Henry John.

Louise Gerfen married George Conrad Jacob Wendler of Collinsville. They had six children, George, Erwin, Rosa, Otto, Walter and Kenneth. (See related family story.)

Christian Friedrich "Fred C." Gerfen and his wife Martha were the parents of Evelyn, Fred, Vernon and John. Evelyn and husband Waldemar Roth's children are Kenneth, Robert, Donna, David, and Dan. Fred, Jr. had one daughter, Gloria. John married Esther Brase and had three children, John R., Sandy and Diane.

Friedrich Wilhelm "William or Bill" and his wife Martha were the parents of Wilma, Dorothy, Eleanor, Orvil and Carl August Gerfen. Wilma married John Regshack and had one daughter Rae. Wilma was also married to John Lunn. Dorothy and her husband Harold Landwehr had three daughters, Joan (Mrs. Robert Drape), Gail (Mrs. William Swaby) and Karen. Eleanor married Thomas Earhart. Orville and his wife Clarice had two children, Donald and Janice. Carl and his wife Bernice Grim had one son, Bruce.

Carl August Gerfen and his wife Estelle Margaret Schroeder settled in Breese, IL, where they had six children, Richard Conrad Henry, Arlene Helena, Earl Frederick, Charles Otto "Bubbles," Jeanne Marie and Gerald Melvin. Richard married Grace Virginia Beardsley and had three children, David, Susan, and Barbara (Mrs. David Culbreth). Arlene married Hugh Miles and had four children, Peggy, Robert, Janis (Mrs. James Cross) and Jeanne. Earl married Joyce Elaine Valek. Bubbles married Margaret Eugenia "Margene" Branch and had four children, Thomas, Charles "Chip" Earl and Christopher. Gerald married Colleen Emma Arnold and had four children: Mark, Leslie (Mrs. Shep Weinstein), Donna (Mrs. Mark McGowan) and Julie (Mrs. McFarland). *Submitted by Anna M. (Wendler) Huckla.*

GERLING FAMILY

- The farm to which Christian and Caroline Gerling moved (see Martin and Lydia Gerling Hecht entry) was directly across the road from the future site of Triad Middle School. As Christian plowed the fields, he turned up many arrowheads from Indians who had lived near the creek there. Locals called them the Lickskillet Indians but no records of them have been discovered. When they moved into Troy to 314 Montgomery Street, he tried to earn his living as a hauler but soon found that feeding his mules without living on a farm left no profits. In January 1922 he was working in the Troy Mine when a runaway coal car inflicted fatal injuries.

Following is a short summary of their children's lives. Paul – see Suzanne Hansel's entry.

Christian III had a metal plate put into his head as result of a WWI wound and, though disabled, lived independently in various cites, but never returned to Troy.

Simon's first assignment was as a Lutheran grade school teacher in NY state where he died

Christian and Caroline (Litchenberg) Gerling, 1884

in the great flu epidemic, leaving his wife and year-old daughter.

Rueben died as a baby from failure to thrive.

Joseph – see Brunworth history.

Caroline lived with her husband and two sons on a farm northeast of Collinsville. In 1944 they moved to a farm a few miles south of Troy. During the 50s they bought a farm about one and one-half miles east of Troy. Their son Theodore built his home on a corner of that farm.

Bethel died of scarlet fever at age three.

Deborah (see Brunworth history).

Theodora moved to St. Louis and died in childbirth, leaving her husband and three-year-old daughter.

Ronald moved to Edwardsville with his wife. He served in the Phillipines in WWII.

Celine became a school teacher and taught in a one-room school between Troy and Marine. After marriage she lived on a farm one mile south of Marine with her husband and two sons. *Submitted by Sharon (Brunworth) Repp.*

PAUL F. AND FANNY P. (CRAMER) GERLING

- Suzanne Hansel's maternal grandfather, Paul Frederick Gerling, was born in 1885 in an area called Blackjack, near Florissant, MO, and died in 1960, Alton, IL. He was the oldest of twelve children, four born in Blackjack and eight born after they moved to Troy. (See photo and the Martin and Lydia Hecht Family info.) A cousin, Bertha Gerling, told the story about the family's move from Missouri to Illinois in the early 1890s. She said that there was snow on the ground, and her father, August Gerling, along with his half brother, Christian, drove the box wagons that had runners underneath to haul their furniture and other belongings. With the help of

Christian Gerling family, 1903-04
(l. to r.) Front: Deborah (on lap), Caroline. Middle: Joseph, Caroline, Christian, Lydia. Back: Paul, Simon, Chris Jr. Two children, Reuben and Bethel, had already died when this photo was taken. Three additional children were born after the date of this photo: Theodora, Ronald, and Celine.

Lickskillet Farm, late 1893 or early 1894
In the upstairs window is mother, Caroline Gerling,
age 28, pregnant with son, Reuben, born 2-94. She
didn't want to come out in the cold. (l. to r.) Standing:
half-brother, August Gerling, age 17, with gun,
Caroline and Christian's sons: Joseph, age 3, Simon
age 5, Christian Jr., age 7 and Paul, age 10 (Suzanne's
grandfather) and father, Christian Gerling, age 39.

a cousin, Rickie Gerling, mother Caroline rode the train to Troy with their four little boys. Their destination was the Siercey Farm at Lickskillet. No one seems to know where the name Lickskillet originated. The farm was 3 1/2 miles east of Troy and 3 miles west of St. Jacob on the Troy/St. Jacob Road (Route 40 across from the old Triad High School). In 1909 the family sold some of their personal property and in early 1910 moved into their new home on Montgomery Street in Troy.

Gerling family, 1930
(l. to r.) Ruth, Clifford, Paul, Fanny, Paul

Paul married Fanny Pearl Cramer in 1913, at the bride's home on Throp Street in Troy. She was born in 1888 in Troy and died in 1953 in Edwardsville, IL. They had four children: William Lewis Paul (b.1914-d.1991); Clifford Joseph (b.1915-d.1989); Frances, who died in infancy; and Caroline Ruth (b.1920-d.1987), Suzanne's mother. (See photo.) Suzanne's great-grandmother, Caroline Lichtenberg Gerling or "Grossmama" as she was affectionately called by her family, was born in 1866 and died in 1942. Suzanne remembers going to visit their home at 314 Montgomery Street, Troy.

There was a letter written by Grossmama in 1932 and recently given to Suzanne by her cousin, Bethel Hecht Hoppas. It began "To my dear ones so far away and yet so very near and dear, " and ended with, "Let's keep on praying for all that don't pray." Cousin Bethel wrote to Suzanne that "we've surely a special lady in our tree." Suzanne's great-great grandfather, Christian Frederick Gerling, had three previous marriages, (all wives died) and three children

before marrying his fourth wife, a widow by the name of Lichtenberg. One of the children from his first marriage was Suzanne's great-grandfather, Christian F. Gerling, who was born in 1855 and died in 1922 from injuries received while working in the Troy coal mine. Four children were born of the fourth marriage. One son, August Gerling, who was a half brother to Suzanne's great-grandfather, was a brick layer. He built many homes and commercial buildings in Troy and surrounding towns, including the home place for the Gerlings on Montgomery Street. Suzanne's great, great Uncle "Gus "came to visit her family many times and was a very kind and affectionate man.

Suzanne stayed and was raised by her grandmother and grandfather Gerling in Edwardsville after her parents' divorced in 1943. They moved to Glen Carbon in 1946. After her father's second marriage ended in 1948, her sister Jeanette and brother Jimmy came to live with their grandparents, too. Suzanne's grandfather Paul did refrigeration work on cooler motors at dairy farms and locker plants all over this area. She remembers going to East St. Louis with him to pick up motors and parts where she always got a soda and a candy bar. Sometimes she and her grandmother rode with him on some of his jobs during the summers and on weekends. Once during World War II when a lot of rationing was going on, a lady passed a plate of cookies around and Suzanne almost choked trying to eat one. She had made them with no sugar!

One of her grandfather's sisters was Celine Hollmann of Marine. Suzanne fondly remembers her great aunt Celine because she was the kindest and most thoughtful person she had ever met in her life. If just one percent of the world's population were like her, the world would be a better place to live. She baked the best cookies ever and always had a big basket of goodies whenever she came to visit. Great Aunt Lena Fedder of Troy, was another sister of her grandfather's that was such a hard worker but always had time for others. There was a time when Suzanne's grandparents were both in the hospital and the Fedder's took her and her siblings into their home to stay for a time. Suzanne remembers going to Fredricktown, MO, and visiting with Great Aunt Lydia Hecht and her family. They lived in the boonies, and everyone had such a good time roaming around the farm and having the cows and one particular rooster chase them. Grandfather's brother,

Four generations of Gerlings, 1941
Paul I, Grossmamma Carolina,
Paul II, Pauly (in front)

Ronald, who lived in Edwardsville, was a really fun person. He liked making things like whistles from tree branches and kaleidoscopes from colored rocks that were just beautiful. What a neat person he was, always kidding and joking with the children.

Gerling clan, 1943
Grossmama, Caroline Gerling, had died the year
before and the Brunworths now lived in the house
on 314 Montgomery, Troy. (l. to r.) Front: Ted
Fedder, Carolyn Hecht, Sharon Brunworth,
Leonard Hollmann, Arthur Fedder. Middle:
August Brunworth, Lena Gerling Fedder, Bethel
Hecht, Lena Hecht Gerling, Barbara Gerling,
Ronald, Gerling, Deborah Gerling Brunworth.
Back: Walter Brunworth, (peeking) Henry
Hollmann, Clifford Gerling, Dorothy Gerling,
Paul Gerling, Fanny Gerling, Celine Gerling
Hollmann. Otto Fedder took the picture.

One of the many friends Suzanne and her grandparents used to visit was Aunt Lizzie Ottwein. She lived in the cutest little house at 106 Webster Street. It was just perfect for her because she was the cutest little old lady. Suzanne remembers seeing her put waves in her hair with a hot curling iron that had been heated on the stove. She had Sunday school pins from Friedens Church that must have been more than a foot long after having taught for over fifty years. Just up from Aunt Lizzie's on Market Street were the Becker's, Les and Hulda. They had the neatest flower garden where Suzanne loved to roam, explore and sit. *Submitted by Suzanne Hansel.*

EDWARD DEWEY AND EDNA LEOPAL STARK GERSTENECKER - Edward Dewey Gerstenecker was born 17 Feb. 1897 in Jarvis Township, Madison County, IL. (Refer to James M. and Catherine "Kate" Maurer Gerstenecker Family.) He married Edna LeOpal Stark on 10 December 1921 in Greenville, Bond County, IL. She was born 8 February 1902, near Elk City, Chautauqua County, KS. She was the daughter of Charles LeRoy & Nancy Ellenore Heltsley Stark.

They had ten children. The first nine were born in Jarvis Township: Berniece Marie, born 7 December 1923, married Edwin Earl Heck on 25 June 1944 in Troy (he died 30 August 1982, Quincy, Adams County, IL), died 27 November 1997 in Quincy, Adams County, IL; Catherine Eleanor, born 25 December 1925, married (1) Clark Rundell Lewis on 23 August 1958 in Troy (he died 6 November 1981), married (2) James William McNiven on 29 November 1986 in Grimsby, Ontario; Dale Charles, born 14

January 1927, married Lyla Marie Thurnau on 15 April 1950 in Troy; Evelyn Mae, born 14 March 1929, married Duane Curtis DeCota on 21 October 1950 in Troy; Edgar Edward, born 7 October 1930, married Nell Elizabeth Standefer on 15 August 1956 in Troy (she died 26 August 1999, Seneca, MO), died 12 November 1983 in Jarvis Township; Milton Roy, born 15 October 1932, married Ethel Graham on 11 November 1957 in Edwardsville; Alvin Frank, born 26 April 1934, married Janet Louise Oestrike on 10 June 1961 in Alton, IL; Grace Edna, born 14 June 1936; Jane Opal, born 10 August 1938, married Robert E. Lee Converse on 19 April 1958 in Troy; Marjorie Sue, born 10 November 1940 in Highland, married Glenn S. Hall on 8 December 1962 in Troy. He died 6 November 1992, Quincy, Adams County, IL.

Ed and Opal occupied the Maurer farm on the south city limits for 20 years until Ed died on 11 February 1945. He was buried in Friedens Evangelical Cemetery, Jarvis Township, near Troy. Ed was a prominent dairy farmer who took great pride in his purebred Holstein herd. He served several terms on the grade school board of education, one term as highway commissioner and was active in Madison County Farm Bureau. At the time of death he was chairman of Troy Local of the Sanitary Milk Producers Association, which he had helped organize.

Opal died 16 March 1976, St. Joseph's Hospital, Highland. She was buried in Friedens Evangelical Cemetery. Opal worked in the cafeteria at Triad School District. She was a member of Rebekah Lodge 544 of Troy, Troy Senior Citizen Club, and Troy Missionary Society. She taught ladies Bible classes at Troy Presbyterian Church where she was a long time member. *Submitted by Frank and Janet Gerstenecker.*

JAMES M. AND CATHERINE (KATE) MAURER GERSTENECKER - James was born 2 June 1862, in Jarvis Township on the farm where he spent his entire life. He was the 8th and youngest child of Gottlieb (born 22 July 1816, in Germany the son of Christian Gerstenecker, married 18 August 1844, in Bay St. Louis, Mississippi, and died 11 March 1870, in Jarvis Township) and Margaret O'Brien Gerstenecker born 20 Nov. 1820, in Cork County, Ireland, and died 21 May 1904, in Jarvis Township). James and Kate were married 25 Dec. 1882, in Collinsville, Illinois.

Their nine children were born in Jarvis Township: George William, born 11 Oct.1883, married Clara Boston on 24 Oct. 1908, died 9 Dec. 1956, at St. Joseph's Hospital, Highland; Nellie Blanche, born 18 Jan. 1885, married Christian W. Gunkel on 14 Mar. 1910, died 1 Feb. 1978, Collinsville; Josephine Margaret, born 30 Oct. 1886, died 29 Dec. 1982; Wilbur Harrison, born 19 Sep. 1888, married Marguerite Bachman on 2 Nov. 1927, died 30 Apr. 1964; Charles Stanley, born 18 Jul.1890, married Frieda Diepholz on 31 Aug. 1916, died May 1971 at St. Elizabeth's Hospital, Belleville; Maude Catherine, born 30 Jan. 1892, married George Carl Leo Wittmann, died 29 Mar.1985; James Adam, born 29 Nov. 1893, married Olive Wiedmeyer, died 31 Jul. 1974, Centralia; Leroy Hobson, born 2 Oct. 1895, married Norma Jarvis on 28 Jan.1928, died 28 Oct. 1960, at St.

Elizabeth's Hospital, Belleville; Edward Dewey, born 17 Feb. 1897, married Edna LeOpal Stark on 10 Dec. 1921, died 11 Feb. 1945, St. Mary's Hospital, Clayton, MO. (Refer to Edward Dewey and Edna LeOpal Gerstenecker Family.)

James died on 14 Oct. 1945, at home in Spring Valley. Kate died on 9 July 1948, at St. Mary's Hospital, Clayton, Missouri. Both are buried in Glenwood Cemetery, Collinsville.

James was a farmer who was ahead of his time. He had a furnace and water piped into the house in the early 1900s. He also operated his own electric generating unit for general lighting and other uses. He was a native and lifelong resident of the Spring Valley area of Jarvis Township. He served as a school director and highway commissioner for many years. He was a director of Troy Grain Company from its organization for 26 years. His chief interests were his home and family.

Kate was born 12 October 1863, in Collinsville to Adam (born 26 November 1821, in Bermbach, Nassau, Germany, married 21 October 1849, in St. Louis, MO, and died 7 October 1887, in Jarvis Township) and Catarine Fischer Maurer (born March 1830 in Reibich, Hessen Darmstadt, Germany, and died 14 March 1912, in Collinsville). She was the 9th of 11 children. Kate was a lifelong resident of the Spring Valley community. *Submitted by Frank and Janet Gerstenecker.*

JAMES AND MARY CATHERINE GERSTENECKER - James Arthur Gerstenecker was born on October 13, 1921, in Madison County on his sister Beulah's eighth birthday. His father was George W. Gerstenecker, son of James and Kate Mauer Gerstenecker. His mother, Clara Boston Gerstenecker, was the daughter of James and Fanny Thorpe Boston who emigrated from England. James had three sisters: Beulah, Helen (Royal) Siefferman and Merle (Edward) Triska. He began a farming career following in the footsteps of many generations of the Gerstenecker family.

James graduated from Liberty Grade School. His teacher for all eight grades was Miss Ora Edwards. He graduated from McCray-Dewey High School. He was a member of the Liberty School Board and the Triad Community Unit No. 2 Board when the schools of Troy, Marine and St. Jacob were consolidated. He was a member of the Board of Directors of the Troy Grain Company, a township trustee and is a member of the Troy United Methodist Church where he has served in various offices. He retired from farming in 1982 and lives in Troy.

James and Mary Catherine Kinder, daughter of Lester M. and Catherine Jones Kinder (refer to Kinder Family, Lester M.), were married on December 25, 1945, in the Troy Methodist Church. Mary Catherine graduated from Troy Grade School and McCray-Dewey High School.

She earned a teaching certificate from Southern Illinois University, Carbondale, a B.A. degree from McKendree College in Lebanon, IL, and a M.A. from SIU in Edwardsville. Mary Catherine taught two years at Maple Grove School, four years in grades 3 and 1 at Troy Grade School and left teaching for several years when they moved to the former Emil Haury farm. Jana Catherine was born on March 15,

Gerstenecker family, 1984
(l. to r.) Front: John, Daniel, Kelly Neudecker
Back: John L. and Kay Neudecker, Mary C. and
James A. Gerstenecker, Jana Gerstenecker

1949, and Kay Ann was born on December 12, 1952. In 1958, Mary Catherine returned to teaching Grades 4 and then 2 at the Troy Grade School. In 1965, Triad Community Schools asked Mary Catherine to help implement a federally funded Title I remedial reading program. She served Marine and St. Jacob schools as a remedial reading teacher and faculty reading consultant for the next 15 years, retiring in 1980 after 30 years.

Mary Catherine joined the Troy United Methodist Church at the age of 7. She taught Sunday School for many years and has held several church offices. Mary Catherine also belonged to the Troy Woman's Club, Pin Oak Home Extension and was Secretary of the Oak Lawn Cemetery Board many years. She was a member of Delta Kappa Gamma, an honorary society for teachers, and the Illinois Education Association. Jana and Kay attended Triad Community Schools and graduated from Triad High School in 1967 and 1971, respectively. Jana, a resident of Troy, graduated from Southern Illinois University in Edwardsville and has worked in the SIU Admissions Office for over 30 years.

Kay married John L. Neudecker, son of Luke and Dorothy Sedlacek Neudecker of Marine on May 27, 1972. John served in the United States Navy submarine service for 10 years, attaining the rank of Petty Officer 1st Class. He earned a Bachelor's Degree from Edison University and is Superintendent of Personnel for Ameren U.E. at the Callaway Plant in Fulton, MO. Kay achieved certification as a Licensed Practical Nurse in Norwich, CT, and is now Office Manager for the Superintendent of Schools in Fulton, Missouri.

John and Kay have lived in Fulton, MO, for 20 years and are the parents of three children: Kelly Janette who graduated from the University of Missouri in Columbia and is a music teacher, John James who is a senior at Truman State University, and Daniel Lucas, a senior at Fulton High School. *Submitted by Mary Catherine Gerstenecker.*

ELMER GINDLER - So the story goes, Henry and Barbara Wittman Gindler bought the Schmidt Farm, across from St. Jerome Catholic Cemetery, in what is called Blackjack, as a wedding present for their son Henry and his wife, Anna Kirsch, when they married on January 17, 1906. Henry and Anna had five children: Oscar (b. February 12, 1907, d. May 17 1993), Walter (b. August

23, 1908, d. September 1980), Irene (b. July 8, 1912), Harold (b. December 5, 1915, d. July 4, 2001) and Elmer (b. June 28, 1918).

All the children left the farm for other jobs or to farm elsewhere, but Elmer stayed on with his parents to farm the home place. Elmer and Loretta Druessel were childhood sweethearts, both attending the local Blackjack School until eighth grade. They both recall enjoying the box socials and their favorite teacher, Elmer's cousin, Paul Dollinger.

Elmer loved music as a child and taught himself to play a used accordion at the age of 12. He later purchased a mandolin at age 16 and still plays that same instrument today.

Elmer and Loretta and their families were members of the St. John Evangelical Church in Blackjack. The church was later destroyed by a tornado in 1936. At this time, most of the church families started attending Friedens Evangelical Church in Troy.

Elmer and Loretta Druessel were married on September 21, 1940, at her home, also in Blackjack, by the Rev. R.H. Mornhinweg. That evening they were honored with a "shiveree." Friends, neighbors and relatives surprised the newly married couple with an impromptu wedding reception, complete with noise makers (pots and pans, cowbells) and gifts. The couple and their folks supplied food and drink for the party.

Elmer and Loretta moved in with Henry and Anna, sharing half of the house. Henry and Anna later moved across the pasture to a small home which was the Fred Druessel place. Henry and Mary Ann Becherer have now built a new home on this site. Elmer and Loretta had one daughter, Beverly, born on August 6, 1945, the same day that the United States dropped the atomic bomb on Hiroshima, Japan, during World War II. It was also at this time Elmer and Loretta were hooked up with rural electricity, and purchased a Philco refrigerator, which is still functioning today. Even the crisper with the glass lid is still intact.

Elmer and Loretta worked as a team on the farm, raising hogs, cattle and chickens. Elmer retired from farming in 1983, and he and Loretta started spending their winters in Florida. One year they tried Arizona and thereafter, they spent their winters as "snowbirds" in Texas with many of their good friends.

As a farmer, Elmer was valued as a member on the Troy Grain Company board and as a trustee for the Troy Fire District. He also spent many years as a member of the church board at Friedens. Loretta gave a lot of her time to the Women's Guild at Friedens. She and her sister-in-law, Irene, had great fun performing plays for the group on special occasions.

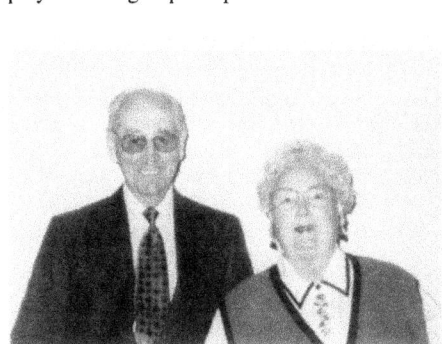

Elmer and Loretta Gindler, 2000

On December 21, 1968, Elmer and Loretta's daughter, Beverly, married Don Turner from Ponca City, OK. Beverly was a vocal music teacher in the Edwardsville school district for 34 years. Don was a buyer at McDonnell-Douglas/ Boeing for 34 years. They are now enjoying retirement from their home in Glen Carbon.

In September 2000, Elmer and Loretta and his brother and his wife, Harold and Fern Gindler, celebrated their 60th Anniversaries together at an open house at Friedens. All of their attendants from both weddings were still living and able to attend the reception.

Throughout their 61 years of marriage, Elmer and Loretta have especially enjoyed music and dancing. Although they are now physically limited, they still enjoy playing cards and dominos with friends and relatives. *Submitted by Beverly I. Turner.*

HENRY GINDLER FAMILY

(l. to r.) Front: Henry, Anna (Kirsch) and Irene (Gindler) Druessel Kotzman. Back: Walter, Harold, Elmer and Oscar Gindler.

OSCAR AND DOROTHY GINDLER - Oscar Gindler was born on February 12, 1907, in Blackjack, south of Troy, IL, the son of Henry and Anna (Kirsch) Gindler. He was the oldest of five children. His siblings were Walter, Harold, and Elmer Gindler, and Irene Gindler Druessel Kotzman. They were hard-working farmers. Oscar graduated from the eighth grade, and then stayed on the farm to work. He and Leonard Schurman then owned a dairy in Troy at 125 E. Market Street.

Dorothy (Ludwig) Gindler was born on February 20, 1909, in Mount Vernon, MO, the daughter of William and Laura (Schmidt) Ludwig. She was the youngest of five children. Her siblings were Albert and Orlando Ludwig, Celia Aydelott, and Lorla Miller. Their father was a Methodist minister, so the family moved around quite a bit in the west and midwest. Her father retired at Troy, and Dorothy taught school there from 1930-1934. She later returned to college and earned her bachelor's degree at age 55, and taught in the Triad School District from 1959-1969.

During her early teaching in Troy, she met Oscar. He was working at the dairy one Sunday morning and saw Dorothy walking on the sidewalk across the street. She had on a gray suit, little gray pillbox hat, and gray shoes and

*50th Wedding Anniversary, 1984
(l. to r.) Front: Nancy Fischer, Dorothy Gindler, Mary Lou Ammann, Judy Gindler. Back: Earl Fischer, Oscar Gindler, Dennis Ammann, Willard Gindler*

purse. He told his friend, "Someday I am going to date that gal!" They were married August 23, 1934. Oscar made powdered milk and hauled milk to St. Louis, and Dorothy worked behind the counter dipping cones for the teenagers who hung out there.

Oscar sold the dairy and established Gindler Sales and Service, selling Studebaker and Packard cars. He was seen on snowy days running his jeep with the snowplow down the streets and sidewalks of Troy. He was mayor of Troy for two terms (1953-1965), putting in the first street signs, and working long hours overseeing the installation of the sewer system. He was an alderman for 12 years, volunteered with the fire department for 40 years, and was a charter member of the Troy Lions Club, having 54 years perfect attendance. He was chairman of the Troy Homecoming for 28 years. Oscar was the former owner of the Blue Haven Restaurant and Motel, east of Troy. He then worked on establishing the Tri-Township Park, putting in the roads, and planting and watering the many trees which look so beautiful today.

Oscar and Dorothy were blessed with three children: Nancy Gindler Oberto Fischer (born January 29, 1941, married to Earl W. Fischer, and living in Glen Carbon); Willard Gindler (born July 7, 1943, married to Judy Blumer Gindler, and living in St. Jacob); and Mary Lou Gindler Ammann (born February 2, 1948, married to Dennis Ammann and living in Highland). Oscar and Dorothy have 10 grandchildren and three great grandchildren.

Oscar and Dorothy retired to Cherokee Village, AR, in 1978, and contributed extensively to activities there. Oscar passed away May 17, 1993, in Arkansas, and Dorothy passed away July 11, 1997, in Troy. *Submitted by Nancy Fischer.*

CAROLYN SCHMIDT GOLFIN - Carolyn Schmidt, youngest child of Harold and Marie Schmidt, was born August 16, 1942, in Highland, IL. She is a graduate of William Woods College, Murray State College, and earned a Master's Degree from Webster College. She taught elementary school and was a reading specialist for 12 years in the St. Louis area. She married Byron A. Golfin, born November 5, 1934, on July 1, 1972. He is a graduate of Washington University and worked as a chemical engineer for Unilever until his retirement in 1997. They reside in Chesterfield, MO, and have two daughters. Diana was born August 5, 1976, and is an attorney for Lashley

Bryon Golfin family, 2000
Byron, Diana, Andrea, Carolyn

and Baer in St. Louis. Andrea was born March 30, 1980, and attends Texas Christian University in Ft. Worth majoring in speech pathology.

Carolyn and Byron enjoy traveling, tennis and classic cars. *Submitted by Carolyn Schmidt Golfin.*

MINNIE LEVO AND JAMES GORETTI

Philamena "Minnie" Levo was born July 23, 1893, (died July 25, 1967) in Collinsville, the oldest daughter of Peter and Laura (Cossono) Levo. She married James Goretti (born in Italy in 1888, died December 22, 1952) on July 6, 1917. They resided in St. Louis. James, or "Jim" as he was known, owned and operated a restaurant in north St. Louis for many years. He was a good cook and when the Levo family came for holiday dinners, he was in charge of the cooking.

Minnie, for a short time, owned and operated a dry goods store in that same area in north St. Louis. One son was born to this union, Edward Goretti who was born June 30, 1918, and died July 1, 1986.

He and his wife, the former Shirley Bryant of Mississippi, had six children. They are Terry Edward, Paulette Goretti Brinker, Leigh Ann Goretti Bowermaster, James Scott Goretti, Karen Dee Goretti Pierce and Kevin Bryant Goretti.

Minnie was a seamstress and enjoyed making garments for family members. She loved her bulldogs and throughout her lifetime had several as house pets. She also raised canaries. She had a room devoted to them on the second floor of her home. Other canaries were spotted throughout her home.

She and Jim lived at 6528 Bartmer Street in St. Louis for many years. In her later life she contacted diabetes and, after the amputation of her leg, only lived for a short time.

Both Minnie and Jim are buried in Laurel Hill Cemetery, St. Louis, MO. *Submitted by Mae Grapperhaus.*

GRANGER-LAWSON-LIEBLER FAMILY

Born on January 4, 1844, Joseph Granger emigrated with his parents from Paris, France, to the United States of America during Joseph's infancy. The family established residence in the French settlement, east of Highland, near the Bond county line. Soon after their arrival, both parents died and left Joseph an orphan at the age of six.

On August 12, 1861, seventeen-year old Joseph Granger enlisted at Greenville and was assigned to Company "D" Third Illinois Cavalry. Col. E.A. Carr organized the regiment at Camp Butler, IL. In 1864, Joseph fought in the Battle of Vicksburg, and a bronze plaque in the Illinois Memorial at the Vicksburg National Military Park bears his name. On October 10, 1868, he was discharged from the service at Fort Snelling in St. Paul, MN, and, by this time, held the rank of First Sargeant.

Joseph Granger wed Mary Lawson on January 16, 1867, in Troy. Miss Lawson, born on November 19, 1843, was the daughter of Joseph and Hannah Lawson of Lorton, England, in Cumberland County. When Mary was nine years of age, the family came to the United States, leaving behind the graves of two children who had died in infancy. Hannah Lawson died on October 8, 1864, and Joseph Lawson died on August 20, 1857.

The Grangers' only child, Cora Mary, was born on December 5, 1875, and the family lived on a farm in Troy. Joseph Granger died on September 14, 1896. Cora married Frederick Andrew Liebler, Sr., of St. Jacob, IL, on August 8, 1900, at the Methodist Episcopal Church of Belleville, IL. Frederick Liebler was the son of Joseph and Katherine Doll Liebler. Joseph was born in September of 1835 in Germany and died in St. Jacob on February 3, 1912; his wife was born in January of 1844 in Germany, and her death occurred on April 29, 1919, in St. Jacob.

Frederick and Cora lived on her parents' farm in Troy. Cora's mother, Mary Granger, died on February 6, 1937, at the age of 93. At the time of her death, she was the oldest resident of Troy and had been a member of the Presbyterian Church for forty years. Cora gave birth to three children, Judd, Helen, and Frederick, Jr. Judd, who was born on January 30, 1902, wed Hulda Emma Langenwalter on March 2, 1929, in Collinsville. A hat-maker, Judd also worked on trains, and his tragic death on May 22, 1944, was the result of a fall from the top of a train car. Frederick Liebler, Sr., died in Highland on January 1, 1956, at the age of 81. Cora Mary died in Highland on October 27, 1959, at the age of 83.

Born on July 8, 1903, Helen Liebler married Raymond Matthews on December 27, 1927. Ray owned a Shell station in Troy, and Helen was a seamstress at the Kay-Lee Dress Factory in St. Louis. Helen died on September 15, 1987. Her brother, Frederick Andrew, Jr., was born on December 19, 1904. He wed Eleanor "Lina" Ashmann on September 2, 1944, in Carlisle, IL. Known as "Hap," Frederick owned Liebler Hardware on 201 E. Market from 1948 to 1981. His death occurred on June 24, 1990. *Submitted by Lori Earnshaw.*

DALE AND KELLY (HASTY) GRAPPERHAUS - Dale Anthony Grapperhaus was born September 17, 1969, and is the son of James and Mae Grapperhaus. Dale graduated from Triad High School in 1987 and is currently employed with the Jarvis Township Road District. He is also a self-employed farmer.

Kelly Jo Hasty was born January 17, 1969, the daughter of Mary Hasty and Jon Hasty. She graduated from Metro-East Lutheran High School in Edwardsville in 1987. She then earned

Grapperhuas family, 2001
(l. to r.) Front: Caleb, Kelsey, Clayton and Colton. Back: Dale, Kelly

her Bachelor's Degree in Special Education in 1991. She worked for several years at Triad High School. She is now the Assistant Director of Special Education for Region II Cooperative.

Dale and Kelly were married in 1993. They are the parents of four children: Clayton Scott Grapperhaus born in 1994; Kelsey Dale Grapperhaus born in 1995; Colton Jon Grapperhaus born in 1998 and Caleb James Grapperhaus born in 2000.

Dale and Kelly are raising their family on a farm southwest of Troy. *Submitted by Kelly Grapperhaus.*

DANIEL J. AND SANDRA I. (KAMP-WERTH) GRAPPERHAUS - Daniel John Grapperhaus, son of James and Mae (Mersinger) Grapperhaus, b. May 21, 1963, and Sandra Irene Kampwerth, daughter of Benedict and Amelia (Wessel) Kampwerth, b. November 18, 1963, were married at St. Paul Catholic Church in Highland on October 26, 1984.

Grapperhaus family, 1998
(l. to r.) Front: Hannah, Sandy, Daniel
Back: April, Jacob

After their marriage, the couple bought the house and farm of the late Josephine Gerstenecker. Following renovation of the home, they moved into it.

They are the parents of three children, Jacob Daniel, April Louise and Hannah Mary. Dan works in St. Louis, MO, and Sandy works in Highland, IL. Dan also enjoys farming and raises cattle, swine and grain.

The family attends St. Jerome Catholic Church in Troy. *Submitted by Sandy Grapperhaus.*

DARELL AND VICKIE (DETTO) GRAPPERHAUS - Darell Charles Grapperhaus formerly of Troy, IL, was born at St. Joseph Hospital in Highland, IL, on April 29, 1966.

Vickie Ellen (Detto) Grapperhaus of St. Jacob, IL, was born at Belleville Memorial in Belleville, IL, on November 24, 1965.

Darell and Vickie were married on May 22, 1987, at St. Paul Catholic Church in Highland. The couple's first home was in St. Jacob at Westglen Apts. In August of 1987, they purchased a hog farm located at 966 Walnut Rd. in St. Jacob. The home was erected in 1927.

They have three children, all girls: Tiffany, Tracy and Tanya. Tiffany "Marie" Galeaz the oldest was born July 2, 1985, at Scott Air Force Base in Belleville. She enjoys hanging out with her friends and shopping. Tracy Mae "Squirt" the middle was born November 12, 1987, at Anderson Hospital in Maryville. She enjoys animals, which includes working with cows for 4-H, and cheerleading. Tanya Michelle "Boomer" the youngest was born June 14, 1989, at Anderson Hospital. She enjoys singing, cooking and also cheerleading.

Grapperhaus family, Oct. 2000
Front: (l. to r.) Tanya, Vickie
Back: Darell, Tiffany, Tracy

Both Darell and Vickie are graduates of Triad High School. In 1984 after graduation Darell went to work for Weyerhaeuser in Belleville, IL, and is currently employed there in the Maintenance Dept. Vickie attended BAC and St. Louis Community College at Forest Park where in May of 1999, she graduated with an Associate of Applied Science in Mortuary Science and is currently employed at Kurrus Funeral Home in Belleville.

Together Darell and Vickie enjoyed remodeling their home, riding their Harley, working outdoors gardening, and spending time with their girls. Darell also enjoys hunting and Vickie enjoys cooking. Darell has been a volunteer with St. Jacob Fire Department since 1989 and currently is a Captain. Vickie is also involved with the Fire Department as an Auxiliary member. The family attends St. James Catholic Church in St. Jacob. *Submitted by Vickie Grapperhaus.*

DENNIS AND MARGARET (LANAHAN) GRAPPERHAUS - Dennis Gerard Grapperhaus b. December 29, 1964, and Margaret Viola Lanahan b. September 16, 1968, were married June 12, 1999, at Mother of Perpetual Help Catholic Church in Maryville. Reverend Steve Janoski performed the ceremony. The couple met at a benefit for Dennis' brother, Danny, in 1996.

They have one daughter, Carolyn Margaret. Dennis graduated from Triad High School, St. Jacob, and Margaret graduated from Edwards-

Grapperhaus family, 1996
(l. to r.) Front: Carolyn, Margaret
Back: Dennis

ville High School and received a BA (chemistry major, mathematics minor and MS (organic chemistry) from SIUE.

Dennis, who was raised and grew up in the Spring Valley community south of Troy, is self-employed. Margaret, who grew up in Edwardsville, is a chemist and works in Chesterfield, MO.

Dennis built a home in Troy and they reside there. They are members of St. Jerome Catholic Church in Troy.

Dennis enjoys riding his motorcycle, hunting and gardening. Margaret enjoys gardening, cooking and home decorating. *Submitted by Margaret Grapperhaus*

JAMES AND MAE GRAPPERHAUS
James "Jim" Herman Grapperhaus was born in 1939 in St. Rose, IL, the son of John Henry and Irene (Kohlbrecher) Grapperhaus. He married Mary "Mae" Mersinger, who was born in 1938, on June 10, 1961. She is the daughter of Oscar and Louise (Levo) Mersinger.

Six children were born to this union. Laura Louise Grapperhaus, born in 1962, married Scott Reilson. They have two children, Jared and Maria Reilson. Daniel John Grapperhaus, born in 1963, married Sandra Kampwerth in 1984. They are the parents of three children: Jacob Daniel, April Louise and Hannah Mary. Dennis Gerard Grapperhaus, born in 1964, married Margaret Lanahan in 1999. They are the parents of Carolyn. Darell Charles Grapperhaus, born in 1966, married Vickie Detto (Schuessler) in 1987. They have three children: Tiffany, Tracy and Tanya. Dean Joseph Grapperhaus, born in 1968, married Carla Jo Suess in 1990. Dale Anthony Grapperhaus, born in 1969, married Kelly Jo Hasty in 1993. They are the parents of four children: Clayton, Kelsey, Colton and Caleb.

Jim and Mae farm south of Troy on the farm on which Mae grew up. Jim, who farms about 950 acres, semi-retired from farming in 2001. Jim is also the Jarvis Township Highway Commissioner and has served since 1977. Mae is the editor of the *Times-Tribune* in Troy and has worked for the newspaper since 1985. Prior to working for the *Times-Tribune*, she worked for the *Collinsville Herald*.

Both are active in the community. Jim is a retired Troy Volunteer Firefighter after 20 years of service; member of the Troy Knights of Columbus 9266 and the Maryville/Troy Knights of Columbus, Fourth Degree Assembly. He is a former director of the Troy Grain Company,

Madison County Soil and Water Conservation and a former Troy Jaycee.

Mae is the founder and charter member of the Troy Historical Society, a member of the Troy Unit of the Madison County Homemakers, Troy Chamber of Commerce, Troy Genealogical Society, Troy Historical Preservation Commission and Troy Main Street.

Early in her life, she was a private music teacher of piano and guitar. Later she became the leader of a 4-H Club for about 11 years, and was very active in her church and with her children's school activities. Jim worked for 11 years at Hunter Packing Company in E. St. Louis early in the couple's married life. They both attend St. Jerome Catholic Church in Troy and were former members of St. John the Baptist Catholic Church in Blackjack, an unincorporated community about 4 1/2 miles south of Troy.

Grapperhaus family, 2001
(l. to r.) Front: Laura, Mae, Jim
Back: Dennis, Dale, Dan, Darell, Dean

They were married at St. John's Church and all of their children were baptized there. Jim and Mae were active in that church until it closed in 1992. They both enjoy traveling and their grandchildren. Mae enjoys local history, genealogy, antiques, reading, music and flowers. She is currently restoring Spring Valley School, the school she attended until the sixth grade when the district was consolidated. The school was built by her grandfather, Valentine Mersinger. Mae co-owned and operated the Tique Shoppe, an antique/collectible store in Troy from 1989 through 1995.

Jim retired from farming in 2001 and is currently helping son, Dale, who has taken over the farming operations. *Submitted by Mae Grapperhaus.*

LOUIS JEAN GRIEVE - Louis Jean Grieve was born on Jan. 14, 1912. He was originally from Collinsville, IL. Lou married Mary Dean Elliott (see Roy Daniel Elliott,Sr.) on March 17, 1932. They resided in Troy for approximately 30 years. Lou and Mary Dean operated The Colonial Upholstery Shop on the corner of Market and Hickory Streets for a number of years.

Lou and Mary Dean had two children: Robert Louis (b. November 9, 1932) and Shirley Dean (b. January 8, 1936). Robert married Shirley Rose Schilling and lived in Troy. They had five children before they divorced: Sharon (1954 - 1972), Jeff (b. Feb. 1955) has a child, Jeff; Bryan (b. Aug. 1956) has three children: James, Chris, and Lindsey; Bobby (b. Nov. 1958) has three children: Brandon, Danielle and

*Grieve family, 1940
(l. to r.) Robert, Mary Dean,
Louis, Shirley*

Jonathan; and Cynthia Dean (b. July 1964) has two children: Russell and Adam.

Robert later married Lenora Garcia and now lives in Madison, IL. They have one son, Raymond Arthur (b. Nov. 19, 1972). Raymond and his wife Kristy live in Granite City with their two sons, Justin (b. May 25, 1993) and Zachary (b. Aug. 21, 1998).

Shirley Dean married Marvin Spengel, from Edwardsville, on March 5, 1955. They lived in Troy for about 20 years. They now live in Nashville, TN. Shirley and Marvin have three children: Michael (lives in California), Mitzi Dean Spengel Malter (b. June 3, 1956) of Collinsville, IL, and Mark (b. Feb. 15, 1962) of Nashville, Tenn.

Mitzi Dean Spengel Malter has two children: Ryan Elliott Malter (b. Apr. 28, 1979) who has a son Chantz (b. Mar. 7, 2000) and Rachel Dean Malter (b. Aug. 22, 1983). Mark Spengel has three children: Ashley and Brandon of NC; and Chelsea (b. Dec. 26, 1990) of Troy.

Lou Grieve died of cancer in October 1967. Mary Dean married Raymond Manuel Cabello of Collinsville on November 1, 1968. They currently reside in Collinsville. Mary Dean is now a great-great grandmother. *Submitted by Mary Dean Elliott Cabello and Kae Elliott Schmitt.*

GRODZICKI FAMILY - The Grodzicki family first entered the Troy area in 1948. John Sr. and Helen moved from East St. Louis, IL, to the Blackjack area, approximately one quarter mile from her parents, Joe and Anna Benak who were farmers. The Grodzickis had four sons: John (Jr.), Joe, Bob, and Richard. Helen died in 1962 and John Sr. died in 1994. All four sons completed their education in the Troy schools. John moved to the St. Louis area in 1966; Joe moved to Collinsville, IL, in 1961; Bob and Richard continue to be Troy residents.

John left the Troy area in 1956 to attend SIU in Carbondale, and after graduation, went into the Army where he served for three years at Fort Carson, CO. Later, he worked in St Louis where he met Mary Ann Honaker. The daughter of an Air Force officer, Mary Ann had recently moved to St Louis from Shreveport, LA, for employment as an Army auditor. On 7-16-1966, they married and later moved to a farm in the Blackjack community in 1967. They have one daughter and three sons. Dianne is married to Marty Peterson of DeSoto, IA; they have two sons, Cody and Tyler; they reside in Lenexa, KS. Dave is not married; he resides in Denver,

CO. Dan is married to Cassie of Harrisonville, MO; they have a daughter, Kayla; they reside in Merriam, KS.

John was a U. S. Government auditor throughout his career. During his Troy residency, he traveled out-of-state frequently. Mary Ann was a homemaker involved with the many activities revolving around their children. She taught preschoolers at St. Jeromes Catholic Church, was a member of the Madison County Homemakers Association, rooted for their boys in little league ball, and volunteered wherever she was needed. They were members of St. John the Baptist Catholic Church, Blackjack.

In 1978, John and Mary Ann and family moved to West Des Moines, IA, for career reasons. They lived there until 1985 when they moved to Lenexa, KS; again, for career reasons. Now that their children were young adults, Mary Ann began employment for a property developer doing accounting and data analysis; she quit in 1994 near the time John retired from the U. S. Government.

*Grodzicki family, 2000
(l. to r.) Front: Cody, Tyler, Kayla
Middle: Dianne, Mary Ann, Cassie
Back: Dave, Marty, John, Dan*

In their leisure time, they spend the winters in Mesa, AZ, where they have a winter home. John is still involved in part time work doing background investigations of people seeking employment. Mary Ann also works part time doing accounting for several business-related families in Mission Hills, KS.

When they are not at their winter home, they travel to numerous dance festivals in the Midwest and West. Avid dancers, they have met many dancers from other states and look forward to reunions with them at the various dance festivals.

Because of family ties, John and Mary Ann are frequent visitors to the Troy area. *Submitted by John Grodzicki.*

THEODORE AND FLORENCE GUEN-NEWIG - Ted and Florence Guennewig lived at 107 West Clay street in Troy, moving from St. Jacob in 1941. Ted was a native of Troy, the son of Theodore and Margarette (Apple) Guennewig. Florence was a daughter of Edwin and Mary (Bachman) Frey of Troy, who, for many years, owned and operated the Troy Telephone Company. They parented Florence's daughter Grace Schmidt, who later married Merrill Ottwein of Troy.

Ted was a railroad telegrapher for the Litchfield and Madison and Illinois Central Railroads, and was very active in the Troy Lion's Club. In the zenith days of that organization,

when they would raffle two new automobiles and other appliances at the annual homecoming, Ted was perennial ticket sale chairman, and usually won the prize for most tickets sold.

Ted was born in 1898 and died in 1958. Florence was born in 1899 and died in 1977. They were married in 1934. Both were members of Friedens United Church of Christ, where Florence was very active in the Ladies Society. *Submitted by Merrill Ottwein.*

GUTTERSOHN FAMILY

Art and Esther (Schurman) Guttersohn were married August 8, 1936, at the Friedens E & R Church parsonage in Troy.

HAMPSTEN FAMILY - Darrell Hampsten and Jennifer Weir bought a house in Troy in June 1998 and were married in O'Fallon on July 18, 1998. Darrell was born in Waukegan and grew up in Robinson. Jennifer grew up in Berlin, IL. They met at Illinois State University in 1986, when both were students.

She is a school social worker in the O'Fallon schools, after graduating from ISU and earning her master's degree in social work from the University of Illinois. He went to SIU-Edwardsville as a full-time student. He began working at the *Times-Tribune* newspaper as a part-time reporter in September 1998.

In October 1999, Darrell and Jennifer started the *Maryville Voice,* a newspaper serving the Maryville area. Within two weeks after publishing, they found out Jennifer was pregnant with their first child. Emma Jayne Hampsten was born on May 22, 2000, two weeks after Darrell finished his bachelor's degree in small business management. The business ended in November 2000, and Darrell went to work full-time at the *Times-Tribune* as an assistant editor.

Since moving to Troy, Darrell was appointed then elected to the Tri-Township Public Library District Board of Trustees, and later as Jarvis Township Collector. He is a past president of the Kiwanis Club of Troy, and serves as treasurer of Friends of the Park and Troy Main Street. Together, they are also members of the Troy Historical Society. *Submitted by Darrell Hampsten.*

ERNEST AND SOLLIE HAMPTON - In the early 1920s the Hampton brothers arrived in Troy from the Collgate, OK, area. Ernest and Sollie were drawn to this area like many others to find work in the local coal mines. Both brothers were said to have been very colorful characters.

Ernest later married Della (no maiden name) of Highland, IL. He worked in the local mines until his retirement. Della was employed by Martha Manning Dress Factory in Collinsville. During the 1930s they owned and operated Hampton's Millinery Store located on Market Street across from the current City Hall Building. The windows of their store displayed beautiful handmade hats. Both Ernest and Della are believed to have died in the early 1960s.

Sollie married Bessie Bunch, a school teacher from Oklahoma, in approximately 1923. She then joined him in Troy. Together they had one child, Omar Russell Hampton born December 20, 1924.

Sollie was known to still be working in the local mines at the age of 72. He died at the age of 87 in January of 1966, and Bessie followed five months later in May 1966 at the age of 74. *Submitted by Valorie Hampton.*

JAMES RUSSELL HAMPTON - James (Jim) was born on March 28, 1957, to Omar and Melba Hampton. He and his older brother Mike grew up on Henderson Street in a neighborhood full of children where playmates were plentiful. One of his favorite thing to do as a child was ride his bicycle to Ma's Cafe, order a cheeseburger and play the pinball machine until he ran out of nickels.

Hampton family, 2001
(l. to r.) Valorie, Jamie, James

Jim attended St. Paul Lutheran Grade School and graduated from Triad High School in 1975. He then enrolled in Ranken Technical Institute and was employed as a welder after graduation.

Jim married Valorie Johnson of Maryville on October 15, 1976. Their daughter Jamie Michelle was born on May 21, 1980. They lived in Maryville and Collinsville for a few years before returning to Troy.

Once Jim was back in Troy, he became an active member of the Troy Volunteer Fire Department. He has served the community as Fire Chief from 1996 to the present. Jim enjoys playing golf and having barbecues with friends around the pool.

Valorie is self-employed as a cosmetologist and is a member of the Troy Fire Department Ladies Auxiliary. She has enjoyed living in Troy and raising their daughter here.

Jamie attended Troy grade schools and was a very active high school student. She was a member of the Knight Moves Pom Pon squad for four years, editor of the 1998 yearbook and co-editor of the 1998 school newspapers. Jamie was a member of the National Honor Society and was named in *Who's Who Among American*

High School Students. One of the highlights of her high school years came when she represented Triad's Pom squad as their Captain and danced in the Macy's Thanksgiving Day Parade in New York City in November of 1997. Jamie graduated from Triad High School in 1998.

Jamie is currently a student at Southeast Missouri State University. She is studying Interior Design and Architecture. She is a member of Gamma Phi Beta Sorority and has held several offices including President. She plans to graduate in 2002 and pursue a career in Interior Design. *Submitted by Valorie Hampton.*

MICHAEL HAMPTON - Michael E. Hampton was born on August 19, 1954. His parents Omar and Melba Hampton also had one other son, James, born on March 28, 1957. Michael married LeAnn Dawson on April 11, 1980. LeAnn, born on February 2, 1960, is the oldest daughter of William and Donna Dawson, Troy natives since 1960. LeAnn also has one brother, William, and a sister, Susan.

Michael and LeAnn both graduated from Triad High School. After their marriage they bought a house at 401 Cook Avenue where they have lived ever since. Michael and LeAnn are the parents of three sons, Michael W., born on October 8, 1991; Jared R., born September 21; and Joshua H., born August 20, 1989.

Michael also graduated from Ranken Technical College in St. Louis as did his father-in-law, brother and his oldest son Michael currently attends. He has worked in construction for over 25 years and currently owns and operates his own electrical contracting business – Hampton Electric. LeAnn has been employed by David Birenbaum & Associates in St. Louis, a management consulting firm where she started working over 20 years ago as a receptionist and executive secretary to currently being director of publications. *Submitted by Michael Hampton.*

OMAR RUSSELL HAMPTON - Omar Russell Hampton, son of Sollie and Besse Hampton, was born on December 20, 1924. He lived in Troy his entire life with the exception of approximately three years that he srved in the US Navy during World War II. He was drafted at the age of 18, while still in high school, and received a deferment until after his graduation. He then reported to the Great Lakes for training and was later stationed in Hawaii until the end of the War.

Omar met Melba Bartles of Edwardsville in 1947 while skating at Moonlight Roller Rink in Troy. They were married the following year on May 23, 1948. They had two sons. Michael Edward Hampton was born on August 19, 1954. James Russell Hampton was born on March 28, 1957.

Omar worked for the Federal Government in Management Analysis until his retirement in 1980. He served as Chairman of Troy's Planning Commission in the 1970s, was an Elder at St. Paul Lutheran Church and a member of Troy American Legion Post #708.

Melba was a homemaker, Den Mother and a member of the St. Paul Lutheran Ladies Aid.

Omar and Melba had many friends in the community. One of their favorite pastimes was

Melba and Russell Hampton, 1988

weekend camping trips with other Troy couples. Omar enjoyed joining in on a good practical joke and was always good natured when the joke was on him.

Omar and Melba were married for 44 years and were blessed with four grandchildren before Omar's death at the age of 67 on September 3, 1992. His wife Melba survives and is still a resident of Troy. *Submitted by Melba Hampton.*

GARI AND THERESA HANALEI - Gari Kahi Hanalei was born on Sept. 19, 1955, in Fort Dodge, IA, to Ralph and Phyllis Hanalei. Gari's father was in the Air Force, stationed at Lincoln AFB, Nebraska. His father returned to Honolulu, Hawaii, in 1958, and his mother remained in Iowa, remarrying Kenneth Mylenbusch in 1966. Gari and his parents and sister Holli then moved to Kansas City, MO. They later moved to Hazelwood, MO, and then to Troy in 1970. Gari graduated from Triad High School in 1973. Gari graduated from Kaskaskia Junior College in 1975 with an Associate Degree in Applied Science.

Theresa was born on March 15, 1964, in East St. Louis, IL, to John Vito Marino and Theresa Elizabeth (Grill) Tassallo. Her father was an engine mechanic stationed out of Amarillo, TX. He died on April 22, 1972, and Theresa's family moved to Colllinsville later that year. She attended SS Peter and Paul grade school and graduated from Collinsville High School in 1982. She attended SIU-E.

Gari and Theresa met at Softball Central through mutual friends Mike and Lori Baumgartner and were married in Collinsville, IL, on March 14, 1987. Gari worked for Lanahan Brothers Construction in Troy as a carpenter, and Theresa worked for Bryan, Cave, McPheeters and McRoberts in St. Louis as a word processing operator. They built their first

(l. to r.) Chad and Gari Hanalei

(l. to r.) Natalie, Theresa, Patrese

home in Troy in 1988, and have lived in it since then.

They have 3 children. Daughter Patrese Pualani was born June 11, 1991. Her Hawaiian middle name means "flower of heaven." Their second daughter Natalie Kuuipo was born July 1, 1994. Her Hawaiian middle name means "sweetheart." Their son Chad Mahi was born March 1, 1996, and his Hawaiian middle name means "strong, energetic."

In January of 1995, Gari and Theresa purchased Kamm's Soft Water from Arthur and Yvonne Kamm and have continued to serve the community of Troy. Gari and Theresa have created many friendships through their business and look forward to meeting and serving new customers throughout the years. (See related Kamm's article.) *Submitted by Theresa Hanalei.*

MERLE M. AND SUZANNE R. (SMITH) HANSEL - In 1964, Merle and Suzanne Hansel moved to Troy from Moro, IL, with their childen Merla Sue (b. 1961) and Steven Willard (b. 1963). To Suzanne it was like coming "back home" to a familiar place from her childhood. Both her maternal grandfather, Paul F. Gerling, and her maternal grandmother, Fanny P. Cramer Gerling, had their roots in Troy. Suzanne visited in Troy with family and friends as a child and tagged along with her great-grandmother, Mattie Cramer, and grandmother, Fanny, to the Travel Club (a game played with dice), Pin Oak Home Extension, and the Troy Methodist Church. Both Paul and Fanny are buried in Troy City Cemetery.

Merle and Suzanne's family grew to five: Sheila May (b. 1967), Carla Jean (b. 1969) and Paula Jane (b. 1971). For 12 years they lived and farmed on what they were told was the old Krejci Farm, north of Troy, off Riggin Road. In 1976 they moved into Troy, buying an older home in Taylor Addition on Elmer Street, formerly known as the J.F. Jarvis Subdivision, No.2. All the children attended Troy schools and graduated from Triad High School and have graduated from various colleges and universities. Merla married Joseph Billquist in 1983, and they have two children, Christopher, 12, and Elizabeth, 9, and live in St. Charles, IL. She earned her nursing degree at Northern Illinois University, DeKalb. Steven married Jennifer Burke in 2000 and lives in Webster Groves, MO. He earned his engineering degree at SIUE, and did his graduate work at the University of MO-Rolla. Sheila married William Michael Maul in 1988; and they have two children, Michael, 5, and Jonathan, 1, and live

in Houston, TX. She earned her associate degree in communications at Lewis and Clark College, Godfrey. Carla married Anthony Schmidt in 1996; they have a daughter, Ellen, 20 months. She attended Eastern Illinois University, Charleston, for two years and then at the University of Illinois in Chicago earned her Doctor of Pharmacy degree. They live in Gallup, NM. Paula married Patrick Coughlin in 1997, and they live in Clayton, MO. She attended the University of Illinois, Champaign-Urbana, where she earned her degree in political science and then attended St. Louis University School of Law, St. Louis, MO, and earned her Juris Doctorate. Paula and Patrick are due to have their first child, July 5, 2001.

In 1965, Suzanne and Merle joined the Troy Methodist Church, transferring their membership from Immanuel Methodist Church in Edwardsville. Besides farming, Merle was a truck driver for construction work throughout the area. Suzanne was a secretary for the Edwardsville School District after high school graduation, but became a homemaker for the next 20 years after the birth of their first child. Merle retired from driving in 1997 and enjoyed puttering with cars, trucks, tractors and lawn mowers. Suzanne went back to office work in 1981 and is still working full time. Merle and Suzanne took square dance lessons, graduated in 1991, and joined the Highland Squares Dance Club, Highland, IL. They enjoyed dancing all over Illinois and Missouri for several years. As their children grew, they were active in many school, church and community activities, especially 4-H and scouting.

Hansel family, 40th Wedding Anniversary, 1995 (l. to r.) Front: Carla (Hansel) Schmidt, Paula (Hansel) Coughlin. Middle: Sheila (Hansel) Maul, Steven Hansel, Suzanne Hansel, Merla (Hansel) Billquist, Elizabeth Billquist, Christopher Billquist. Back: Michael Maul, Merle Hansel, Joseph Billquist

Merle's parents were Mary Alice Bishop Hansel (b. 1889 in Litchfield, IL, d. in 1950 in Staunton, IL) and Willard Elmer Hansel (b.1886 in Montgomery County, IL, d.1939 in St. Louis, MO). They were married in 1909 in Litchfield, IL. Merle was the youngest of ten children. He was born near Raymond, IL, in 1929. Years later, Merle and a brother lived with their mother and farmed until they both entered the military service. Merle was a Korean War veteran. Suzanne and Merle were married in 1955 at Immanuel Methodist Church in Edwardsville, and have lived in Edwardsville, Moro and Troy. Merle passed away March 17, 2000.

Suzanne's parents were Caroline Ruth Gerling Smith (b. 1920, Troy, d. 1987, Tallahassee, FL) and Willard James Smith (b.1917, St. Louis, d.1986, Oklahoma City, OK). They were married in 1937 in Edwardsville, IL. Suzanne Ruth was born in Edwardsville in the house along Route 143, across from the VFW later in 1937. Suzanne has a sister, Sylvia Jeanette Smith Tharp, born in 1940. She lives in Utah with her husband and has four children and five grandchildren. Suzanne has a brother, Willard James Smith, Jr.(b. 1941), who is married and lives in Florida. There is also a half brother, Larry Michael Smith (b.1947 in Chicago), who lives in Oklahoma City. Suzanne attended Leclaire Kindergarten in Edwardsville in 1942-43. After she finished first through third grades at the Columbus School in Edwardsville, her family moved to Glen Carbon. It was there she graduated from eighth grade in 1951. She attended Edwardsville High School and graduated in 1955. *Submitted by Suzanne Hansel.*

DWIGHT AND NADINE HANSON - Nadine (Schultze) Hanson was born in Troy, Jan. 21, 1930, the fourth child of August C. and Hilda (Esenberg) Schultze. Her grandparents were August W. and Louisa (Wendler) Schultze and Charles and Bertha (Heck) Esenberg all of Troy. Her siblings are Vernon (Jean) Schultze, LaVerne (Delbert) Erke, Thelma (Robert) Schmitt, and Erwin (Barbara) Schultze. She attended St. Paul's Lutheran School for eight years and graduated from McCray -Dewey High School in May, 1947.

Dwight Hanson's parents were Everett and Delphine (Rochell) Hanson who lived in Trenton. His siblings are Verona (Delmar) Meier and Ardell (Sandra) Hanson.

Dwight and Nadine were married on May 8, 1954, at St. Paul's Lutheran Church and lived in and around Troy until 1980 when they moved to rural Trenton where they now reside.

They have four children – Debra (Christopher) Zimmer, Marine, IL; Dennis (Veronica) Hanson, Trenton, IL; Kathy (Bruce) Bridgeforth, Peoria, IL; and Kenneth (Sandra) Hanson stationed at Dover, DE.

Their grandchildren are Adam and Aaron Bohnenstiehl, Kimberly and Kristine DeBra, Cody and Dale Bridgeforth, Ashlee, Amber and

Hanson family, 1999 (l. to r.) Front: Nadine and Dwight. Back: Kenneth, Kathy Bridgeforth, Dennis, Debra Zimmer.

Zachary Hanson, Valerie, Rachel, Megan, Lenore and Douglas Zimmer and one great grandchild Gabryl Hanson.

Dwight retired in 1992 after 33 years at Granite City Steel and farmed until 1999 when he had to retire from farming, due to ill health.

Dwight and Nadine enjoy traveling, gardening, fishing, playing cards and embroidering.

They attend Messiah Lutheran Church in Lebanon, IL. *Submitted by Dwight Hanson.*

LEWIS AND ARKANSAS HARRIS

Lewis Byron Harris (b. Mar. 8, 1849, d. Jun. 16, 1932) married Arkansas Cook (b. Sept. 13, 1847, d. Oct. 18, 1905). They had five daughters.

Their first daughter, Emma, was born Dec. 8, 1875. She died July 21, 1939. Anna (b. Aug. 25, 1878, d. Nov. 29, 1959) married Emery Lemen Edwards (b. Jun. 7, 1874, d. Jan. 3, 1954) on March 17, 1903. They had two children. Their eldest daughter was Lois Corinne, born May 4, 1913. Their youngest daughter, Edna Louise, (b. July 16, 1916, d. Aug. 30, 1988) was married Sept. 2, 1944, to James Patrick Trihey (b. Apr. 15, 1910, d. May 26, 1965). Their first child was Rita Barbara (b. Dec. 9, 1946, d. May 19, 1969). Elizabeth Ann was born Aug. 19, 1951, and Molly Leilana on Sept. 27, 1975.

Lewis and Arkansas named their third daughter Ada. She was born Dec. 18, 1880, and died June 13, 1967.

Lewis Harris family, late 1894-95 (l. to r.) Front: Lewis, Lula, Arkansas Back: Emma, Anna, Ada, Grace

Grace, the fourth daughter, was born Dec. 28, 1883, and died May 26, 1967.

Their last daughter, Lula, was born Sept. 19, 1887, and died Jan. 18, 1942. *Submitted by Betty Trihey.*

HARRIS HOMESTEAD FAMILY -
The Harris family has been one of the families that homesteaded in Jarvis township.

Benjamin Harris was born May 27, 1777. He lived on a farm south of Troy, on Liberty Rd. He married Aria (Lloyd) on July 14, 1838. He died June 27, 1853.This union had six children; three died at a very young age. Harriet (the only girl) married a Webber, and Lewis and Elijah were the other two to live for many years.

Records show minutes of a group known as the Liberty Home Protection Society which

(l. to r.) Front: Frances Wilhelm, Mary Strong, Ollie Hall, Clara Weiss, Myrtle Harris, Julia Harris, Myrtle Willimann Back: Walter Strong, Earnest Weiss, Charles Harris, Ben Harris

was dated in the late 1890s and the early 1900s. Dues were $.25 a member, with thirteen members.

Lewis and Arkansas (Cook) had five girls: Ada, Grace, Anna, Emma, and Lula. Ada, Grace and Lula never married. Anna married Emery Edwards. They all stayed in Jarvis township on Kirsch and Formosa Rds. Most of these relatives are buried in the Harris cemetery which is located on Liberty Rd.

When Ben died June 27, 1853, Elijah lived on the farm until the time of his death, June 21, 1938. The sale bill (which still exists) lists the farm acreage, with modern house, double garage, barn, cow barn and other out buildings. The house is about 1/8 mile from a power line, and has its original Deco lighting system. The farm sold for $500.00 an acre. Some items sold at the sale and prices were quart jars $.07, ice box $2.95, rocker $35.00, living room set $19.00, one horse plow $1.40, planter $17.00, and cultivator $5.25. The house is still there.

He and his first wife (Margaret Demint) had two children, Ed and Ellen; with his second wife (Mary Caroline Renfro) he raised seven children, five girls and two boys – Olive May Hall, Clara Maud Weiss, Benjamin Dew Harris, Francis Marie Wilhelm, Myrtle Lily Willimann, Charles Guy Harris, and Mary Eveline Strong. The boys went to eighth grade then went to work. All five girls went on to become teachers. When Elijah died, the farm was sold to Mary Strong. Someone in the family has always lived on the homeplace.

Mary and Walter Strong had four children: Esther, Floyd, Milton, and Joyce. Floyd lived on the homeplace for many years, until his death.. Milton lives on part of the original homeplace.

Ollie, Francis, Myrtle, and Charles "Guy" all stayed in Jarvis township until their deaths.

Ollie and husband (Henry Hall) lived on a farm on Mill Creek Rd. Then David and Gladys Hall lived there until their deaths. They had three children Earl, Eva Mae and James.

Francis and husband (Henry Wilhelm) lived just southwest of Troy on Formosa Rd. They farmed until their

deaths, then someone in the family lived there until recently. It is still owned by family, but rented out. They raised four children: Susie, Marguerite, Agnes, and John.

Myrtle and Louis Willimann lived just down the driveway from the homestead, just across from Liberty School. They had one son Dale who now lives in the old Liberty School. His daughter lives in his home place, across the road.

Guy bought a farm just to the east of where he was raised on Liberty Rd. He farmed his small farm and worked at Lumaghi coal mine. Guy and Myrtle (Goetter) raised four children there. His oldest son Charles Orville lives on their farm now. The others are Verla, Roy (who also lives on Liberty Rd.) and Shirley (Harris) Strake who now lives in New Baden, IL. *Submitted by Shirley (Harris) Strake.*

ROY AND JOANN HARRIS -
Roy and JoAnn (McIntyre) Harris reside on Liberty Road, south of Troy. Joann is from Trenton. They have three children, David Harris, Terry Harris and Kathy Smith.

Roy and JoAnn Harris in 1990 with friend, Annie Struckhoff, between them.

Roy graduated from Liberty Country School and from Troy High School in 1953. JoAnn graduated from Trenton schools. JoAnn is retired from Amoco Travel Plaza in Troy. *Submitted by Mae Grapperhaus*

RANDY AND PAT HART -
Randy Hart was born Sept. 16, 1954, in Staunton, IL, to Leroy and Delores Hart. He graduated from Staunton

Hart family, 1998 – Christy, Pat, Randy, Lisa

High School in 1972. Pat Simpson's parents, Bob and Helen, lived in Millstadt, IL, when she was born on June 22, 1955. Pat graduated from Belleville West High School in 1973.

Pat and Randy met in 1976 when they were both attending SIUE. He majored in psychology and earned his Bachelor of Science degree in 1977 and his Master of Business Administration in 1979. Pat's undergraduate majors were special education and elementary education. She earned her Bachelor's degree in 1977 and her Masters in Special Education in 1981.

After their marriage on May 19, 1979, they settled in Edwardsville. Daughter Christine Marie was born May 16, 1983. Their second child, Lisa Catherine, was born March 11, 1985.

Randy and Pat were impressed with the schools in Troy, so the family moved here in May 1987. Both girls attended the Mother's Day Out program at the Troy United Methodist Church. Later they were involved in the Troy Soccer League for many years, which was a great way for the family to meet a lot of wonderful people in town. Christy graduated from Triad High School in 2001, and Lisa will graduate in 2003.

Pat taught special education in Glen Carbon for several years, and has taught in Troy schools since February 1980. She has taught second grade for many years. Randy is Director of Marketing, Bakery Division, for Bunge Foods in St. Louis. *Submitted by Pat Hart.*

THE MARTIN AND LYDIA (GERLING) HECHT - In the early 1890s Christian Gerling II and Caroline (Lichtenberg) Gerling (see photos) moved from the Blackjack / Shoveltown community near Florissant, MO, to a farm east of Troy, known as the Siercy Farm at Lickskillet. In 1910 the family moved into their new home in Troy at 314 Montgomery Street. Christian and Caroline had a large family, six boys and six girls: (see photo of the 5 girls and of a family gathering in 1919) Paul I – married Fanny Cramer; Christian III – did not marry; Simon – married Magdaline Hecht; Joseph – did not marry; Reuben – died in infancy; Lydia – married Martin Hecht; Caroline – married Otto Fedder; Bethel – died in early childhood; Deborah – married Walter Brunworth; Theodora – married Carl Kopp; Ronald – married Barbara Slemmer; Celine – married Henry Hollmann.

The Herman and Maria (Sudbring) Hecht family lived and farmed east of Troy. In later years Herman (see photo) moved into Troy to

Gerling girls, 1924
(l. to r.) Caroline (Lena) Fedder, Theodora Kopp, Lydia Hecht, Deborah Brunworth, Celine Hollmann

Hecht men, 1914
(l. to r.) Front: Herman Sr., Martin
Back: Fred, Robert, Herman (Bill) Jr.

the Captain Cook home (see historic homes section) where the city park is located today. Herman and Maria's family was Baby Boy Hecht – died soon after birth; Magdaline-married Simon Gerling; Martin – married Lydia Gerling; Fred-married Esther Kane; Robert – married Hulda Meier; Herman Jr. (Bill) – did not marry.

Sometime after Maria Hecht died in 1911, Lydia Gerling was hired to help Magdaline with the household chores. This brought the Hecht-Gerling families into closer acquaintance.

Christian Frederick Gerling, 1885

Caroline Lichtenberg Gerling, 1885

Martin Hecht married Lydia Gerling at Manhattan, KS. He was a sergeant in the mounted engineers stationed at Fort Riley, KS. She worked as a waitress at a local hotel in Manhattan prior to marriage. They had two daughters: Bethel Celine – married Charles Dean Hoppas and Carolyn Marie – never married.

Bethel graduated from McCray-Dewey Township High School and completed her education in nursing at Topeka, KS. After graduation she met and married Dean at Manhattan, KS, where he was attending university. They moved to southwestern Kansas where Dean taught vocational agriculture at the high school. Bethel worked as an R.N. in hospital nursing. There are four children in their family. Douglas Hoppas served a tour in Vietnam and died while a senior in veterinary medicine. David Hoppas engineers and constructs underground irrigation that irrigates only below surface level and served a four-year enlistment in the Air Force. Leslie (Hoppas) Vining oversees hospital housekeeping and was in the regular army. Meredith (Hoppas) Grusing did not aspire to anything military, but has her masters in education and teaches in Wichita, KS. There are two grandchildren. Nathan Grusing

Original photo taken late summer 1919, copy 1/29/ 1971. Mary Voss, Sylvia Gerling and Chris Gerling, Jr. not on photo. (l. to r.) Row 1: Esther Lampe, Celine Gerling Hollmann, Harold (Buddy) Niehaus, Velma Gerling Tyner, Clifford Gerling, Elmer (or Harvey) Niehaus, Paul Gerling Jr., Melba Lampe. Row 2: Ronald Gerling, Amanda Lichtenberg, Deborah Gerling Brunworth, Theodora Gerling Kopp, Selma Lichtenberg, Lena (Lay) Hecht Gerling Schroeder, Mathilda Lampe, (Mrs.Walter) Meta Lampe. Row 3: Herman Niehaus, Caroline Gerling Fedder, Bertha Gerling, Amelia Gerling, Carrie Niehaus, Lydia Gerling Hecht, Fannie Cramer Gerling. Row 4: Henry Lampe, Chris Gerling Sr., Bill Lichtenberg, Paul Gerling Sr., Gus Gerling, Oscar Lichtenberg, August (Gussie) Lampe, Caroline Lichtenberg Gerling (back of post) Joseph Gerling, Walter Lampe.

engineers and constructs underground irrigation that waters above ground level and Katie Lynn Grusing who graduated in 2001 with a degree in elementary education. *Submitted by Bethel (Hecht) Hoppas.*

LARRY AND JANET HELLDOERFER Larry Aloysius Helldoerfer, born August 6, 1951, to Aloysius and Marie Emig Helldoerfer of the Blackjack farming community southeast of Troy, was the oldest of five children: Larry, Mary Jane, Marilyn, Gerard and Barbara. Larry attended Troy grade schools and Triad High School.

While in high school, Larry met Janet Veronica Mersinger born October 11, 1952, the second child of Gilbert and Muriel Lloyd Mersinger, who lived on a farm southwest of Troy. Larry and Janet teamed up when he asked her to attend the Junior Prom at Triad. From that time on, they were a couple. Following high school, Larry went to Louisville, KY, to earn a certificate in electronics. Janet attended SIUE graduating with high honors, earning a Bachelor's Degree in Elementary Education. Right after Janet graduated, she and Larry were married on

Helldoerfer family, circa 1990
Larry, Janet, Jill, Lee, Amy

November 16, 1973, by Rev. Joseph Dineen at St. Jerome's Catholic Church in Troy.

Larry developed a successful career in technical service for Business Products Center in St. Louis, and throughout the years won many awards that were proudly displayed in their home. Larry also began farming the fields owned by Janet's mother – a sideline he truly enjoyed. Janet began her career teaching fifth grade at Molden Elementary School in Troy and later fifth grade at McCray-Dewey School. She went back to SIUE and received her Masters Degree in Education in 1977. Janet received both local and state recognition for her excellence in teaching. Larry and Janet built a home on Janet's mother's farm and raised three children: Jill Jeanette born May 23, 1979; Amy Elizabeth born July 16, 1980; and Lee Lawrence born August 11, 1983. Over the years, they were able to take many family trips together, often when Larry traveled on his job. On one of Larry's assignments to London in 1994, the whole family went along, experiencing sights and history they had studied in school. They created many wonderful family memories.

The children excelled in high school sports – Jill in basketball and softball; Amy in varsity cheerleading; and Lee in track. Jill and Amy were valedictorians of their high school classes.

In 1994, Janet was named Principal of McCray-Dewey School in Troy, a job she worked diligently to get. She happily served in that role until she became ill and died March 1, 1996. During the summer of 1997, Larry became ill; he died March 4, 1998. The children were then cared for by Larry's sisters, Marilyn Taylor and Barbara Dolosic; they continued to live in their family home.

At this writing, Jill has graduated magna cum laude in 2001 from SIUE with a Bachelor's Degree in Electrical Engineering and is completing her Master's Degree. Amy is a senior at SIUE, finishing a Bachelor's Degree in elementary education. Lee graduated in 2001 magna cum laude from Triad High School. He also plans to pursue a career in elementary education.

Larry and Janet are buried in St. John the Baptist Catholic Cemetery in the rural Blackjack community. *Submitted by Gail Wolff.*

TILDEN AND MARY ANN HELMICH

Tilden and Mary Ann were married December 12, 1942. Tilden entered the army on April 24, 1941, and served until October 16, 1945. *Submitted by Tilden Helmich.*

Mary Ann Helmich, at 77 years old, and Tilden Helmich, at 82 years, October 1995.

C.A. HENNING

C.A. HENNING - Clarence and Ethel (Young) Henning moved to Troy in 1942 when Clarence accepted a teaching position at the McCray-Dewey High School. Ethel was the daughter of David and Louise Young of Pin Oak Township. From 1943-1953, Clarence was a science teacher and the coach of all sports. During these years, his teams won more than thirty trophies. The boys' basketball record was 203 and 98.

Ethel and Clarence Henning

Several athletes qualified for state finals in track and cross country. For the next four years, Mr. Henning was the principal of the high school. When Triad became a consolidated district, he became the first principal of the high school. During the years 1959-1961, the curriculum was enlarged, counselors were employed, and football and girls' sports were started.

From 1962-1977, Mr. Henning became the superintendent of Triad Community Unit #2. Triad was one of the first districts in the state to initiate all day kindergarten classes and hire reading specialists. The district grew as new buildings were added: Molden Elementary, Wakeland Center, an agriculture classroom building, a large addition to the high school, and renovations or additions to the Marine, St. Jacob, and McCray-Dewey buildings. All bond issues and tax referendums were passed during these years.

Clarence was also involved in the community of Troy. He served on a committee to install street signs, and helped to survey the community for door to door mail delivery and for city sewer service. He has been a Lions Club member since 1943, serving as president in 1953. Mr. Henning served one term as president of the Troy Civic Improvement Corp. which developed the Troy Industrial Park. He was one of four Lions Club members to provide local money to buy ground for the local park. He also assisted in the formation of the Troy Security Bank.

After retiring in 1977, Clarence served to two terms on the Madison County School Trustees, served for two years on the Southwestern Agency on Aging, and was president of the United Savings and Loan.

Mr. Henning has received numerous honors. In 1953, he was named the Troy Citizen of the Year. The C.A. Henning Elementary School was named in his honor in 1988. He also received the Melvin Jones Foundation Award in 2000.

Clarence has been a member of Alpha Sigma Phi since 1932, the Troy United Methodist Church since 1942, the Troy Lions Club since 1943, Phi Delta Kappa International, the National Association of Secondary Principals since 1955, the American Association of School Administrators since 1962, and the Educational League of Illinois since 1963. He served as president of the Southwestern Illinois Coaches Association for one term.

Clarence and Ethel's children are Carol Taake of Troy, Kay Korte of Lebanon, and Don Henning of St. Louis. They have nine grand-children and two great grandchildren.

Mr. Henning is a 1934 graduate of Ohio Wesleyan with an A.B. degree and the University of Illinois with an A.M. degree in 1952. He has done additional graduate work at Ohio State, SIU-E, and SIU-C. *Submitted by Kay Korte.*

OTHO GARRETT HENSLEY

OTHO GARRETT HENSLEY - Otho Garrett Hensley was born June 20, 1908, to John Christian and Amanda Margaret (Sooter) Hensley of Iberia, MO. Otho lived in Iberia until the age of 18 when he moved to Granite City, IL, to work for General Steel Castings as a welder. He married Genevieve Whitten on Nov. 5, 1927. Genevieve was born in Bingham, IL, on April 1, 1906, to William Woodford and Lavina Elizabeth (Casey) Whitten. Otho and Genevieve lived in Granite City and had one child, Gloria Arlene, born Mar. 4, 1931 (see Roy Daniel Elliott, Jr.).

Genevieve and Otho Hensley, 1927

The family moved to Franklin St. in Troy in 1940. In 1947, Otho bought the Busse farm north of Troy on the Staunton Road. He continued to work for General Steel and farmed on the side until he retired around 1970. Genevieve died Nov. 1, 1975. Otho died Jan. 8, 1990. The farm now has been developed into a residential area called "Oakland Hills." *Submitted by Kae Elliott Schmitt.*

JOHN IRWIN HINDMARCH

JOHN IRWIN HINDMARCH - John Irwin Hindmarch was born Jan. 22, 1892 (d. July 25, 1973). Irwin married Jessie Cade Elliott who was born Nov. 29, 1890 (d. Dec. 24, 1973), of Grant and Clara Elliott (see Grant L. Elliott). They had one child, Dorothy Dee. The family lived in Troy and Irwin practiced law in St. Louis, MO, and Troy.

Dorothy married Clinton O. Scott (b. Dec. 30, 1921, died 1989) on July 31, 1948. Clinton "Scotty" was in the military for seven years and retired from Union Electric after 36 years. They had two sons: Robert Lynn and David Jean. Robert "Lynn" was married to Donna Wasmer and lives in Seattle, WA. Lynn and Donna had a daughter and a son: Kelly Ann (married to Craig Pearsons) and Christopher Elliott Scott.

John I. And Jessie (Elliott) Hindmarch, 1920

Dottie and Scotty's son, David, married Alice Hunt. They live in Denver, CO, and have two children, Bethany and Eric David. *Submitted by Dorothy Hindmarch Scott and Kae Elliott Schmitt.*

DONALD J. AND GAY M. HINNEN -

Gay Madelon McFarland Hinnen was born in Troy, Illinois, to Gordon and Sybil McFarland on April 15, 1932.

Gordon McFarland was born in East St. Louis, IL, and Sybil McFarland was born in Troy, IL. They lived in Troy all their married life. Gordon died in 1979 and Sybil in 1994.

Gay has three brothers – Gordon and Keith of Troy, IL, and Michael (deceased). She has two sisters, Sharon Schlaefer of St. Jacob, IL, and Gina Hays of Glen Carbon, IL.

Gay graduated from Troy Grade School and McCray-Dewey High School (1950). She married Donald J. Hinnen from Glen Carbon, IL, in 1952. Gay and Don Hinnen lived in Troy, IL from 1952 until 1962. Their four sons – Britt, Gregg, Todd, and Reed – were born while they lived in Troy.

Don Hinnen attended St. Louis University while he also worked at Highland Hospital and the Madison County Sanitarium. He graduated from St. Louis University with a degree in Business Administration and a Master's in Hospital Administration. In 1962 Don accepted a position in administration at Mercy Hospital in Denver, Colorado. The family moved to Denver.

Donald and Gay (McFarland) Hinnen family

A daughter, Beth, was born in Denver in 1962.

Don accepted another position in 1965 of director for the Arizona Hospital Association.

The family moved to Phoenix, Arizona. While living in Arizona, Gay started to take college classes.

Don accepted a position as Regional Director for the American Hospital Association

in Denver in 1969. The family moved back to Denver. Gay continued her college classes and in 1971 graduated from Arapahoe Community College with her 2 year degree in Nursing. She worked as a nurse in Colorado for nine years, then retired.

Don accepted a position in 1982 for the Regional Vice President for the Voluntary Hospitals of America in Atlanta and the family moved to Atlanta. After three years he moved the family again when he joined the corporate office of VHA in Dallas, Texas. He retired in 1990.

They moved to Sun City West, Arizona, in 1990 and enjoy golfing, volunteering and building houses for Habitat for Humanity, RVing, and international travel. *Submitted by Gay Madelon (McFarland) Hinnen.*

JOHN AND KATHARINE (BAER) HIRSTEIN -

Katharine Baer was born 27 December 1856, in Blackjack, Madison County, IL, daughter of Jacob and Anna Elizabeth Langenwalter Baer. She was married 25 February 1883, at Summerfield, IL, to John Hirstein, born 25 March 1858, in Missouri, son of Abraham and Barbara Wittmer Hirstein.

Wedding photo, 25 Feb. 1883
John and Katharine (Baer) Hirstein

They lived in Blackjack on her father's farm where most of their children were born.

Anna was born 16 December 1883, married 16 January 1907 to Gustav W. Ruth; died 20 October 1946, buried Summerfield Cemetery, Summerfield, IL. Children: LeRoy, Lucille, Melvin, Ralph.

Selma was born 11 November 1885, died 4 June 1911, buried Summerfield Cemetery.

Emma was born 11 September 1887, died 12 December 1917, buried Summerfield Cemetery.

Samuel was born 8 September 1889, married 19 February 1918 to Clara Stocker. Their daughter was Harriet. Samuel married (2) 9 November 1921 to Alvina Harpstrite, died 19 January 1963, buried City Cemetery, Trenton, IL. Their children were Leslie and Harold.

John was born 22 December 1891, died 21 October 1918 while on furlough from the United States Army, buried Summerfield Cemetery.

Daniel Jacob was born 13 December 1893, married 9 April 1919 to Frieda Berger, died 22 December 1942, buried Summerfield Cemetery. Children: Ethel, Edith, Gerald.

Edward Theodore was born 17 December 1895, married 17 October 1944 to Lynette Basinger, died 19 December 1980; body

donated to St. Louis University Science Research. No children.

Clara Lydia was born 30 August 1899, died 15 September 1899, buried Summerfield Cemetery.

In 1891 John and Katharine purchased farm land two miles southeast of Summerfield and lived there until they retired from farming in 1921. They built their retirement home in Summerfield.

Katharine died 24 January 1940. John died 27 December 1943. Both are buried in the Summerfield Cemetery. *Submitted by Edith Hock.*

ALLEN HOLLOWAY -

Allen Hal Holloway was born on July 26, 1935, in Fillmore, IL, to Jacob Thomas Kessinger Holloway and Charlotte Lona (Prater) Holloway. He had one brother, Norman Curtis (b. Aug. 17, 1940, d. Feb. 27, 1984). His family moved to rural Troy in March 1942, and rented a farm house on Maple Grove Road from Charles and Edna Bangert. While living here, Allen attended Maple Grove School.

The Holloway family rented a house on South Hickory Street in the spring of 1943. Later, the family bought a home at 402 North Franklin. The house had the distinction of being the last house on Franklin Street. The only thing north of the home was the Stanovich farm property. The entire family became members of the Troy United Methodist Church. Charlotte taught Sunday school classes, belonged to the Fidelis Circle, and quilted with the church quilting ladies. Jacob worked the night shift on the railroad, and was unable to attend services on a regular basis, as did the rest of his family.

Allen and Norman attended Troy schools. Allen graduated in June 1953, and Norman, in June 1958. Allen attended Eastern Illinois University at Charleston for one year then transferred to St. Louis College of Pharmacy in 1954. He graduated in June 1958 with a Bachelor of Science in Pharmacy. He passed the Illinois State Board exams in 1958 and has been a registered pharmacist ever since.

Allen and Sue Carol Fults were married on November 23, 1955. Sue was born in East St. Louis on March 12, 1938, to Myron Zeno Fults (b. 11-14-1913) and June Elizabeth (McDonald) Fults (b. 11-29-1916, d. 1-3-1976). Sue attended East St. Louis elementary school and junior high school, but graduated from McCray-Dewey in 1955. She had moved to Troy with her family in 1953. Her father, who worked for Swift Company in East St. Louis, wanted to

Sue and Allen Holloway, 2000

move his family to the country, and chose Troy as their new home. She has one brother, Kenneth Fults, b. Aug. 11, 1941. Sue and Allen have 4 sons: Bryan Keith (b. 1-25-57) m. Constance Joan Wright, son-Austin Louis; Bruce Kent (b. 8-31-59) m. Cheryl Ann Wickert, son-Jacob Allen, daughter-Jessica Brooke; Brent Kevin (b. 10-29-62) daughter Kalah Michelle; Bradley Kenneth (b. 8-23-67).

After graduation from college, Allen worked for pharmacies in Jacksonville and Edwardsville. He and Sue purchased the Kamm Pharmacy in January 1960 from Jule "Bud" and Rosalie Kamm, and changed the name to Allen's Drugs in 1961, a name it still bears today. Allen and Sue operated the pharmacy for 38 years before selling it to Todd Evers and retiring on October 1, 1998.

Both Allen and Sue keep busy and active in their retirement, still living in the same house on N. Charcoal they purchased in 1963. Allen belongs to the NRA and the Edwardsville Gun Club, and enjoys hunting and the outdoors. Sue, an accomplished artist, is a member of the St. Louis Watercolor Society and the Gateway East Artists' Guild, and attends art classes and workshops frequently. *Submitted by Sue Holloway.*

JACOB THOMAS KESSINGER HOLLO-WAY - Jacob Thomas Kessinger Holloway (b. Sept. 15, 1911, in Fillmore, IL) and wife, Charlotte Lona Prater Holloway (b. May 12, 1917, in Fillmore), and their two sons, Allen Hal (b. July 26, 1935, in Fillmore) and Norman Curtis (b. Aug. 17, 1940, in Barrington, IL, where their father managed and operated a grain and dairy farm) moved to rural Troy in March 1942.

The Holloway family rented a farm house on Maple Grove Road from Charles and Edna Bangert. Jacob worked for the Illinois Central Railroad as a telegraph operator and was transferred to the Mont Station office, which was about 2 1/2 miles from their Maple Grove home, and 3 miles southeast of Edwardsville. While the family lived here, Allen attended Maple Grove School, and sadly, Norman was diagnosed with juvenile diabetes at age 2. This early disease contributed to his early death later at the age of 43 1/2 years.

In early spring of 1943, the Holloway family moved to a rent house on South Hickory Street in Troy. After one year there, the family purchased a home at 402 North Franklin, the last house on Franklin Street. North of Jacob's home was the Stanovich farm property. Charlotte lived at the North Franklin home until her death on May 24, 1969.

The Holloway family became members of the Troy United Methodist Church where Charlotte taught Sunday school classes, and was an active member of Fidelis Circle and the quilting group. Jacob worked the 11 p.m. to 8 a.m. shift on the railroad and was unable to attend on a regular basis, as his sons did.

Both boys graduated from Troy schools; Allen, in June 1953, and Norman, in June 1958. Allen later became a pharmacist and Norman was a barber, both in Troy. Norman began his barbering career with Milton "Bud" Klaus in Troy. He later bought the barber shop with partner Ray Ulrich. He worked there until his death on Feb. 27, 1984. Norman married Clara

Louise Johnson on June 9, 1962, and she and son, Michael Todd, live on Blackjack Road.

Jacob worked for several railroads as a result of buy-outs and mergers in the industry. After Mont Station closed, he worked at Glen Carbon and Madison as a telegraph operator and dispatcher. When Chicago Northwestern Railroad bought his employer company, Jacob was offered a promotion as a dispatcher, if he would move to Chicago. He declined because he wanted his family to remain in Troy with their many friends. Jacob married his second wife, Jane White in September 1970, and they lived on Franklin Street until 1978. He retired in 1973. The couple moved to Coffeen, living there until Jacob's death on Jan. 4, 1988. Jane died on June 20, 2000.

Son Allen married Sue Carol Fults on November 23, 1955. They have four sons: Bryan, Bruce, Brent, and Bradley, and four grandchildren. They reside in Troy. *Submitted by Allen Holloway*

CARL HORVATH - Carl and Cora (Schneider) Horvath moved to Troy from Collinsville in September of 1955 to a small farm three miles southwest of Troy, off Troy-O'Fallon Road.

The Horvaths had three children; they are Carl Horvath, Gladys Horvath and Kenneth Horvath. They all live in the St. Louis Metro Area.

Carl graduated in 1957 from McCray-Dewey High School in Troy. Gladys graduated in 1959 from McCray Dewey High School, Troy. Kenneth graduated in 1965.

Young Carl moved away from Troy in 1964 when he married Karen Nischwitz of Edwardsville, IL. They lived in Edwardsville and raised three children. Their names are Wendy, Debbie and Damon. The couple have one grandchild. They all live in the St. Louis Metro area.

In May of 1999, Karen, Carl's wife, died of cancer. Carl still lives in Edwardsville. *Submitted by Carl Horvath.*

HOVATTER FAMILY - Bradley Hovatter was born in Wichita, KS, on April 24, 1956. His parents are Donald and Jo Hovatter of Lebanon, IL. They moved from Kansas to Lebanon in 1960. Brad has one brother, Michael, and wife Deena, of Bethalto, IL.

Teresa (Poletti) Hovatter was born on August 22, 1958, in E. St. Louis to Edward and Bernadine Poletti of Troy, IL. She has two sisters, Marilyn and Judy, and one brother, Wayne. (Refer to the Edward Poletti family.)

Hovatter Family, 1997
(l. to r.) Teresa, Brad, Amanda, Nathan

Brad and Teresa met through a cousin while in high school. They married on September 3, 1977, at St. Mary's Catholic Church in Trenton, IL. They built a home in rural Troy on the family farm, where they still reside. They are members of St. Jeromes Catholic Church in Troy.

Amanda Leigh was a joyful addition to the family on July 6, 1985, in Belleville, IL. She has been involved with dance since the age of seven. She continues to dance as a member of the Triad Knight Moves Dance Team. She will graduate in 2003.

Nathan Bradley was welcomed into the family on July 26, 1988, in Belleville, IL. He enjoys playing soccer, baseball, and football. He will graduate in 2007.

The family enjoys boating and snow skiing with family and friends. *Submitted by Brad and Teresa Hovatter.*

HUCK FAMILY - Francis "Fran" Huck was the son of Blanche Wood and Francis W.A. Huck. He was born July 15, 1923, in St. Louis, MO. Patricia "Pat" Huck was the daughter of Theresa Buehne and Henry Ruesche and was born Nov. 28, 1931, in St. Louis, MO. They were married Jan. 26, 1952, at St. Pius V Catholic Church in St. Louis. They had 4 children-Michael, Nancy, Mark and Paul. They have 4 grandchildren and 5 great-grandchildren. They have lived in Troy since 1970, when the family moved from St. Louis. Fran worked at McDonnell Douglas for 36 years, retiring in December 1984. Fran died Oct. 30, 2001, at Anderson Hospital, Maryville, IL.

Wedding photo, 1952,
Francis and Patricia Huck

Pat has been a member of various community organizations. However, the Tri-Township Public Library is closest to her heart. She was instrumental in its formation and organization and has been a library trustee for over 25 years. She was one of those board of trustees members honored for 25 years of service to the library in 2001 by the Lewis and Clark Library System. She contributed to the design of the new building and was the unofficial foreman on the construction site. She currently serves as the board treasurer, keeping a close watch on all finances.

She has also been a charter member both of the Troy Genealogical Society and the Troy Historical Society, helping to compile this history book. Her interest in history and genealogy is not just centered in Troy, for she is working on the Clinton County history book. She works diligently to preserve history and artifacts. Pat keeps busy with her community interests and family activities. *Submitted by Pat Huck.*

MICHAEL FRANCIS HUCK - Michael was born in St. Louis, MO, on October 23, 1952, to Francis and Patricia (Ruesche) Huck and was the first of four children. He has a sister, Nancy, and two brothers, Mark and Paul. The Huck family lived in South St. Louis.

After graduating from high school in 1971, he moved to Troy. The rest of the family had moved to Troy the previous summer. They lived on the property where they had operated a campground since the summer of 1964. The campground closed in the fall of 1973 due to the gas crisis.

Wedding photo, 1998 Linda and Michael Huck

After working nine months in Springfield, IL, he returned to Troy in 1973 to work at the Blue Haven Service Station, located at the junction of Illinois Route 162 and U.S. 40. Michael worked for Willard Gindler at the station for three years. In September 1987 Michael began working as a reporter for the *Times-Tribune* in Troy. In 1988 he found himself also working as a reporter for radio station WRYT-1080 in Edwardsville. After leaving the *Times-Tribune* for three years, he returned in 1991 and continued to work for both the paper and WRYT until 1995. He was then hired as the editor of the *Journal-Messenger*, which serves the New Athens and Marissa area of St. Clair County. In April 1997 Michael began working for the *Suburban Journals* as a composing room assistant in St. Louis.

While still living in Troy, Michael met Linda Lanning, who lived in Arkansas, through America Online. After visiting back and forth and meeting each other's families, Mike proposed to Linda in August 1997. In November 1997 he began working as a graphic artist for the Arkansas Department of Parks and Tourism. Linda is originally from Rockford, IL, and is a Certified Public Accountant for Ameron Coatings in Little Rock. Mike and Linda were married at the Tri-Township Public Library in Troy on May 23, 1998. They continue to live near Alexander, AR. *Submitted by Mike Huck.*

DAVID AND ANN (WENDLER) HUCKLA David L. Huckla was born on June 9, 1941, the son of Frank and Helen (Saksa) Huckla of Granite City, Illinois. David graduated from Assumption High School in East St. Louis and attended Ranken Trade School were he received a Doctorate of Motors degree. David served on the Madison County Board of Supervisors, farmed, and retired from Granite City Steel with 30 years of service.

Huckla family, 1996
(l. to r.) Mary, David, Jeff Hommert, Ann, Darla, Darla's friend's child

David's eldest daughter, Mary, received a Bachelor's Degree in Interior Design at the University of Missouri at Columbia, MO. She is employed at Treasure Island Casino in Las Vegas, NV.

David's younger daughter, Darla, received a Master's Degree in Early Childhood Education at Southern Illinois University at Edwardsville. She is a kindergarten teacher in Mitchell, IL.

Ann Marie Wendler was born on December 21, 1957, in Highland, IL, the daughter of Erwin Arthur Wendler and Frances Mary Frey of St. Jacob. Her parents moved to Highland in 1963. Ann graduated from Quincy College in 1979. Ann's son, Jeff Hommert, attends Triad High School.

David and Ann were married on July 30, 1995, living in Troy until 1998 when they moved to the home David built on his farm west of St. Jacob. *Submitted by Ann Huckla.*

HULTZ FAMILY - Elizabeth Boskamp was born in Mt. Carmel, IL, on April 14, 1880. She died in Denison, TX, on November 5, 1967. She married William Mueller on March 7, 1905. William was born in Poseyville, IN, on September 21, 1880. He died in Collinsville, IL, on March 24, 1949 He was a miner and also worked at the Brooks Canning Factory. The couple had ten children and lived in Collinsville all of their married lives. One of their children was Mary Mueller.

William's parents were Mary E. (Hoenig) Hultz (b. February 10, 1864 d. May 20, 1931) and Charles M. Hultz (b. October 1, 1886 d. March 17, 1955). They were married on March 25,1885. They were the parents of Louis Philip Hultz, who was born on June 12, 1894, and died on December 25, 1955.

Louie married Helen Mary Mueller about 1930. Louie drove a truck and did general

Hultz family, 1953
(l. to r.) Front: Louie, Charles, John.
Back: Fannie (Hultz) Nemnich

hauling. Helen was a housewife. They were the parents of Mary Elizabeth Hultz (b. September 24, 1933). Some of the family gathered at a family picnic in 1953 at Grandpa Charles Hultz's home.

BILL HUMPHRIES - Bill Humphries and his sister, Geraldine Marie, were children of Clarence A. and Mabel C. (nee Bond) Farris. They were adopted by Thomas and Clara Belle (nee Schwob) Humphries.

Geraldine Marie (married name Losse) died July 31, 1996. They had a brother Charles Farris, who served in WWII in the U.S. Navy and also served in Korea in the U.S. Army. He was killed in Korea. Bill also had a sister, Betty Lou Farris Carlson.

Bill Humphries (8th grade) 1948-1949.

The Humphries family moved to Troy and Mr. Humphries built a brick home on the old John Jarvis place on by-pass 40 (Route 162-Edwardsville Road in 2002). The home still stands and has the original foundation of the old Jarvis home. The original wall can still be seen in the basement of the brick home.

Bill Humphries attended Troy schools. He joined the U.S. Marine Corps and served for eight years. After he was discharged from the service, he lived in southern California until 1994 when he moved back to the Midwest. He now resides in St. Louis, MO. Prior to that, he lived in Arnold, MO. *Submitted by Mae Grapperhaus as told by Bill Humphries*

WILLIAM AND CARLA HYTEN - William M. Hyten was born on May 16, 1947, to Wilbur G. and Geraldine L. Hyten. He spent his first 42 years of life in Edwardsville, IL. Bill was a 1965 graduate from Edwardsville High School. Carla J. Hyten was born on May 28, 1954, to John and Hester Vessell. Carla lived her entire childhood in Belleville, IL. She graduated from Belleville East High School in 1972.

Bill and Carla met in 1977 while teaching together at Glen Carbon School in the Edwardsville Community Unit School District. They married on March 29, 1980. On Valentines' Day in 1990, the Hyten family completed construction on their new home and moved to Troy.

Both Bill and Carla earned undergraduate and advanced degrees from Southern Illinois University at Edwardsville. Carla holds a Bachelor of Science and Master of Science Degree in Speech Pathology. Bill holds a Bachelor of Science Degree in Education, and both a Master of Science and Specialist Degree in Educational Administration.

Hyten family, 1998
(l. to r.) Michael, Olivia, Shelli, Carla, Bill and Ty

After teaching and coaching in the Edwardsville Schools for twelve years, Bill accepted his first administrative position in 1981 with the Triad Community Unit School District as principal of the Troy Grade School (now William S. Freeman School). He served in a duel role as principal at both Troy Grade School and Molden School from 1984 to 1986. From 1986 to 1988, his duel duties included principal at Molden School and District Elementary Curriculum Coordinator. He was appointed the first principal of the newly constructed C. A. Henning School for the 1988-1989 school year. And lastly, Bill served as Triad Superintendent of Schools for thirteen years – 1989 through 2002. During this same period of time, Carla delivered speech and language services to primary students in several Edwardsville Schools: Glen Carbon, Hamel, LeClaire, and N.O. Nelson.

Bill and Carla are proud parents of three children: Shelli (June 1, 1971) and Mike (October 11, 1973) from Bill's first marriage, and Ty (September 10, 1987) from their own marriage. As this information was being published in the spring of 2002, both Bill and Carla were retiring from the field of education – Bill after 33 years; Carla after 23 years due to her battle with multiple sclerosis. Shelli (age 30) was working in the Human Resources Division of Enterprise Corporate in St. Louis with plans to marry in the fall. Mike (age 28) and his wife Olivia were residing in Westminster, CO, where Mike was a Graphic Designer for Conet, Incorporated, and Olivia was employed as a high school guidance counselor. Grandchildren were the family's immediate dreams. Ty (age-14) was to begin his freshmen year at the new Triad High School during the fall of 2002. He was focused on his academics, but was also very interested in track, tennis, computer science, and the guitar.

The Hytens love the people and friendly atmosphere of the rapidly growing Triad communities of Troy, Marine, and St. Jacob. Although somewhat biased, they also think that Triad Schools are extraordinary! *Submitted by Bill Hyten.*

WILBUR JACKSON - Wilbur Jackson was born in 1918, one of the three children of William and Bertha (Baum) Jackson born in Troy.

Wilbur remained in Troy and married a local girl, Norma Rood, daughter of Clinton and Adella Rood of Troy. Wilbur and Norma have four children – Donna (now Kampwerth of Highland, IL) in 1943, Margy (now Voigt of rural Alhambra, IL) in 1947, William (of Marine, IL) in 1950 and Sherry (now Rieken of Troy) in 1952. Sadly, Norma succumbed to breast cancer in 1957. In 1958 Wilbur married Adeline Martin of rural Edwardsville. Wilbur and Adeline have two sons – Daniel (of Troy) in 1959 and Timothy in 1964 (who died too early in 1985).

Wilbur graduated from McCray-Dewey High School in 1936. He attended Ranken Trade School in St. Louis and graduated in 1938 with a degree in Auto Mechanics. Through 1943, Wilbur worked in Auto Parts in East St. Louis and as a trucker for his father. In 1943, Wilbur was drafted into the Army and spent two years with the 756th Engineers in England and France. In 1946, Wilbur returned to Troy and his career in auto parts, until 1948 when he joined McDonnell Aircraft. Wilbur spent 32 years at McDonnell Aircraft (McDonnell-Douglas). Highlights of his career include being a part of both the F-15 and F-18 development teams. Wilbur retired from McDonnell-Douglas in 1980 and still resides in Troy.

Wilbur Jackson, 1999

Each of Wilbur's children is a graduate of Triad High School. Donna is part of the second graduating class at Triad. After high school, Margy attended East St. Louis Beauty Academy, and joined Norene Halleman at Norene's Beauty Shop in Troy, before moving to Alhambra. As a result of an early childhood illness, William suffers from a dramatic hearing loss making his progress through the schools difficult, and these difficulties lead Wilbur to challenge the Triad Board of Education to establish a Special Education Department before beginning a football program – which it did. William followed Wilbur to McDonnell-Douglas (now Boeing). Sherry worked for several years at the Troy Security Bank, before moving on to other financial institutions in St. Louis. Daniel and Timothy attended St. Paul's Lutheran School, then Triad. Daniel graduated from Southern Illinois University at Edwardsville in 1984 with a Master of Science Degree in Economics. Daniel spent eight years on the Planning Commission and four years as an Alderman for the City of Troy. Timothy was a student at Belleville Area College (later called Southwestern Illinois College) at the time of his death.

The Jackson grandchildren have produced yet another generation of Troy residents. Sherry and Gary Rieken have two sons – Joe in 1989 and Jacob in 1994. Daniel married the former Lisa Seres of Collinsville and has three children – Christopher, born in 1987, Megan, born in 1990 and Sarah, born in 1991. All attend Troy schools. *Submitted by Mae Grapperhaus.*

WILLIAM JACKSON - For the past 90 years, for four generations, the Jackson family has been an integral part of the history of Troy. Jackson family members have attended each and every Troy School. Jackson family members have been involved in numerous civic organizations and activities through out Troy's last century. The story of the Jacksons of Troy is in large part a reflection of Troy itself.

Wedding photo, May 1, 1912
William and Bertha (Baum) Jackson

Recently married in Carlyle, William and Bertha (Baum) Jackson left the family farm, at what is now Haslet State Park, and moved to Troy in early 1912. William was attracted to Troy by the possibility of work in the coal mine and by the presence of two of his sisters already living in Troy – May (Jackson) Potts and Maude (Jackson) Schaeffer. William and Bertha have three children while in Troy – Iona (now Moser of Highland, IL) in 1913, Wilbur in 1918 and Vera in 1920 (now Scott of Bloomington, IN).

Mr. and Mrs. Jackson, circa 1940s

William did find work in the Troy coal mine – as a hoisting engineer. After several years in this position, William struck out on his own as an independent trucker. Initially hauling workers to the mines in Maryville, he also became a logger in and around Troy, specializing in walnut lumber. William's trucking business thrived, allowing him to expand into long distance hauling, mostly between Chicago and St. Louis. At its height, William's trucking business included three trucks. Among other employees, William employed Noah Hall who, along with his wife, later owned and operated Noah's Ark and Grace's Grill on the corner of Market and Washington in Troy.

William's trucking business was instrumental in the development of early Troy.

Jackson children, 1920-21
(l. to r.) Wilbur, Iona, Vera

In addition to hauling coal from the mine, he was responsible for hauling much of the material necessary for the construction of U.S. Highway 40, south of Troy. In connection to one of its most prominent citizens, William hauled the supplies for a young Paul Simon when, as a result of his investigations, union drivers refused to carry goods for Mr. Simon's *Troy Tribune*.

William and Bertha left their home at 312 Staunton Rd. and retired to Palmetto, FL, in 1958. Bertha passed away in December 1966, and William returned to Troy. William passed away in November 1976. *Submitted by Mae Grapperhaus.*

RALPH SANFORD JAMESON - Ralph Sanford Jameson was born August 23, 1922, in Granite City, IL, to Issac Sanford and Mary A.(Drake) Jameson. Issac, a chauffeur, was born in Detroit, IL, on November 4, 1881, and died March 4, 1952. Mary, a homemaker, was born in Pearl, IL, on October 3, 1893, and died February 23, 1953. He married the former Lola Virginia Patterson on July 22, 1939, in Granite City, IL. Lola, born in Finley, TN, on September 1,1920, was the daughter of Leonard Samuel and Jewel Arty (Redin) Patterson. Mr. Patterson was born April 30, 1894, and was in the United States Army during World War I where he was awarded the Purple Heart in Argonne, France. He died February 26, 1959. Mrs. Patterson was born September 16, 1898, and died September 24, 1979.

Ralph was an electrician with the United States Navy from 1941 to 1945. He and his wife have three children.

Janet Jean Jameson was born December 21, 1944, in Granite City. She graduated from Triad High School in 1963. On August 5, 1963, she married Richard William Kruse, born October 17, 1945, in Alton, IL. They divorced in April 1990. Three children were born of this union.

Ralph and Lola Jameson, 1990

The eldest is Karen Kay born December 26, 1964, in Highland, IL. She married Douglas Wayne Little on July 2, 1988. Doug was born October 24, 1966. They have one son, Andrew Michael, born in St. Louis, MO, on October 12, 1990. In the middle is Kelly Kae who was born June 20, 1969, in Highland, On July 15, 1989, she married David B. White who was born September 7, 1967. They have a son, David Benjamin, Jr., born September 11, 1991, in San Francisco, CA, and a daughter, Alexandra Kaye, born at Scott Air Force Base, IL, on July 18, 1995. The Kruse's son, David Matthew, was born July 14, 1970, in Highland. David died March 28, 1997, in Springfield, IL.

Cynthia Susan Jameson was born February 29, 1948, in Granite City. She married Gary Richard Adams on September 16, 1967. Gary was born July 14, 1948.They also have three children. The eldest is Susan Elaine, born September 4, 170. On June 9, 1990, she married Charles Lancaster Moore, born November 22, 1963. They have three children: Bethany Lane, born May 28, 1994; Chelsea Amelia, born August 3, 1995; and Mallory Marguerite, born January 19, 1999, on her great-great-grandmother Adams' 91st birthday. In the middle is daughter Julie Ann, born January 1, 1972. On March 18, 2000, she married Brian Martinson who was born December 17, 1966. Their son Gary Richard Adams, Jr., was born June 6, 1977. He teaches English as a second language to the French in South Africa.

Ralph Sanford (Rusty) Jameson, Jr., was born December 26, 1953. On August 8, 1983, he married Patricia Lynn Ackerman who was born May 30, 1962. They have thre daughters: Nicole Elaine, born March 13, 1984; Natalie Elizabeth, born August 13, 1985; Megan Lola, born July 27, 1987; and one son Patrick Sanford, born February 14, 1990.

Mr. Jameson moved his family from Granite City to Troy in 1956. At that time he was a salesman for St. Louis Plumbing and Heating. When that company was destroyed by fire in 1965, he operated his sales business from his car. The business name, R & L Supply, was made up of his name, Ralph, and that of his wife, Lola. In October 1968, when he located to what is now the dentist office of Dr. Mark Friederich, his inventory was being stored in his basement at the John Wilhelm farm, at the former Watson Lumber Co., and at several other nearby places. In 1972 he moved the business into the building on Edwardsville Road that was the original mine shaft to the Troy Coal Mine, and operated there until his death August 15, 1990. Son Rusty ran the business until he sold it in February 1999, to Plumber Supply. *Submitted by Lola Jameson.*

JARVIS FAMILY - In 1632 three Jarvis brothers — Daniel, James, and John — came to America from England. John eventually settled in Virginia. Many of his descendants moved westward, and one of them, also named John Jarvis, came to the Illinois Territory in 1803.

This fourth generation John had been born July 28, 1754. He married Mary Fields (born Nov. 22, 1780), and they had two children: a son (Fields) and a daughter. Mary died in

Jarvis family, 1985
(l. to r.) Anita, James, John, and J.D.

Virginia in 1788, and Fields then accompanied his father to Illinois. They settled in Turkey Hill, a settlement southeast of present-day Belleville, and remained there until 1813.

John Jarvis then moved further north and made the first entry of government land in what is now Jarvis Township. As others settled around him, they named the area Columbia. In 1819 a town was laid out and the name was changed to Troy.

As was the custom of the time, when John had reached "his majority," he had been given a slave. This slave (whose name was Steve) had not come to Illinois with John, but he remained devoted to him. In 1823 Steve set out to search for John. When he found him, John was an invalid. So Steve placed a cot at the foot of John's bed and became his nurse. John Jarvis died a few months later, and Steve died shortly thereafter. They are buried in the same plot in Troy.

John Jarvis and his second wife, Sarah Gilham Waddle, had had three sons: John G. Wesley, and Fletcher. Wesley married Mary (Polly) Kinder, and they had a son, James Nelson, who was born June 1, 1849. James Nelson married Elizabeth Donoho, and their son, Benjamin Wesley (B.W.), was born June 15, 1877.

B.W. married Lena Peters on June 22, 1904, and they had four children: Russell and Sarah (who died in infancy), Benjamin Edward, and James Wesley. B.W. owned and published *The Troy Call* for 50 years before poor health caused him to sell the weekly newspaper to Paul Simon. B.W. also enjoyed automobiles, and he owned one of the first in the area. When he made a long trip to Indianapolis, he was invited to drive his automobile around the race track (now known as the Indianapolis Motor Speedway). This was quite a thrill for him and was a story he loved to tell. Benjamin Wesley Jarvis died Oct. 13, 1948.

B.W. and Lena's son Benjamin Edward married Ellen Whiteside Kranz, and they had two children: Edward Lee (who died March 27, 1967) and Jane Ellen (who married Max Kaegy of Greenville; they have two sons, Kevin and Michael). Ellen died on Oct. 20, 1967, and Benjamin Edward died July 20, 1982. (His second wife, Anne Borst — whom he married in 1969 — died Dec. 14, 1999.)

B.W. and Lena's son James Wesley married Anita Schneider on Aug. 14, 1938. He died on Oct. 9, 1992. James and Anita had two sons, J.D. and John Michael. J.D. married Myriam Lozada and lives in Las Cruces, NM. John Michael married Valerie Lanter and lives in Troy with their two sons (James Wesley and Evan

Michael) in a home once owned by Mrs. Nan Baglin, a cousin to B.W. Jarvis. *Submitted by Anita S. Jarvis.*

BENJAMIN EDWARD JARVIS

BENJAMIN EDWARD JARVIS - Benjamin Edward Jarvis, second son of Ben W. and Lena (Peters) Jarvis was born Jan 19, 1908, and he passed away July 20, 1982.

Ben E. attended Troy Schools and Blackburn College at Carlinville. During his lifetime he was a member of both the Typographical Union and the Machinists Union. He worked at numerous companies in St. Louis and in Illinois, including several area newspapers. He began working at *The Troy Call* for his father Ben W. Jarvis. Ben E. worked many years at the *Edwardsville Intelligencer* and the *Belleville News-Democrat.*

Ben E. was married July 19, 1930, to Ellen W. Kranz of Troy. She was the oldest daughter of John and Jennie (Whiteside) Kranz of Troy. Ellen W. was born June 11, 1909. Ben E. and Ellen built their home at 231 East High Street in 1933, and resided there for their entire married life. They had two children. Jane-Ellen, married Max D. Kaegy, July 1960. They have two grown sons, Kevin and Michael, and one grand-daughter, Beth Ann, daughter of Kevin and Patti Kaegy. They all live on Route 4, Greenville. Edward Lee Jarvis, born Nov. 13, 1938, died March 27, 1967. Ed attended Troy area schools, Rankin Trade School, and he worked as a machinist at McDonnell-Douglas Corporation, St. Louis, for some years.

Ellen W. Jarvis died Oct. 20, 1967. In June, 1969, Ben E. married Mrs. Annie (Borst) Poston in Lemay, Missouri. Annie was raised in Troy and was the daughter of Marshall and Mattie (Riggin) Borst. The Riggins were also among the pioneer Madison County families. Annie B. Jarvis presently resides with her sister Martha Linenfelser in Collinsville, IL. *Submitted by Jane Ellen Kaegy.*

BENJAMIN WESLEY JARVIS

BENJAMIN WESLEY JARVIS - Ben W. Jarvis was born in Troy in the family home – presently 223 East High Street. He was the only suriving son of James Nelson and Elizabeth (Donoho) Jarvis. Ben W. was born June 15, 1877, and he died at home in Troy on Oct. 13, 1948. The family home was built by his father, J.N. Jarvis.

J.N.'s parents, Wesley and Mary Jarvis, donated the site for the Presbyterian Church in Troy and helped organize it. They also donated the land for the Troy City Cemetery.

B.W., as he was called, went to work at age 12 for his father, J.N. Jarvis. J.N. started the first newspaper in Troy, *The Commercial Bulletin*, in May, 1872. B.W. also worked in a coal mine and in the general store of August Droll. Mr. Droll later bought the *Troy Star* newspaper, and established the *Weekly Call.* B.W. worked for Mr. Droll, then went into business with A.W. Bounds, Mr. Bounds being 70 years old, and B.W. 20 years old. In March, 1899, B.W. bought *The Troy Call* from Mr. Droll. He updated the equipment and was in business with a weekly newspaper. B.W. attended Troy public school, and took a night business course at McCray-Dewey Academy.

B.W. was married June 22, 1904, to Lena Peters of Greenup, IL. After their marriage they took a trip to the St. Louis World's Fair. B.W. and Lena had four children: Russell Peters Jarvis (b. Aug. 2, 1905, d. March 23, 1910); Benjamin Edward Jarvis (b. Jan. 19, 1908, d. age 74, July 1982) resided his entire life in Troy just down the street from his parents' home; James Wesley Jarvis (b. Sept. 15, 1912, d. October 9, 1992); Sarah Elizabeth Jarvis (b. Oct. 18, 1914, d. Oct. 24, 1915).

B.W. was an avid outdoorsman and loved to fish and hunt. In 1931 they built a summer home that they called "Cozy Camp." It was near Prairie du Rocher on the Mississippi River. They vacationed there for many years. Lena had a lovely flower garden there, as she had in Troy. The summer home was built on the same floor plan as their home in Troy.

The last issue of *The Troy Call* was published Sept 26, 1947. B.W. died Oct 13, 1948. He had been an editor and publisher for 48 years. He was active for many years in the Southern Illinois Editorial Association, holding several offices.

Lena Jarvis died May 21, 1964. She and Ben and many of the family are buried on the Jarvis lot in Troy City Cemetery.

In February 1948, the newspaper was sold to Paul Simon. He changed the newspaper's name to *The Troy Tribune. Submitted by Jane Ellen Kaegy.*

JAMES WESLEY JARVIS

JAMES WESLEY JARVIS - James Wesley Jarvis was born Sept. 15, 1912, the 3rd son of Ben W. and Lena (Peters) Jarvis, at the family home in Troy. He died Oct. 9, 1992. He attended Troy area schools, and on Aug. 14, 1938, married Anita Schneider of rural St. Jacob. (She is the daughter of the late Emil Schneider and Esther (Schien) Schneider.) Jim and Anita celebrated their golden wedding anniversary in Troy in August 1988. They have resided their entire married life in their home in the eastern part of Troy.

Jim was employed by his father at the *Troy Call.* During World War II, he worked at Curtis-Wright Aircraft in St. Louis; then, at *Granite City Press* and *Collinsville Herald* newspapers. He retired from Shell Refinery after 27 years in November 1974.

Their sons are James David (J.D.), born June 9, 1950, and John Michael, born May 13, 1953. J.D. now resides in Las Cruces, New Mexico. J.D. is employed as a Communications teacher at New Mexico State University, and he is also manager of the P.B.S. station, both in Las Cruces.

John Michael Jarvis is married to Valerie Lanter of St. Jacob. They reside east of Troy and have two sons: James Wesley II, born Aug. 4, 1989, and Evan Michael, born March 7, 1992. John works in Troy for Flo-Systems and Valerie is a homemaker. *Submitted by Jane Ellen Kaegy.*

JOHN JARVIS

JOHN JARVIS *(for whom Jarvis Township was named)* - John Jarvis was born in Virginia on July 28, 1754. He and his family were early pioneers and fighters of the Revolutionary War and ventured westward. He married Mary Fields in 1780, and they had five children. She later died in Virginia. The one most familiar with the Illinois families is Field Jarvis (b. 1782.)

John and his family came to Indiana territory at an early date. He soon followed the footsteps of his brother, Franklin Jarvis, who settled in St. Clair County (Turkey Hill) with the William Scott family in 1797. Three families and others formed the beginning of the little Shiloh Methodist Church. John and Field soon ventured a little distance more.

John married a second time to Sarah Gillham Waddle in 1809. Sarah also was from an early pioneer family, William Gillham and Jane McDow. Sarah had four children, and John and Sarah became parents of five, one dying in infancy. Alexander, Thomas, Andrew and William Gillham, John G., Wesley, Lucinda and Fletcher Jarvis grew up together.

On September 10, 1814, John and Titus Gregg filed for land in Madison County. He entered 160 acres in northeast section nine, and began his homesteading. In 1819, John was given this land by President Monroe. Later, in 1821, he bought an additional 200 acres from Titus Gregg in section four. The town of Troy is mainly built on the entry land of Jarvis.

John kept a house of entertainment for the accommodations of the emigrant travel moving westward. In 1816, a hand mill was built. This was a big convenience for all early settlers. Rowland P. Allen wrote in 1817 into his diary about his journey to Illinois: "On Monday, December 22nd to our astonishment drove seventeen and a half miles this day. Put up at night at Troy with a Mr. Jarvis, a very fine man. In Troy we saw the first real marks of civilization since we left Shawneetown. Before retiring for the night, Mr. Jarvis gathered his family and the strangers around the family altar, read a chapter from the Bible, sang a hymn and offered up to the Almighty God a most feeling, excellent and appropriate prayer." Both John and Sarah were well liked and highly respected in the community.

Jarvis Township, at the close of 1818, had 21,713 acres. Of these, 11,325 acres had homesteaders or owners. A Pennsylvania German, Abraham Vanhooser, owned 1,040 acres. By 1818, the little settlement was called Columbia. This was the year Illinois became a state. In the year 1819, John Jarvis sold ten acres of land for $10 an acre to James Riggin and David Henderschott. Columbia became Troy, a name given by James Riggin.

In Virginia he had released a slave, Ben, who longed for his Master, as he grew older. Ben walked from Virginia to Illinois, found John Jarvis and was granted a request. The body of John Jarvis lies somewhere in Brookside (it is thought near Wayland Street and Barnsback – the grave hasn't been found) with the slave, Ben, at his feet.

After John died an invalid on October 29, 1823, Sara raised his children alone. John G., the eldest son, was born April 28, 1810. He married Ellen Brown, later Emily Brown. Nine children were born to this union. Most of this family lived around Troy. Sidney Jarvis was a Civil War veteran. Wesley Jarvis was born August 16, 1812. He married Mary Kinder, and they had five children. This family was raised in Troy and still has a lot of descendants here. William Jarvis served in the Civil War.

Lucinda Jarvis was born in November 1814 and married Thomas Bolton. Three children were born. One, John Bolton, was a leader in the Kansas early settlers. Lucinda married a second time to Henry P. Hayes. All of this family went to Kansas and eventually scattered all the way into Canada and throughout the states.

Fletcher Jarvis was born January 24, 1816. He married Ann Eliza Brown and had 13 children. The two eldest sons, Confederate Army soldiers, wagon-trained it to Washington State. Some of the others went to California, others to Missouri and Kansas. So, this whole Jarvis line has left early pioneer footsteps. Sarah lies in Troy City Cemetery. John Jarvis filed the following will: "I, John Jarvis of Madison County and state of Illinois, after solemnly recommending myself with all my concerns unto the hands of my Blessed Redeemer, do make my last will and testament in manner and form of following, viz. That after all my lawful debts are paid I do hereby bequeath unto my beloved wife, Sara Jarvis, the use of the farm whereon I now live, with all its appurtenances with all my household and kitchen furniture, farming utensils, ten head of cattle including her choice of two milk cows, ten head of sheep, one yoke of steers and cart; one horse called Ball and gray mare, with all my stock of hogs; during her life. I bequeath the land I purchased of Daniel Parkinson to be sold, and the money arising therefrom to be equally divided between my five first children and my daughter Lucindia Jarvis; and after the death of my wife, Sara, all the property shall be sold and equally divided among said six children, except the farm which I bequeath unto my three youngest sons, John, Wesley and Fletcher Jarvis. As Witness Whereof, I do hereby set my hand and seal this twenty-fifth of October 1823. John Jarvis (Seal) Signed, sealed and delivered Attest: Thomas Baker in presence of Moses Twist, Lloyd Belt." *From an article in a 1962 issue of the Troy Tribune written by Hilda Ebl.*

PAUL AND SUE JARVIS - Paul Gordon Jarvis was born 12-27-52, in St. Louis, MO, son of Ernest A. Jarvis of Putnam, CT, and Jane Voelker (Jarvis, Fisher) of Troy. Grandparents were maternal, Frank Voelker and Vera Dillingham (Voelker, Price) and paternal, John Baptiste Jarvis and Phoebe La Chance of St. Hyacinthe, Canada.

Paul had an older brother John Marshall, 4-30-51; sister Nancy Ellen, 5-22-54; and brother Alan Francis, 11-19-55.

Paul became Troy's first Eagle Scout in 1969 with Troop 38. He also started music under Darwin Schmitt in 1963, 5th grade, playing tuba, and he went on to be a lifelong musician, singer, songwriter, playing drums and 7 other instruments. Boulderdash, Medusa, Broken Arrow, High Horse and James R. are some of Paul's bands. He now heads St. Louis's 1st Zydeco Band, the "Zydeco Crawdaddys," with Paul on accordion.

Paul began taxidermy in 1966 and still has a shop in Troy. Hunting, fishing, history, reenacting, flintknapping, bow-building and turkey calling are some of Paul's interests. He became Illinois State Champion Turkey Caller in 1995 and placed 7 times in that contest.

On June 16, 1979, Paul wed Susan Ann Phelps from St. Louis at Bangert's Grove in

Paul and Sue Jarvis family
(l. to r.) Front: Paul, Sue, Abbie Lynn.
Back: Adam Franklin, Amanda Sue

Troy. Sue's Mom is Laverta Phelps (Obrian) of St. Louis and father (deceased) was Forrest Edger Phelps of St. Louis. Sue has 2 brothers: Dave, 4-26-1949, and Bob, 1-13-1953.

Paul and Sue's first born, Amanda Sue, 2-9-81, second, Adam Franklin, 10-20-83, and third, Abbie Lynn, 7-26-96, were all born at O.A. Hospital, Maryville.

Sue is an electrical worker at Basler Electric, Highland. Being a good wife and mother keeps her busy. Amanda finished Triad and graduated from Hickey Business School and now works at Stout Marketing in St. Louis.

As of this writing, Adam is a junior at Triad and plays football and the drums. He also enjoys hunting and fishing. He works at Troy Pizza Hut.

Abbie is going to pre-school at First Step in Troy and keeps Mom and Dad young.

Paul and Sue have been married for 22 years and have lived on Lower Marine Road for 23 years. Paul is a lifelong resident of Troy. *Submitted by Paul Jarvis.*

JONES FAMILY

Jones family, Feb. 18, 1912
(l. to r.) Gwendolyn, 8, Dannie, 15, Esther, 17, Florence, 19, Catherine, 21, Ritchie, 23

Jones family, early 1900s
(l. to r.) Front: Gwendolyn, Mary (Morgan) Jones
Back: Esther, Florence, Daniel, Catherine, Ritchie

VINCENT AND SYLVIA (ARTH) KAUHL
Sylvia Elaine Arth was born March 6, 1942, the daughter of Albert and Bernice Arth. Sylvia attended Formosa school for three years, then went to Troy Public Grade School and McCrayDewey High School. She graduated in 1959.

On September 2, 1961, she married Vincent Joseph Kauhl of Marine at St. Jerome Church in Troy.

Vincent helped his father-in-law, Albert Arth, farm most every evening after work and weekends, if needed, until Albert retired from farming. Albert and Vincent did many things together: hunting, going to the Indianapolis 500 races, etc. Vincent has many memories of the Arth farm. When Albert died, Vincent got everything ready for the sale by cleaning up all the equipment and going through everything and putting it on hay wagons, and cleaning all the buildings out. This took many months. Vincent submitted the name of Triad High School as the name for the new school district in 1958. He won the contest and a 35mm Kodak camera. Now that high school is a middle school and a new high school was built closer to Troy along Route 40.

Vincent and Sylvia are the parents of three sons: Brian, Bruce, and Barry.

Brian Michael Kauhl (b. June 18, 1962) married Jana Kay Bayer of Edwardsville. They reside in Edwardsville. Albert and Elizabeth Bayer are her parents.

Bruce Joseph Kauhl (b. October 20, 1963) died on October 20, 1963.

Barry Joseph Kauhl (b. November 24, 1965) married Shelley Ann Riffel of Highland. Her parents are Dennis and Cindy Riffel. They are the parents of two children, Taylor Jordan, b. August 18, 1993, and Brendan Joseph, born September 30, 1996. They reside in Highland. *Submitted by Sylvia Kauhl.*

ARNIM ADAM AND ESTHER (FRUTIGER) KECK - Arnim Adam Keck was born in Madison County, IL, on February 15, 1907. He was the sixth of seven children born to Martin Keck Jr. and Emma (Hobein) Keck of Troy. He married Esther Marie Caroline Frutiger, daughter of Louis and Lula (Noll) Frutiger of St Jacob, IL, on February 10, 1931, in Alhambra and then moved into the "Hagler Residence" in Troy. Esther was born February 16, 1908, in St Jacob. Esther and Arnim lived at 209 Bryn St. in Troy until Arnim's death on February 9, 1984, in Edwardsville. Esther continued living in their home until 1995 when she moved to the retirement home in Highland and then later to Faith

Arnim and Esther (Frutiger) Keck, 1981

Countryside Nursing Home in Highland. She died on July 27, 2000, at St Joseph's Hospital in Highland.

"Arni" worked at Mobil Oil Company in East St. Louis and also farmed on the family farms in Madison County. Esther was a homemaker. They were married for fifty-three years and were members of Friedens United Church of Christ in Troy. They were also members of Troy Senior Citizens and Lebanon Senior Citizens where they both enjoyed playing cards. They are both buried in Friedens Cemetery.

Ralph and Doris Keck family, 2000
(l. to r.) Front: Ralph and Doris (Paul) Keck
Back: Michael and Catherine Keck, Rodney, Brenda,
Taylor Capelle, Brian, Patrick, Teresa, Lauran May

Esther and Arnim had two children: Ralph Louis Keck (b.February 23,1932), currently of St. Jacob, married Doris Jean Paul, daughter of Frieda and George Paul of Worden, IL, on August 9,1958.

Gene Keck family, 2000
(l. to r.) Steven, Gene, Pamela (Beaver), Stacey
(Keck) Mank, Benjamin Mank

They have four children: Brian Joe Keck married Teresa Gehrs. Teresa has four children, Danielle, Nicole, Nathan, and Lauren May. They live in Edwardsville, IL. Rodney Louis Keck lives in Pacific, MO. Brenda Sue Keck lives in St. Jacob and has one daughter, Taylor Layne Capelle. Michael Paul Keck married Catherine Johnson. They live near Edwardsville and have two children, Patrick Reno and Kathleen Marie Keck.

Gene Arnim Keck (b. January 15,1947), currently of Lebanon, IN, married Pamela Gayle Beaver, daughter of Lyda and Howard Beaver of O'Fallon, IL, on August 2, 1969. They have two children: Stacey Lynn Keck married Benjamin Aaron Mank and lives in Indianapolis and Steven William Wesley Keck lives in Highland, IN. *Submitted by Pamela Keck and Doris Keck.*

LAURINA (SLIVA) AND LOUIS HENRY KECK - Louis Henry Keck was the third of seven children born to Martin Jr. and Emma (Hobein) Keck of Troy, IL. He was born April 30,1900, and died August 18, 1966, at home in Troy.

He married Laurina Josephine Sliva on February 8, 1921, in Edwardsville, IL. She was the daughter of Frank and Josephine (Sedlacek) Sliva. Laurina was born in Blackjack, IL, on June 13, 1902, and died in Troy on August 18, 1953. Laurina's brother was Robert Sliva who was married to Edna Keck, Louis's sister. He then married Lauretta Schildknecht Wick (1910-1977) on June 17,1957. She had two sons, Dennis and Ronald Wick. She was the daughter of Phillip and Jenny (Sedlacek) Schildknecht. Louis was a farmer in his younger years and then became the owner and operator of Keck's Tavern in Troy. Louis' home was at 809 S. Main St. in Troy.

Lauretta continued operating the tavern after Louis' death. Louis and his wives were members of the Friedens United Church of Christ in Troy. Louis and Laurina are buried in Friedens Cemetery in Troy. Lauretta is buried in College Hill Cemetery, Lebanon. Laurina and Louis Keck had two children: Dorothy Keck married Gustiv Edward Suter (1920-1996) on September 18, 1940, and had one child, Lee.

Lee Alan Suter married Terri Warner March 29, 1974, in Troy. Terri was the daughter of Margie (Gaines) and Richard Warner. Lee and Terri had two children, Tobey and Corey.

Ethel Mae Keck was born March 28,1923, in Madison County, IL and died May 28, 2000. She married Eldon Herbert Loehring on September 19, 1942, in Troy. Eldon was born in Caseyville, IL, on January 6, 1919, and died on January 25, 2000. He was the son of Mary (Ohlendorf) and William Loehring. Ethel and Eldon are buried in Summerfield Cemetery. They had three children: Donald, Wayne, and Roy.

Donald Lee Loehring was born January 14,1947, in Highland. He married Lyda Ruth Fleehart on June 22, 1969, in Lebanon, IL. Lyda was the daughter of Fred and Cornelia (Zeeb) Fleehart. They currently live in Kansas City, MO. Donald and Lyda had three children: Donya Leigh, Sonja Re' and Trent Alan. Donja Loehring, married David Crichlow and has a daughter, Brianna Nicole. Sonja Loehring, married Earl Lanier and has three children: Corrin, Ethan and Sierra. Trent Loehring married Jennifer Marie Brown.

Wayne Edward Loehring was born November 2, 1950, in Madison County and married Claudia Ann Chapple. Wayne and Claudia had two children, Megan Elizabeth and Brian Todd Loehring who married Tonya Bohnensteihl on October 19, 1996, in Lebanon, IL.

Roy Louis Loehring was born on October 26, 1956, in Highland, IL. He married Patricia Ann McCormick on July 3, 1982, in O'Fallon, IL. Patricia was the daughter of George and Mayme (Hogee) McCormick. Roy and Patricia had three children, Scott, Misty and Jeffrey Loehring. Misty has three children: Leann Welsh, Cody Lee Burcham and Autumn Stasberg. Misty is married to Dave Stasberg. *Submitted by Pamela Keck and Lyda Loehring.*

LOUIS AND LAURINA KECK/GUS AND DOROTHY SUTER/ELDON AND ETHEL LOEHRING - Louis and Laurina (Sliva) Keck were life-long residents of Troy. Louis, better known as "Louie," was born on April 30, 1900, in O'Fallon, IL, the son of Martin Jr. and Emma (Hobein) Keck. Louie was one of seven children (four sisters and two brothers). He married Laurina Sliva on February 8, 1921.

Louie was a farmer for most of his adult life while Laurina was a homemaker who frequently tended bar part-time at several local taverns along Illinois State Route 40 between St. Jacob and Troy. Louie and Laurina had two children, Dorothy (Suter), born September 25, 1921, and Ethel (Loehring) born March 28, 1923. On September 8, 1945, unable to care for his farm anymore, Louie purchased a tavern at the intersection of Illinois State Route 40 and South Main Street in Troy. "Keck's Tavern" quickly became a favorite watering hole for the local population and for those visitors traveling along busy Route 40 between St. Louis and Indiana.

In her daily journal, written between the years 1923-1953, Laurina recorded numerous social events of local interest held at the tavern. Fish, coon, and rabbit fries were common as was the making of turtle mulligan stew. Euchre and pinochle card games were daily occurrences amongst the locals who stopped by to share a drink or farmers who had just completed their stop at the elevator nearby. She faithfully recorded significant weather-related events, traffic accidents, marriages, births, and deaths. Laurina died of cancer on August 18,1953.

Louie married Lauretta (Schildknecht) Wick of O'Fallon on June 17, 1957. They continued to operate the tavern and Lauretta expanded the business to include food and sandwich service. Louie died August 18, 1966, but Lauretta continued to operate Keck's Tavern until her death in 1975. Keck's tavern was a local landmark for 30 years.

Dorothy Keck married Gustiv Suter on September 18, 1940. She and Gus had one child, Lee Alan, who was born on September 21, 1950. Dorothy was a homemaker while Gus became a heavy machine operator. Both Gus and Lee were Troy Volunteer Firemen serving faithfully for over 20 years each. Gus died on January 17, 1996.

Ethel Keck married Eldon Loehring on September 19, 1942. They were married by Reverend Mornhinweg in the Evangelical & Reformed Church parsonage at 2 p.m. in the afternoon. During the ceremony, the cuckoo clock struck twice, and the rest they say, is history.

Ethel and Eldon had three sons. Donald Lee, born on January 14, 1947, is married and currently resides in Kansas City, MO. Wayne Edward, born

Keck family, circa 1940s
(l. to r.) Front: Louis and Laurina
Back: Dorothy (Keck) Suter, Eldon Loehring,
Ethel (Keck) Loehring, Gus Suter

November 2, 1950, is married and currently resides in Troy. Roy Louis, born October 26, 1956, is married and currently lives in O'Fallon, IL.

Eldon Loehring died January 21, 2000, while Ethel passed away on May 28, 2000, after a twelve year battle with cancer. *Submitted by Wayne Loehring.*

IRMA E. (SCHNEIDER) AND EDWIN MARTIN KECK -

Edwin Martin Keck was born on December 25,1908 or 1909, to Emma H. (Hobein) and Martin Keck, Jr. of Troy. He was the youngest of seven children. He married Irma E. Schneider on April 9,1930, in Troy. She was born on November 28,1908, in Highland, IL, and died on February 25,1985. Edwin died an August 7, 1980. Edwin and Irma are buried in Keystone Cemetery, St. Jacob, IL.

They had two children, Carl Robert and Glenn Edward.

Glenn Edward Keck (January 17, 1931 -March 15, 1949) is buried in Keystone Cemetery, St. Jacob, IL.

Carl Robert Keck married Jeanette Florence Swengross on December 7, 1952. They currently live in the Lebanon, IL, area. They had four children:

1. Carl Robert Keck Jr. (Bob) was married first to Barbara Ann Leman. They had a daughter, Calesta Ann Keck who lives in Phoenix, AZ. Carl is currently married to Rose Ann Todd.

2. Kathleen Marie Keck was previously married to Richard Frisby and they had two sons, Jeremiah and Joshua Frisby. Kathleen Keck lives in Ft. Collins, CO.

3. Michael Edwin Keck was married to Connie Roedle. They had two sons, Michael Edwin, Jr. and Andrew Thomas Keck who live in the Edwardsville, IL, area. He is currently married to Guene LyBerger.

4. Randy George Keck was married to Cindy Stevens. They had two children, Jacob Martin and Morgan Elise Keck and live in the Frogtown and Breese area. *Submitted by Pamela Keck and Jeanette Keck.*

MARTIN AND EMMA H. (HOBEIN) KECK

Martin Keck Jr. was born May 29, 1866 or 1867, in the area known as Prairie Ridge, O'Fallon Township, St. Clair County, Illinois. He was the sixth of the eleven or twelve children born to Martin Keck Sr. and Eva (Remelius) Keck of O'Fallon. Martin Keck Sr. was born November 30, 1831, and died February 19, 1906, in

Children of Emma and Martin Keck, Jr. circa 1950s Front: Edna Sliva, Louise Porter, Susan Diepholz, Evelyn Fehmel. Back: Louis, Edwin, Arnim

O'Fallon. Martin Keck Sr. was the fifth of seven children born to Abraham and Appolonia (Schneider) Keck. They were from the Darmstadt, Rhein Pfalz, area of Germany and emigrated to the USA in 1846. Eva (Remelius) Keck's parents, Jacob and Appolonia or Ablana (Storck) Remelius or Rummelius were also German immigrants who settled in the O'Fallon area. Martin Sr. and Eva (Remelius) Keck are both buried in the Keck-Remelius Cemetery near O'Fallon.

Martin Keck Jr. married Emma H. Hobein on February 20, 1894. She was one of the seven children born to William and Elizabeth or Wilhelmina (Steinborn) Hobein of O'Fallon. They were immigrants from Hanover, Germany. Emma was born August 10, 1870, in St. Clair County, Illinois. Emma and Martin Jr. moved to the Troy area shortly after their marriage. They lived and farmed two miles east of Troy for thirty-four years. He was the former director of the Troy State Bank and an official of the Troy Lumber Company. At one time he operated a sawmill and a threshing business near Troy. He was a rural school director of the Gilead School for thirty years and served several terms on the Troy Township School Board. They moved to the town of Troy in 1928. Martin died on February 10, 1934, in Troy. Emma was a homemaker. She died on December 13,1955, at St Joseph's Hospital in Highland, Illinois. Martin and Emma were active members of Friedens Evangelical and Reformed Church. They are both buried in the Friedens Cemetery in Troy.

Emma and Martin Keck had seven children – Louise Elizabeth (Keck) Porter, Susan Louisa (Keck) Diepholz, Louis Henry Keck, Edna L. (Keck) Sliva, (Eve) Emma (Keck) Fehmel, Arnim Adam Keck and Edwin Martin Keck (see related articles). *Submitted by Pamela Keck and Lyda Loehring.*

GEORGE HERMAN AND KATHERINE (MCENANEY) KESSEL -

George Herman Kessel was born February 26, 1859, in Massachusetts. On October 10, 1879, he married Katherine McEnaney who was born March 14, 1855, in Mongahan, Ireland. They had six sons – George, Henry, Edward, Walter, Frederick and Louis. George died November 15, 1912, and Katherine died December 17, 1919, in New York.

George played a cornet in John Philip Sousa's band. Katherine played the violin and was a seamstress for the Metropolitan Opera in New York. Their musical talents carried forth to the next generation as their son Henry played piano for silent moves; when talkies came, he lost his job and was hired as a pianist by Igor

Stravinsky, the Russian composer. Sons Louis, who also played piano, and George each had dance bands.

Louis Kessel was born February 3, 1890, in New Haven, CT. He married Almeda Orben February 14, 1914, in New York. Almeda was born September 28, 1896, in Port Jervis, NY, and died May 15, 1938. In 1937 they moved to Alton, IL, from Philadelphia where he was a superintendent for Union Tank Car; he had worked 42 years on the railroad. In 1938 he moved to Edwardsville. Louis and Almeda had 11 children: Edith born October 10, 1915, in New York and died September 17, 1975, in California; Dorothy born April 22, 1917, in New York, and died February 14, 1973, in Illinois; Floyd born October 22, 1918, in Pennsylvania and died October 20, 1982, in California; Louis born September 24, 1920, in Pennsylvania and died December 6, 1964, in Illinois; Albert born December 17, 1921, in Pennsylvania and died June 21, 1987, in Pennsylvania; Eleanor born September 20, 1923, in Pennsylvania and died August 20, 1926; Lillian born July 26, 1925, in Pennsylvania; George born January 17, 1928, in Pennsylvania; John born July 22, 1930, and died October 23, 1992, in Georgia; Charles born February 17, 1932, in Pennsylvania and died November 19, 1953; and William, the youngest, was born November 16, 1934, in Pennsylvania. Louis married a second time to Catherine Reber Richard of Alton on November 5, 1940.

Lillian Kessel married H. Bensa August 7, 1944, in Edwardsville, IL. He was born August 30, 1924, and died November 1, 1980; he worked for the railroad for 36 years. Lillian was a member of Eden Church in Edwardsville, sang in Friedens Choir, charter member and past vice president of the Madison County Genealogy Society, past president of Shut-Ins, past president of American Legion Aux. 199 in Edwardsville, past president and board member of the Senior Citizens, Home Extension, Moose Lodge in Edwardsville, Noble Grand Rebecca's Troy Pride of the West Lodge 544 and director of Merry Makers Band for 22 years in Edwardsville. In 1992 she met Alvin Frey with whom she now shares a home.

The Bensas had three children. Marie born February 27, 1947, in Alton, IL, married Richard Giebe who died September 2, 1971. Their children were Dawn, Diane and Debra. Marie married Roger Dubach and had sons Robert and Roger.

Martin Keck, Jr. family before 1934 (l. to r.) Front: Emma (Hobein), Martin, Jr. Back: Louisa Porter, Edna Sliva, Arnim, Edwin, Louis, Evelyn Fehmel, Susan Diepholz

Kessel brothers, 1902 (l. to r.) Front: Louis, George, Frederick. Back: Walter, Henry, Edward

Sharon was born July 12, 1949, in Highland. She married Michael Flaugher May 25, 1984. Their children are Tara, born June 22 1985, and Christopher, born November 17, 1987.

Michael, born March 13, 1957, in Highland, married Michele Fencel on August 28, 1979. Their children are Cole, born March 23, 1982, and Brooke, born August 23, 1992. *Submitted by Lillian Bensa and written by Reba Mathis.*

WILBUR EMERY KIMBERLIN - Wilbur Emery "Kimmy" Kimberlin was born on August 5, 1912, and died on February 27, 1997. His parents were Emery Charles and Mary (Young) Kimberlin of Troy. Kimmy's father, Emery Charles, was one of four children born to Charles and Elizabeth (Maurer) Kimberlin of Troy. Emery's siblings were George, Arthur and Anna. Kimmy's mother, Mary, was one of four children of Ephriam and Sarah Jane (Ford) Young of Troy. Mary's siblings were Earl, James, and Bertha Young.

Evelyn (Elliott) and Kimmy (Wilbur) Kimberlin, 1947

Kimmy was raised in Troy with his sister Ardath and brother Dale. He retired from W.H. Dyer in St. Louis, MO. Kimmy married Evelyn Lucille Elliott (see Roy Daniel Elliott, Sr.) on August 8, 1934. They had three children: John Emery (b. August 31, 1939), Jay Daniel (b. August 15, 1949) and Carla Jane (b. April 16, 1952).

John and his wife, Mary (Pepe), live in CT. They have one daughter, Jennifer (b. Feb. 22, 1972), who is married to Andrew Lambeth and lives in Alexandria, VA.

Jay and his wife, Doris, live in Troy. Jay has one son, Jacob (b. Oct.9, 1979), who lives in Texas and has two children.

Carla and her husband, Robert D. Arnold, of Indianapolis, IN, were married in April of 1991. *Submitted by Evelyn Elliott Kimberlin and Kae Elliott Schmitt.*

KINDER FAMILY - The Kinder family probably came from Germany and settled first in Pennsylvania before the Revolutionary War. After the war they settled in Kentucky where Jacob Kinder was killed by the Indians. His son, George, came to Illinois in 1812 with his wife Isabella Roseberry and children. The children rode horseback and George and Isabella walked, herding their livestock before them. They settled on a section of ground located near present day Anderson Hospital.

One of their sons, Captain Jacob J. Kinder built the "Kinder House" about the time of the Civil War, which still stands.

*Kinder children
(l. to r.) Nelson Roy, Mary Samuella, Edna Alice, Mattie Posey, Lester Morrison*

George and Isabella's sixth child, Nathaniel Buckmaster Kinder, married Phoebe Ann Morrison. Her father was from Scotland. Nathaniel's fifth child, Nelson Montgomery Kinder, married Catherine Maud Shaffer on 3/29/1877.

Nelson and Catherine's children were Phoebe Ann who married James Osburn; children were Edith and Martha. The second child was Nelson Roy who married Bertha Dorsey. The third child, Lester Morrison, (nicknamed "Buck" because he resembled his grandfather Buckmaster), married Catherine May Jones; children were Lester Morrison Jr. and Mary Catherine. Fourth child was Mattie Posey who married Franklin Reaves. Fifth child was Mary Samuella who married Clarence Anderson; children were Phoebe, Merlin, Catherine, Robert, Laura, Amy, George, and Lester. The sixth child was Edna who married Edgar Absher; children were Frank and Mary Lou.

The Kinder family from George and Isabella to the present generation are buried at Oaklawn Cemetery in Glen Carbon. *Submitted by Mary Catherine Gerstenecker.*

ROGER PAUL AND KAREN "COOKIE" LESLIE (ADELHARDT) KING - Roger was born to Charles "Paulie" and Agnes (Davis) King on September 24, 1942. Until he was eight years old, the family resided on a farm in rural Marine, IL, then moved into Marine proper. Cookie was born to Lester and Ruby (Kirsch) Adelhardt on September 28, 1943. She grew up in Troy, first in their home on Windy Hill, then on Staunton Road.

Roger and Cookie met in 1957 at what was then McCray-Dewey High School. They dated until April 20, 1963, when they were married at Friedens United Church of Christ in Troy. Their first child, Michelle "Shelly," was born the following March 11, 1964. Three more children followed: Jeffrey, born October 9, 1966; Melinda "Mindy," born June 7, 1970; and James, born April 5, 1972.

Roger was a hard-working young man. When he was just 13 years old, he landed his first job.

After graduating from Triad High School in 1960, as a member of the first graduating class from the newly formed Triad District, he attended and graduated from Rankin Technical School in St. Louis, MO. Roger worked as a draftsman for several architectural/engineering firms in St. Louis. Then, at the age of 26, he opted for a career change and began working

with the Louisville Nashville Railroad in E. St. Louis, IL, working his way up from switchman to brakeman, to conductor, to fireman and eventually engineer. Roger has proven that railroading is in his blood. In 1988 after 16 years of service, Roger was elected to office with the Brotherhood of Locomotive Engineers.

He has served the union in several different capacities, including Vice General Chairman. Roger has volunteered as Cub Scout Leader and Khoury League Coach, and has served on a board at Friedens United Church of Christ.

Cookie started her career in her father's, Les Adelhardt, grocery store. After graduating from Triad High School in 1961, she attended Marketing Training Institute in St. Louis, MO. She worked as a cashier at Adelhardt's IGA until her first child was born. She dedicated the next years to full-time parenting of her four children. Cookie volunteered as a Girl Scout Leader, served as Vice President of the Triad Band Boosters, and was one of the founders of the Triad Pom-Pon Moms' Booster Club for the Triad High School Pom-Pon Squad. She was voted Triad Band's Volunteer of the year in 1982. When Cookie returned to work, she chose the banking industry. She has been a financial friend to Troy residents through many bank acquisitions and mergers for the past 15 years.

Roger and Cookie continue to reside in Troy in the same house in which they raised all their children. As grandparents to their six grandchildren, Danica and Hattie (Shelly's children), Amy, Matthew and Casper (Jeff's children), Gabriel (Jim's son), and Mindy's soon to arrive seventh grandchild in February 2002, they are looking forward to retiring, traveling, and spending time enjoying their growing family. *Submitted by Roger King.*

ARMIN AND HELEN (NIX) KIRSCH - The sixth child of John and Emma (Bauer) Kirsch, Armin Andrew Kirsch, (b. 07/11/1908, d. 04/25/1985) was a plumber. He married Helen Mar-

*Wedding photo, March 12, 1939
Armin and Helen (Nix) Kirsch
with flower girl Jan (Kirsch) Albertina.*

garet Nix (b. 01/25/1914, d. 07/25/1994). They had two children: 1. Judy (Kirsch) Epperson, special education teacher, married John Epperson, farmer, three children — Jean, Jason and Julie, and one grandchild; 2. Dale Kirsch (b. 03/07/1947), U.S. Navy veteran, businessman. *Submitted by Janet Albertina.*

GUSTAV KIRSCH - Johannes Kirsch (1827-1911) was born in Bavaria, and moved

Wedding photo, 1896
Gustav and Emma Kirsch

to the Alsace Lorraine region of France as an adult. While in Germany, he made his living as a cooper (barrel maker). He moved to America and went to St. Louis where he met Louise Roth (1835-1913). They married in the mid 1850s and moved to Troy and settled on land just south of Troy, off the present Troy-O'Fallon Road. They had eight children: Gustav, Martin, William, Henry, Jacob, John, Barbara (Langenwalter) and Louis (who died as a teenager).

Gustav Kirsch (1868-1932) married Emma Lueke (1874-1947) of Missouri on May 3, 1896, in the Evangelical church (no longer in existence) in Blackjack, south of Troy. Emma had two half brothers and two half sisters: Henry; Edward (married Genevieve Harrison of Troy, has one son Jack); Sophie; and Mary Schotemeier Voelker (married Adam Voelker of Troy), has two sons Robert and Roger). Henry, Sophie, and Mary were life-long residents of Troy. Edward and Genevieve moved to Belleville. Gustav and Emma farmed the ground that is now in and around the intersection of Troy-O'Fallon Road and the Conrail railroad tracks, 2 miles south of Troy. They had eight children: Elmer, Olinda, Augusta (died at the age of 2), Clara, Ruby, and three children who were stillborn.

Elmer Kirsch (1897-1966) married Edna Weinacht of Lebanon in 1931. They had one son Donnie who married Delores Willmann of Highland in 1960. They have two children, Cory and Gina Olinda Kirsch (1901-1994). Olinda married Francisco Galli (1899-1985) of Modena, Italy, in 1934. They had one daughter, Nelda, who married Harry Mussman of East St. Louis in 1963.

Augusta Kirsch (1904-1906) died at age two of whooping cough.

Clara Kirsch (1906-1991) was a life-long resident of Troy. She taught school for 43 years beginning in Blackjack and Formosa country schools and then on to the Troy Public School.

Ruby Kirsch (1912-1994) married Lester Adelhardt (1913-1980) of Troy on June 2, 1933. Just after marriage they moved to Edwardsville for a short time and then moved back to Troy. They lived in several homes before settling on Staunton Road where they raised three children: Karen (Cookie), Terry (Bud), and Sherry. Cookie married Roger King of Marine in 1963, and they have 4 children: Michelle, Jeffery, Melinda, and James. Bud married Tami Souther of Springfield in 1967, and they have two children, Chad and Krista. Sherry married Rick Smith of Troy, and they have three children, Luke, Jennie, and Jacob. *Submitted by Sherry Smith.*

JOHN AND EMMA (BAUER) KIRSCH - The second child of Johannes and Louisa (Roth) Kirsch, John Kirsch, married Emma Salome Bauer.

Wedding photo of John and
Emma S. (Bauer) Kirsch

(l. to r.) Walter C. Kirsch, Ella (Kirsch) Best, John
Gustav Kirsch, Armin Andrew Kirsch

They had seven children: 1) Arthur F. (b. 1890, d. 10/15/1918), served in WW I; 2) Ella Barbara (b. 01/27/1893, d. 08/20/1973), spouse Clarence Best (b. 01/13/1894, d. 01/07/1969), who served in WW I, worked at the Stock Yards in E. St. Louis, and loved to sing; 3) Ernst Jacob (b. 11/10/1894, d. 09/07/1925), served in WW I; 4) Walter Christian (b. 01/30/1899, d. 08/18/1967), sheet metal worker for Gifford & Co. in St. Louis and an accordion player; 5) John Gustav (b. 08/04/1905, d. 03/05/1973); 6) Armin Andrew Kirsch (b. 07/11/1908, d. 04/25/1985); and 7) Ruth Josephine Kirsch (b. 04/29/1912, d. 09/06/1913). *Submitted by Jan Albertina.*

JOHN GUSTAV AND IOLA (FULTON) KIRSCH - The fifth child of John and Emma

Kirsch family, circa 1960
(l. to r.) Front: Iola (Fulton)
Kirsch, John G. Kirsch.
Back: Janet R. (Kirsch)
Albertina, John W. Kirsch.

Kirsch, John Gustav married Iola Frances Fulton (b. 08/24/1910). He was a sheet metal worker for Gifford & Co. in St. Louis. Iola worked at the Troy Locker Plant for 5 1/2 years, then became a beautician and operated Kirsch's Beauty Shop in her home for 22 years. They had two children: Janet Ruth and John Walter. *Submitted by Janet Albertina.*

JOHN AND SUE (KOONCE) KIRSCH - The second child of John Gustav and Iola (Fulton) Kirsch was John Walter Kirsch (b. 03/03/1938).

John and Sue (Koonce) Kirsch, 2000.

He served in the U.S. Army, operated John's Auto Repair in the old Schmitt Chevrolet building on Market St. in Troy from 1963-1967 and Kirsch Heating and Air Conditioning at 111 S. Main Street in Troy from 1974-1986, and retired as an insurance claims analyst.

John Kevin Kirsch family, circa 2000
(l. to r.) Amanda, Lana, John Kevin, John Andrew

He married on August 17, 1957, G. Sue Koonce (b. 09/30/38). She retired as a supervisor of loss report unit for an insurance company. They had two children: 1. John Kevin Kirsch (b. 01/11/1959), instrument calibration inspec-

Larry Hicks family, 1999
Kelli Nicole, Pamela Kay (Kirsch), Larry

tor, married Lana Sue Gusewelle (b. 09/20/59), vending company delivery driver, two children – Amanda Sue Kirsch (b. 12/31/1983), student, and John Andrew Kirsch (b. 06/08/1987) student; 2. Pamela Kay Kirsch Hicks (b. 09/21/1964), attorney, married Larry Hicks (b. 11/02/1951), landscaping business, one child — Kelli Nicole Hicks (b. 11/30/1995), student. *Submitted by Janet Albertina.*

JOHANNES KIRSCH - Johannes Kirsch was born September 27, 1827, in King of Prussia, Germany. In 1854, he came to the U.S. via a port in New Orleans, moved to the north, and settled in Troy, IL, where he purchased property and began farming. On February 14, 1857, he married Louisa Roth who was born in Hanover, Germany, on August 20, 1835. Both died in Troy: Johannes, on 09/24/1911; Louisa, on 12/26/1913.

Johannes and Louis (Roth) Kirsch family, before 1900

Together they had eight children: 1) Martin (b.1857, d. 1934), spouse Elizabeth Bernhardt; 2) John (b. 04/22/1860 in Troy, d. 07/14/1939 in Collinsville), spouse Emma Salomi Bauer (b. 04/29/1869 in Troy, d. 09/26/1920 in St. Louis, MO), who was the daughter of Ferdinand (b. 1867, d.1947) and Mary Huber Bauer (b. 08/15/1843, d. 06/10/1926); 3) William J. (b. 1863 in Troy, d. 07/1939 in Troy), spouses Lizzie Langenwalter (b. 1872, d. 1921) and Susan Keck; 4) Barbara (b. 1866, d. ?), spouse Jacob Langenwalter; 5) Gustav L. (b. 1868, d. 1932), spouse Emma L. Schotemeyer (b. 1874, d. 1947); 6) Louisa S. (b. 1874, d. 1887); 7) Jacob (b. 10/06/1876, d. 12/1960), spouses Maria Deimling (b. 1879, d. 1960) and Emma Herbst; 8) Henry Kirsch (b. ?, d. ?). *Submitted by Jan Albertina.*

WILHELM KLEIMEIER - Wilhelm Kleimeier was born on January 12, 1831, and died August 13, 1905. He married Maria Klausing, born October 21, 1832, and died December 23, 1891. Both are buried in the Lutheran Cemetery, Troy. Mr. Kleimeier was one of the men who started St. Paul Lutheran Church and school in 1867.

Mr. Kleimeier was a farmer. The brick house on Schmalz Road is still standing in good shape and is occupied. It is over one hundred years old.

Wilhelm and Maria had eight children, 3 boys and 5 girls. Four girls married and lived in Troy. They were Mary Beutel, Sophia Peters, Elizabeth (Lizzie) Diepholz, Katherine (Katy) Sims, and Hannah Rubin (St. Louis). All are deceased.

Two boys married and lived in St. Louis; one boy married and lived in Wentzville, MO.

Home of Wilhelm Kleimeier family on Schmalz Road, 1970.

The offspring of this family can be traced living in seven states. Sophia Keimeier Peters is the mother of Dale H. Peters. *Submitted by Dale H. Peters.*

JOHANN KLEIN - Johann, b 12 Feb. 1795, in Dornbach, Rheinland Pfalz, Germany, died in 1873/4 in Madison Co., on 2 Aug. 1829, in Gehrweiler, Rheinland Pfalz, married Henrietta Frey (b. 1803 in Gehrweiler, Rheinland Pfalz, d. 1883 in Madison Co.) and had 5 children, who came from Germany to southern Illinois, settling in Troy. Volentine (b. 6 Oct. 1835) and Parmelia Etheridge (b. 11 Dec. 1834) were married in Greenville 30 Sept. 1860, and eventually took over his father's farm and lived in Troy. Friedericke (b. 6 Oct. 1837, d. 10 Apr. 1920) married Gottfreed Heinrich on 17 Feb. 1856, then later married Peter Geibel and settled in Belleville, IL. Elizabeth (b. 20 Mar. 1840) married John Kelling/Kuehling on 29 Jan. 1860, and settled in Smith County, Kansas.

Johann (b. 23 Apr. 1843, d. 28 Nov. 1917) married Verena Kuehling on 4 June 1868, and settled in Belleville. Jacob (b. 28 Oct. 1845, d. 29 Mar. 1924) married Elizabeth Gabriel on 23 Sept. 1872, lived in Pocahontas then settled in Baden Baden/Millersburg, now called East Pierron, IL.

Johann Klein's ancestors had lived in the Rhineland Pfalz area of Germany for many generations, mostly as shepherds, and sometimes as swineherders, migrating slowly from village to village with their animals. Johann Klein had been living in the town of Rockenhausen for many years as a swineherder supplying the pork for sausages, etc., but with living conditions steadily deteriorating after the 1848 Revolution, something had to be done. Their hometown had heard much in letters from others who had emigrated to southern Illinois not far from the Mississippi.

They had written about the great personal freedoms, economic conditions and opportunities presented there. Johann decided that the future for his family would be best in America. They would, over time, sell their house and animals and proceed overland 350 miles in about 10 days to La Havre, France, for the boat trip.

They set sail in the fall of 1853 on the ship *European*, with Robert C. Turner as Captain, with a passenger list of 365 along with 50 gallons of cherry brandy in bottles and 55 gallons of wine. The ship followed the trade wind route down the north west coast of Africa then west across the Atlantic to the Caribbean then northwest into the Gulf of Mexico, taking about 6 weeks for the journey. Johann, Henrietta (Frey) his wife, and 5 children, Volentine,

Friedericke, Elizabeth, Johann, and Jacob landed at the port of New Orleans on 9 December 1853.

After a nine day steam paddle-wheeler boat trip up the Mississippi River, the family arrived in the St. Louis area. They spent several years around Greenville, Marine, St. Jacob, and Troy, IL, since many other German families from their homeland area had gotten their start there. Johann then bought acreage in rural Troy near the East Fork of Silver Creek. Many descendants of this family are in the area yet. *Submitted by Richard L. Cline.*

BEATRICE MARIE (ARTH) KLEM Beatrice Marie (Arth) Klem (b. March 14, 1918) married William Edward Klem (b. December 2, 1921) on December 31,1941. Beatrice attended McCray-Dewey High School and then finished her high school years at St. Theresa Academy in Belleville. She also went to Rubicam Secretarial School in St. Louis, MO. The couple had two children, Constance Marie and Mary Kim; four grandchildren and five great-grandchildren.

William served in the U.S. Navy, worked for the Veterans Administration, and worked with his wife in the Dairy Queen on Vandalia Street in Collinsville. They became sole owners of the Dairy Queen later on. Beatrice worked for Dr. Joedieckie also. She inherited 31 acres adjoining Marguerite's (her sister) along US Hwy 40.

Constance Marie (Klem) Schneider, Starzyk (b. October 11, 1944) married Robert George Schneider (now deceased). They were the parents of Scott Robert Schneider, b. September 2, 1962, and d. August 2001. He had one daughter, Christine Marie (Schneider) Prince (b. February 13, 1966). She has two children, Joshua Cole (b. October 22, 1991) and Kenneth Kreiger (b. March 29, 1999).

Stacey Lee (Schneider) Scheib (b. March 27, 1969) has two children, Neil Riley and Jacob Travis.

Beatrice's daughter Mary Kim (Klem) Ingle (b. March 27, 1952) married Tim Ingle and together they had Ashley Marie Ingle (b. April 1, 1985). *Submitted by Sylvia Kauhl.*

EUGENE KLENKE - Eugene Harold Klenke was born December 19, 1951, at St. Joseph's Hospital in Highland, to Harold and Beulah (Meier) Klenke. He is the second of five children. He attended St. Paul's Lutheran School and graduated in 1970 from Triad High School. He was active in FFA and ran cross country. In 1972, he married Lois Keilbach of rural Highland. They lived for seven years in Highland and then returned to Troy in 1982

(l. to r.) Gene, Henry, Lois & Denise Klenke

231

to operate the family farm. Gene farms around one thousand acres, mostly rented farmland. His crops include, hay, corn, soybeans and wheat. He also has 35 head of Simmental beef cattle. Gene has two children, Denise Willis, born October 17, 1973, and Henry Klenke, born February 20, 1978.

Both children graduated from Triad High School. Denise currently lives in Troy. She graduated from the University of Illinois with a degree in animal science. Henry is currently a United States Marine stationed at Camp Pendleton in California. Gene was named Madison County Outstanding Young Farmer by the Madison County Farm Bureau in 1981 and the family was named Great American Family by the Madison County Association for Family and Community Education in 1995. Gene also served on the Young Farmer's Committee. He is currently serving as a director for the Hamel Cooperative Grain Elevator Board. He is also a member of Friedens United Church of Christ, having served as usher and youth leader, and worked at chicken and sausage suppers. Lois is a Sunday School teacher at Friedens. He also belonged to 4-H and exhibited animals for many years at the Madison County Fair, dairy cattle, swine, and beef cattle. He is an avid hunter and enjoys watching sports. *Submitted by Lois Klenke.*

HAROLD ROBERT KLENKE & BEULAH ANN (MEIER) KLENKE - Harold Robert Klenke was born in Pin Oak Township July 31, 1925, to Henry F. and Alice (Ziegler) Klenke. He grew up in rural Alhambra and attended Salem Evangelical Church in Alhambra and graduated 8th grade from Siebert School.

Beulah A. and Harold R. Klenke, 1997

Beulah Ann Meier was born in Collinsville Township April 20, 1926, to Louis H. and Rosa (Kleppisch) Meier just east of Maryville. She attended St. John's Lutheran Church at Pleasant Ridge. She attended school in Maryville and graduated from Collinsville High School.

Harold and Beulah were married September 14, 1947. They lived near Alhambra until they moved to their farm and home north of Troy in 1949. They milked Holstein cows and raised pigs, chickens, hay, straw, and field crops. The farm became a home for five children: Marilyn Elaine, Eugene Harold, Dianne Faye, Barbara Ann, and Kenneth Dean. Harold, Beulah and family were members of St. John's Lutheran Church in Pleasant Ridge through 1971. At that time, the family joined St. Paul's

Lutheran Church in Troy. All of the children attended and graduated from St. Paul's Lutheran School and Triad High School.

Harold had always been active with farming and farming activities. He had been director for nine years for Hamel Cooperative Grain Co., and a Pin Oak Township Trustee for 40 years, from 1961 to 2001. He also gave many hours of service to the church as a voting member. Beulah was very active with the Madison County Genealogical Society. She researched the family history. She was well known for her bread pudding, embroidery, and laugh. She gave her all as wife and mother and she drove the grain truck at harvest time. With children in 4-H, Harold and Beulah were always there to help with livestock, cooking, and sewing projects. They had many hay rides and a few barn dances on the farm and liked bowling, dancing, and card playing. A good game of horseshoes was always a summer activity.

Sadness was part of the family, as well as joy. Beulah was burned in a pressure canner accident; yet, she was blessed with minimal scars. Everyone recovered from a vehicle accident in 1965 that put Harold in a leg/body cast and hurt four of the children. On December 2, 1984, death came to Kenny in a vehicle accident. Throughout their lives, God has always been their provider of love and joy and peace.

Marilyn is a farmer's wife, Gene farms the land that Harold farmed for more than 50 years, Dianne directed the choir at St. Paul's Lutheran Church and is a CFO's wife, Barb is a contractor/farmer's wife, and Kenny was instrumental in promoting the Simmental breed at the Madison County Fair.

Harold and Beulah are blessed with eight grandchildren and two great grandchildren. The grandchildren are Robert and David Gerstenecker, Denise (Klenke) Willis and Henry Klenke, Kevin and Chad Miller, and Tyler and Leslie Unterbrink. *Submitted by Marilyn Gerstenecker.*

ERNEST PHILIP KNECHT - Ernest Philip Knecht was born on August 19, 1911, on a farm in Pin Oak Township, to Charles Conrad Knecht (1887-1917) and Edna N. Steinehaege Knecht (born 1889). He had two brothers, Charles Knecht and Walter Knecht, and two sisters Julia Knecht Taake and Mary Knecht Hickok.

Ernest Philip went to Sylvan Hall School, a country school in Pin Oak, and was in the last

(l. to r.) Front: Julia (Knecht) Taake, Mary (Knecht) Hickok. Back: Charley Knecht, Phil Knecht, Walter Knecht

*Wedding photo, circa 1900s
Charles and Edna N. (Steinehaege) Knecht*

graduating class (Class of 1929) of the old McCray-Dewey Academy in Troy. Thirteen students graduated from the class, 3 boys and 10 girls.

His first wife was Dorothy Minoni of Edwardsville. His second wife is Mildred Hartnagel.

He has 4 stepchildren, 12 stepgrandchildren and 14 stepgreat-grandchildren.

He worked for the L and M Railroad, U. S. Radiators, in construction for a time in Mattoon, Illinois; and Dunlap Construction. He worked on Route 143 from Edwardsville to Marine and at Shell Oil Company. His last job before retirement was for an Edwardsville firm, owner and operator of Edwardsville Machine and Welding Co.

Mildred and Philip Knecht

His family moved from one farm to another farm 3 miles away in Pin Oak when he was 2 1/2 years old. The family moved in a box wagon and made their own road to the farm located on Old Staunton Road in Pin Oak.

His mother's second husband was Herbert Busse.

Mr. Knecht remembers snow over the fences as he walked 2 1/2 miles through the fields to school. Mr. Knecht is a life member of the Masonic Lodge; Shriners; Ainad Temple of E. St. Louis, IL; Scottish Rite Bodies, Valley of Southern Illinois; Order of Eastern Star, Edwardsville Chapter 667; M.W. Grand Lodge of A.F. and A.M.; and the Moose Lodge, Edwardsville.

Mildred, who came from the State of Virginia then grew up in Belleville, was a self-employed beautician in Edwardsville for 30 years. She is an artist and took lessons from Max Autenrieb.

Her grandson is Robert Rizzi, a Troy Police Officer.

At this writing, the couple makes their home at 237 Third Avenue in Edwardsville, IL.

Written by Mae Grapperhaus following an interview with Ernest and Mildred Knecht in February, 2001. *Submitted by Ernest Knecht.*

KLOPFER FAMILY - Mike Klopfer was born on September 12, 1946, in Alton, IL. His parents were Joseph B. and Audrey B. Klopfer (nee Deck). He graduated from Alton Senior High School in June, 1964. Terry Kochersperger was born May 3, 1946, in Alton. Her parents were Edward J. and June L. Kochersperger (nee Tomlinson). She graduated from Alton Senior High School in June 1964.

Mike and Terry graduated together in 1964 and then went their separate ways. He served in the Army from 1965 until 1967 serving in Germany and Viet Nam. They met again in October, 1968, started dating, and married in March, 1969. He worked for Illinois Bell Telephone as a lineman in Maryville, IL, and she worked for Associates Finance, Inc., as a loan clerk in Wood River, IL. They lived in Alton until their move to Troy on May 15, 1976.

Their daughter Kelly Lynn was born August 2, 1979, and graduated from Triad in 1997. She played on a softball and soccer team before going to Triad. While at Triad she was on the Flag Drill Team, played clarinet in the band for several years and also played soccer. She is currently employed at Anderson Hospital as an ER admitting clerk is and also studying to be an EMT.

Kelly and her dad are avid drag racers. Her dad has been drag racing since high school and she has been racing since her senior year of high school. They race a 1967 Chevelle. In her first year of racing (1997) she qualified to represent Gateway International Raceway in the High School Division and raced at Indianapolis, IN, for Sears Craftsman E.T. Finals. Although she came in second, it was quite an honor to qualify and race at Indy.

The Klopfers are members of Troy United Methodist Church. They enjoy drag racing, fishing, camping and bowling. *Submitted by Terry L. Klopfer*

A.M. KOCH - August M. Koch of Jackson, MO, received a "call" in March, 1927, from St. Paul's Congregation of Troy to be the principal of St. Paul's School. The Rev. C. Lange was the pastor of the Congregation. He accepted the "call" and the family moved to Troy, in August, 1927. The

Koch family, 1943
(l. to r.) Front: Lydia, Markus
Back: August, Virginia

A.M. Koch, 1950

family included Mr. Koch, his wife, Lydia, and two children, Markus, age 8, and Virginia, age 3.

The home they lived in was the teacherage, on Throp Street, which was behind the school. Mr. Koch graduated from the Addison Normal School in Addison, Illinois, in 1913. Previous placements or "calls" were in Des Plaines, IL., St. Louis County, MO, and Jackson, MO. Mr. Koch was the principal of St. Paul's School from 1927 until 1956 when he retired from teaching.

He taught grades 5 through 8, and played the organ for church services. Mr. Arthur Stahmer taught grades 1 through 4. One accomplishment of Mr. Koch during those teaching years was letters of commendation from principals of the high school that St. Paul's students were outstanding in academic achievement. He also was instrumental in starting a Sunday School at St. Paul's. Many times he would be seen playing softball with the students during lunch and recess.

During many of those years, there were pastoral vacancies, and Mr. Koch took care of the many duties required to secure pastors, as well as helping with other activities.

Markus, son of the Kochs, attended St. Paul's school and spent one year at McCray-Dewey High School. He then spent the rest of his high school and college years at St. Paul's College in Concordia, MO. Further education included Concordia Seminary St. Louis, graduating in 1944. He also attended Washington University and was awarded the Master's Degree in history. After several placements in the parish ministry, he spent the rest of his life in farming in Sikeston, MO. He married Doris Geske of Sikeston, MO. They have three children: John, a veterinarian in Cape Girardeau, MO; Timothy, a farmer in Sikeston; and Rebecca, a teacher in Sikeston Schools. Markus died in April 1987.

Virginia attended St. Paul's school and graduated from McCray-Dewey High School in 1941. She worked in St. Louis as an executive secretary in an insurance company until her marriage in December 1950 to Robert Kamprath of Maplewood, MO. He was a teacher in a Lutheran School in Maplewood, and later attended Concordia Seminary where he graduated in 1954. Their calls took them to placements in South Dakota; Beecher, IL; Collinsville, IL (Holy Cross Lutheran); Omaha, NB; Portland, OR; and Eugene, OR. Robert died in July 1980.

Their children are Tom, a pastor in Michigan; Tim, a pastor in Klamath Falls, OR; Deborah, an executive with a development firm;

Sara, an executive director of a Christian help organization in Salem, OR; Michael, a manager in a food industry in Portland, and Peter, pastor in Ohio. There are fourteen grandchildren.

Mr. Koch retired in 1956 and with his wife, Lydia, moved to Sikeston, MO. He died in January 1959 in Sikeston, of a perforated ulcer. Lydia then moved to live with daughter Virginia, in Beecher, IL, to make her home with the family. Lydia died in Eugene, OR, at the age of 96.

Some memories growing up in Troy: The many ball games behind the school — corkball, softball and baseball; Walther League (youth organization) activities, picnics, wiener roasts; walking to high school across town; the Homecoming parades in July; the neighbors- the Kuekers, the Hankes, Waldens, Taakes, Driques, Andrews, and others; commuting to St. Louis to work; the bells of St. Paul's Church announcing a funeral and tolling according to age for members who died; children's Christmas Eve programs at St. Paul's Church; Lela Polwort-Sesock's beauty shop to get hair "marcelled;" St. Paul's school picnics in June after school was out; the plays the children gave; the fishing booth and other stands; the family style chicken supper served by the ladies of St. Paul's; special ladies – Mayme Taake, Sophia Schultz, Lena Wendler, Lena Fedder, Frieda Kueker, Anna Flath, Anna Kueker; going to Collinsville and E. St. Louis to shop the dime stores – FW Woolworth and Newberrys; the Bunco Parties given by the Pleasant Hour Club at church; and the Troy Skating Rink and the skating parties there. *Submitted by Virginia Kamprath.*

JOHN RICHARD KRANZ - John R. Kranz was born July 28, 1882, on a farm east of Troy and north of the present Triad School. He was the youngest son of George V., Sr., and Emma Bertha (Kohlmeier) Kranz.

John left school at age 9 to work on the farm, due to his father's death. Later he and his mother moved to a home on Staunton Road, Troy. John was married on Dec. 19, 1905, to Jennie M. Whiteside. She was born July 26, 1881, and was the daughter of Andrew Jackson and Ellen Jane (Waxham) Whiteside, all of Pin Oak Township.

John's mother sold John and Jennie the back of her lot for their home; John built it and they lived there until their deaths in 1965.

John farmed and was the mine carpenter at Troy Mine. He built many barns that are still used in the area, and he built the Troy Elevator.

Jennie passed away May 25, 1965, and John passed away June 23, 1965.

They had three children. The first was Ellen Whiteside Kranz who married Ben E. Jarvis. They had two children: Jane-Ellen Kaegy (now of Greenville) and Edward Lee Jarvis, who died in 1967. Ellen died in October 1967, and Ben E. died July 1982.

The second child was Mary M. Kranz who married Clifford Zinkgraf in June 1942. They lived at O'Fallon in his family home until his death in August 1946. Mary returned to Troy in 1948. She taught school in O'Fallon and Troy, retiring in 1972. She resides in Troy at this time.

The third child was James Lewis Kranz who married Edna Prott of Marine. They presently reside on their farm south of Troy.

Their daughters are Carolyn (Mrs. Ron Klaustermeier) and Laurie Ann (Mrs. Patrick Mersinger). Ron and Carol own and operate A & R Paints and Crafts in Troy. They have a son, Kristopher, and a daughter, Mandy. Laurie Ann and Patrick farm in rural St. Jacob. Laurie works at the Troy Elevator. Their children are Steven, Adam and Jennie. *Submitted by Jane Ellen Kaegy.*

HENRY C. KUEKER -

Henry C. Kueker was born January 6, 1885, in the Troy community, to Henry F. and Christina Kueker. At the age of 16 years, Henry F. had immigrated to southern Illinois from Germany.

After studying at an embalming and mortuary school in Chicago, Illinois, Henry C. was employed by and later purchased the J.H. Steinhans and Sons Undertaking business in Troy. In the early 1920s, it was newly named the Henry C. Kueker Undertaking and Embalming Business.

His purchase included the Troy Home Furnishing and Hardware store, also owned by the Steinhans family. Both businesses were located in the same building on Market Street that now houses the Troy Tribune office. Henry F. was owner of the local lumber company and Troy Mfg. Co., makers of a household oil, which sold for 25 cents a bottle.

Two of Henry C.'s four sisters, Anna Kueker and Clara Stahmer, were life-long residents of Troy. During his early years in Troy, Senator Paul Simon made his home with them, and often referred to Anna as his "second mother." Henry's other sisters were Linda Kueker and Louise Kueker Fischer.

Henry C. married Frieda Peters, daughter of August and Mary Wilke Peters, whose brother, Charlie Peters, was a grocery store owner in Troy. They had two daughters, Arline and Fern. Arline married Kenneth Lyons, son of Richard and Martha Buhrmester Lyons. Kenneth died April 25, 1993, eleven days after their 50th wedding anniversary. Fern married Ray Taake, son of Mr. And Mrs. William Taake (both are deceased). The Lyons had two sons, Jim (Doris) of Troy and Terry (Ruth Anne) of Oklahoma City, Oklahoma. The Taakes had a daughter, JoAnn (Jim) Kesterson, and a son, Larry Taake, both of Troy.

Henry C., who died June 12, 1941, sold his funeral home to Jewel Edwards in the late 1930s. That business today is Troy's Laughlin Funeral Home. The hardware merchandise and building were sold to Fred "Happy" Liebler, a Troy resident, now deceased. *Submitted by Arline Lyons.*

MERRILL (SAM) AND BETTY KUEKER

Merrill (Sam) F. Kueker was the 5th child of Charles Henry and Dora Louise (Wilkening) Kueker both of Ruma, IL. Sam was born in Troy on February 8, 1921. He had three brothers, Gilbert, Lester and Earl, and a sister Lorene Schultz. All are deceased. A sister, Dorothy Holshouser, resides in Troy.

Betty J. (Thomas) Kueker was born in Troy on May 4, 1924. She was the first daughter of Arthur J. and Anita (Droll) Thomas of Troy. Arthur worked for the *Edwardsville Intelligencer* and Anita was a former schoolteacher,

Merrill (Sam) and Betty Kueker, 1943

and a bookkeeper for Famous and Barr. Arthur was also on the Troy Board of Education. Betty had a brother, William, now deceased, who resided in Godfrey, and a sister Marge (Thomas) Porter of Troy.

Sam and Betty met at the Moonlight Roller Rink in Troy and were married on December 12, 1943, at the Troy Presbyterian Church. They had two children: Jane Ann (Noll) Brandel, born on January 24, 1947, in Highland, and Thomas Merrill, born on December 18, 1949, in Highland.

Jane now resides in Wildwood, Missouri, and is the mother of three sons: Todd, Kyle and Matthew Noll. Tom has been a lifelong resident of Troy. He is married to Kay (Landolt) of Alhambra and they have two children, Angela and Brandon.

Sam served in World War II and was a participant in the Battle of the Bulge. His brother Earl also served in the war and was killed in the South Pacific. After returning from the service, Sam worked at Moderne Linen, Bill Pitt's Soda Company, Adelhardt's Grocery Store and Troy Grain, all in Troy, and also for Bruno Bread in Collinsville before becoming disabled.

Betty worked at Troy Snack Bar and Bill Pitt's Soda Company in Troy, and also for Jere's (Glik's) in Collinsville.

They both worked at bingo and Saturday night dances at the Firemen's Hall in Collinsville until Betty's death on February 10, 1985. Sam died on April 19, 1993. *Submitted by Kay Kueker and Jane Brandel.*

THOMAS AND KAY KUEKER -

Thomas M. Kueker is the son of the late Merrill (Sam) F. and Betty J. (Thomas) Kueker of Troy. He was born on December 18, 1949, in Highland. He has one sister, Jane A. (Kueker) Noll Brandel. He graduated from Triad High School in 1968. He served in the U. S. Army from 1968 to 1971 and is a Vietnam veteran.

Kay A. (Landolt) Kueker is the daughter of Lawrence O. and Shirley M. (Casper) Landolt of Alhambra. She was born on June 8, 1954, in Highland. She has two brothers, Michael and Jack, and a sister, Pamela. She graduated from Highland High School in 1972.

Tom and Kay met in October 1972, in Highland and were married October 12, 1974, in Livingston. After their marriage they made their home in Troy. They have two children: Angela K. was born on February 4, 1979, in Highland and Brandon T. was born on November 16, 1980, in Highland. Angela is a senior at Southern Illinois University-Edwardsville with a major in Early Childhood Development. Brandon is in his second year of the Carpentry

Kueker family, 1998
(l. to r.) Front: Tom, Kay, Angela. Back: Brandon

Apprentice program of Local 295 with Throm Construction in Collinsville.

After graduation and prior to entering the Army, Tom was employed at Jakel Manufacturing in Highland. Upon returning from the Army he worked for Conalco Aluminum in Venice, Sunset Hills Country Club in Edwardsville, and Southern Illinois University-Edwardsville. Tom is a member of the Troy VFW and Troy American Legion.

After graduation, Kay was employed at Basler Electric Company in Highland, Southern Illinois University-Edwardsville, Our Lord's Lutheran Church in Collinsville, Lutheran Brotherhood in Edwardsville, and Michael A. Burstadt & Associates in Glen Carbon. Kay is an auxiliary member of both the Troy VFW and Alhambra American Legion.

Kay and the children are members of St. Jerome Catholic Church in Troy. After having spent many years involved in their children's activities, Tom and Kay are involved with the Randy's Over 40 softball team. *Submitted by Kay Kueker.*

WILLIAM KUEKER -

William Kueker was born on December 28, 1945, to Victor and Josephine (Sartoris) Kueker of Troy, IL. His wife Jane, born on February 13, 1948, was the daughter of Luke and Dorothy (Sedlacek) Neudecker of Marine, IL.

Bill and Jane met at Triad High School. Bill graduated in 1965 and started the apprenticeship program for carpenters at night school while he worked as a carpenter during the day. On June 3, 1966, Jane graduated and Bill gave her an engagement ring. One year later to the day they were married at St. Elizabeth's Catholic Church in Marine, IL.

Very soon after the wedding a lot was purchased north of Troy in Bangert's Grove and

Kueker family, 1997
(l. to r.) Jill, Jane, Bill, Carol, Julie

the building of their own home began. The basement was dug on September 30, 1967, and they moved in on February 29, 1968. Bill, with the help of friends and family, did most of the work at night and on weekends as he worked all day and went to school two nights a week.

Bill was a member of Carpenter's Local #295 in Collinsville, working out of the union hall for eleven years. In 1976 he went to work at Standard Oil Refinery in Wood River, which later became Amoco Chemical Petroleum Additives. He worked there until the plant closed in 1995.

Bill was a member of the Troy Volunteer Fire Department for 24 years and the fire department at Amoco for 15 years. Amoco sent him to Fire School at Texas A & M and also to hazardous material training.

Jane went to work at Ralston Purina in St. Louis and later at Southern Illinois University Edwardsville Graduate School Office. She quit working to raise her children. In 1979 she took a job as a school bus driver for Triad School District, driving until she took a position as custodian at the St. Jacob Elementary School in 1996.

Carol Ann was the first daughter born to them on April 24, 1968. She attended the Troy schools, Triad High School, and Belleville Area College. Carol is a legal secretary in St. Louis, MO. and is engaged to Gary R. Ross of Little Rock, AR. Their wedding is planned for October 12, 2001.

The second daughter born to the Kuekers was Julie Kay on February 24, 1973. Julie also attended the Troy Schools, Triad High School, University of Missouri at St. Louis and Nova Southeastern in Davie, FL. In May of 2000 Julie graduated as a Doctor of Optometry from Nova and later in the summer she became engaged to Bryan Barfield of Melbourne Beach, FL. They plan to be married in the spring of 2002.

Jill Marie is the third daughter born on August 28, 1980. She attended the Troy Schools, Triad High School, Belleville Area College, and Southern Illinois University at Edwardsville.

Bill and Jane still live in the house they built north of Troy, soon approaching 34 years. *Submitted by Jane Kueker.*

GERALD AND THERESA LANAHAN

Gerald Lanahan (b.9-2-29) and Theresa Decker (b. 11-24-28) were married on June 24, 1950. When newly married, they lived in a house on Rt. 162 that Jerry was building. His mother Viola had given each of her 3 sons one half acre to build on near the old home place, the log house on Rt. 162.

On December 3, Jerry was recalled to serve in the Korean War. Six months later Theresa joined him in Camp LeJeune, NC. Here their first son, Gerald Joseph, Jr. (Joe), was born in the Naval Hospital on April 29, 1953.

After his honorable discharge in December of 1953, Jerry worked on construction, building houses in St. Louis before starting his own company later. Five more children were born during these years: Mary Kathleen (b. 4-20-55, d. 6-1-58), Kenneth Patrick (b, 12-17-56), Cynthia Marie (b. 8-2-59), Nancy Ann (b. 1-10-61), and James Edward (b. 5-14-62).

The family lived on Rt. 162 and in Edwardsville (now Maryville) before moving to Troy in November of 1960. They bought

Lanahan family, June 2000
(l. to r.) Cindy, Joe, Jerry, Theresa, Kenny, Nancy, Jim

ground from John and Mary Voelker, developing it over the years into Lanahan Addition, with five total additions. They named the streets after their children. The family moved into the first house in the First Addition on Mary Drive. The second house was built for City Treasurer Carl Taake, later mayor of Troy, and his wife Julia. In later years other subdivisions were developed, and the Concept 2000 homes were introduced.

Jerry and Theresa celebrated their Golden Wedding Anniversary in June of 2000 with their family, which includes: Gerald (Joe) and Susan Jean Meyer Lanahan and children Joshua Michael, Janelle Katherine, and Justin Edward; Kenneth (Kenny) and Debra Kay Thomas Lanahan and children Matthew Aspen and Kari Lynn; Cynthia (Cindy) and Jeffery Perkins and children Jennifer Ann and Elizabeth Marie; Nancy and Bobby Douglas and children Kimberly Ann, Laura Nichol, and Joshua; James (Jim) and Juliane Nichon Thuller Lanahan and children Jesse and Nicki.

Although he retired from building in 1990, Jerry still serves his community as Alderman. Theresa and Jerry enjoy traveling and being active in many organizations. *Submitted by Theresa Lanahan*

ANDREAS L. AND ANNA MARIA (WIDICUS) LANGENWALTER -

Andreas L. and Anna Maria Widicus Langenwalter and their children came to the United States from Ruchheim, Germany, around 1845. They came to New Orleans and then traveled up the Mississippi River to St. Louis.

Andreas was born 30 October 1791, in Weisenheim am Sand, Germany. Anna Maria was born 21 June 1800, Ruchheim, Germany. They married 25 March 1822, Ruchheim, Germany, where they were farmers.

Anna Maria's brother, Johann Jacob Widicus, and family had come to the United States in August 1840 and settled on land they had purchased in Jarvis Township, Madison County, IL. This same area was the Langenwalter family's destination. In 1847 Andreas purchased 120 acres of land for $1,400, also in Jarvis Township, about two miles northeast of the Widicus farm. Andreas built a two story brick house on his land. The farm stayed in the family for many years until 1975 or 1976. The house is still used as a residence.

Their children were all born in Ruchheim, Germany. Jacob, born 9 January 1823, married 28 March 1849, Elizabeth Baer, died 20 July 1852, buried Baer Family Cemetery, Ridge Prairie, St. Clair County, IL, had two children; Elizabeth, born 26 July 1827, married 31 May 1848, Alexander Wilson, died 12 February 1888,

buried Island Creek Cemetery, Jasper County, IL, had seven children; Anna Elizabeth, born 7 January 1831, married 28 March 1849, Jacob Baer, died 6 May, 1904, buried Summerfield Cemetery, Summerfield, St. Clair County, IL, had twelve children; Catherine, born 31 May 1833, married 15 February 1855, John Widicus, died 10 January 1898, buried Widicus Family Cemetery, Blackjack, Madison County, IL, had ten children; Andreas, born 21 February 1836, married 1858, Anna Margaretha Wohlgemuth, died 26 November 1882, buried Langenwalter Family Cemetery, Blackjack, Madison County, IL, had nine children; Samuel, born 29 July 1838, never married, died 8 June 1877, buried Langenwalter Family Cemetery, Blackjack, Madison County, IL; Katherine Elizabeth, born 7 August 1841, married 26 October 1858, Peter Riebold, died 3 January 1917, buried Fairview Cemetery, Grangeville, ID, had ten children.

Anna Maria Widicus Langenwalter died 11 July 1852, at her home in Blackjack. Andreas died 19 July 1860. Both were buried in the Langenwalter Family Cemetery. *Submitted by Edith Hock.*

LANGENWALTER FAMILY -

The Langenwalter family came to Jarvis Township in the mid 1840s . The first to arrive were the parents, Andreas, born 30 October 1791, in Weisenheim am Sand, Germany, and Anna Marie Widicus, born 21 June 1800, in Ruchheim, Germany. They were married 25 March 1822.

Their children, all born in Germany, were Jacob 1823-1852; Elizabeth 1827-1888; Anna E. 1831-1904; Katharina 1833-1898; Andreas 1836-1882; Samuel 1838-1877; Katherine E. 1841-1917.

Son Andreas was married about 1859 to Anna Margaretha Wohlgemuth, born 10 November 1838, in Ruchheim, Germany. Their children were Maria, Samuel, Johannes, Andreas, Jacob, Samuel, Anna E., Wilhelm, and Anna.

In the next generation, Johannes, born 21 March 1864, married the daughter of their neighbor to the south. Maria Schmitt was the seventh child of Johannes Wendel and Anna Barbara Schneider Schmitt. She was born 6 March 1866. John and Mary, as they came to be called, were married on her birthday, 6 March 1887. They, too, had a large family. Daniel, Regina, John, Anna, John Samuel, Maria, Frieda Rosa (who died as an infant), Wilhelm, Paul, Karita (Corida), Olinda, and Irene. These children all attended

Wedding day, 6 March 1887
Johannes Langenwalter and Maria Schmitt

Blackjack School at the corner of Blackjack and Mill Creek roads.

The family farm in Blackjack was in the Langenwalter family from the 1840's until the 1970s. The last of the family to live on the farm was Arnold, son of the second generation, Jacob. The sturdy German style brick home still stands on Mill Creek Road and is occupied by a generous family who gives access to the cemetery without restriction. The Langenwalter Cemetery is the resting place of nineteen family members, including the first and second generation Andreas' and their wives.

The parents of Maria Schmitt are buried just a short distance away in the tiny Schmitt Cemetery just to the south of the Langenwalter farm. John and Mary Schmitt Langenwalter moved from Blackjack to Collinsville in the early 1900s. One of their younger daughters, Corida, married Anton Fuetsch of Collinsville. They had three children, Vernon (died in infancy), Adele, and Betty. Betty married Arvil W. Wrigley 19 April 1947. Arvil has a connection to Troy as well.

His great grandfather Michael Voisin had a farm on Spring Valley Road in the 1850s. Michael and three of his children are buried in the Watt Cemetery in Fawn Meadows subdivision. Arvil's father, William H. Wrigley was born in Troy to Isaac Samuel and Mary Voisin Wrigley.

Betty and Arvil Wrigley were blessed with twins born 27 February 1951, Robert Alan of Moscow, ID, and Kathryn Jean Wrigley of Athens, IL. Betty and Arvil are retired but very active as community volunteers in Collinsville.

Robert is the father of three. He is a poet and a professor at the University of Idaho. His wife is Kim Barnes. Their children are Philip, son of Robert and Vana Berry, Jordan and Jace.

Kathryn married Ted Rucker and has two children, Adam and Hannah. Kathryn is Health Services Librarian at St. John's Hospital in Springfield, Illinois.

In July of 2000 a Langenwalter reunion was held in Collinsville with about one hundred people attending from 14 states. The highlight of the reunion was meeting at the cemetery and doing some necessary clean up of trees, etc. This was the first time most of the family had ever been to the cemetery. *Submitted by Betty A. Wrigley.*

LANGENWALTER FAMILY - The following names are taken from the Langenwalter Cemetery. Children born to Jacob and Anna Elizabeth (Langenwalter) Baer were Anna (b. June 1858, d. Sept. 1858), Daniel (b. Jan. 1862 d. Nov. 1862), Elizabeth (b. 1855, d. 1858), Jacob (b. 1850, d. 1865), Katharina (b. 1852, d. 1852) and Maria (b. 1853, d. 1884).

Louis and Maria (Langenwalter) Gindler had one son John (b 1883, d. 1884). Andreas Langenwalter (b. 1792, d. 1860) and Anna Maria (Widicus) Langenwalter (b. 1800, d. 1852) were parents of Samuel (b. 1838, d. 1877) and Andreas (b. 1836, d. 1882).

Andreas Langenwalter and his second wife, Margaretha (Wohlgemuth) Langenwalter were parents of Anna (b. 1872, d. 1877), Samuel (b. 1862, d. 1869) and William Tobias (b. 1871, d. 1876). Children of Andrew and

Barbara (Dausman) Langenwalter are Arthur C. (b. 1895 d. 1896) and Ida M. (b. July 15, 1896, d. July 16, 1896.)

Children of Johannes and Marie (Schmitt) Langenwalter are Frieda Rosa (b. 1896, d. 1897) and John Samuel (b. Apr. 1892, d. July 1892). *Submitted by Carol Langenwalter Bell.*

LANGEWISCH FAMILY - Wilhelm Langewisch and Johanne (Hoffman) Langewisch lived on a farm on Zenk Road about one-half mile west of Riggin Road. They had ten children: Sophia (2/13/1867-12/26/1936), Wilhelmina (Minnie) (8/11/1868-9/26/1949), Wilhelm (9/5/1871-12/18/1950), Johanna (Hanna) (10/29/1873-4/14/1955), Agnes (9/12/1875-1/9/1946), Amalie (Mollie) (12/10/1878-12/26/1931), Charles (2/13/1881-8/29/1966), Eleonore (Laura) (2/15/1883-4/28/1949), Augusta (Gustie) (5/1/1885-10/8/1946), Theodore (Teet) (12/23/1887-10/8/1961).

In October 1898, Sophia married August Brunworth (see Brunworth history), Wilhelm (Bill) Langewisch married Elise Eberhardt (9/1/1870-9/15/1954), and three children were born to them: Florentine (Maudie) (2/15/1900-7/28/1984), not married, Edna (3/8/1901-1/20/1911), Edward (6/2/1907-4/10/1963).

They lived on a farm on Staunton Road about one-half mile north of the Lutheran cemetery. Maudie did housekeeping in St. Louis.

Agnes married George Flath and they lived on a farm about one and a half miles east of Troy. They had five children: Olinda married Hilbert Koenig of Edwardsville, Alma married Robert Sudbring of Collinsville, George (1908–1976) married Frieda Meier (1907–1989), (sister of Hulda (Meier) Hecht), Eleonore – remained with parents, Theodore (8/27/1915-3/11/1982) married Clara Bode (9/15/1912-11/23/2000).

Agnes died soon after she, George Sr. and Eleonore moved to a house they built in Troy. George Jr. remained on the family farm. Theodore and his family lived on a farm approximately two and one-half miles northeast of Troy in Pin Oak Township.

Of the senior Wilhelm Langewisch family Wilhelmina, Johanna, Eleonore, Charles and Theodore lived on the family farm. One of the cash crops was broom corn with which they made brooms and sold locally. Hanna had customers in Troy who bought her eggs and butter. Augusta worked and lived in St. Louis and came home periodically to visit. They all had a close family relationship with the George Flath and August Brunworth family nieces and nephews.

Wilhelm was a German immigrant. Johanne's mother was a stow-away dressed as a man on one of the ships which brought the Saxon immigrants (and Lutheranism) from the Saxony area in Germany to Perry County, MO. Wilhelm and Johanne Langewisch and all descendants were lifelong members of the Lutheran church and educated their children in the Lutheran grade school in Troy. *Submitted by Sharon (Brunworth) Repp.*

DELMER AND VIOLET LAUNIUS - Delmer was born on May 24, 1921, to Jeff and Delica Launius in Franklin County, IL. He graduated from McLeansboro High School in 1940; and he

Launius family, 1971
(l. to r.) Front: Gregory, Violet, Delmer.
Back: Sherry, Steven

later served in WWII from 1942 to 1946, working as an aircraft instructor, air inspector, and aerial engineer on B-24 bombers. He was stationed in the Philippines and Japan.

Violet was born on April 24, 1930, in Washington County, IL, to Ben and Louise Groennert. She graduated from Nashville High School in Nashville, IL. Her family history includes farmers and teachers, two occupations that influenced her own life and career choice later. Vi earned her B.S. in elementary education at SIUE, and later her M.S. in Instructional Technology there. During her professional career, she taught grade school in Roxana, and in Fairview Heights, taught English in junior high, and served as librarian there until her retirement in 1994.

Delmer retired in 1982 after teaching for 39 years in this area. He received his B.S. in 1948 and came to Troy to teach Vocational Agriculture, teaching at McCray- Dewey High School in the morning, and at St. Jacob High School in the afternoon. During his career as Vocational Agriculture instructor for the Troy and Triad schools, Delmer served as the advisor for the Future Farmers of America, receiving the Honorary American Farmer Degree.

He also taught night classes and served as coordinator for Belleville Area College and acted as Illinois Crop Inspector for ten years. He appeared in the 15th edition of *Who's Who in the Midwest* in 1975-76. Among his community activities, he has served on the St. Paul Lutheran Church school board, served as President of the Troy Savings and Homestead Association for 19 years, was a member of the Senior Citizen Board, and is currently a member of the Troy American Legion Post 708 and V.F.W. Post 976.

Violet and Delmer have three children and three grandchildren. Dr. Steve Launius was born on January 21, 1954, in Highland and is

Delmer and Vi Launius, 2001

presently Superintendent of Schools in Seward, Illinois. He lives and farms in Nashville, Illinois. Sherry Launius Manley was born on November 24, 1956, in Highland. She married Lawrence Manley and is presently employed by the Troy Post Office and lives in Troy. She is the mother of the 3 Launius grandchildren, Christopher, Dana, and Keri Schlemer. Dr. Gregory Launius was born at Highland Hospital on December 24, 1959. He is currently a Pediatric Radiologist in Louisville, Kentucky, and travels widely when time permits.

With their children grown and prospering, Vi and Delmer have time to devote to other interests. Vi is interested in genealogy and antiques, while Delmer continues to sell real estate and serve on various boards. Both are currently involved with land development and have built a new house, which they hope to occupy in summer of 2001. *Submitted by Delmer Launius.*

ED LESICKO -
Ed Lesicko was born in Worden, IL, in September 1908. He died in Troy in 1988 and is still survived by two sisters, Ad Zimmer and Mary Eaton, both in Oregon. His wife, Dellora Allen, was born in 1912 and died in 1954. After her death, Ed rasied 5 kids (Donna, Jim, Ann, Kathy and Sue) alone and never remarried. Although his children all tried to find another wife for him, he always said, "Why would I want someone else after your mother?"

Ed Lesicko

He was a volunteer fireman in Troy for 20 years. He was an electrician in the coal mines (along with his brothers, Joe and John) for close to 50 years. His children can remember many phone calls at all times when people needed electrical work done or something fixed. He helped wire the city of Troy when electricity came.

He was also a strong Catholic and never lost faith in the church. He helped Father Dineen many times and the children remember him coming to their home many times.

Ed told his children when he was young he thought about working at the Princess Gardner factory in St. Louis. He went there one day and watched these big machines slicing leather for wallets and purses and noticed people with no fingers, no hands, no arms, and decided the coal mines didn't look so bad.

He loved his family. At the time of his death, he had five grandchildren (Michael, Corey, Curt, Tracie, and Sara). He also had many true friends in Troy (just to mention a few-Russ Wiesemeyer, Warnie Spencer, Les Adelhardt,

Freeman Porter, Puz Weider) and some of these friends even helped him build his house on 106 Henderson.

Ed Lesicko was an inspiration to all. He was the true meaning of love and unselfishness. His children think of him often and feel so fortunate to have had him in their lives. *Submitted by Kathy Talbert.*

LETURNO -
The Leturno family, Joseph and Theodocia, arrived in Madison County, IL, sometime after 1843 and prior to 1847.

Joseph Mitchell Leturno was first found in the 1850 Census of Madison County, IL, as a three year old child in the household of Jesse Renfrow. Family tradition had always indicated that Joseph, as well as his mother and father, were all born in Minnesota. Perhaps the family Renfrow with which he was residing had some Minnesota connection and Joseph picked up on that. Also, his brothers were found in the 1850 census to have been residing in the households of others: Henry in the household of James B. Andrews, and Calvin in the household of John W. Hagler. Their mother was deceased, 1848-1850, and possibly their father could not provide the proper care for his children. The father was still living at this time.

The family migrated to Madison County from Ohio through Indiana. The earliest record of the Leturno family that can be verified is Francis Leturno and his wife Sarah Edwards. Francis died in Montgomery County, OH, about 1814. The only known offspring of this marriage was Joseph Leturno b. 1811-1813 in Montgomery County, OH. Joseph married Theodocia Hill 31 March 1836, in Hamilton County, IN. Children born to this marriage were Henry F., 1838, Indiana; Calvin Fletcher, 1841, Marion County, IN; George, 1843, Indiana; Joseph Mitchell, 1847, Madison County, IL. *Submitted by Vernon L. Lacey.*

EDWARD TOBY LEVO -
Edward "Ed" Toby Levo was born April 16, 1896, the oldest son and third child of Peter P. Levo, Sr., and Laura (Cossano) Levo. He was born in Collinsville and never married. He served in World War I. After the war, he operated the family store in Troy, which later became the Levo Bakery.

His brother Peter later owned and operated the bakery and Edward owned and operated a tavern, next door, called the Homestead Tavern located at 108 West Market Street. The building is built around a log cabin which was a stage coach stop in the early days of Troy.

Ed Levo behind the bar at his tavern, the Homestead Tavern at 108 West Market Street on March 22, 1953.

In the late 1940s, he built a home under the Troy water tower just a few doors down from the tavern. He and his mother, Laura Levo, lived there a short time when she fell and broke her hip. She died November 8, 1949.

Edward lived in the house alone until the mid-1960s when he suffered a stroke. His sister, Louise Mersinger, cared for him in her home south of Troy for about two years. He then moved to the Rockwood Nursing Home in Troy where he died September 17, 1967.

He is buried in SS Peter and Paul Catholic Cemetery, Collinsville, IL.

He was a member of St. Jerome Catholic Church, Troy American Legion Post 708 and a retired Volunteer Firefighter. He was a well known businessman in the town of Troy and was the first business in Troy to own a television set in 1948. *Submitted by Mae (Mersinger) Grapperhaus.*

ELMER AND EMMA (WYATT) LEVO
Elmer Levo, son of Peter and Laura (Cossano) Levo, married Emma Wyatt on January 4, 1941, in Troy. Best man was Joseph J. Mersinger, and maid of honor, Laura Ann Romeo. Emma's parents were John Wesley and Ora (Hurst) Wyatt.

Wedding, Jaunary 4, 1941
(l. to r.) Joseph J. Mersinger, Laura Ann Romeo, Emma (Wyatt) and Elmer Levo.

Elmer served in WW II and was killed in action in Vire, France, in August of 1944. He is buried in France. Emma worked at Armour and Company in East St. Louis for several years.

Several years after Elmer died, Emma married R.C. Kamm. She is now living in Collinsville. *Submitted by Mae Grapperhaus.*

KIRK AND RACHAEL LEVO -
Kirk Allen Levo was born on March 25, 1969, to Paul and Bonnie Levo of Troy. He graduated from Triad High School in 1987 and from SIU-Carbondale in 1991 with his Bachelors of Science in Accounting. Kirk is currently an auditor with US Bank Business Credit in St. Louis.

Kirk married Rachael Michaels, of Scott Air Force Base, IL, on May 28, 1994. They have three children, Sean Patrick Levo born July 26, 1991, Courtney Elizabeth Levo born September 9, 1994, and Jared Michael Levo born June 9, 2000. They currently reside at 611 Whippoorwill in Troy. Sean and Courtney attend St. Paul Lutheran School in Troy. *Submitted by Kelli Ponce.*

PAUL LEVO -
Paul was born in Troy, IL, on December 14, 1936, to Peter and Vera (Wild) Levo of Troy. He joined a sister, Marilyn, age

11 and a brother, Ronald, age 7. Paul loved to help his dad at the Levo Bakery and play basketball as a young man. He graduated in 1954 from McCray-Dewey High School in Troy.

On July 1, 1961, he married Bonnie Moeller and they had two children, Kelli Ann Levo born October 15, 1965, and Kirk Allen Levo born March 25, 1969. They both still reside with their families in Troy. Paul and Bonnie were married for 28 years and have five grandchildren.

Paul is best known around town for being the "Insurance Man." He worked for Prudential Insurance Company for 25 years before retiring in 1991. Paul has also officiated countless basketball and football games in the area for the past 45 years and continues to do so today. Paul now works for Charter Communications selling cable and writes a column entitled "Sportalk" for the *Troy Times-Tribune* each week. *Submitted by Kelli Ponce.*

PETER PAUL AND LAURA COSSANO LEVO -

Peter Paul Levo Sr. (born June 26, 1858, in Italy, died April 9, 1945, in Troy, IL) and his wife Laura Cossano (born October 1871 in Alexandria, Italy) came to America in December 1892 from northern Italy. Laura was from Alexandria and Peter from a nearby village. When they came to America, they settled in the Collinsville area. Their first child was born in July 1893. Her name was Philomena (Minnie). Other children born to the union were Caroline "Carrie," Edward Toby, Mary, Peter J., Louise Laura, Elmer C. and Octavia.

Levo family 1942
(l. to r.) Front: Laura (Cossano), Peter Paul
Back: Edward Toby, Peter Jr., Philomena "Minnie,"
Caroline "Carrie," Mary, Louise, Octavia, Elmer

Peter Levo Sr. was an entrepreneur of sorts. He was a farmer, a storekeeper, a wine maker and builder of homes. He also worked for a time in the Collinsville coal mines.

He began a grocery store on Vandalia Street in Collinsville across from SS Peter and Paul Catholic Church. The family lived next to the store. Most of the children were born there. He built a stone home on a farm in Collinsville township and moved the family there. He raised grapes and other fruits and vegetables which he sold to different stores and individuals.

He bought a store in Troy (108-110 West Market Street). It was a confectionery store that later became a bakery shop operated by his sons. Later Edward operated a tavern in 108 W. Market and Peter Jr. took over the bakery. The tavern had a small apartment upstairs where the family lived briefly. Later, he built a home south of Troy on West Kirsch Road.

He was an avid wine maker, selling some, and enjoyed his grape vineyards wherever he lived. He enjoyed serving wine to his guests, making them stay longer by serving more wine.

He had a long white beard in his later years and was tall and thin. He kept "balsam" whiskey high in a cabinet for "medicinal" purposes. Two of his favorite songs he would sing to very young granddaughter Mae were "My Bonnie" and "Old Black Joe."

Laura was a short somewhat stocky woman, but was pretty lively. She managed to take good care of her eight children. A typical Italian woman, she enjoyed her family and loved looking at photos. When the family moved to Troy, daughter Carrie married Peter Pelligrini, and they bought and lived on the Loyet Road farm.

Peter Sr. died in the W. Kirsch homestead after a lengthy influenza type illness. Following his death, the family had an auction. Laura then went to live with her son, Edward, in Troy.

Mary Levo Romeo and her husband James Romeo bought the farm (18 acres) on West Kirsch Road and moved there.

Laura, after only living with Edward a few short months, fell and broke her hip. She was unable to take care of herself after that and spent the last few years of her life residing at the homes of three daughters, Mary, Louise and Carrie.

When Carrie was killed in a tragic train-auto wreck, Laura came to live with Mary and Louise. She died on November 8, 1949, at the age of 78 at the home of her daughter, Louise Levo Mersinger.

Both Peter P. and Laura Cossano Levo are buried in SS Peter and Paul Catholic Cemetery, Collinsville, IL. *Submitted by Mae Grapperhaus.*

PETE AND VERA LEVO -

Peter J. Levo of Collinsville, IL, was born in 1900. In 1921, Pete married Nina Vera Wild from Troy, IL. They resided in Troy and Pete worked at Mothers Way Bakery in Troy until 1933, at which time he bought the bakery and changed the name to The Levo Bakery. Pete and Vera had three children: Marilyn Dee Levo born in 1926, Ronald Gene Levo born in 1928, and Paul William Levo born in 1936.

Vera and Peter Levo, Jr.

Marilyn married James Bergstrom on October 16, 1949, and they left the Troy area. They had three children: David, Doug and Holly Bergstrom LeMay. Ronald (known by most as Moe) married Mauda Trueblood-Looser in 1956, and they moved to St. Louis. They had

two children, Tom and Terry. Paul married Bonnie Moeller in 1961, stayed in Troy and had two children, Kelli Levo Ponce and Kirk Levo, who both still reside in Troy.

Pete Levo died in 1964 and Vera died in 1974. Vera lived in Troy all of her life and was an active member of the Troy Methodist Church. She loved to quilt and be with her grandchildren. Pete and Vera had 3 children, 7 grandchildren and now have 11 great grandchildren. *Submitted by Kelli Ponce.*

TOM AND MINTA LEWIS -

One of the founding families on Windy Hill was that of Tom and Minta Lewis. Affectionately known as "Bootch," Tom was one of the members of the large Lewis family important in Troy's history, and Minta, the daughter of one of Troy's early merchant families, the Seligmans. Tom was to became a miner and worked many years in the Troy mines.

Lewis family
Front: Lew. Back: Earl, Pete, Beth, MaryBeth, Paul

The couple raised three children, Earl, Beth, and Paul, who became known about town for their friendly natures and musicality, performing singly and together at many Troy functions.

Earl graduated from the University of Illinois in business and went on to serve in the Chicago area in sales management with Sunbeam and other major companies, raising his own family in suburban Chicago, including Jack and Marilyn. Earl also served in World War II.

Beth was the subject of another sketch, having married Clarence Frey.

Paul also served in World War II, primarily as an entertainer. An accomplished pianist and vocalist, he entertained first at home, and then in uniform, entertaining troops in many countries, with a long stint in England. Taking a job in Philadelphia after service life, he became active in the SPEBQSA, the Society for the Preservation and Encouragement of Barbershop Quartet Singing in America. He arranged music for, and directed the Philadelphia SPEBQSA chorus for many years, and sang in an elite barbershop quartet. As a youth, he was very active in the Walther League at local, state and national levels. *Submitted by Beth Lewis Frey and M. Ottwein.*

LINDNER AND BUGGER FAMILIES

The Lindner and Bugger families lived in the area of Troy and Blackjack, IL. They originally came from Bavaria, Germany. John Adam Bugger was a linen weaver there and emigrated to the U.S. in 1844 with his wife Katharine and four children.

John bought a log cabin on the Troy-O'Fallon Rd. in Madison County, IL, from John Flory in 1856 and sold it to Frederick Mersinger in 1859. This cabin was dismantled and reassembled behind Southern Illinois University near a lake there and is now being moved to the Town Park in Troy, IL. John had six children who, for the most part, married and stayed in the area. The three sons married Schwartz, Wittmann and Schwend girls. The three daughters married into the Schwartz, Mersinger, and Bechtlofft families. His oldest daughter, Marie Barbara Bugger, married Philip Schwartz and they had three sons and five daughters. The sons married Liebler and Miller girls. One son died as an infant. The daughters married into the families of Liebler, Niehaus, Brendel and Hellings. One daughter died as a child.

Mary Ann Hellings married Conrad Lindner after the death of her first husband, Joseph Hellings. She had four children, Josephine Hellings, Arthur, John and Augusta Lindner. Most of these families lived on farms in the Blackjack area at one time. In 1907 the Lindner family homesteaded in OK. In 1912 they returned to Troy. The family moved to St. Louis, MO, after the death of Conrad Lindner. Arthur worked as a laborer for the Combustion Engineering Co. there for 32 years. He had three sons, Glenn, Donald and Jerome, the youngest and the last of that generation still living. *Submitted by Jerome Lindner.*

DENNIS WAYNE LITTLE - Dennis Wayne Little is the second son born to Vernon W. and Judy McGlamery/Weidemann Little. Dennis was born May 29, 1968, at St. John's Mercy Hospital in Creve Coeur, MO. He moved to Troy with his parents and older brother Douglas when he was 4 years old. The year he started school, he was joined by a younger brother, Dusty.

Dennis Little, 2002

Dennis went to Triad schools and attended BAC. He played little league baseball and went on to play 4 years of football at Triad High School. Dennis has always liked to make things with his hands and really enjoyed all of the shop classes throughout high school. He is also a computer buff like the rest of the family and spends much of his leisure time on the internet learning new and better ways to build anything he can.

Dennis has been the building maintenance Engineer for O'Fallon Health Care Center in O'Fallon, IL, for the past three years and finally moved to O'Fallon after moving from Troy in 2001. Dennis is a "dyed in the wool" Rams fan, never missing a game; and when he can't get tickets to the game, he watches them on TV with his brothers Dusty and Doug. He is currently in school part time.

Dennis enjoys spending time with his nephew Andy, and he and his brothers have some awesome paintball wars. *Submitted by Judy Little.*

DUSTIN WAYNE LITTLE - Dustin Wayne Little is the third son of Vernon and Judith (McGlamery/Weidemann) Little. Dustin was born June 7, 1975, at St. Joseph's Hospital in Highland, IL.

Dusty Little, 2002

"Dusty" went to Triad schools and BAC, and SIUE where he got an Associates degree. He played little league in grade school and was a member of the football team for 2 years at Triad. He found his niche in drama, performing in several plays and musicals. Two of his most memorable characters were Ito in *Mame* and the Mayor in *Bye, Bye Birdie*. Drama allowed his natural comedic talents to shine, earning him the Drama Award his senior year.

He became interested in computers while in grade school, even then wanting to work for I.B.M. He achieved his goal, for he later worked for I.B.M. in St. Louis. He now works for Boeing at its St. Louis facility. Although still single, Dusty is a home owner in Troy. Dusty always greets everyone with a ready smile, and all enjoy his great sense of humor. In his leisure time he enjoys cheering for the Cardinals and supporting the Rams. *Submitted by Judy Little.*

VERNON W. LITTLE - Vernon and Judy Little moved to Troy in 1972 after living in Black Jack, MO, for the first nine years of their marriage.

Vernon W. Little was born in Du Quoin, IL, on December 23, 1942, the son of Edgar "Vernon" and Ruby "Lucille" nee Pritchett

Judy and Vernon Little, 2002

Little. Vernon's sister Doris Jean Purcell and husband Bill live in Centralia, IL, and his brother Robert Allen Little and wife Jan (Kuhn) live in Glen Carbon, IL. Vernon graduated from Du Quoin High School in 1960 and attended SIUC.

On March 14, 1964, Vernon married Judith E. McGlamery/Weidemann at the First Christian Church in DuQuoin, IL. Judy was born March 30, 1944, in Tampa, FL, and was the daughter of Joseph E. McGlamery II and June Elizabeth (Ayer). Judy has one older brother, Joseph E. III and his wife Gloria (Nieto), living in Washington D.C. and a younger brother, Louis H. Weidemann and wife Judy (Behrns), living in Kansas City, MO. Louis is the son of June and Clement L. Weidemann and has two sons, Scott and Brian Weidemann.

Upon graduating from SIUC, Vernon began work at McDonnell Aircraft Co., then continued at McDonnell-Douglas and finally at Boeing, performing failure analysis work and nondestructive testing throughout his career, retiring after 37 1/2 years. As a young man, Vernon was intrigued by motors and motorcycles and how they worked. He spent countless hours taking apart and reassembling engines and volunteered to help many friends who needed help. Vernon's volunteerism still holds true today, and he still works on wheels, although not cars or motorcycles. Since retiring, Vernon devotes time to Shriners Hospital in St. Louis, keeping all of their wheel chairs in working order.

Andy Little, age 11, 2002

Judy has had a variety of jobs but loved her job as children's storyteller at the Tri-Township Library the most. Judy is currently serving on the Tri-Township Public Library Board as its Secretary. She is the founding President of the Troy Genealogical Society and is a genealogist at heart and is in the process of helping the Society index the City Cemetery. Judy also belongs to the Troy Historical Society, Daughters of the American Revolution and is a member of Beta Sigma Phi Sorority. She has had many creative endeavors including the scanning of all of the pictures for this History Book of Troy. She also enjoys trout fishing and sewing.

Vernon and Judy have taken several long trips since their retirement, but they enjoy being at home close to their children and grandchild, Andy.

Andrew Michael Little, born in 1990, will attend Triad Middle School in the fall of 2002. He enjoys soccer and swimming and is a whiz at computers, even helping his dad construct a see-through computer. Like his Uncle D, he is a great Cardinal fan, too. *Submitted by Judy Little.*

WAYNE AND CLAUDIA LOEHRING

Wayne Loehring was born November 2, 1950, in Highland, IL, to Eldon and Ethel Loehring. He attended Summerfield Grade School and graduated from Lebanon High School in 1968. Wayne graduated from McKendree College in 1972 with a BA degree in history and education. He later earned his Master's degree from SIU-Edwardsville in Public Administration.

Claudia Chapple was born in East St. Louis, IL, on April 27, 1952, to Ralph and Harriet Chapple. She attended grade school in Lebanon through the fourth grade when her parents moved to Fairview Heights, IL. Claudia attended Grant Grade school and later graduated from Belleville East High School in 1970. Claudia graduated from McKendree College in 1985 with a BSAD degree in elementary education.

Wayne and Claudia met at a local football game in 1969 and were married on April 22, 1972. They settled in Lebanon where Wayne taught social studies at the local high school and coached basketball. Wayne was on active duty with the Army when son Brian was born on November 23, 1972. Daughter Megan was born on February 11, 1977. In 1986 the Loehrings moved to Troy after Claudia was hired as a kindergarten teacher within the Triad School District.

Loehring family, circa 1990s
(l. to r.) Wayne, Claudia, Brian, Megan

In 1990, Wayne was hired as a civil service employee by the Department of the Army. He continued to serve in the Army Reserve and eventually retired as a Command Sergeant Major in April 1999, having successfully served for 27 years. He is currently employed as a Personnel Specialist with the U.S. Army Reserve Personnel Command in St. Louis, Missouri.

Claudia continued to teach kindergarten and her classroom was eventually moved into the new C.A. Henning school in Troy in 1987. She has been an active teacher participating in numerous school and community committee efforts in addition to assisting in the development of curriculum initiatives over the years. She also has been a presenter at numerous local and state-wide workshops and seminars.

Brian graduated from Lebanon High School in 1990 and from McKendree College in 1994. He married Tonya Bohnenstiehl from Lebanon on October 19, 1996. Brian teaches social studies at Belleville East High School and completed his Master's Degree in school administration from Southern Illinois University-Edwardsville in 1999. Tonya graduated

from McKendree College in 1993 with a BA degree in criminal justice. She is currently working as a Correctional Officer at the St. Clair County Juvenile Detention Center.

Megan graduated from Triad High School in 1995 and from McKendree College in 1999.

She currently teaches 6th grade at Triad Middle School. Megan is engaged to Doug Raymond, Bunker Hill, IL. An April, 2001 wedding is planned. *Submitted by Wayne Loehring.*

LOWENSTEIN, HACKMAN, AND PLAGEMANN FAMILIES -

The connection to the city of Troy began with the family by the name of Hackmann. Information passed down said that Frederick Hackman came from Prussia, in Germany. The exact dates or what port of entry that he came through is not known.

The family first lived on a farm 2 miles north of Troy on Staunton Road. Then they bought a farm 4 miles northwest of Troy in Pin Oak Township. The brothers operated a saw mill located on the farm.

The family consisted of 8 children, Herman or Harman born 1851, Fred born 1853, Hannah born 1854, William born 1856, Jane 1858, Laura born 1859, Sophia born 1862 and Katie born 1867.

Jane married George Lowenstein in 1880; and two children were born of this union, George F. and Annie both born in 1883. Annie passed away in 1932 and George in 1946. George and Annie went to school at the old Sylvan Hall school located in Pin Oak Township.

Katie married John Plagemann in 1906 and moved to St. Louis, MO, and one son was born of this union, Harvey Plagemann, born in 1908 (d.1960). Katie died in 1934. Harvey married Agnes Burrichter and they had two children, George Plagemann, born in 1936, and Katie Plagemann Leach, born 1938. After the death of George Lowenstein, Harvey moved his family to the farm in Pin Oak Township.

These were the only children born to the Hackmann's. The brothers never married. Sophia married Louis Plagemann, a brother of John Plagemann, from St. Louis; no children were born of this union. Laura married a Charles Kasper. Hannah never married.

George Plagemann married Judith Kidd from Edwardsville, and two children Todd Plagemann and Tammy Plagemann Edwards were from this marriage. Todd married Tracy Greenfield; they live in Troy, and Tammy married Randy Edwards and lives in Maryville, IL. Randy and Tammy have two children, Jonathan and Christine. George is married to Francis Schaffer and resides in St. Louis County, MO.

Katie Plagemann married Billy Joe Leach from Glen Carbon in 1957, lived in Granite City until 1975 then moved to Colorado Springs, CO, and they had one son John E. Leach. John married Debbie Simpson and they had one daughter Torie Marie Leach. *Submitted by Katie Leach.*

ALVIN LOYET -

Alvin and Mildred "Millie" Loyet have been residents of Jarvis Township for almost 60 years. They raised their family on a farm southwest of Troy where they also raised dairy cows and pigs.

Loyet children, circa 2000
(l. to r.) Front: Joan Schreiber, Mildred Loyet, Alvin Loyet, Teresa Oakley. Back: Charlotte Hamill, Anita Howard, Gerald Loyet, Marlene Loyet, Curt Loyet.

Their children were Charlotte Hamill of Las Vegas, NV; Anita Howard of Troy, IL; Gerald "Terry" Loyet of Collinsville, IL; Marlene Loyet of St. Louis, MO; Curtis "Curt" Loyet of Maryville, IL; Joan Schreiber of Troy, IL; and Teresa Oakley of Glen Carbon, IL.

BEN LOYET -

Through the years the name Loyet has had many spellings – Lojet, Lojeth, Loitet, Loyed, Loget and Loyet – from Maxdorf, Germany to Madison County, Illinois, U.S.A. By 1786 the Loyets had moved on to Ruchheim and then to Oggersheim. They departed Europe at the port of Antwerp and entered the U.S. at New Orleans. After a time at Primm Street, Belleville, Illinois, they settled in the Blackjack area south of Troy in Madison County, Illinois. These hard working people farmed the fertile land surrounding St. John the Baptist Catholic Church on Lebanon Road near the junction with Blackjack Road. This is the story of the people who made that journey.

In 1807 Johannes Lojet, the son of Joannes Lojet and Anna Mersinger, married Philippina Fouquet, the daughter of Joseph Fouquet and Maria Kubler. They had a family of ten children – seven sons and three daughters. Five children died in Germany. Johannes died there in 1844. On July 8, 1851, Philippina and her three remaining children, George Adam, Melchior and Philippina followed her two oldest sons to the U.S. Jean had migrated to the U.S. in September, 1840, and Johannes Georg at an unknown date. After the death of Melchior, a subsequent owner of his farm, Mr. Guettermann, donated one acre of the land for a church, school and convent.

Franz Bertram, father-in-law of John Louis Loyet, gave eight acres for a cemetery, where most of these early settlers are buried.

On April 20, 1843, Jean married Elisabeth Loos the daughter of Johannes Loos and Dorothea Lojet. They were the parents of three sons, John, George and Adam, and one daughter, Francisca.

On June 24, 1866, their son George married Barbara Krehers, the daughter of John Krehers and Barbara Liebler. Their family grew to include nine children - five sons: Michael, George Paul, John, Frederick and Peter; and four daughters: Anna Maria, Anna Barbara, Rachel and Barbara Josephine. The new brick church was built in 1883. When stained glass windows from Europe were procured in 1895, George donated the front window on the right side in honor of his family.

In 1892 their son George Paul married Catherine Bugger, the daughter of John Bugger and Elizabeth Wittmann. Their farm was on Blackjack Road west of the junction with Lebanon Road. To this union were born eight children: Clara married Louis Obernuefemann; Ben married Ella Scully; Mayme married William Siegel; Edna married George Fohne; Arthur married Lorene Meyer; Freemont married Mabel Lehm; Earl married Bertha Hohrein; Emma died shortly after birth. The year 1917 was sad for George Paul. His father, wife and infant died, and his oldest son, Ben, was serving in the U.S. army in France in WW I against Germany, the homeland of his ancestors. In 1927 George Paul was named to the board of directors of Troy State Bank.

Ben, now a letter carrier, married Ella Scully on May 18, 1927, at SS Peter & Paul Church in Collinsville. He had a new home built at 733 Maple Street in Collinsville. In 1933 George Paul came to live with Ben and Ella and their growing family. In 1938 Ben and Ella bought a large home at 406 Vandalia Street. Their seven children are Genevieve married Gildo Varda; James married Juanita Meadows; Virginia married William Stephens; Helen married William Graham; Marilyn married Robert Catalpa; Robert married Carol Hoke; Nancy married Vernon Deason. Ella's elderly aunt, Ella Enright, also came to live with them. George Paul died at 406 Vandalia on May 16, 1955.

After more than thirty years on the job, Ben retired from the post office in 1960, returning more than one year in unused sick leave. This hardworking man was a devout Catholic who attended daily mass with his wife. He enjoyed the outdoors – hunting, fishing and beautiful trees. He was a baseball fan – preferring the St. Louis Browns. But the leisure activity his family remembers most is his pleasure in playing cards - especially pinochle. His great memory and ability to keep track of cards played made him a preferred partner, but he always seemed to pick Ella as his partner in everything. On May 18, 1985, Ben died on the 58th anniversary of his marriage to Ella. On April 21, 1995, Ella died. After being the Loyet home for 57 years, 406 Vandalia Street was sold.

Besides their seven children, Ben and Ella are survived by twenty-two grandchildren and twenty-one great-grandchildren, who are scattered across the U.S. in eight states. Ben's descendants have added the following surnames to his legacy: Varda, Hitch, Hicks, Silverwood, Ehlschlaeger, Stephens, Jay, Graham, Yelton, Ulery, Keplar, Kelly, Catalpa, Massa, Warren, Schlotter, Deason and Reed. *Submitted by Juanita Loyet.*

CLAUDIUS LOYET - The progenitor of the many Loyet descendants was a Claudius Lojet, who was born about 1710 and died in Maxdorf, Germany. He lived a long and prosperous life and had 4 wives and a total of 8 children. His great-great grandsons immigrated from Oggersheim, Germany, over an 11 year period

and resided in Madison County, IL. The first to come was John (Loyd Jean) Loyet who immigrated to Illinois on September 15, 1840, landing in New Orleans and then coming to St. Louis and then across to Madison County.

He purchased land in Jarvis Township, around the area of Blackjack. Other brothers soon followed. Joh. George came in 1848 on the ship *Oregon*. Melchior brought his mother Phillipina Fouquet Loyet and other sisters to the United States in 1851. On the 20th of April 1843, John married Elisabeth Loos in Belleville. They had 4 children, of whom only 2 sons lived to adulthood. Cholera killed John and many other relatives between 1849-1852. There is a mass gravesite and marker naming many of these individuals on the land originally owned by the Loyets and now in the possession of Joe Mersinger. After the death of John, Elisabeth married John's brother Melchior and had 6 more children. Many times brothers married their brother's widow to make sure the family was taken care of. Joh. George married Maria Schroth in Germany. They had 5 children. After he died, she married his brother, George Adam Loyet in 1849 and had 2 more.

The family grew considerably over the years and farming was their mainstay. During the Civil War, Joseph Loyet served with the 82nd Regiment of Illinois Volunteers. He was captured in North Carolina and held as a prisoner of war for over a year before being released. Ill treatment caused his early death in 1878. He is buried at the Old City Cemetery in Troy. Joseph married Appolonia Becki on the 21st of April 1866 in St. Louis. From this union came 8 children: Joseph Charles who married Emma Reidlinger; Frederick who married Katherine Greifuz Louis; George who married Irene Hettel; Francis; William John who married Augusta Bornhauser; Louisa Maria who married John Reed and Hedwig Loyet. When Joseph died, he left his wife with 8 children under the age of 12. Appolonia had to "farm out" the oldest 5 to other families since she was left without any means of support and give up the land her husband had purchased from her parents.

Apollonia (Becki) Loyet

All but two of their children married and moved either to St. Louis, Missouri, Highland or East St. Louis, IL. Frederick and Hedwig stayed at the family home and took care of their aged mother.

The Loyets married into many German lines that ended up in Madison County- Bugger, Fohne, Mersinger, Siegel, Arth, Hettel, Becki, Reed and Schaefer. These families made their

homes in Madison County up to 160 years ago and many descendants still remain. *Submitted by Kathleen D. Cormack.*

FRED AND EMMA LOYET - Fred Loyet and Emma Niehaus were the parents of Herbert, Erwin, Victor, Gertrude, and Cecilia Loyet. Herbert married Mary; Erwin married Ann (first

Wedding photo, Feb. 6, 1907, Emma and Fred Loyet

wife) and Dee (second wife); Victor married Ella Meier; Gertrude married Adrian Mersinger; and Cecilia married Michael Katich. *Submitted by Donald Mersinger.*

GEORGE AND BARBARA LOYET - Barbara and George Loyet lived in Blackjack on East Lebanon Road. They were the parents of

Barbara and George Loyet, pre-1900

Michael and Frederick Loyet. George was called the "wheat king" because he could grow wheat well and bought several tracts to expand his farm. *Submitted by Donald Mersinger.*

RAYMOND LOYET - Michael Loyet was the oldest child born to George and Barbara Loyet in 1866. They were both of German descent, originating from the Alsace- Lorraine region on the Rhine River.

Michael married Barbara Arth in 1893. They moved to their own farm in rural Troy, where they raised their seven children, two daughters and five sons. Michael became blind in his early sixties and lived to be 101 years.

Raymond Loyet was the fourth child born to Michael and Barbara in 1901. He married Christine Schlemer of rural Collinsville in April, 1926. Christine was the third child of six born to Joseph and Laura Schlemer, both of Bohemian descent.

Upon their marriage, Ray and Christine moved into a new bungalow on 80 acres of land belonging to his father. (Today it remains the

Loyet family, 1986
(l. to r.) Front: Ray Loyet, Christine Loyet, Gladys Weider, Marian Wakeland, and Doris Schultheiss. Back: Arthur (Puz) Weider, Ray Wakeland, Peter Schultheiss.

original home and barn in the Steelecrest Subdivision, south of Troy.) They worked hard, as they had learned from their parents, raising corn, wheat, oats and alfalfa. They always had a dairy herd, shipping milk to a St. Louis dairy daily.

They had no conveniences, such as running water and electricity, when they began their life together, but took advantage of them as they became available. When the tractor replaced their horses, it was a great day!

They had four children: three daughters, Gladys, born April 1927; Marian, born September 1928; and Doris, born December 1933; and one son Nelson, born August 1942. He died at 23, in July 1965, due to accidental death during his college summer vacation while working on Interstate 55-70 construction just north of Troy.

Gladys married Arthur "Puz" Weider and lives in Troy. They have four children, two sons and two daughters. Curtis, first born, died at age 23 of a malignant brain tumor in 1973. Stuart married Paula McMahon, lives in Troy and has three daughters – Lauren, Sarah and Chelsea. Karen married Darrell Becker, lives in Highland and has two daughters – Amanda and Angela. Annette married Lowell Mills, lives in Marine and has a daughter Emily and a son Eric.

Marian married Ray Wakeland, who died in August 1998. She lives in Michigan and Florida. They have four children, three daughters and one son. Barbara married Steve Berry, lives in Owosso, MI, and has two daughters, Megan and Molly. Susan married Craig Kowal, lives in St. Joseph, MI, has a son Michael and daughter Morgan. Michelle married Sam McLaren, lives in Owosso and has a son Matthew. David married Pam Boesiger, lives in Williamston, MI, has two daughters, Paige and Erin, and a son Grant Robert.

Doris married Peter Schultheiss and they live in Green Valley, Arizona. They have five children, one son and four daughters. Bradley married Jackie Daly, lives in Cork, Ireland, has a daughter Sara and son Shane. Laurie Wingender has a son Brian and lives in Jacksonville, Florida. Sara married Craig Lancaster, lives in Austin, TX, and has two sons, Drew and Jake. Karen married Eric Cadle, lives in Crown Point, Indiana, and has three sons, Josh, Zachary and Brett. Maribeth married Keith Jezek, lives in Austin, TX, has two sons, Walker and Weston and a daughter, Audrey.

Ray and Christine, along with their work on the farm, took part in their children's activities, also enjoyed their Sunday outings with family, played cards, danced, and, in their retired years, travelled. They were married about 65 years when Christine died in January, 1991, at age 85. Ray died in March, 1996, at age 95. *Submitted by Gladys (Loyet) Weider.*

LOYET, BECKI, AND HETTEL FAMILIES

The Loyet, Becki, and Hettel families lived in the Troy vicinity for many years. The Cormack family is found living in that vicinity in 1820 but moved into Macoupin County and then into Arkansas by the 1850s. (Illinois got too civilized for them and the tax man was close to their heels.) Collateral families include the Vanhoosers and Renfros who first settled that area in the early 1800s. *Submitted by Kathleen D. Cormack.*

MARGUERITE DOROTHY (ARTH) LUCIDO -

Marguerite Dorothy (Arth) Lucido was born on January 17, 1916, and died on June 17, 1997. She went to Formosa school and graduated from McCray-Dewey High School. She married Andrew Lucido, who is deceased.

At first, they lived in East St. Louis; then they moved to Belleville. They had a daughter, Nancy Lynn (Lucido) Beltran. She is living in Florida. Nancy married and had three children, Andrea, Jessica and Brandon. Andrea has one son, Cole; Jessica had two sons and two daughters. A son and daughter are deceased in 1992. Brandon has one child.

Marguerite inherited 31 acres along U.S. Hwy. 40 and the small house and three acres in Collinsville where Lewis and Mary, her parents, had lived. They owned the Dairy Queen in Belleville for many years after selling their half of the one in Collinsville on Vandalia to Beatrice and William Klem. Marguerite and the Klems were part owners. *Submitted by Sylvia Kauhl.*

ALBERT AND IRMA OTTWEIN LUDWIG

Irma Ottwein was born on August 3, 1907, in the Formosa area, and raised in Troy (see George and Carrie Ottwein). Irma, her sister Helen, and brother-in-law, Les Becker, assisted their mother, Carrie Ottwein, who owned and operated the Confectionery on Main St. It was in the confectionery that Irma met Albert. After a courtship, they were married August 8, 1932.

Albert Milton Ludwig was born March 29, 1907, in Mt. Pleasant, Iowa. His parents were William Peter Ludwig and Laura A. Schmidt Ludwig (See Wm. P. and Laura Ludwig). Albert

Irma and Albert Ludwig, 1963

attended high school at Wapello, Iowa. He went to college at Central Wesleyan, Warrenton, MO; Washington University; Illinois University and Chicago Kent College of Law. He taught school in St. Louis County and Troy for a total of 20 years.

Albert moved to Troy in 1929 to serve as basketball coach at McCray-Dewey High School. According to a special edition of the *Troy Times*, November 7, 1985, "The school had not won a game the previous year to his arrival as coach. At the conclusion of the time he was coach, the team had won 75 percent of the games played." A daughter, Virginia Ann, was born on February 16, 1935. After leaving Troy, Albert, Irma, and Virginia lived in Jacksonville, IL; Oak Park, IL; Jefferson City, MO; and Clayton, MO.

For 22 years Albert was associated with Farm Bureau Insurance Services of Illinois and Missouri. Albert started the Missouri Farm Bureau Insurance Company in 1946 in Jefferson City, MO. He spent twelve years as the Missouri Insurance Manager. During Albert and Irma's years in Jefferson City, they were very active in the Central United Church of Christ and other community organizations and activities. Albert was a member of Kiwanis and held various offices in this club. He was on the first Board of Directors of the Memorial Community Hospital, and was instrumental in starting this institution.

In 1959, Albert and Irma moved to Clayton, Missouri, where he worked for the BMA insurance company. They moved to Troy in the '60s, where he was a real estate broker. He served as principal in a grade school, and then taught math at Triad High School until his retirement.

Albert and Irma were active members of Friedens United Church of Christ. Albert was a member of the Troy Lions Club and held various positions, including president.

After a lengthy illness, Irma passed away on December 26, 1964.

Albert married Esther Kruse on June 10, 1966. Esther was born and raised on a farm near Edwardsville, and was previously married to Hermann Kruse. They had two sons, Robert and Richard. She worked as a secretary for the County Farm Advisor. Esther died on May 9, 1992.

In 1993, Albert moved into the retirement center in Highland. In 1994, Albert moved into Hampton Nursing Home in Alhambra, where he passed away on August 24, 1996. *Submitted by Virginia Bailey.*

WILLIAM PETER AND LAURA A. (SCHMIDT) LUDWIG -

William Peter Ludwig was born January 6, 1863, in Arnheim, Brown County, Ohio. His parents were Philip Peter Ludwig II and Mary Elizabeth Bohl Ludwig. He was one of 13 children.

W.P. was married in the 1880's to Cecelia Winkler. They had one child, Clara, who died at the age of 2. Cecelia also died not long after.

On November 2, 1893, W.P. married Laura A. Schmidt in Farina, Illinois. Laura A. Schmidt Ludwig was born November 17, 1873, in Tarp, near Apenrade, Schlesswig-Holstein, Germany. Unfortunately, there is not much known about the genealogy on Laura's side of the family.

Ludwig family circa 1915
(l. to r.) Front: Celia, William P., Laura
Back: Albert, Orlando, Lorla, Dorothy

They had the following children: Celia Agnes Ludwig Aydelott, b. September 6, 1895, d.October 1, 1976; Lorla Lydia Ludwig Miller, b. May 15, 1899, d. June 22, 1991; Orlando Ellison Ludwig, b. June 8, 1903, d. May 26, 1964; Albert Milton Ludwig, b. March 29, 1907, d. August 24, 1996; Dorothy Elizabeth Ludwig Gindler, b. February 20, 1909, d. July 11, 1997.

William or "W.P." or "Willie" was a minister in the German Methodist Conference and served in churches in Nebraska, Appleton, MO, Farina, IL, Burlington, IA, Gordonville, MO, Wapello, IA, Emden, IL and Troy.

For reasons of health he dropped out of the ministry for several years to farm and can tomatoes at Mt. Vernon, MO, and to operate a dairy at Glendale, Arizona. The Ludwigs also operated a boarding house for students at Iowa Wesleyan College at Mt. Pleasant, IA.

W.P. was educated at Central Wesleyan College, Warrenton, MO. Laura had some training at the Academy there, also.

The Ludwigs moved to Troy in the 1930s after he retired from the ministry due to poor health. Reverend Ludwig assisted in some of the ministry work at the Troy Methodist Church. It is remembered that W.P. preached the last Sunday of the month in German. Since most of the younger generation could not understand German, they did not have to go to church on those days.

W.P. and Laura lived in three houses in Troy. The one most remembered by their grandchildren was the house on Center Street. This house had a summer kitchen and breezeway, where the couple spent a lot of their time, as it was much cooler than in the bigger house. Both W.P. and Laura loved to garden,

Ludwig family
(l. to r.) Albert, Lorla (Ludwig) Miller, William P.,
Dorothy (Ludwig) Gindler, Laura (Schmidt)
Ludwig, Orlando, Celia (Ludwig) Aydelott

and in their "retirement" raised prize dahlias. It was in this house that W.P. died September 7, 1944, after listening to a speech by presidential candidate, Wendell Wilke, and commenting "that was a good speech." It was said by his son Albert, that William P. was a very devout man.

After W.P. died, Laura lived with her daughter, Dorothy Ludwig Gindler and her family for a number of years. She then moved to St. Louis and lived with her daughter, Celia Ludwig Aydelott, for 13 years. Laura was known as a very loving woman. Laura died November 21, 1967, in St. Louis, MO. Both W.P. and Laura are buried in Friedens Cemetery in Troy. *Submitted by Virginia Bailey.*

JIMMIE LYBARGER - In 1938, Chas. A. Lybarger Construction Company of Granite City, IL, was contracted to build the Troy Grade School (now the William S. Freeman School) on Staunton Road. Ten years later, Charles Alexander and Nancy Ellen (Jones) Lybarger's son, Jimmie (the third oldest of 10 children), Jimmie's wife Lela (Lockley) Lybarger (born to Augusta [Dillow] and Martin Otis Lockley, Sr.), and their 2-yr.-old daughter Karen Lee moved from Madison, IL, to Troy. In August 1946, the Lybargers moved to their 2-story house on S. Main St., an area then known as "Brookside." The story goes that a train depot once stood at the corner of S. Main and Rt. 40. When it was torn down, some of the 100-yr.-old materials were used to construct part of the house the Lybarger's purchased. Now, 55 years later, Jimmie and Lela (married June 28, 1941) still reside there.

Lybarger family, 1981
(l. to r.) Front: Lela, Patti, Karen
Back: Jimmie, Jimmie, Jr.

Four months after moving to Troy, daughter Patti Jean was a spcial "gift" to the family – being born Christmas Day, 1946.

When they moved to Troy, Jimmie was in the construction industry with his father and four brothers and Lela was a homemaker. Both became active in their new home town, participating in church (Troy Methodist), community, and school affairs (Lela acted in a PTA play that also starred the future U.S. Senator Paul Simon).

1959 was important for Jimmie Lybarger, Jr., was born March 22. In that same year, Jimmie, Sr., was appointed to the school board (replacing Milton Strong) after Troy, Marine and St. Jacob were consolidated into one district, and

a new high school was under construction (opening fall, 1959).

Along with his involvement in the completion of the high school, Jimmie was on the board when the new addition to the high school was built in the mid 1960s and the Wakeland Center and the Molden School were built in Troy. He worked with 3 superintendents: Fred Wakeland, C.A. Henning and Robert Rogier. He served as president of the board during his last 4 years, but did not seek re-election when his term ended in April, 1976 (he was followed by Robert Purcell).

In 1979, Jimmie, Sr. joined the Madison County Corrections for Christ Ministry. He has been a member 22 years and served as president for 16. The 35 members of this group minister to 5 counties (6 complexes, including 2 juvenile facilities), visiting 4 of the complexes twice a week. Jimmie has also been a volunteer chaplain at Anderson Hospital since 1985.

Jimmie, Jr., is a third generation involved in the consruction industry. He resides in Troy and is the father of 4 children- Ryan, Christopher, Jordan and Marissa.

Their youngest daughter, Patti, is married to Dennis Amsden. They live in Collinsville, IL, where they are the pastors of Son Life Church. Dennis and Patti have 5 children: Dawn (Mrs. Tim) Stark; Dennis, Jr.; Deedra (Mrs. Paul) Mager; David and Dallas.

Their oldest daughter Karen is married to Robert Freeman, the son of William S. Freeman, for whom the Troy Grade School is now named, and the granddaughter of Charles A. Lybarger, the general contractor who built Troy Grade School. Bob and Karen are the parents of three children: Kristan Leigh (Mrs. Warren) Byrd, Kyle William (Amy Strong) Freeman, and Kane Michael (Jennifer York) Freeman.

Jimmie and Lela are also the proud great grandparents of Caitlin, Devynn and Cali Byrd; Lydia Stark, Jake Robert Freeman, and Cole Mager. *Submitted by Jimmie and Lela Lybarger.*

JIM AND DORIS LYONS - Jim Lyons was born September 18, 1944, to Kenneth and Arline Kueker Lyons. A life-long resident of Troy, he was a graduate of St. Paul's Lutheran School and Triad High School.

On July 3, 1965, Jim married Doris Hartmann, daughter of Emmanuel and Hulda Schlaefer Hartmann. They have a son, David, and a daughter, Jan. David and his wife Susan live in Rockville, MD. He is a computer consultant and she is an archivist for the U.S. government. Jan lives in Bethalto, IL. She is a reading specialist in the Alton, IL, school district.

Jim has one brother, Terry Lyons, who is the facility director at he Marriott Hotel in Oklahoma City, OK, where he resides with his wife, Ruth Anne. Doris has one sister, Norma Jean Peter Grist, of Windsor, CA.

Jim has been an insurance agent since 1967. In 1980, he opened his own agency in Troy, following in his grandfather, Henry C. Kueker's footsteps as a local insurance agent. For the past 25 years, Jim and Doris have owned and operated the Trojan Nursery, east of Troy. They have now changed from a retail to a wholesale operation. *Submitted by Jim and Doris Lyons.*

LYPE FAMILY - The Lype family name can be traced to Hans Leipp, who married Ursula Vogelsanger of Switzerland in 1635. Their son Melchoir married Margaretha Mueller circa 1666 in Germany. Their grandson Johannes Leipp (Leib) left Germany and sailed to America in 1727, where he settled in North Carolina and raised seven children. One of these children was Godfried Johannes Lype (Lipe, Leib), who married Barbara Rudisell in 1762. They had seven kids of their own, at least three of whom fought in the Revolutionary War. Four of Barbara Rudisell's brothers, in fact, spent the long cold winter with General Washington at Valley Forge.

Lype family, 1994
(l. to r.) Front: Jerrylene, Crissy
Back: Bob H., Cathy, Jeff, III, Tom, Cori, Dan, Mary K.

Two of the Lype brothers, John and Leonard, moved west to an area just south of current Murphysboro, IL, in 1819. Other Lypes had already settled in the area as evidenced by the officially recorded death of Peter Lype, who was killed by Potawatami Indians near Kaskaskia in 1793.

The Lype brothers brought their families with them, including a son named Daniel (born 1808). Daniel would marry Charlotte Etherton and have a large family before his death at age eighty. One of their children was a son named John, who was born in 1831. John would marry Delila Walker in 1853 and have four boys of his own when, in the summer of 1862, he enlisted in the Union Army (IL 81st) at the age of thirty-two to fight in the American Civil War. Less than a year later he would fall dead in the trenches outside Vicksburg, just a few days before the city fell. He left Delila a widow with four boys and personal property valued at $227 (which included a wash kettle worth $2.50 and 100 lbs. of bacon valued at $8.00). She was

(l. to r.) Jeff, Mary K., Bob, Tom,
Jerrylene, Dan, Crissy, Cori

given a widow's pension of $8.00 per month and never remarried.

Daniel Lype, one of John and Delila's sons, was only three years old when his father left for the war. Perhaps this lack of a father when growing up contributed to his own failed marriage with Molly Davis. Daniel worked as a hired hand on Molly's father's farm and would marry her in 1882.

Molly's father, Abel Cartwright Davis, had also been a Civil War veteran (31st MO) who would hold many public service positions, including sheriff, tax collector, and judge of Jackson County, Illinois. Abel's grandfather was John Logan Sr., who was a medical doctor in the late 1700s and early 1800s. This meant that Abel's cousin was John Logan Jr., who was the Civil War general and politician who would eventually run unsuccessfully for the vice presidency of the United States. Having a general for a cousin apparently didn't help Abel Davis, since his rank was a lowly infantry private.

Daniel and Molly would have four children before they divorced, one of which was Jefferson Cartwright Lype (born in 1890). Molly had remarried by the time Jeff was nine, and he apparently resented his father's absence as he would never discuss his father in later life. Jeff was a born salesman; and he used this skill to become a successful businessman (owning J.C. Lype Tailoring Co.) and eventually a popular Baptist minister in E. St. Louis, Illinois. If he knew anything about his grandfather's death at Vicksburg, he never told his only son, Jefferson Cartwright Lype Jr., about it. Jeff would grow up in E. St. Louis and attend William Jewel College before becoming a decorated pilot in World War II and marrying Jerrylene Benton of Mississippi in 1952. Jerrylene was the 1951 Miss Mississippi College as well as the homecoming queen. She also had a father who was a Baptist minister (Bob Hollis Benton).

After moving to Troy in 1968, both Jeff and Jerrylene would teach school for many years and rear two sons, Jefferson Lype III and Bob Hollis Lype. The two would attend Triad High school in the early 70s, where Jeff would meet Mary Kay Bostrom. Jeff would graduate from Western Illinois University and marry his high school sweetheart, Mary Kay. They have two sons Daniel and Thomas. Jeff built a successful insurance agency in E. St. Louis and lives in nearby Shiloh, Illinois. After graduating from Southern Illinois University, Bob married Cathleen Hogan, also from Troy. After living in Chicago for four years while completing his post graduate degree, Bob had two daughters Corinne and Christine. Bob moved his family to the Farmington, Missouri, area in 1992 where he is a practicing optometrist. Jerrylene Lype still resides in Troy. *Submitted by Jerrylene Lype.*

AUGUSTA HOENIG AND EDWARD MAEDGE - Augusta Dorothy Hoenig was born on September 15, 1910, the daughter of Andrew and Dora (Werner) Hoenig. She married Edward Maedge of Marine in 1931, and they lived together in a farmhouse in Blackjack, an area south of Troy. Edward was a coal miner, and Augusta was a homemaker. They also sold pears from their orchard, as well as potatoes and produce.

Augusta (Hoenig) and
Edward Maedge, 1931.

The Maedges had eight children, one of them dying at the age of four. During the scarce money years of the Depression, the family lost the farm to back taxes and moved to Troy (pop. 1154) in 1943, first living in a show (movie) house at the corner of Washington and Clay Streets. With the help of Aunt Minnie, a year later the family moved to a home on Kimberlin Street. The couple's last daughter was born in March 1948, followed by the death of Edward in May of that same year, leaving Augusta to raise her children alone.

To help make ends meet, Augusta laundered for other people and made a garden in the lot next to her home and sold vegetables. Her children would help her shell lima beans and peas, which she sold for 25 cents a pint. She raised chickens for the family, and her children had a paper route to help with expenses.

The people of Troy helped Augusta's family throughout the years. For a short while, the family was on State Aid, and the State Aid people constantly came to make sure there was no telephone or television in the house. Augusta thought she would get along without State Aid, and it was a struggle for her, but she made it through those years.

Augusta was proud of her children, and she took an active part in their lives as a member of the PTA, remaining a member even until some of her grandchildren were in school. She was a woman of faith, making sure that even if her children were up late on a Saturday night, they still attended church the next morning. She made sure that each of her children got an education and stayed out of serious trouble.

She passed away in December of 1992 at the age of 82. Her children are Dorothy Maedge (1931-1935), Edward Maedge (1933), Charles Maedge (1935), Frieda (Maedge) Kuhn (1936-2001), Clara (Maedge) Lang (1938), Ruby (Maedge) Schultze (1940), Janet Maedge (1942) and Ruth Ann (Maedge) Ostendorf (1948). *Submitted by Emily Ostendorf.*

MANNZ FAMILY - On 1 January 1839, George and Barbara (Beck) Mannz left Hesse Kassel in Germany and emigrated to America. They arrived in Baltimore, Maryland, with daughters Martha (Haury), Katharine (later Mrs. Conrad Eisenberg), and Maria (later Mrs. John Michael Beck). They moved westward and settled in Madison County, Illinois. Later they moved to Blackjack, a settlement south of Troy.

George and Barbara's fourth child was born on 28 April 1841. John Mannz became the first

Mannz born in America. In 1861, he enlisted in the Civil War. He served two enlistments for two other men and used the money they paid him to buy more farm land.

John married Caroline Susanna Busch on 11 April 1875. John and Caroline had Kathryn on 28 April 1878, and she married Christian Widicus on 11 March 1902. John Henry was born on 18 April 1883, and married Josephine Marie Guttersohn on 11 April 1917. Hannah was born on 26 September 1886, and married Henry Hecklinger on 24 April 1906. Gottlieb Ludwig arrived on 14 October 1888 and married Louisa Laura Adelhardt on 23 October 1913, in Moscow Mills, Missouri. (Twenty-five years earlier, on 24 October 1888, Louisa's parents, Frank and Katharine Druessel Adelhardt were married at Blackjack, Illinois. The Adelhardts moved to a farm near Moscow Mills, MO, after their marriage and now their oldest daughter would move back to Blackjack).

Kathryn and Christian Widicus farmed her parents' farm, but when Christian was given a farm near Lebanon, IL, by his father, they left the Mannz farm. Gottlieb was working at Willard's Stove Foundry at O'Fallon, IL, but Gottlieb came back to the farm near Troy.

Gottlieb and Louisa (Adelhardt) Mannz had three children: Ella Katherine, Pauline Louisa, and Henry Gottlieb. Ella was born on 4 September 1914, and married Vilray (Bill) Frank Fulton, Sr. on 7 July 1937. Pauline was born on 3 October 1916, and married Leigh Gordon Gass on 26 April 1940. Henry was born on 18 November 1920. He married Virginia Lee Meyer on 1 June 1947.

Henry continued the family farm, but it was becoming harder for two families to make a living on the family farm. So, Henry became a substitute rural letter carrier and eventually a full time rural letter carrier. He carried mail for over twenty-four years. He also served as a Jarvis Township Road Commissioner for five years.

Henry and Virginia's children left the farm and both earned college degrees. Gloria Lynn earned a Bachelor of Arts degree from McKendree College in Lebanon and then a Master of Science in Education from Southern Illinois University Edwardsville. Gloria lives and teaches fourth grade in Troy. Richard Henry earned Bachelor degrees in Zoology and Environmental Biology from Eastern Illinois University and later his Masters in Environmental Studies from Southern Illinois University Edwardsville. He married Theresa Scheiper on 15 September 1978. They make their home in Town and Country, MO, with their daughter, Laura Anne, who was born on 25 May 1986. *Submitted by Gloria Mannz.*

RICH AND DEE MASON - Joseph Richard (Rich) Mason was the only child born to George (b. 1906 d. 1985) and Katherine Mechella Mason (b. 1912 d. 1954) in 1932 in Pocahontas, IL.

In 1934 Dolores (Dee) Paoletti Mason was the third child born to Gino (b. 1904 d. 1949) and Anne (Vairo) Paoletti (b. 1905 d. 1990), also in Pocahontas.

Both Rich and Dee grew up in Pocahontas and attended school there. Rich graduated from high school in 1950, and Dee, in 1952. Rich attended Greenville College, receiving his B.S.

Mason-Cange families, 2000
(l. to r.) Front: Todd, Ted, Kathy, Kate, Mark
Back: Jeff, Kirk, Rich, Dee, Rob

Degree in Education. He then attended the U of I receiving his M.S. in Educational Administration in 1958. His undergraduate work was interrupted by another commitment, however. He was drafted into the Army and spent the next two years as a paratrooper and a member of the 508 Regimental Combat Team, the forerunner of the Green Berets. Dee attended SIU-C and Greenville College, and completed her undergraduate degree at SIUE with a B.S. in Elementary Education.

Rich and Dee were married while Rich was still in the service. They lived at Fort Benning, GA, and Fort Campbell, KY, until he was discharged. They returned to Pocahontas to live until Rich finished his degree at Greenville College. Their daughter Kathy was born during this time, and their son Bob was born two years later. By this time, the family had moved to Highland, IL.

Kathy and Bob attended grade school at St. Paul's in Highland. In 1969 the family moved to Troy where Kathy attended Triad High School, and Bob attended McCray-Dewey Junior High. Kathy graduated from Triad in 1972, and Bob, in 1974.

After graduation, Kathy attended BAC and then SIU-E and received her B.S. in Elementary Education. She then married Edward (Ted) Cange of Belleville, IL. Both are presently teaching in the Triad District. Kathy teaches 4th grade at Molden Center, and Ted is an assistant principal and athletic director at Triad High School.

Upon completion of high school, Bob attended BAC and also worked on construction. His life came to an abrupt end in 1980. He died in a motorcycle-automobile accident at the age of 24.

Rich and Dee have 6 grandchildren, the children of Kathy and Ted. They all presently

Bob Mason, 1974

live in Troy. Kirk, the oldest, is a student at SIU-E. Todd is presently attending SWIC. Rob, a senior, will be graduating from Triad in 2002. Jeff, a sophomore, and Mark, a freshman, are also students at Triad. Kate, the youngest, is an 8th grader at TMS.

Rich has had a very interesting career. He began teaching and coaching in 1956 at St. Paul High School in Highland. He taught there for 5 years and then taught and coached at Assumption High School in E. St. Louis, IL, for 1 year. Rich then accepted a position as teacher and basketball coach at Triad High School in 1962. He remained at Triad until his retirement in 1994. Rich spent 45 years in education. During that time, he was a classroom teacher, athletic director and assistant principal for 7 years, a coach for 34 years, and a principal for 18 years. Since 1994 he has been serving as Co-Transportation Director for the Triad District.

Dee's career has not been as extensive. Aside from being a mother, a grandmother, and a basketball coach's wife, she also spent 36 years in education. She began her career at St. Paul Grade School in Highland. Dee taught 5th grade for 15 years and then accepted a position at McCray-Dewey Junior High. She taught in Troy for 21 years, retiring in 1994.

The Masons are thoroughly enjoying their retirement. Both enjoy traveling, sporting events, outdoor activities, and spending time with their family and friends. *Submitted by Dolores Mason.*

HAROLD AND REBA MATHIS - Harold and Reba Mathis began their life in Troy, IL, in February 1961 when they purchased a home at 304 North Franklin. After 13 years at that location they moved to Pin Oak Township where they still reside.

Harold and Reba Mathis

Harold Marshall Mathis was born 7 April 1936 in Pine Lawn, MO, to Otha and Ruth (Whitworth) Mathis. Otha was born in 1903 in Knights Prairie Township, Hamilton Co., IL, and Ruth was born in 1903 in Brushy Mound Township, Macoupin Co., IL. Harold's early childhood was spent in the Gillespie, IL, area and then east of Carlinville, IL, where he attended a one-room school. In the spring of 1948 the family moved to Litchfield, IL, where Harold became very active in the Boy Scouts for many years. He was a newspaper carrier for the Litchfield *New Herald* and during his high school years he worked at the B & M Bakery, delivering bakery items in a Model A panel truck. In 1954 he graduated from Litchfield Community High School.

Harold worked 31 years on the railroad as a tower operator, ticket agent, and traveling representative. He began with the New York Central Railroad in 1955 at Litchfield Tower and retired in 1986 from Willows Tower in East St. Louis, IL. The New York Central became the Penn Central and later Conrail. Since his retirement, he has enjoyed amateur radio, emergency services, woodworking, model railroading, and restoring older vehicles.

Reba Louise Niemann was born 11 December 1935 in Litchfield, IL, to John and Agnes (Barlow) Niemann. John was born in 1900 and Agnes in 1902, both in Walshville Township, Montgomery Co., IL.

Reba's early childhood was spent living in the country south of Litchfield, later moving into town. Reba was active in Girl Scouts for many years. In 5th grade she began playing clarinet which she continued to do throughout high school, while attending college, and in the Troy Community Band. She also played piano and organ at church. In 1953 she graduated from Litchfield Community High School and attended Southern Illinois University in Carbondale, IL. She worked for the Illinois Division of Highways in Springfield, IL, General Contracting Co. in Granite City, IL, and Holzinger Real Estate and *The Times Tribune* in Troy, IL. Her interests have been amateur radio, gardening, genealogy, and quilting.

Harold and Reba were married 6 June 1959 at Zion Lutheran Church in Litchfield, IL. They are the parents of two children. Their son, Charles (Chuck) and wife Tammie, of St. Jacob Township, IL, have two sons, Kevin Sweet currently serving in the U.S. Marine Corp., and Geoff Conner Mathis. Their daughter, Karen, and husband Scott Stippich live in Brownsburg, IN. *Submitted by Harold and Reba Mathis.*

JANE STORMENT MAYHEW - Jane Mayhew originally moved to Troy in April 1950 with her family, James and Susie Storment and a twin sister, Ann, and a sister, Carolyn. Ann and Jane were in the fifth grade; Carolyn was in the first. Ann and Jane had Imogene Auwarter for a teacher and Carolyn's teacher was Mrs. Newberry.

The family lived on Charcoal Street at the corner of Charcoal and Montgomery. There were three acres and a large barn. Prior to living in Troy, the family had lived in Caseyville, IL, and prior to that on a farm in Texaco, Illinois.

Ann and Jane Storment graduated from McCray-Dewey in 1957. Jane married Kenneth Fritschle in 1958. Ken was in the same class as Jane and had moved from Utah Street in south St. Louis in 1951. The family lived in several homes in Troy: an apartment on Park Street; a rented house from Dave and Gladys Skeens on Hickory Street, when the Skeens were in Japan; and a small home on Hazel Street which they rented from Frank and Carrie Adelhardt.

The family purchased their first home on Bryn Street on the north side of the street from the elementary school. The house was purchased from Everett and Laverne Poulson, who had three daughters. Ken worked at Granite City

Steel for nine years, then in the steam/pipe fitters for about five or six years. Jane was a stay-at-home Mom.

Ken began working for Ralston Purina Company in 1972. He trained as maintenance supervisor in Vandalia for one year and then was transferred to Omaha, NB, in 1973. From there the family transferred to Pocatello, ID, where Ken was production manager and then continued as manager at Montgomery City, MO; Jackson, MS; and Macon, GA. He left Purina which had become Purina Mills.

Then they moved to Cartersville, GA. The couple divorced. Jane went to Plymouth, IN. Two children were born to Ken and Jane Fritschle. They are Charles Glenn born in 1959 and Carole Ann born in 1961. Charles Glenn is married to Robin Schoenecker of St. Louis. They have two children, Ellen Lorraine who is married to Anthony Freed and Evin Charles. Carole Ann married Billy Goza in Pearl, MS. They have one daughter. They divorced and Carole is remarried to Jerry Johanan.

Jane Storment remarried in 1997 to David Mayhew of Warsaw, IN. They currently reside there. *Submitted by Jane Mayhew.*

BRANDON AND SUSAN (BAUMGARTNER) MAZUR - Brandon Mazur of Glen Carbon and Susan (Baumgartner) Mazur of Troy were married on September 21, 1996, in Maryville. After their honeymoon to Padre Island, they moved into their new home which Brandon built.

Mazur family, 2001
Brandon, Maverick, Susan

Brandon was born on September 14, 1973, in Belleville to Edward Mazur of Blanchard, OK, and the late Linda (Lewis) Mazur of Glen Carbon. Susan was born on July 29, 1972, in Belleville to Otto and Sharon (Daiber) Baumgartner of Troy.

Brandon graduated from Blanchard High School in Blanchard, OK, in 1991. Brandon also attended grade school in Robertsville, MO. Brandon played many sports, tennis, soccer, baseball, basketball, football and hockey. Brandon graduated from Rankin Technical College in St. Louis in 1995. Brandon is the owner of Mazur Construction. Brandon loves motorcycle riding, golfing, and playing Play Station 2.

Susan graduated from Triad High School in 1990. She graduated in 1992 from BAC with an AA and AS, and then earned a BS in Mathematical Studies with Secondary Education at SIUE (1995). She is a math teacher at Hazelwood East High School in Missouri. Susan was active in

Girl Scouts, 4-H, soccer, gymnastics, track, band, cross-country and cheerleading. Susan loves swimming and gardening.

Brandon and Susan were blessed with a son Maverick Michael born on January 4, 2001. Brandon and Susan are busy building another new home and enjoying parenting. *Submitted by Susan Mazur.*

DANIEL E. McALEY JR. - Daniel E. McAley Jr. was born in Providence, RI, and is a native of Warwick, RI. He is the son of Marion (Marsh) Quinn of West Warwick, RI, and the late Daniel E. McAley, Sr. After graduating from Warwick Veterans' Memorial High School, he joined the U.S. Air Force. Following basic training in San Antonio, TX, Dan's first duty assignment was Scott Air Force Base, IL. While stationed there, he met Mary "Sharon" Childress. They were married at Scott Air Force Base Chapel, near Belleville, IL, on April 30, 1966.

Sharon is a Collinsville, IL, native. She was born in St. Louis, MO, to Mary (Guaglio) Childress and William H. Childress. Sharon attended SS Peter and Paul School (K-8) in Collinsville and graduated from Collinsville High School. Her maternal grandfather, Joseph Guaglio, was a coal miner who worked in the Lumaghi and Bunker Hill Coal Mines in Collinsville, and the Troy Coal Mine in the 1950s.

In July of 1966, Dan reported for duty at Iraklion Air Station, Crete (Greece). The island of Crete was home for Sharon and Dan until April 1969. Their first son, Daniel E. McAley III, was born at Wheelus Air Force Base in Tripoli, Libya, Africa, on May 15, 1967.

In June of 1969, Dan was sent to Bolling AFB in Washington, D.C. and the family lived in District Heights, Maryland. When the assignment was completed, Dan was discharged from the Air Force in November 1969. The family moved to Collinsville, IL. Upon graduation from Belleville Barber College in December 1970, Dan started working at Darrell's Barber Shop, Collinsville, in January 1971.

Sharon graduated from Southern Illinois University, Edwardsville, IL, and taught for the Department of Defense School while she was overseas with her husband. She has been a teacher in Collinsville Unit #10 since December 1969.

A second son, Patrick W. McAley, was born to the McAley family on March 17, 1977, at Anderson Hospital in Maryville, IL.

On March 31, 1979, the McAleys and sons, Dan III (age 12) and Patrick (age 2) moved from

McAley family, 1999
(l. to r.) Front: Mary "Sharon."
Middle: Daniel E., Jr., Patrick. Back: Dan, III.

Collinsville to Troy. Their new home was at 512 Riggin Road. Twenty years later, the McAleys built a home off Staunton Road in Taylor Lake Estates. Their current residence is 112 Taylor Lake Drive.

After 13 years with Darrell's Barber Shop, Dan Jr. purchased Jake's Barber Shop, Troy, in April 1984.

The shop became Danny's Barber Shop. (Refer to Danny's Barber Shop) Seventeen years later, Dan continues to operate the shop.

Dan McAley III attended McCray Dewey Jr. High in Troy and graduated from Triad High School, St. Jacob, in 1985. He worked at Troy Security Bank from September 1984 to June 1987. On June 19, 1987, he enlisted in the U.S. Air Force. At the present time, he resides in East Alton, IL.

Patrick McAley attended the Troy schools and graduated from Triad High School, St. Jacob, in 1995. From 1993 to 1997, he worked at McDonald's Restaurant in Troy and became a manager while he was there. He attended Belleville Area College in Belleville, IL. He currently resides in Troy, IL. *Submitted by Sharon McAley.*

RANDY AND REATA (RIEBOLD) McALLISTER - Reata Jo Riebold was born in East St. Louis, IL, (Christian Welfare Hospital) on February 19, 1956. Reata is the daughter of Paul and Catherine "Kay" (Schmisseur) Riebold. She has one brother, Mark, who now is the 5th Generation Riebold to live on the family farm south of Troy. The State of Illinois honored the Riebold family farm with a gift of a Centennial Certificate and Plaque to Paul and Kay Riebold. Reata grew up on the farm and lived in the Blackjack community all her life with the exception of seven years when she resided in St. Louis, Missouri.

Reata attended Troy Grade School, Molden School, McCray-Dewey, and graduated from Triad High School in 1974. She double majored in marketing and business administration and graduated with a B.A. Degree from McKendree College (Lebanon, IL) in 1978. She received her M.B.A. Degree from Lindenwood College (Lindenwood, Missouri) in 1985. She was employed with G.E.C.C. Financial Services as a management trainee during and after graduation from McKendree College. Subsequently, she worked with McDonnell Douglas Corp. (Boeing) and was employed as a purchasing agent and subcontracts administrator for 11 years. After Reata and her husband started their family, she worked an additional 7 years with Boeing as a part-time and contract-hire employee. Reata holds a substitute teaching certificate in Madison County.

Randal McAllister was born in Breese, IL, on April 5, 1955, and is the son of Garneau and Alice (Venhaus) McAllister. He attended St. Joseph Grade School, Lebanon Grade School, and graduated from Lebanon High School in 1973. He double majored in accounting and business administration and graduated with a B.A. Degree from McKendree College in 1977. Randy received his M.B.A. Degree from S.I.U. (Edwardsville, IL) in 1986. He is employed in financial planning with Boeing Company.

Randy and Reata were married on October 11, 1985, in Las Vegas, NV, at the Guardian Angel Cathedral and lived in St. Louis, MO, until they built their home in 1986, southeast of Troy in the Blackjack community. They continue to live there and now operate a small grain farm.

Randy and Reata are the happy parents of two children: Lauren, born June 22, 1989, and Kyle, born August 21, 1992, at Anderson Hospital in Maryville, IL. Lauren and Kyle are both students attending St. John Neumann Catholic School in Maryville, IL. The family attends St. Jerome Catholic Church in Troy. *Submitted by Reata McAllister.*

GORDON AND SYBIL MCFARLAND
Gordon was born in St. Louis on November 1, 1907, to Gordon McFarland and Augusta (Elsbeck) McFarland. Gordon's father came to America from Germany in 1888. Gordon's parents separated when he was two. His father moved to California and never again contacted him. His mother raised him with help from her family who were in the Troy area. He spent a lot of time with his uncles, George and John Mills.

McFarland family, 1976
(l. to r.) Front: Sharon, Regina, Sybil, Gordon, Gay
Back: Keith, Gordon

Sybil (Garland) McFarland was born in Troy, IL, on Aug. 1, 1911, to Arthur "Sport" Garland and Drusilla (Mashek) Garland. Sybil graduated from McCray-Dewey High School in 1929. Sybil's grandfather came to America from England in 1889.

Gordon and Sybil were married on Oct 3, 1931, at St. Jerome Catholic Church, Troy, IL, by Rev. George Hobbs. They had 6 children: Gay, 1932; Sharon, 1935; Gordon Jr., 1941; Mike, 1944; Keith, 1951; Regina, 1953.

Gay married Don Hinnen, and they have 5 children: Britt, Gregg, Todd, Reed, and Beth. They now reside in Sun City West, AZ.

Sharon married Larry Schlaefer, and they have 4 children: Wayne, Linda, Laurie, and Steve.

Gordon married Janel Wyatt, and they have 3 children: Kimberly, Sidney and Gordon.

Michael (deceased) married Janice Klaus, and they had 1 daughter, Pamela.

Keith married Annie Woods, and they had 1 son, Keith. He later married Andrea Cox, and they have 1 son, Dakota.

Regina married James Hays, and they have 4 children: Jennifer, Jeremy, Justin and Tara.

Gordon was a well-known laborer in the Troy area. He also worked construction and at the refineries in Granite City area. He served in the U.S. Navy in 1944-1945. He was active in his church and the Troy American Legion. Gordon died in 1979.

Sybil stayed home when her children were young then worked at the Troy Post Office for Postmaster Wheeler Davis. Later she owned and operated the old Davy Sims store in Brookside. When her youngest child started school, she went to work as a dietician at St. Joseph's Hospital, Highland, IL. She worked till her death in 1984.

Sybil loved to entertain. She did many great skits at St. Jerome as a member of St. Ann's, and for Troy Senior Citizens, Tops, bowling banquets and St. Joseph's Hospital dinners.

Everyone remembers Sybil; she either made you laugh or cry. She was a wonderful person.

Gordon and Sybil lived in Troy all of their married life. *Submitted by Sharon Schlaefer.*

GORDON RICHARD MCFARLAND - Gordon Richard McFarland was born in Troy, IL, to Gordon and Sybil McFarland on Aug. 8, 1941.

Gordon has two brothers, Keith of Troy and Michael (deceased 1966), and three sisters, Gay of Sun City, AZ; Sharon Schlaefer of Troy; and Gina Hays of Glen Carbon, IL.

Gordon attended Troy Grade School and McCray-Dewey High School and graduated in 1959.

Gordon attended Central Missouri State College in 1959-1963 and graduated in August of 1963 with a B.S. in Education. Gordon married E. Janel Wyatt of Buchner, MO, in 1963. Their two daughters, Kim and Sidney, and one son, Gordon W., were born in Troy.

Janel attended Central Missouri State 1961-1962 and SIUE in 1967-68 and graduated with a B.S. in Education in 1968. She was a teacher at Triad High School and Troy Grade Schools from 1968 to 1999, retiring in June, 1999.

Gordon was a teacher and coach in the Jacksonville, IL, school district in 1964-65.

McFarland family, 1996
(l. to r.) Row 1: McLaine White, granddaughter. Row 2: Sidney. Row 3: Janel, Kim (McFarland) White. Row 4: Gordon Wyatt, Gordon R.

Gordon attended graduate school in 1965-66 in Warrensburg, MO, C.M.S.C. He graduated in Aug. 1966 with a Masters Degree in Physical Education.

Gordon returned to Troy in 1966 and taught school and coached in the Edwardsville School District until he retired in 1994. *Submitted by Gordon R. McFarland.*

ADAM MERSINGER - The fourth of nine children, Adam Mersinger was born January 16, 1868, in a log cabin on the northwest corner of Mill Creek and Troy-O'Fallon Roads to Frederick Mersinger and Anna Bugger. Grandparents to Adam were Johan and Philipina Mersinger who emigrated to the United States in 1834 from Bavaria, Germany. They settled northwest of O'Fallon, IL, and their log cabin still stands today.

Adam Mersinger, 1890

Adam married Elisabeth Riebold, daughter of John and Mary Kraher Riebold. It is interesting to know that two Mersinger brothers married two Riebold sisters. Adam married Elisabeth and his brother, Valentine, wed Catherine Riebold. This caused a strong bond with their children and grandchildren which continues to the present.

A brass band was formed circa 1890, consisting of several Mersinger brothers and cousins along with a few neighbors. Adam became the leader of this group and his discipline to their practice was consistent. He insisted on practice even during impassable snow storms – by way of the 8-party telephone line. He would get them all on the telephone and loudly say: "1 -2 -3 together ....!" One year at the State Fair in DuQuoin, Illinois, Adam was selected to be director over all the gathering bands, and his family has always been happy to tell of this event.

Sometime around 1900, Adam bought the building on the northwest corner of South Main and Market Streets in Troy. It housed a tavern with a hotel upstairs. Travelers could keep their horses in the stables and rent a room for the night before moving on in the morning.

Nine children were born to Adam and Elisabeth on their farm on East Mill Creek Road in Blackjack: Martha (Bayer), August 28, 1894-April 12, 1995; Peter, March 28, 1896-September 19, 1982; (see Peter Mersinger family), Agatha (Conley), February 8,1898-January 17, 1976; Aloys, April 14,1900-August 9, 1992; twins: Cordelia (Valadie) still living and Louise, born February 19,1902-April 27, 1993; Jacob, July 7, 1904-December 29, 1995; Fred, February 19, 1906-April 20, 1998 and Augusta, November 30, 1908-December 27, 1980.

Elisabeth died in 1909, probably from pneumonia. Farming and caring for a baby and the other eight children became difficult for Adam. Martha, the oldest, took on the 'mother-role' but after two years, she and Adam decided to look to St. Louis for raising the family. They moved to the 3900 block of Michigan near St. Anthony of Padua Church and

School where the children younger than Peter all attended. Adam became the 'trustee' for the Parish and there his love for God flourished. His examples of hard work and his love for family drew his children together for their life-time of closeness.

He worked in several different trades and when he retired, lived with some of his children until he settled in with Agatha and her husband Edward Conley. Adam died in their home in South St. Louis County on September 2, 1957, at the age of 89. *Submitted by Dorothy (Mersinger) Bartnett.*

ADRIAN AND GERTRUDE (LOYET) MERSINGER - Adrian Philip Mersinger and Gertrude Loyet were married November 6, 1946, at St. John the Baptist Catholic Church in Blackjack.

Gertrude and Adrian Mersinger

They lived on Adrian's family home place (along West Kirsch Road). Adrian farmed and in 1960, due to illness of children, Geraldine and Catherine, the family moved to Tucson, AZ, where Adrian worked for a bread company as a route driver. Gertrude worked in the school cafeteria. They returned to Illinois in 1963 and lived on the same farm. Gertrude worked for a number of years at the old K-Mart in Collinsville (State Park area). In 1976, they built a new brick home on the same farm.

Mersinger family, 1974
(l. to r.) Geraldine, Donald, Gertrude, Adrian, Joseph M., Catherine

The couple enjoyed ballroom dancing and competed in and won several dance contests.

They were the parents of four children: Donald Oscar, Geraldine Mary, Catherine Ann and Joseph Michael.

Gertrude died May 2, 1983, and Adrian died October 25, 1994. They both are buried in St. John the Baptist Catholic Cemetery in

Blackjack. *Submitted by Mae Grapperhaus for Don and Mary Mersinger.*

ALOYS (OLLIE) F. MERSINGER - Aloys (Ollie) F. Mersinger, born April 24, 1900, was the fourth child of Adam and Elisabeth Riebold Mersinger. He was born on their farm on East Mill Creek Road in Blackjack (See story of Adam Mersinger). Ollie was baptized Catholic and attended school at St. John the Baptist Church on Lebanon Road in Blackjack where there was a one-room schoolhouse. All classes were taught in the German language and the school extended only to the fourth grade.

Aloys (Ollie) and Pearl (Garber) Mersinger, 1965

While Ollie had eight brothers and sisters, his best friend was his cousin, Ben Mersinger, son of Phillip and Mary Mersinger. Ollie and Ben ran in the fields and woods, played and sometimes even wrestled together and "got into trouble." Their relationship of love continued all of their lives with Ollie and his family's many visits to Ben's farm.

Ollie's Mother, Elisabeth Riebold Mersinger, died July 21, 1909, shortly after the birth of her daughter, Augusta. Ollie was nine years old and he always remembered with sorrow the time after he heard this sad news. He just ran out into the cornfield and kept running as long as he could. Throwing himself down on the ground, he cried and cried.

He also remembered all the fun and loving times he spent with his grandfather, Jacob Riebold. He played and helped with chores on his farm and sometimes even was able to stay the night. With joy and love he recalled that this was a real treat.

The Adam Mersinger family moved to St. Louis after Ollie's Mother died when Ollie was 11 years old. He was proud to finish his schooling by graduating from the eighth grade at St. Anthony of Padua Catholic School in South St. Louis, where he also sang in the church choir.

On September 12, 1925, Ollie married Pearl Garber and they had one child, Betty Jane. She was a talented, fun-loving, and beautiful daughter. She danced and played the piano by ear and so did Ollie. He seemed to inherit his musical ability from his father, Adam. Tragedy struck on November 22, 1947, when Betty Jane, 20 at the time, was killed in an automobile accident.

Ollie had worked for several years in the warehouse of Shapleigh Hardware and then Anheuser-Busch Brewery until he retired. He and Pearl loved to travel. They were proud of the fact that they visited all 50 states, the last one being Alaska when Ollie was 84 years old.

Their home was on Jefferson Avenue in South St. Louis until 1956 when they moved into a new home in Crestwood, Missouri. Ollie died August 9, 1992, of a heart attack at the age of 92. He never lost his beautiful, easy-going and very loving personality. He is buried beside his wife, Pearl, and daughter Betty Jane, in Resurrection Cemetery in St. Louis. *Submitted by Dorothy Mersinger Bartnett.*

AUGUSTA (GUSSIE) MERSINGER -
Gussie was born November 30, 1908, at the family home on East Mill Creek Road in Blackjack. She was the youngest of nine children of Adam and Elizabeth (Ella) Riebold. She was 8 months old when her mother died so she was essentially raised by her father and sister, Martha.

Augusta "Gussie" Mersinger

Gussie was about 2 years old when the family moved to St. Anthony's Parish in St. Louis where she attended school. She worked for Pet Milk Company for over 40 years. She died in December 1980 and is buried in Resurrection Cemetery in St. Louis. Her family called her "Honey." *Submitted by Arlene Vien.*

BEN AND EDITH MERSINGER -
Ben and Edith Mersinger were married on Oct. 26, 1927. Ben was born Nov. 22, 1900, the son of Philip and Mary (Fohne) Mersinger in Blackjack. Edith (Noeltner) Mersinger was born July 30, 1901, the daughter of William and Emma (Ahlmeyer) Noetlner of St. Jacob.

After their marriage, they lived their entire life on a farm west of St. Jacob in Jarvis Township. They had a dairy and farm operation. Ben was a active member on the Qui Vive County school board and also took part in the consolidation of the Triad School District. Edith was a homemaker. Both were active in the St. James Catholic Church. They had two children, Leroy and Delores.

Leroy (now deceased) married Betty Bellm on Oct. 14, 1950, and had three children, David, Joan, and Janet. David married Kathy Trame and they had two children, Greg and Aaron. Joan married Wayne Anderson and they had two children, Michael and Chris. Janet married Brion Boeshans and they had two children, Cory and Rachel.

Delores married Orville Daiber (now deceased) on Oct. 18, 1958, and they had three children, Sharon, Dennis, and Judy. Sharon married Daniel Dickman and they had three children, Todd, Adam, and Lisa. Judy married Kevin Brendel and they had two children, Ashley and Benjamin. Dennis married Lori O'Laughlin and they had three children, Dawn, Garret and Brett.

Ben died March 22, 1977, and Edith died May 20, 1991. Leroy died Oct. 1, 1995. Orville died May 22, 1991. Delores remarried Stanley Luczak and he died April 12, 2001. *Submitted by Delores Daiber Luczak.*

DONALD AND MARY MERSINGER
Donald and Mary (Bossler) Mersinger were married December 28, 1974, at St. Clare Church in O'Fallon. Don is the oldest son of Adrian and Gertrude (Loyet) Mersinger. The couple has two children, Nick and Sara. Nick graduated from Southern Illinois University Carbondale with a degree in industrial technology and is living in Sanford, Florida. Sara graduated from DePaul University with a degree in business and is living in Chicago, Illinois.

Don is an ag-business instructor at Wabash College in Mount Carmel, Illinois. Mary is also a school teacher and is currently working at the college in the ESL Program. She is also a math and reading tutor.

Mersinger family
(l. to r.) Mary, Nick, Sara, Don

Since 1990, the family has hosted numerous foreign exchange students from South America, Europe and Asia. The family enjoys participating in the exchange program and has learned a lot from the students. *Submitted by Donald and Mary Mersinger*

FRANK AND ROSE (ARTH) MERSINGER

Wedding day, circa 1900
Frank and Rose(Arth) Mersinger

FRED P. MERSINGER - Fred P. Mersinger was the eighth child born to Adam and Elisabeth Riebold Mersinger (see Adam Mersinger family). He was born in 1906 on his older twin sisters' birthday, February 19, making it convenient to celebrate three birthdays on the same day.

Sally and Fred P. Mersinger 1950

He was only three years old when his Mother died and five when the family moved to St. Louis where he attended St. Anthony of Padua Catholic School. His childhood was filled with adventurous stories with the neighborhood boys. One time, while riding his bicycle, he fell and broke his leg. The family doctor 'set' the bone right in their home on the dining room table.

Fred was most proud of the few years he groomed and cared for a pony that was boarded in a stall in the shed at the rear of the Mersinger property. The pony belonged to a doctor who bought it to entertain his children and their friends. Fred felt his job was important and took it very seriously.

He was a natural salesman and never had a problem finding employment. He sold shoes and quickly was advanced to management in the retail shoe business. While being in charge of a store in Peoria, Illinois, he met his sweetheart, Sally (Ella Salsavage) and married her in Quincy, Illinois, in 1929.

Later he was transferred back to St. Louis and eventually was employed by Falstaff Brewery Company where he worked until he retired in 1971. They had no children and bought a new home in Webster Groves, Missouri, where they often entertained their family and friends. Sally and Fred were warm and fun-loving. They always were able to have other people experience a good time as well as their love.

Sally converted to the Catholic faith and they both were actively involved in parish life at Curé of Ars Church. Fred did much work for them, such as planting and caring for their rose garden and building a manger for their Christmas scene. He assembled it every Christmas until he died. It is erected each year and they have a plaque in his honor, commemorating this work. When Fred was 91, he was still serving as usher at his church and continued to live and take care of himself in his home.

After a two-month period of illness, Fred died of pancreatic cancer on April 20, 1998, at the age of 92 and is buried with his wife, Sally, in Resurrection Mausoleum in St. Louis, Missouri. *Submitted by Dorothy Mersinger Bartnett.*

FREDERICK AND ANNA (BUGGER) MERSINGER -
Frederick Clemet Mersinger was the son of Johan Mersinger and Phillipine Wagner-Schroeder, born December 10, 1835. He married Anna Agatha Bugger on October 3, 1858. Anna was the daughter of Adam Bugger and Katharina Walier. A year later, in 1859, he

Mersinger family, circa 1879, in front of house on farmstead south of Troy. (l. to r.) On the porch: Frederick and Anna. In the yard: unkown male, Phillip, Lena, Caroline, Valentine, Frank, Barbara, Adam, John

purchased the farmstead from John A. Bugger three miles south of Troy.

They had nine children: John J. (b. April 6, 1859); Frank Joseph (b. July 4, 1861); Barbara (b. July 14, 1863); Adam (b. January 18, 1868); Valentine (b. October 19, 1869); Phillip (b. June 26, 1871); Caroline K. (b. February 22, 1874); Lena (b. August 1877); and Rose (b. May 3, 1884).

Frederick and his brothers, Valentine and John, were among those responsible for building the present brick church in Blackjack in 1883. The stained glass windows in St. John the Baptist Catholic Church still bear their names. Daughter Rose was the first person baptized in the new brick church in 1884.

Three of the four girls became nuns. Caroline became Sister Aloysia of the Precious Blood in Ruma, IL. She taught for 27 years in the Belleville diocesan schools. Lena entered the Order of the Good Shepherd as Sister Mary Cherubim. She was elevated to Mother Superior around 1935. And Rose became Sister Mary Joseph in the Carmelite Order. *Submitted by Sharon Petty.*

GARY AND SUE (WALMSLEY) MERSINGER

After graduating from Triad High School in 1967, Gary Mersinger, son of Ted and Helen Mersinger, attended SIUE for two years. He then enlisted in the Army for two years. He completed basic training at Fort Leonard Wood, MO, and AIT at Fort Ord, CA, before being assigned to the Old Guard, the Army Ceremonial Unit, stationed outside of Washington, D.C. at Fort Meyer, VA.

Gary and Sue Mersinger family, circa 2000 (l. to r.) Kevin Tiernan, Aimee holding Theodore (Teddy), Wendy, Sue, Gary and Todd

While at Fort Meyer, Gary met Sue Walmsley, from Pontiac, MI, who was serving in the U. S. Navy. Sue, who was working on special assignment at the Bureau of Naval Personnel, turned down Gary's first request for a dance the night they met. Gary's response of "Please" to her rejection caught Sue off-guard. She not only agreed to a dance with the stranger from "Blackjack" but also eventually married him on November 11, 1971.

After both were discharged from military service, they moved to Carbondale, IL, where Gary completed his education, obtaining a degree in Agricultural Economics. Gary then took a job with the Farmers Home Administration, an Agency of the US Department of Agriculture. This job required they move to Freeport, IL, then to Kankakee. When a new office was finally opened in Edwardsville in 1978, Gary and his family were able to move back "home."

Gary and Sue had four children: Aimee Marie (b. in 1976), Wendy Anne (b. in 1979), Mary Elizabeth (b. and d. November 20, 1981), and Todd Gary (b. in 1983).

After the move back "home," Sue decided to go back to school. She graduated from BAC and then enrolled at SIUE. She obtained a Bachelors degree in Speech and Audiology and then obtained a Masters degree in Speech Pathology. She graduated with honors in 1986 with Gary, who completed his MBA at the same time. Sue eventually took a job with the Collinsville School District where she taught Speech and Language at Kreitner Grade School in Fairmont City.

All three of Gary and Sue's children graduated from Triad High School. Aimee went on to obtain a college degree in primary education. She married Kevin Tiernan and currently lives in Glen Carbon. Kevin is a computer programmer who works for A. G. Edwards. Aimee currently works for the Triad School District. They have one son, Theodore (Teddy) John, who was born August, 2000. Wendy attended BAC, graduating with an associate's degree. She currently lives in New Port Richey, FL, and is pursuing an education in the marketing field. Todd entered the Army on August 9, 2001. He has completed his basic and advanced training as a Combat Engineer. Having just completed specialized training to operate heavy equipment, Todd will be assigned to an Army unit in Germany.

Gary and Sue live south of Troy on property that has been in the Mersinger family for 3 generations. They enjoy traveling, gardening, and maintaining "Sleepy Hollow" the name they have given their home and property. *Submitted by Gary Mersinger and Sharon Petty.*

GERALDINE MARY MERSINGER

Geraldine Mary Mersinger, born April 10, 1951, was the second oldest of four children – two boys and two girls. Her parents were Adrian Phillip Mersinger and Gertrude Elizabeth (Loyet) Mersinger. Her brothers and sister were Donald Oscar, the oldest; Catherine Ann, the younger sister; and Joseph Michael, the youngest. Gerry and her brothers and sister were all baptized at St. John the Baptist, a little country church in Blackjack.

Adrian Mersinger family, 1974 (l. to r.) Gerry, Don, Gertrude, Adrian, Joe, Cathy

Geraldine soon became known as "Gerry" to both family and friends. Born in E. St. Louis, IL, she grew up on a farm three miles south of Troy, belonging to her grandmother Kate Mersinger, her father's mother. Both Gerry and her sister Cathy were born with a lung condition that required a daily routine of breathing treatments; so the two sisters developed a special bond, as they endured their nightly breathing treatments together.

Gerry attended the Troy schools. She attended Troy Elementary through the middle of third grade, when the family moved to Tucson, AZ, attempting to improve the sisters' health in a drier climate. The family stayed three years and returned in 1963. Gerry attended McCray-Dewey Junior High. In 1969 she graduated from Triad High School.

Gerry then attended the University of Arizona in Tucson, graduating with a B.A. in English and Language Arts. Her English teaching career began on the Navajo Indian Reservation in northern Arizona in Kayenta. There she taught Native Americans until 1978 when she moved to New Mexico for one year to teach at a junior high in Kirkwood. A year later she returned to Kayenta where she continued teaching and working as the Language Arts Department Chairperson until January 1984.

In January 1984, she moved to Mancos, CO, and taught at Mancos High School for two years. Next, she taught five years in tiny Dove Creek, CO.

In 1991 Gerry moved to northeastern Colorado where she bought her first home in Brush. She taught three years at Fort Morgan Middle School. In the summer of 1992, friends returned from teaching in South America; and Gerry began to think that she, too, would enjoy teaching abroad.

Soon Gerry began telling the family that she was investigating the idea of working overseas. After attending a Teacher Fair in 1994, she was interviewed by 5 schools. Later, Gerry was offered a teaching job in Turkey; and she accepted it. She taught from 1994-1996 in Tarsus, Turkey. In 1995 Gerry learned of the DODDS program – Department of Defense Dependents Schools – with schools world wide. She completed the voluminous application and hand carried her application to Arlington, VA.

In July 1996 when she came back to the states, she learned that she had the opportunity to teach in Seoul, South Korea. After teaching four years there, she received a transfer to

Kaiserslautern, Germany, in the spring of 2000. *Submitted by Geraldine Mersinger.*

GILBERT AND MURIEL MERSINGER

Gilbert Henry Mersinger, born in the rural Troy area February 26, 1909, to Valentine and Kate (Riebold) Mersinger, was the fifth of seven children: Olivia, Veronica, Ludolph, Oscar, Gilbert, Joseph and Adrian. He attended Troy Grade School before studying at The Pontifical College Josephinum Seminary in Columbus, OH. After leaving the seminary, he helped his mother, brothers and sisters on the family farm south of Troy. His father had died at age 49 in 1919. Kate died in 1950 at age 70.

Gilbert Mersinger, corner of South Main and Center, Troy

Muriel Betty Lloyd was born March 4, 1913, in Carlinville, IL, to William Thomas and Nellie Beatrice (Hall) Lloyd. Her family moved to her grandparent's (John and Ellen Lloyd) farm on Lebanon Road east of Collinsville and southwest of Troy. She had one older brother, Everett Hall Lloyd. They attended schools in Collinsville. Her family's farm property adjoined that of her uncle and aunt's, (George and Emma Lloyd) on the southwest and Eulah and Jennie Lloyd Close on the east. Jennie died in 1937 and Eulah in 1941, leaving a young son Thomas William to be raised by his Uncle Will and Aunt Nellie. Will Lloyd was killed by a train at Lumaghi Coal Mine as he was walking to his car on the day of his retirement in January 1945. Nellie died in 1969.

Gilbert and Muriel had met at a dance, courted, and then were married June 26, 1940, by Rev. B.N. Manning at St. John the Baptist Catholic Church in Blackjack. Gilbert's brother Adrian Mersinger and Muriel's good friend, Mary Pickoraitis (Doran), were their attendants. They honeymooned at Piasa Chautauqua resort near Grafton. The newlyweds built a home on an acre of the Lloyd farm. In 1943, Gilbert was drafted into the Navy and was assigned to the U.S.S. *Lexington* Aircraft Carrier in the South Pacific until November 1944. Before and after the service, Gilbert farmed with horses and also worked off the farm at various jobs. These included running a filling station at the corner of South Main and Center Streets in Troy and working at the American Car Foundry. He finally returned to farming, this time with tractors, and hauling grain to Troy Grain Company. He was a good mechanic and carpenter – continuously repairing and building things. Muriel worked at the Martha Manning dress factory in Collinsville the first several years of their marriage. She became a homemaker after Gail and Janet were born, always preparing delicious meals, keeping a tidy house and raising chickens on the side.

Daughter Gail Louise was born in Highland, IL, on February 6, 1946. Then on October 11, 1952, Janet Veronica was born in East St. Louis. While living at home, Gail and Janet attended Troy Grade Schools and Triad High School before earning Bachelors' degrees at SIUE.

Life on the farm was typical, with crops of grain and hay, cattle, chickens, sometimes hogs, and a steady stream of dogs and cats over the years. A highlight was acquiring Sugarfoot, a beautiful, but sometimes spirited and mostly stubborn, palomino horse in the late 1950s. Family recreation included picnics, visits to the zoo, attending large family gatherings, celebrations and reunions. The growling arrival of the road grader (oftentimes driven by cousin Cornelius "Corny" Schmitt), the ominous oil trucks, and then being temporarily cut off from the outside world until the road was again made driveable always added some late summer excitement.

Gilbert and Muriel were active at St. John the Baptist Catholic Church. Gilbert was a member of the Knights of Columbus and Muriel worked with the Ladies' Sodality quilting and helping with the many card parties and church picnics. Gail and Janet occupied themselves with Scouts, 4-H, schoolwork, playing games and doing chores.

Muriel returned to work part time in 1968 as a housekeeping inspectress at the Bel-Air Hilton Hotel in St. Louis. It was about this time that Gilbert suffered a stroke and became partially disabled. His sister Veronica stayed with him on the days that Muriel was scheduled to work so that she could retain her job.

Wedding photo, June 26, 1940
(l. to r.) Gilbert Mersinger, Muriel (Lloyd) Mersinger, Mary Pickoraitis, Adrian Mersinger

Gilbert died April 12, 1971, on Easter Monday night – the day after the family had been together to celebrate the holiday. It had been a warm spring day, and he had relaxed out on the porch that afternoon, waving to the folks he knew on their way home from work.

Gail had moved to Collinsville in 1970. Janet married her high school sweetheart, Larry Helldoerfer, in 1973. They followed the family tradition and built their home on the Mersinger farm.

Muriel continued to work until after her first grandchild, Jill Jeanette, was born; then she retired from the hotel. Muriel babysat Larry's and Janet's children, Jill, Amy Elizabeth, and Lee Lawrence, and continued to help the family through the years and after Janet's untimely death in 1996. Muriel became ill early in the next year, and she died July 29, 1997.

Gilbert and Muriel are buried in St. John the Baptist Catholic Cemetery in the rural Blackjack community beside Janet and Larry. *Submitted by Gail (Mersinger) and Richard E. Wolff.*

JACOB MERSINGER - On July 7, 1904, Jacob Mersinger was the seventh child to be born to Adam and Elisabeth Riebold Mersinger on their farm on East Mill Creek Road in the Blackjack area of Troy.

Jacob Mersinger

Jacob was only five years old when his mother died and age seven when his family moved to St. Louis, MO. He attended school near his home at St. Anthony of Padua on Meramec Street. He was called Jake by all who knew him.

Jake was a very talented and ambitious boy who decided he would rather work than go to school and, therefore, did not graduate from grade school. Not only did he work at many different types of jobs, but he also taught himself to play the banjo. He excelled with this, as well as singing, all through the years and even played with several bands at nightspots in St. Louis. About the age of 85, he made an audio tape filled with his joyful music and songs that has been cherished by his family.

Sometime in the late 1920s, Jake married Elsie (maiden name unknown) who was a very pretty young lady from Crystal City, MO. They lived in St. Louis and had no children. After approximately seven years of marriage, they separated and divorced. However, it is important to note, that what Jake was to discover next helped to form the rest of his life. When he was applying for a Catholic church annulment, he found that Elsie had been previously married and had not gotten a divorce, which automatically made their marriage invalid in the first place.

Jake was so hurt from this separation that he had a difficult time adjusting. He, therefore, decided to move far away from his home in St. Louis and relocated to Hawaii where he went to work for the shipyards at Pearl Harbor. He was there during the Japanese attack on December 7, 1941, and spent days putting out fires. The memories of this were very difficult for him, and his family never heard him talk of his experiences there until his visits home fifty years later.

Shortly after that harrowing experience, Jake moved to San Francisco, CA, where he met the love of his life, Juanita Guigda. She was a young lady from San Salvador, El Salvador, where her family owned a coffee plantation. Jake and she moved there when Jake was hired to manage the plantation, but after many years of being away from the States, they decided to move back to San Francisco where they adopted a sweet little girl, Erma.

To list Jake's talents and involvements is impossible. He was extremely active and very interesting up to the day of his death. Only hours before he died at home of a sudden stroke, he had been playing pool and talking with his friends at the nearby senior center. Jake was loved by all who knew him. He died at the age of 91 and is buried in Daly City, California. *Submitted by Dorothy Mersinger Bartnett.*

JOHN MERSINGER - John Mersinger was born July 30, 1795, in Freinsheim, Germany, to Jacob Mersinger and Francisca Klein. John married Philipina Schoeder, and with their 3 children, Mary K., Frances, and Valentine, sailed to America about 1832. They took the southern route, which is longer but not as rough, to New Orleans, then came up the Mississippi River to St. Louis. They bought a team of oxen and a cart, and emigrated to O'Fallon, IL, then called Ridge Prairie. They settled there about 1832, building a log house (which still stands today). They had 2 more sons, John and Fred.

Joseph and Lucille Mersinger family, 2001 (l. to r.) Front: Katie Benhoff, Mary Benhoff, Joseph Mersinger, Molly Mersinger. Back: Steve Benhoff, Margaret Benhoff, Rozann Mersinger, James J. Mersinger, Joseph J. Mersinger and Lucille Mersinger.

Fred Clement Mersinger married Anna Bugger and settled in Jarvis Township about 4 miles south of Troy. They had 9 children – John, Frank, Barbara, Adam, Valentine, Philip, Kate, Lena and Rosa.

Valentine Mersinger married Kate M. Riebold Oct. 12, 1888, at St. John the Baptist Church at Blackjack. He farmed south of Troy all of his life. He served as trustee of Spring Valley School and played in the Blackjack Brass Band at concerts, weddings and marching events. He died at the early age of 49, leaving his wife Kate with 7 children- Olivia, Veronica, Oscar, Ludolph, Gilbert, Joseph J., and Adrian.

Olivia E. Mersinger never married and died at age 40.

Veronica Mary Mersinger served in the military at Fort Dix as a WAC and never married.

Oscar Frank Mersinger married Louise L. Levo Jan. 30, 1937. He served as a trustee of Spring Valley School and McCray-Dewey Township School, and served many years on the Troy Grain Board. He sang with the Collinsville Barber Shop group for many years. He loved to entertain: Fourth of July was a big day at his home.

Ludolph A. Mersinger married Lenora Hess.

Gilbert H. Mersinger married Muriel E. Lloyd on June 26, 1940, and they had 2 daughters, Gail and Janet. Gilbert served in the Navy on the aircraft carrier *Lexington.*

Joseph J. Mersinger married Lucille M. Strieker May 28, 1957, at St. Francis of Assissi, Aviston, IL. He worked at Chas. A. Pfizer for 30 years until he retired. He took piano lessons from Bert Weber and graduated from McCray-Dewey High School in 1935. He joined Robert Taylor's Orchestra in 1935 and played and entertained for 40 years before retirement. Joe and Lucille had two children, Margaret and Jim.

Margaret Mersinger married Steve Benhoff and has two daughters, Katie and Mary.

Jim J. Mersinger married Rozann P. McClinnen, and has two children, Joseph James and Molly Mersinger. Joseph James is the seventh generation in the Mersinger family.

Adrian P. Mersinger married Gertrude Loyet and had four children – Donald, Geraldine, Catherine, and Joseph M.. Adrian served on the Triad School Board and on Jarvis Township Board of Trustees. *Submitted by Joseph J. Mersinger.*

JOSEPH AND KAREN (FREY) MERSINGER
Joseph M. Mersinger, son of Adrian and Gertrude (Loyet) Mersinger, was born on July 8, 1954, at St. Mary's Hospital. He graduated from Triad High School in 1973. He was a member of the FFA Club. On February 18, 1984, he married Karen A. Frey at Immaculate Conception Church in Pierron. She is the daughter of Alvin H. and Shirley Espenschied Frey. Joseph was raised on the family farm south of Troy. In 1960 his parents decided to move to Tucson, AZ.

They lived in Tucson for three years and moved back to the family farm in 1963. Joseph started to help his dad farm when he was in the 6th grade. In 1984 when Adrian retired from farming, Joseph and his wife took over the family farm. Their son, Jonathan, is now involved with helping on the farm. The family enjoys going to the kid's school activities. Joseph, Karen and family are members of St. Jerome Church in Troy. Joseph belongs to the Knights of Columbus and Karen is involved with the youth group at church.

Mersinger family, 2000 (l. to r.) Front: Lynn. Back: Jonathan, Joseph M., Karen, Katie.

Mersinger wedding, February 19, 1984. Karen (Frey) and Joseph M. Mersinger

Their children are Jonathan, b. November 19, 1986; Katie, b. January 28, 1990, and Lynn, b. November 13, 1991. Justin (March 21, 1995) Bobbie Joe (February 16, 1997) and Kyle (October 12, 2000) are deceased. *Submitted by Joe & Karen Mersinger.*

LOUISE C. MERSINGER / CORDELIA MERSINGER VALADIE - Twins were born, fifth in line, to Adam and Elisabeth Riebold Mersinger, (see Adam Mersinger story) on February 19, 1902. They were named Louise (Lula) and Cordelia (Dula). The dresses they have on in the accompanying picture were made by their mother, who made the delicate embroidery and tiny pleating by hand. She died when the twins were 7 years old. They attended school at St. John the Baptist Catholic Church in Blackjack until the third grade when they moved with their family to St. Louis. They finished their education at St. Anthony of Padua Catholic School on Meramec Street in South St. Louis.

Mersinger twins, 1909 (l. to r.) Louise C. and Cordelia

Louise helped to care for the house chores for her Father, Adam, and family for several years as she grew into adulthood. She was a very beautiful young lady. Later, she worked at several office jobs, but especially liked being a telephone operator and receptionist for a group of doctors until she retired. While Louise had a long-time beau, she never married and lived with her sisters, Augusta (Gussie) Mersinger and Martha Mersinger Bayer in South St. Louis. She died of cancer at the age of 91 on April 27, 1993.

Likewise, Cordelia grew in loveliness, met and married a business-gentleman, Lloyd Valadie who was from New Orleans. They made their home in Mobile, Alabama, and had no children. It is interesting to note that through Lloyd's business, they became very social and actively participated for many years in the Mardi

Gras balls and parades. Lloyd had been crowned King Rex one year, and Cordelia had been mighty proud of this honor for him.

While Cordelia has some dementia, she is so physically healthy that she takes absolutely no medication at this time and is still living in Mobile at the age of 99. It is also noted that of her other eight siblings, five of them lived over the age of 90; Martha Mersinger Bayer was almost 101. *Submitted by Dorothy Mersinger Bartnett.*

LUDOLPH MERSINGER - Ludolph "Lud" Mersinger was born in February 1907, the second son of Valentine and Kate (Riebold) Mersinger.

Lud and Ruth (Malwitz) Mersinger, circa 1930s

He married Ruth (Malwitz) Epps in the late 1930s. She had one son, Dale Epps, from a previous marriage. They lived in Collinsville. Lud worked for and retired from the City of Collinsville. Ruth died in the early 1970s.

Lud then married Lenore (Heim) Hess in September 1975. They reside in Highland.

Lud and Lenore (Heim) Mersinger, 1975

An avid hunter and fisherman all his life, he was an excellent gardener as well. In his later life he enjoyed hunting deer, but as of 2002, has not yet bagged one. At one time in the 1940s and 1950s, he owned a clubhouse in Grafton, IL. He and his first wife, Ruth, spent many weekends "up the river at the club house."

Both Lud and Lenore are members of St. Paul Catholic Church in Highland. *Submitted by Mae Grapperhaus.*

OLIVIA MERSINGER - Olivia Emma Mersinger was born August 14, 1900, the first child of Valentine and Kate (Riebold) Mersinger on a farm in the Blackjack community (address is West Kirsch Road, Troy).

She was a member of the Troy Drum and Bugle Corps for several years, a member of the

Olivia Mersinger, 1900-1940

St. John the Baptist Catholic Church in Blackjack, the Altar and Rosary Sodality there, and a member of the Highland Daughters of Isabella-Sacred Heart Circle 237.

She enjoyed working outside and was known to work at anything: carpentry, chopping wood, or anything physical out-of-doors. She milked the family cows, but also helped on other parts of the farm. Following the death of her father, she assisted her mother with the many farm and house chores. She also enjoyed garden work.

In the late 1930s she and her sister Veronica took a trip to Wisconsin to see the Dells and other points of interest. She came down with cancer shortly after returning from the trip. She was able to see rural electricity installed in her community before she died. On or around her goddaughter's (Mae Mersinger) birthday (June 1940), she was able to attend a little party for Mae and was delighted to see the electric lights work in the house her brother Oscar had built just down the road from where she was born. This was the last time she was at Oscar's house, it was told later.

She never married. Friends who knew her in the Drum and Bugle Corps said she was a nice person and was very attractive.

She died at her home at the age of 40 in September 2, 1940, after a long period of suffering with the dreaded disease. She is buried in St John the Baptist Catholic Cemetery in Blackjack. *Submitted by her Goddaughter, Mae Mersinger Grapperhaus.*

OSCAR AND LOUISE (LEVO) MERSINGER Oscar Frank Mersinger was born in 1904, the son of Valentine and Catherine (Riebold) Mersinger. He married Louise Laura Levo on January 30, 1937. Louise was born in 1904, the daughter of Italian immigrants, Peter and Laura (Cossano) Levo.

Prior to their marriage, Oscar purchased the Wilbur Edwards farm. The farm had been run down and no one had lived on it since the house had burned years before. Oscar built a house with the help of Adolph Boulanger, a local carpenter and friend of the family.

The couple had one daughter who was christened Mary Olivia, but was known as Mae.

Oscar and Louise met at dances. Oscar lived a short distance from Louise on what was later to become West Kirsch Road, south of Troy.

A dairy farmer, he milked Holstein cattle and raised hogs, chickens and sheep. He was also a grain farmer raising corn, wheat, alfalfa and soybeans. In 1954, the barn that he built burned to the ground. After the fire, he went into the Hereford beef cattle business.

At retirement, he turned the farm over to his son-in-law, Jim Grapperhaus.

He liked music and he and Louise enjoyed dancing. In their later years, they traveled and spent time at their vacation home in Cherokee Village, AR. Louise enjoyed working outside in the lawn and garden. She grew beautiful flowers in her yard, raising zinnias, petunias, roses and other flowers. She canned vegetables and fruits every summer. Until she was 89 years old, she did canning for the family.

They were members of St. John the Baptist Catholic Church in Blackjack, where they were married. Oscar served as church trustee for 30 years; was a member of Holy Name and St. Joseph society; served on the Spring Valley School Board (1930s and 1940s); and the McCray-Dewey High School Board of Education in Troy (1948-1950).

He served as a director for the Troy Grain Company and was a lifelong member of Troy Knights of Columbus Council and the Maryville/Troy Fourth Degree Assembly Knights of Columbus. In his retirement years, he joined the Mississippi Valley Barbershop Chorus in Collinsville.

Oscar and Louise Mersinger,
50th Wedding Anniversary, 1987

Louise was a member of the St. John Altar and Rosary Society and served as its president twice and worked on many committees.

In the Spring Valley neighborhood, she and several of the neighboring ladies organized a pinochle club and named it "The Tongue Tied Pinochle Club." The group played cards at a different member's home each month. They enjoyed an annual outing to St. Louis to dine and to see a movie. Louise was also a member of the Troy Democratic Women's Club.

In 1951, the couple began hosting an annual Fourth of July party held near the holiday for relatives and friends. Musical entertainment, potluck supper and fireworks were features of the day. The U. S. flag lowering ceremony was always held at dusk. The party continued every year for the next 30 plus years.

Oscar died July 6, 1990. Louise died July 31, 1994. They are buried in St. John the Baptist Catholic Cemetery, Blackjack. *Submitted by Mae Grapperhaus.*

PETER HENRY MERSINGER - This is the story of Peter Henry Mersinger, the second of nine children, born on March 28, 1896, to Adam and Elisabeth Riebold Mersinger on their farm on East Mill Creek Road in Blackjack (refer to story of Adam Mersinger). Peter was baptized

Mersinger family, 1975
(l. to r.) Front: Florence Stockglausner, Marian
Jansen, Dorothy Bartnett, and Arlene Vien
Back: Peter and Agnes Mersinger

and attended school at St. John the Baptist Catholic Church in Blackjack. Through the fields, he walked with his siblings to school and then returned home to help with his farm chores. After completing the fourth grade, he was needed fulltime and farming became his life at this very young age of ten.

Peter's Mother died July 21, 1909, leaving nine children under the age of 15. Farming and the care of these young children became such a burden on Peter's father and the oldest daughter, Martha, that they decided St. Louis might provide more conveniences in rearing this family. They eventually made this move in 1912 to South St. Louis and lived in the 3900 block of Michigan near St. Anthony of Padua Church.

At age 16, this transition was not easy for Peter. He missed farming. For several summers, he returned to live and work on the farm of his Aunt Kate Riebold Mersinger after her husband, Valentine, died. He grew very close to his seven cousins and to this day, Peter's family is still in close relationship with the next generation in the Troy area.

In 1917, he met Agnes Bruemmer (born August 26, 1897, died August 15, 1986) at a St. Francis deSales Church social. However, he was drafted into the army for World War I. The war ended just as he arrived in France. While there, he continued to stay in touch with his Aunt Kate Mersinger in Blackjack and his letters are still precious keepsakes of his daughters.

Peter became a tool and die maker by trade and he married Agnes, November 3, 1920. They had four daughters: Florence, born December 23, 1921, died December 28, 1989, married Lester Stockglausner; Marian, September 3, 1924, married Clement Jansen;

Will, Peter and Otto Mersinger – visit to St. John the
Baptist Cemetery, Lebanon Road, Blackjack, 1979.

Dorothy, February 20, 1929, married Roland Bartnett; and Arlene, March 10, 1937, married Francis Vien.

Until his death on September 19, 1982, from prostate cancer, Peter lived with Agnes for 60 years at 4031 Eichelberger Street in the Bevo Mill area of St. Louis, where his gardens flourished as well as his daughters. Each was born in this house and lived there until she married.

As life continued in St. Louis, he was always drawn back to Blackjack. His family had yearly extended visits with his cousins and Aunt Kate on their farm. After her death, the visits did not stop, only moved. By this time, her son, Oscar, and Louise Mersinger had their farm nearby on West Kirsch Road and their warm hospitality welcomed Peter's family annually, again for an extended time. What loving and cherished memories these fun 'adventures' were for all. However, Peter always managed to find some kind of work that needed to be done. It was his way of being back on a farm. His attachments to Jarvis Township were so strong, that he and Agnes are buried in St. John's Cemetery in Blackjack.

Their daughters all married and have children and grandchildren. The members of Peter's family feel very closely connected to their Mersinger relatives in Illinois. They see them regularly and truly appreciate their Troy/ Blackjack heritage. *Submitted by Dorothy Mersinger Bartnett*

PHILLIP AND MARY P. (FOHNE) MERSINGER - Phillip Mersinger was born June 26, 1871. His wife Mary P. Fohne was born October 22, 1880. Both were born and raised in the Blackjack area. On October 17, 1899, they were married in St. John's Catholic Church in Blackjack. They lived on the family farm three miles south of Troy, in the home that had belonged to his parents Frederick and Anna (Bugger) Mersinger.

Wedding day, October 17, 1899
Mary (Fohne) and Phillip Mersinger

By 1915 Philip and Mary had 8 of their 9 children, including 15 year old Benjamin J., Ottmer V., Cecelia A., Elmer J., Emil J., Urban J., Marie P., and one year old Bertha B.

In January of 1915, a horrible epidemic of scarlet fever broke out in the Blackjack community. Two families in particular suffered unbelievable losses. Some of the Mersinger and Riebold children were riding home together under the blanket of a wagon. The disease spread to at least six of their children. Emil, aged 8,

Mersinger family, circa 1909, in front of house on farmstead south of Troy. (l. to r.) Ottmer, Ben, Phillip, Emil, Urban (under 1 year), Elmer, Mary, Cecilia

was the first to die on January 31. His 10 year old brother Elmer died the very next day. A week later, February 7, little Marie, aged 4, died. Ten days later, 12 year old Cecelia was in her mother Mary's arms when she told her mother that she saw the angels coming. Mary knew, at that moment, she had lost her fourth child to the disease. It was also feared that 15 year old Ben would not survive, but somehow he managed to pull through. Phillip and Mary Mersinger had lost 4 of their children in 18 days.

During that period, the family had been quarantined. Food was brought and left for them by family and neighbors, and the young bodies were picked up and buried without family present. Clothing and bedding were buried in a hole dug far away from the house. The standard method used in those days to treat those affected with scarlet fever was to try and shock their systems with hot and cold. They would wrap the children in heated sheets to heat their bodies and then re-wrap them in cold sheets, that had been left outside, to lower their body temperature.

Theodore G., "Ted," was born three years after the tragedy.

Phillip, Mary and their 5 children all worked on the family farm until the children married. Farming was a hard life and all were needed to make the farm work. They had milking cows and raised corn and wheat. Acres of potatoes were planted to be sold as a cash crop. They would go to town near the Adams store and sell potatoes from their wagon. For enjoyment, Phillip, as did his father Frederick, played the fiddle and was a member of a local band.

Ben, Urban and Ted each took up the family trade of farming, one in St. Jacob, Highland and the family homestead respectively. Ottmer married, but died at the age of 30 of a heart attack. When Bertha married, she moved to Collinsville.

When Ted married in 1943, Phillip and Mary moved to Collinsville. In 1945 Phillip died of a heart attack. Mary lived another 30 years. She swore by St. Joseph's aspirin and rubbing alcohol to ward off arthritis. She died in 1975 at age 95. Grandma Mersinger can be remembered as grandmas should be remembered. She was a very short woman, a little stocky, with gray hair pulled up in a bun at the top of her head. She always wore small flowered, print housedresses and wire-rimmed glasses. As she got older, she would sit for hours in her rocker, saying her rosary. *Submitted by Sharon Petty and Helen Vieth.*

RUSSELL AND TERRI (PAULSON) MERSINGER - Russell P. Mersinger, son of Ted and Helen Mersinger, was born in 1957, and attended Triad High School, graduating in 1976.

Mersinger family, 2001
(l. to r.) Front: Megan and Aaron
Back: Terri and Russ

Russ started taking over the family farm as a sophomore since his father Ted was ill. He farmed and attended SIUE for two years. When his father died in 1977, he took on the full duties of the family farm. By renting neighboring ground, Russ expanded the acreage farmed to about 700 acres. Crops included were corn, beans and wheat, following in the footsteps of his father and grandfather. Livestock consisted of hogs; he no longer dairy farmed.

Although he had expanded the acreage, farming was extremely financially difficult in the 1980s. He decided to take a second job to support the farm. He started working at Southwestern Electric Co-op as a tree trimmer in 1982. He took a lineman's position in 1984.

He met Terri D. Paulsen of O'Fallon in 1984, and married her August 24, 1987. They expanded the livestock to include sheep and pigmy goats – a first for the farm. The sheep were a wedding present. Terri wanted one sheep and Russ got her the whole herd.

Their first child, Aaron Paul, was born in 1988. Megan Darlene was born in 1993.

Russ is now a foreman of a line crew at Southwestern Electric Co-op. Terri is a pension plan representative for District #9, International Assoc. of Machinist and Aerospace Workers.

They still raise sheep and goats today, which can be seen near the pond on the family farm three miles south of Troy.

Russ and son Aaron are avid deer hunters and the whole family enjoys boating. Both Russ and Terri are active in the Cystic Fibrosis Foundation. *Submitted by Russell Mersinger.*

TED AND HELEN MERSINGER - In 1940, Theodore (Ted) G. Mersinger met Helen M. Kapp of Highland at a dance at Highland Park. It was something special from the beginning, and on October 27, 1943, they were married. Ted had grown up on the family farm located three miles south of Troy. His father, Phillip Mersinger, and great-grandfather, Frederick Mersinger, had lived and worked the farm before him. Being the youngest son, when he married he and his wife moved into the family farmhouse and started raising a family.

Wedding photo, Oct. 27, 1943
Helen (Kapp) and Ted Mersinger

Their first born, Dennis, died in 1945, from pneumonia at three weeks old. In 1947 their second child, Sharon Marie, was born, in 1949 their son Gary Lee, in 1950 their daughter Connie Jean and finally Russell Paul in 1956.

The family worked the 160-acre farm raising hogs for market, milking cows, raising chickens and selling eggs, as well as growing corn, beans, wheat, and bailing hay or silage for the livestock. Every winter Ted's brothers and brothers-in-law would help butcher several hogs in the old wash house for sausage and meat for the coming year.

Ted and Helen Mersinger family, 1968
(l. to r.) Front: Ted, Helen, Sharon, Russell
Back: Gary, Connie

In 1975 Ted and Helen decided the old farmhouse had seen its better days and they needed to tear it down. In doing so, the structure revealed its inner skeleton, a log cabin. The cabin had been moved from the timber area to its current location by Ted's grandfather, Frederick Mersinger. The cabin had been added on to several times and covered with white painted weatherboards and took on the appearance of a typical large farmhouse. The log cabin was donated to the Madison County Historical Society, but they were unable to erect the cabin. SIUE transported the logs and erected the cabin at the Tower Lake site. The cabin stood at SIUE for at least 10 years and finally in the fall of 2001 it was taken apart again and moved to the Tri-Township Park where it is to once again be resurrected.

Ted and Helen never took many vacations due to the demands of the farm until Gary and Russ were old enough to handle the livestock. They did however, love to dance. Probably every Saturday night of the last 15 years of their marriage, they would go out to dances with friends. Ted was a smooth dancer and Helen

Mersinger family, Christmas 2000
(l. to r.) Row 1: Sharon, Aaron, Kevin Baka (Wendy's boyfriend), Wendy, Megan. Row 2: Helen, Sue, Aimee holding little Teddy Tiernan, Todd. Row 3: Russ, Gary, Kevin Tiernan. Row 4: Terri, Connie, Mike.

always loved to dance. They had met on the dance floor and they continued to enjoy dancing all the days of their lives.

After a long fight with cancer, Ted died in 1977. Helen stayed on the farm and son Russ farmed the ground. In 1981 she married Leonard J. Vieth and moved to Hamel.

After 15 years of marriage, Lenny died in 1986. Helen ultimately moved back to Troy where she resides today. *Submitted by Helen Mersinger Vieth.*

VALENTINE AND KATE (RIEBOLD) MERSINGER - Valentine Mersinger married Kate M. Riebold at St. John the Baptist Catholic Church. They lived and farmed in Blackjack on West Kirsch Road about 2 1/2 miles south of Troy.

Valentine Mersinger, early 1900s

Seven children were born to the couple. They were Olivia, Veronica, Oscar F., Ludolph, Gilbert, Joseph J. and Adrian P.

Hard working and musically inclined, Valentine played the bass (baritone) horn in the Blackjack Band. When weather prevented the band from practicing, the members would call on the party telephone line and play their instruments.

Valentine died at the age of 49 in 1919, leaving Kate with the seven children. The youngest was 18 months old; the oldest, 18 years.

Oscar, at the age of 14, helped his mother run the farm. He and his brother, Lud, took care of the horses. Olivia milked the cows and Veronica helped her mother with the housework.

An interesting story that Oscar always told was the time an influenza epidemic was running

Mersinger family circa 1930
(l. to r.) Front: Olivia, Kate, Veronica
Back: Adrian, Ludolph, Oscar, Gilbert, Joseph

rampant in the countryside. An uncle and aunt, Phillip and Mary (nee Fohne) Mersinger, lived on Troy O'Fallon Road on a farm. Their children were all very ill and needed assistance, but Valentine and Kate were discouraged from going to their house for fear of carrying the dreaded disease back to their own children. Kate made food for Valentine to take to the sick household. Valentine would go as far as the corner fence post at the far corner of Phillip's land to set the containers of food. When Valentine was out of sight, Phillip would go and get the food. These gestures of good will prevented Valentine's family from catching the contagious disease. The Phillip Mersinger family lost several young children from the disease.

Olivia, who never married, died at age 40 of cancer; Veronica never married. Oscar married Louise Levo and bought the Edwards place west of the Valentine Mersinger homestead.

They had one daughter, Mae. Ludolph married Ruth Malwitz, his first wife, then married Lenore Heim Hess, his second wife. Gilbert married Muriel Lloyd and they lived on Lebanon Road. They had two daughters, Gail Louise and Janet Veronica. Joseph married Lucille Strieker. They had two children, Margaret and James Joseph. Adrian married Gertrude Loyet. They had four children, Donald, Geraldine, Catherine and Joseph Michael.

Kate took good care of their children and was a very religious woman. She belonged to St. John the Baptist Catholic Church; was a member (and long time president) of the church altar society; and the Daughters of Isabella, Sacred Heart Circle 237, Highland. She enjoyed working in her garden, quilting and doing things for other people. She was a generous woman who gave vegetables and fruit from her garden to neighbors and to those who had less than she. She enjoyed having a little fun while she did it, by making her gifts a little special with different decor or gift wrappings.

Both Valentine and Kate Mersinger are buried in St. John the Baptist Catholic Cemetery, Blackjack. *Submitted by Mae Mersinger Grapperhaus.*

VERONICA MARY MERSINGER

Veronica Mary Mersinger was born November 1, 1902, the second child of Valentine and Kate (Riebold) Mersinger on a farm south of Troy near Blackjack.

When she was 16, her father died, and she and her sister, Olivia, and brothers, Oscar,

Ludolph, Gilbert, Joseph and Adrian, were left to help their mother on the farm. Veronica's job was to assist her mother in the house with the housework.

At an early age, about 17 or 18, Veronica took a job in St. Louis doing housekeeping for Mrs. Burg. She worked there for several years and often told, in her later years, that she prepared and served huge dinner parties for the Burgs who were wealthy people. The parties often included high society guests. On several occasions she served Clark Clifford who went on to become a statesman for the U.S. Government. Veronica learned many of the wealthy people's traits and in later years used those ideas and recipes in her entertaining.

Veronica Mersinger, circa 1920s

Later, she became employed at the Alton State Hospital in East Alton, IL, as a practical nurse. She worked there for about 35 years. In WWII she joined the U.S. WAC . (See military section).

In the late 1940s or early 1950s, Veronica took on a project of building a "spec" home and actually helped hammer nails along with the contractor as the house was being built.

After retiring from the State of Illinois, Veronica or "Fronie" as family and friends called her, worked for a short time for the Weinell family in O'Fallon. The family was developing a subdivision north of O'Fallon. Her job included cleaning houses after they were built. Veronica also worked for a short time at the Rockwood Nursing Home in Troy.

She bought a piece of ground along West Kirsch Road from her brother, Oscar. After retirement in 1968, she built a home, and lived there the remainder of her life.

Veronica was a generous person. She never married but did a lot for family and friends. Whenever the need arose for help in the way of medical or financial needs, Veronica was willing to chip in for the cause. On weekends she came back to Troy (she lived in the nurses' quarters on the hospital grounds) to help the family. After her mother died, she came home every weekend to assist Joseph, her brother with his household chores.

She bought a car and learned to drive when she was in her late 50s and enjoyed traveling. On March of 1956, during one of her adventures to northern Illinois, she had a severe auto accident, which left her hospitalized with two broken legs. Following recovery, she again began doing for others.

Later, when her brother, Gilbert, was ill, she helped him by taking him on day

trips to pass the time while Muriel, his wife, worked in St. Louis.

Veronica loved parties and preparing for them at her little house. One such party was a western party. Everyone came dressed in western costume. Another was the "Flag Pole Raising" party in which a big ceremony was held on her front lawn around the flagpole.

She served her church, St. John the Baptist Catholic Church in Blackjack, as president of the Altar Society and did it with style. She also served as sacristan at the church. She had a flare for decorating and presenting meals. This she learned from Mrs. Burg.

After she built her home, she held camp outs on her lawn for her nieces, nephews and great-nieces and nephews. She loved Halloween and called that her "special holiday." She enjoyed having the children come for treats on that holiday.

She enjoyed working in her yard and could be seen outside in the summer tending to her lawn or planting rows and rows of vegetables in her niece Mae's garden.

She helped her niece Mae (who lived next door to her) with her children. She did baby-sitting, baking, cleaned house and did a multitude of chores for Mae and her family. She also helped brother, Adrian's, family.

On December 8, 1992, she died in her home. Mae found her lying on the floor in her hallway with hands crossed on chest. She always said, "Mae, you will find me some day."

She had pre-arranged her funeral luncheon with napkins that read "I'll Be Seeing You" and left written instructions for the table décor. She was a unique person and enjoyed life, but was always ready to assist others. *Submitted by Mae Mersinger Grapperhaus.*

GARY AND CARRIE (DEEREN) METZE

Gary and Carrie (Deeren) Metze enjoy living on the family farm on the western city limits of Troy with their son, Kyle.

(l. to r.) Gary, Carrie, and Kyle Metze

Gary, the son of Carolyn (Veath) and Kenneth Metze of Belleville, attended the Belleville schools and then earned a degree in music from Southern Illinois University at Edwardsville.

Formerly the manager of the Ponderosa Restaurants in Cahokia and Belleville, he is now the Regional Training Manager for Healthcare Services Group, Inc. Carrie, the daughter of James and Audrey (Ottwein) Deeren of Troy, attended the Troy schools and received a certificate of completion from Patricia Stevens

Career College. She then earned her Bachelor's degree from Southern Illinois University at Edwardsville. She taught business subjects at Patricia Stevens for several years, and then in 1987 joined the faculty of Triad High School. She teaches keyboarding, computer skills and related business subjects. She is a member of Friedens United Church of Christ, the Southwest Area Business Education Association, and the Illinois Business Education Association.

Music has played a large part in the life of this family. Gary, a gifted tenor, sings with a professional southern gospel group, The Gateway Quartet. Gary and Carrie both sing with the Black Tie Affair, a semi-professional group based in Edwardsville. Gary plays bass guitar, and Carrie has played piano since childhood and plays the French horn with the Troy Community Band. Gary has been featured as tenor soloist with the SIUE Concert Chorale and at many other community and church events. It looks as if son Kyle will continue the family talents and interests as he is studying piano and loves to sing almost as much as he loves karate, baseball, soccer, swimming and golfing with his dad. *Submitted by Audrey Deeren.*

DAVID AND VALERIE MEYER - David and Valerie Meyer were married on Nov. 10, 1984, at St. James Lutheran Church in Columbus, MT.

Meyer family, 2002
(l. to r.) David, Valerie, Hannah, Kathryn

David is the son of LtC. (USAF, Ret.) James F. Meyer, reared in Prairetown, IL, and a graduate of Staunton High School, Staunton, IL, and Orralee (Womeldorf) Meyer, formerly of Decatur, IL. His parents currently reside in Lebanon, IL. His parents are alumni of the University of Illinois. David was born at Clark AFB, Philippines, Oct. 28, 1960. David is a graduate of the University of Nebraska, Lincoln, with a Bachelor of Arts Degree in History and Embry Riddle Aeronautical University with a Masters of Science Degree in Aviation Management. He is currently employed as an Officer in the USAF. He spent summers at the family farm near Prairietown, IL, with his grandparents Edwin and Lucille (Gusewelle) Meyer.

Valerie (VanEvery) is the daughter of Bernard and Lois (Lien) VanEvery of Columbus, MT. Both of Valerie's parents were born and reared in the Stillwater River Valley of Montana. Her mother, Lois, is a graduate of Absarokee High School in Absarokee, MT, and her father, Bernard, is a graduate of Columbus High School

in Columbus, MT. They currently reside on the family ranch located on the Stillwater River, 5 miles east of Absarokee, MT. Valerie is a graduate of Carroll College, Helena, MT, with a Bachelor of Arts Degree in Nursing, and the University of Texas at Austin with a Masters in Library and Information Science. She is currently employed as the Library Director at Tri-Township Public Library District in Troy. Valerie's middle name is Ruth and she shares that middle name with her daughter Kathryn, her mother, her grandmother Violet (Anderson) Lien, and her great-grandmother Mattie (Shortridge) Anderson.

David and Valerie have two daughters. Kathryn was born in Anchorage, AK, Nov. 25, 1987 and will graduate from St. Paul's Lutheran School May 2002. She plans to attend Triad High School and has aspirations of being an architect. Hannah was born in Hampton, VA, Jun. 1, 1990, and is a student at St. Paul's Lutheran School. *Submitted by Valerie Meyer.*

EDWIN L. AND INEZ P. (SEIBERT) MEYER - Edwin Lester Meyer was born February 1, 1904, in Pin Oak Township, Madison County, IL. He was the eldest child of John W. and Hattie (Porter) Meyer. Inez P. (nee Seibert) Meyer was born March 31, 1913, on a farm east of Shiloh, IL. She was the eldest child of Charles B. and Amanda C. (Renner) Seibert. Inez started her school years by attending Grass Land School, south of Scott Field. She graduated from Belleville West High School and went on to school to become a hairdresser. Both Lester and Inez belonged to Shiloh Valley Grange, St. Clair Pomona Grange, and Madison County Farm Bureau. Lester belonged to St. Clair Odd Fellows Lodge, the Samaritans Lodge, and Lebanon Singers Association. Inez belonged to Pride of the West Rebekah Lodge.

As a child, Lester started school at Sylvan Hall School, north of Troy. The family moved around in various communities like Pierron, Pocahontas, Trenton and Lebanon. In 1932, they bought a farm southeast of Troy in the Blackjack community, Jarvis Township. It was here that Lester turned to farming after his marriage. The farm was in the family until 1990 when it was sold.

In his early days, Lester was a trucker by trade. He hauled milk to Highland Dairy Company and then later to St. Louis Dairy. He also hauled coal and livestock for various farmers around the area. It was through the grange that he met his wife, Inez. At the time, Lester was a member of Emerald Mound

Edwin Lester and Inez (Siebert) Meyer

Grange. There was a function at Emerald Mound one evening which Inez and her parents attended. Lester had his eyes on his future wife. He mentioned to them that Emerald Mound was going to have a chicken dinner on the following Sunday and invited Inez and her parents to attend the dinner. Lester and Inez dated for four years before Lester popped the question. They married on January 13, 1937, in Belleville at the Parsonage of St. Johns United Church of Christ. After her marriage, Inez became a housewife. She enjoyed working in her flower garden and truck patch. She was an excellent cook, often being complimented on her cooking. Her daughter often said that her mother was the best cook on the East side of the Mississippi. Inez entered the Madison County Fair for several years in the culinary division and took many prizes, with one year taking Grand Prize on her Cherry Chiffon Cake.

To this union are two children: Donald L., born on April 30, 1939, and Joyce I., born on September 6, 1945. Donald started his school year at Virgin School, south of St. Jacob. After the school was closed in the early 1950s, he attended school in the Lebanon School District. Joyce started her schooling in Lebanon School District, also. Both graduated from Lebanon Community High School. Lester died on January 16, 1986, and Inez died on June 10, 2000. Both are buried at College Hill Cemetery, Lebanon. *Submitted by Joyce Meyer.*

JOHN W. AND HATTIE M. (PORTER) MEYER - John W. Meyer was born in Lebanon on December 5, 1878, and was the son of John N. and Elizabeth (nee Amsinger) Meyer. He married Hattie Mariah Porter, daughter of Robert M. and Mary Elizabeth (nee Isaac) Porter on March 24, 1903, at the Methodist Church in Troy.

John W. and Hattie M. (Porter) Meyer, circa 1903

In John's early life he attended school in the Blackjack Community. After he became older, his parents moved to a farm a few miles north of Lebanon. After his schooling, he became a farmer by trade, renting farm land in various communities in the area. They settled on a farm north of Lebanon and later moved to a farm north of St. Jacob. After his retirement in 1954, John and Hattie moved into Troy. In Hattie's early life she was raised in the Troy-St. Jacob community.

After she graduated from high school, she became a school teacher until her marriage when she became a housewife.

John and Hattie belonged to Friedens United Church of Christ and were charter members of the Lindley Grange.

To this union there were eight children: Lester, Raymond, Irvin, Mary (Martin Pomatto), Hilda (Kenneth Heim), Lavern, Clifford and Ella (Victor Loyet). Lavern died in infancy and is buried in Augusta Cemetery, St. Jacob. John died June 25, 1959, at Highland, and Hattie died May 24, 1975, in Macoupin Co., IL. Both are buried at College Hill Cemetery, Lebanon. *Submitted by Joyce Meyer.*

MARY ANN MILLS - Mary Ann Mills, daughter of Walter John and Florence Ward Mills, was raised on the family farm on Spring Valley Road with her sister Nancy and brother Bill. She graduated from Troy Public School in 1959 and Triad High School in 1963. After high school graduation, she went to work in St. Louis, learning a great deal about how the world really works off the farm.

Her first job was with a travel agency, whetting her desire to see more of the world. The second job was with a stock broker, learning about how money is made (and lost) on the stock exchange.

Since she was still "footloose and fancy-free," she decided to move on and took a third job with Peabody Coal Company. Here she really found her niche! Typing, filing, answering phones and keeping records in the Land Department held her interest for the next 11 years.

In 1969, she met "the right guy," Jerry Grow, an accountant from Salt Lake City, UT, and married him on April 18, 1970. He was also working at Peabody. Eventually, they bought a home in south St. Louis County, where they lived for about four years. Then, the chance came to move to Arizona and off they went. They both moved up in the company, Mary Ann to Office Manager of the Western Division office and husband Jerry to Vice President - Sales. The years in Arizona were full of hard work, travel and adventure! Mary Ann retired from Peabody in 1985 and Jerry in 1995. They decided now was the time to return to Illinois to be near Mary Ann's mother and sister, so they packed up their household, sold their home in Flagstaff and returned to Illinois in 1996. Now they reside very happily in Glen Carbon within easy reach of family and friends. *Submitted by Mary Ann Grow*

WALTER AND FLORENCE (WARD) MILLS - Walter Mills and Florence Ward were married in Christ Episcopal Church in Collinsville on January 27, 1934.

Their families had lived in the Troy area for several generations. Both their fathers were coal miners. Florence's father, Albert Ward, went to work in the Lumaghi Coal Mine in Collinsville when he was ten years old and worked there until he was sixty. And Florence's grandparents, Martin and Elizabeth Herbst, had a blacksmith shop in Blackjack southeast of Troy in the late 1800s.

Walter's parents, John and Mary Anna, lived in Collinsville Township and, in their later years, Maryville. Walter had seven sisters and three brothers. Florence had one brother.

Walter and Florence moved to a farm south of Troy on Spring Valley Road in the late 1940's.

There Florence kept busy with a big house and garden while Walter farmed. In addition to farming, Walter worked for the State grading roads and plowing snow.

The couple had three children, William (Bill), Mary Ann and Nancy. They moved into town in 1960, living in a house constructed by Walter and Bill on Weston Street.

Bill and his wife Judy (Boyd) Mills live in Kimberling City, Missouri. Mary Ann and her husband Jerry Grow live in Glen Carbon, and Nancy and her husband Don Barsch live in Troy.

Walter passed away in 1978. Florence now lives in town and maintains a lively interest in antiques and flea markets. *Submitted by Nancy Barsch.*

WILLIAM AND JUDY (BOYD) MILLS
William (Bill) Mills, the son of Walter and Florence Mills, was five years old when the family moved to a farm south of Troy on Spring Valley Road. His first school years were spent at Spring Valley School House, a one room country school not far from his home.

In 1959 he graduated from McCray-Dewey High School and continued to live and work in the area.

On December 9, 1966, William married Judith Boyd, the daughter of Tom and Lou Boyd of Thomasville, MO. The couple raised five children: Rhonda, Tony, Bobby, Tommy and Randy. Rhonda, Bobby and Tommy have blessed them with six grandchildren. They have also been blessed with their first great grandchild.

William works for Rinehart Trucking in Branson, MO, as a diesel mechanic, and Judith works for the Family Dollar Store in Branson West as an Assistant Manager. *Submitted by Judith Mills.*

JEFF AND TAMMY (BAUMGARTNER) MITCHELL - Tammy's grandparents, Otto and Gertrude Baumgartner, moved to Troy in 1952 from Grantfork, IL. They had 11 children; all graduated from Troy school district.

Their first child was Leonard Baumgartner born January 7, 1937. He married Betty Rose Heller on February 8, 1958, at St. Jerome Catholic Church in Troy. Betty was born on March 20, 1939, and died November 16, 1986. She was the daughter of John and Florence Heller of Troy.

Leonard and Betty had 5 children: Leonard, Michael, Tamara, Julie, and Daniel, all born in Troy and graduates of Triad High School.

Tammy graduated from Triad High School in (1982). She married Jeffery Mitchell on September 6, 1986, at St. Jerome Church in

Troy. Jeff is the son of Bernard and Shirley Mitchell of Troy, previously of Granite City. Tammy and Jeff still reside in Troy with their 2 children: James Andrew Mitchell, b. September 24, 1987, and Maggi Rose Mitchell b. June 6, 1992.

Jeff has been a printer for Graham-Pierce Printing of O'Fallon, IL, for 13 years. Tammy is currently City Clerk of Troy. *Submitted by Tammy Mitchell.*

JOSEPH MITCHELL - Joseph Mitchell was a private in Company K, 140th Regiment, Illinois Volunteer Infantry (100 days). He joined and was enrolled for service at Perry, Pike County, Illinois, with his residence listed as Troy, Madison Co., IL, on 28 May 1864. He was mustered out of service 20 October 1864 at Chicago, IL. Joseph Mitchell's father, Joseph, as well as his brothers Henry and Calvin also saw service in the Union Army during the Civil War. Henry served in Company C, 48th, IL Inf., Carlyle, IL. Calvin and the father, Joseph, served in Company K, 30th Reg. IL Vol., Carlyle, IL. It is not known if the Leturno family was residing around Carlyle at the time or not. Calvin was treated in General Hospital in Cairo, IL, from November 1861 to April 14, 1862.

Joseph Michell married Letitia Perlina Bardsley abt 1871/72. Four known children were born to this union: Cassius Scott, 15 December 1873; Hannah Theodocia, 15 December 1875; Carrie Perlina, 18 June 1878; and Joseph Robert, 8 March 1882. Cassius married Mollie Hare; Hannah Theodocia married Samuel Bracken; Carrie Perlina married William Turnbull and Joseph Robert married Epsa Ball. *Submitted by Vernon L. Lacey.*

SAMUEL MIX - Samuel Mix married Grace Dee Elliott in 1941. Grace Dee was born Dec. 29, 1892, the daughter of Grant and Clara Elliott (see Grant L. Elliott). They lived in St. Louis, MO, until his death in 1945. Dee continued to live in St. Louis, caring for her maiden aunts, Maude (1877-1951) and Blanche (1875-1956) Cade.

Samuel L. and Dee (Elliott) Mix

Dee returned to Troy in 1955 to live with her brother "Babe" and his family on 511 S. Main St. in Troy. She lived there until her death in 1974. *Submitted by Kae Elliott Schmitt.*

THOMAS AND CATHERINE (SIMS) MORGAN - Thomas Morgan and Catherine Sims were married January 2, 1856, in the Capel y Cwm Methodist Chapel at Llansamlet, near

Mitchell family, 2001
(l. to r.) Front: Maggi, Tammy
Back: James, Jeff

Swansea, Wales. They had nine children, six sons and three daughters. They emigrated from Wales in 1868 with children William, Thomas, Hannah, Hopkin, and Mary and her twin. While at sea, Mary's twin died and was buried at sea.

The family located first in St. Louis, Mo., then O'Fallon, IL and Fairfield, IL, and in 1883, came to Troy, IL. They lived in the area of Troy known as Brookside. Their home stood where Route 40 is now located. They also owned two smaller homes in Brookside which they rented out. Catherine Morgan's brother, Hopkin T. Sims, also became a resident of Troy.

Catherine Morgan was 80 years of age when she died, Thomas was 84. Both are buried in the Troy City Cemetery.

Their daughter Mary married Daniel R. Jones, a Welsh immigrant, on Nov. 30, 1887. Daniel was a blacksmith. Daniel died in 1903, Mary in 1954. Both are buried in the Troy City Cemetery.

Their children are Ritchie Annette (married to William Frangen, children Paul, Clyde, Catherine, Marjory and Lester), Catherine May (married to Lester Morrison Kinder, children Lester Morrison Kinder Jr. and Mary Catherine), Florence Belva, Esther Jane, (married David Jones, child Bernice), Daniel (married to Lillian Pyatt, children Marcella and Betty Jane) and Gwendolyn Narcissus (married to Fred Coad, children, twins Robert and Thomas). After Fred's death, Gwendolyn married William Schmitt.

After Daniel's death Mary raised her children with the rent from one of the homes her parents owned. She had to be very thrifty and was a very resourceful person. In later years, while living in St. Louis with Esther and Florence, she owned two rental flats.

The only son, Daniel, died at the young age of 32. The sisters were very close and with their children spent every Sunday together. All of the grandchildren called their grandmother "Mama Jones" following the lead of the eldest, Paul Frangen. The sisters all "mothered" all of the children and the children loved to spend holidays and vacations with all of them. *Submitted by Mary Catherine Gerstenecker.*

REV. RICHARD H. AND HERNA MORNHINWEG -
New Braunfels, TX, was the home to Richard Mornhinweg until he went to college in Elmhurst, IL. He went to Eden Seminary in St. Louis, MO. Rev. G. Mornhinweg, his father, ordained him in New Braunfels.

Herna Mornhinweg was born in Collinsville, IL, to Henry and Bertha Derwelis. Herna and Richard were married by his father in Collinsville. They traveled all the way from Hookdale, IL, (their first church) and they arrived in Troy in 1932. They ministered to Friedens Evangelical and Reformed Church, which is now Friedens United Church of Christ.

Naturally they were active in the Church , however, they also participated in many community projects. "Rev," as he was affectionately called, was very proud of his membership in the Lions Club .

After his early morning walk he would stop at the Shell "filling station" (next to Adams Store) and talk to whoever was there. He would also wave to everyone on their way to work. It

Herna and Richard H. Mornhinweg, 1960

was said that some felt the day wasn't right if they didn't wave to "Rev."

The nearest hospital was in Highland, and he would go there often to visit members from the church who were sick. There was no privacy act in those days, so he would check the list of patients. If there was a patient he knew and they were from Troy, he would stop in to say "Hi" and offer a prayer if they wished; if he knew them, he would visit. A year or two after Paul Simon became the publisher of the *Troy Tribune*, "Rev" was named "Citizen of the Year."

Herna was not as active in the community but liked to quilt. She was very proud of her bell collection. Several of her prized bells were from a Buddhist temple, the Collinsville Bell Factory, and a bell for a turkey.

Richard and Herna were parents of a daughter, Jacquelyn, born in 1933. The Mornhinwegs lived in Troy for forty-three years. They retired from the ministry in Troy in 1975 and moved to the Edwardsville-Glen Carbon area. "Rev" passed away in 1990 and Herna in 1996. *Submitted by Jackie Estes.*

EDWARD MORRISS - Edward Morriss and his wife Margery (Hardwich) emigrated from their home in Nodaway County, VA, in December 1838, to the Belleville, St. Clair County, IL, area where they remained until the spring of 1849. They then moved and settled on Section 12 of Collinsville Township. Here they resided several years, engaging in farming, and later moving to Section 18 in Jarvis Township, where they remained until his death in the fall of 1848. Edward and Margery had six children: Hillis, Serena, Rodeville C., Eusebious, Timenia (married Henry Roper) and Eurethra (married Green Roper). *Submitted by Millie (Collins) Shaffer.*

GEORGE C. MORRISS - George C. Morriss, a son of Rodeville and Arminda (Hamilton) Morriss, was born in the Formosa area on April 8, 1865. He married Margaret Rose (Hampton), daughter of Frank L. and his wife of Troy. To this union was born one child, a daughter, Ethel Wright Morriss, who married John H. Collins of Troy.

Margaret, know as Maggie, died at 26. Several years later George married Caroline Sprick of the Formosa area. To this marriage were born three daughters: Viola Marie (who married Keith L. Edwards of Troy), Beulah (who died in infancy), and Gladys Millie (who married Alfred Pape of Edwardsville).

George engaged in dairy farming and horse trading in the Formosa area until about 1901

when he built a home and livery stable in Troy at the corner of West Clay and Powell Streets. He also engaged in the grain, feed, and trading business until 1933. He was also active in local politics and served as Tax Assessor for several terms. He served on the local school boards and was involved in many other community activities until, in 1933, ill health curtailed his participation. Mr. Morriss died in 1939.

All three of his daughters, Ethel, Viola, and Gladys, became school teachers, teaching in the local area country schools (Liberty and Formosa), Troy Grade School and Troy High School, and later in the communities of Glen Carbon, Maryville, and Granite City. *Submitted by Millie (Collins) Shaffer.*

RODEVILLE CLINTON MORRISS
Rodeville Clinton Morriss was born in Nodaway County, VA, on June 19, 1820, and came with his parents to IL in 1838. On Oct. 26, 1843, he married Arminda Hamilton, daughter of William and Jane (Robinson) Hamilton who were early settlers of Madison County.

To this union were born five sons and two daughters: Margery (married Joseph Fix of Collinsville), John H., Mollie, Louis, Henry, Robert, and George. John moved to Collinsville, and Louis and Henry, to St. Louis. Robert and George remained in the Troy area.

Rodeville farmed in the Formosa area. After the death of his wife, Arminda, he married Fannie Landon. Several years after the death of her husband, Fannie had moved to Troy purchasing a dwelling at the northwest corner of S. Main and Prospect Streets, which she later traded to the Baptist Church for their parsonage property at the NW corner of Charcoal and Byrn, where she lived until her death in 1924. *Submitted by Millie (Collins) Shaffer*

TED AND DAWN MUSHILL - Ted and Dawn Mushill built a house in Troy in February of 2000. Ted and Dawn were both born and raised in Granite City, IL, and moved to Troy because

Ted and Dawn Mushill

they enjoy the "country feel" of Troy. Ted is employed as a Foreman at GKN in St. Louis and Dawn in employed as the Executive Director of the Troy Chamber of Commerce. *Submitted by Dawn Mushill.*

JON AND NANCY NEMNICH - Jon Joseph Nemnich and Nancy Jean Frutiger were married on May 3, 1975, at Friedens United Church of Christ in Troy, Illinois. They met during their high school years at Triad High School. Jon was

Nemnich family, 2000
(l. to r.) Front: Jon, Nancy, Nathan. Back: Jennifer.

born March 12, 1952, at St. Joseph's Hospital in Highland, IL. He is the son of Joseph and Ella (Barth) Nemnich, Jr. Jon graduated from Triad High School in 1971. He has lived in Troy his whole life.

Nancy was born August 28, 1955, at St. Joseph's Hospital in Highland, IL, the daughter of Delmar and Mildred (Kirsch) Frutiger. She lived in St. Jacob, IL, and attended St. Jacob Grade School. Nancy graduated from Triad High School in 1973.

They are the parents of two children, Jennifer Ann and Nathan Jon. Jennifer was born on June 9, 1980. She graduated from Triad High School in 1998, and Hickey College in St. Louis, MO, in 1999 with a diploma in Graphic Design. Jennifer is presently working in St. Louis.

Nathan was born on March 9, 1984. He will graduate from Triad High School in 2002. Nathan enjoys playing basketball. *Submitted by Jon and Nancy Nemnich.*

JOSEPH AND FRANCES HULTZ NEMNICH, SR. - Joseph Nemnich, Sr., was born February 12, 1896, the son of John and Amelia (Wentz) Nemnich. Frances Ella Hultz was born June 3, 1901, in a house which still stands on the corner of Staunton Road and Thorp Street. (Jerry Kueker lives there now.) She was one of three girls and three boys – Elizabeth, Louis, Mamie, Frances (Fannie), William and John Hultz (another son Charles died in infancy), all born in Troy to Charles and Mary Hultz. Fannie attended grade school and two years of high school before quitting to go to work like lots of young people did in those days. She worked at the bakery-same location as today. The owners were Henry and Mary Schneider. Fannie called Mrs. Schneider "Aunt Mary."

Fannie met and dated a young man from Marine, Joseph Nemnich, before he was drafted

Fannie and Joe Nemich, Sr., early 1960s

into the Army and served in WWI and saw overseas action in Europe. He returned in May of 1919, and they dated again. One day, at the bakery, Aunt Mary suggested to Fannie, "I hope you marry that nice young man before the winter months and he would have to come through those bottoms!" Joe and Fannie were married in Springfield, IL, (by a judge) on September 24, 1919. They started out in Edwardsville on Denny Avenue. On July 31, 1920, they had a daughter, Charmion, known as Dottie.

In December of 1923, they were burned out of their flat and had to live with relatives for a short time. They moved to Collinsville and lived there until 1926. In Collinsville a son, Joseph Nemnich, Jr., was born on February 7, 1925. Joe Jr. was born on the site where the Collinsville library now stands. They lived in an upstairs apartment in a house owned by John Renfro at the time. Joe married Ella Barth on June 19, 1949.

In September of 1926 they moved to Troy. (Charmion was 6 days late for school in the 1st grade.) Joe worked at his mechanical job in Troy at the Ford Garage-the site is now City Hall. Many years he worked out of town in E. St. Louis at Brodhead Motors. In the late 40s and 50s, Joe and Fran both worked for Oscar Gindler in the Studebaker Garage, located where the 5 Star Billiard Parlor now stands.

Joe and Fannie were married 53 years before they both passed away. Their daughter Charmion married Andy Semanisin and had two sons, Robert and David. Joe Jr. and Ella had two daughters and one son, Cheryl, Jon, and Debra. They had three great-grandchildren, Daniel and Susan Semanisin and Mat Boster.

In 1969, Fannie had her right leg amputated (diabetes). Until 1973 she spent her time in a wheelchair, being taken care of by her mate. Joseph died on March 3, 1973, at 5:30 a.m., and Frannie died on July 3, 1973, at 5:30 a. m. They were two good Troy citizens! *Submitted by Charmion Nemnich Semanisin and Nancy Nemnich.*

JOSEPH NEMNICH, JR. - Joseph Nemnich, Jr., was born February 7, 1925, the son of Joseph and Frances (Hultz) Nemnich, Sr. He married Ella Barth on June 19, 1949. Ella was the daughter of Fred and Emma (Wille) Barth born on April 11, 1919. They lived most of their married life in Troy.

Joe and Ella Nemnich, 1991

Joe and Ella had three children. Cheryl Lynn was born on April 4, 1950. Cheryl and her husband, Dan Howard, live in O'Fallon, MO. Cheryl has two children: Mat Boster and Andrea Howard.

Jon Joseph, the second child, was born on March 12, 1952. He and his wife, Nancy (Frutiger), live in Troy. They have two children: Jennifer and Nathan Nemnich.

The third child, Debra Jean, was born on March 13, 1955. She lives in Belleville, IL, and has four children: Loretta (Lori), Joseph (Joe), Mark Jr., and Christopher (Chris) Rice.

Joe Nemnich died on July 10, 1997, and Ella died on September 15, 1997. *Submitted by Jon and Nancy Nemnich.*

ELMER H. AND ROSE M. NIEDRINGHAUS
Elmer H. "Bud" Niedringhaus Jr. was the son of Elmer H. and Mabel A. (Hatfield) Niedringhaus Sr. He married Rose M. Enos, the daughter of William and Johanna (Sautoff) Enos on November 29, 1940.

Rose and Bud Niedringhaus, April, 1985

Three children were born to this union. They are William E. who married Patricia Strom; Richard G. who married Linda Wiesemeyer and Joann M. Niedringhaus, who is single.

Mr. Niedringhaus had one brother, William B. Niedringhaus, and one sister, Elizabeth Studebaker.

Mrs. Niedringhaus had one sister, Mrs. Agnes Watts, and two brothers, Richard and William Enos. Mrs. Niedringhaus owned and operated a beauty shop in Granite City and was secretary for Troy Homestead Savings and Loan for 20 years. She was associated with the real estate/insurance firm owned by her husband, Bud Niedringhaus.

The couple lived in Granite City then moved to Lakeview Acres in Maryville in 1950. They came to Troy in 1985 and moved to the Creekside Addition.

Mrs. Niedringhaus enjoyed needlepoint and hand crafted things. She was a member of the First United Presbyterian Church in Collinsville. She was a member of the Women's Club of Troy and was a member of the Anderson Hospital Auxiliary in Maryville. She also enjoyed bridge and was a member of a bridge club.

Mr. Niedringhaus owned and operated Niedringhaus Agency, which was located on 107 E. Market Street in Troy. He was a member of the Troy Lions Club. He liked to play tennis and take care of his many properties. He also was an appraiser and enjoyed that kind of work.

Joann, their daughter, enjoys swimming, kick boxing and working in her yard. She has a dog "Snuggums." She attended Maryville North Grade School and graduated from Edwardsville High School in 1973. She currently lives in Troy.

Mrs. Niedringhaus was born July 24, 1916, and died April 22, 1990. Mr. Niedringhaus was born January 11, 1916, and died January 21, 1999.

Mr. And Mrs. Niedringhaus have four grandchildren and two great-grandchildren. The couple is buried in Sunset Hill Cemetery in Glen Carbon, IL. *Submitted by JoAnn Niedringhaus and written by Mae Grapperhaus.*

ARNOLD AND ELLA NIEHAUS - When John Henry Niehaus came from Germany to America in 1847 with $35 in his pocket, he proved himself a self-made man. By 1851 he was in Troy and the next year he was a farmer. He married three times. His first wife, Anna Marie Beckering, died while giving birth in 1855 along with their newborn child. He then wed Martha Paulina Steinert and together they had 3 children. Their firstborn died at 6 months old. The next two children, Henry and Joseph grew to be adults and resided in Troy. He and his third wife, Elizabeth Rad, had 3 more children, Charles, Frank and William.

Henry married Barbara Schwartz (the third daughter of Phillip Schwartz and Barbara Bugger) in 1882. They had 6 children. Dora died as an infant. Emma married Fred Loyet. Elizabeth married Joseph Green. Theo died at 26 years of age. Arnold married Ella Noeltner. Oscar never married and lived on the Niehaus farm all of his life until his death at the age of 49.

Arnold Joseph Niehaus, born August 3, 1896, was married on September 8, 1920, to Ella Emma Noeltner, who was born January 7, 1899. They lived and farmed the Niehaus homeplace along with Oscar where the brothers had been born and raised. Arnold died on March 19, 1963, at the age of 66. His wife Ella moved to Collinsville after his death. Ella died on December 18, 1989, at the age of 90.

Arnold and Ella parented 6 children on the Niehaus farm in Troy. Ella was fortunate to know all of her grandchildren and was very proud to tell others that she had 26 grandchildren.

Melvin, born September 3, 1921, married Marian Knebel in 1954 and farmed the homeplace until he retired. They have one son, John Henry and his wife Dana. John now farms the land.

Lorine, born July 25, 1923, married Omar Bugger in 1943. They had 4 children, Edward (Judy), Luella (Dennis) Hollenkamp, Elmer (Pat) and Shirley (Lloyd) Roberson. After the death of Omar in 1974, Lorine then married Paul Tonnies in 1976.

Marcella, born November 27, 1925, married Herbert Heim in 1948. Their 4 children are Harold (Nancy), Rita, Janice and Dennis (Julie).

Twins, Bernadine (older by six minutes) and Bernice, were born December 10, 1927. Bernadine married Ed Poletti in 1950. They had 4 children, Wayne (June), Marilyn (Don) Meyer, Teresa (Brad) Hovatter and Judy (Bruce) Steele. After the death of Ed in 1988, Bernadine moved into Troy from the family farm.

Bernice married Melvin Friederich in 1947. They had 8 children, Carol Ann (Jim) Meyer, Gene (Connie), Marianne (Bill) Hicks, Joanne (Jim) Kalla, Russell (Kim), Robert (Shelly), Susanne (Jim) Osterhout, and Joseph (Cristal). After the death of Mel in 1975, Bernice married Leonard Dickerson in 1989.

Arline, the youngest Niehaus child, was born March 30, 1930. She married Vincent Fohne in 1954. They had 5 children, Gary (Debbie), Donna (Duane) Albers, Dianne (Steve) Morton, Mary Ellen (John) Comell, and Sharon (Jerry) Buckley. After the death of Vincent in 1995, Arline married Arthur Donald Fohne in 1999.

Arnold and Ella enjoyed many family gatherings on the farm. Keeping with tradition, many holidays were kept in the same spirit as generations before them. Before days of "great rooms" or "family rooms," the Niehaus family would gather in all parts of the house to play cards or board games. Summertime always included fried chicken, homemade ice cream and, of course, delicious baked pies. Winter brought the big day of butchering when family and neighbors would help prepare the meats. Arnold and Ella were active members of St. John the Baptist Catholic Church in Blackjack and, along with Oscar Niehaus, donated a new organ for the Church. Arnold was a church trustee and Ella, a member of the Altar and Rosary Sodality. The annual church picnic was a social event that again brought families together to work, support and enjoy the picnic.

Life has been very good for the Niehaus family in Troy. And the Niehaus family thanks Troy for many happy memories. *Submitted by Bernice Niehaus (Friederich) Dickerson.*

NIEHAUS TWINS - On December 10, 1927, Arnold and Ella (Noeltner) Niehaus were awaiting the birth of their fourth child at the family homeplace and were surprised with the birth of identical twin daughters, Bernadine and Bernice. Bernadine was born 6 minutes before Bernice. Dr. Molden, who charged a total fee of $25.00, delivered the twins. Four days later they went for their first horse and buggy ride. The twins were going to be baptized at St. Jerome Catholic Church in Troy.

The twins attended their first few years of schooling at a one-room school house at the Catholic School in Blackjack (settlement just outside of Troy) along with their siblings, Melvin, Lorine, Marcella and Arline. Later they attended Gilead School in the country to finish their grade school education. The twins graduated from McCray-Dewey High School in 1946. Both were members of the marching band with Bernadine playing the cornet and Bernice playing the trombone. The twins occasionally

Niehaus Twins, 1931
(l. to r.) Bernice, Bernadine

switched classes and were amazed that no one could tell the difference.

There were many fun times for the twins; however, life was hard growing up on a farm with many chores such as milking cows and gardening. Going to the store was a rarity, since most of the food was grown on the farm. Fresh fruit from the market was a luxury given to them by relatives who came to visit from the city.

Bernadine married Edward Poletti on April 18, 1950. Together they worked their farm in Troy. The family attended St. John the Baptist Catholic Church in Blackjack. Ed was a trustee of the Church and Bernadine, a member of the Altar and Rosary Sodality.

Bernadine and Ed had four children. Wayne married June Wessel and their children are Kathryn, Timothy, Luke and Michael. Marilyn and her husband Don Meyer have two sons, David and Robert. Teresa and her husband, Brad Hovatter, have two children, Amanda and Nathan. Judy and her husband, Bruce Steele, have two children, Christina and A. J.

Niehaus Twins, 1946
(l. to r.) Bernice, Bernadine

After the death of Ed in 1988, Bernadine moved from the family farm into Troy.

Bernice married Melvin Friederich on June 3, 1947. They were active members of Saints Peter & Paul Catholic Church in Collinsville. Mel was a Fourth Degree member and past Grand Knight of the Knights of Columbus and Bernice, a member of the Altar and Rosary Society.

Bernice and Mel had eight children. Carol Ann (Timmermann) is married to Jim Meyer and she has one son, Joseph Timmermann. Gene married Connie Carl and has four children, Shawn, Brandy, Autumn and Nicholas. Marianne and her husband, Bill Hicks, have two sons, Michael and Matthew. Joanne and her husband, Jim Kalla, have two children, Thomas and Jennifer. Russell married Kim LaDue and

Niehaus family
(l. to r.) Front: Melvin, Ella (Noeltner), Arnold. Back: Bernadine Poletti, Bernice Friederich Dickerson, Lorine Bugger Tonnies, Marcella Heim, Arline Fohne.

they have two children, Rachel and Kyle. Robert married Shelly (Bluemner) White and they have two children, Jaclyn (White) Allison and their son Zachary. Susanne and her husband, Jim Osterhout, have three sons, Daniel, Andrew and Ryan. Joseph married Cristal Foulk.

Mel died in 1975 at the age of 47. Bernice then married Leonard Dickerson on April 7, 1989, at St. Jerome Catholic Church in Troy. The Dickersons now live in Collinsville.

The twins have enjoyed keeping up with their friends and attending their high school class reunions. Bernadine and Bernice, as identical twins, have always shared a special bond and often think the same thoughts (at times somewhat eerie). However, the twins are individuals; Bernadine knew she wanted the farm life and Bernice preferred to live in town.

Growing up on a farm in Troy was an adventure with plenty of stories to tell. Family and friends mean everything to the twins and here in Troy is where it all began. *Submitted by Bernadine Poletti and Bernice Dickerson.*

DON AND MARILYN NIHISER - Donald Nihiser was born Sept. 19, 1941, in Decatur, IL, to Louis and A. Maxine (Rich) Nihiser Oberdalhoff. He grew up in Pocahontas and graduated from Highland High in 1958. Marilyn (Tensineyer) Nihiser was born December 9, 1944, in Hoyleton, IL, to Raydeen and Pauline (Kasten) Tensineyer. She grew up in rural Carlyle and graduated from Carlyle High in 1962 and in 1986 received 1000 credits from Bryan Institute, Bridgeton, MO, in computer science. Don worked at Neubauer's Market in the meat industry; Marilyn worked primarily at Basler Electric in the secretarial field until 1966.

Don and Marilyn met on a blind date in 1959, married August 4, 1963, and settled in rural Highland, building their home themselves. Don was drafted in October, 1966, and was sent to Vietnam in 1968, leaving Marilyn behind, five months pregnant with their first child, Todd, who was born in Breese, IL, May 26, 1968. While in Vietnam, Don served in the First Infantry Division in the Siagon area during the Tet Offensive. He gained rank from a PVT to E-6 in a short time and won medals, including two Bronze Stars. Don returned home in October, 1968, and Terry was born in Breese, IL, October 7, 1969.

In 1969 Don and Marilyn owned and operated the meat department in Van's Discount Store (presently Highland TruBuy) in Highland. In November, 1971, they purchased Troy Frozen Foods from Earl and Harold Schmidt. In

Nihiser family, 2000
(l. to r.) Front: Marilyn. Middle: Todd, Don. Back: Terry.

1972-73 they discontinued the meat department in Highland and put all their efforts into Troy Frozen Foods.

Todd and Terry graduated from Highland High and both attended SIUE. Todd attended two years and Terry, six. Todd continued working at their family business, completed a meat cutting trade school course at Penn State University, and purchased his own home in Troy in 1992. Terry worked at college and the family business; however, the 1993 fire of Troy Frozen Foods occurred just at the time when Terry was ready to work on his project for his Masters in electrical engineering. Terry "dropped his hat" to work with the family. By the time everything got "back in line," the professors, computers, and software had all changed at college. Terry worked totally on his own at night on the Troy Foods' computer to design and build a smokehouse micro-processor, a project he had dreamed of making while still in junior high. He had hopes of building and patenting the "new" computerized invention for the meat industry; however, with computer technology moving fast there was a similar program on the market when the Nihisers were building, so Terry even helped that company install it into the new Troy Frozen Foods' smokehouse system. He completed his project which qualified him for his thesis, presented it to the professors and received his Masters degree. *Submitted by Marilyn Nihiser.*

LAWRENCE C. NORBURY - Lawrence Charles Norbury was born in East St. Louis, IL, on August 2, 1943, to Charles William and Agnes Ann (Petry) Norbury. He grew up in the neighboring community of Collinsville. His parents were both born and reared in Troy. Larry graduated from Collinsville High School in 1961. In March 1963, he went to work at Granite City Steel. He began his career there in the Cold Strip on the shipping floor. Presently he is a Furnace Operator in the BOF. From 1965 to 1969 he served in the United States Army and is a Vietnam veteran.

On September 4, 1970, he married Susan Kay Ringley in Collinsville. Sue was born on April 18, 1948, in Macomb, IL. In 1952 her parents moved to Collinsville where she grew up. She graduated from Collinsville High School in 1966 and attended Southern Illinois University and Belleville Area College.

Larry and Sue moved to Troy in 1995 with their two sons and one daughter. Paul Lawrence Norbury was born December 5, 1972. He is an assistant manager with Bob Evan's Farms, Inc., and has served in the United States Air Force Reserves since 1993. He currently resides in Pontoon Beach, IL.

Mark Thomas Norbury, born December 6, 1974, is a Driver/Representative for CCX Transportation in Salem, IL. He married Tracy Ann Santel on September 30, 2000. Tracy was born December 1, 1974, and is an accountant with Big River Zinc, Inc. They reside in Trenton, IL. They have one child, Abigail Nicole Norbury, born Oct. 31, 2001.

Kelley Denise Norbury was born January 12, 1978. On June 11, 1999, she married Peter Edward Schultz who was born August 6, 1978. They currently reside at Scott Air Force Base

Larry and Sue Norbury, 1995

where Pete is serving with the United States Air Force. Kelley graduated from Belleville Area College and attended Southern Illinois University. She is employed by Bob Evan's Farms, Inc.

In 1995 when Larry and Sue decided to build a new home in the quiet, friendly town of Troy, it was in anticipation of retiring here. They are both active members of St. Jerome Catholic Church. Larry is also a member of the Troy Knights of Columbus Council 9266 and the 4th Degree Assembly. *Submitted by Sue Norbury.*

ROBERT AND KAREN OBERNUEFE-MANN - Karen is the daughter of Benedict and Amelia (Wessel) Kampwerth of Highland, IL. Robert is the son of David and Mildred (Fohne) Obernuefemann of Troy, IL.

Robert's grandmother was Edna (Loyet) Fohne of the Blackjack area. Robert's grandfather was George Fohne of the Blackjack area.

Robert and Karen were married on February 17, 1973, and have lived in the Blackjack area since then.

They are the parents of two children, Dr. Kelly Obernuefemann, born 7/7/73, lives in Charleston, SC. Timothy Obernuefemann, born 3/16/77, lives in Troy, IL. *Submitted by Karen Obernuefemann.*

GEORGE AND VERNA (GAERTNER) OTTWEIN - The marriage of George Ottwein, Jr. and Verna Gaertner took place on April 30,1941, at Friedens United Church of Christ by Rev. R.H. Mornhinweg. The date was also the 25th wedding anniversary of Verna's parents, Arthur and Minnie (Bangert) Gaertner. Verna was born on May 23, 1919, in Troy. She had one brother, Albert Gaertner. George was born on March 24, 1913, the son of George and Carrie (Wilhelm) Ottwein. He had one brother, Oscar, and three sisters, Hulda Becker, Helen

George and Verna (Gaertner) Ottwein, 2000

Voss and Irma Ludwig. George and Oscar farmed and operated the Fairview Farm Dairy.

George and Verna still live on the family farm just west of Troy. George is a retired Troy fireman. He was active on the boards of Troy Savings & Homestead, Troy Grain Company, Troy Senior Citizens, and Illinois Grain Dealers' Association. He likes to garden, play Euchre, and go fishing. They are members of Friedens United Church of Christ where George served on the church council. Verna is active in the women's guild. She likes to cook and collect recipes, and watch cooking shows on TV.

They have one daughter, Victoria Fischer, married to Tom Fischer, and a granddaughter, Rebecca Fischer. *Submitted by Verna Ottwein.*

GEORGE AND CARRIE OTTWEIN, SR.

In March of 1911, the George and Carrie Ottwein family moved to a farm on the outskirts of Troy, and for the balance of the century, the family enjoyed life on "Fairview Farm" while practical citizens of the City of Troy.

George and Carrie Ottwein,
Wedding January 15, 1901

George and his brothers, Valentine and Jacob, also lifelong residents of Troy, were sons of Karl Ottwein, a German emigrant of the 1850's who settled in Blackjack, marrying Philippina Schroeder of O'Fallon. Jacob died in 1926, unmarried. Valentine married Elizabeth Weber and lived his entire life on Webster Street. Sister Anna Marie married Adam Petry and lived on a farm south of St. Jacob. Philippina married Johan Heinrich Menke and moved to St. Louis.

When George was not even a year old, his mother died, and all of the children were placed into other families in the Troy area. George lived first with cousin Mary Ernst and then a Cook family but stayed the longest with the Goetz family west of Troy, where he lived until he married.

These relationships required George to work as a hired hand for his board, and allowed little time for school.

George married Carrie Wilhelm, the daughter of John and Johanna (Holtmann) Wilhelm, who farmed just north of Formosa, a neighbor girl and a member of Friedens, in 1901. Until the move to the Troy farm, they first lived on a farm owned by Carrie's father at Formosa, a farm bought from the heirs of General William T. Sherman. General Sherman had St. Louis roots and a strong interest in railroads, with the Pennsylvania Railroad bisecting this farm.

Intending to buy a farm of their own, and then having three girls and a boy, the family chose this location next to town because of the

George and Carrie Ottwein family, 1933
(l. to r.) Irma, Helen, Carrie, George, Jr.,
George Sr., Hulda, Oscar

proximity to the services and social life of the city. Those children making the move were Hulda, Oscar, Irma and Helen. Two years later, George, Jr. was born.

Family folklore tells of how the family moved by horse and wagon the two miles from the old farm, driving or herding their livestock along the road. This family of 7 enjoyed an active happy life in the old home during the '20s and '30s, sharing the joys of a large and active family, participating in the Roaring '20s, as well as suffering through the ills of the depression in the '30s.

One can imagine the activity surrounding daily life. The family developed various livestock enterprises on the farm, especially a milking herd of Brown Swiss Cattle. Producing Grade A milk for the St. Louis market, they also started a retail milk route in the city of Troy, known as Fairview Farm Dairy.

When Oscar married in 1927, he and his wife Hilda occupied the family home, and George Sr. and Carrie briefly retired to the city of Troy. They bought a home on Market Street, and operated, with the girls of the family, a "confectionary" on Main Street in Troy, in a building that later became Rood's Paint Store.

But George Sr. didn't like "city life," and so in 1929, he and Carrie built and occupied a second home on the farm, which they occupied for several years, or until George Jr. was married.

Then, the younger George Ottweins moved into the second home, where they still reside today. George Sr. and Carrie returned to the home on Market Street, where they spent the remainder of their long lives, living with Hulda and Lester Becker, their daughter and son-in-law.

George died in 1961 at the age of 90, and Carrie lived to an astonishing 105 years of age. At the time of her death in 1984, she was the oldest resident of Madison County. They had been married 60 years at the time of George's death in 1961.

In her younger life, Carrie was an extremely active farmwife, doing the cooking and housework for a large family and many guests, making much of their clothing, doing lots of gardening and canning, and even making soap.

But Carrie had an important avocation that she followed all of her life, making quilts. The family estimated that she was involved with making more than 1000, either individually, or in Friedens Church. In later life, she had several shows where the best of the quilts she made were shown to the public.

George and Carrie were both active in the life of Friedens Church and passionate supporters of the Republican Party. George Ottwein Sr., being taught to read and write German and English by his wife after they were married, became an avid reader and a staunch supporter of education. For a period of time, he served on the board of trustees of McCray-Dewey School.

George and Carrie lived as the core of the family well into the next generation, and established the farmstead as the center of the family's life for the greater part of a century! *Submitted by Merrill Ottwein.*

MERRILL AND GRACE OTTWEIN

Merrill Ottwein and Grace Schmidt, both natives of Troy, were married in Friedens Church in 1950. Merrill, the son of Oscar and Hilda Ottwein, grew up on the family farm. Grace, the daughter of Florence (Mrs.Theodore Guennewig) of Troy and Roland Schmidt of St. Jacob grew up in the Guennewig home on Clay Street, at the north end of Main. Merrill and Grace spent the first 6 years of their marriage in Champaign, IL, where Merrill finished degrees in General Agriculture, Animal Science and Veterinary Medicine. Grace worked at the University of Illinois, where they owned and operated a rooming house, facetiously called, "Grace and Joe's Flophouse."

Ottwein family, 1969
(l. to r.) Front: Amy. Middle: Grace
holding Emily, Paul, Merrill. Back: Ann.

Returning to Edwardsville/Glen Carbon, Merrill practiced veterinary medicine, founding Hawthorne Animal Hospital. During calendar year 1967, after ten years of practice, the family lived in San Pedro Sula, Honduras, Central

George and Carrie Ottwein and 10 grandchildren.
(l. to r.) Front: Merrill Ottwein, Leslie Becker and
Victoria Ottwein Middle: Dick Voss, Bobby Voss,
Darrell Voss, Marie Voss. Back: Audrey Ottwein,
Carol Mae Voss, Virginia Ludwig.

America, where Merrill worked as a veterinarian and agriculturalist in a self-help project called "Diakonia," a division of Church World Service. In 1969, Merrill was elected as a Republican to serve in the Illinois Senate, but lost his bid for reelection to that body.

He subsequently developed residential and commercial real estate in Glen Carbon., Edwardsville and Troy, developing projects including Cottonwood Station, Cottonwood Junction, Ginger Creek, Lakewood, Kettle River, Airport Plaza, Maryville Office Center and Troy Junction.

After practicing traditional commercial and residential real estate brokerage, Merrill currently operates, with his son Paul, a "buyers only" relocation company, Home Buyers Relocation Service. Relating to that role, Merrill was a charter member of the National Association of Exclusive Buyer Agents, serving on the Board of Directors for a number of years, as treasurer and then president of the national organization.

During high school years, Grace and Merrill had both been active in choral and instrumental music, an avocational involvement continued to this date. Merrill and his sister, Audrey, along with friends, Bob, Floyd and Dick Rogier and Gene Adams, became locally popular entertainers, doing show-style and barbershop tunes. Merrill and Grace's children, along with sister Audrey's children have continued this family involvement in a variety of settings, including church, a secular show group called "The Black Tie Affair," community theatre, and the Triad Community Band. Merrill still plays trombone in that band.

Merrill and Grace have four children, seven grandsons, another seven step grandsons and one step granddaughter. Two daughters, Ann (Mrs. Michael) Culp and Emily (Mrs. Wally) Osika, currently live in Glen Carbon. Ann has sons Rick and Brent Leh, and works as an executive secretary in St. Louis. Ann's husband Michael is an instrument specialist with Tosco Refinery in Wood River. Emily is a representative for Merck Pharmaceuticals, while her husband practices dentistry in Edwardsville. Another daughter, Amy (Mrs. Keith) Zagar, now lives in Southlake, Texas, and has two sons, Matthew and Patrick. (Keith Zagar also grew up in Troy and is an attorney.) Ann and Emily sing with "Eden," the contemporary music program at Eden United Church of Christ. Emily is active in community musical theatre. Son Paul lives in Edwardsville, and has sons John, Adam and Tyler. Paul and Merrill operate the family realty relocation business. Grace is an insurance specialist for Dr. Richard Coy's chiropractic practice in Edwardsville. Merrill and Grace currently live in Glen Carbon and have just celebrated their 50th anniversary. The family is active in United Church of Christ. *Submitted by Merrill Ottwein.*

OSCAR AND HILDA OTTWEIN - Oscar John Carl Ottwein moved with his parents, George and Carrie Ottwein, to the Ottwein farm just west of Troy when he was just 8 years old, in the year 1911, and spent the rest of his long life in the same home. He married Hilda Bardelmeier, daughter of William R. and Emma

Ottwein family, 1941
Merrill, Oscar, Hilda, Audrey

(Engeling) of Pin Oak Township, in 1927. Together, they occupied the hilltop home for another 69 years. They had two children, Merrill and Audrey.

Oscar and Hilda spent their entire lives supporting the livestock and grain operations on the farm, in partnership with Oscar's brother, George Jr. But related business activities brought greater prominence to both families. Of special note was Fairview Farm Dairy, a retail milk production and delivery service to the citizens of Troy, a separate story here.

Oscar also served on the local school board for a number of years, during the period that the grade school now known as Freeman School was built. He was in the group that incorporated the Troy Security Bank where he served on the Board of Directors, and as President for many years. George, Jr. served on the Board of Directors of Troy Grain Company and Troy Savings and Homestead Association. Oscar was an active member of the Troy Lions Club, and was proud of the fact that he was the last surviving charter member of that prominent local organization, noted for its good works and for its fun. George, Jr. was a volunteer fireman in Troy for many years. Oscar also served on the Board of Directors of the Madison County Extension Service and the brothers were always at the forefront of agricultural innovation.

Avocationally, Oscar and Hilda enjoyed an amateur musical heritage, with Hilda playing the piano and Oscar the violin, and both of them were active church and community singers.

Oscar's father and uncle, George Sr. and his brother Valentine, even before, had been prominent as accordion players for local dances and entertainment. Hilda had learned to play the piano at some sacrifice on the part of her father. Growing up in rural Pin Oak Township, her father, Wm. R. Bardelmeier insisted that the family have a piano and that Hilda, coming to

Oscar and Hilda Ottwein, 60th Anniversary, 1987

be an only child after the death of her sister, learn to play the piano. So every Saturday morning, usually by horse and buggy, he took her into Edwardsville, 5 or 6 miles away, for a piano lesson. In the rich musical period after World War I and of the early twenties, Oscar told the story of dating once a week, visiting Hilda in the family's Model T Ford, and usually taking a piece of sheet music to Hilda as a gift.... always one of the more popular songs of the period. Consequently, Hilda came to possess a wonderful library of sheet music of the period.... all of the popular songs of the early part of the century could be found there. Merrill and Audrey were thusly encouraged to enjoy musical involvements, with Audrey becoming a teacher and performer, also the subject of separate sketches.

Even after retiring from active farm operations, Oscar and Hilda continued to live in the big white farmhouse on the hill....enjoying a large extended family and many friends, their children, grandchildren and even great grandchildren, as all frequently returned to the family fountainhead.

Oscar died in 1996, just after the couple's 69th anniversary, at the age of 93, and Hilda died two years later, at the age of 91. They were both active in the life of Friedens United Church of Christ. *Submitted by Merrill Ottwein.*

VALENTINE AND ELIZABETH (WEBER) OTTWEIN - On May 22, 1902, Miss Elizabeth Weber was married to Valentine Ottwein at Friedens Evangelische Kirche in Troy. The bride, born on April 5, 1873, was the daughter of Sebastian and Margaret Weber of Blackjack. The groom, born on October 20, 1868, was the son of Karl and Phillippina (Schroeder) Ottwein of rural Blackjack. The couple lived their married lives in the little house at 106 Webster Street. Behind the house, like most houses in Troy, was a garden, chicken house, outhouse, and a shed or two to house the horse and buggy, wood or coal, and tools.

Valentine and Elizabeth Ottwein
in front of their house at 106 Webster in 1904

Valentine was a painter and paperhanger and helped relatives with farm work.

Although the two were childless, they were beloved by their nieces and nephews and very much a part of the family of Val's brother, George Ottwein. Everyone called them "Uncle Val" and "Aunt Lizzie". Since Aunt Lizzie taught the toddlers' Sunday school class at Friedens Church most of her life, she was "aunt" to several generations. At the time it was the custom for a pin and subsequent bars to be given for each year of perfect Sunday school attendance. Aunt Lizzie's pin was at least a foot long and she wore it proudly on her coat lapel to the awe of all the children.

Aunt Lizzie had a misshapen ankle as a result of a childhood illness-probably polio. She limped and walked with a cane but never lost her cheerful and helpful attitude.

Uncle Val had quite a sense of humor and with brother George, usually the straight man, the two were quite a comedy team at times. Of course, about half the repartee was in German to the good-natured disgust of the rest of the family.

Valentine and Elizabeth Ottwein, 1943

Aunt Lizzie told that on her wedding day she wore a lace-trimmed dress and a little flowered hat. Her papa took her into town to the church in a horse-drawn buggy. She made him promise not to race as he was usually inclined to do, but when a neighbor caught up with them and wanted to race, the temptation was too great. Off they went, Lizzie holding on to her hat and the buggy. She arrived at the church windblown and dusty and quite angry with her papa.

Family members tell of a wonderful Christmas custom: On Christmas Eve, after the Sunday school program at Friedens Church, the entire family would make the rounds with a stop at each home to see the tree and if Santa had arrived. The first stop, however, was always at 106 Webster where Aunt Lizzie and Uncle Val would light tiny candles in holders clamped to the branches of a small artificial tree, all of which had been brought from Germany by an ancestor. Uncle Val stood ready with a bucket of water and all other lights were doused. To the awe-struck children this was a magical Christmas moment.

Valentine Ottwein died in 1944, and Elizabeth died in 1958. They are buried in Friedens Cemetery. *Submitted by Audrey Deeren.*

GLADYS MORRISS PAPE - Gladys Morriss, born March 31, 1904, the daughter of George C. and Caroline (Sprick) of Troy, graduated from the Troy grade and high schools and attended college at Normal, IL, for a couple of years before becoming a teacher in the Troy Grade School.

She married Alfred Pape in 1930, curtailing her teaching career, since married women were only allowed to do substitute teaching in those days. They moved to Edwardsville, where Alfred was employed as a butcher. Gladys later returned to the classroom, after the ban was lifted on married women as teachers, teaching classes

*25th Wedding Anniversay, 1955
Gladys and Alfred Pape*

in Stallings, Glen Carbon, and Granite City, until her retirement. She, too, achieved a Masters in teaching by taking many summer and night school classes.

At the present time (2002) she lives alone in her own home at the age of 98; her husband died in 1978. She enjoys people and participating in church activities and women's groups. She even still drives her own car at 98. *Submitted by Millie (Collins) Shaffer.*

PETER AND CAROLINE V. (LEVO) PELLIGRINI - Peter Pelligrini was born in Italy and came to Collinsville in the early 1900s from LaSalle, IL. He came to Collinsville to seek work in the coal mines. He met Caroline "Carrie" Levo. They were married and lived on a farm in Collinsville Township. The farm was purchased from Carrie's father, Peter P. Levo Sr. Her mother was Laura L. (Cossano) Levo. The couple had no children. On the farm they milked cows, had a garden and did some small farming, mainly grape vineyards. The farm was located at the end of Loyet Road. The house was built by her father and was a large two story stone house.

They enjoyed the neighbors and played pinochle with a card club in the neighborhood. Peter, or Pete as he was called, liked his booze. He was a little man with a loud booming voice that made his presence known wherever he went. He continued to work in the Lumaghi Mines in Collinsville for a time.

Carrie was a mild mannered woman who loved to laugh and often teased her nieces and nephews. She could get a little upset with Pete sometimes, but basically, she was a sweet person and was willing to help everyone in the family when help was needed. She enjoyed cooking and tending to her garden.

Pete and Carrie Pelligrini, 1942

The couple never owned a vehicle and didn't know how to drive. In about 1948, they bought a pick-up truck and Pete learned how to drive, but wasn't the best driver in the world according to family sources.

On February 10, 1949, while Pete was taking Carrie to a Valentine Day card party at St. Jerome Catholic Church hall in Troy (the church in which they were members), their truck was hit by a freight train just about 1/8 mile from their home. Carrie, age 57, was killed immediately and Pete was badly injured. He recovered and lived in the farmhouse with a friend, Cornelius Schmitt, for a number of years. Schmitt came to stay with him to help with milking the cows.

The two men "batched" for about 16 years. As Pete was getting up in years, his health was getting poor. He moved in with his wife's sister and husband, Louise and Oscar Mersinger. He died in July 1968 after suffering a stroke in the farmyard of the Mersinger residence.

Pete and Carrie Pelligrini are buried in St. Jerome Catholic Cemetery, Troy. *Submitted by Mae Grapperhaus*

SOPHIA KLEIMEIER PETER - Sophia Kleimeier (b. May 29, 1869, d. May 24, 1955) married William F. Peter (b. May 29, 1864, d. December 26, 1912). Both are buried in Friedens Cemetery.

Mr. Peter was City Clerk of Troy sometime before 1912. Sophia was well known in and around the community. Her father was one of the founders of the Lutheran Church and School. Her husband died in 1912, and she was left with three children. In order to keep her family and home together, she went to work. She did house work and was a nurse's aid. She was recommended by doctors to those ill or with childbirth. She was a very hard-working person. She never avoided a duty or a task. Her spirits were low at times, but she was never bitter about her lot in life.

No pampered child of today could ever begin to fathom what she set out to do with three boys to rear, Wilbur, Harold, and Dale. Her faith and trust in the Lord's word and promise was very strong. Her boys never knew they were poor. Her husband had operated a barber shop next to *The Troy Call* where Ben Jarvis was owner and editor. After Mr. Peter's death in 1912, his son, Wilbur, operated the shop for some years. He later moved to St. Louis and operated one of the largest barber shops downtown. Harold sold insurance and lived in St. Jacob. They are both deceased. Dale operated a super market in Webster Groves, MO. He sold it to Kroger and became an executive with Kroger until early in 1953. *Submitted by Dale H. Peters, son of Sophia Kleimeier Peter. Harold and Dale added an "s" to their last names.*

DENNIS L. AND LINDA A. PETRY - Dennis L. and Linda Petry reside on the Petry Family farm south of Troy on West Kirsch Rd. Dennis is the third generation of the Petry family to live on the family farm. He is the son of Edmund A. (Dick) Petry and the grandson of Philip Petry.

Dennis was born on April 6, 1944, in E. St. Louis, IL. His parents are the late Edmund and Emma (Baltruschat) Petry. He is a lifelong resident of Troy and graduated from Triad High

Petry family, 1998
(l. to r.) Front: Heather, Regina Ann, Geetu, Jeffrey Michael, Linda. Back: Joel and Dennis.

School in 1962. Dennis attended SIU-E and earned a bachelor's degree in Business Management in 1968. He is a past president and currently the senior member of the Triad Board of Education, having served on the board since 1977. One of the greatest rewards of Dennis' tenure on the Board of Education was to be able to present each of his three children with both their 8th grade and high school diplomas. Dennis is also a past member of the Board of Trustees of the Troy Fire Protection District, a past moderator of the annual town meetings of Jarvis Township and a past ASCS Community Committeeman. He is a member of the Troy Council Knights of Columbus and recent past Grand Knight.

Linda is the daughter of Mary L. (Chism) Giles of St. Jacob and the late Melvin R. Giles. She was born on October 6, 1947, in E. St. Louis, IL. Linda is a graduate of Collinsville High School in 1965. Prior to having a family, Linda worked in the accounting department of Boatmen's National Bank in St. Louis.

Dennis and Linda were married on September 9, 1967, at Ss. Peter and Paul Catholic Church in Collinsville. They have three children: Jeffrey Michael and his wife, Geetu, residing in Round Rock, Texas; Joel Robert and his wife, Heather, residing in Troy; and Regina Ann residing in Seattle, Washington.

Dennis is employed by the U.S. Postal Service in Glen Carbon, IL. Linda is employed at Allen's Drugs in Troy. *Submitted by Linda Petry.*

EDMUND A. AND EMMA L. PETRY

Edmund A. (Dick) Petry was born and raised on the Petry family farm south of Troy on West Kirsch Road. The farm was purchased by Edmund's father, Philip Petry. Dick was born

Wedding photo, 1941
Edmund A. (Dick) and Emma L.
(Baltruschat) Petry

on January 8, 1907 to Philip and Mary (Probst) Petry. He is the third of five children.

Like all farm children, Dick grew up working on the farm and took over the operation of the farm completely at the age of 20 for his mother when his father passed away. The family recently learned that Dick served as a truant officer for some time at the old Spring Valley School south of Troy.

On November 8, 1941, Dick married Emma L. Baltruschat at St. Jerome Catholic Church in Troy. Emma was born on January 10, 1913 in Collinsville, IL, to John and Martha (Steffenhag) Baltruschat. Emma worked for many years at the dress factory in Collinsville prior to her marriage and moving to Troy. Dick and Emma were the parents of one son, Dennis L. Petry.

Dick and Emma were loyal and dedicated members of St. John the Baptist Catholic Church in Blackjack. Dick was a member of the Holy Name Society and Emma was a member of the Altar and Rosary Sodality.

Dick passed away on January 24, 1978, as a result of injuries related to a farm accident. Emma passed away on July 22, 1994. Both are buried in St. John the Baptist Catholic Cemetery in Blackjack. *Submitted by Linda Petry.*

JEFFREY M. AND GEETU G. PETRY

Jeffrey Michael Petry is the oldest son of Dennis L. and Linda A. Petry of Troy. Jeff was born on July 23, 1969, in Highland, IL. He is a 1987 graduate of the Triad School District. Jeff received a bachelor of fine arts degree in industrial design from the University of Illinois in May 1991. He earned a masters degree in business administration from Washington University in St. Louis in May 1996. He is currently employed by Question Technologies as a solutions marketing manager in Austin, Texas.

Jeff married Geetu G. Batheja on September 5, 1998, in St. Louis, MO. Jeff and Geetu had a double wedding ceremony on their wedding day. A Catholic ceremony was held at 2:00 p.m. followed by a traditional Hindu wedding ceremony. Geetu is the daughter of Gobind and Rekha Batheja of San Antonio, Texas. Geetu graduated from Parkway North High School in 1991 and received a medical technology degree from University of Missouri-St. Louis/Jewish Hospital in May 1997. *Submitted by Linda Petry.*

JOEL R. AND HEATHER M. PETRY -

Joel Robert Petry is the second child of Dennis L. and Linda A. Petry of Troy. He was born on January 28, 1973, in Highland, IL. He is a 1991 graduate of the Triad School District. Joel attended the University of Illinois for 2 1/2 years and also attended SIUE where he earned a degree in history in December 1999 and is currently working toward a teaching certificate. At the present time he is employed as a resident services director at Edwardsville Terrace.

Joel married Heather M. Simmons on August 5, 1995, in Troy. Heather grew up in St. Jacob and is the daughter of Steve Simmons and Nancy Simmons. She graduated from Triad High School in 1991. She has attended Belleville Area College and also SIUE. She is currently employed at Rita Marie's Florist in Troy. *Submitted by Linda Petry.*

PHILIP PETRY -

Philip Petry was born in Darmstadt, Germany, on September 18, 1859. As a young man he came to the United States with other family members who settled in the area surrounding Troy. Until his death September 7, 1927, he farmed on Kirsch Road south of Troy. The farm is still owned by a grandson, Dennis Petry.

Mr. Petry married his first wife, the former Barbara S. Mersinger, on February 15, 1887. She was born July 14, 1863, and died April 12, 1894, shortly after the birth of their third child. The children born of that union were Fred C. Petry, born January 7, 1888; Leo A. Petry, born March 26, 1890; and Barbara C. Petry, born April 5, 1894. Fred married and had six children whom he reared in St. Louis. Leo never married and lived on the farm. Barbara married Robert Loyet on January 8, 1917. They lived in Troy with their eight children.

Petry family in the field on their farm on Kirsch Road south of Troy, 1914. (l. to r.) Front: Edmund "Dick", Clara, Barbara, Philip, Clem. Back: Mary (Probst) holding Agnes, Enno, Leo, Fred.

He married his second wife on November 19, 1901. Born Mary Hedwig Probst on February 1, 1875, she was adopted from a Chicago orphanage by the Niehaus family. Mary died November 17, 1960. There were five children born to them: Enno H. Petry, born September 15, 1902; Clement V. Petry, born August 30, 1904; Edmund A. (Dick) Petry, born January 8, 1907; Clara E. Petry, born October 12, 1909; and Agnes A. Petry, born August 18, 1912. Enno lived in the Belleville area with his wife Eleanor O. Klohr and two children. Clement married Johanna Voegele and they lived in Grantfork with their three children. Edmund (Dick) was married to Emma L. (Baltruschat) and lived on the family farm along with their son Dennis, and Dick's brother, Leo. Clara never married. Agnes married Charles William Norbury and had three children. (Refer to the Henry Joseph Becherer and Lawrence Charles Norbury biographies.) *Submitted by Mary Ann Becherer.*

PHILIP PETRY -

Philip Petry was a farmer who came to this area as a young boy from Darmstadt, Germany, with his family in 1863. His parents were Johann and Barbara (Schwartz) Petry. Philip was the fifth child, having 4 brothers and one sister. His brothers were Adam, Michael, John and Val; his sister was Anna.

Philip married Barbara Mersinger on February 15, 1887. They had three children: Fred, Leo and Barbara. Fred married Bertha Drees and lived in St. Louis. They had 6 children. Leo never married. He served in the army in WWI

Wedding photo, 1887
Philip and Barbara (Mersinger) Petry

and then worked as a mechanic for Gilbert Buick in St. Louis before retiring and moving to the family farm in Troy. Leo told stories of how he once worked on Babe Ruth's car. Barbara married Robert Loyet of Troy and they had 8 children.

Philip's wife, Barbara, died one week after the birth of their daughter in 1894. On November 19, 1901, Philip married Mary Probst who lived in the Blackjack area, and who had been raised by the Niehaus family after the death of her mother. Philip and Mary moved to a farm south of Troy on West Kirsch Road. They had 5 children: Enno, Clem, Edmund, Clara and Agnes. Enno married Eleanor Klohr and had a son and a daughter. Clem married Johanna Voegele and had three children. Edmund married Emma Baltruschat and had one son; Clara never married; Agnes married Charles Norbury and had three children.

Philip died September 7, 1927, and Mary died November 17, 1960. They are both buried in St. John the Baptist Catholic Cemetery in Blackjack. *Submitted by Dennis and Linda Petry.*

REGINA A. PETRY - Regina Ann Petry is the third and youngest child of Dennis L. & Linda A. Petry of Troy. Gina was born on July 7, 1977 (7-7-77), in Highland, IL. She graduated from Triad School District in May, 1995. She then attended SIUE for two years. Gina transferred to Illinois State University in Bloomington- Normal, IL, where she received a bachelors degree in social work in May, 2000.

In October, 2000, she moved to Seattle, Washington. She is employed by the YWCA as a program specialist in a self-sufficiency program. *Submitted by Linda Petry.*

PETTUS FAMILY - Homer Pettus was born in Bonne Terre, MO, September 19, 1926, to William and Waneetie Pettus. He grew up in that area, where lead mining was the leading industry for many years.

He served in the Marine Corps during WWII and was stationed in Japan after the Atomic Bomb was dropped. After his discharge, he returned home and met and married Helen Banes from Leadwood, MO, on June 3, 1950.

Helen was born in Leadwood on March 4, 1932, to Harold and Betty Banes. She lived there until she married, and then moved to the St. Louis area. In 1952 they moved to East St. Louis and their first son, Jim, was born June 4, 1953. Two years later their son Bill was born on June 5, 1955. Then on October 11, 1957, their youngest son, Randy, was born. As their children

grew and were entering junior high, East St. Louis schools started declining. The family was searching for a town with good churches, schools and a friendly atmosphere. They found this and more in Troy.

Jim graduated from Triad in 1971, Bill in 1973, and Randy in 1975. Jim married Karen Rosenbalm from Knoxville, TN. They have two children, Michael and Jennifer.

Jim has served twenty years in the Army and Karen works at the University of South Carolina.

Bill married Pat Brendel from Marine, IL. They have three children, Dan, Jason and Trevor.

Bill works at Ameren UE, and Pat is the secretary at Triad Middle School. Randy married Karie Peterson from Yuma, AZ. They have three children, Chris, Joshua, and Jakob, and a granddaughter, Alexandra. Randy served 23 years in the Marine Corps.

Pettus family, 2000
Front: (l. to r.) Jakob, Chris, Alex, Homer, Helen, Pat, Bill, Janna (Dan's fiancee). Back: Michael, Karen, Jim, Josh, Karie, Randy, Jason, Trevor, Dan.

Homer retired from Ameren UE in 1986. He is a member of Bethel Baptist Church and the VFW. Helen retired in 1994. She was the secretary at Triad Middle School. She is a member of Bethel Baptist Church and several organizations there. They both enjoy flower gardening and traveling. They also enjoy living in Troy and are glad they moved here 34 years ago! *Submitted by Helen Pettus.*

SHARON (MERSINGER) PETTY - After graduating from Triad High School in 1965, Sharon (Mersinger) Petty, daughter of Ted and Helen Mersinger, attended SIUE in the first year of the new campus. She began teaching at Edwardsville High School in the fall of 1969. She helped establish the girls' athletic program at EHS in the fall of 1973. She coached girls' basketball for 12 years and had a number of great teams, but her real coaching love was field hockey. Although she had never before seen a game, she took on the coaching responsibilities in the fall of 1974.

In 1976 she made her first trip to the state playoffs and came back with the second place trophy. In 1978 her field hockey team won the Illinois State Title, the very first in Edwardsville High School history. In 1980 and 1981 her teams again placed second in the Illinois State Tournament. In 1988 her field hockey team won the St. Louis Bi-State Championship, the equivalent of State Title.

She has had over 40 players attend college on field hockey scholarships.

Sharon Petty, back row, left.

Three players played on Jr. Olympic teams and two participated in the U.S. Olympic Games.

In 1991 she received the Excellence in Teaching Award from SIUE.

She is in her 33rd year of teaching and her 10th year as department chair. This fall was her 28th year of coaching field hockey. *Submitted by Sharon Petty.*

DAVID PEVERLY - The Peverly family moved to Troy in 1979 after purchasing one of Troy's oldest homes at 306 East Market Street. Both David and Patricia are advocates of the preservation of historical properties and saw an opportunity to bring this same philosophy to the Troy community. The home was built circa 1870 and was in need of significant repair and renovation. The Peverlys had been active in the Historical Society of Lakewood, Ohio, previous to their move to Troy and share both knowledge and appreciation of old structures from the years they lived in the New England area. David Emery Peverly was born in 1940 in Decatur, IL, and Patricia Shea Peverly was born in E. St. Louis, IL, in 1943. Patricia grew up in Collinsville, IL, and met David in 1964 in St. Louis, MO. After their marriage in 1965, the couple lived at several locations throughout the United States during David's military career in the U.S. Coast Guard. They planned to eventually relocate to the Collinsville area.

The Peverlys have three daughters. Christine Peverly Kovach was born in Massachusetts in 1967; Heather Peverly Fournie was born in California in 1970; and Janet Peverly was born in New Hampshire in 1972.

The daughters attended St. Paul's Lutheran School and Triad High School.

David retired from active duty in 1981 and began his "second career" as a Real Property Administrator in downtown St. Louis. Patricia was employed as a registered nurse in several states and has been the Administrative Director of Patient Care Services at Anderson Hospital since 1982. The couple are active members of St. Paul's Lutheran Church in Troy. David is a member of the Troy Lions Club and Pat is a member of several civic and service organizations in Collinsville. The couple are also known for their love of Black Labrador Retrievers.

After purchase of the Market Street residence, the Peverlys worked to get national recognition for the historical structure. Because of the home's architectural significance (Italianate Country Villa), their efforts were successful and the "John Carney House" was officially placed on the National Register of Historic Places on July 28, 1983. David and Pat were given a certificate of appreciation by the City of Troy in December, 1983, for "their efforts at establishing Troy's first official historic landmark." This home continues to be an example to residents of Troy that historic preservation is necessary and vital to the town's successful future.

David also consulted with the owners of the Jarvis home and assisted with a second successful National Register application. Largely due to the Peverlys' leadership, these two structures remain the only properties in Troy to be honored with this national recognition. Both David and Patricia are members of the Troy Historical Society and actively contribute to the ongoing preservation efforts of the Troy community. *Submitted by Patricia Peverly.*

EDWARD AND BERNADINE POLETTI

The Poletti family started when Eddie was born on November 18, 1919, to Peter and Francis (Adelia) Hepplewhite Poletti of Collinsville, IL. He graduated from Collinsville High School in 1937. He served in WW II as a medic where he was awarded several medals, including the Purple Heart. Bernadine Niehaus Poletti was born on December 10, 1927, to Arnold and Ella (Noeltner) Niehaus of Troy (refer to Niehaus Family).

Edward and Bernadine Poletti

Eddie and Bern met at a local dance and courted several years. They were married on April 18, 1950, at St. John the Baptist Catholic Church in Blackjack. Bernadine always wanted to stay living on a farm. They were fortunate to purchase one in 1951 that joined her family farm where she grew up. They worked together at dairy and grain farming. They raised four children. Their first child, a son, Wayne, was born on January 6,1954. On September 12,1955, a daughter, Marilyn, was born. Three years later on August 22, 1958, Teresa arrived and was the baby of the family for 4 years. Judy, a pleasant surprise, arrived on November 11, 1962, completing the family.

The family life revolved around the family farm. A normal day included milking and feeding cows, raising chickens, collecting eggs, tending a garden, raising crops and riding ponies. Grandparents, aunts, uncles, and cousins frequently visited. Butchering in the early winter was an annual event.

The family belonged to St. John the Baptist Catholic Church, where they always

Poletti family, 1981
(l. to r.) Front: Marilyn Meyer, Teresa Hovatter, Judy Steele. Back: Wayne, Bernadine, Edward.

looked forward to the Blackjack Picnic once a year. They belonged to the Mid-America Dairy Association and periodically took a tour with the A.O. Smith Harvester Company. Eddie was a charter member with the Knights of Columbus Council #9266. Bern belonged to the St. Ann Altar and Rosary Sodality.

The family enjoyed boating at Indian Hills Lake in Cuba, MO, Horseshoe Lake in Illinois and, in the early years, on the river.

Teresa was the first to marry on September 3, 1977, to Bradley Hovatter of Lebanon,IL. They have 2 children, Amanda and Nathan (refer to Bradley and Teresa Hovatter Family). Wayne married a year later on August 19, 1978, to June Wessel of Highland, IL. They have 4 children: Kathryn, Timothy, Luke and Michael. A son Matthew, passed away at birth in 1980. On January 23, 1981, Judy married Bruce Steele of Troy. They have 2 children, Christina and A.J. (refer to Bruce and Judy Steele Family). Marilyn married Donald Meyer of Trenton, IL. They have 2 children, David and Robert.

During the early retirement years they enjoyed visiting Eddie's Army buddy in Georgia. They also looked forward to the warm sunshine of Florida each winter when they traveled with Bern's twin sister Bernice.

The family was devastated when Eddie passed away on July 16, 1988. A few years later Bern built a house and moved from the country to town. Wayne moved onto the family farm. Bern was a constant, positive influence to her family until she unexpectedly passed away on June 11, 2001.

The entire family has shared many special occasions and continue to have countless fond memories. *Submitted by Teresa Hovatter, Judy Steele, Wayne Poleti, and Marilyn Meyer.*

MARK AND KELLI PONCE

MARK AND KELLI PONCE - Mark and Kelli Ponce were both born and raised in Troy, Illinois, and now reside at 603 Whippoorwill, Troy. Mark is the son of Lawrence and Donna Ponce of Troy and was born on April 15, 1961. Mark joined two older brothers, Larry and Gary at 106 Weston, Troy. Mark graduated from Triad High School in 1979 and worked for many years at Adelhardt's and then later, Bernhardt's Food World in Troy. Mark received his Bachelors of Science Degree from SIUE in 1991. Mark has owned and operated a Wild Birds Unlimited franchise for the past 8 years in St. Louis.

Kelli is the daughter of Paul and Bonnie (Moeller) Levo who were both also raised in Troy. She was their firstborn and was born October 15, 1965, at Highland Hospital and brought home to 304 Bryn St., Troy. Kelli graduated from Triad High School in 1983 and from SIUE in 1986 with her Bachelors of Science in Business Administration. She received her Masters in Business Administration in 1991 and her teaching certificate in 1996. She is currently a business teacher at Collinsville High School.

Mark and Kelli were married on September 14, 1991, and have two sons, Jordan Patrick Ponce born on March 17, 1993, and Joshua Parker Ponce born on February 8, 1997. Jordan and Joshua attend St. Paul Lutheran School in Troy where their family are active members. They enjoy playing baseball, soccer, and are members of the CMT YMCA. *Submitted by Kelli Ponce.*

LOUISE ELIZABETH (KECK) AND IRVIN E. PORTER

LOUISE ELIZABETH (KECK) AND IRVIN E. PORTER - Louise Elizabeth Keck was the oldest child of Emma H. (Hobein) and Martin Keck, Jr. of Troy. Louise was born on September 9, 1895, in Jarvis Township, Madison County, Illinois. She married Irvin E. Porter on February 16, 1916. Irvin was born in 1890 and died in 1956. He was a farmer. Louise died on December 2, 1986, at Faith Countryside Nursing Home in Highland where she had lived for four years. They are both buried in Friedens Cemetery in Troy. Louise and Irvin had four children: Helen Porter married Glen Hagemann on October 6, 1943. They had two children, Janet and James. Janet Hagemann married Richard Quinn on April 20, 1968. James Hagemann (December 27, 1948-January 2, 1997) is buried in College Hill Cemetery, Lebanon, Illinois. Robert Porter (1919-1974) is buried in Friedens Cemetery in Troy. He had married Vera Wilkins on October 8, 1944, and they had two children, Robert and Alan. Robert Porter Jr. married Patricia Moore and they have two sons, Brent and Robert. Alan Porter has 3 children, LaTonya (married to Russel Bousquet), CaTina and Troy. Marie Porter never married. Grace Porter married Jack Leder on October 15, 1949. They had three children: Carol, LuAnn and Edward.

Carol Leder married Wendall Adams on June 6, 1972. They had three children, Zachary, Ann and Taylor. Ann is married to Mark Rollinson and they have a daughter, Allison Grace. Lu Ann Leder married Rick Bennett (deceased) and they had three children, Kevin, Bryan and Richard. Edward Leder married Sharon Curtis and they have two daughters, Ashley and Christina. *Submitted by Pamela Keck.*

JOSEPHUS PORTER

JOSEPHUS PORTER - Josephus Porter was born at Greenup, IL, on May 21, 1837, and when eight years of age accompanied his parents who moved to Marine. His father died shortly after the move and his mother moved into Troy.

At the age of 25 years he volunteered for service in the Union Army in the Civil War and served three years. He served as first sergeant in Capt. D.G. Todd's Company G, 117th Reg. of Illinois Infantry, and was discharged at Camp Butler, IL, on August 5, 1865.

Josephus and Melissa (Giger) Porter

He married Melissa Ann Giger on January 6, 1876, at the Augusta Chapel in the country west of St. Jacob, where the present Augusta Cemetery is today. Justice George M. Searcy of St. Jacob performed the marriage. Melissa was born in Marine on November 2, 1857. She was the daughter of William and Susan Giger. Her father was a veterinarian in Marine for many years.

Josephus and Melissa made their home on a farm in Jarvis Township for a number of years and then moved to St. Jacob where he ran and owned a grocery store and was mayor of St. Jacob.

The family moved back to Troy about 1909. Some years later, after the death of Josephus, Melissa moved to Oakland, California, to live with her granddaughter.

To this union were born two children: a daughter dying in infancy, and a son, William, who died in 1945. Josephus, Melissa and their children are buried in the Augusta Cemetery. *Submitted by Joyce Meyer.*

ROBERT M. PORTER - Robert M. Porter was born at Marine, IL, on April 14,1845, and in 1867 was united in marriage with Nancy Ellis. To this union were born two children, both of whom died in infancy. Nancy, his wife, also died a short time later.

His second marriage was on March 16, 1870, to Mary Isaac, daughter of Joseph and Mary Ann Isaac of near Troy. Eleven children were born to this union with ten surviving to adulthood. They are Robert "Monroe"; Mary Elizabeth (Philip Stock); Nancy Irene "Rene" (Hampton Long); Joseph Isaac (Emma Riggin); William Barnett "Barney" (Dora Cline); Hattie Mariah (John W. Meyer); Daniel Ethen(Lillie Wells); Bertha Eta (Emil LeBegue); Irvin Elmer (Louise Keck); Roland Leo (Ella L. Gaertner). There was a child who died in infancy and is buried in Augusta Cemetery.

Family of Robert and Mary (Isaac) Porter, circa 1900

Robert was a farmer in the Troy-St. Jacob Community for many years. He lived on a farm about two miles east of Troy and it is here that Robert and Mary raised their family.

One day, Mary drove into St. Jacob with a horse and buggy to do some trading and to call on one of her sons before heading back home. After making her visit, she started for home. But a little later the horse was seen wandering aimlessly down the street and finally halted before a hitch rack. Mary was found lying in the buggy and was hurried home, but died before being carried into the house. She died January 14, 1914, and is buried in Augusta Cemetery. Robert died May 10, 1915, and is also buried in Augusta Cemetery.

Robert united with the Augusta Methodist Church in his boyhood; and when that church was abandoned, he transferred his membership to the St. Jacob church where it remained all his life. *Submitted by Joyce Meyer*

LLOYD PROCTOR - In 1947, Lloyd and Verna Proctor moved from Maryville, IL, to 1 1/2 acres on Arth Avenue about 2 miles outside the Troy city limits. Lloyd worked for the railroad, and Verna was a homemaker. Their daughter, Joanne Marie, was 8 years old. An older daughter, 21 year old Margaret Louise, was in college and married soon after graduation. An older son, Virgil, had died in 1935 from pneumonia at the age of 7.

Archer Lloyd Proctor and Verna Mae Peters had married in Arkansas in 1921 but had moved north to Illinois in search of work for Lloyd. He worked in the coal fields and during the Great Depression had worked for CCC.

The home on Arth Avenue would be the only house they would ever own. They built a basement living area first and this is where the family moved. The house was completed and they settled in. Indoor plumbing came along later, as did a son, Archer Lloyd, born in 1948.

Joanne attended the one-room schoolhouse in the area for three years. When that school closed, she attended the elementary school in Troy and eventually graduated from McCray-Dewey High School in 1957. Archie, as he was called, graduated from Triad High School nine years later.

Lloyd loved to work the land and every year planted an extensive garden. Many fruit and other trees were planted and some of those grace the yard of the house, which is still standing. Joanne and Archie learned to love gardening from him.

Verna Proctor worked at Blue Haven Restaurant for many years. She was active in the Baptist Church in Troy. Lloyd continued to work for the railroad until his unexpected death in January 1962 at the age of 64. After Lloyd's death, Verna and Archie lived in the Arth Avenue house for some period of time, but moved from there and into a mobile home.

After the death in 1968 of her second husband, William Carrington of Maryville, Verna began a vagabond life, living in Illinois in the summer season and "snow birding" in California in the winter, where sisters and daughter Joanne, lived. In 1994, she was unable to return to California after a summer stay with daughter Margaret in Bloomington, IL, and

Proctor family, circa late 1940s
(l. to r.) Louis Soeldner, Margaret (Proctor) Soeldner, Joanne (Proctor) Kleppe, Verna (Peters) Proctor holding Archie Proctor, Lloyd Proctor

entered McLean County Nursing Home, where she lived until her death in 1999 at the age of 97 1/2.

Joanne still lives in California, where she moved shortly after graduation. She was married in 1957 to Robert L. Kleppe. Archie is divorced and lives in Calgary, Alberta, Canada. Margaret Proctor Soeldner, a widow, died shortly before her mother in 1999.

Joanne has two sons, Robert William and Anthony Lloyd, both married and living in California. Margaret had 6 children, 4 of them still living in Illinois, 2 live in the Bloomington area, 2 live in the Chicago area, 2 preceded her in death. Archie has no children. *Submitted by JoAnne Proctor Kleppe.*

DAVID AND FLORENCE REES - David and Florence Rees were both of Welsh ancestry. David's family came to America in 1850, and Florence's family arrived in the 1870s. They met while each of them was living with relatives in Collinsville, Illinois.

On September 18, 1907, David Rees and Florence Thomas were married at the Madison County Courthouse in Edwardsville. They moved to Troy the same day so David could begin work at the Brookside Coal Mine, which was located along the present Rt. 40 west of Troy Grain Co. Later he would be employed at the Donk Brothers Mine.

The new bride also had a brother, William, and a sister, Elizabeth, already living in Troy. Her brother, William, and his wife Mary Ann Thomas still have grandchildren living in Troy: Mrs. Don (Elaine) Ackerman, Dale (Ping) Wille, and Mrs. Duane (Geraldine) Zobrist. Florence's sister, Elizabeth, and her husband, Otis Crystal, do not have any direct living descendants.

Rees family
(l. to r.) Henry, David, Florence, Mary Elizabeth

David and Florence Rees first lived in a small three-room home at 1578 Troy O'Fallon Rd., just several houses south of the Rt. 40 intersection. This home has been extensively remodeled in the past years.

Exactly one year after their marriage on September 18, 1908, their first child, a son named for his paternal grandfather, Henry William Rees, was born.

About 1909, the family moved to a house on the corner of Market and Border Streets. This house has been torn down and is now part of the Laughlin Funeral home parking lot. It is interesting to note that in the back yard of this residence was a small brick building which served as the City Jail. While the family lived at this location another child, Mary Elizabeth Rees, was born on July 27, 1910.

About 1915, David and Florence purchased a home in a part of Troy which at that time was known as Brookside. This home is on Lorean Drive just off of South Main Street.

In 1920, David's father, Henry Rees, came to live with the family as he was quite elderly and in ill health. Henry Rees passed away just two weeks after his arrival. He is buried in the Troy City Cemetery.

Around 1925, the family purchased a home at 307 Troy Avenue where they lived for about eighteen years until they moved to a house on 102 Sarah Street. The children attended the Troy Schools. Henry dropped out of high school to begin work at the local coal mine. In 1928, Mary Elizabeth graduated in the first class of the new McCray-Dewey High School.

The family was affiliated with the Troy Methodist Church. They were also active in other community organizations. David was a member of Neilson Lodge #25 I.O.O.F., and the Troy Masonic Lodge A.F.A.M. Florence was a member of the Rebekah Lodge and the Ladies' Aid at the Troy Methodist Church. David served several terms on the Troy City Council during the 1920s and early 1930s. He was mayor of Troy in the late '30s. During his term as mayor, the city put in the first City Water Works.

During the mid-forties, David retired from mining and worked as a security guard at Granite City Steel. In 1948 the couple again moved to their final home in Troy on 116 Center Street, where the couple lived until David's death in 1956. Florence passed away in 1964. They are interred in the Troy City Cemetery. *Submitted by Jack Rees.*

HENRY WILLIAM AND VURLA DORA REES

HENRY WILLIAM AND VURLA DORA REES - Henry William Rees and Vurla Dora Marcham were married at the home of her mother in Carlyle, IL, on June 25, 1932. Their attendants were Vurla's brother, Arnold Jacob Marcham of Carlyle, and Henry's sister, Mary Elizabeth Rees of Troy. They were married by the Rev. Crawley, pastor of the Carlyle Methodist Church, who had also previously been the pastor of the Troy Methodist church.

They took up residence at 102 Sarah Street on the day of their marriage. Henry was born and raised in Troy, and some facts about his early years are covered in the history of David and Florence Rees. Vurla was born and raised in Carlyle, the daughter of James Buchanan and Kathryn Ann Marcham, on January ,1911. She had two older half brothers and two older half

Henry William and Vurla Dora Rees

sisters. Her parents operated a grocery store in Carlyle. Vurla attended Carlyle schools and graduated from Carlyle High School in 1929. She worked for her parents in the grocery store until her marriage.

At the time of their marriage Henry was employed by Lungstras Cleaning Co. in St. Louis, MO. He began work there in 1931 and left in 1948. He had previously worked as a hatter making men's hats, and at the coal mine in Troy. For a period of about one year, in1928, he worked in the automobile plants in Detroit, MI. During the early years of their marriage, Vurla was a homemaker.

In 1933 they moved from 102 Sarah Street to 106 Dewey Street. This same year Vurla's mother, Kathryn Marcham, a widow, moved from Carlyle and made her home with Henry and Vurla in Troy. She remained with them until her death in 1947.

In July of 1936 they purchased a home at 313 S. Hickory Street. On August 28, 1936, their only child, John William (Jack) Rees was born at St. Joseph's Hospital in Highland, Illinois.

Henry and Vurla were active members of The Troy United Methodist Church, as well as other groups in the community. Henry was a member of The Troy Fire Dept. from the early 1930s until about 1950. He served on the McCray-Dewey High School Board of Education from 1942 to 1946. He was also a member of Neilson Lodge #25, I.O.O.F., having served as Noble Grand of that organization during its centennial year in 1948. Vurla was a member of the Rebekah lodge, and various ladies organizations of the Methodist church.

In 1953, they purchased Clean Craft Cleaners in Granite City; both operated this business until about 1964.

Henry worked at various other laundry and dry cleaning establishments in St. Louis until he retired, and Vurla worked at Allen's Drug Store and The Troy Schools Cafeterias until she retired.

Their son John William (Jack) Rees attended the Troy Schools, and graduated from McCray-Dewey Township High School in 1954.

Henry died on September 26, 1985, and Vurla died on August 21, 1998. They are interred in the Friedens Cemetery in Troy. *Submitted by Jack Rees.*

JOHN WILLIAM (JACK) AND DOROTHY JUNE REES

JOHN WILLIAM (JACK) AND DOROTHY JUNE REES - John William Rees and Dorothy June Diveley were married at the Troy Methodist Church on October 26, 1957. Their attendants were Robert Henry Baglin, a cousin of John's, and Elinor Marie Hall, Dorothy's sister. They

were married by the Rev. Carrol Morris, pastor of the Troy Methodist Church.

Jack was born and raised in Troy, the son of Henry and Vurla Rees. Dorothy came to Troy at the age of six, when she became the daughter of John and Irene Cullen, who resided at 500 S. Main St. in Troy. Both Jack and Dorothy attended Troy schools and graduated from McCray-Dewey High School. Jack graduated in 1954, and Dorothy in 1956.

After their marriage, they moved into an apartment on Edwardsville Rd. in Troy, which was owned by Bill and Molly McCormick. Jack was working for Sutherland Lumber Co. in East St. Louis, and Dorothy was working for The Seven-Up Co. in their corporate office in St. Louis. In June of 1958 they both quit their jobs and moved to Carbondale, IL, where Jack re-entered Southern Illinois University. He had previously attended the University in 1954 and 1955. Jack secured part time work at a local Veterinary Hospital, and Dorothy worked at Dill Investment Co. Just a couple of months after this move, they discovered that Dorothy was expecting their first child.

John and Dorothy Rees

On May 4,1959, John William (Bill) Rees Jr. was born at Holden Hospital in Carbondale. It soon became evident that Jack would have to interrupt full time student status and secure steady employment. In June of 1959, they moved back to Troy. Jack entered summer classes at McKendree College, so that he could take the two necessary classes to be eligible to take the examination for a provisional teaching certificate. In August of that year, he was issued a teaching certificate, and secured a job with Triad Community Unit District #2. He was assigned to teach a self-contained seventh grade class at Marine Grade School.

In November of 1959 Jack and Dorothy moved to Marine. Shortly after this move they found out that Dorothy was expecting their second child. On August 17,1960, Michael Henry Rees was born at St. Joseph's Hospital in Highland. With two children and the meager salary of a teacher in the early '60s, Jack secured summer employment with Sutherland Lumber Co. and Dorothy got a job with The First National Bank in Marine.

In June of 1962, Jack graduated from McKendree College with a degree in biology.

On July 25,1963, a third child, David James Rees was born at St. Joseph's Hospital in Highland.

In June of 1965, Jack was transferred to Troy to teach science in the junior high school.

They moved back to Troy, and purchased a parcel of land at 414 S. Main Street. Construction of a new home was started on June 8, 1965. Jack, his father, Henry Rees, and a good friend, Kenny Ziegler, did the construction work. It was only possible to build this home because Mr. Leeds Watson, owner of Watson Lumber Co. in Troy, volunteered to carry a large lumber bill until construction was far enough along to secure a construction loan.

Jack had been taking graduate classes at SIUE since 1963, and in June of 1967 graduated with a Master of Science Degree, in Education Administration.

Dorothy decided to start taking college classes in 1967 and entered SIUE that same year. After two years of college, her education was interrupted by the birth of the couple's fourth child. Allen Matthew Rees was born on January 26, 1970, at St. Joseph's Hospital in Highland.

In 1972 Dorothy started back to school at SIUE with books under one arm and a two year old boy under the other. She graduated with a Bachelor of Science degree in elementary education, in June of 1975. She started teaching that year in the Triad School District, teaching at the third, fifth, and seventh grade levels.

Jack completed course work for the sixth year specialist degree in 1977, and in 1979 was transferred to Triad High School as Assistant Principal.

Jack and Dorothy both retired from Triad Community Unit #2 in 1994. Jack continues to work part time for the school district as Co-Transportation Director with Richard Mason, who had been Principal of Triad High School, and also retired in 1994. Dorothy continues to substitute teach in the Triad Schools.

The Rees boys all attended school in Troy, and all graduated from Triad High School. John William Jr. attended St. Louis College of Pharmacy for two years. He then transferred to Logan College of Chiropractic where he graduated in 1982. He resides in Cambridge, MD, and is the father of six children. Michael Henry attended SIUE and is the owner of PLM Inc., a parking lot maintenance company. He is married to the former Lynn Harris. They have two children and live in Edwardsville. David James attended Belleville Area College. He lives in Bethalto, IL, and has two children. David works for Bruckert Chevrolet in Bunker Hill. Allen Matthew received two associate degrees from Belleville Area College. He is married to the former Tina Sidener of Glen Carbon, IL. They have two children and live in Denver, Colorado. Allen owns PLM Co. a parking lot maintenance company. At this writing Jack and Dorothy have twelve grandchildren.

Jack and Dorothy have been active in various organizations. Jack is a Past Noble Grand of Neilson Lodge #25, a past master of Marine Lodge #355 A.F.& A.M. in Marine. He is a member of The Valley of Southern Illinois Scottish Rite Bodies. Dorothy is a former member of the Eastern Star. Both were members of various school organizations. Jack and Dorothy are members of St. Matthews United Methodist Church, in Maryville, IL. *Submitted by Jack and Dorothy Rees.*

SCOTT AND LAURA (GRAPPERHAUS) REILSON - Laura Louise Grapperhaus, born March 31, 1962, the oldest child of James and Mae (nee Mersinger) Grapperhaus, married Scott Russell Reilson, born May 24, 1962, youngest son of Bill and Marian (nee Guentensberger) Reilson, were married March 18, 1983.

Reilson family, 1992
(l. to r.) Maria, Scott, Laura, and Jared

They have two children, Jared Scott Reilson and Maria Christina Reilson. They reside in St. Jacob.

Laura works for the Lammert Building Ptr. in downtown St. Louis, MO. Scott works for Greyhound Bus Lines, St. Louis.

Laura enjoys antiquing and watching Triad football and wrestling. She is a member of the St. James Altar Society at St. James Catholic Church in St. Jacob and is current president of St. Jacob Firefighters Auxiliary.

Scott also has interest in the school activities of the children, likes bicycling and participated in RAGBRI, a cross-state event held in Iowa. He is a St. Jacob Volunteer Firefighter and is a member of the St. Jacob Community Park Board.

Jared and Maria both work at Ponderosa Restaurant in Highland, IL, on a part-time basis. They attend Triad High School.

Jared is on the Triad Varsity Football (Class of 2002) team, the wrestling team, enjoys sports and collects sports memorabilia. He is also a Junior Firefighter for the St. Jacob Volunteer Fire Department, Maria is in the Triad French club and is active in many other activities. She enjoys socializing with her friends and shopping.

The Reilsons have lived in St. Jacob since 1984. The family is a member of St. James Catholic Church in St. Jacob, IL. *Submitted by Laura Reilson.*

JESSE RENFRO - Jesse Renfro was born in Kentucky September 22, 1796. He came to Madison County, Illinois, in 1810. In the spring of 1814, when he was not yet 18 years old, he enlisted as a mounted ranger in Captain Whiteside's Company. Their purpose was to protect settlements from Indians. He served for a year and a half. On September 4, 1817, he and Letty West were married. Letty West was the daughter of Isaac West, one of the early settlers of Collinsville Township. They became the parents of thirteen children, eight daughters and five sons. They lost a few children while they were young.

When Jesse was about 30 years old, he became interested in religion and joined the Methodist Church. At a conference in St. Louis

on October 8, 1843, he became a deacon. On September 17, 1848, in Belleville, he was ordained an elder.

The first building for religious purposes in the Troy area was the Gilead Methodist Church. It was also a school. Gilead is a few miles east of Troy. The building was a square, 20 or 30 feet. The outside was weather-boarded with rough clapboards. The inside was plastered. The benches were made of logs split in half with pins driven in the rough side for legs. This was the first school in Jarvis Township, and the first classes held there were in 1824. School was for six months, and Jesse furnished the books. He used the old *U.S. Speller*, *Pike's Arithmetic*, and the New Testament of the Bible. He received $100 for the school term. The last year Jesse taught, he had 40 pupils.

Jesse was also a preacher at Gilead, and was still preaching when he was 85 years old.

Before regular churches, they had circuit riders. They covered many miles to speak often in someone's home. In 1852, Jesse Renfro was the circuit preacher in the Edwardsville Circuit. Jesse strongly opposed secret organizations such as the Masons and Odd Fellows.

Jesse and Letty lived to celebrate their golden and diamond (60) wedding anniversaries. At their diamond wedding celebration, there were 100 of their descendants and many friends and neighbors.

Jesse and Letty were married almost 65 years before Letty passed away. She was 81 years old. Jesse was 85 years old when he passed away. They are buried in the Gilead Cemetery, which was established in 1821, near Gilead Church and School, and their home. *Submitted by Sue Wopat and Agnes Helmkamp.*

WASHINGTON DEW RENFRO - Washington Dew Renfro, son of Jesse and Letty Renfro, was born April 12, 1832, and died March 26, 1918. He married Frances Eveline Black. They were the parents of ten children: William Preston, born 1852; Letica (Letty), born January 9, 1854; Andrew Theodore, born March 12, 1855; Sarah Delphia, born December 21, 1856; Mary Caroline, born April 9, 1858; Susan Lily, born November 17, 1859; Jesse Romulous, born May 25, 1862; Cyrus Washington, born February 1, 1864; Fanny May, born January 7, 1866; and infant daughter, born March 21, 1869; One story his granddaughter, Frances Wilhelm, told about her grandfather was that he was missing ear corn from a hole in his corncrib. He set a steel trap in the crib. One morning, when he went out to milk, a neighbor had his arm in the hole. Grandpa Renfro said, "Good morning." The man replied, "Good morning." Grandpa Renfro went on to the barn and milked the cows.

Washington Dew and Mariah Adaline (Dees) Renfro

On his way back to the house, he said to the man, "Come on in and have breakfast with us." The man said, "I can't. I'm caught." Grandpa Renfro said, "Why didn't you tell me? I would have let you out." This he did, but still insisted the neighbor come into his home for breakfast. Grandpa never missed any more corn.

Grandpa Renfro was very opposed to drinking any alcoholic beverages. He told his family, "If a drink of whiskey would save me, let me die."

Grandpa Renfro's first wife died April 8, 1869. He then married Mariah Adaline Dees on May 8, 1872. They had six children: infant daughter, born March 12, 1873; George Dew, born July 17,1874; John Wesley, born February 28, 1876; Harriet Adeline, born December 20, 1877; Harry, born December 20, 1877; Dora Maude, born October 30, 1880.

Washington Dew Renfro's daughter, Mary Caroline, married Elijah Dodson Harris.

Washington's son, Jesse Romulous, married Katherine May Baker. They were the parents of five girls: Lela Renfro Shelton McDermott, Eveline (Eva) Renfro Buhrmester (Edward), Bessie Renfro Sweeny (Sidney), Mandy Renfro McMakin (Clyde), Ella Renfro Keller (Clate).

Lela Shelton had two sons, Willard and Wesley. Willard had a daughter, Dortha.

Eva and Edward Buhrmester, former Troy residents, had two children, Audrey and Edward Burdette. Burdette was killed in France on November 16, 1944, in World War II.

Audrey married Edward Scheck. They had one daughter, Veronica.

Bess and Sid Sweeny had two daughters, Maxine Sweeny Hartman (Fred) and Virginia Sweeny. Maxine and Fred had a son, John.

Mandy and Clyde McMakin had a son, Clyde Elmo, and a daughter, Lemoine. Ella and Clate Keller had five children. They lived in the state of Washington.

After Jesse Romulous Renfro's wife died, he married Maude Williams. Jesse Romulous (Uncle Rome) is buried in Gilead Cemetery. *Submitted by Sue Wopat and Agnes Helmkamp.*

JASON RICHTER - Jason Aaron Richter born September 18,1968, was raised on his family farm located at the corner of Rt. 4 and Faust Rd., outside of Lebanon, IL. On December 5, 1992, he married Tanya Kay Walter who was born June 18, 1971, and raised in Mascoutah, IL. They have

Richter family, circa 2000
(l. to r.) Benjamin, Abigail (on lap), Tanya, Hilary, Jason, Allison (on lap), Holly.

5 children, Hilary Kay (b. May 25, 1993), Holly Kathlen (b. December 7, 1994), Benjamin John Aaron (b. March 4,1996) and twins Allison Ann and Abigail Rayette (b. June 5, 1998).

The couple decided to raise their family in Troy and moved here in September 1999. They purchased the home at 1003 Troy O'Fallon Road and have enjoyed getting to know people in the community.

Jason is a graduate of McKendree college with a degree in Math and Computer Science. Tanya is an education major. The family enjoys fishing, crafts and creating scrapbook albums. In the winter the children love sledding on the hill in their yard and in the summer they have fun playing ball in the back yard. They enjoy being part of such a big family. The family also has a shi tzu puppy named Muffin who was born August 8, 2001. Their family motto is "Experience is not what happens to you; it is what you do with what happens to you." (Aldous Huxley) *Submitted by Tanya Richter.*

MARY ELLEN SCHMIDT RICHTER
Mary Ellen Schmidt, daughter of Marie and Harold Schmidt, was born on November 19, 1936. She is a graduate of McCray-Dewey High School and William Woods College in Fulton, MO. On December 27,1960, she married Charles H. Richter of Baltimore, Maryland, who was the principal architect and chairman of the board of the architectural firm of Richter, Cornbrooks, Matthai, Hopkins. They have one daughter, Ellen Kirk, born August 19,1962. She is a graduate of Hollins College and The Maryland Institute of Art. She is married to Patrick D. Jarosinski, a graduate of Catholic University School of Architecture. They have one daughter, Ellen Kirk Richter Jarosinski, born August 8,1996. *Submitted By: Mary Ellen Schmidt Richter.*

RITCHER/MATTHEWS FAMILIES - August Ritcher came from Bohemia and settled in Troy. He volunteered from Madison County for a 3 year tour in Company F, 117th Regiment, IL Infantry, on Aug. 15, 1862, at Camp Butler in Springfield, IL. During his tour, he was promoted to corporal and engaged in battles in Tennessee, Mississippi, and Arkansas. He was mustered out on Aug. 5, 1865.

His description at time of muster-in was 28 years old; height 5'4"; complexion, light; eyes, blue; hair, brown; where from, Bohemia; occupation, farmer.

August Ritcher married Mary Catherine Hollis (born in Kent Co., DE, May 15, 1841) on Dec. 27, 1870, in Troy. Six children were born in Troy to them, five boys and one girl.

Charles Edmond Ritcher was born on Sept. 28, 1871, and died Feb. 5, 1941, in Omaha, NE.

Adda May Ritcher was born on Oct. 5, 1873, and died June 12, 1966, in Troy.

Henry Adelbert Ritcher was born on May 26, 1875, and died Match 15, 1965, in Pontiac, MI.

Stanley Jerome Ritcher was born on Aug. 22, 1877, and died May 27, 1910, in Troy.

Franklin A. Ritcher was born on Sept. 25, 1879, and died Dec. 1, 1899, in Troy.

George Clyde Ritcher was born Sept. 25, 1881, and died Jan. 4, 1974, in Alton, IL.

The daughter, Adda, married Velorus A. Matthews (b. Aug. 27, 1871, in Montgomery Co., KS, d. Mar. 10, 1904, in Troy) on June 24, 1896, in Troy. Adda was a school teacher in the Troy schools, and Velorus was a carpenter. To them two sons were born.

(Clyde) Raymond Matthews was born on Oct. 24, 1898, in Princeton, KS, and died June 29, 1988, in Edwardsville, IL.

Frank Veldrus Matthews was born Aug. 11, 1903, in Troy.

Ray Matthews married (Cora) Helen Liebler, also of Troy on Dec. 27, 1927, in Greenville, IL. For many years Ray owned and operated the Shell Station in Troy. Helen worked for many years as a seamstress at Karlee Dress Factory as well as a homemaker. To them, one son was born – Robert Ray Matthews.

Frank Matthews married Dora Barbara Langenwalter on Sept. 1, 1928, in Charleston, IL.

Frank worked as a meat salesman for Hunter Packing Co. in E. St. Louis, IL, for thirty-two years. To them one daughter was born – Joan Elaine (Matthews) Farenzena. *Submitted by Sheila Ziegler.*

JACOB RIEBOLD - Jacob was born on the Riebold farm in Blackjack on March 15, 1843, to Johann and Margaret (Koch) Riebold. Jacob was the youngest of five living children. His siblings were Peter, John, George and Elizabeth. Jacob married Anna M. Kraher sometime in the 1860s. Anna was the daughter of Johannes and Unknown (Liebler) Kraher. Her birthdate was Oct. 18, 1848. They began married life in a two-room log cabin. As the family grew, additions were made to the cabin, transforming it into the Victorian farmhouse shown here.

Jacob Riebold family, 1882-83
(l. to r.) unknown hired hand, Anna M., Catherine "Kate", Jacob, Henry, Elisabeth, Emma

Jacob and Anna were the parents of 10 children. The first child died shortly after birth, name and date unknown. The surviving children were Emma B. (b. 1868, married Frank Mersinger, d. Oct. 23, 1949), Elisabeth Louise (b. 1870, maried Adam Mersinger), George Joseph (b. 1874, d. 1881), Johann Jacob (b. 1877, d. 1879), Henry (b. 1878, married Emma Bugger, d. March 17,1959), Catherine (Kate) M. (b. 1880, married Valentine Mersinger, d.1950), Anna (b. 1883, married John J. Schmitt, d. December 24, 1918), John Michael (b. 1885, married Claudine Hilby, d. July 24, 1945), and Mary (b. Jan. 1, 1887, d. July 2, 1888).

Jacob raised his family on the farm, which today is located at 9131 E. Mill Creek Rd. He was active in community life. Jacob is remembered as kind, gentle, and uncomplaining in his later years. He never raised his voice except when the grandsons would get a little noisy. He would entertain the kids by telling stories. Jacob became blind late in life, having previously lost one eye in a farming accident. He was well respected by the community and dearly loved by his family. Jacob was a member of the German Evangelical and Reformed Church. Anna was a member of the St. John the Baptist Catholic Church. She was a charter member of Altar and Rosary Sodality formed around 1890. Jacob hauled brick from the railroad in Troy to Blackjack for the building of the new brick Catholic Church in 1883. Both churches were located in the Blackjack community. Jacob died on Oct. 7, 1931, and is buried in the New St. John Evangelical Cemetery, located on Lebanon Road. Anna died on Nov. 14, 1899, and is buried in the St. John the Baptist Catholic Cemetery, also located on Lebanon Road in Madison County. *Submitted by Mark and Chris Riebold.*

JOHANN RIEBOLD - Johann and Margaret (Koch) Riebold emigrated from Germany in 1838. They purchased an eighty acre farm, log house, and livestock for $700. This was located at what is now 9023 and 9131 E. Mill Creek Road. Johann and Margaret were the parents of five living children. There were four sons: John, Peter, George, and Jacob, and one daughter, Elizabeth. John, Peter, and Elizabeth were born in Darmstadt, Germany. George was born on March 14, 1838, at Pete Stiefel's place, located near Matthew's Crossing on Troy Road. Jacob was born on March 15, 1843, on the Riebold farm in Blackjack. Johann died sometime between 1843 and 1850 and he is believed to be buried in the old German Evangelical and Reformed Cemetery on Lebanon Road. Margaret remarried a man named Michael Housam, sometime around 1850. They were the parents of one daughter, also named Margaret.

Elizabeth married Harry Schieler. Harry was shot and killed in Idaho. He had traveled out west with George Riebold, his brother-in-law. George had gone out west after the Gold Rush to try to find his fortune. He never married and he is believed to be buried on the Platte River. Elizabeth later remarried a Wunderlich (first name unknown). Peter Riebold married Katherine Langenwalter. They lived east of Troy

Jacob Riebold circa 1900,
youngest son of Johann Riebold

for a short time before moving to Grangeville, Idaho. Their children were Emma, George, Mary, Jacob, Sam, and Sylvia, all raised in Idaho. Peter Riebold died July 22,1921. Jacob kept in touch with Peter through letters after his move to Idaho. John married a Burke (first name unknown) and had a blacksmith shop in Troy. This blacksmith shop was located at what is now known as the "Wedge" on Edwardsville Road. He had at least 5 children: George, who moved to Texas Co. MO; Fred, whose wife had a bakery in Troy; John A. (known as Doc) married Dodie Allen, lived in Troy, and also owned a blacksmith/repair shop after his father John; Emma married a Robert Morris; Kate married a Percy Davidson; Jacob remained on the farm his entire life and raised his own family there; Margaret Housam married a John Meyer. Johann and Margaret were members of the German Evangelical and Reformed Church. *Submitted by Mark and Chris Riebold. Information complied from notes taken by Claudine Riebold as told by Jacob Riebold before 1931 and notes from Corinne Riebold Sedlacek.*

JOHN M. RIEBOLD - John Michael Riebold was born March 4, 1885, to Jacob and Anna (Kraher) Riebold. He was one of ten children born to this union. John was born on the family farm, what is now known as 9131 E. Mill Creek Road, located in the Blackjack community south of Troy. He lived his entire life on this same farm. John made a living by farming but also took a keen interest in business and civic movements. He served as Treasurer of the Troy Grain Co. and Director of the Helvetia Mutual Insurance Co. He helped obtain right-of-way for the rural electric company. John also served as a trustee and usher for the St. John the Baptist Catholic Church where he was a life-long member. In 1923, John served as School Director for the St. John Catholic School.

Wedding photo, 1914
Claudine and John M. Riebold

John married Claudine B. Hilby on September 22, 1914, at the St. Jacobus Catholic Church (now known as St. James) in St. Jacob, IL. Claudine was the daughter of Daniel and Caroline (Gau) Hilby of St Jacob. She taught school in St Jacob, several years before her marriage. They lived on the Riebold farm with Jacob, John's father. John purchased the farm and equipment after Jacob's retirement from farming. John and Claudine took care of Jacob in his declining years. Five chilren were born to this union, with two dying in infancy: Mabel Caroline (b. Aug. 1, 1915, d. Aug. 5,1915); John

John M. Riebold family, 1940
(l. to r.) Front: Corinne E., Claudine B.
Back: John H., John M., Paul O.

(b. Sept. 14, 1916, d. Sept. 19, 1916); Corinne Emma (b. July 9, 1918, married Leo Sedlacek on Nov. 29, 1941); John Henry (b. May 2, 1921, married Evelyn Ruppel on April 15, 1947, d. Dec. 14, 1991); Paul Oscar (b. Aug. 12, 1924, married Catherine Schmisseur on Nov. 28, 1951, d. April 15, 1992).

The family attended St. John the Baptist Catholic Church. Claudine was a member of the Altar and Rosary Sodality. Corinne was an organist at the church. John Michael died at the age of 60 years on July 24, 1945, after a long illness, Claudine built a house on Main Street in Troy in 1951. She lived there until her death on May 11, 1966. John M. and Claudine are both buried in the St John's Catholic Cemetery, Blackjack. *Submitted by Mark and Chris Riebold.*

MARK P. RIEBOLD - Mark Paul Riebold is the 5th generation Riebold to live on the family farm located in the Blackjack community south of Troy. Son of Paul and Catherine (Schmisseur) Riebold, he was born on December 15,1953, at Christian Welfare Hospital in East St. Louis. Mark has one sister, Reata Jo Riebold McAllister. Mark attended Troy schools, graduating from Triad High School in 1972. He attended McKendree College in Lebanon, IL, graduating in 1976 with a degree in Sociology. While attending McKendree, Mark met his future wife, Christine L. Miller. Mark worked summers with the Madison Co. Highway Dept. on a survey team. After graduation from college, he worked for Olin Corporation, Madison Co. Housing Authority and McDonnell-Douglas Astronautics Division (currently known as Boeing Co.) Mark has been employed as a Government Property Specialist with Boeing for over 18 years.

Wedding Day, 1982
Mark and Christine Riebold

273

Christine was born at Illini Hospital in Pittsfield, IL, on January 28, 1953. She is the daughter of John Edward Miller and Janice Gay (Weaver) Miller. Christine grew up in the Pleasant Hill and Rockport, IL, area with 3 sisters: Gail Elaine (Miller) Anderson, Sherry Diane (Miller) Brendel, and Ellen Kay (Miller) McDade. The Miller family also lived in Louisiana, MO, from 1965-1967. Christine graduated from Pleasant Hill High School in 1971. She attended and graduated from McKendree College in 1975 with a degree in Biology and Psychology. Christine worked summers as a waitress at the Dairy Dip in Pleasant Hill. While in college, she worked one year as a resident assistant in the dorm and later worked at the Farm Fresh Milk Stores in Fairview Heights and Belleville, IL. Christine has been employed as a Medical Technologist with Memorial Hospital in Belleville for over 25 years. She currently works part-time in the chemistry department.

Riebold family, 1998
(l. to r.) Front: Christine, Jennifer. Back: Mark.

Mark and Christine were married at St. Joseph's Catholic Church in Louisiana, MO, on May 1, 1982. They made their home at 9023 E. Mill Creek Road, also on the Riebold family farm. After the death of Mark's parents in 1992, they moved into the family home at 9131 E. Mill Creek Road in 1994. They are the parents of one daughter, Jennifer Christine, born on October 6, 1988. Jennifer attended Henning, Freeman, and McCray-Dewey schools in Troy. She represented McCray-Dewey in the *St. Louis Post Dispatch* Spelling Bee in March 2000. Jennifer currently attends 7th grade at Triad Middle School where she is on the softball team.

Mark, Chris, and Jennifer attended St. John the Baptist Catholic Church in Blackjack until it was closed in 1992. They are currently members of SS Peter and Paul Catholic Church in Collinsville. Mark is also a member of Knights of Columbus, Troy Council. *Submitted by Chris Riebold.*

OSCAR AND MARIE RIEBOLD - Oscar Riebold and Marie Kohne were married Nov. 26, 1930. Marie was born Dec. 18, 1909, the daughter of William and Martha (Haenni) Kohne of St. Jacob, IL. Oscar was born Oct. 15, 1907, the son of Henry and Emma (Bugger) Riebold. Henry and Emma lived in Blackjack 1910-1947. Henry and Emma are buried in St. John's Catholic Cemetery in Blackjack. Henry and Emma had five children: Hilda (b. 1902 d. 1920), Lester (b. 1903 d. 1915), Oscar (b. 1907 d. 1987), Paul (b. 1909 d. 1915) and Henritta (b. 1913 d. 1915).

Oscar and Marie (Kohne) Riebold, circa 1980

Oscar and Marie lived in Blackjack (1936–1949); they then moved to a farm just north of Lebanon, IL, on Route 4. They retired from farming in 1973 and moved to Highland, IL. Oscar passed away May 15, 1987, and is buried in St. Joseph's Cemetery, Lebanon. Marie still resides in Highland in her home.

Oscar and Marie had two sons, Orville and Melvin. Orville was born March 1, 1932. He married Leona Knebel on June 30, 1959. They had one daughter Leann born June 20, 1966, who lives in Belleville, IL. Orville passed away Aug. 16, 1982, and Leona passed away on March 22, 2000.

Melvin was born Jan. 2, 1934, and married Elvenia Frey on May 30, 1956. They live south of St. Jacob, IL. They have two sons, Carl and Russell.

Carl, born Jan. 26, 1960, married Karen Weis of St. Jacob on April 17, 1982, and they have two sons, Michael (b. Aug. 4, 1984) and Andrew (b. March 22, 1989). They live west of Troy.

Russell born Sept. 14, 1961, married Tina Littlefield of St. Jacob on July 11, 1981. They have a daughter and son, Amy (b. Feb. 3, 1982) and Eric (b. Dec. 7, 1984). They reside in St. Jacob. *Submitted by Melvin and Elvenia Riebold.*

PAUL O. RIEBOLD - Paul Oscar Riebold was born August 12, 1924, to John M. and Claudine (Hilby) Riebold on the Riebold farm in Blackjack. His siblings were Corinne Emma and John Henry. Paul lived his entire life on this same farm. He attended country schools in Blackjack and graduated from McCray-Dewey High School in 1942. Paul managed the farm for his mother after the illness and death of his father from 1944-1950. Paul met his future wife Catherine May Schmisseur at the wedding reception of Norman and Doris Brendel in 1948.

Wedding photo, 1951
(l. to r.) Jo Nash, Russell Hess, Kay and Paul Riebold

Catherine was born May 19, 1918, to Edward and Angeline (Melgrani) Schmisseur in Centreville Station, IL. She had one brother Wilson Edward Schmisseur. Catherine attended school at St. Mary's in Centreville and was a 1936 graduate of Belleville Township High School. After graduation she traveled for two years throughout the entire United States with her parents. She also graduated from Rubicam Business College in 1941. Catherine was employed as a secretary in the Judge Advocate Office at Scott Air Field until her marriage to Paul.

Catherine (Kay) and Paul were married on November 28, 1951, in East Saint Louis, IL. They made their home on the family farm. Paul served as Director with Helvetia Township Mutual Insurance Agency from 1946-1982. He received his Illinois broker's license in 1958. Paul owned and operated the Riebold Insurance Agency in his home from 1958 until his death in 1992. Kay served as secretary for the agency. Paul was elected Jarvis Township Supervisor in 1961. He was also elected to the Madison County Board to represent Jarvis, Marine, St. Jacob, and Pin Oak Townships. He served in these elected positions from 1961-1977.

Paul O. Riebold family, 1988
(l. to r.) Front: Kay and Paul Riebold, Reata McCallister, Randy McCallister. Back: Mark and Christine Riebold.

During his political career he formed friendships with Paul Simon and Melvin Price. Paul also met President-elect John F. Kennedy. He served as VP of Illinois Association of County Board Members, 1972-1975, and as President of Illinois Township Officials Association, Zone 1, 1968-1972. He served on many committees both as chairman and as a member while in office. As chairman of the Madison County Environment Committee, Paul received an award for the first state licensed water testing laboratory. Both Paul and Kay were active in the local community as members and officers of the Jaycees/Jaycettes, Troy Lions/Lioness, and the Troy Democratic Club. Paul also served as land agent for Ziegler Coal Company in the early 1980s. Paul and Kay were avid bingo players and enjoyed trips to Las Vegas beginning in the 1970s. They were the parents of two children, Mark Paul, born December 15, 1953, and Reata Jo, born February 19, 1956. Their biographies are listed separately. Paul and Kay were members of St. John the Baptist Catholic Church in Blackjack. Kay was a member and officer of the Altar and Rosary Sodality and past president of the Alton Deanery. Paul died April 15, 1992, and Kay died July 5,

1992. They are both buried in the St. John the Baptist Catholic Cemetery in Blackjack. *Submitted by Mark and Chris Riebold.*

ALBERT AND EMMA RIEDER - Albert

Rieder was born in Baden, Germany, in February 1859. He was the oldest son of Joseph Rieder and Anna Maria Swense. When he was eight years of age, his parents emigrated to this country, landing in New York. They remained there for several years before moving west and located in Belleville, IL. In the fall of 1872 they moved to a farm between Marine and St. Jacob where Joseph Rieder died a few years later.

After his father's death, Albert moved to Troy and on 25 December 1879, he married Emma Gaber. They located on a farm in the Blackjack community where they remained for a number of years before moving to Troy where he engaged in the saloon business and built an opera house. In 1901 he retired from both endeavors and moved to a farm on the northeastern limits of Troy. He then followed the occupation of an auctioneer for a number of years.

Mr. and Mrs. Rieder had two sons, August Rieder of Troy and George Rieder of near Fairmont City. They had a daughter, Mrs. Sophie Kurth of Nokomis, and two adopted daughters, Mrs. Philip Schultze of Troy and Mrs. Charles Beaver of Collinsville. One child born to them died in infancy.

Albert Rieder had a wide acquaintance throughout other towns and communities in this immediate vicinity. He had a jovial disposition and the faculty of making and retaining friends wherever he went. He possessed keen judgment and business ability; as a result he amassed considerable property and competency. Hospitality and charity were always two outstanding characteristics of his nature, and his country home was the scene of many social gatherings. His home life was that of a devoted husband and father. He was long remembered by a legion of friends. He died in 1927. *Submitted by Pat Rehg.*

AUGUST AND MARGARET RIEDER

August F. Rieder, the second son of Joseph and Anna Rieder, was born in 1862 in Germany. When he was three years of age his parents came to this country and located near Troy. He was married to Margaret Christman. They farmed near Troy, but around 1900 they moved into town where he worked in the mines as long as his health permitted.

August and Margaret had eight children, six of whom survived to adulthood. Their sons are John M. of Troy and August, Jr., of Peoria. Their daughters are Mrs. Charles Novak of Chicago; Mrs. E.H. Heller of Sikeston, MO; Mrs. Walter Troeger of Detroit, MI; and Mrs. Charles Beaver of Troy. They had nine grandchildren.

August had one sister, Mrs. Mary Kurth of Troy, and three brothers, Albert and Joseph of Troy, and George of Collinsville.

He was a devout member of St. Jerome's Catholic Church in Troy and was a devoted husband and father. His wife, Margaret, preceded him in death by 27 years. He died in September 1935 after an extended illness of asthma and complications. He is buried in St. Jerome's Cemetery. In his obituary in *The Troy Call* it was stated, "His nature was quiet and unassuming and withal he was a true friend and good citizen." *Submitted by Pat Rehg.*

MARIE ROGIER - Marie Rogier, daughter of

Robert and Kate Horsely Dawson, was born April 1, 1902. She was the oldest in a family of five children.

Marie Rogier, 1965

Marie grew up in Troy, attended the local schools, and worked for a time at the Switzer Candy Co. in St. Louis. She was a self-taught musician, and after learning to play the piano, organ, and guitar, became very active in church and community musical groups.

On December 24, 1928, she married Floyd Rogier of Highland, who was a ministerial student at the time. After he completed his studies in Chicago, the couple moved back to the Troy area where their first son, Robert, was born in November, 1929. In February of 1930, Floyd was appointed pastor of a Methodist church in Longpoint, IL, where he served for four years.

While living there, the couple had two more sons: Floyd, Jr. was born in January of 1931, and Richard in February of 1932.

In 1934, Floyd was assigned to a church in Osman, IL. While serving there he began to experience health problems, and died in February 1939 at the age of 29. Marie, with her sons aged 7, 8, and 9 moved back to Troy in the summer of 1939.

As a single mother, Marie worked hard to support and raise her three sons. They successfully completed their education in the Troy schools, and all later served in the military during the Korean War.

In 1956 Richard married Rose Farmer of Troy. They had three children, all graduates of the Triad Schools. Richard, Jr. married Karen Gerling of Maryville and now lives in Kettering, OH. Rene married Kent Robinette of Bethalto and lives in Edwardsville. Rhonda is married to Norman Fohne of Lebanon and lives in rural Troy

Floyd married Eunice Kaltenbacker of Old Ripley in 1956. They made their residence in Highland. Robert married Diana Dettmer of Edwardsville in 1963. Their son, Michael, graduated from Triad and lives in Glen Carbon. He is married to the former Dynette Shrader. Jennifer, their daughter, is married to Thomas King. Both are Triad graduates. They presently live in Maryville.

Marie Rogier was a very active member of the Troy Methodist Church. She served as pianist/organist for thirty years – rarely missing a service. She was also much in demand as an accompanist. She accompanied numerous soloists, ensembles and choirs as they performed at church, school, civic and social functions in Troy and the surrounding area. Even as her health declined, she continued to serve – playing organ for the Sunday service only two days before she died at her home in Troy on April 22, 1969.

Her son, Robert, retired from the Triad District, still lives with his wife, Diana in Troy. Floyd, retired from government work, lives in Highland with his wife, Eunice. Richard, also retired from government service, resides with his wife, the former Jean Schmidt, in Glen Carbon.

Marie's other descendants are her great grandchildren: Kyle and Monica Rogier of Kettering, Ohio; Zachary and Erin Robinette of Edwardsville; Stephen and Laura Fohne of Troy; Joel and Lydia Rogier of Glen Carbon; and Lucas King of Maryville. *Submitted by Robert Rogier.*

JAMES AND MARY (LEVO) ROMEO

Mary Levo was born July 23, 1898, in Collinsville, IL, the fourth child of Peter P. and Laura (Cossano) Levo.

She married James Romeo born October 18, 1892, in Sicily, Italy, on October 18, 1916. They lived in Collinsville in the Morris Hills addition. Three children were born to them. They were Vincent, Laura Ann and William "Billie."

After Mary's father died, she and James "Jim" bought the Levo farm south of Troy (house and 18 acres) from Mary's mother and brother. Mary was a big talker and quite a joker. She had lots of friends and enjoyed making her spaghetti and meatballs and other Italian dishes for them. She enjoyed being with people and entertaining. She loved to have "company."

Jim didn't talk much. Mary did all the talking. Jim would make fun of her in his Italian brogue, he would say, "I say one word, she says a thousand."

Jim and Mary attended St. John the Baptist Catholic Church in Blackjack while they lived in Troy.

In later years, while they lived in the Troy community, Jim worked in the Troy Mine for a while until it closed, then worked at Emerson Electric. They grew strawberries for a time and also grew vegetables. One year, Mary laughed about her "large" strawberries and said they were as big as a coffee cup. She made jokes about those large strawberries. Jim enjoyed a

Wedding day, October 18, 1916
Mary (Levo) and James Romeo.

little farming with a few swine and calves. Jim died in 1956 and Mary lived alone for several years after that.

She worked for an invalid neighbor, Anna Edwards. She helped take care of her and did her housework on a daily basis.

For a short time she went to live with her brother, Edward, at his home in Troy, but eventually decided to sell her house and farm. She moved into a small home in Collinsville on Sunset Drive, off St. Louis Road. Later her son, Vincent, lived with her. She died in the late 1980s.

Both Mary and Jim are buried in SS Peter and Paul Catholic Cemetery in Collinsville. *Submitted by their niece, Mae Mersinger Grapperhaus.*

DELBERT RUSSELL - The slow migration to Troy began in 1960 when Delbert Lawrence Russell of Collinsville purchased the old Lutheran parsonage and property on what was called "The Old Mill Pond" on Clay Street. He then had the parsonage moved to sit closer to the pond. (What a sight to see: that big house raised up on wheels.) Part of the original land is now the baseball field at St. Paul's. After re-modeling, the home was leased to Wilma Sparlin who used it as a rooming house. (The population was about 1,500.)

Delbert Lawrence (1914) was the son of Lawrence David and Anna Mae (Shuttleworth) and was born in Collinsville. He married Carmen Wallace in 1918 and had two children: Betty Jeanne (1941) and David Lawrence (1946). Delbert and Carmen owned and operated Russell's Flowers in Collinsville for sixteen years.

Delbert passed away in 1962 and Carmen moved to Troy to live in the home with daughter Betty and husband Herman Cothran. Betty has two daughters, Shawndel (1962) and Shelby (1966), who both attended Triad schools. Shawndel married Scott Rose of Collinsville and has one son, Joshua (1992), and a daughter, Abbey (1994). They currently live in St. Jacob, IL. Shelby married Mike Gaultney from Troy, and she and her son, Tyler (1997), are residing in Troy.

David and Stephanie (Wright) live in Mason City, IL. They have one daughter, Pam

Russell family, 1998
(l. to r.) Front: Abbey Rose, Shawndel Rose, Joshua Rose, Betty Cathran, Carmen Russell, Stephanie Russell (holding Davey Kunkel), Jack Kunkel, Matt Russell. Back: Scott Rose, Mike Gaultney (holding Tyler Gaultney), Shelby Gaultney, David Russell, Pam Kunkel, Scott Kunkel.

(1969) and one son, Matthew (1970). Pam is married to Scott Kunkel from Dallas, TX, and lives with their two sons, Jack (1994) and David (1998) in Champaign, IL. Matthew is living in El Dorado, AR, where he is enjoying the outdoors, being employed by Arkansas State Forestry System.

During the years in Troy the crisp ice skating on the pond and the cool summer breezes blowing off the water were unforgettable. There were also a few times when the pond overflowed the spillway and flooded the streets. It was also relaxing to sit by the water and look across and see the many beautiful collies raised for years by Dale McMackin. Mr. Kueker used the back of the property to grow peanuts. What a treat for city folk who had never seen a peanut plant, or knew how they grow under the soil, on the roots. Each year, he would share a sample of the fresh, roasted crop.

Betty is now retired, and she and her mother still live in Troy in a much smaller home.

They are members of the Troy United Methodist Church. *Submitted by Betty Cothran.*

MAJOR AND MRS. JAMES SABELLA
The Sabella family relocated to Troy in the summer of 2001. Before moving to Troy, Jim had spent 12 months at Osan Air Base, South Korea, while Kim and the kids rented a house in Belleville, and spent the year house-hunting. They moved into the home at 506 Lakewood Drive, surrounded by oak trees and sharing a portion of the lake. They brought with them Figaro, the cat.

Jim and Kim met in 1986, while he was stationed at Tinker Air Force Base in Midwest City, OK, and Kim was a senior at Carl Albert High School. They married December 30, 1988; Jim was commissioned in the AF in 1989, received his pilot wings in 1990, and they've been "flying" ever since. Jim is in his 18th year of his Air Force commitment, flying the C-9 Nightingale. Scott AFB will be the final military assignment, with retirement coming in 2004, hoping to keep Troy as the "retirement" home.

Anthony is in the ever-popular Mrs. Ackerman's final fifth grade class. He plays trumpet, enjoys soccer, reading, fishing and camping. Hannah is in 4th grade with Mrs. Nussbaum. She sings in the school chorus, attends gymnastic class, and aspires to cheer with our awesome Triad cheerleaders in the future. Rachel is 2 1/2, loves to go for walks, play with play-dough, and "talk" on the phone. The street on which they live is busy with kids playing kickball, building snowmen, and having water fights-whatever the season allows.

Kim is a funeral director. The Sabellas attend St. Jerome's Catholic Church, where the kids are altar servers with Father Steven Janoski. *Submitted by the James Sabella family.*

RICHARD W. AND LORNA L. SCHAUBERT
Lorna Lee Schmidt, daughter of Earl and Leola Schmidt of Troy, and Richard W. Schaubert, son of Richard and Emma Schaubert of St. Jacob, IL, were married Aug. 19, 1950, at Friedens E&R Church in Troy.

Lorna was born in Highland, IL, Aug. 7, 1928, and moved to Troy in 1929. She attended grade school and McCray-Dewey High school

Wedding day, August 19, 1950
Richard and Lorna Schaubert

in Troy. After graduation in 1946, she went to modeling school in St. Louis and became a model for the Daryl Dress Co., also of St. Louis, and at the same time was employed as a secretary at the Mercantile Insurance Agency in St. Louis.

Some of Lorna's activities and hobbies over the years include playing the piano, tap dancing, playing French horn in the high school band, roller skating, and singing in the church choir from 1943 until the present.

Richard W. (Bill) was born Apr. 26, 1927, in Granite City, IL, moved to St. Louis, MO, to Summerfield, IL, and then to St. Jacob where he attended grade school and high school. He enlisted in the Army in July, 1944, and went into active duty immediately upon graduation from high school in May 1945. He served in Germany with the 508th Parachute Infantry Regiment, 82nd Airborne Division and was discharged in Nov. 1946. Bill attended SIU at Carbondale, IL, transferring to Washington University in St. Louis and received a B.S. in Civil Engineering in 1953 and an M.S.C.E. in Structures in 1958. He was Vice President of Eason, Thompson & Assoc., Inc., a Consulting Engineering firm in Clayton, MO, until retirement in 1993. During this time he taught at Washington University in the engineering school, evening division, for 31 years. Hobbies include baseball, hunting, fishing and singing in the church choir.

They have three children: a daughter, Nancy Lee Meier, born Jan. 29, 1954, and identical twin sons, Richard Eric (Rick) and William Earl (Bill), born March 2, 1960. Nancy lives in Chicago and is Chief Financial Officer for Hutchinson, Shockey, Erley & Co., a municipal bond broker dealer in Chicago. She has one daughter, Tiffany Lee, who lives in Newport Beach, CA. Rick married Jeanie Cook

Schaubert family
(l. to r.) Richard E., William E., Lorna, Richard "Bill", Nancy

Graves of Troy, and lives in Conroe, TX. They have four children: Michaela Christine and Richard Corey Schaubert and Pamela and Elaina Graves. Rick is a pilot for Continental Airlines and is based in Houston, TX. Bill married Cynthia Eitrem of Sault Ste. Marie, MI, and they live in Fresno, CA. They have one daughter, Loren Paige. Bill is a pilot for Southwest Airlines and is based in Oakland, CA.

Bill and Lorna are members of Friedens United Church of Christ in Troy and reside in the Twin Lakes Subdivision. Both enjoy traveling and spending time with their family. *Submitted by Lorna Schaubert.*

HENRY AND DINA SCHLAEFER - Henry Schlaefer married Dina Reimler in the 1880s. They had four children: Henry Jr., Louis, Hulda and Norman (He died very young from eating the coloring that they mixed in margarine: it was poison.)

Henry and Dina settled on a farm east of Troy which his father Valentine purchased when he came to America from Germany in the 1850s. Also coming to America at that time was a brother Heinrich and a sister Catherine. The ships they came on were the *Haure* and the *Ouinonebaugh.*

Henry Schlaefer Jr. married Dorothy in Michigan and they had one daughter Henrietta.

Louis married Fern Niggli and they had one son, Larry. He later married Mary Bell and they had one son Louis.

Hulda married a Peters and they had one daughter Normajean. She married Emanual Hartmann and they had one daughter Doris.

Henry was born in 1861 and died in 1941. Dina was born in 1878 and died in 1930.

The Schlaefer farm was then taken over by Louis Schlaefer after his father's death and later purchased by Larry and Sharon Schlaefer. They still own the farm. It's located on Schlaefer Road east of Troy. *Submitted by Sharon Schlaefer.*

LARRY AND SHARON SCHLAEFER
Larry Louis Schlaefer was born on Aug. 18, 1936, to Louis Schlaefer and Fern (Niggli) Schaefer. Sharon (McFarland) Schlaefer was born on Aug. 11, 1937, to Gordon McFarland and Sybil (Garland) McFarland. Larry graduated from McCray-Dewey High School in 1954. Sharon graduated in 1955.

Larry and Sharon were married in 1955 and had 4 children: Wayne, Linda, Laurie and Steve.

Wayne was born 11-18-55. He married Barbara Hediger and they have 3 children: Randi, Traci and Barkley. They live on a farm in St. Jacob.

Linda was born 1-13-59. She married Kevin Byrne and they have 2 sons: Shawn and Ryan.

Laurie was born 10-9-61. She has been a teacher in Bethalto for 17 years. She lives in Troy.

Steve was born 11-18-64. He married Dana McCarey and they had 3 sons: Scott, Shane, and Shae. Steve and Stacy, his second wife, have 2 children, Stephen and Samantha. They live in Greenville.

Larry and Sharon moved east of Troy after they were married and purchased the Keck homeplace and had a large dairy farm there for 40 years. They built a new home on the Schlaefer

Schlaefer family, 1994
(l. to r.) Front: Sharon, Larry, Linda.
Back: Laurie, Steve, Wayne

family farm in 1995 and reside there now. It is located on Schlaefer Road.

Larry was a farmer all his life. He and his family milked cows for many years and he also bought and sold dairy cattle. Larry really enjoys his cattle. When he was younger he and his father Louis rode in the horse shows in the area taking ribbons in many events. He also rode with his father in the parades in the area on their beautiful white horses.

Larry served on the Madison County Farm Bureau Board, supported the F.F.A. of Triad High School, and is a member of the Troy Senior Citizens.

Sharon helped on the dairy farm and also drove a school bus for the Triad schools for 25 years. Sharon has played softball for many years and participated in the last four National Senior Olympics. She played at the one in 2001 at Baton Rouge, LA. Sharon is a member of St. Ann's C.C.W, Troy Senior Citizens, Adult Fellowship, quilts at her church and volunteers for the Food Bus.

Larry and Sharon are active members of St. Jerome Catholic Church, Troy. They enjoy watching their grandchildren play sports. They like to travel some. They love family events and getting together.

Larry and Sharon have been married 45 years. In the year 2000 they were chosen as Grand Knight and Lady for the Troy Homecoming. That was a great honor. They love Troy and are happy to be a part of the history of Troy. *Submitted by Sharon Schlaefer.*

LAURIE SCHLAEFER - Laurie Ann Schlaefer was born October 9, 1961, at St. Joseph's Hospital in Highland, Illinois. She is the daughter of Larry and Sharon Schlaefer. Laurie grew up on a dairy farm and enjoyed

Laurie Schlaefer, 1992

working on the farm. She has two brothers and one sister: Steve, Wayne, and Linda. She graduated from Troy Grade School, Triad High School, and Southern Illinois University Edwardsville. She received a Bachelor and Master's degree in education. She has worked as a teacher for 17 years. *Submitted by Laurie Schlaefer.*

LOUIS SCHLAEFER - Louis Schlaefer was born in Troy, IL, on March 13, 1908, to Henry Schlaefer and Dena Reimler Schlaefer. Louis lived on a farm east of Troy all of his life. His grandfather, Valentine Schlaefer, came to America from Germany in 1850 and settled on the farm which is still in the family today. Larry and Sharon Schlaefer now own the farm.

Louis Schlaefer was a very interesting person and a very hard worker. He farmed, milked cows and bought and sold cattle all his life. He truly enjoyed every minute of it.

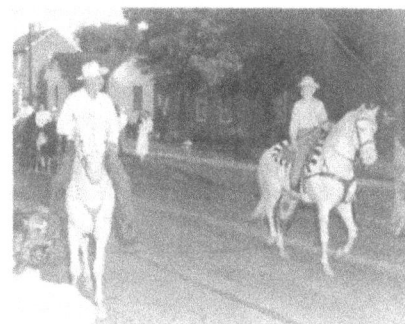
(l. to r.) Louis and Larry Schlaefer, 1948

Years ago, when they farmed with horses and mules, Louie had a pair of mules named Jack and Jerry that he not only farmed with, but were also used to build Old Rt. 40 and dig basements in Troy. During the depression Louie cut props for the coal mine for money to help his Dad pay the taxes.

Louie went to the Troy Lutheran School until the eighth grade. Louie never could read or write too well because when he went to school it was in German not English. He never continued his education because he had to work on the farm.

Louie also loved horses. Throughout his lifetime he had many horses. He and his son Larry competed in many horse shows in the area. They took many ribbons in barrel racing, calf roping and showmanship. For many years they had two white horses that they rode in many parades in this area. They had beautiful saddles and all the accessories for the horses. Folks around here still remember Larry and Louie and their white horses.

Louie married Fern Niggli and they had 1 son, Larry. Louie married Mary Bell and they had 1 son, Louis, Jr. Louie passed away in 1989. *Submitted by Sharon Schlaefer.*

STEVEN SCHLAEFER - Steven Louis Schlaefer was born November 18, 1964, St. Joseph's Hospital, Highland. He is the son of Larry and Sharon Schlaefer. He graduated from Troy Grade School and Triad High School.

He has five children: Scott, Shane, Shae, Samantha, and Stephen.

Steve Schlaefer, 1983

He worked on a dairy farm for many years and now is employed as a driver for a trucking company. *Submitted by Steve Schlaefer.*

WAYNE AND BARBARA SCHLAEFER

Wayne Larry Schlaefer was born in Highland, IL, on Nov. 18, 1955, the son of Larry and Sharon McFarland Schlaefer of St. Jacob. He moved to 10553 Keck Road in 1974.

On Aug. 31, 1979, he married Barbara Hediger who was born Nov 12, 1960, the daughter of Mildred (Bohnenstiehl) Hediger of Highland, IL. They lived in the existing farm house for 4 yrs. and then built a new house. They have 3 children: Randi Lynn was born July 10, 1981. She is a sophomore at S.W.I.C. Traci was born Sept. 5, 1983, and is at Triad High School. Barkley was born May 28, 1985. He is at Triad High School. Wayne and Barbara like to watch their children play sports and travel.

Schlaefer family
(l. to r.) Seated: Barkley, Wayne.
Standing: Randi, Traci, and Barbara.

Wayne is a farmer and a livestock dealer as is his father Larry Schlaefer. Wayne's grandfather, Louis Schlaefer, was also a livestock dealer.

Barbara is the accounting manager at Terra Properties – a real estate/management company in Highland. *Submitted by Wayne Schlaefer.*

SCHMALZ-GIGER FAMILY -

George Schmalz, son of Mamie and Richard Schmalz, married Lucille Hildebrandt in 1937. They had 3 children: Dale (b. Aug. 2, 1939), Helen (b. 1942), and Jon (b. April 16, 1956).

George and Lucille farmed until George's death in 1974. George also served as Jarvis Township Assessor for 24 years. After his death, Lucille was elected to his position and served as assessor from 1974 to 1989.

Their eldest son Dale currently lives in Highland, having retired from Highland High

Schmalz-Giger family, 1990s
(l. to r.) Front: Helen (Schmalz) Buchta, Debbie (Giger) Hardy, Mrs. George (Lucille Hildebrand) Schmalz. Back: Dale Schmalz, Jon Schmalz, Terry Giger, Shirley (Giger) Schmitt.

School after 30 years. He is also co-owner of Terry's Appliance Center.

Helen married Jay Buchta. They are both retired and reside in Glen Carbon. They have 3 children: Bob Abel, Michelle (Abel) Haynes, and Emile (Buchta) Flowers. Michelle married Ken Haynes and has a daughter Madison. Emile married Steve Flowers and also has a daughter Payton. Jon married Debi Oestringer in 1980. They live on and now own the farm, purchased by George Dressel over a century ago. They also own and operate Jon's Appliance Repair. They have 2 daughters, Heather and Kristen.

Fredricka and Fredrick's daughter, Mamie Spies, married Ray Giger in 1940 and had 3 children: Shirley (b. 1951), Debbie (b. 1957), and Terry (b. 1965). Tragically, Mamie died two weeks after Terry's birth. After Mamie's death, George and Lucille raised the three Giger children along with their own, making a family of 8.

Shirley married Dale Schmitt in 1974; they live in Highland. Shirley teaches at St. Jacob Elementary School; Dale is employed by Systems and Electronics Inc. (SCI).They also have 2 children, Amy and Bryan.

Debbie married Edward Hardy in 1982; they live in Towanda, IL. They both work for the Federal Government.

Terry is co-owner of Terry's Appliance Center in Troy and Collinsville and has 1 daughter, Autumn, and lives in Troy. *Submitted by Terry Giger.*

EARL L. SCHMIDT -

Earl L. Schmidt was born August 2, 1899, in Highland, IL, to Fred and Caroline (Britt) Schmidt and was raised on the family farm west of Highland.

Earl and Leola (Meyer) Schmidt, circa 1977

On February 19, 1927, Earl married Leola Meyer (b. April 21, 1903) of St. Jacob, IL, daughter of Hugo and Louise (Adler) Meyer. They moved to Troy on October 1, 1929, at which time Earl and his brother Harold purchased the Newport Soda Co. in Troy from Irwin Hindmarch. They operated it until they sold the business in 1944 to William "Bill" Pitt and started the Troy Frozen Foods. The "locker plant," which it was commonly called, was located at the southeast corner of Main and Center and provided Troy with freezer capabilities and the opportunity to purchase meat in quantity as home freezers were quite rare at that time. The business was sold in November, 1971, to Don and Marilyn Nihiser. A fire destroyed the building in August of 1993, and the Nihisers relocated the plant on Highway 40.

Earl and Harold were also the developers of the Twin Lakes Subdivision, located 1/2 mile east of Troy on Illinois Rt. 162. Earl and Leola lived at 109 Wayland Ave. for many years before moving and building a home in the Twin Lakes Subdivision in 1958.

Earl was a charter member and past president of the Troy Lions Club and also served as a board member of McCray-Dewey High School for some years. Leola was a past president and member for many years of the Troy Women's Club. She was also a member of the Collinsville Business and Professional Women's Club. Both were members of Friedens United Church of Christ and Leola was a member of the Women's Guild.

Earl and Leola had two children, Lorna Lee (b. August 7, 1928) and Lorraine Louise (b. Dec. 22, 1932). Lorna married Richard Wm. Schaubert Aug. 19, 1950; they reside at Twin Lakes in Troy and have three children, Nancy, Richard and William, identical twins. Lorraine is married to James Murray and lives in Tequesta, Florida. She has two daughters, Laurie and Lisa.

Earl and Harold were avid hunters of ducks and geese and were especially fond of pheasant hunting in the Dakotas. Earl passed away Nov. 27, 1980, and Leola on Dec. 10, 1990. They are buried in Friedens Cemetery at Troy. *Submitted by Lorna (Schmidt) Schaubert, daughter of Earl and Leola Schmidt.*

HAROLD A. SCHMIDT -

Harold A. Schmidt was born December 12, 1903, in Marine Township to Fred and Caroline (Britt) Schmidt. When he was around six years of age, his family moved to a farm one mile west of Highland where they were engaged in farming. In 1929 he and his brother, Earl, purchased the Newport Bottling Works in Troy from J. Erwin Hindmarch. Newport Soda was delivered throughout the metro area. In 1931, Harold married Marie Meyer, daughter of Hugo and Louise (Adler) Meyer of St. Jacob. In 1936 they built their red brick residence at 107 Wayland Street which now serves as offices for the St. Jerome Catholic Church. In 1944 Earl and Harold sold the business to William "Bill" Pitt and started Troy Frozen Foods. The "locker plant" which it was commonly called provided Troy with freezer capabilities and the opportunity to purchase meat in quanity as home freezers were quite rare at that time. The business was sold in November 1971,

Harold and Marie Schmidt, 1981

to Don and Marilyn Nihiser. A fire destroyed the building in August of 1993 and the Nihisers, relocated the plant on Highway 40. Harold and Earl were the developers of Twin Lakes subdivision located just east of town on Route 162.

Harold was a Charter member and past president of the Troy Lions Club. Marie was a long time member of the Troy Women's Club, Collinsville Business and Professional Women's Club and a Girl Scout Leader. They were active members of Friedens Evangelical and Reformed Church which later became Friedens United Church of Christ. Harold served as president of the church board, and Marie was an active member of the Women's Guild.

Harold and Marie sold their home on Wayland in 1961 and purchased the Jarvis home from Mrs. Bessie (Jarvis) Keller located at 317 East Center Street. That home was placed on the National Register of Historic Places in 1988. Harold and Marie had three children: Harold who resides in Denver, Mary Ellen who resides in Baltimore, and Carolyn who resides in St. Louis.

Harold passed away September 15, 1989, and Marie on October 12, 1998. They are buried in Frieden's Cemetery in Troy. *Submitted by Carolyn Schmidt Golfin, daughter.*

HAROLD, JR. AND PEGGY SCHMIDT

Harold Andrew Schmidt, Jr., the son of Harold and Marie Schmidt, was born August 22, 1934, in Highland, Illinois. Harold attended Troy Grade School and McCray-Dewey High School.

He has a B.A. in Geology from DePauw University and an M.S. in Geology from the University of Kansas. He married Peggy A. Wasson of Garden City, KS, June 25, 1960. Peggy graduated from the University of Colorado with a B.A. in Psychology.

Harold worked as a petroleum geologist for Chevron Oil Co., Union Texas Petroleum and Exeter Drilling Company in the Rocky Mountain region. Since 1973 he has been a self-employed consulting petroleum geologist/ geophysicist, working on various oil and gas projects throughout the western United States. Peggy is a self-employed medical transcriptionist for several medical clinics in Denver, CO. They make their home at 10 Heather Way, Golden, CO.

Harold and Peggy have three children. Harold Andrew Schmidt III was born March 25, 1964, in Wheat Ridge, CO. Andrew has a B.A. in Political Science with emphasis on Eastern Europe and Russian from the University of Wyoming and an M.S. in Public Administration

from the University of Colorado. He is presently employed as the Director of Public Works for Milliken, CO, and resides in Greeley, CO.

Anne Marie Schmidt was born May 15, 1967, in Casper, WY. Anne is a graduate of Stephens College, Columbia, MO, with a B.A. in Science and Art with emphasis on photography for which she has won awards. After graduation she served two years in the Peace Corps as a teacher in Western Samoa. Anne married Tovio Petelo of Apia, Western Samoa, on September 4, 1994, and they reside in Denver, CO. They have two children, a girl, Mesepa Arabella, born May 30, 1998, and a boy, Depores Oliver Andrew, born May 5, 2001. Anne is a self-employed medical transcriptionist, Tovio is an automotive sales associate for Sears. He also composes, produces and performs his own original music.

Jennie Alison Schmidt was born January 18, 1975, in Wheat Ridge, CO. Alison is a student at Metro State College in Denver, CO majoring in History and Behavioral Science. She has also studied Russian at the University of Colorado and has a Certificate of Achievement from the University in St. Petersburg, Russia. *Submitted by Harold A. Schmidt, Jr.*

LAVERN (MUELLER) AND WILLIAM F. SCHMIDT - LaVern Mueller was born on August 2, 1924, in St. Louis, MO, and moved to Troy in 1932 when she was eight years old. Her parents, Joseph and Lydia (Druessel), sister Lillian, and brothers Gilbert, Russell, and Joseph, Jr., accompanied her. LaVern participated in the Troy Junior Drum and Bugle Corps and performed in Pittsburgh, Pennsylvania. She attended McCray-Dewey High School, but did not graduate as her father became too ill to work, and she had to contribute to the family income. She worked at Adams Dry Goods store in Troy. She later worked as the Assistant Postmistress of Troy, and then married William F. Schmidt in 1945.

William F. (Bill) Schmidt was born on July 14, 1924, in Gillespie, IL, to Martha (Stunkel) and Louis H. Schmidt. The family eventually moved to a small farm on Poag Road, Edwardsville.

Bill met Troy girl LaVern Mueller at a dance at Lindendale Park in Highland. Dates in the 1940s consisted mostly of going dancing, to the movies, or roller skating at Moonlight Roller Rink. The romance was interrupted by Bill being drafted into the U.S. Infantry. A Corporal Technician, Bill was sent to Africa as a tank corpsman because he could drive a tractor! From Tunisia in Africa he was sent to Salerno and then to Casino, Italy, where he was wounded by a sniper. After recuperation he was sent back into battle where he was hit by a shrapnel shell and received 15 entry wounds. After another recuperation he was sent to Anzio where he was eventually hit by four bullets, which fractured an arm and a leg, putting him permanently out of the fighting. He was awarded three Purple Hearts and a Bronze Star.

Bill's three brothers were also in the Army and actually met each other in both Africa and Italy. A total of 16 of his family members served in the war. Some were injured, some became POWs, but all survived to come home.

50th Wedding Anniversary, 1995
Bill and LaVern "Buzzy" Schmidt

Sent back to a base at Columbus, GA, in 1945, Bill promptly notified LaVern back in Troy who got on a train to Georgia to get married. After a couple of hours of travel, LaVern found she was on the wrong train.

The couple settled in Troy after Bill's discharge from the Army. Bill worked for Moderne Linen as a route supervisor and LaVern began raising the family, consisting of daughters Connie and Suzanne, and sons William F., Jr., and Jeffrey. In 1947, Bill and LaVern opened "Smitty's Confectionary" in the Brookside Dairy Building at 717 South Main. William was elected Alderman of Troy, and ran for Mayor, but was defeated by Oscar Gindler. At age 34, LaVern returned to Troy High School and attended classes fulltime and completed her junior year and most of her senior year. Finishing at Edwardsville High School, she earned her diploma at age 35.

The Schmidt Family moved to Edwardsville in 1961. LaVern worked at Edwardsville High School, and William worked for Dow Chemical and Consolidated Aluminum. William and LaVern are retired and currently live in Edwardsville. Connie lives in Pentwater, MI; William F., Jr., lives in Seattle, WA; and Suzanne and Jeffrey live in Edwardsville. *Submitted by Jeff Schmidt.*

EDWARD SCHMISSEUR - Edward A.

Schmisseur was born March 29, 1874, to Eugene and Elizabeth (Beatrie) Schmisseur on a farm in Belleville, IL. Angeline Melgrani was born on June 26,1877, in Centreville Station, IL. Edward and Angeline were married on November 28, 1912, at the Immaculate Conception Catholic Church in Centreville Station.

Edward was a rural mail carrier and Angeline was the postmistress for Centreville Station. At that time the mail was delivered by the mail carrier in a horse and buggy.

Edward A. & Angeline (Melgrani) Schmisseur, circa 1940

They were the parents of two children, Wilson Edward (b. August 29, 1913) and Catherine May (b. May 19, 1918). Edward also maintained rental houses in Centreville. After his retirement around 1936 from the postal service, Edward, Angeline, and daughter Kay traveled the U.S. in an Airstream trailer. They traveled for two years visiting all 48 states. In the mid-1950s Ed and Angeline moved to Troy to be closer to their son Wilson and daughter Kay Riebold, who both lived in rural Troy, They lived in a house on Main Street next door to Claudine Riebold, Kay's mother-in-law. Edward and Angeline attended St. Jerome's Catholic Church at that time. Angeline and Claudine often went to daily mass together. Edward died on November 16, 1957, and Angeline died on October 2, 1964. They are both buried in the St. John the Baptist Catholic Cemetery in Blackjack. *Submitted by Mark and Chris Riebold.*

WILSON SCHMISSEUR - Wilson "Sam" was born on August 29, 1913, to Edward and Angeine (Melgrani) Schmisseur of Centreville Station, IL. He had one sister, Catherine May, who was born on May 19, 1918. He married Evelyn W. Whetstone on August 21, 1938. Evelyn was born on June 13, 1918, to Harry and Lillian (Westmorland) Whetstone. Evelyn had one sister, Neva. Wilson and Evelyn were the parents of one daughter, Sandra K. Schmisseur Binder of Mexico, MO, and three sons, Wilson Edward "Ed" of Corvallis, OR; Thomas Craig of Collinsville, IL; and Richard Dean who is deceased. Richard died on November 16, 1960 at the age of sixteen years. Wilson and Evelyn moved to a farm south of Troy, located on Troy-O'Fallon Road several years after their marriage. Wilson owned and operated a dairy farm while also working for the Mobil Oil Corporation. During the Great Depression in the early 1930's, Wilson traveled west to work on the construction of the Hoover Dam. He had many colorful stories of this time period. He and his friend "rode the rails" to return to Illinois and told stories of the hobo camps they encountered along the way.

Evelyn and Wilson Schmisseur, 1950s

Evelyn was a 50-year member of the Women's Club of Troy, past president of the I.L.G.F.W.C. She was a LPN and worked as an assistant for Dr. H.H. Hurd. Evelyn also worked ten years for Watson Lumber. Evelyn was a charter member of the group instrumental in forming the first library on Market Street in Troy.

Wilson was a member of St. Jerome's Catholic Church and Evelyn was a member of the Troy Christian Church. Evelyn died on

December 2, 1998, and Wilson died one month later on January 9, 1999. They are both buried in St. John the Baptist Catholic Cemetery in Blackjack. *Submitted by Chris Riebold.*

SCHMITT FAMILY

Wedding photo, May 8, 1912
(l. to r.) Front: Lori Schaefer, Anna (Schaefer) Schmitt. Back: Val Schmitt, Joseph Schmitt.

ADAM SCHMITT

Grandma and Grandpa Schmitt and family, 1910
(l. to r.) Front: Adam, Appolonia (Eberle) Schmitt. Back: John, Mame, Elizabeth, Rose, Val, Julia, Joe.

B.J. (NOBBY) AND BETTY SCHMITT

Nobby was born on September 19, 1923, in Troy to William S. and Louise (Langenwalter) Schmitt. His grandparents were Sam and Rosa (Meyer) Schmitt and Jacob and Barbara (Kirsch) Langenwalter. He has a sister Ruth Geraldine and brother Jack Lee Schmitt.

Schmitt family, 2000
(l. to r.) Front: Susan (Schmitt) Martz, Nobby, Betty. Back: Steve.

Betty was born on August 1, 1923, in Highland to Othmar and Minnie (Meyer) Raeber. Betty and Nobby were married in Odessa, Texas, on August 7, 1943, while he was serving in the U.S. Air Corps. Nobby became the Chevrolet dealer in Troy upon the retirement of his father. In 1948 their son, Steve, was born.

In 1961 Chevrolet Motor Division closed the Troy dealership, and Nobby became the Chevrolet, Buick, and Oldsmobile dealer in Greenville, IL. Nobby, Betty, and Steve moved from Troy to Greenville. While there a daughter, Susan, was born on August 6, 1962. Steve presently owns the dealership which he purchased in 1980. Nobby and Betty have lived in Highland since 1988. *Submitted by Betty Schmitt.*

CORNELIUS A. SCHMITT - Cornelius "Cornie" A. Schmitt was born September 19, 1907, the only child of John and Anna (Riebold) Schmitt.

Cornelius A. Schmitt, 1948

Never married, he lived at the home of his uncle, John Riebold and worked as a hired hand. Later he lived and worked on the farm for his cousin, Oscar Mersinger.

He was employed by Jarvis Township Road District and could be seen in his truck working on the roads. For a time he worked for the county highway department. He always signed his name C.A. Schmitt.

A large framed man, he tipped the scales at nearly 400 pounds and was six feet or more tall. He liked to bowl in his spare time and was a member of several leagues. When asked where he was going on bowling night, he would answer, "New York." He was also very light on his feet and was a good dancer.

His birthday was a big deal for him and he was known to celebrate it every year with his buddies. Oscar Niehaus, Melvin Niehaus and other friends would join him in celebrating.

He had a cartooning talent and would draw pictures when "baby sitting" for Oscar's daughter, Mae. He enjoyed reading western mysteries and accumulated hundreds of books while living at his cousin Oscar's house. He also enjoyed listening to the radio and "The Lone Ranger."

In 1949, he went to live with a friend, Pete Pelligrini, after Pete's wife was killed in a tragic auto accident. He helped Pete milk the cows and also continued working on the roads.

In his retirement years, he lived in the cottages at Moonlight Roller Rink. It was there that he died July 7, 1982. He is buried in St.

John the Baptist Catholic Cemetery, Blackjack. *Submitted by Mae Grapperhaus*

JACK LEE SCHMITT - Jack Lee Schmitt was born June 16, 1937, to William Samuel and Louise (Langenwalter) Schmitt of Troy. Jack lived in Troy with his parents and two older siblings, B.J. "Nobby" and Ruth Geraldine. He graduated from McCray-Dewey High School in 1955. Jack began developing his interest in the automobile business as he grew up. Not a surprise, considering his father was an automobile dealer and his older brother, Nobby, and brother-in-law, Jack Weir, were already in the business.

Jack married Evelyn Louise Niebruegge on Sept. 9, 1961. Evelyn was born Feb. 5, 1939, to August H. and Enda C. Sudhoff Niebruegge of Troy.

Jack and Evelyn moved to Nokomis, IL, for two years. They then moved to Red Bud, IL, in 1963 until 1967, when they relocated in Jacksonville, IL. Their last move was to Belleville, IL, in 1975, where they currently reside.

Jack and Evelyn have two children: Kathy Marie (b. Sept. 27, 1966), and John William (b. Sept. 11, 1968). Kathy is married to Robert Federico, who has two children, Tony and Danielle. John is married to Dawn Eyman, and both couples live in the Belleville area. *Submitted by Kae Elliott Schmitt and Jack Lee Schmitt.*

JOHN J. SCHMITT AND CORNELIUS A. SCHMITT - John J. Schmitt was born on February 13, 1879. He married Anna Riebold of Blackjack. Anna was born on July 27, 1883, to Jacob and Anna Mary (Kraher) Riebold on the Riebold farm. After John and Anna married, they lived with her father Jacob and brother John. Anna's mother was deceased, and she took over taking care of the household.

Corney Schmitt and his dog, 1912

John and Anna were parents of one son, Cornelius "Corney" A. Schmitt. He was born on September 19, 1907. John and Anna moved from the Riebold farm to a home on Lebanon Road after the marriage of her brother John to Claudine Hilby in 1914. John and Claudine continued to live with his father Jacob on the Riebold farm. Anna died during the influenza epidemic on December 24, 1918.

It was very difficult for Corney, who was only 11 years old, to lose his mother at Christmas. John J. Schmitt died July 8, 1949. Corney spent much of his childhood and young adulthood on the Riebold farm. He worked as a

farm hand and later worked on the State Highway Department. Corney never married and later lived in Troy. He held a special place in the Riebold family. Corney died on July 7, 1982. He is buried next to his parents in St. John the Baptist Catholic Cemetery in Blackjack. *Submitted by Mark and Chris Riebold.*

STEVEN SAMUEL SCHMITT, SR. - Steven Samuel Schmitt, Sr. was born May 9, 1948, in St. Louis, MO. He was the first child of Billy Junior (Nobby) and Betty (Raeber) Schmitt of Troy. Until he was five years old, Steve and his parents lived in Troy; then the family moved to Highland (home of his mother) for one year. They returned to Troy and lived there until Steve was 13. His family moved to Greenville, IL, in the summer of 1961 where his parents began Nobby Schmitt Motor Company.

Schmitt family, 2000
(l. to r.) Front: Sara Marie, Kae, Steven S., Jr. Back: Steve.

Steve graduated from Greenville High School in 1966. He earned a Business degree from Western Illinois University in 1970. He married Kae Ann Elliott (from Troy) on June 11, 1971. She is the daughter of Roy Daniel and Gloria (Hensley) Elliott of Troy.

Kae grew up in Troy and graduated from Triad High School in 1968. She attended William Woods University, in Fulton, MO, for two years. She then transferred to Southern Illinois University at Edwardsville, where she graduated with a degree in Special Education and Elementary Education.

Steve and Kae lived in Greenville from 1971 to 1985. During this time Steve became the automobile dealer at Nobby Schmitt Motor Company. Their two children, Sara Marie (September 25, 1975) and Steven Samuel, Jr. (June 17, 1978), were born in Greenville. The family moved to Highland in June of 1985, after purchasing Genteman Chevrolet, now Steve Schmitt, Inc.

Sara graduated from Highland High School in 1993. She earned a Bachelors Degree in psychology and history from Indiana University in 1997. She earned her Masters in social work from Saint Louis University in 2000.

Steven, Jr. graduated from Highland High School in 1996. He earned a Bachelors Degree in psychology and business from Indiana University in 2001. Steven has continued the family involvement in the car business. He is the fourth generation to be a part of the "Schmitt" automobile business. *Submitted by Kae Elliott Schmitt.*

WILLIAM S. AND LOUISE (LANGEN-WALTER) SCHMITT - William Samuel Schmitt was born on July 23, 1892, to Samuel and Rosa (Meyer) Schmitt. His siblings were Anna (Schmitt) Gornet, Ottillia (Schmitt) Davidson, John W. Schmitt, Henrietta (Schmitt) Liebler, Edna (Schmitt) Schoon, and Vernetta (Schmitt) Young.

Schmitt family, 1949-50
(l. to r.) Front: Grandma Louise, Jack, Grandpa Wm. Holding Steve. Middle: Judy and Joy Weir. Back: Gerry and Jack Weir, Nobby (B.J.) and Betty Schmitt.

Louise (Langenwalter) Schmitt was born on November 18, 1894, to Jacob and Barbara (Kirsch) Langenwalter. Her siblings were Arnold Langenwalter, Dora (Langenwalter) Matthews, Hulda (Langenwalter) Liebler Seets, Helen (Langenwalter) Renfro, and Bertha (Langenwalter) Kramer.

William and Louise had three children: B.J. (Nobby) Schmitt, Ruth Geraldine (Gerry) Weir Stevenson, and Jack Lee Schmitt.

William was the Chevrolet dealer in Troy from 1929 through 1959. William and Louise were both active members of Friedens E & R Church and other civic organizations. William passed away on November 25, 1967, and Louise on July 29, 1978. *Submitted by Betty R. Schmitt.*

CATHERINE ANN (MERSINGER) SCHMOLL - Catherine Ann (Mersinger) Schmoll was born on December 26, 1952. She was the daughter of Adrian Phillip Mersinger and Gertrude Elizabeth (Loyet) Mersinger. Cathy lived on a farm south of Troy. She had an older brother, Donald Oscar, and sister, Geraldine Mary, and a younger brother, Joseph Michael.

Catherine was best known as Cathy to everyone. One of her family's close friends remembers holding Cathy as a young child and saying, "This child has trouble breathing." Though she was never physically strong because of her lung condition, she enjoyed being outdoors. She enjoyed playing short games of

Gertrude and Adrian Mersinger kids, circa 1990
(l. to r.) Joe, Cathy, Gerry, Don

tennis during high school and college, and she played the clarinet in high school.

Cathy and her family moved to Tucson, AZ, in 1960 for three years to see if the drier climate would help improve her health. There she attended St. Peter and Paul's parochial school. What to wear to school was never a problem because the school required uniforms.

She finished school back in Troy where she attended McCray-Dewey Junior High School and Triad High School. She wanted to become a teacher in the sciences, so she attended Southern Illinois University at Edwardsville.

Her first teaching job was back in Tucson, AZ, but she missed her family very much. So she returned to Illinois and taught near Redbud, IL. What she wanted most of all was to be teaching in her school district. She was hired to teach middle school at Molden School.

In 1993 she met Robert Schmoll at a Valentine dance. They continued dating and married on June 11, 1994. When she married Robert, she gained two stepchildren: Jeremy and Michelle. The following year Cathy and Robert built a home outside of Baldwin.

Cathy stopped teaching in Troy in the spring of 1999 because her health was worsening. After being hospitalized numerous times for pneumonia and lung infections, her doctor said he would not release her from the hospital until she resigned from her teaching job. She resigned. It broke her heart to stop working, but she searched for other interests. She became involved in the Lutheran Church where she wrote cards and letters to the shut-ins in Baldwin. She also flew to Colorado in the summer of 1999 and 2000 to visit her sister Gerry. At this time Cathy was using oxygen more and more. Her health was declining rapidly.

Cathy died on April 10, 2001, at St. Elizabeth's Hospital in Belleville, IL. *Submitted by Geraldine Mersinger.*

J. FREDERICK AND ANNA SCHRAMECK

Fred Schrameck was born in Troy, IL, to his parents Charles and Barbara (Ruff) Schrameck, on October 6, 1896. He had one brother, Francis (Frank), and one sister, MaryAnn (Mayme). Mayme married Carl Davis of Troy and they had three children: James, Jerome, and Dorothea. Frank married Loretta Daly of Collinsville, IL. They had one son, Francis Michael.

Schrameck family, 1940
(l. to r.) Front: Gladys Marie, Imelda Catherine, Barbara Claire, Ann Teresa. Back: Eugene C., J. Fred, Anna (Feeney), Virginia Marie.

Fred Schrameck was called to serve his country as a young man in the Army during World War I — 1914-1918. He served as a PVT. 1st Class overseas until the war ended. Fred had met Anna Feeney of Collinsville, IL, before leaving for overseas and they corresponded during the war. When WWI ended and the soldiers returned home to the states, Fred asked for Anna's hand in marriage. She and Fred were married 10-20-1920 at SS Peter & Paul Catholic Church in Collinsville. To the couple were born six children: Eugene Charles, Virginia Marie, Ann Teresa, Barbara Claire, Imelda Catherine, and Gladys Marie.

Fred attended school in Troy through the eighth grade, then went to work at Troy's main industry, Troy Domestic Mining Co. located in the west end of town. His dad Charles was already employed there and also his brother. Fred became Mine Superintendent serving at that job for 20 years or more until the mine closed. He then became a mine inspector for the State of Illinois, and worked at area mines in Collinsville, O'Fallon and Livingston. Fred was well-known by the nickname "Bryan and Brynie" by his co-workers and served as Secretary-Treasurer of Troy's Labor Union #382, served as a Troy Alderman of Ward Two for three terms. During the growth of Troy after World War II, Fred joined the battle to get sewers installed to replace septic tanks in new Troy subdivisions being built, as well as all over town. This was very controversial as many citizens and home owners did not want progress.

Fred served on the Troy Elementary School Board of Education for twelve years. He also was a steady volunteer at St. Jerome as the priest Father Hobbs called on Fred to help "next door" with many projects through the years.

Anna and Fred bought a home at 103 Wayland Street in Troy and lived there (raising their six children until marriage) for their entire lifetime. Eugene served in World War II with the Army in Europe and returned home to Troy after the war ended.

Fred and Anna's children all married. Eugene married Arvella Roy of St. Louis and their children were William, Janet, Kay, Paul, Susan. Virginia married James Crites of St. Louis.

Ann Teresa married John Thomas Taylor of Troy, IL, and they had five children: Patricia Ann, Kathleen, Jo Ann, Nancy and James Arthur. Ann later married Francis Florek. Barbara married William Lowery of Edwardsville, IL, and their children were Michael and Cynthia. Imelda (Cathy) married Rudolph Rivas of Whittier, CA, and their children were Theresa and Ricardo. Gladys married Robert Long of Edwardsville, IL. Their children were Linda and Anne.

Fred and Anna have 24 great-grand-children, some of whom still live in Troy. However, their home no longer exists in Troy as it was sold to St. Jerome's Church and was torn down to make room for a parking lot for church.

Fred and Anna were also active members of American Legion Post #708 and World War I Barracks #286 in Troy, serving as officers of the Legion and Auxiliary for many years. They and many other members worked hard and steady to raise the money to build and pay for the present American Legion Building in Troy by having fund raisers such as Friday fish fries. *Submitted by Ann T. Florek.*

JOHN AND HELEN SCHULTZE - John, youngest son of Charles and Mary (Fisher) Schultze, was born in Troy 3-30-1907. He married Helen Schroeppel of Collinsville on 11-28-1928. John worked for railroads most of his life – Mo. Pacific, NYC and IC. They lived most of their lives in Troy. John died 7-28-1981; Helen, 12-18-1986.

John and Helen Schultze family, 1954
(l. to r.) Front: Patricia, Joe, Mary. Middle: Lois, Jean, Helen, John Sr. Back: Paul, Jim, John.

They had 9 children: Jean, born 8-26-1930, married Bill Kebbel of Collinsville 6-24-1950, divorced after 17 years. They had 3 children: Gary, Alexandria, VA; Dennis (Sherry) has 3 children, Winter Park, FL; Karen Bieda, 1 child, St. Louis. Jean married Joe Wallace 2-14-1976 and lives in Granite City.

Lois, born 5-7-1932, married Oliver Hughes of Collinsville on 6-27-1953. Oliver will be remembered as having the first TV repair business in Troy. They have 4 children and live in Lenexa, KS: Donna (Paul Boenisch), 2 children, Columbia, MO; Dr. Mark (Kris), 4 children, Peoria, AZ; Neil (Glennis), Loveland, CO; Gregory (Kaye), Acworth, GA.

John Jr., born 12-4-1933, served 4 years in the Navy. He married Betty Seymore of Troy on 11-7-1959. John was in the printing business for many years before going back to school to become a mortician. They live in Ashley, IL, where he has the funeral home. They have 4 children: Todd (Julie), 3 children, Centralia; Ross (Stacie), 2 children, Ashley; Wendy Kachuba, 4 children, Ashley; Holly (Shawn Dinkelman), Ely, IA.

James, born 6-12-1938, married Rosemary Knecht of Troy on 3-16-1963. Jim served 4 years in the Air Force. He has a Consulting Appraisal Management business, serves as an expert witness, and a closed corporation expert. They live in Staunton, have 2 children – James Andrew "Andy" (Jennifer), Troy, and Jessica, Edwardsville,

Paul, born 4-11-1940, married Vera Bock of Godfrey on 5-18-1963. After many years as a theater manager and vice president of Wehrenberg Theaters, he is now employed in Guest Services at Alton Belle Casino. They live in Godfrey and have 3 children: Shane (Lisa), 2 children, Alton; Tammy (Gary Neese Jr.), 2 children, Godfrey; Shawn (Kristy), 3 children, Cottage Hills, IL.

Mary, born 10-25-1943, married Charles Loyet of Troy on 9-1-1962. Mary has been a legal secretary for many years. They live in Carrollton, IL, and have 2 children – Lisa (Bryan Oliver), 2 children, St. Louis; Jeff, 1 son, Carrollton.

Patricia, born 9-21-1946, married Donald Take 3-13-1965, lived in Troy and Glen Carbon, divorced after 12 years. Pat was a postal employee. They had 2 sons: Randy (Cheryl), 2 children, Downers Grove, IL; Duane (Patti Meyers from Troy), expecting a baby in June, Alhambra. Pat married Aaron Hinton of Glen Carbon on 5-28-1977. Aaron had 3 children – Karen (Mark Beasley), Glen Carbon, 2 children, Mark has 3; Kevin (Terri), 1 child, Pana; Karla (Dee Bullock), Alta Loma, CA; Aaron died 11-11-1996.

Richard, born 9-6-1948, died several hours after birth.

Joseph, born 3-5-1950, married Karen Prott of Marine on 5-16-1970. They live in St. Jacob, and have1 child, Tiffany (engaged to Victor Duncan), Marine. Joe is in Federal Building Security.

The family members say they will always remember the time in their lives growing up and living in Troy. *Submitted by Lois Schultze Hughes*

AUGUST F. SCHURMAN - August Schurman, orphaned at the age of three, was raised by the August Brockmeier family on the "bluffs" along Illinois State Route 157, south and west of Edwardsville. August married Emma Wickert of Marion, Illinois in 1905 and farmed in the "bluffs" area. In 1913 August and Emma purchased approximately 120 acres for $17,500 from Enly F. Tilley, granddaughter of Samuel Wood. Wood had homesteaded the farm from the U.S. Government in 1850. Enly Tilley was the mother of William Tilley, who lived in a house atop a hill (now excavated) on the current site of the Troy Center.

The 120 acre Schurman farm ground was bordered (roughly) by Illinois Route 162, Riggin Road on the east and extended north to the John Meier farm and west to the Ben Zenk farm. The home place is on Zenk Road and is easily recognizable by the large gambrel-roofed barn with red siding. Emma and August had six children: Leonard, Esther, Edgar, Helen, Hilbert and Wilma. Leonard married Eula Hart and had three children; current Troy resident Marian

This picture of Emma and August Schurman was taken about 1940 on their farm on Zenk Road during the last summer they lived there.

Lewis is their oldest. Esther married Arthur Guttersohn and moved to Collinsville. Edgar moved to California in the early 1930s, married and made his home there. His son Lee Schurman and grandson Clay Schurman are the family namesakes and also make their home on the West Coast. Helen married Clifford Michael and moved to Highland, Hilbert married Elva Bruechaud and they live in Greenville. Wilma married A. Thomas Edwards and still resides in Troy. Their daughter Linda and son-in-law William Ingersoll likewise live in Troy. A total of 10 grandchildren, 21 great-grandchildren and great-great grandchildren were able to trace their roots to Emma and August Schurman.

The Schurmans retired from farming in 1940, moved to South Dewey Street in Troy, and turned the operation of their farm over to their eldest son Leonard. August passed away in 1950 and following Emma's death in 1971, the 27 acres on the north side of Zenk Road were sold to James Laughlin and Herbert Lochmann. The remaining acreage was later sold to Harvey Schultz who developed the land into residential and commercial property. The Schurman gravesites are in Troy's Friedens Cemetery.

Emma lost her wedding band after she placed the ring in her apron pocket while milking. Some 30 to 40 years later Leonard found the shiny ring in the barnyard.

August used two teams of mules to perform the "horse power" for farming implements; the teams were named Jule and Kate and Sally and Jack. Wilma can recall chicken thieves striking the hen houses during the night. During the early '30s gypsies camped west of the farm in the area of the Langwisch and Zenk farms, causing concern for the Troy merchants as they were noted for stealing (they also stole Wilma's doll, Annie). Wheat harvest was done using wagons to bring the sheaves from the fields to the steam powered threshing machine which was moved from farm to farm in the threshing circuit. The farmers in the circuit helped each other with the harvest; the women provided a morning and afternoon lunch which was carried to the threshing site usually in the wash basket. At noon a hearty dinner was served to the workmen. *Submitted by Wilma (Schurman) Edwards.*

JOSEPH SCHWEND - In 1851 a terrible cholera epidemic was in progress in St. Louis, MO. Ferderich Dennler arrived with 10 of his 13 children. His wife Katharina Brugger had died at sea and was buried there. Three of the children died of cholera and were buried in a mass grave with other victims. Mary, the oldest girl, had met Joseph Schwend, a.k.a. Anton Schwendemann. They decided to marry in St. Louis and take her youngest brother, John Ulrich (3yrs.), and youngest sister, Rosina (7 yrs.), with them to Blackjack, IL, where they became farmers. In Blackjack they remained 12 years then moved to Saline Township near Highland, IL. Joseph died in 1878. Mary married two more times, first to Conrad Eisenberg and then to Carl Meier.

Joseph and Mary's children were all born in Blackjack, except for Conrad and Charles being born at Highland. Marie Annie, the oldest, married Sebastian Joseph Bugger, had 11 children, and they lived their entire lives in

Blackjack. (See John Adam Bugger Story). Joseph Adam, the next child, married Veronica Geiser and they moved to Dowell, IL, but later moved back to Highland.

After Veronica died, Joseph married Stephana Tholmann. They later divorced and he married his widowed sister-in-law Sophia Billeter Schwend. He fathered 12 children. Katherine, the third child, married Michael Petry. In the early 1880s they moved to the Dowell area. They had 11 children. Barbara, the fourth child, was a twin. She married John J. Mersinger. They moved to Dowell briefly but returned to Blackjack, and raised 9 children. Caroline, the other twin, married Michael Endres. They also moved to Dowell to spend their entire married life. They had 7 children. Conrad the sixth child was born in Highland. He married Sophia Billeter. Conrad died in a wagon-train accident and left 5 children. Charles the youngest was also born at Highland. He and Louisa Gilgen married and had 8 children.

A Schwend/Dennler Reunion is held yearly in Highland. *Submitted by Whitney Papproth Wisnasky*

DONALD SCOTT - Donald Scott is the son of Laverne (Porter) and Donald Scott. His mother was the daughter of Roland and Ella Porter.

40th Wedding Anniversary, 1998 Don and Pat Scott

Donald had a sister, Paula. Donald attended Troy Grade School in Troy, then moved to Japan with his mother and sister where his father was stationed. Don went to school in Tokyo, Japan, for several years then returned to the USA where Don graduated from Colorado Springs High School in Colorado Springs, CO. He married Pat on April 4, 1958, in Colorado Springs. She was a sister of a friend of Don's and they went to the same high school together. They now reside in Texas. *Submitted by Mae Grapperhaus.*

MICHAEL AND CONNIE (MERSINGER) SEDLACEK - Connie Mersinger grew up on her parents' (Ted and Helen Mersinger) farm south of Troy. One of her daily chores was feeding and watering the 1000 caged chickens as well as gathering, candling, and sorting eggs. Riding the family ponies was one of the fun things to do. She was a member of the Merry Makers 4-H Club and developed her sewing interest.

Connie participated in sports as a cheerleader starting in the 8th grade and continued through her senior year of high school. Connie met Michael R. Sedlacek of Marine in

Michael and Connie (Mersinger) Sedlacek, 1994

1965 – her freshman year at Triad. Mike was an avid hunter, trapper, and fisherman. He had played basketball in grade school in Marine and he was eager to play football when it was introduced into the sports program his freshman year at Triad. He also participated in track.

They were high school sweethearts. They were not only selected "Most Friendly" by their classmates, but Connie was crowned Homecoming Queen and Mike was her escort their senior year in 1969. On April 24, 1971, they were wed.

Since 1978, they have resided in rural Collinsville, just southwest of Troy. After working briefly at General American Life, Connie began her career with the Government in 1969 in St. Louis. She was a secretary with Farmers Home Administration (USDA), worked 1.5 years with the General Accounting Office (1975-1976), and returned to FmHA. After returning to school, she became a computer specialist in 1991. Since 1995, she has been working for Rural Development.

Mike has worked from 1977 to the present at Monsanto Chemical Company – now Solutia, in Sauget, IL.

Connie and Mike's family has always included at least one dog, starting with three Dobermans, then a Weimaraner, and now a Vizsla.

Connie and Mike enjoy bicycling, boating, diving, fishing and other water activities, as well as nature and wildlife. They have plans to retire on Norfolk Lake near Mountain Home, AR. *Submitted by Connie Sedlacek and Sharon Petty.*

CHARMION NEMNICH SEMANISIN Charmion Nemnich of Troy and Andy Semanisin of Maryville became engaged when she was 21, right before Andy was drafted into the Army, as was her only brother, 18-year-old Joseph Nemnich, Jr. Both served in the South Pacific. Charmion and Andy were married after the war in 1947.

Charmion's parents were Joseph Nemnich, Sr., born in Marine, IL, in 1896, and Frances (Hultz) Nemnich, born in Troy in 1901. They married in 1919.

Andrew's parents were John Semanisin, a coal miner from Maryville, who was born in Czechoslovakia, and Susan Bacha, who was born in Austria. Both had emigrated to this county in the early 1900s and met in this area. Andy had 3 brothers and a sister who died in childhood.

Andy and Charmion bought the house where Charmion still lives on W. Center Street

in 1949, and where they raised their two sons, Robert (b. 1948) and David (b. 1952). Robert married Marsha Clenney, and they have 2 daughters, Susan and Mary Ann. David married Barbara Boyce; they had a son, Daniel. Later he married Lisa Curtis. They have 2 children, Thomas and Leslie.

Charmion has wonderful memories of her school days in Troy, graduating from the 8th grade between 2 future doctors. James G. Adams, Validictorian, became one of Troy's beloved M.D.s. Charmion was salutatorian and 3rd highest was Charles Arthur Molden, later a doctor, too.

After graduation, Charmion worked at Pete Levo's Bakery, Hosto's Linen Service, Kelly's Kroger Store, Watson Lumber Company, in the city's water department, and as city clerk. She retired from being the City Clerk in 1982.

She was active in Jarvis Township Senior Citizens and Friedens Church, where she was President of the Women's Guild. Andy worked at the Granite City Army Depot for many years. He belonged to the American Legion and St. Jerome's Church, where he was active in the K. of C. Andy died in July 1999. Charmion loves to reminisce about Troy's good ole days and enjoys her family and many friends and activities. *Submitted by Charmion Semanisin.*

G.A. AND MILLIE SHAFFER - George Allen Shaffer was the 8th child of James P. and Maud Jackson Shaffer. Born in Troy on 12/23/20, he graduated from the Troy Grade School and McCray-Dewey High School. In 1940 the Shaffer family moved to St. Louis to find better employment for Allen and an older brother, Jim. Allen went into the Ploeser-Watts Insurance Agency as an office boy, learning the business he was later to have as a lifetime career. On New Year's Day, 1943, he received his notice to be a member of the U.S. Army Air Force, reporting to Jefferson Barracks a few days later for induction.

Millie Marie Collins also graduated from the Troy Grade school, McCray-Dewey High School, and Miss Hickey's Training School for Secretaries in St. Louis. Upon graduation, she was employed by the Commercial Dept. of AT&T as a secretary and teletype trainer.

On June 18, 1944, Allen, as he was generally called, and Millie were married in the Troy Presbyterian Church where they had grown up together. They returned to New Hampshire where Allen was stationed. He was later transferred to San Francisco, CA, where she joined him until his discharge in March 1946.

Millie and George A. Shaffer, 1975

Upon returning to the area, Allen returned to the insurance business in St. Louis and Millie, to Southwestern Bell there.

Mr. John E. Hindmarch, a local Troy insurance agent with a long established business, became ill; and the opportunity arose for the Shaffers to purchase his accounts, so the G.A. Shaffer Agency was born in Sept. 1947. It was the only insurance business with a SIGN! (A couple of other agents were selling insurance but did not have offices, as such.)

In 1950 Allen took the Illinois Real Estate exam and became Troy's first licensed Real Estate Broker. The office was at 213 S. Main St. The building was remodeled into their office and residence until 1962 when they moved into a separate residence. In 1963 the Agency rented quarters in the United Savings & Loan's new building at 120 W. Market St. Allen was the managing officer of the United Savings Loan Assn. which had evolved from the merging of the Home Bldg. & Loan and Keystone Bldg & Loan Associations in the mid-'50s.

The United Savings & Loan was in the process of merging with Granite City's Madison County Federal S & L when Allen suffered a stroke from a brain aneurism; and surgery left him an invalid. Millie continued the business to complete the merger in 1979 and then sold the G.A. Shaffer Agency to Madison County Federal in 1984 to retire. After 37 plus years, the sign went down.

The Shaffers were very active in the community of Troy, serving as officers of the Troy Lions Club, The Women's Club of Troy, the Troy Presbyterian Church and were ready volunteers in community projects. Allen belonged to the American Legion and the IOOF. Millie continues to be a volunteer at Anderson Hospital on a weekly basis. *Submitted by Millie Collins Shaffer.*

GEORGE AND MARY SHAFFER - George Shaffer was the son of David and Martha (Posey) Shaffer. Martha was the daughter of Jubilee Posey, an early settler of the Pin Oak Township area. George married Mary Blakeman, foster daughter of Dr. and Mrs. Angeline McCray Dewey, who bequeathed their property for the education of youth and for whom the old high school was named.

George was a farmer for many years on the north side of Pin Oak Road and east of Staunton Road. He and Mary had five sons and three daughters: James, Roy, David, Gordon, Stanley, Nona, Catherine, and Edna (died in infancy).

James stayed in the Troy area and married Bessie Maud Jackson of Carlyle and was a topside engineer at the Donk Bros. Coal Mine in Troy. They had nine children. All graduated from McCray-Dewey High School in Troy except Robert, who graduated from Beaumont High School in St. Louis after Maud and the boys moved to St. Louis in 1940 so Jim and Allen could more readily find employment. The girls were either married or living away from Troy by that time.

Georgia Ruth married Arthur Adams of Collinsville; Gladys Marie married Clyde Yocum, Cleveland, OH; Edna Alberta married Henry Linder, Cleveland; Grace Winifred married Albert Roeth, Chicago; Norma Maud married Raymond Dee Stephens, Collinsville; Wilma May married Homer Cline, Troy; James Posey married Betty Padjen, Jeanette Orme, St. Louis; George Allen married Millie Marie Collins, Troy; and Robert Wilton married Carolyn Hafner, Chicago.

Mr. Shaffer suffered ill health for many years and died on March 19, 1936, at age 54.

Maud returned to Troy in the late 40s, where she died on July 16, 1974, at age 89. *Submitted by Millie Collins Shaffer.*

GENERAL WILLIAM TECUMSEH SHERMAN -
Civil War General Sherman, known for his famous march through Georgia, once owned land near Troy in Jarvis Township. At one time, he owned 98 acres near the junction of I-70 and 55. This land was eventually purchased by Mr. and Mrs. Henry Wilhelm.

General William T. Sherman

On August 14, 1880, the sale was completed, and Sherman became the owner of a portion of the northeast quarter of section 18, containing 88 acres. It was sold from the estate of William R. McKeen for $6720. An additional 10 acres was added on April 11, 1881, located in the southeast corner of the southwest quarter of section 7, which adjoins the other property. The sale was made from the Taylor estate for $700. In March of 1884, Sherman sold a 3.6 acre tract to William Cook for $300.

A house stood on the property, built sometime before 1873. Sherman visited the farm and perhaps stayed overnight in the house, but he never had permanent residence there. He had previously visited several times in Troy with his friend William W. Jarvis, whom he had met during the Civil War, and stayed with him. Perhaps these Troy visits lead to his interest in the area and his eventual land purchase.

At one time, a mill was supposedly built on the farm, near the Vandalia Railroad right-of-way. No one knows exactly where it was located. A mill stone did stand in the Wilhelm's yard, but the other was missing.

Upon Sherman's death in 1891, his son Philemon inherited the land. Philemon later sold it to George C. Morriss on March 15, 1892, for $9000. Sherman, never really too successful in financial matters, had realized a 12-year profit of $1880 on his speculation of Jarvis Township land. *Information taken from* The Collinsville Herald *and* The Bulletin, *the Troy newspaper in 1875.*

DIANA AND HAROLD SHREVE -
Diana and Harold Shreve were high school sweethearts at Soldan-Blewett High School in St. Louis.

They married in 1953, and shortly thereafter, Harold was drafted into the army and served in Korea. When Harold returned to civilian life, they moved across the river to Illinois.

The couple has 2 daughters, Holly and Tami. Holly married Garry Gilbert and lives in Rochester Hills, MI. Tami married Gregory Schmidt and lives in O'Fallon, IL. Happy for their children and delighted by the new additions to their family, Diana and Harold spent the next several years spoiling six grandchildren and planning for retirement.

Harold completed his 42 years at Emerson Electric in 1992, and Diana typed her last letter for the law firm of Keefe and DePauli in 1995, after working there for 22 years.

In 1993, they searched for a home in a smaller community, and in 1994 they moved to Troy, buying the historic Deimling House from former Mayor Ron Criley. They enjoy restoring and redecorating their Victorian home and have had the pleasure of making new friends and of becoming a part of a warm, welcoming community.

Diana serves as secretary of the Troy Historical Society. She especially enjoys learning about the city's history, as well as, learning about its fascinating residents. *Submitted by Diana Shreve.*

PAUL AND JEANNE SIMON -
Paul Simon was born November 29, 1928, in Eugene, OR, to the Rev. Martin and Ruth Simon. He grew up in Eugene and entered the University of Oregon in 1945 at age 16 to study journalism. In 1946, his parents moved to Highland; he transferred to Dana College in Blair, NE, where he studied for two years.

Paul came to Troy in 1948 after finishing his junior year of college, at the age of 19. The *Troy Call*, published by Ben Jarvis, ceased publication when Ben learned he had cancer, then almost always a fatal diagnosis. However, the community wanted a newspaper. The Superintendent of Schools, Fred Wakeland, learned through his friendship with Paul's father that Paul wanted to get into the newspaper business. With the leadership of the Troy Lions Club, the Troy Security Bank offered Paul a full mortgage on the equipment, and Paul started the *Troy Tribune* in July of 1948.

The newspaper took on local causes, like the need for a sewer system and the visible problem of corruption in the offices of sheriff and State's Attorney in Madison County. The newspaper grew and Paul and his associates,

Simon family, circa late 1970s
(l. to r.) Paul, Sheila, Martin, Jeanne

Ray Johnsen and Elmer Fedder, eventually acquired 12 other newspapers around the state. Paul was elected State Representative at the age of 25, and while serving, met State Representative Jeanne Hurley of Wilmette, IL. They married in 1960 and bought the home owned by the Robertsons, widely called "The Towers," at 306 East Market Street. Upon their marriage, they became the first husband-wife team in history to serve in the Illinois General Assembly.

Jeanne and Paul had two children, Sheila (b. March 13, 1961) and Martin (b. May 21, 1964). Both are married and both couples have two children. Sheila teaches at the Southern Illinois University Law School in Carbondale and Martin is a news photographer in the Washington, D.C., area.

The entire family campaigned together. Paul was elected State Senator in 1962; Lieutenant Governor in 1968; lost a narrow race for Governor in 1972; and then served in the U.S. House for 10 years and U.S. Senate for 12 years. In 1988 he narrowly lost the race for the Democratic nomination for President. Earlier, because the district lines for the vacant House seat were a few miles outside of Troy, Paul and Jeanne had moved to Makanda (near Carbondale).

They continued to live in this area until Jeanne's death in February 2000. *Submitted by Paul Simon.*

EDNA L. (KECK) AND ROBERT WILLIAM SLIVA -
Edna L. Keck, born October 31,1902, to Emma H. (Hobein) and Martin Keck Jr. of Troy, married Robert William Sliva on May 27,1923, in Troy. She was the fourth of seven siblings.

Wedding photo, circa 1920
Edna (Keck) seated and Robert Sliva (back right)
Bride's maid is Edna's sister.

Edna graduated from McKendree College in Lebanon, Illinois, and taught school for 42 years at Gilead School, Goshen School and the Le Claire School in Edwardsville. She was a 50 year member of the Troy Women's Club, a member of the Troy American Legion Auxilliary Post 708, and Beta Sigma Phi. Edna died on November 28,1988, at St Joseph's Hospital in Highland. "Bob" was born September 30, 1895, in Troy to Frank and Josephine (Sedlacek) Sliva. Bob was employed as a finisher at the General Steel Casting Co. of Granite City until his retirement in 1960. He served on the Troy City Council for 12 years. He was a Charter member of the American Legion of Troy, a Charter member of the WW I Veterans of Troy, a member of the Fisher-Weeks American Legion Post 1299 of Edwardsville and a member of the Troy Laborers Local 382. He saw action in WWI in France where he was gassed which kept him coughing all his life. Bob died on October 10, 1968, at St Joseph's Hospital in Highland. Edna's brother, Louis Henry Keck was married to Bob's sister, Laurina Josephine Sliva. Edna and Bob had no children of their own, but were the favorite Aunt and Uncle of their many nieces and nephews and great nieces and nephews. They were members of Friedens United Church of Christ and lived at 106 S. Dewey St in Troy. Edna and Robert are buried in Frieden's Cemetery, Troy. *Submitted by Pamela Keck.*

TOM SLIVA - The brick farmhouse, once known as the Sliva Farm, a mile and a half east of Troy, was acquired by Frank Sliva, Sr., and his wife Magdalena (Ebermayer) in 1906, and sold to his son, Frank Sliva, Jr., and his wife, Josephine (Sedlacek). Frank and Josephine had three children: Tom, Laurina, and Bob, who all grew up on the farm.

Tom and Maggie Sliva, at their daughter's wedding, May 20, 1950

Laurina married Louis Keck. Their children were Dorothy, who married Gus Suter, and Ethel, who became Mrs. Eldon Loehring.

Bob married Edna Keck (Louis' sister). They were childless, but their home was always open to nieces and nephews.

Tom married Margaret (Maggie) Brendel in 1919. When they married, they stayed on the farm, and his parents, Frank and Josephine, moved into town. Tom and Maggie raised two daughters on the farm. Viola was born in 1922, and Normagene in 1929. Viola married Jack Taylor of Troy in January 1942, and moved to town. Sad to say, in December of that same year, she died in childbirth. Normagene married Richard Jenks and moved to Collinsville. The Slivas were all active members of St. Jerome's Catholic Church in Troy. In the last years of his life, "Grandpa" (Frank, Jr.) Sliva, returned to his old home on the farm to live with his son, and died there in 1955.

The 100-acre farm had been part of a 160-acre land grant to Jess Renfro in January of 1817. It was truly a brick house, with even the interior walls made of brick. This made wiring for electricity in the 1940s interesting, for all receptacles had to be mounted on the baseboards.

Running water was not added until the mid-'50s. Even without the amenities taken for granted now, growing up on a farm was a

Wedding photo, May 1, 1894
Josephine (Sedlacek) and Frank Sliva, Jr.

wonderful experience. Loneliness was not a problem as town kids were frequent visitors. Either bikes were used for transportation or "shank's mare," the kids' legs. All the Slivas and their relatives have wonderful memories of the historic old homestead and of good times on the family farm. *Submitted by Normagene Jenks.*

LABAN SMART - Laban Smart, one of two sons of Peter Smart, was born on Nov. 9, 1758, in North Carolina. His father, born in North Carolina, served in the French and Indian War. While serving in the Revolutionary War, Amos, Laban's brother, died from camp fever.

After his military service in the Revolutionary War, Laban settled in Chatham County, NC, where he married Susannah Simmons. They had 10 children. In 1806 they migrated to Warren County, KY. After ten years, they continued to Madison County, IL. A Lubon Smart is listed in Madison County on the 1818 Territorial Census for Illinois. In the family are 2 males over 21 yrs. of age and 3 females. Some of the family were members of the Canteen Creek Baptist Church. Three of his children who came with him from Kentucky were Wiley, Peter and Henry B.

They made their home in section 1 of Jarvis Township. It became known as "Smart's Prairie." He received land grants for his military service in other areas and a pension in 1834 of $20 yearly for his service in the North Carolina Continental Line.

Laban farmed until 1838, when his wife passed away. Then, he went to live with his children until his death on March 28, 1840. He was buried along with his wife in section 2 of Jarvis Township. A special Revolutionary War marker was placed in the Hagler-Keown Cemetery. *Submitted by the Troy History Society. Information was taken from an article in the* Troy Tribune *of June 10, 1976, and the* Brink's History of Madison County, Illinois.

RICHARD SMITH JR. - Richard C. Smith Jr. was born in St. Louis, MO, on August 21, 1952. When Rick was two years of age, his family moved to Troy. His parents are Richard and Mary Smith now of Belleville. Rick was one of six children all who grew up in Troy and attended the Troy public schools. Rick was the oldest child and the only boy of the family. He has five sisters, Patrice, Margaret, Catherine, Rebecca and Maria.

Richard married Sherry Lynne Adelhardt on August 31, 1973, in the old St. Jeromes

Catholic Church in Troy. After a few years of traveling with Rick's job, they settled back down in Troy and built a home on Sherry's mother's home place (Gustav and Emma Kirsch farm, south of Troy).

Rick graduated from Parks Air College in Cahokia in 1973, and worked for General Electric in Schenectady, NY, and Kansas City, MO. He then became a carpenter/millwright out of the St. Louis hall and worked for Accurate Construction of St. Louis, after which he worked as a steel erection estimating engineer and then owned and operated his own construction company. He now works for C.J. Smith Machinery in St. Louis as a Sales Engineer and holds a certificate as a Certified Sales Engineer. Rick is currently seeking an MBA degree from SIUE.

Rick and Sherry Smith

Sherry traveled with Rick until they settled down to raise their three children. Over the years she has worked at many different jobs from grocery store clerk, to bank teller, from public school aide to punch press operator at Christian Wolfe, a communion wafer factory in Troy. Currently she is working at SIUE as a copy operator while pursuing her bachelor degree in Industrial/Organizational Psychology.

Smith children
(l. to r.) Front: Heather (Cummins).
Middle: Luke, Jennie. Back: Jacob.

Rick and Sherry have three children: Luke Charles, Jennie Lesetta, and Jacob Frank. Luke, born June 5, 1978, married Heather Cummins of Troy on December 30, 2000, and lives in Mexico MO, where he teaches English and Journalism at the Missouri Military Academy and where Heather is a student at William Woods University.

Jennie, born March 16, 1982, is a college student and is interested in art and travel and resides at home.

Jacob born April 18, 1983, just graduated from Triad, is living at home, working and exploring college options. *Submitted by Sherry Smith.*

JOHN SOMRATY III AND GERTRUDE ESTELL POWERS

Troy, IL, became home for Gertrude Estell Powers after she was widowed. She lived for fifteen years in Troy until her death in 1997. Her family history began in mid-1600 colonial America. The history for her

Gertrude Estell Powers and John Somraty, III, 1977

husband, John Somraty III, began in the Austrian-Hungarian Empire. The couple came from very diverse cultural and historical backgrounds. They married in 1934, beginning their life journey together in America. John was born in 1909 in Tiszadada, Szabolcs Co., Hungary, and Gertrude was born in 1916 in Denison, Grayson Co., TX. They were the parents of eleven children who lived to adulthood and who beget nineteen grandchildren and thirty great grandchildren. Their children are Rose Marie (Ron) Yarbrough, b. 1936; Mary Jane (Bill) Aegerter, b. 1938; Helen(e) June (Karl) Stone, b. 1940; John Arthur (Jean), b. 1942; Thomas Paul (Joyce), b. 1944; Shirley Ann (Jewell) Pennock, b. 1946; Lawrence Edward (Pat), b. 1948; Bonnie FloElla (Bill) Tucker, b. 1950; James Andrew (Guinevere), b. 1952; Barbara Ann Holifield (Dean), b. 1954; and Candice Lorraine, b. 1957.

During the Depression years, John Somraty's family traveled to Michigan and Indiana for work. They moved to Highland, IL, and settled in rural Bond Co., Pocahontas, IL, in February 1944. The family moved to the St. Jacob area in 1957. A home located in Trenton was purchased in 1966. They resided there until John Somraty's death in 1981.

The parents of John Somraty, III, were Janos (John) Szomrati, II, b. 1886-d. 1966, and Borbala (Barbara) Pap, b. 1890-d. 1919, in

Somraty family, 1981
(l. to r.) Front: Bonnie, Barbara, Candace, and Rose. Back: Lawrence, Mary, John, Shirley, Thomas, and Helen. Absent: James.

Tiszadada, Szabolcs Co., Hungary. Both parents are buried in Mount Hope Cemetery, Belleville, IL. John II arrived at Ellis Island on the *Carpathia*, March 29, 1912. He found a job with Aluminum Ore Company in E. St. Louis and retired August 1, 1953. He saved money to send for his family in Hungary. His two sons, Janos (John, III) and Sandor (Alexander II), born in Tiszadada, Hungary, arrived at Ellis Island with their mother Barbara Pap Szomrati, November 9, 1912, on the *Pannonia*. They settled in Washington Park, IL. A brother, Andrew, was born 1914 in E. St. Louis, IL.

The parents of Gertrude moved to Illinois from the Popular Bluff area, Missouri. Her father, Elbert DeWitt Powers, was born in 1885 in Fair Dealing, Butler Co., MO, and died 1962 in Oceola, Mississippi Co., AR. Her mother, Clara Elzada Griffith, was born in 1895 in Asherville, Stoddard Co., MO, and died in 1943 near Highland, IL, in a train auto-collision. Gertrude was the third of nine children born to Elbert and Clara Powers.

Powers-Somraty, four generations, 1991
(l. to r.) Front: Gertrude Estell (Powers) Somraty, b. 1916. Back: DeAnna Chiste Kasich, b. 1960, Rose (Somraty) Yarbrough, b. 1936, Christina Chiste Digby, b. 1980

The Power(s) family history can be traced to John Power, b. 1710, and Mary Holloway, b. ca. 1714, in Wilmington, DE. They were married in the Wilmington Old Swedes Church in 1735. Rose's fourth great-grandmother, Naomi Pennington Power, wife of John Wesley Power, is laid to rest in Locust Creek Cemetery near Nashville, Washington Co., IL. The Pennington family history can be traced to Abraham Pennington in 1690, Cecil Co., MD, and finally to England. *Submitted by Rose Powers Somraty Yarbrough.*

BRUCE AND JUDY STEELE

The Bruce and Judy Steele family started when Bruce was born to Daniel and Myrna Steele on August 6, 1960. His parents moved to Troy in September of 1964. He has one brother Keith and two sisters, Janet Wilson and Annette Menchak, who also live in Troy. Bruce graduated from Triad High School in 1979. He met Judy Poletti, because she was a friend of his sister Annette. They didn't date until he was out of high school and mutual friends were getting married. Judy had car trouble, so she had to ride with Bruce from the photographer to the reception.

They have been together ever since. They have two children Christina (Chrissy) who was born on the Friday of Troy's Homecoming, July 24, 1981. Their son Andrew James (A.J.) was

Steele family, 1999
(l. to r.) Front: A. J. Back: Chrissy, Bruce, Judy.

born on July 9, 1985. Their lives include boating and camping with the family and trying to vacation whenever possible. Going to church and enjoying time with friends and family are very important to all of them. (For related information refer to the Edward and Bernadine Poletti Family). *Submitted by Judy Steele.*

STOCK-DRUESSEL FAMILY

Ruth Lydia Druessel was born March 13, 1922, to Fred Druessel (1885-1942) and Marie Anna (Pollman) Druessel (1888-1974). Fred was a carpenter and Marie, a housewife. Ruth attended the one-room Blackjack School, where her father before her had studied. Later she attended SIU-C and McKendree College. She started her teaching career by teaching for one year in the same Blackjack School. She later taught kindergarten in the Troy schools from 1962-1985, when she retired.

In 1943, she married Orlo Calvert Stock who was in the Army Air Force at the time. Orlo (1920-2001) was the son of Robert and Nola Anderson Stock. Before entering the army, he had worked as an auto-body man. After 4 years in the service, he became a mechanic and a farmer.

Ruth and Orlo had three sons: David, Duane, and Dale. David was born Dec. 18, 1943. He graduated from SIU-C, married Marsha Smith, and lives in Benton, IL. He is employed by Rend Lake Conservation. David and Marsha have three children: Erin Elizabeth (b. 1978), a graduate of Purdue University in 1959 and currently, a pre-med student; Adam Todd (b.1981), and SIU-C junior, studying to be a court reporter; and Ryan Timothy (b.1985), a high school junior.

Duane Robert was born in 1949. He graduated from Triad High School and attended

Wedding photo, March 13, 1943
Ruth and Orlo Stock

287

SIU-E, where he later taught economics. He obtained his doctorate from U of I, Urbana. In 1978 he joined the University of Oklahoma as professor of finance. His first marriage was to Jana Gerstenecker (1971-1976). In 1980 he married Rhonda Autrey. They have two daughters, Lauren Elizabeth (b. 1984) is a junior in high school; and Leah Michelle (b. 1987) is in the 8th grade.

Dale Fred was born in 1951. He graduated from Triad High School, like his brother, Duane. He married Janet Spicker in 1977; they divorced in 1998. Robert Edward was born to them in 1979. He graduated from Triad and works at the Humane Society in St. Louis, MO.

Since retirement, Ruth continues to be active. She is a member of Delta Kappa Gamma and Friends of the Library, helping at their book sale twice a month. *Submitted by Ruth Stock.*

ANNIE STRUCKHOFF - Annie Struckhoff, born April 24, 1913, the daughter of Charles and Elizabeth (Hoenig) Sruckhoff, died May 20, 1994. She had five brothers, Charles, August, Raymond, Melvin and Elmer Struckhoff, and one sister, Mamie Kropp.

Annie Struckhoff, 1981

She was born in Troy and grew up there. In her later life, she lived in Edwardsville in a modest apartment above a drug store. She was a woman of unpretentious means, who thought of everyone else's needs more than her own.

She left one half of her estate ($100,000) to the Hoyleton Children's Home in Hoyleton, IL. The people at the Hoyleton Home never knew her, but wished that they would have. She had made arrangements long before her death to leave the money to the home, but no one knew of this.

She never married, but always did wonderful things for her friends. She helped many in the time of need. When Annie was a young woman, she walked from Troy to the country south of Troy many times to help friends in need. She often visited with the late Miss Ora Edwards, who lived in the country and would pitch in to help with any chore at hand. If there was a new baby or a funeral somewhere in the neighborhood, Annie was there to assist. When a neighbor (Lousie Mersinger) lost her mother (Laura Levo), Annie came to her aid during the funeral days and helped with serving lunch and cleaning the house. Annie was a real kind person.

She was instrumental along with the late William S. Freeman, Triad's Assistant Superintendent, in placing Kathy Harris Smith, daughter of Roy and Joann Harris, into school.

Kathy was deaf, and Annie kept trying until she got Kathy into school. She took care of Kathy and took a liking to her.

In her early years, Annie did domestic work and for a time was employed at Moderne Linen Laundry in Troy. After moving to Edwardsville, she cared for twin boys and was janitress at the N.O. Nelson School.

She collected stamps for her church to help overseas. This was only one of the many things she did for her fellow man.

She is buried in Friedens Cemetery in Troy. *Submitted by Mae Grapperhaus from recollections, newspaper clippings and information received from JoAnn Harris and Kathy Flarris Smith.*

WILLIAM TAAKE AND LOUIS AND MILDRED (TAAKE) HUSTON - William "Bill" Taake's father, Henry Taake, moved his family from Norbern, MO, to a farm east of Troy on Old 40, now Route 162. The farm had the barns, pigs, and cattle on the south side of the road and the house on the north side. The Taake family farmed there for over 80 years until the farm was sold to the Schmerbauch family in the 1950s.

Bill Taake (Carl William Frederick Taake) grew up on the farm, but as a young man went "out west" and worked as a cowboy on his brother's ranch in Kansas. Eventually, he moved back to Troy where he courted and married a neighbor girl, Mary (Mayme) Schultze on June 4, 1916. They had known each other most of their lives and loved to tell the story that, as the oldest school boy in the neighborhood, Bill had taken her to her first day of school at the Troy Lutheran School that they all atttended. Of course, the children walked to school each day from the country.

The couple had four children: Carl, Raymond, Russel, and Mildred.

Carl served Troy in elected positions, including being mayor. He married Julia Knecht who was a school teacher in the Troy schools. They had one son, Terry.

Raymond saw service and was wounded in World War II. He married Fern Kueker and, with their two children, JoAnn and Larry, lived their entire lives in Troy.

Russel served in WWII as a gunner on a supply ship, which was torpedoed, and he spent time in the ocean before being rescued. He married Dorothy Howerton, and they had a son, Tracy.

Mildred, born in 1920, married Louis Huston, who had just returned from service in World War II, on October 25, 1945. Louis, born in 1916, was the son of Josephine (Richardts) and George Huston who had moved their family to Troy from Mattoon in the 1940s. Mildred and Louis lived their entire 53 happily married years in Troy. They had four children: Carol, Robert, William and Brian.

Daughter Carol Campbell now lives in Highland. She is a government employee and has two daughters, Mary and Shannon.

Robert (Bob) Huston is married to Carma. They have three teenage daughters. He works for the city of St. Louis.

William (Bill) lives in Kansas City with his wife, Linda, and their three children: Heather,

who is in the Army; Billy, whose wife is in the Air Force; and Nicole, who works with a space and aeronautical company in St. Louis. Bill installs and repairs computerized hospital equipment. His job has taken him around the world to places such as Siberia, Spain, France, England, China and Japan, as well as to every state in the U.S.

Brian works at a computer-related job, was married to Rachel, and has two sons – Shaun, whose work is also in computers, and Ryan, who is in high school. *Submitted by Mildred (Taake) Huston.*

BOB AND JERI (KNICKEL) TELLMANN
Bob and Jeri were born and raised in St. Louis, MO. They were married in 1965.

Their only son Bobby was also born in St. Louis, and has worked at Fontbonne College since his graduation from high school in 1985.

The family moved to Troy in 1988. They bought a house and barn on five acres to be able to keep their four horses.

Bob worked for Ford Motor Co. for thirty years, retiring in 1996. Jeri works at Firstar Bank and has been at that locaton since 1991.

Bob enjoys owning a Honda Shadow and a Ford T bucket hot rod. Jeri enjoys her horses, community service and activities with her friends. *Submitted by Jeri Tellmann.*

WARREN AND SHIRLEY TREKELL - Warren Reid Trekell and Shirley Ruth (Livingston) Trekell moved to Troy, IL, December 1977, when the Air Force moved the Air Force Communications Command from Richards-Gebaur AFB, MO, to Scott AFB, IL. Warren, the eldest son of Milton E. and Floy May (Jett) Trekell of Hunter, OK, retired from the Air Force in 1974 after serving 28 years. He served in Texas; Japan; Mississippi; Oklahoma; Thule, Greenland; Patrick AFB, FL; Wichita, KS; Clinton-Sherman AFB, OK; Ankara, Turkey; Castle AFB, CA; Bien Hoa, South Vietnam; and Richards-Gebaur AFB, MO. Warren's grandfather and great-grandfather, George Washington Jett, were early settlers of Greenville, Bond County, IL.

Warren was born in Hunter, OK, 26 June 1928. After attending a country school, he graduated from Hunter High School in 1945. He attended Texas A & M College, College Station, TX, prior to enlisting in the U.S. Army in 1946, then joining the U.S. Air Force when it became a separate service. Following his military career, he worked for the U.S. Air Force as a civilian, working military accession programs.

Warren and Shirley Trekell, 2000

Shirley was born in Pond Creek, OK, 25 November 1934. She attended a private school her first three years, then completed her education in the public school system, graduating from Pond Creek High School in 1952. She attended Draughon's School of Business, Oklahoma City, OK. After graduation, she worked in Oklahoma City and Enid, OK, prior to her marriage to Warren on 11 June 1957.

They had two daughters, Laura Jean, on 25 October 1958, while Warren was stationed at Vance AFB. When Jeannie was 7 weeks old, he transferred to Thule, Greenland. While stationed at Wichita, KS, their second daughter, Shari Ann, was born on 6 September 1962.

Following Warren's assignment to Thule, the Trekells lived in Florida, Kansas, and Clinton-Sherman AFB, OK, prior to his assignment to Ankara, Turkey, where they lived for two years. While in Turkey, Shirley began working for the U.S. government.

In 1969 Warren was transferred to Castle AFB, CA, then to Vietnam in August 1970. Shirley and the children remained in California while she worked for the Farmers Home Administration, U.S. Department of Agriculture, Merced, CA, until Warren returned in August 1971. The family then moved to Richards-Gebaur AFB, MO. While there, Shirley worked for the Office of the Inspector General, U.S. Department of Agriculture, before transferring to the Air Force communications Command, Richards-Gebaur AFB.

While living in Belton, MO, Laura Jean graduated from Belton High School in May of 1976. She then attended Central Missouri State University, Warrensburg, MO, graduating in 1980 with a Bachelor of Science degree in Clothing, Textiles, and Merchandising. She currently works for the H.D. Lee Company as a Pattern Designer. She married Donald Douglas Kohler of Harrisonville, MO, 19 July 1980. He also graduated from CMSU, with a Bachelor of Science Degree in criminal justice, and now works with the Belton Police Department. They have one son, Patrick Douglas Kohler, born 7 July 1985. They divorced in 1986.

When the Trekells moved to Troy in December of 1977, Shari Ann was a sophomore at Triad High School, graduating in May 1980. She attended SIUE and received a Bachelor of Science Degree in Management Information Systems in 1984. She worked at the university when a student, became a member of the Information Technology staff following graduation and was awarded her MBA in 1992. Shari married Bryce Lindley Renken on the 23 September 1996, and they are residents of Troy. Bryce, also a graduate of SIUE with a Bachelor of Science Degree in Management Information Systems, works for the May Company. They have one child, Madeleine Jeannine, born 26 March 1998, and are expecting their second child in March/April 2002. Shari also sings with the St. Louis Symphony Chorus.

Both Shirley and Warren continued to work for the Air Force Communications Command following its move from Richards-Gebaur AFB to Scott AFB. Shirley later transferred to Military Airlift Command (now

Air Mobility Command). Warren retired in June 1993 from his civil service position, and Shirley retired in January 1995.

Warren has two children, Warren Reid, Jr., 14 May 1951, and Mary Ellen, 15 Nov. 1952, from a previous marriage. Warren Reid, Jr., is married and lives in Baton Rouge, LA. He has three children by his first wife, Rochelle: Justin is married with one child, Matthew is unmarried, and Amanda is a college student. Mary Ellen married Pedro Guerrero, and they have two daughters. Trina is married with two sons; Tabitha married and had one daughter. Mary and Pedro divorced, and she then married Jose Zepeda. They have three children: Jose, Jr. (deceased), Gracia, and Adrian. *Submitted by Shirley Trekell.*

RAY AND CAROL UNGER - In 1929 Kurt and Margaret Unger sailed from Berlin, Germany, to New York, NY. They settled in St. Louis and in 1938 moved to Collinsville with their son Raymond, age two. William and Laverne Voss, originally from South St. Louis and O' Fallon, MO, raised their daughter Carol and son William in Collinsville. Ray and Carol married and had three children: Tim, Tom and Terri in 1960, 1962 and 1965 respectively. In 1967 they built a house in a new Troy subdivision, Twin Lakes. Their children attended St.

Ray and Carol Unger family, 1969
(l. to r.) Carol, Tom, Tim, Terri and Ray

Paul's Lutheran School and Triad High School.

Tim Unger graduated from the University of Illinois with a master in Civil Engineering. He lives in Ballwin, MO, and has a civil engineering firm in Kirkwood, MO. He is married to Kim (Ditzler) Unger and has three children: Kyle, Page, and Chase, born in 1991, 1994, and 1998.

Tom Unger graduated from the University of Illinois with a BS in Biology and from the University of Missouri-St. Louis Optometry with a doctorate in optometry. He moved back to Troy in 1991 and established a home and optometric practice in Troy (see "Tom and Alice Unger Family" and ""Unger Eye Care"). He is married to Alice (Schmitz) Unger and has three children: Kurt, Drew and Grant born in 1990, 1992 and 1995.

Terri (Unger) Slaby graduated from Southern Illinois University at Edwardsville with a BS in elementary education. She married Troy native Jeff Slaby and lives in O'Fallon, IL. She is a practicing vision therapist at Unger Eye Care in Troy. Terri and Jeff have two children: Jacob and Kaitlyn, born 1992 and 1994. *Submitted by Tom Unger.*

TOM AND ALICE UNGER - Tom Unger was born in Troy, IL, to Ray and Carol Unger (see "Ray and Carol Unger Family") November 13, 1962. He graduated from St. Paul's Lutheran School and Triad High School. He graduated from the University of Illinois-Champaign/Urbana in 1984 with a Bachelor of Science degree in Biology. In 1988 he graduated from the University of Missouri-St. Louis, School of Optometry with a doctorate of optometry.

The Unger family, 2000
(l. to r.) Kurt, Drew, Alice, Grant and Tom

It was while attending optometry school he met Alice (Schmitz). Alice was born in Minneapolis, MN, to Janet and Fred Schmitz. But soon after, at the age of two, her family moved back to their native Kansas City area and settled in Prairie Village, KS. She attended the University of Kansas and graduated with a Human Biology degree in 1987 and completed her optometry doctorate in 1991.

Tom and Alice first met at a social function at the beginning of her first year of optometry school, 1987. Two years later, in May 1989, they married. The following year things got very busy. In October 1990, they had their first son, Kurt. The following spring in 1991 they bought their first house in Troy and opened their optometric practice, Unger Eye Care (see "Unger Eye Care").

As their practice grew, so did their family. Kurt was born October 2, 1990; Drew, October 3, 1992; and Grant, April 1, 1995. The boys attend St. Paul's Lutheran School and Church as their father did while growing up in Troy.*Submitted by Tom Unger.*

EDWARD GENE UPTON - Edward Gene Upton was born July 11, 1958, in Fairfield, IL. His parents were Keith Edward Upton and Charlotte Holstein. He attended grade schools in Wayne County, IL.

Wedding photo, 1994
Edward and Perrian Upton

Upon graduation from the eighth grade, he came to Troy to live with his dad and step-mom.

Ed graduated from Triad High School in 1976. During his teen years he became a pilot, learned to scuba dive, and became an avid photographer. As a cadet explorer with the Collinsville Fire Department, he was able to go to Europe for the first time.

After high school, he attended the University of Illinois on a Naval Scholarship. During the summers he served on various U.S. Naval ships and, for one summer, served on a German Naval ship. During college he worked part-time in the Naval computer lab there. In 1981 he graduated as a Naval Officer. He served for 20 years in the U.S. Navy.

While serving at the Pentagon in Washington, D.C., he met Perrian Prokopchak, who was from Butler, PA. They were married on November 5, 1994, at St. Conrad Roman Catholic Church. They reside in Hughesville, MD.

Upon retirement Ed worked for defense contractors and Perrian, who has a financial degree, works in a bank.

They enjoy traveling, skiing and teaching their pet birds to talk. *Submitted by Joy Whitson Upton.*

JOY WHITSON UPTON - In the fall of 1964 Joy Whitson came to Troy. Like her parents Edward Whitson (1923-1986) and Leona Fulk (1924-), she was born (11 August 1941) in Perry County, IL. Her siblings are John Whitson of Tamaroa, IL; Jerry Whitson of DuQuoin, IL; Janet Benbenek of Carbondale, IL; Jeffrey Benbenek of Edwardsville, IL; and James Benbenek of DuQuoin.

Joy Whitson Upton, 1991

She graduated from Pinckneyville High School, SIU-C with B.S. in Education, and the University of IL with a M.S. in Library Science. In 1994 she retired as Collinsville High School librarian. During that time she also taught courses for SIU-C, SIU-E, BAC and Lewis & Clark Junior College.

On Feburary 26, 1966, Joy married K. Edward Upton in the First Christian Church in Collinsville, IL. Edward G. Upton, her step-son, came to live with them in the summer of 1972. Since 1968 Joy has been an active genealogist doing family research for her family and friends. She helped form the Madison County Genealogical Society, became active in the Illinois State Genealogical Society, was the society's president in 1986 and 1987, chaired many state conferences, and is its archivist. She has written

several syllabuses and articles for societies' quarterlies. She transcribed and published the *Madison County 1860 Federal Census*, which contains over 33,000 persons who lived in the county before the Civil War. She teaches genealogy to steel workers in their computer lab at their Learning Center in Granite City and others in her home.

In her family tree, her paternal names include Rush, Plumlee, Moss, Hiestand, Boehm, Mosier, Pennington, Boone, Uppey, Maugridge, Milton, Morgan, Freiley, Harding, Wright, Frame, Russell, Jolliff, Trout, McCaleb, and Slade. Daniel Boone is an ancestral uncle.

Her maternal family names are Volck, Merckel, Romich, Herner, Berndt, Moser, Fiscus, Schwind, Schmidt, Smedley, Barnett, Pierce, Robbins, Vanarsdall, Moore, King, Cotterell, Peebles, Mackie, Owen, West, Spinks, and Brashar. She enjoys meeting new "cousins."

She has researched in several states, the National Archives and even in the Stat Archives in Worm, Germany, where her Fulk (Volck) family immigrated. Joy enjoys traveling to ancestral homes, visiting the churches her ancestors attended, and doing research in the area.

Another main interest is designing and creating original quilts. When she was 16 years old, she hand-pieced a bow tie quilt, her great grandmother (Cora Moore Robbins) set it together, and her grandmother (Veva Robbins Fulk) and her mom quilted it. This four-generation hand-sewn quilt and others from her mother and grandmothers are among her prized possessions. With the electronic age, she is delving into digitizing and computerized sewing of ancestral quilts making each one an original based on the family history.

Jeanette Dothager and Joy's ancestors lived in the same county in North Carolina in the early 1700s and in 1964 the two of them met in Troy. On a school snow day they designed on graph paper the duplex where they reside and which Joe and Kenny Lanahan built. The duplex is home to her pet Bichon Frise, Kalee Pencoed, whose sister, Grabriel Mercedes, lives next door. *Submitted by Joy Upton.*

OCTAVIA (LEVO) AND GEORGE VACCARO - Octavia C. Levo, born July 26, 1909, was the eighth child of Peter P. Levo, Sr. and Laura Cossono Levo. She married George Vaccaro and lived in University City, MO, most of their married life.

Wedding day, circa 1940
(l. to r.) George Vaccaro, Octavia (Levo) Vaccaro, Francis Vaccaro, Leo Vaccaro

George was a cook in the U.S. Army in World War II. Octavia worked at the Madison County Court House before she and George were married. George was a painter by trade and owned a painting business with his brother Leo Vaccaro.

They had one daughter, Donna Kay.

Octavia died July 20, 1989, and is buried in St. Louis, MO. George is still living at this writing and resides in St. Louis. *Submitted by Mae Grapperhaus.*

JOHN H. AND MARY (SCHOTEMEYER) VOELKER - John H. Voelker (b. 1878) was the son of Adam and Catharine (Schriber) Voelker. He married Mary Schotemeyer (b. 1886) on December 14, 1915, in Edwardsville. Mary's parents were Hy. Schotemeyer and Sophie Sofalo. John had been born in Troy and worked as a miner.

Mary had been born in Fenton, MO, but had later moved to Troy. They had two sons, Robert and Roger, who were born and raised in Troy. Robert graduated from Troy schools in 1935. John and Mary sold land to Gerald Lanahan for the development of Lanahan Addition. *Submitted by Bonnie and Emmett Pfeil.*

MILTON AND HELEN VOSS - Milton H. Voss was born March 11, 1906, in Edwardsville, IL. He was the son of Henry and Matilda (Bardelmeier) Voss. They lived in Pin Oak Township. He had one brother Harvey who lives in Florissant, MO. Milton graduated from Edwardsville High School where he played on the football and basketball teams. Milton sometimes rode his pony from Pin Oak to Troy to court Helen.

Helen (Ottwein) Voss was born June 25, 1905, in Troy. She was the 3rd of 5 children born to George and Carrie (Wilhelm) Ottwein. Helen was baptized and confirmed at Friedens Evangelical Church. The Ottwein family owned and operated a confectionery in Troy from 1927 to Jan. 28, 1929. Helen and her sister Irma (Ottwein) Ludwig helped in the confectionery. Helen's brothers, Oscar and George, were farmers in Troy.

Helen and Milton were married September 14, 1930, in Troy. They lived at 217 E. Market where a son, Darrell, was born July 13, 1931, and a daughter, Carol Voss Stough, was born September 3, 1934. Milton was employed as a petroleum serviceman near Highland. They moved to Sparta, IL, in 1935 where Milton was manager of Randolph Service Co. They moved to Quincy, IL, where he was manager of Adams Service Co. Three more children were born in Quincy: Marie (Voss) Smith on November 14, 1939; Bob on November 25, 1941; and Richard on January 29, 1944. Their oldest son, Darrell, died in a car accident in 1951.

They were members of Trinity United Church of Christ where they served as Sunday School teachers and Youth Fellowship leaders. Milton was an elder on the board of trustees.

Helen was active in the Woman's Guild, was a 4-H leader and was active in the Home Extension. She also was a volunteer with the Red Cross, Blessing Hospital and Good Samaritan Home. Her hobbies were sewing and crafts.

Milton and Helen Voss

Milton was a Farm Bureau member, on the Good Samaritan board and a 4-H leader. After retiring, he was Safety Director of Farm Service at Bloomington. He loved to fish, golf and bowl.

Helen, Milton and their five children loved to come back to Troy to visit family and friends. Over the years they would come to family reunions, for holidays, Troy Homecomings, etc. Several of their children and grandchildren participated in the Homecoming parades. Their son Bob, and his wife, Sue, named their son TROY.

Helen and Milton lived in Quincy until they died; Milton, on November 14, 1989, and Helen, on September 5, 1995. Helen, Milton and their son Darrell are buried at Friedens Cemetery in Troy. *Submitted by Carol Voss Stough.*

DIANA WALINE - Diana Waline was born June 29, 1953, in Waukegan, IL, to Theresa and Frank Waline. Theresa Perez's parents had come from Mexico. Family members were lost or killed during the Mexican Revolution. Gramma Rosa Puente Perez was raised in the convents of Mexico. When the war broke out, she came to the U.S. with an aunt who had been a "street woman" in Mexico. Stories have it that they crossed murky waters to cross over to the United States. Rosa Perez is known to have settled in Coffeeville, KS. Rosa lived also in Libertyville, Wadsworth, Zion and eventually settled in Waukegan, IL.

Later, Edward Perez would also come to the United States. Edward Perez met Rosa Puente and they married. Gramma would say, "You must work twice as hard to have anything and live in a free country. Do good always. Always work and you will have something." They had eight girls and four boys. Gramma said

Aunts and uncles from the Perez family, 1961
Front: (l. to r.) Emily, Jennie, Rosa, Edward,
Delores, Helena, Rose. Back: Linda, Theresa,
Richard, Julia, Angelo

those times were very hard. She would have friends and workers save flour sacks to make skirts for the girls. In those days the sacks were decorated. Grampa owned the Star Restaurant in the 1940s in Waukegan and the 400 Cafe from the 1950s to the mid 1960s. They lived on five acres of farmland in Zion, IL, where they raised pigs, chickens, geese, goats, dogs, and one horse. Gramma canned and worked in the garden. Many times her granddaughter, Diana, took her fresh "hot tortillas" and the salt jar to the garden and ate tomatoes. What a treat!

Frank Waline was from the upper, northern peninsula of Michigan. Photographs show he was an avid cougar hunter and played the accordian quite well. He passed away sometime in the 1960s. Years later Theresa married John D. Gorman, and they had two daughters. Diana graduated from Waukegan High School in 1972 and moved to the Washington, D.C., area to work for the Department of Justice. After working in criminal investigations in various states, Diana settled back into Illinois. Her interests include oil painting, camping, canning and cooking, but, most of all, taking care of a wonderful husband, George Bauer of Troy. She is now Operations Director of a construction company and has one daughter, Rachel Ann Korte. *Submitted by Diana Bauer.*

CLAUDINA HELEN (JARVIS) WATTS
Claudina Helen (Jarvis) Watts was born in Troy, IL (Jarvis Township), on May 31, 1904, to Charles Elmer Jarvis (b. 3/3/1876-d.3/31/1922) and Margaret B. (Henke) Jarvis, (b. 1/21/1874-d. 1/19/1936). Her parents were married in Nashville, IL, on February 7, 1899. She had 2 brothers, the late Lee W. Jarvis, who died in October of 1901, and Elmer Joseph Jarvis, born September 12, 1899, and who died January 18, 1960. At one time, the family lived at Kimberlin and High Street. Claudina attended the Troy Public School and St. Jerome's Catholic School.

Margaret B. and Charles Elmer Jarvis, circa 1900

Claudina's father, Charles Elmer Jarvis, was a weighman at the Donk Coal Mine and also served one term as Township Clerk. He frequently visited the "Original Mineral Springs Hotel," Okawville, IL, established in 1867, where he was given a "Bath Prescription Ticket" on July 28, 1921, which was necessary for admission. The hotel is still in operation today.

Claudina's grandparents were John F. Jarvis and Nancy J. (Montgomery) Jarvis. Some of the Montgomery descendants were engaged in horse breeding. One of the Montgomery prize horses was "Joe Joker,"

Claudina Helen (Jarvis) Watts, 1926

Guidless Harness Wonder, World's Champion in His Class – 2:16-3/4.

Claudina was the niece of the late Nancy O'Dell Baglin, nee Jarvis (b.8/30/1879 – d.4/l/1974). She was the great-granddaughter of John Jarvis of Virginia, who reportedly was the first entry on a list of persons who purchased land in what is now Jarvis Township, Madison County.

Mrs. Baglin had 6 brothers: Thomas Cleveland Jarvis, William Hazel Jarvis, Charles Elmer Jarvis (Claudina's father), Wesley Weston Jarvis, Nelson Montgomery Jarvis and John Stanley Jarvis.

Claudina Jarvis, 1929

Claudina, at the age of 18, and with her widowed mother and her brother, Elmer Joseph, moved to East St. Louis, IL, in 1923. In 1926 Claudina went to Chicago to visit her very close friend, Frances A. (Arth) Smith, also, from Troy. There she met Fred B. Watts from Chicago. They were married on December 6, 1926, in Chicago. Their only child, Marillyn Elaine Watts, was born in Chicago on September 16, 1927. She survives and lives in Belleville, IL.

Claudina died on December 27, 1983, and her husband, Fred B. Watts, died on July 25, 1982. *Submitted by Marillyn Elaine Watts.*

JACK CLIFTON WEIR - Jack Clifton Weir was born April 4, 1924, to Daniel and Ethel Weir. He was an only child, and grew up in the Troy-Collinsville area.

Jack married Ruth Geraldine Schmitt in 1946. After Jack finished college, he and Geri lived in Troy, and worked for Geri's father, William, in the automobile dealership. Jack and Geri later moved to Nokomis, IL, and then to Red Bud, IL, in 1967. Jack died in September 1975.

Jack and Geri had four children: Joy (b. Apr. 7, 1947, d. 1997), Judy (b. May 19, 1948), Jane (b. July 19, 1961), and James (b. Jan. 17, 1963).

Joy married Norman Roy, and they have three children: Jennifer, Suzanne, and Brad. Judy married Steve Flowers, and they have two children: Tammy (Mark Rose, husband) and Patrick. Jane married Mark Johnson, and they have two sons: Jacob and Timothy. James married Mary Jo Renzaglia, and they have three children: Alex, Jack, and Carlie.

Geraldine continues to live in Red Bud, IL. *Submitted by Kae Schmitt.*

ARTHUR F. WENDLER - Arthur F. Wendler was inducted into the 1950 Class of Senior Counsellors for 50 years of service to the Troy area on June 24, 2000.

Arthur F. Wendler, 2000

Born and raised in Pin Oak Township near Troy, Wendler enlisted in the Air Force to receive a four-year college deferment. In his second semester at University of Illinois, he was called to active duty because of World War II.

Although Wendler trained as a bomber pilot, he was never sent overseas. Wendler began schooling in agricultural education, then switched to government law and finally private law. He passed the bar exam almost a full year before graduation.

Before graduating, Wendler married a young dietitian from Iowa named Elaine Pinckney. The couple returned to Wendler's hometown where he began working in the office of Edwardsville attorney James Reed before opening a private practice in Troy.

His office has represented the villages of Marine and St. Jacob and he has served as the city attorney for Troy, and township attorney for Jarvis and Pin Oak townships. In addition, he works as a real estate broker and an income tax preparer.

He and Elaine are the parents of one son, Eric Wendler. *Submitted by Arthur F. Wendler*

GEORGE AND LOUISE (GERFEN) WENDLER - Louise Gerfen was born on October 27, 1870, in Frotheim, east of Minden in Westphalia, Germany, the second of six children born to Caroline Marie Aspelmeier and Henry C. Gerfen.

When Louise was eleven her father brought the family to Troy, IL. Louise married George Conrad Jacob Wendler at the Holy Cross Lutheran Church in Collinsville on November 8, 1891.

Wendler family, 1907
(l. to r.) Front: Otto, Kenneth, George, Louise, Walter. Back: George, Erwin.

Having farmed with his father for 10 years since ending his formal education at age 15, George took over the managment of his father's 81 acre farm in Section 35 of Collinsville Township. George was born April 27, 1866, the youngest of seven children of Johann Wendler and Rosina Kalbfleisch of Collinsville. George also came from a German heritage, his father having immigrated to America with his parents Jacob and Margaretha (Rauk) Wendler in 1847. George's parents remained on the farm with their son and his bride. The farm included a picturesque century old sawmill and the first corn mill, run by water power. Pioneer settlers came forty to fifty miles to have their corn ground at the mill. Earlier Indian habitation is evident by the abundance of Indian artifacts. George was a successful farmer and a member of the Pleasant Grove school board for twenty-seven years. Louise was known for her pleasant disposition and was an excellent cook. She was known especially for her lemon meringue pie, which always had a mysterious brown streak running through it. When George retired they sold the family farm and moved to a neighboring farmhouse before settling in Collinsville in their later years. George died in 1950, after which Louise made her home with her children until her death in 1955.

Louise and George were blessed with six children, George, Erwin, Walter, Otto, Rosa and Kenneth. The boys attended school and settled in the area except for Erwin, with the two eldest acquiring excellent business training at the Commercial College at Collinsville.

George Johann Heinrich was born September 11, 1892, choosing farming as his life's work. He had one son, Robert Hall Wendler, from his first marriage to Grace Hall. Robert married Helen Marian Lovern and had three children, Kirk Robert, Mark Duane and Anita Louise (Mrs. Roger Mason). Grace passed away December 5, 1940, and George later married Ruth Gatchel.

Erwin Arthur "Jack" was born 13 May, 1894. Erwin married Myra Smith. Their children Erwin Arthur "Jack" and Betty Jane were born in Washington. Following Myra's death in Alaska in 1951, Erwin returned to Illinois where he married Frances Mary Hopfinger and had one daughter, Anna Marie (Mrs. David L. Huckla).

Rosa Margaretha Louise was born May 7, 1896, and died when she was four.

Walter Albert was born December 9, 1899. Walter was a chemist and pharmacist, operating his own drug store in Collinsville. He married Henrietta "Yetta" Schoetter. They had two sons, Todd Albert and Walter Kenneth "Buster." Todd has one son, Steven Edward, from his marriage to Billie Dervallis, and one daughter, Karen Jean, from his second marriage to Dorothy Parmentier.

Otto Carl was born November 26, 1902. Otto and his wife Eleanor Kunneman raised eight children on their Collinsville farm: LeRoy, Fae Marie (Mrs. Gil Jaramilla), Dixie Jean (Mrs. Floyd Baker), David, Donald, Marvin Otto, Crawford and Darlene (Mrs. Steven Lesicko). LeRoy married Theresa Viviano and had three sons, Leroy James, Robert and Randy. Fae married Gil Jaramilla. Dixie married Floyd Baker and had Robin, Lisa (Mrs. Daniel Hearn), Melody and Weily. David has a daughter, Carey, by his marriage to Michelle Crosby. David has one son, Colten Steven. Donald has three children, Allen, Cathy (Mrs. Craig Scwartztrauber) and Christina (Mrs. Richard Grieve). Marvin has four sons by his marriage to Sandra Gnavi, Jeffrey Scott, Brian Marvin, Joel and Reagen Eric. Darlene and her husband, Steven Lesicko, have one daughter, Jennifer.

Kenneth Richard was born November 1, 1905. Kenneth married Hattie Belle Donnelly and had one son, Kenneth Terry. Terry married Patricia Sanders and had one son, Michael. *Submitted by Anna M. (Wendler) Huckla.*

MARILYN AND BEN WESSELMANN - Ben Wesselmann was born to Aloys and Dorothy Wesselmann in Breese, IL, and was raised on several farms in Clinton County.

Marilyn and Ben Wesselmann, 2000.

Centralia, IL, was where Marilyn Aussieker was born to Ezra and Gladys Aussieker, and she was raised in the Hoyleton area.

Ben and Marilyn were married in Centralia where they lived for two years. They then moved to Mt. Vernon, IL, for the next year, and later, to Hoyleton, IL, for 30 years.

They moved to Troy in November 1997 from Hoyleton. They looked at several communities in Clinton and Madison counties and chose Troy due to the size of the city and accessibility to the different interstates.

They have two daughters, Michelle, married to Doug Buss of Glen Carbon, IL, and Danelle, married to Erich Maschhoff of Jackson, MO. They have three granddaughters: Madilyn and Megan Maschhoff and Anna Marie.

They are members of Friedens United Church of Christ in Troy.

Ben has been employed at Lange-Stegmann Co., St. Louis, MO, since June 1986 and Marilyn has worked at the Troy *Times-Tribune* since March 1998. *Submitted by Marilyn Wesselmann.*

JOHANNES AND ANNA MARIA (SCHNEIDER) WIEGAND -

Johannes was born on August 3, 1802, in Schenklengsfeld, Hesse, to the Mayor and Parish Elder Heinrich Wiegand. He married Anna Maria Schneider, the daughter of Asmus Schneider, on July 21, 1826, in Schenklengsfeld. She was born on December 9, 1809.

After their marriage, their first son, Heinrich Wiegand, was born on Deceber 22, 1833.

Johannes and Anna had a second child on September 15, 1836, named after her mother, Anna Maria Wiegand. Johannes and Anna Maria stayed in Germany a few more years before braving the trip to the new world.

On August 11, 1840, Johannes and family arrived in Baltimore, MD, on the *Dorothea Louise*. After landing in Baltimore, the story goes that Johannes had to rescue his wife by grabbing her hair as she fell off the gangplank while disembarking the boat. Johannes and family proceeded to Troy, where their third child, Peter Wiegand, was born on August 8, 1841. Johannes bought farmland around Troy and began farming.

Peter Wiegand, circa 1880

Elizabeth Wiegand was born in 1844 and Melinda Wiegand in 1848. Heinrich Wiegand died in June of 1850 after contracting cholera; he had only been sick three days when he succumbed to the disease. Shortly after his son's death, Johannes moved his entire family to Fosterburg in Madison County.

Anna married John Hoehn on March 3, 1854, in Fosterburg; they later left Madison County and moved to Iowa. Peter married Marie Elizabeth Paul on November 8, 1866, after returning from serving in the Civil War. Peter went on to become a successful businessman and farmer in Alton and Bunker Hill. Melinda Wiegand married Charles Schaefer and resided in Fosterburg until her death on February 11, 1928.

During the years after moving the family to Fosterburg, Johannes began acquiring land around Fosterburg in Madison and Macoupin Counties. It is believed that he was a generous man, always willing to help his fellow citizens. Johannes died on January 24, 1881, and was buried in Fosterburg Cemetery. Before Anna Maria's death on May 5, 1901, she had been living with her daughter Melinda. *Submitted by Laura Wiegand.*

DEBORAH AND KEVIN WIESE -

Deborah (Deeren) and Kevin Wiese have lived in Troy since 1994. They have two children, Kathryn (b. February 7, 1990) and David (b. October 21, 1992.)

Wedding photo, 1986 (l. to r.) Deborah (Deeren) and Kevin Wiese

Kevin is the son of Edgar (Bud) Wiese and Jean (Williams) Wiese of Highland. He attended Highland schools and the University of Illinois where he received a degree in Electrical Engineering. He is employed in the Military Aircraft and Missiles Systems Division of the Boeing Company. Kevin is an Eagle Scout and Vigil Honor member of the Order of the Arrow. He gets to the golf course as often as possible.

Deborah (Deeren) Wiese was born and raised in Troy, attended Troy schools and SIUE where she received a degree in Physics. After graduate school, Debbie worked for McDonnell Douglas as an engineer. A stay-at-home mom for several years, she has just completed studies for teaching certification and plans to teach math or science in the public schools.

Both Mr. and Mrs. Wiese are interested in music and have sung in choirs all of their lives, most notably the "Black Tie Affair," a semi-professional group based in Edwardsville. They both play in the Troy Community Band — Kevin, the baritone horn and Debbie, the clarinet. Every year Kevin participates in "Tuba Christmas" in St. Louis. Daughter Katie carries on the tradition, studying the flute.

The Wieses are members of Friedens United Church of Christ. They are also active in the Troy PTO, and Debbie is a Market Day co-chairperson. David is interested in soccer, basketball, karate (where he has earned 6 belts) and baseball. Katie plays the flute and is interested in art, drama, karate, gymnastics, and swimming. She will graduate from Triad High School in 2008 and David in 2011. *Submitted by Debbie Wiese.*

PAUL B. AND ANNA M. WILD -

In the late 1800s Paul B. Wild from Belleville, IL, and Anna M. Pfeifer from Highland, IL, married. They lived in a house where Dr. Lopatin's parking lot is now.

To them were born three children: Orville J.T. Wild, Aug. 6, 1900; Paul W.A. Wild, March 27, 1903; and Agnes M. Wild, Jan. 19, 1913.

Orville died April 14, 1919. Paul died April 17, 1919, and the mother, Anna, died April 17, 1919, all from the flu. They are buried at the Friedens Cemetery in Troy.

Agnes was the first baby born in 1913 in Troy, and she received a silver cup with her name on it from the *Troy Call.*

Paul B. Wild was a coal miner in Troy.

Agnes went to the Troy Public School in the lower grades and finished grade school in St. Paul's Lutheran School and high school at McCray Dewey. Agnes worked at Martha Manning dress factory in Collinsville, IL, until she met Carl L. Gieseking from Pin Oak. They married on March 25, 1935. They had two children: Dorothy Ann born April 6, 1938; and Kenneth Carl, born June 7, 1939.

Agnes and Carl quit farming in 1957 and moved to Troy. Carl was a self-employed house painter, and Agnes became a nurse.

Carl passed away April 25, 1983. Agnes passed away Sept. 6, 1996.

Their daughter, Dorothy Ann, married Raymond Hasty Oct. 8, 1955. They live in Troy and have three sons, eight grandchildren and one great-grandchild.

Their son, Kenneth, married in 1961 and lives in Highland, and has three sons and nine grandchildren. *Submitted by Dorothy Hasty.*

HENRY AND FRANCES WILHELM

Henry John Wilhelm was born June 7, 1886, in Pin Oak Township, a son of John and Johanna Holtmann Wilhelm. He had seven siblings in his family: Carrie Wilhelm Ottwein (married George Ottwein), Emma Wilhelm (died at age 18), Lydia Wilhelm Blumberg (married Fred Blumberg), Hannah Wilhelm Dettmer (married Edward Dettmer), Louisa Wilhelm Bohnenstiehl (married Robert Bohnenstiehl), Augusta Wilhelm (born June 22, 1890, died September 5, 1890) and George Wilhelm (married Berniece Paust).

Wilhelm family, circa 1940 (l. to r.) Front: Henry and Frances Middle: Agnes, Sue, Marge Back: John, Fred Wopat

The family moved to a farm in the Troy area when he was young. He attended a rural school and a German school in Troy for two years. Following German school, he was confirmed at Troy Friedens Church.

Henry farmed with his parents for a number of years. As a young man, he enjoyed dancing, especially the waltz. He also liked to play pinochle.

Henry met Frances Harris when she taught at Formosa school. They were married September 15, 1915, at Grandma and Grandpa (Washington Dew) Renfro's home in Troy.

Henry farmed most of his life, but worked a short time in construction at Lumaghi Coal

Mine #2 in Collinsville in 1922. He was seriously hurt in a fall from a scaffold. After recovering, he never returned to the mine.

Henry served a number of years on Formosa school board. He sold insurance a few years for Country Companies. He worked on Jarvis Township roads, running the grader.

Henry was a member of Troy Masonic Lodge until it closed. He then became a member of Collinsville Masonic Lodge. He was a member of the Ainad Temple in East St. Louis and a member of the Scottish Rite Bodies of East St. Louis.

Henry and Frances Wilhelm were the parents of four children: Sue (married Fred Wopat), Marge (married Eric Strickland), Agnes (married Oscar Helmkamp), and John Henry Wilhelm (married LaVera Ballinger). John died January 11, 1973.

There are 14 grandchildren, 24 great grandchildren, (Steven Iberg is deceased), and 4 great-great grandchildren.

Frances taught in rural schools four years before she married Henry. She returned to teaching in 1933. She taught in the Blackjack, Formosa, Columbia, Bond, Hedgemound and Pleasant Grove rural schools. She also taught in the Collinsville School District. After retiring from the public schools, she taught in Granite City and Highland at the Catholic schools. She taught a total of 40 years.

After retiring from teaching, Frances became an avid quilt maker. She made and gave her children, grandchildren and great grandchildren a total of 54 quilts. She only sold seven quilts and gave three dear relatives each a quilt, which made a total of 64 quilts. There were 17 quilts stored at her home when she passed away. She also embroidered many scarves, pillowcases and pictures. Her crocheted afghans have kept many warm on a cool evening. Many of these items were given to others as gifts.

Henry died September 8, 1956, at the age of 70. Frances died June 26, 1991, at age 97. *Submitted by Agnes Helmkamp and Sue Wopat.*

JOHN AND JOHANNA WILHELM - John Wilhelm, son of Joseph and Mary Winz Wilhelm, was born January 29, 1853, in Lawrenceburg, IN, or Kentucky. Soon afterward, he and his family moved to St. Lois, MO. He attended parochial school until he was eleven. After his mother died in 1864, John and his siblings were placed in a Catholic orphanage. At age fourteen he worked for an uncle making combs from cattle horns. Later, he came to Illinois and worked on farms in the American bottoms, Pin Oak Township and near Troy.

John and Johanna (Holtmann) Wilhelm, 1915

John married Johanna Holtmann on September 6, 1878, in a double ceremony with her sister, Freiderika, and Ernest Hoelscher. Johanna was born near Warrenton, MO, on January 17, 1857, and, as a small child, came to Pin Oak Township, Madison County, with her parents.

John and Johanna had less than a dollar after the wedding ceremony. They started married life with a house on five acres, a team of horses and a wagon. They raised potatoes, which were hauled and sold in St. Louis. John enjoyed reading his German newspaper. Johanna worked very hard in the fields beside her husband.

On winter evenings, John spun wool into yarn, while Johanna and the older children knitted the yarn into stockings and gloves. While fixing breakfast, Johanna would cook a pot of sauerkraut, potatoes, and pork for dinner and keep it warm in a feather bed. Bread dough was also kept warm in the feather bed. During her life, Johanna made 26 quilts, one for each grandchild.

John and Johanna enjoyed playing cards and loved to dance, especially the waltz. John was proud of his black horses, and the surrey he bought at the 1904 World's Fair in St. Louis. He was a school director and a road overseer.

The family was very active all their lives in the German Evangelical Church in Troy.

By 1911, John owned two farms, consisting of 317 acres near Troy. After John and Johanna's death, Robert and Louisa Bohnenstiehl purchased one farm. Henry and Frances Wilhelm bought the other farm. Later, the Bohnenstiehl farm was sold and developed into the Country Village subdivision. At one time General William Tecumseh Sherman owned the other Wilhelm farm. This farm is still in the Wilhelm family.

John and Johanna Wilhelm had eight children: Caroline, born June 8, 1879, married George Ottwein, died September 29, 1984; Emma, born February 22, 1882, died October 1899; Lydia, born April 16, 1884, married Fred Blumberg, died October 30, 1981; Henry, born June 7, 1886, married Frances Harris, died September 8, 1956; Hannah, born August 19, 1888, married Edward Dettmer, died January 29, 1968; Louisa, born March 5, 1890, married Robert Bohnenstiehl, died August 4, 1985; Augusta, born June 22, 1896, died September 1896; George, born August 2, 1898, married Berneice Paust, died May 10, 1999. Surviving today are 15 grandchildren, 60 great-grandchildren, 78 great-great grandchildren, and 37 great-great-great-grandchildren. *Submitted by Agnes Helmkamp and Sue Wopat.*

JOHN AND LAVERA WILHELM - John Henry Wilhelm was born January 13, 1923, and died January 11, 1973. John was born on the family farm in Jarvis Township. The delivery was by Dr. Charles Molden. John attended high school in Troy and Collinsville. In order to take shop classes that were only offered in Collinsville, he had to speak with every school board member from both schools.

Luck had it that another student wanted to attend in Troy, so a trade was granted. World

War II started before he graduated, and John attempted to enlist but was turned down. After graduating, he rode the train to Chicago to meet the draft board and again was refused because he was running the family farms, deemed an essential job.

LaVera Ruth (Ballinger) Wilhelm Hogg was born August 19, 1924. LaVera's present husband is Stephan Hogg of Lebanon. LaVera is the daughter of Edith (Allan) Ballinger Winterringer.

Edith was the oldest of three children born to Martha (Pearson) Allan and Joseph Allan. Alvin Allan and Virginia (Kraft) Brunnworth were her siblings. The Allan family owned a cornerstore in Collinsville. Joseph Allan was a crane operator for the coal mines. Joseph built a barn and house on the Formosa Road. The home was not finished, but the family moved into the barn and hung sheets to create rooms. As summer changed to fall and fall to winter, Martha grew restless, and the family moved from the barn into the unfinished home.

On January 15, 1944, John and LaVera were married in the Collinsville Methodist Church. Their attendants were Agnes (Wilhelm) Helmkamp and Milton Strong. They made their first home southwest of Troy on the Walter Strong farm. John built a home on the family farm in 1949, where the county salt house now sets. John worked at Socony Vacuum and had a shop at home where he welded and sharpened plow shears for neighboring farmers.

When the state decided to build I-55-70 in 1955, the family had to leave their home. They purchased the farm where the family currently resides on Troy-O'Fallon Road.

Four children were born to the couple. Patricia Lee Iberg Hindle was born May 12, 1945. She had one child, Steven Lee Iberg, born September 9, 1966, died Sept. 28, 1988.

John Berdell Wilhelm arrived on April 17, 1949. He married Mary Bauer from Freeburg and has one daughter, Hannah Rose, born December 3, 1980.

Sharon Kay Jasper, born April 8, 1952, married Thomas Jasper of Belleville in 1970. Two children were born: Bryan, born June 5, 1976, and Dawn, born July 30, 1977.

Barbara Jane Stark was born February 14, 1964. Barbara married Brian Stark from New York. They have a daughter, Ashley, born July 26, 1996.

John served as Road Commissioner and on the school board. John and family were active in the Troy Methodist Church, Lions Club, and Masonic Lodge in Marine and Highland, where he was a 32nd degree Mason. *Submitted by Sharon Jasper and Pat Hindle.*

RICHARD AND GAIL (MERSINGER) WOLFF - Gail Louise Mersinger, the oldest of two children, was born in Highland, IL, on February 6, 1946, to Gilbert Henry and Muriel Lloyd Mersinger who lived on a farm southwest of Troy. She was joined in 1952 by a sister Janet Veronica. Gail attended Troy grade schools and Triad High School. After earning a Bachelor's Degree in business from SIUE, she worked at Ralston Purina Company as a secretary for five years, then left to teach business courses at Patricia Stevens Career College in

Dick and Gail Wolff

St. Louis. Gail returned to Ralston Purina in 1974 where she built a career in human resources. She earned a Master's Degree in Management from Webster College in 1979, and later achieved the ratings of Certified Administrative Manager and Senior Professional of Human Resources. Gail served on the Board of Directors of The Vanderschmidt School in St. Louis for ten years. After leaving Ralston Purina in 1995, she joined Wehrenberg Theatres, Inc., in St. Louis as its first Director of Human Resources.

In early 1981 at a professional meeting, Gail met Richard Edward Wolff. He was born December 20, 1937, the third child of Robert Thomas and Grace Constance (Ward) Wolff, joining a brother Robert Thomas Jr., and sister Barbara Jean. Richard's mother had died in 1979, his father, later in 1986, and then his sister in 1988. Richard grew up in St. Louis County, attended Brentwood schools and earned a Bachelor's Degree in Business Administration from the University of Missouri in Columbia. He worked at McDonnell Aircraft Corporation and Monsanto Company before starting his own records management consulting business, Wolff and Associates, in 1970. Richard is also a "sports fanatic" with particular interests in baseball, football, ice hockey, basketball, golf and tennis, having excelled in several of these sports in earlier years.

On September 5, 1981, Gail and Richard were married in St. Louis County and purchased a home in Ballwin. Richard has four daughters: Pamela Jeanne (Thomas) Yeaple, Jennifer Hope Wolff, Eleanor Constance Querry and Elizabeth Wright Wolff. He has eight grandchildren.

Following Gail's mother's death, they purchased her country home where Gail and Janet grew up. They like to spend time in the country, where they can relax and visit Gail's nieces and nephew, Jill, Amy and Lee next door. In addition to spending family time, Richard and Gail enjoy spectator sports, ballroom dancing and travel. *Submitted by Gail Wolff.*

WUENCH FAMILY - Carl and Cleola (Bugger) Wuench were married June 24, 1961, at St. John's Catholic Church in Blackjack. Cleola was Carl's second wife. *Submitted by Carol Rives.*

Carl & Cleola Wuench

CARL WUENCH - Carl Dale Wuench and Florence Mayme Schmitt were married May 8, 1937, in Collinsville, IL. After living in Collinsville a few years, they moved to the Henry Segelken farm, northwest of St. Jacob, IL. Carl worked for the Illinois Railroad, Brooks Catsup, and later for the Illinois Highway Department under the Eisenhower Administration. He also operated his own sorghum mill on Kirsch's farm at west Kirsch Road, south of Troy, where they moved to in 1948. They later moved to St. Jacob on May 7, 1955.

Florence (Schmitt) and Carl Wuench, 1937

Three daughters were born to them: Joann Marie on April 25, 1939; Carol Jean on March 21, 1943; and Dorris Florine on May 12, 1948.

Florence Wuench passed away June 11, 1951. On June 24, 1961, Carl married Cleola Bugger of Troy, IL. He died on November 12, 1980. Cleola works for Strackeljohn Farms in St. Jacob.

Joann attended the Spring Valley School on West Kirsch Road from 1948-1950. Carol attended the school, also, being the only one in the first grade in 1949-1950, the last year before the school closed. The girls then attended Troy Grade School.

On September 23, 1961, Joann married Wesley Krause of Belleville. She is a homemaker in Swansea, IL. They have four children: Ed of Freeburg, IL; Debbie Thompson and her son, Zachary, of Columbia, IL; Karen Dick of Belleville; and Beverly Eckele and her son, Cameron, of Franklin, TN.

Carol was in the second class to graduate from Triad High School on May 26, 1961. She married Larry Sugg of Greenville, IL, on October 3, 1965. They have one child, Diana, of Meadowbrook, IL, and a grandson, Dylan, who was born May 5, 1998. Carol is employed at the Carbondale, IL, Post Office. On August 20, 1987, she married Richard Rives, who died on July 8, 1996.

(l. to r.) Joann Krause, Dorris Meisenheimer and Carol Rives, 1992

Dorris graduated from Greenville High School in May, 1966. She married David Griffin of Fieldon, IL, on February 5, 1974. They have one child, Cathy, and a grandson Michael of Bethalto, IL. Dorris also has another daughter, Christy, and a granddaughter, Kaleigh, of Staunton, IL. Dorris married George Meisenheimer of Alton, IL, on May 9, 1985, and is a homemaker. *Submitted by Carol Rives.*

DR. WALTER ZIELONKO

Zielonko family, 2002. (l. to r.) Front: Florence and Walter Zielonko. Back: Bill, Tom, Marty, Fred, Steve.

Butchering on the Riebold farm, 1910-1920s.

(Below) Cornelius "Cornie" Schmitt driving a W-C Allis Chalmers tractor and pulling a Woods cornpicker; Adrian Mersinger on right, 1940. The tractor and picker belonged to Oscar Mersinger.

(Left) Silver Creek flood, Riebold farm, 1946. George Waters, Kenneth Loyet, Oscar Riebold and Melvin Niehaus.

(Right) Andy Semanisin on bumper; Oscar Gindler behind Andy.

Businesses of Today

Intersection of Edwardsville Road and Riggin Road with traffic signal, early 1990s.

(Below) Edwardsville Road (Route 162) looking east, circa 1967.

101, 103, 105, and 107 East Market Street, 1995. Allen's Drugs on corner.

Troy, Illinois Area
History and Families

Times-Tribune
History of Troy Newspapers

Local newspaper history had its origin in Appleton City, St. Claire County, Missouri, then a town of less than 1,000 people. It was the winter of 1871 when James N. Jarvis, a lad of 22 years, upon the recommendation of a St. Louis music supply house, went to be the instructor of the Appleton City Cornet Band.

It so happened that A.L. Stone and D.C. Meyers, members of the band, were the publishers of the *Appleton City Argus,* a weekly newspaper that had been launched 22 weeks previously. It also happened that the Argus office was a favorite hangout for band members. In fact, the practice meetings were held there.

Young Jarvis, in hanging around the Argus office, became interested in the printing business; and although he was by nature left-handed, he learned to set type right-handed. In the few months that followed, he became thoroughly inoculated with printers' ink – an infection which would persist for three generations.

When his engagement as instructor of the Appleton City Band came to an end in February 1872, Jarvis was anxious to return to Troy. There were two reasons: one was to start a newspaper of his own and the other was Miss Elizabeth Donoho. The first issue of Troy's first newspaper, *The Commercial Bulletin,* made its appearance on May 18, 1872.

Jarvis stated in the first issue, "It is a great pleasure to us that we are able to place the *Commercial Bulletin* before the citizens of Troy and vicinity. It is our intention to publish 500 copies on the first and fifteenth of every month, except when those dates fall on Sunday, then on the Saturday preceding.

The new Times–Tribune *sign at 201 East Market Street. (1990s)*

We shall endeavor to fill our paper with reading matter that will be instructive and entertaining and will also keep a market which will be corrected every time we publish, and

The old Troy Tribune *building on North Main Street. The newspaper was published here by Paul Simon, Ray Johnsen, Paul Ping and Howard Wood from 1948 to 1987. Photo was taken in 1988 after the two newspapers merged.*

The Troy Times *was located in the rear of this building at 201 East Market Street from Feb. 1985 to June 1987 when it merged with* The Troy Tribune *to become the* Times–Tribune. *This photo was taken in 1987.*

we promise our patrons and readers that when it will pay us to do so, we will enlarge our paper."

Advertising rates at the masthead were as follows: "Advertising rates, 75 cents per square." In 1873, the name of the newspaper was changed to *The Weekly Bulletin.* It was published by James N. Jarvis until April 1881, when the paper and plant were sold to George M. Armstrong and Joseph Umberger. This firm lasted but a few months. Umberger took a position with the *Edwardsville Democrat* and Armstrong, not being a printer, sold the paper to Henry B. Morriss. The latter published the paper for two years, then sold it to Dr. F.A. Sabin, who, after a few months, leased it to Edward Bigelow. By this time the paper had rundown due to being in inexperienced hands; however, there continued to be a demand for a paper and printing establishment in Troy.

In 1885, Jarvis established the *Troy Record,* bought the *Bulletin,* and merged the two papers under the former name. The paper was independent.

It was sold a year later to L.K. Pauley, who conducted the paper for three months, and the plant was then taken back under a foreclosure of mortgage.

The Record was suspended; Jarvis continued in the printing business until October 25, 1886, when the plant was sold to Henry A. and Fred W. Miller, who established *The Troy Monitor.* After a short time, the plant was moved to Collinsville and *The Collinsville Monitor* was launched. After several years the paper was sold to Samuel W. Rawson and George C. Hartung, who continued to publish the *Monitor,* but a short time later Rawson sold his interest to Hartung who discontinued the business in Collinsville, removed the plant to Troy and established *The Troy Star* on March 29, 1893. On March 21, 1894, Hartung sold the paper to Joseph F. Edwards and August Droll who completed the first volume of the *Star* and then established *The Weekly Call.*

The partnership of Edwards and Droll as owners and publishers of *The Weekly Call* lasted nine months; Edwards then sold his interest to Droll, who continued to publish the paper until November 12, 1896, then leased the plant to Anderson L. Bounds and B.W. Jarvis, both of whom had been employed by the paper. The partnership was unique in that the senior partner was 75 years old and the junior partner, 19, and it lasted but three months.

Jarvis then leased the plant for another three months, then threw in the sponge. The plant was idle for several months, then was leased by R.V. Moran from Missouri, who put out two issues of the paper and was glad to be afforded an opportunity to withdraw. After another interim of several months, the paper was revived by the owner who continued to publish it until March 13, 1899, when it was sold to B.W. Jarvis.

When *The Call* was purchased on March 13, 1899, it was with an understanding that it was to be moved from the Droll building to a more central location.

The late M.F. Auwarter was interviewed and consented to provide a location by closing up the gap between his store building and the post office. It was not until December that the building was ready, and then the equipment of *The Call* was moved into it. One of the first improvements to be made was to discard the Washington hand press and install a Country Campbell cylinder press and enlarge the paper from a five to six column publication. The press was at first turned by hand, which was a sweat-producing and back-breaking job. This continued for several years, and then horsepower was installed with more or less success, mostly less. After that came a gasoline engine, which in those days was none too reliable and which, with the coming of electricity to Troy, was succeeded by an electric motor.

Two new job presses, a newspaper folder and other more up-to-date printing material was added from time to time. The Country Campbell finally gave way to a Cransten cylinder press and attachable Omaha folder, which does the printing and folding of the paper in one operation.

Paul Simon, 19, as the young publisher/editor of The Troy Tribune. *(late 1940s, pre-bow tie)*

The Call was the first weekly newspaper in the county to install a typesetting and linecasting machine. *The Call's* first machine was a Roger's Typograph – likewise a noble experiment – purchased second-hand from the Bay City, Michigan, *Tribune*. It was so complicated and wonderfully and fearfully made, that not one complete issue was ever gotten out with it.

The Improved American Typograph followed and some years later was succeeded by a Model 15 Linotype and later a more modern Model 14 Linotype. Later the Typograph came into being at *The Call* office.

Sen. Paul Simon, Arlene Bellmann and Paul Ping at Bellmann's 40 years at the newspaper celebration.

It was the longest continuously running newspaper in the county when Jarvis closed the doors in 1946 due to poor health. Troy was out of a newspaper again for about one year. In 1948, a young man by the name of Paul Simon, 19, with the help of the Troy Lions Club, purchased the paper and began printing under the name *The Troy Tribune*. The plant was located at 105 East Market Street. Later, Simon moved his newspaper to the 106 North Main Street location.

Simon continued as the youngest newspaper publisher/editor in the nation until he began his public political life in the early 1950s. At that time the newspaper was sold to Ray Johnsen, who married a Troy girl, Nancy Watson.

In July 1967, *The Troy Tribune* was sold to Paul R. Ping of O'Fallon, who, in October 1978, sold it to Howard Wood, a sports reporter at the newspaper. Wood ran the

Arlene Bellmann, longtime employee of The Troy Tribune, *worked for 40-plus year and was an Editorial Assistant.*

newspaper until it was merged with *The Troy Times* in 1987.

In February 1985, Paul R. Ping under the Newsprint Ink, a corporation, began Troy's second newspaper and named it *The Troy Times*. It was a small office and was located in the rear (201-E) of the building at 201 East Market Street. Ping was the publisher/editor; Mae Grapperhaus was the reporter; and Susan Ping was the typesetter.

About 18 months later, the newspaper was moved to the front of the building on the east side. The two newspapers, *The Troy Tribune* and *The Troy Times* were competing for the same news and advertising turf. It was inevitable that the two would merge.

This took place in the 201 E. Market Street address in June of 1987. The newspaper's new name was the *Times-Tribune*. Paul Ping was Executive Publisher, Arlene Bellmann, who had worked for *The Tribune* for 30 years, was the editorial assistant and Marvin France was the editorial reporter.

The tabloid insert named *The Illinoisian* was printed for a short while along with the regular weekly edition. In 1990, the newspaper office expanded to the west side of the building. Employees included Judy Suess, Mike Huck, Mae Grapperhaus, Sue Yates and Arlene Bellmann.

In 1994, Don Lehnhoff was hired as editor. In 1998, Lehnhoff resigned and Mae Grapperhaus was promoted to the editor's position. In 2001, Darrell Hampsten became the assistant editor.

In 2002, Paul Ping is CEO/Publisher; Mae Grapperhaus is editor; Darrell Hampsten is assistant editor; staff members are Reba Mathis, receptionist/typesetting; Marilyn Wesselmann, bookkeeper/typesetting; Susan Yates, production assistant; Amy Moorleghen, sales representative; Lisa Barras, sports reporter; Derek Crain and Gene Barnard, reporters; Brett Ramsey, summer help; correspondents include Lil Maedge for Marine, Joyce Lininger for Maryville, Sheri Whitaker for St. Jacob and Mike Leonard as sports correspondent.

The *Times-Tribune* is printed at the *Edwardsville Intelligencer* on Tuesday evenings for a Thursday edition each week. Modern computers are used to set type. The newspaper has over 4,000 subscribers.

Allen's Drug Store

Allen's Drug Store, 2002

Allen's Drug Store occupied part of the historic Auwarter Building at the corner of Main and Market. Built in the 1800s, the large building housed various businesses over the years – tavern, merchandise store, Kingston Drug Store, Schoon Rexall Drug and Embrey's Hardware Store. Accounts report at one time that people even rented rooms or apartments over the store when M.F. Auwarter ran his merchandise store there in 1885.

Later, Fred Auwarter ran the store from 1931-1934. In 1945 John and Edna Schoon purchased the Auwarter Building and retained their ownership of the building, even when Jule Kamm ran a drugstore there.

John Schoon owned the building until 1960 when he sold it to Allen and Sue Holloway. Allen and Sue ran Allen's Drug Store until their retirement. Both Sue and Allen grew up in Troy, lived and raised four sons here. They gave friendly, small town, personalized service to their many friends. It didn't matter if a customer was a Troy native or a new resident. He would enter as a customer, but always returned as a friend. Arthritis medicine or poster board, band-aids or a gift, cough syrup or Beanie Babies – it was available at Allen's, along with a smile and a friendly greeting. Many students also recall getting off the activity bus or meeting the fan bus at Allen's. The store was an important part of the community.

It still retains its importance and name in the community, even though Allen and Sue sold it to Todd Evers in 1998 upon their retirement. The friendly, personalized service still remains, and Allen's Drug Store continues to be an important part of the Troy community.

302

Tradition • Innovation • Community Service

Founded in 1868, TheBANK has anded itself on providing customers with quality personal service and innovative products while focusing on community involvement as a locally-owned independent bank.

In 1990, TheBANK became a member of the Troy community, serving residents here with a convenient full-service location. In 1999, TheBANK moved to a newly-constructed Center along Route 162, raising its service to an even higher level.

TheBANK has continually offered cutting edge, innovative services such as a free debit card, free telephone banking, free online banking, online bill paying, and more.

As a member of the community, TheBANK actively supports civic and charitable organizations such as: Troy Chamber of Commerce; Troy Kiwanis; local schools; youth sports; Ministries Unlimited; and Friends of the Library, among others.

TheBANK has a rich tradition of history that is strongly based in service to its customers and its community.

TheBANK
of Edwardsville
Troy Center

507 Edwardsville Road
618/667-6702

www.4thebank.com

303

Kamm's Soft Water

Gari and Theresa Hanalei in front of Kamm's Soft Water.

Gari and Theresa Hanalei, who opened their doors for business on January 1, 1995, at 619 South Main Street, operate Kamm's Soft Water. They purchased the business from long-time owners, Yvonne and Arthur "Swiss" Kamm, who had originally purchased the business on September 1, 1969, from R.0. Matsel. Matsel was located within the Western Auto Store at the southwest corner of South Main and Center Streets. The Kamms then moved the business to their home located on Collinsville Road and continued there until December 1994. Now, as a consultant, Swiss Kamm keeps in close contact with the Hanaleis and continues to offer support.

The business offers installation of water softeners for rent or sale, as well as installation of filters, chemical feeders and water purifiers. It also offers delivery of solar salt and potassium, or they can be purchased at the store. Gari repairs and services most makes and models of water softeners.

A typical water-softening system removes calcium and magnesium ions from hard water and replaces them with sodium ions. Calcium and magnesium ions interfere with the action of household soaps and detergents, but sodium does not. The water-softening process helps detergents to more effectively remove dirt and oils from clothing and dishes. Most manufacturers of water softeners recommend reduction of the amount of soap and detergents used after installing a water softener.

Store offers pool chemicals

In the summer of 1995, Gari decided to add a swimming pool chemical line to his shop. Customers would ask Gari about chemicals for their pool because there wasn't a nearby pool chemical supply

The business sells Pool Pride Chemicals and offers competitive prices for a good brand of chemicals. Their best sellers are the five-gallon liquid chlorine for $15.95 and the 16-pound container of three-inch chlorine tablets for $45. Often customers will purchase the 8-pound container for $19. But Gari and Theresa generally try to sell them the 16-pound bucket because of the great savings. The larger the quantity, the better the deal. Tip to remember: "The cheaper chemicals dissolve quicker and you use more in the long run." Keep an eye out for "bargains." You need to watch for the "active ingredient percentage" when you purchase any chemicals for your pool.

Kamm's has had great success with the chemicals, and customers have commented on how well-maintained their pool has been since switching over to Pool Pride. Several customers said they were using chemicals from the discount stores and could not maintain their pool with those brands. The pool was either cloudy or it turned green frequently. Gari has helped several customers to maintain a great, crystal clear pool all summer long. Stop by and try these products. We can order anything you need, including any pool equipment, parts, lines and /or accessories. The store only carries standard size liners, but any size liner can be ordered and delivered within a week.

Gari and Theresa have brought a great deal of business experience to their company. Gari worked in the construction business for many years and then worked with Swiss Kamm in the water conditioning business. He is a dedicated, independent dealer who is well known for his honest workmanship.

Theresa worked in the computer field for larger corporations throughout St. Louis and uses her computer experience, as well as administrative knowledge in managing the office and daily bookkeeping. The couple have three children, Patrese, 11; Natalie, 8; and Chad, 6. They reside in Troy where Gari Hanalei has lived for the past 30 years. Theresa is originally from Collinsville.

Things to Know

Kamm's year round service hours are Tuesday through Saturday from 8 a.m. to 5 p.m. Office hours are Tuesday through Thursday from 1 p.m. to 5 p.m.; Friday from 9 a.m. to 5 p.m. and Saturday from 8 a.m. to noon. Summer Saturday hours are from 8 a.m. to 4 p.m. The telephone number is 618-667-9316.

Submitted by Theresa Hanalei

St. Louis East Truck Plaza, Inc.

Troy Truck Plaza "76".

St. Louis East Truck Plaza, Inc. (aka Union 76 Truckstop from 1972-1996 and Amoco Travel Center from 1996 to current), located on the northeastern corner of Route 162 and Interstate 55-70, opened November 8, 1972. At that time, the property was owned by Union Oil Company of California, supplying the 76 brand refined fuel and oil products. St. Louis East Truck Plaza, Inc. retails fuel to truckers and over-the-road passengers, along with a full-service family restaurant, garage and shop services, convenient store/gift shop, motel rooms, barber shop, propane fills, and many other services.

This truckstop was part of a 140 full-service truckstop chain from coast to coast. Mr. Irvin J. Grimes and partners owned and operated the business from the start. Mr. Grimes, married with four children, originally from Cincinnati, Ohio, moved to the St. Louis County area in 1972. In 1984, the Grimes family moved their home to Edwardsville, Illinois, when he became sole owner of the business. In 1985, Mr. Grimes hired a University City police officer, also his son-in-law, Mr. Ronald L. Flynn, to become General Manager over the business. Shortly after, he hired another son-in-law, Paul A. Thalhammer, as Comptroller of the business. In 1988, with the business doing exceptionally well, Mr. Flynn became President.

In 1990, Irv, Ron, and Paul decided to purchase another truckstop located in Oklahoma City, Oklahoma, to be operated by Mr. Flynn. Mr. Thalhammer was then promoted to President of St. Louis East Truck Plaza, Inc. By 1991, Mr. Thalhammer originally from the St. Louis County area, moved his wife, Barb, and their three children, Lisa, Nicholas, and Amanda to Edwardsville, Illinois. Shortly afterwards, Mr. Grimes decided to retire.

In 1993, Union Oil Company of California decided to sell their truckstop division. A group of truckstops and their owners, including St. Louis East Truck Plaza, Inc., decided to form a company called National Auto Truck Stops, based in Nashville, Tennessee, to purchase all 140 truckstop locations from the Union Oil Company of California.

In 1996, St. Louis East Truck Plaza, Inc. replaced all their underground storage tanks, re-branded with AMOCO gasoline, and built a free standing Hardee's Restaurant. Also, during 1995-1996, with merger mania going strong in corporate America, National Auto Truck Stops was being acquired by Truck Stops of America, another truckstop chain with 60 truckstops. During this transition, Ron and Paul decided to sell their location in Oklahoma City and purchase the St. Louis East Truck Plaza, Inc. property and buildings, located in Troy, and try this business as an independent location. This transaction was completed in 1997. Mr. Flynn, now Vice-President and head of operations, is living in Maryville, Illinois, and Mr. Thalhammer continues to be President and Comptroller.

In the fall of 1998, Hardee's closed. In the spring of 1999, the former Hardee's Restaurant became home to Paco's Mexican Restaurant, locally owned and operated by Adrian (Paco) Huergo. Paco's remained open until the fall of 2000. Since the summer of 2001, Mama Mia's Italian Restaurant has been open and is locally owned and operated by Memet Dincer.

Although the years 2000 and 2001 have been tough years on the economy, Paul and Ron believe St. Louis East Truck Plaza, Inc. is positioned well for the future! "One great reason we've been successful in the past and are positioned well for the future is due to the dedication of our employees."

Over 20 Years: Barb Avers, Greg Carter Sr., Howard Chamberlin, Vicky Jason, Eva Leath, Veronica Neighbors, Joan Niebruegge, Nancy Scheyer, Larry Strauss, Jo Tate, Randy Trebing, Joann Harris-Ret, Carol Jones-Ret, Rick Kossakoski-Ret, Pat Laswell-Ret, Paula Yount-Ret.

11-20 Years: Sue Frey, Harley Hildreth, Kent Trebing, Warren Jenkins, Dennis Alvis, Paul Becker-Ret, Ed Chamberlin-Ret, Rick Dickerson-Ret, Tom Elmore-Ret, Angela Hydron-Ret, Sonny St. Cin-Ret, Linda Storey - Ret, Nanette Trebing-Ret.

5-10 Years: Greg Carter Jr., Dennis Gardner, Shila Faulkner, Connie Henke, Lorrie Jones, Becky Knabe, Larry King, Gloria Leadley, Doug Leone, Jim Merrell, Ed Rollberg, Ron Stanley, Jose Valdez, Barb Woody, Luke Capps-Ret, Nancy Combs- Ret, Brenda Cusanelli-Ret, Tracy Distler- Ret, Kadie Ernst-Ret, Lenny Elmore-Ret, Peggy Jordan-Ret, Gary Pfister-Ret, Bill Sedlacek Sr.-Ret, Bill Sedlacek Jr.-Ret, Kim Vincent-Ret.

1-4 Years: Carol Bequette, Jacob Brenkendorff, Nathan Case, Chris Cobb, Jason Cook, Jeremy Ealy, Lee Ernst, Willie Fifer, Velta Ford, Kathy Grotsky, Crystal Hill, Sandra Hurd, Debbie Jans, Russ Jarman, Robert Keller, Leslie Klaus, Craig Klingelhoefer, Lorell Krenning, Patricia Launer, Karen League, Erica Lewis, Tara Little, Ronna McGauley, Thomas McNeil, Dana Muller, Justin Niebruegge, Christopher O'Dell, Tiana Petri, Joe Raymond, Linda Raymond, Caroline Rincker, Scott Rodrian, Pam Tamburello.

Looking north, St. Louis East Truck Stop, September 1997.

State Farm Insurance Agency
David M. Margherio, Agent

Equipped with his Chevy Nova and a briefcase of blank applications, David Margherio opened his State Farm Agency on October 1, 1977. His office was located in the pavilion of what was once a rootbeer stand, now the site of the 4-0 Quick Shop. When Century 21 Realty moved out, Agent Margherio moved in. The rent was only $125 a month including utilities, but the building had neither plumbing nor windows. His wife Nancy and Brenda Rechlein, a Triad High School co-op student, comprised the office staff. The population of Troy at that time was approximately 1700. Dave's first applicants were Troy residents Kathy and Mike Nemsky. His first walk-in customer was Doug Goodwin.

In May of 1978 Dave and his staff moved the State Farm Agency to the oldest building in Troy, the log cabin that served as a stage coach stop in former days at 108 West Market. Dave purchased the building from Dorie Williams. The daily business of the agency was handled by Dave, his wife, and Debbie Rippy. A playpen became an

Current location at 540 Edwardsville Road.

office fixture in 1980 when Kristen Margherio, now a junior at Murray State in Kentucky was born. Dana Margherio, a junior at Edwardsville High School, was born in 1984 and made use of that same playpen. The girls joined their father's team approach to the business by licking stamps and envelopes as soon as they could reach the top of his desk.

Karen Gire joined the staff in June of 1982 at the Market Street location. Another Triad co-op student Lisa (Tarjany) Dobson worked there from 1984 until September of 1990. Nancy Boyd was hired in September of 1990. As the city of Troy grew, so did the number of residents who looked to Dave for their insurance needs. As a result, in 1992, David Margherio built a new office building at 540 Edwardsville Road, the agency's present lcoation.

Agent Margherio, his wife Nancy, Karen Gire, and Nancy Boyd were the full-time staff members. Tara (Farrell) Newcombe worked part time as a co-op student and continued to work

Second location at 108 West Market.

until her college graduation. In June of 1999 Linda Ingersoll joined the staff as a full-time employee. Over two thousand households currently call upon Dave and his staff for their insurance services. Though offered the chance to go into management with State Farm, Dave has always chosen to remain on the agency side over the past twenty-four years as he enjoys interacting with the individuals who hold the State Farm policies.

Troy's only State Farm Agent has contributed to many civic organizations and projects including the library, local schools, and sports teams over the years. Likewise, Dave has made an effort to speak to high school students at Triad about the insurance business, especially as it relates to insuring a first car. Over the years people, places, and faces may have changed, but David Margherio's State Farm Agency's Good Neighbor Service has remained a constant in the history of Troy, Illinois.

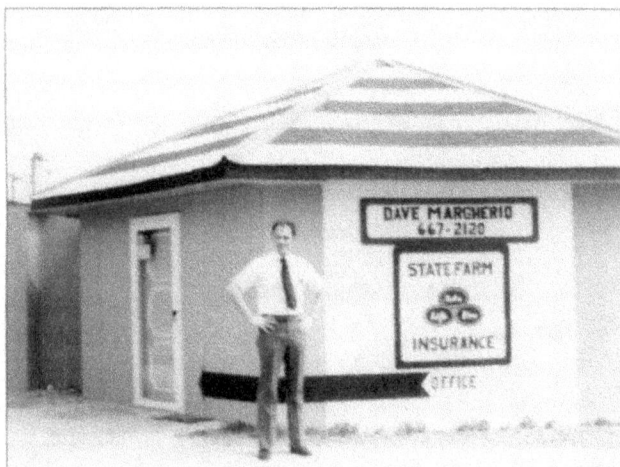
Dave's first office.

Troy Family Dental
Dr. Richard R. Boatman Jr., D.M.D.

Troy Family Dental office, Richard R. Boatman Jr., D.M.D., PC located at 606 Edwardsville Road, Troy, IL.

Dr. Richard R. Boatman Jr. opened his first dental office at 334 Bargraves Boulevard in the newer western end of Troy on January 10, 1989.

The new construction at the time was 1,200 square feet with four dental chairs. As the town and Dr. Boatman's practice continued to grow, the office on Bargraves Boulevard became inadequate.

Dr. Boatman purchased a lot along Route 162 (Edwardsville Road) between Holzinger Realty and the hardware store in 1998. He built a new office with 3,000 square feet and six dental chairs. He named his practice Troy Family Dental, and it is located at 606 Edwardsville Road in Troy.

Dr. Boatman is a kind and considerate dentist with a pleasant personality. He uses all of the latest dental equipment for his patients. He and his wife have six children, one boy and five girls.

Troy Foods, Inc.

Marilyn Nihiser, center, and friends, Mary Ann and Craig Lecce inside the old store. Notice the deer and moose trophies on the wall. Marilyn is a taxidermist. (April 1992)

In November 1971, Earl and Harold Schmidt and their wives Leola and Marie sold Troy Frozen Foods to Don and Marilyn Nihiser and young sons, Todd and Terry. The employees, "Mickey" Wyatt, Dorothy Holshouser, and Ray Loyet, continued to work for the Nihisers. The main business was that of processing hogs and beef with the option of placing those products in customers' lockers, ready for pickup; fruits and vegetables were still offered. As time progressed into the 1970s, home freezers became more prevalent and the lockers were eventually reduced from 492 to 200 as families changed their way of living, and as more fast food businesses grew up.

Troy Frozen Foods had to diversify. The rental apartment was used for more freezer and office space; the main source of refrigeration was that of a 30 HP ammonia York compressor with the Schmidt's 10 HP compressor as a back up, along with various Freon compressors. They added a retail case and refrigerated trucks. Since they were state inspected, they started manufacturing products for wholesale routes and serving such events as picnics, barbeques and other festivals. The Nihisers worked together as a family to make Troy Frozen Foods successful and it was their whole family's livelihood.

All aspects of the business grew, including the wild game processing. Because of the hundreds of deer being processed, and with Marilyn's childhood farm-life with her father,

she developed an interest in servicing that part of the business with taxidermy of mammals.

On August 11, 1993, at 4:31 p.m., with four employees finalizing their end of day duties, 911 had to be called for a fire emergency. In a matter of a few hours, the facility at 200 S. Main was destroyed by fire. All was suddenly lost. The business was such a part of the Nihisers' family life that it was a MUST to rebuild. The location at 200 S. Main Street was a sentimental location; however, current city building ordinances did not make it possible to rebuild on that location. Five sets of architectural drawings were made up before the final location at 404 East U.S. Hwy. 40 was reached.

It took over a year to get the doors open again and return to a normal flow of business. Even though over a year had gone by, the customers were still faithful and returned.

(Left) Inside the first Troy Frozen Foods. Marilyn and Don Nihiser, owners, and Catherine Byrne, employee.

More products were manufactured, and the plant upgraded their inspection system to become a Federally Inspected Meat Plant, thereby permitting selling over state lines. At the end of 1995, the family incorporated it in order to make it easier to pass it on to the next generation – so it emerged with the new name of Troy Foods, Inc.

During the years, two Belleville distributors and a Highland retail market, Neubauer's, have all been bought and incorporated into Troy Foods.

In 1999 the Illinois Department of Agriculture recommended and honored Troy Foods with an International Pork Producers Tour. It was the only meat plant tour in the U.S., with delegates attending from China, Philippines, Mexico, Brazil, Honduras, Italy, Ireland and all over the world.

With the many meat scares of the late 1990s, the Clinton Administration enforced Hazard Analysis Critical Control Points (HACCP) for the meat industry. As of January 25, 2001, Troy Foods, Inc. (and federally licensed meat plants) had to have written its own HACCP plan or it would have been barred from producing products for resale. In order to comply, all products were flowcharted throughout the plant, noting tracking numbers and hazards (temperature checks, restricted ingredients, thermometer calibrations, etc.) of every ingredient, with identification numbers of batches of products and records indicating where batches are sold. Troy Foods' 300-350 different items are all registered with the USDA, inspected daily, tested often and are within the state and federal guidelines to redistribute items for retail, wholesale and interstate distributors.

Troy Foods, Inc. current location at 404 East U.S. Hwy. 40, Troy, Illinois.

Troy Grain

Troy Grain has a long history of serving the farming community in Troy. Established near the railroad at or before 1900, it has seen several owners, managers, employees and directors. Currently it is owned and operated by Everett and Pam Bohnenstiehl.

A Brief History

Although the Troy Grain Company (or mill) has a long history, it isn't certain just when the company began. It is thought that it began when the railroad came through Troy in the late 1800s. In 1927, W.A. Elam Grain Company of St. Louis owned the Milling Company. At that time the company also purchased grain elevators in Vandalia, Mulberry Grove and Hagerstown.

W.A. Elam, Sr. was a former resident of Fayette County and was with the Vallier and Spies Company for a number of years as general manager of its warehouses and elevators. At one time Vallier-Spies owned the mill in St. Jacob.

A partial list of names of those men who served on the board of Troy Grain Company during the 1940s, 1950s, 1960s and 1970s includes Herb Busse, Arnold "Cap" Langenwalter, Oswald "Jim" Druessel, George Ottwein, Oscar Mersinger, Oliver J. Schlemer, Ted Flath and Jim Grapperhaus. Managers include Harry Taake, Ted Flath and Howard Jett.

The board of directors held various feed/seed meetings and seminars at the Sunset Inn in Troy several times a year. Nutrena and Eclipse feeds and Funk's Seed Company were a few of the brand names sold at the elevator.

An annual meeting was held each February at which dividends were paid to the stockholders. The dinner meeting was held at St. Paul Lutheran School auditorium and cafeteria. The ladies of St. Paul's cooked and

Early rail station at the Troy Grain Company mill, 1906.

Troy Grain Co. circa 1940s. Now known as Troy Grain, it is owned and operated by Everett and Pam Bohnenstiehl.

served the meal. A picnic was held each year for the directors and employees and their families.

Troy Grain Company entered a float in the Troy Homecoming parade in most years during the 1940s through the 1970s. The directors and their families would get together to build and decorate the float the week before the homecoming.

In the 1960s, when the railroad threatened to discontinue the rail spur for shipping grain, the directors went to Springfield to negotiate it. The spur was kept for a short while, but was eventually discontinued. Grain then had to be shipped out by large grain trucks.

As the agriculture scene changed, business tapered off considerably in the Troy community. The proximity of Troy to the Mississippi River encouraged many local farmers to transport grain directly to the river for a better price. In the mid-1980s, the Troy Grain Company sold its mill to the Toberman Grain Company of East St. Louis. Toberman owned several small mills in this part of the state. Rich Crain and Pat Bernreuter were managers while it was Toberman's.

In 1988 Everett Bohnenstiehl bought the business. His daughter Karen worked in the office for a few years. In recent years, Mrs. Everett (Pam) Bohnenstiehl manages the office.

In 2002, services and products provided there include grinding, mixed feeds, custom feed mixes, bulbs and garden seed, fertilizer, mulch (bulk and bagged), grass seed, bird seed, horse supplies, horse feed, straw, deer supplies, fish food, bird houses and feeders, general pet supplies and food products. Recently the sale of storage sheds, gazebos and windmills has been added.

Troy Grain's address is 108 West Highway 40. The telephone number is 667-6232.

Loading feed at Troy Grain Company, circa 1970s.

(Right) Troy Grain today.

Troy Savings & Homestead
A Division of
Collinsville Building and Loan Association

Troy Savings & Homestead, a division of Collinsville Building and Loan Association, is Troy's oldest chartered financial institution still in operation. In 1985 Troy Savings and Homestead merged with Collinsville Building and Loan Association, one of the oldest financial institutions in Madison County. The merger allowed the association to offer a wider variety of financial products and services. The Board of Directors, officers, and employees continue to dedicate themselves to serving the financial needs of the ever growing and changing community of Troy.

On June 28, 1886, Citizens Building and Loan Association and Troy Building and Loan Association were consolidated to form Citizens Building and Loan Association. The President of the newly formed Association was J.J. Brown, M.D. Board members included Jarvis, Auwarter, Taylor, Seligmann, Seele, Burk and Padon who were business owners in Troy. The early offices were located in various businesses such as a feed store, furniture store, barber shop and general store,

In 1904 the association was reorganized due to the expiration of the charter of Citizens Building and Loan Association. The new association became Troy Savings and Homestead. The newly

Troy Savings & Homestead building, 100 W. Market Street, September 1997.

elected President of the association was J.W. Steinhaus. Other officers at that time were Frank Collins, vice president; M.T. Auwarter, secretary; and W.W. Jarvis, treasurer.

David Sims was elected to the Board at the annual shareholders meeting in 1932. The next year he was elected president and served in that position until 1955. Mr. Sims continued to serve in an active role on the Board of Directors until his retirement in 1978.

Mr. Niedringhaus, Secretary/Treasurer; Mr. Helmich, Retiring President; Mr. D.D. Launius, President, 1966.

Delmer Launius was elected to the Board of Directors at the annual shareholders meeting in 1957. In 1966 Mr. Launius was elected President when Mr. Ed-

ward Helmich retired. Mr. Launius served as the President of the Association until 1985 when the association merged with Collinsville Building and Loan Association. He continues to serve on the Board of Directors of Collinsville Building and Loan Association as Director Emeritus.

Mr. E.H. "Bud" Niedringhaus, Jr. was elected to the Board of Directors at the annual shareholders' meeting in 1961. He was elected secretary at the annual meeting in 1963 and continued to serve in that position until the merger with Collinsville Building and Loan Association in 1985. Mr. Niedringhaus retired in 1986 but continued to serve on the Board of Directors of Collinsville Building and Loan Association until his death in January 1999.

Shirley Schnoeker began her career at Troy Savings and Homestead in 1976 as a part-time teller. At the 1984 annual shareholders' meeting Mrs. Schnoeker was elected to the Board of Directors. She was the first woman to be elected to serve as a board member for Troy Savings.and Homestead Association. In 1985, with the merger with Collinsville Building and Loan Association, Mrs. Schnoeker became the Branch Manager and Assistant Secretary to the Board of Directors until her retirement in 1999.

Troy Savings & Homestead has had offices at several locations in downtown Troy. Their current office at 100 West Market was completed in 1973.

Troy Savings & Homestead, 107 E. Market Street.

Troy Super Valu

In 1870 Peter Schuette started a general store in St. Rose by relocating a building which had formerly been a Methodist church at Shoal Creek. Peter's two sons, Joseph and Frank, began working at the general store in 1897. In 1902 they built an addition to make a total of 7,000 square feet of floor space on two floors, which comprises the current building today. The store had the reputation of being one of the best markets along the railroad of any area town in its day. It stocked dry goods, notions, shoes, ranges and stoves, tailor-made clothing, groceries, harnesses, shelf hardware, sewing machines, woven and barb wire fencing, carpets and linoleums, etc. Coffee, tea, spices, beans and rice were hand weighed and put in paper bags tied with string. Sauerkraut, herring, vinegar and liquor came in barrels. The St. Rose General Store also dealt in live animals such as horses and cows. Farmers brought in their chickens, ducks and geese, which the Schuettes would dress and ship as far away as New York. At one time the Schuettes were the largest suppliers of fresh eggs in Clinton county...and these eggs also were shipped to the East Coast.

In these years, food and goods were "bartered" (traded) because money was not commonly available to purchase items. The Schuette family eventually established the first banking business in this area to facilitate expanded commerce.

Frank Schuette's sons, Francis and Peter, joined in the business in the 1930s and expanded operations with additional grocery stores in other nearby towns. At one time Schuettes were operating some 14 Schuette Stores in surrounding towns in addition to dairies in Okawille and St. Rose and a meat processing house and general warehouse located next to the original general store in St. Rose. Locations at that time included Breese, Lebanon, Greenville, Carlyle, Highland, Beckemeyer, Trenton, Collinsville, two stores in Belleville, two stores in Centralia, Nashville and Okawville in addition to the original St. Rose General Store.

Finally, Peter's sons, Mike and Tom, joined the business full time in the 1970s and are the fourth generation to operate the business. Today the company employs over 250 associates and operates a total of six modern SuperValu grocery stores in addition to the original general store in St. Rose. The current Troy SuperValu Foods was opened in 1989.

In the fall of 2002, Schuette Stores, Inc. of St. Rose celebrated its 139th anniversary in the grocery business. Although the Schuette family has owned and operated these stores for all four generations, the name has changed numerous times over the 139 years. The original store name was Schuette Bros., then Califo Markets, then SSS Markets, then Tom Boy, then Piggly Wiggly and, for the last 33 years, SuperValu Food Stores. The company is one of the oldest continuously operating family businesses in the State of Illinois and is accordingly listed in the Illinois State Historical Society. The business stands as a real testimony to the hard work and dedication of so many generations of area associates who have maintained such a distinguished tradition of customer service and satisfaction. Schuette SuperValu Food Stores were recently ranked as the third oldest on-going supermarket business in the United States by *Chain Store Magazine*.

(Below) Original store, circa late 1800s

Troy Super Valu, 2002.

Troy Tri-Auto, Inc.
430 Edwardsville Road
Troy, Illinois

In August of 1992, Otto and Sharon Baumgartner purchased Tri-Auto, Inc. at 430 Edwardsville Road and changed the name to Troy Tri-Auto, Inc. Otto is the manager and Sharon is the bookkeeper. On August 27, 2002, they will celebrate being in business for ten years. Otto has been working at this place of business since 1969. He worked previously with his brother, Leonard Baumgartner, who had purchased the business in the 1960s from Oscar Gindler. Leonard named the business Len's Gulf and later changed the name to Len's Service. Leonard and Otto worked several years together repairing vehicles, towing vehicles and pumping gasoline. Together they worked side-by-side long hours, building the business into what it is today. Otto has worked over thirty-two years at this automotive repair shop and has seen many changes in the repair business. What used to be simple repair work with help from repair manuals now takes computer knowledge and top of the line repair equipment. Otto's dream came true when he purchased the business he loved so much.

Otto Baumgartner, Owner, Troy Tri-Auto, Inc., in the office.

Otto Baumgartner, Owner, Troy Tri-Auto, Inc.

Unger Eye Care
"Modern Eye Care, Old-Fashioned Caring"

Dr. Tom Unger, a native of the Troy area, recognized the vibrant and growing community of Troy represented a unique opportunity to establish an eye care practice. In April 1991, Drs. Tom and Alice Unger (see "Ray and Carol Unger Family" and "Tom and Alice Unger Family") established a private optometric practice in Troy. This likely represents the first full time eye care office in Troy's history. They practiced at their original location of 118 West Market (formerly Brown Reality and Dr. Littlefield, orthodontist) for nearly ten years. The growth of their practice necessitated a larger office, additional parking space and handicap accessibility. January 2, 2001, Unger Eye Care opened the doors of their new facility at 534 Edwardsville Road.

board member of St. Paul's Lutheran School. They have donated eye care services through various programs including the Back-to-School Program with Anderson Hospital and the Goshen Rotary and through Vision USA.

Unger Eye Care is an eye care practice with specialties in contact lenses, children's vision and ocular diseases. They carry a wide selection of eye care and eye wear products, including exclusive frame lines, high tech lens treatments and specialty contacts. They are committed to being at the forefront of eye care technology and having a highly trained staff. They strive to have the reputation of providing the most thorough eye care and the highest quality products while attending to each patient's individual eye care needs.

The following is their mission statement:

WHAT: To provide the most thorough, personalized eye care available.

HOW: By listening and understanding each of our patient's unique visual needs; by educating our patients on all aspects of their vision and preventative eye health; by remaining at the forefront of our profession through continuing education; by utilizing the latest in technology and instrumentation.

WHY: We enjoy the relationship which develops with our patients and we want our patients to enjoy a lifetime of healthy eyes and clear vision.

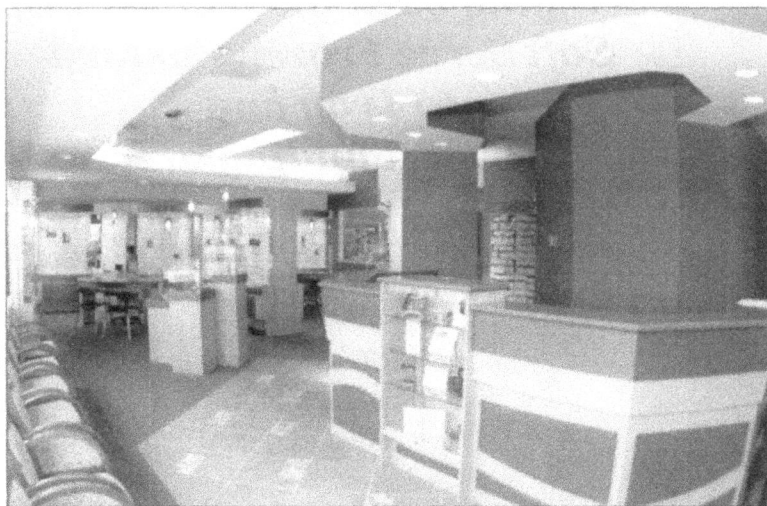

Interior view of new Edwardsville Road location, 2001.

Dr. Tom and Dr. Alice Unger appreciate the opportunity to serve the eye care needs of the same community in which they live and raise their family. They have been active members in the community including past president of the Troy Chamber of Commerce, member of the Troy Lions Club, member of the Goshen Rotary and school

Exterior view of new Unger Eye Care located at 534 Edwardsville Road, Troy, Illinois.

Building with Every Bloomin' Thing on the left and J's Frozen Custard on the right.

Every Bloomin' Thing Floral Gift Shop

Providing fresh, silk and dried floral arrangements for any occasion.

Wedding • Funeral
Anniversary • Birthday • Prom
Gifts • Balloons
Custom silk and dried arrangements
Plants • Plush Animals
Wide selection of gifts & indoor/outdoor decor

Deliveries to surrounding area and
Worldwide Wire Service available.

Phone: 618-667-8300

306 Edwardsville Road
Troy, Illinois 62294
Owners Joan Spencer & Mark Ponce

Hours:
Monday thru Friday 9:00 to 6:00
Saturday 9:00 to 3:00
Sunday 12:00 to 4:00

J's Frozen Custard

Bringing back the tradition of Soft Serve Frozen Custard to Troy and the surrounding area.

Now Serving
Concretes
Smoothies
Sundaes
Shakes/Malts
Cones

Featuring:
Fresh Roasted Pecan Turtle Sundae
Homemade Cookie Dough Concretes
Cheesecake • Peach Pie • Cherry Pie Concretes
Seasonal Specials

Located at
306 Edwardsville Road
Troy, Illinois 62294
Phone 618-667-8300
Owners Joan Spencer & Mark Ponce

Hours of operation:
Monday thru Sunday 11:30 to 10:00

Croffoot Heating and Air Conditioning, Inc.

Croffoot Heating and Air Conditioning, Inc. began in 1981 in a little room in a mobil home owned by Kirk and Susie Croffoot. They had one truck. In 1982 they leased a room from Thompson Designers, architects in Troy, and ran two trucks. In 1984, they built their own building and have doubled their volume and number of employees every year since, even expanding into St. Clair county. Throughout the years, they have been accessible to their customers and have provided honest and dependable service.

CROFFOOT HEATING & AIR CONDITIONING, INC.

1121A E. Main
Belleville, Ill.
(618) 277-2587

302A W. Hwy. 40
Troy, Ill.
(618) 667-2587

SUSIE CROFFOOT
President

CROFFOOT HEATING & A/C

Susie & Kirk

Susie and Kirk Croffoot, Croffoot Heating & Air Conditioning, Inc.

Edward Jones

Neil Goodwin

Neil Goodwin set up an Edward D. Jones office at 710 South Main in 1992. The name of the company was later changed to Edward Jones.

Edward Jones, an investment firm, is located from coast to coast. Jones operates in a niche that's all its own – selling traditionally low risk securities, such as insured tax-free bonds, mutual funds, certificates of deposit and common stock, from one broker office like that of Goodwin's.

The office employs Diane VanBuren who is the senior branch office administrator. Goodwin is from a small town, West Salem, where he grew up with a farm background. He is married to Julie. They have two children, Nicholas and Natalie.

A CPA, Goodwin has 20 years of experience in the stock market field. He worked in St. Louis prior to opening the office in Troy. Very active in the community, he is a member of the Troy Chamber of Commerce, serving a term as its president, and the Troy Kiwanis Club, also serving a term as its president.

Good natured, Goodwin is a well-liked and a trusted Troy businessman.

Madison County Farm Bureau
Service to Agriculture Since 1918

Township Officers and Directors

John Sedlacek, President	*St. Jacob*	Louis Koeller	*Godfrey*
Gary Knecht, Vice President	*Pin Oak*	Irvin Helmer	*Helvetia*
Kenneth Wiseman, Secretary	*Omphghent*	Glenn Gindler	*Jarvis*
Kyle Brase, Treasurer	*Hamel*	Steven (Jake) Geiger	*Leef*
Brent Suhre	*Alhambra*	Gene Daiber	*Marine*
vacant	*Chouteau*	Hilmer Schoenbaum	*Moro*
Craig Engeling	*Collinsville*	John Relleke	*Nameoki/Venice*
Michael Campbell	*Edwardsville*	Ross Hermann	*New Douglas*
Patric Martin	*Ft. Russell-Wood River*	Melvin Paul	*Olive*
Eugene (Bob) Gvillo, Jr.	*Foster*	Steven Plocher	*Saline*

**900 Hillsboro Avenue
P.O. Box 10
Edwardsville, Illinois
Phone: 656-5191**

"Where Membership Means Value"

Quad-County Ready Mix

Quad-County Ready Mix's Troy location.

In the early 1900s, Frank Hustedde and his father, Henry, operated a small building materials company making concrete blocks and pouring concrete for people around the Breese area. Frank and Henry manually loaded the rock, sand and cement on a wagon and delivered it to the job site with a team of horses. They would mix the materials in a wheelbarrow and dump it out at its on-site destination.

In the 1920s, Jaeger Machine Company developed a small mixer powered by a 3-HP, one-cylinder engine. Hustedde and Son purchased one of these mixers, which held approximately two wheelbarrows of mixed concrete. Materials still had to be shoveled into the mixer, but this small mixer saved time dramatically.

In 1952, Frank and Henry Hustedde saw the need for a ready-mixed concrete plant in Breese. They teamed up with Jack Heimann, who was a local construction contractor, and Paul Nettemeyer, who at the time was owner of Aviston Lumber Company, to form Clinton County Ready Mix Corporation in Breese, Illinois. The ready-mixed concrete plant was constructed, and a 1952 International Truck with a 4-cubic-yard Jaeger Mixer was purchased to deliver concrete.

In 1955, Frank's son, Herb, started driving a mixer truck for Clinton County Ready Mix. Herb's brother, Anthony (Butch) Hustedde, was involved in the business from 1961 until his retirement in 1993. In the late 1960s, Herb became manager of the Breese plant and today is the owner and president. In addition, Herb's sons, Neil and Kent, are actively involved in the fourth-generation family business as plant managers.

An affiliate company, Clinton County Materials Corporation, was incorporated on July 1, 1976. This company hauls material needed for the ready-mixed concrete facilities as well as various materials for construction jobs. The fleet is currently comprised of 40 tractor-trailer units, 20 dump trucks and 5 stone slinger trucks.

In April 1992, Clinton County Ready Mix was renamed Quad-County Ready Mix, having expanded from one plant in Breese to six plants in a four county area. Today this company has 75 mixer trucks and 11 facilities spanning six counties.

Employees at Quad-County Ready Mix and Clinton County Materials take personal pride in giving dependable service, and they have gained the respect of local contractors throughout the area.

Steve Schmitt Sales and Leasing

Steve Schmitt Sales & Leasing, 439 Edwardsville Road, Troy, IL 62294 (phone: 618-667-2800)

Steve Schmitt Sales and Leasing was established in February 1999, at 439 Edwardsville Road (Rt. 162, west of Market Street) in Troy. Steve is the third generation of the Schmitt family to be in the automobile business. He is the grandson of William S. Schmitt, who began Schmitt Chevrolet in Troy in 1929, and the son of B.J. "Nobby" Schmitt, who was the dealer of Schmitt Chevrolet in 1959 (see Schmitt Chevrolet). The Schmitts began selling automobiles in Troy, moved to Greenville, IL, added a business in Highland, IL, and recently returned to Troy where they began.

After 25 years of experience with a variety of heavy equipment and construction projects, Terry Hime decided to start his own business. Terry brought all of his knowledge, experience and contacts that he had made throughout the years and established Spring Valley Contracting in 1997. Spring Valley Contracting specializes in underground utility installation, trenching, backhoe, directional boring and grade work.

Terry Hime, owner, has been a member of Operating Engineers Local 520 since 1972. Terry is married to his wife of 29 years, Tina (nee Semith). They have two children, daughter Tiffany (Dan) Kohl and son Kenneth (Dena) Hime, and one granddaughter, Jordyn Kohl.

Sunnyside Nurseries, Inc.

Borrowing money from family and friends, Joseph Foucek purchased the property where Sunnyside Nursery is located from Herman Hecht in 1932. Zdenka Fiala and Joseph Foucek were married on June 7, 1933. There was no honeymoon; the day after the wedding, the new Mrs. Foucek was sent out to hoe the sweet potatoes. In the early years, the Fouceks truck farmed, raised pigs and chickens to make ends meet to pay off their debt and buy the various trees and shrubs to start their nursery. Mr. Foucek would get up in the wee hours of the morning and deliver a load of produce to the market in St. Louis. Sometimes he would get a mere five cents for a whole bushel of green peppers. They also raised pansy plants which they wrapped and delivered to the Woolworth store in Alton on consignment.

In 1941 Mr. Foucek, with the help of his brother and a team of horses, put up two greenhouses which he had purchased from a lettuce grower in Granite City. The greenhouses were dismantled in Granite City and then rebuilt in Troy. The benches were made from concrete mixed in a wheelbarrow with stovepipes used as forms for the legs. These are still standing today. The business expanded to include another farm in Glen Carbon, Illinois, in 1945.

Mr. and Mrs. Foucek had three daughters, two of whom still run the business today. Mr. Foucek's motto was always, "The secret to success is hard work" which is certainly what both of them always did. Mr. Foucek was a charter member of the Troy Lions Club and an avid supporter of the Tri-Township Park. He passed away in 1987; Mrs. Foucek is 90 years old and still living in the house she moved into as a bride.

Sunnyside Nursery

318

Terry's Appliance Center

Terry Giger of Terry's Appliance stands by a new refrigerator inside his store (1990s).

Terry's Appliance at 125 East Market Street opened its doors on January 1, 1989. Terry Giger and his brother, Dale Schmalz, purchased the business from Carl Embrey.

Terry Giger was 23 when he went into the appliance business. He came with sales experience from working several years for Sievers Equipment Company in Hamel.

A graduate of Triad High School, class of 1983, he attended Belleville Area College for two years and farmed the family farm in rural St. Jacob from 1978 until 1985.

Active in school organizations, Giger served as president of the Future Farmers of America for two years and served on numerous FFA committees while a member during his high school years. He was the recipient of the State Farmer Degree his senior year.

The Center is a family enterprise; Terry, along with his two brothers, Dale and Jon, and his mother Lucille Schmalz, kept the tradition of Embrey's Appliance. They continue to do so today. Lucille worked at the store for several years after her retirement from her duties as the Jarvis Township Assessor. Dale is the bookkeeper and Jon handles the repair service for the store.

Terry's Appliance is the authorized dealer for most of the leading brands of appliances. In the mid-1990s, Terry's Appliance expanded to a second location in Collinsville. The company serves both communities in all home appliance needs.

U.S. Bank
100 E. Market Street
Troy, Illinois

Matt Kotzamanis, Branch Manager
Phone: 618-667-4030 • Fax: 618-667-2339

U.S. Bank branch office. In 2001 U.S. Bank was bought out by Firstar – but the company took the U.S. Bank name in 2002.

Carehand P.C.

Dorothy M. Loderstedt, M.D.
Successor to Dr. Walter Zielonko

Adult Family Practice
Most Health Care Plans Accepted

**On staff at Anderson, St. Elizabeths and
Memorial Hospitals**

**102 N. Main Street
Troy, IL 62294
618-667-7007**

Danny's Barber Shop

B ud Klaus built and operated a barbershop at 105 South
Main Street, Troy, IL, in 1960. He operated the shop
along with two other barbers, one of whom was Norman C.
"Jake" Holloway. Then in 1973, Bud sold the shop to Norman
C. "Jake" and Clara Holloway. Norman Holloway operated Jake's
Barber Shop on the same premises from June 1973 until his death
in February 1984.

On April 24, 1984, Daniel E. McAley, Jr. opened Danny's Barber Shop at 105 South Main Street. He and his wife, Mary Sharon,
purchased the shop
from Clara Hollo-
way in 1984. Dan
was formerly with
Darrell's Barber
Shop in Collins-
ville, Illinois, for 13
years. For 18 years,
Danny's Barber
Shop has been in
business, and Dan
continues to oper-
ate the shop at the
same location.

D.L.E. Insurance Agency Corp.

O n March 14, 1995, Diana L. Eiskant opened a scratch
Insurance Agency at 408 West U.S. Highway 40, Suite
#100, Troy, IL 62294. Diana L. Eiskant is the president and 100%
owner of the company, holding licenses for Illinois and Missouri
with various insurance designations. Diana's experience came from
a family-run business, started in Collinsville, IL, which ran from
1981 to February 1995. She acquired new contracts with carriers
due to her extensive experience and insurance knowledge. New
clients were obtained through advertisement and involvement in
various community and other related industry organizations. Since
1995 the business has grown significantly to include clients such
as respected contractors and businesses in the area. Spring of 2001,
Diana's son, Nathan Eiskant, became fully licensed and a full time
employee of the agency. Summer of 2001, a fully licensed office
controller was added to the full time staff. The agency is affiliated
with the Professional Independent Insurance Association, the Troy
Chamber of Commerce, the National Federation of Independent
Businesses and the National Association of Women in Construction. The agency is a full line agency which offers all types of
insurance, including specializing in commercial insurance for contractors who need bonding capabilities. The agency has become a
part of the community. The agency recently moved to a new home
on Troy-O'Fallon Road.

320

Dr. Mark Friederich
Family Dental Practice

Serving Troy
for over 25 years.

Dr. Mark Friederich was in the first class graduating from the School of Dental Medicine at Southern Illinois University in Alton. He started his practice in 1975 in Granite City, IL. After moving to Troy in 1976, he considered opening a practice in Troy as well. In 1980 he purchased the then Jr. Chamber of Commerce Building, formerly Embrey's Hardware Store and before that the Samuel Kingston's Drug Store. The outside of the building was redesigned, and, with the help of his father, the interior was partitioned and remodeled. Dr. Friederich kept some of the square nails removed from the original structure. Dr. Friederich opened his practice in Troy full time in 1986.

Family Dental Practice, 2002

Grapperhaus Construction

Dean J. Grapperhaus, a contractor in Highland, formerly of Troy, owns Grapperhaus Construction. Dean was raised on a farm south of Troy. His parents are Jim and Mae Grapperhaus. He graduated from Triad High School, class of 1986. While in high school, he was in the co-op program and worked for a Troy construction company. He continued to work for the company for several years.

In 1994, he began his own business. Building new homes is his major priority; however, he does some remodeling as well. His motto is "You haven't had a house until you've had a Grapper 'haus.'"

Dean is particular about his work and gives quality workmanship on each and every job. His phone number is 618-654-5813.

Dean Grapperhaus, Grapperhaus Construction, 2002

Bonnie Levo
Levo Law Office

After clerking for the Illinois Supreme Court and working for a private law firm, Bonnie Levo became partners with Richard Tognarelli with offices in Collinsville and, eventually, Troy. On January 1, 1999, Bonnie opened her solo law practice at 112 East Market Street in Troy where she still practices law. Her practice is a general practice involving family law, adoption, wills, trusts and probate, real estate matters, personal injury, worker's compensation, business transactions and miscellaneous legal matters. Bonnie has been Associate City Attorney for the City of Troy since she began practicing in Troy, and is a member of the Madison County Bar Association, Illinois State Bar Association Troy Kiwanis Club and Troy Chamber of Commerce.

John Long

Republican for
Appellate
Court Judge
Fifth Judicial
District of Illinois

*Law Office
Established in 1983*

205 South Main Street
Troy, Illinois 62294
(618) 667-2122

WhiteMountain Financial

539 Troy Plaza
Troy, Illinois 62294
618/667-1638 • Fax: 618/667-1646

Robert Esch, CFP, CSA
Candace Esch, CSA
Donald Schrader, CSA
Cindi Weedon, Office Manager

Visit our website at
www.WhiteMountainFinancial.com

**NO-MARKET-RISK
FINANCIAL PLANNING–
FOR YOU!**

We Wish to Recognize
the Following Patrons
for their Support

4-0 Quick Shop, Bob Harrison, owner, 804 S. Main, est. 1977

Kelly's Deli/Butcher Shop, Mike Klueter, owner, 804 S. Main

Brase Enterprises, Norris Brase, owner, 408 W. US Hwy. 40

Jim Lyons Insurance, Jim Lyons, owner, 420 W. US Hwy. 40

Troy Auto Parts, Jim Fahey, manager, 802 S. Main, est. 1988

Plaza Cleaners, Walt Guller, 326 Bargraves Blvd.

Country Companies Insurance/Financial Services,
Bob Koonce, agent, 415 Edwardsville Rd.

Arnold's Concessions, Arnold Blewer, owner, 2323 Staunton Rd.

A&L Construction Co. & Sons, Inc., Al Hemann, owner,
8558 Hemann Dr., est. 1972

A&L Family Partners, Inc., Linda Hemann,
204 Liberty Square Dr., est. 1999

Thompson Designers, Inc. (arch.), Bill Thompson, owner, 815 Lyons Dr.

Smith Home Improvement, Sam Smith, owner, 8779 Old Lebanon Rd.

News Print Ink, Inc.

Troy Kiwanis Club, Jeri Tellmann, president, est. 1992

Index

Town Square, center of Market Street, looking north, 2002.

Town Square, center of Market Street, looking west, 2002.

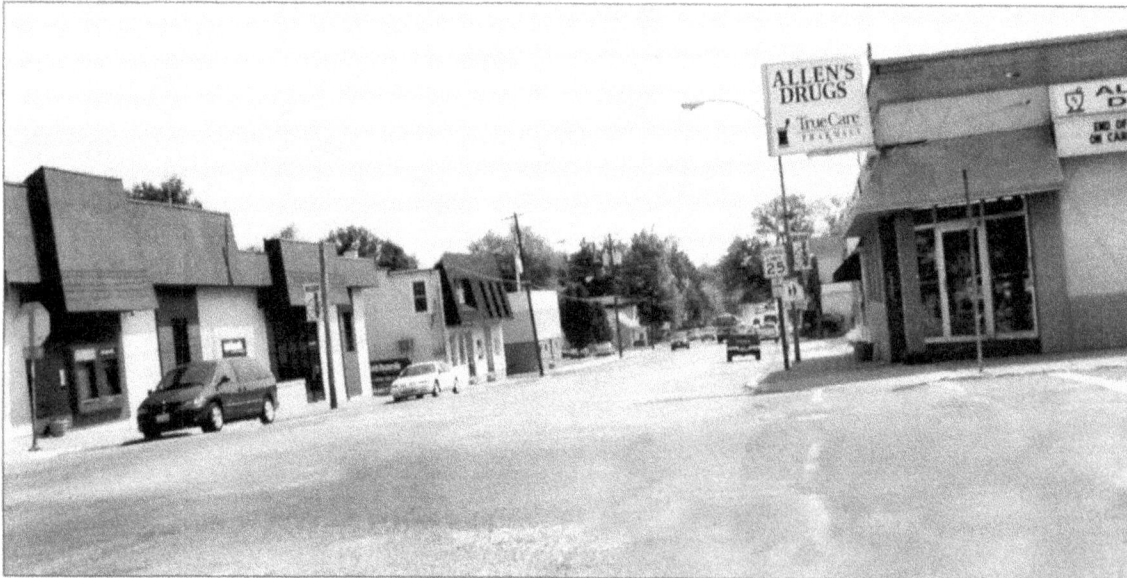

Town Square, center of Market Street, looking east, 2002.

Town Square, center of Market Street, looking south, 2002.

Aerial view of west edge of Troy along Route 162 before growth from 1970 until the present, looking south from Riggin Road on right.